# The Broadway Musical

# THE
# BROADWAY
# MUSICAL
## A Critical and Musical Survey

JOSEPH P. SWAIN

New York   Oxford
OXFORD UNIVERSITY PRESS
1990

## Oxford University Press

Oxford   New York   Toronto
Delhi   Bombay   Calcutta   Madras   Karachi
Petaling Jaya   Singapore   Hong Kong   Tokyo
Nairobi   Dar es Salaam   Cape Town
Melbourne   Auckland

and associated companies in
Berlin   Ibadan

## Copyright © 1990 by Joseph P. Swain

Published by Oxford University Press, Inc.,
200 Madison Avenue, New York, New York 10016

Oxford is a registered trademark of Oxford University Press

Library of Congress Cataloging-in-Publication Data
Swain, Joseph Peter.
The Broadway musical: a critical and musical survey /
Joseph P. Swain.
p.   cm.   ISBN 0-19-505434-2
1. Musicals—United States—History and criticism.   I. Title.
ML1711.S95   1990   782.1′4′0973—dc20   89-70907   CIP   MN

The following page is regarded as an extension of the copyright page.

2  4  6  8  9  7  5  3  1

Printed in the United States of America
on acid-free paper

For Jan
who taught me
to love this music

# Preface

The writer of the critical survey owes a good many debts, intellectual, practical, and personal, to those who have done essential groundwork in historical research and critical thinking and to those who have helped with the innumerable tasks that make the final work possible. In this sense, criticism is never entirely original, for it depends on an environment composed of intellectual tradition and the works, in this case certain American musical plays, to which it calls attention.

Many good books and articles stand behind this book, but its principal formation comes chiefly from a select few. Joseph Kerman's *Opera As Drama* (New York: Vintage Books, 1956; rev. ed., London: Faber, 1989), still the best exposition of the notion of the composer as dramatist, contributed the main premise, which is that in the best examples of American musical theater the music acts as a dramatic agent. Francis Fergusson's *The Idea of a Theater* (Princeton: Princeton University Press, 1949) helped refine more precisely what that means, as did *The Life of the Drama* (New York: Atheneum, 1964) by Eric Bentley, which also acted as chief reference for the various traditional dramatic genres. The only historical survey of Broadway to investigate what makes a good musical is Lehman Engel's *The American Musical Theatre: A Consideration* (New York: Macmillan, 1967), and although his arguments are not based on musical analysis, as is the case here, his observations are full of common sense and have much to teach. Other more purely historical surveys of the American musical theater were relied upon as essential references: Stanley Green's *The World of Musical Comedy* (New York: Barnes, 1974); Abe Laufe's *Broadway's Greatest Musicals* (New York: Funk & Wagnalls, 1969); Ethan Mordden's *Better Foot Forward* (New York: Grossman, 1976), and Gerald Bordman's *American Musical Theatre* (New York: Oxford University Press, 1977) are the principal ones. Beyond those are many biographical books, works of literary criticism, and articles of a specific nature which aided the writing of particular chapters, and for these items the reader is referred to the Notes for each chapter given at the end of the book. Missing even from those lists are the hundreds of periodical reviews of shows, other assorted newspaper features and interviews, and some writing in the scholarly literature that were duly consulted but which proved irrelevant or had nothing to contribute to the issue at hand.

As sketchy as this bibliographical summary may be, the acknowledgment of practical debts must be yet more inadequate, so many are they who helped out with favors large and small. The research for the book received an enormous boost at its outset from the National Endowment for the Humanities, which supported the initial bibliographical collection with a Summer Research Stipend in 1986. The Colgate University Research Council supported the work at a later stage. To both institutions I am deeply grateful.

My chief aide in collecting bibliography was Ms. Susan M. Cooney. Further help was provided by the reference staff at Case Library at Colgate University who patiently processed a large number of inter-library loan requests in fine humor. In this new age of computers there is no typist to thank, but the music department staff of Ms. Roberta Healey and Ms. Marilyn Jones helped me with many other administrative tasks and the entire department at Colgate gave me encouragement throughout the project. I must also thank Mr. Sheldon Meyer, Senior Vice-President at Oxford University Press, and his able and professional staff. Mr. Meyer supported this project enthusiastically when only two chapters were drafted and made many valuable suggestions en route.

The heart and soul of this study—indeed the reason for writing it when many other books on Broadway are available—are the musical examples contained in it. The detailed analysis of these examples provides the lion's share of the evidence and illustration for the critical arguments. Appreciation is due all the agencies which own the reprint rights to this music (listed on the copyright page) for carrying out the necessary negotiations with understanding, fairness, and efficiency. The one exception in this search for permissions was the Wren Music Co., which refused all permission to reprint the music and lyrics from *A Chorus Line* because of the critical nature of the attending discussion. I apologize to the reader for the inconvenience and somewhat convoluted writing the omission of those examples causes.

The examples were formatted using Dr. Keith A. Hamel's *Notewriter,* run on a Macintosh SE computer and printed with Macintosh's Laserwriter II NT. They were then reduced for final printing. In general I have copied the piano-vocal scores, the principal musical sources for this study, as closely as possible. Occasionally, in the interests of visual clarity, I omitted details of orchestration, stage directions, or other matters that had no bearing on the discussion, but in all cases I hoped to represent fairly the essence of what is heard in the theater in a format that keeps the discussion manageable.

Personal debts are harder to recognize sometimes but are no less real. The three most important ones I trace back to my undergraduate days at Dartmouth College. There two music teachers, Professors Steven J. Ledbetter and Charles Hamm, showed by the example of their own research in American music and, more important, by their wholesome open-mindedness to music of all sorts that a critical survey such as this was not beyond imagining. The last debt I trace to a young woman named Janice Lee, my classmate, best friend, now my wife of ten years, who insisted on dragging a high-brow music student again and again to musical theater productions to see and hear the magic there.

J.P.S.

*Hamilton, New York*
*Fall 1989*

# Contents

# The Broadway Musical

# CHAPTER 1

# Introduction

The intention here is not to write a comprehensive history of the American musical theater, but to survey the achievements of its music as a dramatic element. In the best musical plays of the Broadway tradition, songs are embedded in a drama to which they contribute mightily. They are more than simple decorations or diversions. Rather, they establish characters, move the plot, intensify conflicts, and constitute other events that would be expected of a spoken play. Without the songs these plays would be considerably poorer, even incomprehensible.

The perspective adopted in this survey, then, is one as old as the very idea of combining music and drama. The music of a good musical play informs the drama that contains it, and the composer is a dramatist in his own right, more important sometimes than the person who writes the words. This perspective is perhaps best articulated in modern times by Joseph Kerman in his *Opera as Drama*,[1] a critical survey of serious opera of the European tradition.

Whether music in the theater can really be an essential dramatic force has been a matter of some contention. If drama is a product of words alone, then any musical adaptation must weaken the drama, because music is in general abstract, without explicit semantic reference. "When drama takes on the abstract character of pure music or pure dance it ceases to be drama; when, as a compromise, it tries to combine the abstract with the concrete it is invariably the drama, the words, that suffer," writes theorist Eric Bentley.[2] But if actions are the stuff of drama, as Aristotle would have it, then words are just one way to articulate "the underlying structure of incident and character."[3] Anything else that can express the thread of the action has just as much right to dramatic representation as words. When the important actions are actions of feeling, or emotion, then music not only suffices but surpasses the power of words to define the action. As Kerman has it:

. . . even the most passionate of speeches exists on a level of emotional reserve that music automatically passes. Music can be immediate and simple in the presentation of

3

emotional states or shades. In an opera, people can give themselves over to sensibility; in a play nobody ever quite stops thinking.[4]

The lack of explicit semantic reference in Western music, the very quality that makes it unsuitable for conveying fact and idea, makes it an ideal symbol of psychological or emotional action. The first association of a musical phrase with a character or situation carries over throughout the drama, and so not only the overt actions of the characters but also their thoughts and states of feeling become sensible to the audience. That is the rationale behind the leitmotif, a fragment of music that comes to represent a character or object of importance. Bentley advises the dramatist to imitate action by finding "objective equivalents of subjective experience."[5] He means the subjective experience of the audience, but in music there is the equivalent of the character's experience as well, which in turn may be felt directly by the audience.

It is possible to deny music a dramatic role, then, only if one insists that drama is a product of words alone. Once anything else—stage gestures, facial expressions, lighting—is allowed to contribute, then music too must be admitted as a powerful and subtle analogue to the emotional and psychological action.

To understand how music performs as a significant dramatic element in the Broadway tradition, a musical analysis is needed that connects the songs in their detail with the dramatic elements of plot, character, and action. In the second act of Leonard Bernstein's *West Side Story*, for example, it is not enough to point out that when Maria persuades a bitter, bristling, and disillusioned Anita to intercede in behalf of the man who just killed her lover, a dramatic climax has occurred. Such persuasion seems incredible. On the other hand, any technical analysis of the music without reference to plot and character misses the essential meaning of the duet. In the contrasting section or "release" of Anita's opening solo, she sings the following:

**Ex. 1–1**  Bernstein and Sondheim,, "A Boy Like That," mm. 18–20.

Her bitterness and hatred of Tony come through in the minor mode, accented offbeats, and the chromatic and diminished melodic intervals that her phrases outline. But why then should the same music be taken up by Maria when she enters?

**Ex. 1–2**  Bernstein and Sondheim, "A Boy Like That," mm. 38–40.

It fits because this is more than telling Anita that she is dead wrong. The song here makes explicit a serious accusation: that Anita's animosity is rooted in the shallowness of her own relationship with her lover Bernardo, a shallowness made painfully clear by the depth of Maria's commitment to Tony. Maria, in quoting this theme with the words "It's true for you, not for me," takes Anita's denial of love and turns it back on her. But this is confrontation, not persuasion. Persuasion begins with the onset of the last section of the duet:

**Ex. 1–3**  Bernstein and Sondheim, "A Boy Like That," mm. 68–72.

Maria's melody is much transformed and yet the same as before. Shorn of its chromatic anacrusis to the central G, the strong offbeats and the diminished intervals, and translated into the major mode, the song that once stood for the denial of love now becomes the expression of love. This transformation of the melody mirrors the change in Anita, and makes such a moving and drastic character change quite believable. Maria convinces her that the love she feels has a depth far beyond anything that Anita has known, and therefore worth saving. She does this in terms that Anita understands, reshaping her own musical argument, as it were.

Musical gestures can take on dramatic meanings and functions because they have only general semantic connotations, unlike words, whose referents are usually quite specific. Musical meanings become specific only when associated with the words of the libretto. The chromatic phrase in Example 1-1 reflects Anita's emotional state by its association with the text, whose meaning is obvious. Music, however, is not so devoid of semantic references that just any gesture will do for a particular expression. The abstractness of music is limited by its home culture, which overlays various musical effects with meanings accumulated over many generations. Bitterness and hatred are not necessarily expressed by the minor mode and diminished intervals of Example 1-1, but those emotions are certainly within the expressive range of those effects; a composer would not use them to express love or joy except in the most contrived circumstances, or in a non-tonal idiom. The composer's art as a dramatist consists of choosing gestures appropriate for the expression required in a dramatic situation. These gestures then take on specific meaning when associated with the words in a musical texture. The most astonishing aspect of this scheme is that the music then amplifies incomparably the dramatic situation from which it takes its own meaning. There is a sort of feedback system that operates quite like certain other mechanisms of human perception.[6]

In short, the critical survey which this book comprises regards the traditional tools of composition—melody, its harmonization, change of key, rhythm, and texture—as elements of dramaturgy. This sort of analysis has never been applied to Broadway stage music before. There are fine surveys and histories of Broadway, to be sure, even ones in which dramatic criticism is the principal aim, but none have music as the principal focus of the criticism. Leaf through the pages of a volume by David Ewen, Stanley Green, Ethan Mordden, or Lehman Engel: there are no musical examples. This situation allows only the most general statements about the role that music can play; the particular musical solutions to dramatic problems and the rare moments of true musical-dramatic insight can only be recalled, never described. The direct analysis of music surely narrows the scope of this book—no one could discuss every important moment of every show in such detail—but in return it may provide a deeper understanding of the composer's craft as a dramatist.

One troubling question remains. Isn't this critical approach a bit lofty for Broadway? Is the popular tradition really worth this sort of attention?

It would be fair to say that the products of Broadway have not had much success in the annals of scholarly criticism. The musical theater has received virtually no attention from serious music critics at all, and what little it has received has been patronizing at best. In his *The Playwright as Thinker* of 1946, Eric Bentley states that the dramatic content of one of the most reknowned examples of American musical theater is essentially trivial:

> Perhaps Mr. Oscar Hammerstein is a fair specimen. His work *Oklahoma!* . . . has been "hailed" as establishing a new genre, praised in at least one literary quarterly, awarded a Pulitzer Prize by special dispensation, and compared, not unfavorably, with *The Magic Flute*. It was the outstanding theatrical success of the war period; and it is entirely representative of current trends. In fact, it belongs with the "new Americanism" in being folksy and excessively, ostentatiously wholesome; also in being trite, cocksure, sentimental, and vacuous. On the stage it is decked out in gay color and from time to time enlivened by tricky dancing. But in all drama . . . color and dancing are only embellishments; in this case they are the embellishment of a scarecrow.[7]

If only the outline of the *Oklahoma!* story is recalled, this judgment might seem to be fair, but Mr. Bentley has not accounted for an essential element. In identifying the play as Hammerstein's, he disregards completely the contribution of the other dramatist, Richard Rodgers. This stems from his belief, somewhat muted in later writing, that music rarely contributes anything worthwhile to the drama of words. In its extreme form, it is a position that denies the claims that opera makes on dramatic art.

Even when it is agreed than any critical assessment of the American musical stage must include its music, it is entirely possible that the musical talent of Broadway is unequal to the ideal of music drama. In his speculation on the future of the musical stage in *Opera as Drama,* Kerman raises the possibility of popular musical theater as a source for new works of merit, but quickly dismisses such a thought:

> Popular art has other channels. One of them is musical comedy. Theoretically this might serve as a proving-ground for art, just as *opera buffa* did in the eighteenth century; but in over a hundred years operetta and musical comedy have come forth with not a single serious dramatist. . . .[8]

The context of this judgment, in particular Kerman's rather Olympian standards for "serious dramatists" as set out in his book, should perhaps be recalled. His pantheon admits but two members: Mozart and Verdi, and even their works have imperfections. Monteverdi, Handel, Gluck, Wagner, Debussy, Berg, and Stravinksy, among others, stand just outside the small inner circle. All others are simply undramatic.

The problem is complicated by two additional factors. One is the simple fact of popular success. The view from the end of the twentieth century affords a perspective unavailable to Bentley and Kerman, namely, that there is now a repertoire of American musical theater pieces, a repertoire that has undergone a process of classicization just as other repertoires have done. From the thousands of shows composed since the turn of the century, perhaps two or three dozen have survived to be regularly performed. Some critics recognize a "golden age" of the American musical theater centered on the decades of the 1940s and '50s, when many of them were composed. This observation defines a group of important forerunners, including Jerome Kern, Cole Porter, George Gershwin, and Rodgers and Hart, and a period of "decline" setting in by the late 1960s. More important, the shows of the golden age are two generations old at least, which means that their appeal has survived some rather radical changes in society and in the style of popular music. The rise of a repertoire that behaves like other serious repertoires in the culture is difficult to dismiss.

Even so, it is often dismissed because the music seems to be rooted in popular styles rather than "serious" or "cultivated" or "classical" styles. This origin is the second factor that complicates the judgment of Broadway's ultimate value.

Whether Broadway in modern times remains a purely popular tradition is open to question, but that its origins are popular is undeniable. The theatrical elements were entirely drawn from the traditions of vaudeville, burlesque, and popular stage plays; the theater songs of the early 1910s and 1920s were written by the same men who composed for the publishers of Tin Pan Alley. Both

Jerome Kern and George Gershwin began their careers as song pluggers in music publishing houses. The training of many of even the greatest talents of Broadway was of such a happenstance nature that their musical facility was limited in ways that seem incredible today. Richard Rodgers, who always composed at the piano, never learned enough technique to play classical chamber music, despite an effort with formal lessons in the middle of his career.[9] Irving Berlin, it is said, composed all his songs in the key of F-sharp. He had to hire a musical secretary to transpose them to more suitable keys afterward.[10]

On the other hand, elements of the art music tradition of the West can be discerned creeping into Broadway from the late 1910s onward, a harbinger of the increasingly serious intentions of certain composers. Victor Herbert was a fine classical cellist, and the principal operetta composers of the 1920s, Sigmund Romberg and Rudolf Friml, were trained in Europe. Gershwin had formal training in harmony and counterpoint, although not before he was well established on Broadway, and of course his *Porgy and Bess* is known as an ''opera'' in the serious sense. Cole Porter studied with Vincent d'Indy in Paris. Such examples proliferate later in the century: Leonard Bernstein's brilliant career need not be detailed here, but it is less well known that Stephen Sondheim studied composition with Milton Babbitt, or that Andrew Lloyd Webber was trained from boyhood in classical horn, violin, and piano.

Certainly there are many who would view the domination of the Broadway tradition by popular interests as a constraint so overwhelming that any artistic value must be choked off. Bentley admits the possibility of a dramatic art that is admired by both critic and public:

> Until the modern period great drama has possessed not only those deeper and subtler qualities which reveal themselves to the careful analyst and which constitute its greatness, it has also possessed more generally available qualities. It has appealed on different levels. It has appealed to the connoisseur *and* the public.[11]

But his overall assessment of the state of modern theater is that ''it is almost inconceivable that any drama could satisfy the canons of the most exacting criticism and also be popular.'' [12] The ''commodity theater,'' as he terms it, appeals to the lowest common denominator in its audience and therefore excludes the deep and the subtle aspects of dramatic art.

In an absolute sense he is right about Broadway. The tyranny of the financial motive in the early decades is there for all to see, in the endless parade of mindless ''formula'' shows, in the reliance on superficial devices such as chorus lines and comedy routines quite unrelated to any story, and in the producers' resistance to the slightest innovation. The style of Broadway's music is eclectic by nature, able to absorb and put to dramatic use a variety of different sorts of music, but its contributing sources then were always popular. Experimentation with the new and various styles of art music coming out of Europe early in the century was impossible. These developments progressed at a rapid rate and left

the entire world of popular music far behind for the first time in the history of
Western music. If high art resided only in those cultivated developments of Debussy, Schoenberg, and Stravinksy, then certainly Broadway must have been cut
off from such ambitions.

But Stravinsky argued that "The more art is controlled, limited, worked over,
the more it is free."[13] Because they had to please their public, and were thus
denied from the advances and pretensions of the European avant-garde, Broadway composers were left free to continue to explore the possibilities of a musical
style which in learned circles had become old-fashioned and, in the individualistic world of the twentieth century, unacceptable. They were free to draw on
the newer popular styles of jazz and rock. The most ingenious of these composers found that they could sell their creations without sacrificing their dramatic
ideals. And there was substantial departures from the norm, amid the tight-fisted
producers and unsophisticated public. *Porgy and Bess* was produced and did run
for several months; *Oklahoma!* did begin without a chorus number; *Carousel* did
have a few odd-sounding chords during its prelude and did kill off its main
character. Gradually, the Broadway composers came to realize that if their musical dramaturgy was convincing enough, they could include most anything they
wanted.

Stravinsky's point that conscious limitations of art can paradoxically liberate
the artist is well to keep in mind, but such limitations also have their price. The
most important constraints imposed on Broadway by the popular tradition were
the technical ones. Popular songs can be most expressive, and composers learned
to make them dramatically effective as well, but their expressive and dramatic
range is limited, first of all by their length and second by the musical languages
to which they have recourse.

American popular songs are simple in form and are generally quite short.
These features limit not so much what can be expressed but to what degree it
can be conveyed. It is vain to hope for the affective climaxes that one hears in
the classical operas because there is not enough time to prepare them in a Broadway song. Mozart can prepare a climactic finale for twenty minutes, and Wagner
for an entire act, but a theater song must make its point and quit within a very
few minutes. Only by constructing musical relationships across the entire drama
could Broadway composers create similar effects, and that level of composition
was beyond all but a handful of the best musical plays of the tradition.

The tradition assimilated a number of different popular styles during the course
of the century, but at its core was a rather simplified nineteenth-century Romanticism. Like its glorious ancestor, this style made expressive use of chromaticism
and of the systematic delay of the cadence, but these were never developed to
the extent heard in large Romantic classical works because of the limitations of
popular taste and of the popular song form. Musical expressions and constructions based on melodic phrasing and motivic or thematic processes are common
in Broadway songs, but extreme chromatic effects are not, and the tonal center
is generally clear at any point. Composers were free to mix in elements of jazz

and rock when those styles became popular, but they turned out to be useful only in certain types of dramatic situations.

That the Broadway tradition is in its roots and through much of its history a popular tradition, then, is a factor that has constrained the tradition in significant ways, but has yet left room for achievement. The significance of the achievement can be seen in the resilience of the repertoire grown up over the last six decades and in the attraction that the tradition has had for "serious" musicians such as Gershwin, Bernstein, and Weill.

The popular nature of the tradition does not undermine the search for a real musical dramaturgy, although it may limit the scope of the dramaturgy. Certainly the composers themselves seemed to understand their role: Kern spoke of himself as the "musical clothier" of a dramatic situation,[14] and Rodgers and Hammerstein spent weeks and weeks discussing dramatic problems of organization before a single word or note was written. That Stephen Sondheim actually researched the historical and cultural setting of his *Pacific Overtures* (1976), as did Webber and Rice for their *Evita* (1979), indicates how much the dramatic acumen of the most serious composers has developed.

Yet, Richard Rodgers and Sondheim cannot be equated with Verdi and Wagner just because their ideals of musical drama are similar. There is an essential difference that lies not so much in whether there is success or failure as in what is attempted. The most compelling Broadway show has a certain sense of limited scope never heard in a masterwork of European opera. It is not that the show has failed; it simply did not try to do as much. Perhaps here the element of sophistication comes in at last. Paradoxically, it could be argued that such a show is more valuable than the second-rank opera of Bellini or Meyerbeer which sets higher artistic goals of much greater sophistication but fails to live up to them. Certainly many shows of Broadway hold the stage better.

An aesthetics of popular art is clearly wanted here. The small New England church, the Greek household vase, and "Greensleeves" have won high esteem for generations, but how are they to be compared to the Gothic cathedral, the temple sculpture, and the Dowland lute song? The problem is reminiscent of certain ideas of Leonard Meyer about "value" and "greatness" which might offer at least a working solution.[15] His argument attempts to solve the difficulty musicians have when they recognize that a Chopin prelude seems to be a flawless and completely satisfying work, but one which cannot be compared with the Beethoven "Hammerklavier" Sonata. The Chopin, as perfect as it seems, simply does not attempt the same structural dimensions and content as the sonata. Yet no one derides the prelude for this inequity. Both have value because they both succeed in fulfilling the terms of their conceptions, but only the Beethoven piece is great, because its conception is great. Edward T. Cone argues similarly that "for fullest enjoyment we want the medium of an art to be saturated—used to the fullest extent in every dimension."[16] As with the short song forms of Broadway, what is at issue here is not what may be conveyed, but to what degree.

Broadway is worth criticizing because its best works can have this sort of value without attempting the dimension of the European operatic masterworks, what Francis Fergusson calls "the limited perfection of the minor dramatic genres."[17] The achievements are simpler and the expectations are smaller. The abiding popularity and undeniable position of these plays in American culture warrants a more serious look than they have been given in the past.

Any critical survey must be selective by nature. Because its focus is on the American musical theater, plays not of American origin are excluded. Kurt Weill's The *Threepenny Opera* and Lionel Bart's *Oliver* are important works in Broadway's history, but do not originate in that tradition.[18] Because this is not a history, works which are important primarily because of some historical reason are not included unless they are musically valuable as well. Marc Blitzstein's *The Cradle Will Rock* and Galt MacDermott's *Hair* come to mind.

Even with these exclusions, too many plays remain to be discussed between two covers. The final list of musical plays to be discussed in detail has been drawn up to demonstrate not only the quality of dramatic achievement in the Broadway tradition but also the variety of the achievement. The tradition has successfully adapted romantic novels, frame stories, Shakespearean plays, and classical myths. It has promoted religious experience in a theatrical setting, produced a morality play, and included the characteristics of various ethnic groups. All of these facets need to be included in the selection if the wide variety of dramatic achivement within the tradition is to be appreciated.

There are some plays whose quality so impressed their contemporary audiences that they influenced the course of the tradition in their own right. *Show Boat* and *Oklahoma!* demanded their places for this reason. Others such as *Carousel* and *West Side Story* have been recognized by the rest of the world as worthy of presentation in their own languages, in their world fairs, and as part of operatic repertories, so that they required inclusion not by virtue of immediate recognition but by a more sustained admiration.

The rest were included because they turned a particular interest into drama very well, and because they represent certain key personalities of Broadway's history. Cole Porter's *Kiss Me, Kate* was neither the first nor the last to use a Shakespearean model, but it comes at the end of his long career and is by far his best show, and one which uses that model most explicitly. Like Porter, Frank Loesser wrote his own lyrics as well as music, and in *The Most Happy Fella*, for which he also adapted his own libretto, he realized one of the very few neglected musical plays of highest merit. The chapter on Lerner and Loewe includes two of their most famous plays, *My Fair Lady* and *Camelot*, because they both dramatize important Western myths. George Gershwin's *Porgy and Bess* comes closest to the ideal of European opera. There are a number of plays using ethnic settings to choose from, but Bock's *Fiddler on the Roof* is the most famous and the only one that attempts to make a dramatic issue of ethnic values.

The period of the last twenty years, being most recent, is most difficult to evaluate, and the choices were made with more an eye to qualities that make a play stand apart, with less confidence of esteem that will last for generations. Stephen Schwartz has had a good career and his *Godspell* is a dramatic presentation of a seemingly anti-dramatic subject. Hamlisch's *A Chorus Line* has a novel approach to plot, and its complete commercial success makes it difficult to ignore, as are the historical dramas of Webber and Rice. Most problematic of all perhaps is the work of Stephen Sondheim, which has such astonishing variety that choosing a single play of his is bound to be a misrepresentation. His setting of a thrilling story in *Sweeney Todd,* however, offered dramatic problems and solutions that are particularly engaging.

Some readers will be disappointed in the lack of any consistent attempt to fix the most "authentic" version of each play through an examination of original sources, orchestra parts, conductors' scores, and other documents. Apart from the simple consideration that any such attempt would expand the book beyond all practicality and usefulness, the fact is that judging authenticity, of any music but particularly theater music, is an enormously complex issue. Leaving aside the technical matters, there is the basic question of what is to be considered, in general terms, the "authentic" version, even if every different stage of creation could be reconstructed. Is it to include all the composer's songs for a play, including those later discarded with his consent? Should it be the show before out-of-town tryouts, or the one that opened in New York, after changes and cuts were made? What if later changes came about at a later date? The problem has been visited anew with a new recording of Jerome Kern's landmark musical *Show Boat,* which includes all the music Kern ever wrote for it, including about forty minutes that he and Oscar Hammerstein agreed had to go well before the play opened in New York.[19] In only two cases, *Porgy and Bess* and *Carousel,* has it been necessary to include concerns of origin and authenticity in these essays, since in only those two plays are essential critical matters affected by them. In all the others the quest for the authentic version has proved irrelevant. After all, the American musical theater is a living tradition. There is no need to authenticate any of these plays in order to justify their production today; on the contrary, these musicals live on despite cutting, orchestration simplified down to a single upright piano, and singing that ranges from the unbearable to the operatic. The best musical plays of Broadway clearly own qualities which transcend the particular versions in which they are performed. Those qualities are the concern of this survey.

For this reason, the illustrating musical examples are taken, with appropriate permission, of course, from the standard published piano-vocal scores. These are the most accessible and most efficient documents of the music, and are therefore the sources of most contemporary productions.

All of the plays included in the study are well known or, indeed, renowned. Bentley's arguments about commercial art notwithstanding, continual admiration for a play sustained over generations seems more trustworthy than the esteem of an individual writer.

This is not to say that the selected plays are to be accepted as unqualified artistic successes. Certainly the most compelling moments in these plays warrant attention if the variety of dramatic achievement is to be understood, but none these plays is without significant weaknesses or flaws. The evaluation of these flaws can be just as instructive, in terms of the overall assessment of the Americal music theater, as the analysis of the high points. The opposite perspectives of success and failure enhance an understanding of musical dramaturgy. Beyond the serious recognition of the value in the Broadway tradition, it is this sort of understanding that this book seeks to promote.

# CHAPTER 2

# First Maturity

*It is my opinion that the musical numbers should carry the action of the play and should be representative of the personalities of the characters who sing them.*[1]

JEROME KERN

In virtually every historical study of the American musical theater, *Show Boat* is recognized as an important landmark. It is the summit of Jerome Kern's career as a stage composer, and the first critical success of the young lyricist Oscar Hammerstein II, who would follow it with many more in the coming decades. The comments of Wilfred Sargeant, classical violinist turned *New Yorker* critic, in reviewing the 1954 revival by the New York City Opera, reflect the general consensus:

> The work is, of course, a masterpiece of its kind, and a much more genuine example of American musical theatre than most self-consciously American operas that I can recall. Its tunes remain entirely enchanting, and, as musical shows or light operas go, it has a very effective book—a far more effective one than, for example, that classic of the species "Die Fledermaus."[2]

The journalists, writing about particular performances, point to the individual characteristics of the show that are outstanding: the quality of the music, the lyrics, the realism of the plot, the unabashed American character. Serious historians of Broadway have a different reason that is more fundamental and yet subsumes all of the above characteristics. *Show Boat* is the first American musical that integrates the elements of a musical theater into a credible drama. The songs, the generous amount of instrumental music, the dancing, the crowd scenes, all arise from events in a rather serious plot. Nothing is extraneous.

The play grew out of the novel *Show Boat,* by Edna Ferber, who although little remembered today was once a highly popular novelist. She wrote *Show Boat* after having spent some time living on an active showboat that played the Mississippi in the mid-1920s. The book was published in 1926 and immediately became a best seller. Jerome Kern, an avid rare-book collector who liked to keep abreast of literary developments, read it and saw its possibilties for the musical theater at once. He spoke to Ferber about it in person after meeting her at the theater, secured the rights, and then interested Hammerstein in the project. Best of all, he convinced the redoubtable Florenz Ziegfeld to produce it.

In retrospect it seems that the composition of *Show Boat* came about as the result of a series of fortunate coincidences. No other Broadway composer with sufficient clout to begin such an outlandish project would have looked twice at the novel. Kern in the mid-1920s was the dean of Broadway composers, and although his plays immediately preceding *Show Boat* are as unremarkable as those of his contemporaries, except perhaps for the quality of their music, it is clear that he had a much loftier conception of what the popular musical stage could be. He found a kindred spirit and an enormous talent in Hammerstein, who was to become one of the foremost lyricists of the Broadway stage for the next thirty years. Hammerstein had had his share of frivolous musical comedies, but gained valuable experience with some of the luminaries of the 1920s Broadway theater: Vincent Youmans (*Wildflower* of 1923), Rudolf Friml (*Rose Marie* of 1924), Sigmund Romberg (*The Desert Song* of 1926), and with Kern himself (*Sunny* of 1925). Together they fashioned a vision of musical theater unique for its day.

The fashioning required a prodigious amount of work. The novel, a rambling piece that takes in five decades, two cities, and thousands of miles, had to be streamlined to fit the conventions of the musical theater. An entire decade and many characters were cut out; other characters were combined into a single stage character, and in general the cast "around the showboat is much more consistent than in the novel, in which they come and go realistically."[3]

This sort of patient adaptation indicates how well Kern and Hammerstein understood their craft. Operas in general have smaller casts than spoken plays, since the dramatic action revolves around singing characters, and singing takes up much more time than speaking. A small cast is virtually a prerequisite of significant character development in a musical play.

Composer and lyricist labored with revisions and improvements for nearly twelve months, a length of time unheard of in the 1920s. It opened at the Ziegfeld Theater on December 27, 1927, and ran for 572 performances.

The achievement of *Show Boat* impresses not only on its own terms, which it continually must do in order to last, but also in view of the reigning traditions of musical theater in the 1920s. There were two principal genres of musical theater: musical comedy and operetta.[4] They were as different in construction, tone, and effect as could be, but they both failed to contribute a single lasting work for the stage for the same reason. They failed to present their audiences with credible drama.

The musical comedy that flourished on Broadway in the early decades of the century was a casual and happenstance affair. Constructed as it was from traditions of vaudeville and burlesque combined with some of the procedures of European operetta, a musical comedy was little more than a succession of songs, comedy routines, and dance numbers that as often as not had nothing to do with the progression of a story. If one was fortunate enough to encounter a plot, it was with rare exceptions a silly situation comedy without any dramatic complications that might interfere with the various acts. That the *New York Times* critic in 1927 described *Show Boat,* which seems quite straightforward today, as "crammed with plot" gives some idea of the norm.[5] And even when there was a reasonable plot, the collaborators often took no notice of it. Jerome Kern, from early on in his career, stood out as somewhat of an oddity because he demanded to know the entire story of the play before he began to compose the songs for it.

Indeed, from 1915 to 1918 he composed a series of shows for the small Princess Theater which combined small casts and simple plots with the aim of achieving significant continuity between story and song. Here Kern's reputation was made. If the very occasional revivals of some of the better "Princess" musicals reveal the awkwardness and strains of an adolescent growth, perhaps most of all in the plots of Guy Bolton, it is growth nonetheless. Kern's dramatic instinct would eventually result in *Show Boat,* but the Broadway outside the Princess was burdened by stifling conventions and contract requirements, and they forced Kern to revert to older production standards in the early 1920s. Oscar Hammerstein recalled his collaboration with Kern on the musical *Sunny* in 1925 this way:

Our job was to tell a story with a cast that had been assembled as if for a revue. Charles Dillingham, the producer, had signed Cliff Edwards, who sang songs and played the ukelele and was known as Ukelele Ike. His contract required that he do his specialty between ten o'clock and ten fifteen! So we had to construct our story in such a way that Ukelele Ike could come out and perform during that time and still not interfere with the continuity. In addition to Marilyn Miller, the star, there was Jack Donahue, the famous dancing comedian, and there was Clifton Webb and Mary Hay, who were a leading dance team of the time, Joseph Cawthorn, a star comedian, Esther Howard, another, Paul Frawley, the leading juvenile. In addition to the orchestra in the pit we had also to take care of George Olsen's Dance Band on the stage.[6]

To be sure, *Sunny* was a hit, which suggests that those producers knew something about public expectations. On the other hand, *Show Boat* too was a hit, which perhaps indicates that audiences will not hesitate to embrace good theater when they have the chance to experience it.

The more serious operettas of Victor Herbert, Rudolf Friml, and Sigmund

Romberg, all Europeans with classical training, offered the coherent plot and musical integration that the musical comedy lacked, but undermined any significant dramatic effect by removing the story far away from the real experience of the audience. They are typically historical fictions or fairy tales set in exotic places, such as a European court or the Sahara desert, and involve disguised heroes, mistaken identities, and the like. In its tone the operetta parallels nineteenth-century melodrama, which, according to Eric Bentley, was designed to arouse a little bit of anxiety in the audience without direct confrontation or involvement:

> One can see which elements of melodrama aroused anxiety: the hideous happenings of the plot, the terrible dangers, the wickedness of the world and of the villain. How were these things kept under control?
> By a remoteness and exoticism, both of geography and style, which told the spectator: we don't mean you.[7]

In short, audiences were fascinated but seldom moved. It is an interesting point that not a few of the lasting musicals of the 1940s and 1950s are also set in exotic environments: *South Pacific, Brigadoon,* and *Fiddler on the Roof* come immediately to mind. Yet these avoid the trap that claimed nearly all American operettas. The difference is this: though these latter plays may be set in faraway, even mythical, places and times, the dramatic issues in them do not depend on the exotic at all, but derive from the commonest of experiences. How many have wrestled with the sort of social prejudice that confronts Nellie and Lt. Cable, with the choice between security and the ultimate risk of loving that Charlie Dalrymple must make, and with the generation-gap problems of Tevye? At least, sympathy for such characters comes easily. It is much more difficult to take so seriously Margot Bonvalet's dilemma in *The Desert Song* (1926), when she agonizes over loving a disguised outlawed revolutionary whom she has never really met.

The quality of the music in both of these genres is really not at issue. Victor Herbert, Romberg, and Friml, as well as Kern, Gershwin, Rodgers, and others, wrote many, many songs which long outlasted the shows that first presented them. They were picked up by arrangers and jazz musicians to be played again and again as standards. The failure was entirely dramatic, a failure of courage, really, on the part of composers, librettists, and producers to confront their audiences with real dramatic situations. "Tea for Two" is a good song by Vincent Youmans which has attracted listeners for generations, but if that is the deepest expression of love that the young couple in *No, No, Nanette* can manage, then no one need be surprised that the audience comes away merely amused, at best. The viewers were never seriously engaged.

*Show Boat* has had at least one revival in New York City in each decade since its first performance, and countless revivals elsewhere. It has attracted the attention of even serious opera companies; in 1954 it was performed by the New York City Opera, with Julius Rudel conducting, and in 1983 by the Houston Grand Opera.

With the exception of the first one in 1932, each major revival has occasioned revisions of the play, and some of these have been significant. The 1946 revival cut three scenes, added Jerome Kern's last composition ''Nobody Else But Me,'' and replaced his motivically constructed prologue to Act I with a traditional medley overture composed by orchestrator Robert Russell Bennett. The song was dropped thereafter, but this 1946 version is generally the one marketed and performed today.

Critical assessment by journalists has varied little in the sixty-year history of the show. There is some consensus in the later decades that the dialogue is dated and that there is some awkwardness in the plot, especially at the end, but all writers point to the continuing freshness and appeal of the music.

The one part of the musical that was never changed in any of its major revivals is the first scene of the first act, and it is this scene that is Kern and Hammerstein's best achievement in musical dramaturgy. The musical theater has precious little time to establish its characters and main plot premises because musical expression takes up so much more time than speech. This scene's significant success is its integration of plot and character exposition with dramatic action, so that in barely fifteen minutes the audience is introduced to five main characters, three conflicts, two social norms, and a love story which is already developed in the music. All this is unified by a frame defined by the music.

The curtain rises to reveal the river levee at a Mississippi town crowded by black stevedores who are stacking bales of cotton. The showboat *Cotton Blossom* is moored upstage. The opening ''crowd scene'' was virtually required by the conventions of the 1920s; this one, however, is boldly unconventional in its immediate portrayal of racial inequity. After a brief introduction based on a chromatic leitmotif associated with the Sheriff Vallon, the tempo becomes *animato* and the stevedores begin to sing:[8]

**Ex. 2–1** Kern and Hammerstein, *Show Boat,* "Opening" (No. 1), mm. 13–20.

The musical setting for this uncompromising lyric is as simple as could be, employing mainly tonic and subdominant harmony, and yet Kern manages to evoke an ethnic flavor in the melody by recalling the "gapped" scale, missing the seventh step, on the word "Mississippi." The texture is enlivened somewhat when the women's chorus (the "gals") joins the men's with a contrasting section in G-sharp minor based on the same motives. The men sing a counterpoint of a work call motive beneath.

A cynical listener could well remark that the music does not come close to expressing the sentiment of the lyric. The melody is set in E major and its rhythm seems just too cheerful. This criticism must be dismissed, however, when the original tune returns, now sung by both men and women. Kern reharmonizes the refrain with a chromatic bass, whose "blue" sixth and seventh steps not only heighten the ethnic flavor of the chorus but express the black community's feeling of resignation about its position. This reharmonization is all the more effective for having been denied on the first hearing.

**Ex. 2-2**   Kern and Hammerstein, *Show Boat,* "Opening" (No. 1), mm. 29–36.

The first musical section of the scene then concludes with another motive emphasizing the gapped scale.

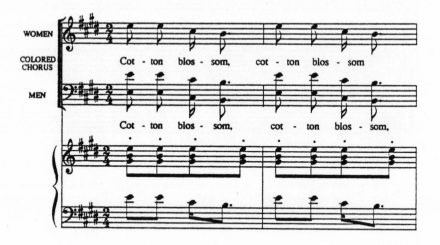

**Ex. 2–3**  Kern and Hammerstein, *Show Boat*, "Opening" (No. 1), mm. 37–44.

At this point the orchestra plays under a brief dialogue, in which the audience is introduced to Steve, the leading actor of the showboat troupe, Pete, the villianous engineer, and Queenie, the black cook. The orchestra plays a leitmotif which stands for Julie Laverne, the leading actress, even though she does not appear. The rationale for this is that Steve and Pete will soon quarrel over Julie, but on the whole the rapid introduction and alternation of motives in this interlude is rather clumsy.

The crowd on stage is then increased by the entrance of a white women's chorus playing the local town beauties ("mincing misses" in the libretto) and a white men's chorus of "town beaux." The men begin with this salute.

**Ex. 2–4**  Kern and Hammerstein, *Show Boat,* "Opening" (No. 1), mm. 93–101.

The slower rhythm and smoother lyricism of the tune makes a clear differentiation between the racial groups, which of course is Kern's purpose, but the new music is not without connections to the old. Clearly, the motive in measure 93 recalls the first black chorus tune (mm. 13–14) both in rhythm and in shape, and the sixth step of the scale is emphasized ("bevy") because of the following rest, again recalling the gapped scale so characteristic of the opening chorus. The women respond with the same tune, then modulate to F major, the mediant key to D-flat, the same relationship constructed by the E – G-sharp modulation of the black chorus.

When the music returns to D-flat, the beaux introduce a new melody.

**Ex. 2–5**  Kern and Hammerstein, *Show Boat*, "Opening" (No. 1), mm. 118–24.

Here the dotted rhythms so characteristic of the black chorus are reintroduced, but even the more lyrical first two measures recall the *Cotton Blossom* motive in its shape and emphasis on the sixth step of the scale.

These motivic connections are not frivolous. They make possible the climactic joining of the four singing groups that finishes the choral number of the first

**Fig. 2–1**  Comparison of motives from Exs. 2–3 and 2–5.

scene. As the white people sing in anticipation of the evening's show, Kern adds the black choruses singing a work call outlining a dissonant E minor seventh over a pedal of A. Finally all the singers are united by the *Cotton Blossom* motive.

**Ex. 2–6**  Kern and Hammerstein, *Show Boat,* "Opening" (No. 1), mm. 142–49.

The ironic lyric maintains the distinction between the two social groups, but the ensemble makes musical sense because of Kern's careful preparation of the motivic material. In an audible way, the two groups, black and white, have shared the same material throughout.

The next section of this opening scene shows much less musical integration; its function is to introduce the main characters and conflicts as efficiently as possible. Hammerstein fashions the scene around a typical arrival of the showboat to a new river town. There is a parade and, once a crowd has gathered, a short presentation of the principal actors. This ploy familiarizes the audience with most of the main characters at a single stroke: Captain Andy, the troup leader; Parthy Ann, his shrewish wife; Julie, the leading lady; Frank and Ellie Chipley, the comic actors and dancers. In the course of the scene, the quarrel between Pete and Steve over Julie erupts suddenly; Pete is fired from troupe, and leaves swearing revenge. Except for one chorus number for the admiring townspeople ("Captain Andy"), the music here functions as a prop: the march of the parade, the dance music for the short presentation.

Two characters remain to be seen: Magnolia, Captain Andy's daughter, and Gaylord Ravenal, an aristocratic river gambler who will soon join the showboat troupe. They are introduced singly, in such a way that the audience instinctively and immediately recognizes them as the principals of the play.

Magnolia is only mentioned in dialogue at first, and, more important, is associated at once with a piece of music. A simple tune, played on the piano, is heard coming offstage from the interior of the *Cotton Blossom*.[9] One of the awestruck children asks of Parthy Ann:

GIRL: Is that your little girl playing the piano?
PARTHY: Yep—ain't so little any more—eighteen this comin' August.[10]

This occurs before the parade and quarrel. Shortly after Pete's departure, Ravenal strolls onstage to the accompaniment of a new theme in the orchestra, which is quickly interrupted by the chromatic sheriff's motive when Vallon appears. He and Ravenal converse:

VALLON: Back in town, Gay?
RAVENAL: For a short stay.
VALLON: Can't be more than twenty-four hours, you know.
RAVENAL: Give me time, can't you? I haven't been 24 hours stepping off the gangplank to this wharf, have I? . . . I can get on just as quickly.
VALLON: No offense, Gay. Jest though I'd remind you in case of trouble—it'd be terrible to have you locked up—all the purty gals on the river front'd be cryin' their eyes out. Where you aim to go from here?
RAVENAL: Who cares? Who cares where I go?
VALLON: Seegar?

(*As he proffers it, Ravenal takes it, sniffs at it and raises his eyebrows disdainfully*).

RAVENAL: What did you call it?
VALLON: Seegar!
RAVENAL: Optimist![11]

This exchange sketches Ravenal's character very quickly. He has no roots and is in some kind of legal trouble; he is also handsome, even dashing, and has aristocratic tastes. When Vallon leaves, Ravenal begins to sing a song which plays on these characteristics, and begins the most important dramatic development of the first scene.

Ravenal begins by singing two four-bar periods which make up an antecedent phrase of a melody.

**Ex. 2–7** Kern and Hammerstein, *Show Boat*, "Opening" (No. 1), mm. 351–58.

The harmonization of this antecedent could hardly be simpler, limited as it is to tonic and dominant harmony. The consequent phrase, which begins with exactly the same melodic gesture, takes quite a different turn.

**Ex. 2–8** Kern and Hammerstein, *Show Boat,* "Opening" (No. 1), mm. 359–70.

The plain authentic cadence in the third measure is now turned into a more expressive deceptive cadence (V-vi), adding an urgent continuity that requires an extra four-bar period at the end of the tune for its proper resolution. The antecedent phrase of eight bars is therefore balanced by a convincing consequent of twelve. This added weight at the end causes the listener to doubt Ravenal's rhetorical queries at the outset and to pay more attention to his wondering "where's the mate for me?" A change of character not at all implied by the lyric has been suggested quite firmly by the music.

Ravenal's musings are interrupted by the sound of a piano coming from the *Cotton Blossom*. The audience knows the tune already, and who is playing it, but Ravenal, unaware of this, turns to listen. The first encounter with Magnolia is made.

**Ex. 2–9**  Kern and Hammerstein, *Show Boat,* "Opening" (No. 1), mm. 370–86.

The little tune is set in G major, in subdominant relation to Ravenal's melody. At this point, the orchestra takes up the phrase and effects a very distant modulation to F-sharp major (mm. 381-86). This cadence is turned into a dominant and Ravenal resumes his singing, taking up the piano motive in the key of B minor, the relative minor of his original D major, and immediately enters upon an expressive descending melodic sequence.

Ex. 2–10   Kern and Hammerstein, *Show Boat*, "Opening" (No. 1), mm. 386–94.

The sequence never really leaves the key of B minor, but since it is the descending minor scale that is heard, the pitches used are the same ones of Ravenal's original key of D. The piquant lowering of the A-sharp to A natural in the very last phrase thus makes explicit what was already implied: a return to the local tonic.

Kern has turned again to the same procedure he used in Ravenal's first address, and made it more expansive. The harmonization of the orchestral transition and Ravenal's new phrases is so startling in comparison to the relatively simple harmonies heard earlier that the expression of his true feelings about the conflict of freedom and love is unmistakable. Moreover, because of the motivic connection with the little piano tune, the audience realizes the cause and solution of these longings even before he realizes them himself.

The A major chord, acting as dominant, makes the transition back to Ravenal's original theme for the song's conclusion.

**Ex. 2–11** Kern and Hammerstein, *Showboat,* "Opening" (No. 1), mm. 395–409.

Now the cadence in the third measure (m. 396) is made more expressive than ever by the use of the deceptive in minor (V-VI7), undermining any remaining allegiance to the freedom about which he sings.

Ravenal is taken aback by her address; she seems naïve, not knowing that she should wait for the gentleman to speak first. The interlude music behind their dialogue is neutral, except for a brief recapitulation of the piano tune, the modulation to the leading tone key by the strings, and the following sequence in minor, all of which reinforces the musical connections between the two characters. The audience learns that Magnolia wishes she were an actress, since actresses may make believe they are various exciting characters. She starts to leave because she realizes that she and Ravenal have not been properly introduced, but Ravenal suggests that they make believe, as actors do, that they have been introduced and that they have fallen in love at first sight!

make be-lieve that you love me. Oth-ers find peace of

mind in pre-tend-ing; Could-n't you? could-n't

I? could-n't we? Make be-lieve our lips are

**Ex. 2–12**  Kern and Hammerstein, *Show Boat,* "Make Believe" (No. 2), mm. 5–37.

In its form, use of chromaticism, and melodic sequences, the song is a typical example of a popular song of Tin Pan Alley. Again, the musical interest is directed forward, toward the end, this time by careful placing of chromatic harmony. The first phrase has no trace of chromaticism; the second ("Others find

. . .'') introduces a touch, mostly in the interest of setting up an important dominant chord at the end. The emotional intensity is suddenly and forcefully increased at the beginning of the third phrase, however, when the opening motive is set with diminished harmony (VI +) instead of the vague tonic with which the song began. This phrase too ends with chromatic alterations, but the most explicit chromatic writing is saved for the fourth and final phrase. The climactic lyric is set to rising chromatic lines in both bass and in the inner parts. The song ends with the same melody with which it began, now retaining its diminished harmony.

This emphasis on the end of the song encourages the audience to take Ravenal's last words more seriously than the first, as before in his soliloquy. Clearly his expressions of love are more than play-acting, more than ''make believe.'' To say so explicitly, as he does, however, is a breach of etiquette, and so even as he makes the cadence to his song, the music slips into a mild waltz and he begins to apologize.

**Ex. 2–13**  Kern and Hammerstein, *Show Boat*, "Make Believe" (No. 2), mm. 37–53.

Magnolia, in her first musical entrance, however, interrupts his apology, finishing his melody by reminding him that they were only pretending to be lovers. In this she shows a maturity far beyond her years. She has saved Ravenal, who as an aristocrat prides himself on his sense of propriety, from a very embarrassing situation with consummate grace. She relieves the situation further by elaborating on the joys of pretense, to a much lighter theme than Ravenal's waltz.

**Ex. 2–14**  Kern and Hammerstein, *Show Boat,* "Make Believe (No. 2), mm. 53–69.

This theme recalls the music of the offstage piano both in its melodic shape and its placement in the key subdominant to the principal key of "Make Believe." The music, then, succeeds in maintaining her ingenue character while resolving this difficult situation, since the little piano tune was her introduction to the action.

Ravenal, relieved, echoes her sentiments by repeating the new theme. This is the sort of quick, reflexive agreement that always occurs when two people are trying to paper over an obvious faux pas. The music now moves into a disjointed, accompanied recitative texture in which Magnolia reaffirms the rational basis for make believe. The real purpose of the passage seems to be to return to the original "Make Believe" tune, this time set a semitone higher than before.[12]

The recapitulation of "Make Believe" not only rounds out the form of this musical section, but also fulfills a dramatic necessity by allowing Magnolia to offer her own love in the same terms as has Ravenal. These sentiments, of course, grow logically out of her excuses, but as before, the music contradicts the characters' professions of "make believe." After Magnolia sings the first two phrases (same as Ravenal in Ex. 2-12), Ravenal sings the third, and finally, both sing together in the fourth phrase, the one with the most intense rising chromaticism.

**Ex. 2–15** Kern and Hammerstein, *Show Boat,* "Make Believe" (No. 2), mm. 111–19.[13]

During the climax of the chromatic progression, the two break into parts, and Magnolia rises to the high G, the highest sustained note of this section.

Although this duet is the center of the opening scene, it is not its conclusion. As soon as the lovers have finished singing, Vallon returns to escort Ravenal away for a conversation with the local magistrate. At the same time, Joe, a black stevedore, enters carrying a sack of flour. Magnolia, entirely enchanted, asks Joe whether he saw the young "gentleman," and he allows that he has seen many like him on the river. She runs off to tell her best friend Julie, and Joe muses to himself about what he has seen:

JOE: Better ask de ol' man river what he thinks. He knows all 'bout dem boys . . .
He knows all 'bout ever' thin.[14]

The introduction of Joe as the Everyman figure of the play is perhaps somewhat awkward, but his musical number is a superb conclusion to the first scene
of *Show Boat*. His introductory quatrain is set to exactly the same music as the
very beginning of the scene ("Niggers all work on de Mississipi . . ."), but
the words are different, the tempo is greatly slowed, and with only strings accompanying, the tune seems quite transformed to the point that many would not
recognize it as a recapitulation. This is followed by the famous refrain (see Fig.
2-2). The middle section of the refrain again recasts music from the opening
number, this time the "gals'" song which is set in the mediant key.

**Ex. 2–16**  Kern and Hammerstein, *Show Boat,* "Ol' Man River" (No. 3), mm. 25–32.

This passage is dignified much more than its first occurrence by the slower tempo
and by the transition back toward the tonic of C major. The moment of modulation (m. 32, "jail") is made clear by the D minor chord, negating both the

leading tone and supertonic of the mediant key of E minor, and is always emphasized by the singer. During the last phrase of the refrain, Joe is joined by the
chorus of stevedores that opened the scene. Now the reference to that opening
becomes explicit in the lyric:

JOE: Niggers all work on de Mississippi
    Niggers all work while de white folks play.
    Pullin' dem boats from de dawn to sunset,
      Gitten' no rest till de Judgment Day.
MEN: Don't look up an' don't look down,
    You don't dast make de white boss frown;
    Bend yo' knees an' bow yo' head,
    an pull dat rope until yo're dead. (etc.)

The music then returns to the refrain of "Ol' Man River" for a climactic choral
rendition.

This song was almost instantly acclaimed by critics as the leitmotif for the
entire play, and indeed it is used in just such a manner throughout the remainder.
Its first occurrence, however, by recalling the essential themes and even the same
performers from the play's beginning, provides a convincing structural close to
this lengthy and dramatically ambitious opening scene. The musical recapitulations in "Ol' Man River," however, are not just a structural rounding for the
scene, but constitute yet another dramatic development. Each theme is transformed in a simple yet effective way. The unavoidable impression at the scene's
end is that although the love match is to be the primary dramatic focus, social
injustice will provide a most serious backdrop for that story and affect its course
in important ways.

Even if the song had not been placed in the larger musical context so effectively, "Ol' Man River" would still be counted as the most important musical
achievement of the play. Certainly a number of technical details contribute to
this impression: the mild syncopation in the main motive, the emphasis again on
the sixth step which gives the tune such an ethnic flavor, and the weak beat
chords in the winds which effectively paint the swell of the Mississippi. The real
power of the song, however, derives from its overall melodic design, without
which these details would seem like mere decorations.

Kern's melody is a triumph over the standard form for an American popular
song, a form that has survived to some extent to the present day: A A B A. The
advantages of such a form are immediately obvious; there is some repetition and
some contrast. It is really an elaboration of the centuries-old ternary form (A B
A). For dramatic uses, however, the form has one clear disadvantage, in that the
song must end with the same music with which it began. In other words, a
melodic idea conceived as a beginning must also function as an ending. In many
examples less fortunate than "Ol' Man River" the effect is one of a static or
even anti-dramatic emotion.

Clearly there must be some adjustment in the final phrase, and such adjustments were part of the expert songwriter's craft. Richard Rodgers often solved this problem by an extension of the phrase. Here is an example from *Oklahoma!*.

**Ex. 2–17** Rodgers and Hammerstein, *Oklahoma,* "I Cain't Say No", mm. 22–29, 54–77.

The fourth phrase, based on the same melodic idea as the first, is more than twice as long. The extension begins when the melodic course to the fifth degree of the scale is delayed, first by changing the harmony so that the tune goes up only to the fourth degree, and then by chromatic elaborations on the notes around the fifth degree. This extension intensifies the comic effect of the song by mak-

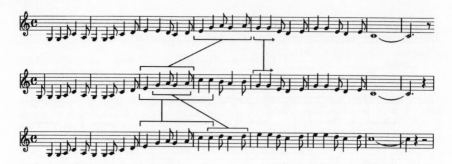

**Fig. 2-2**  Diagram comparing the first, second, and fourth phrases of Kern and Hammerstein's "Ol' Man River."

ing Ado Annie seem more flustered and unstable than ever, because the chromaticism makes the music seem unstable. More important, the extension turns what would be a disappointing return into a climax. The dramatic development of the character has moved forward in the face of a form that should compel retreat.

Kern's solution is quite different from the device of extending the final phrase. Instead, he incorporates into his melodic design subtle changes which produce a climax in the final phrase without giving up any sense of balanced proportion (see Fig. 2-2).

The first phrase has a typical arch contour, rising a major ninth from G up to A, the sixth degree of the scale. Quite untypical of a popular melody is the motivic consistency of the phrase; every measure has exactly the same rhythmic pattern until the cadence on the low C. The second phrase, which is supposed to echo the first one according to the A A B A pattern, does indeed sound the same. The diagram makes clear, however, that Kern has shifted the fourth measure of the first phrase to become the third measure of the second phrase. Thus, what the listener takes to be the peak of the first phrase occurs earlier, and this inspires the continuation up to the high C on "soon forgotten." The subtlety of this alteration in the melody is such that one barely notices any change at all. It is made possible by the motivic consistency, so that one measure seems so easily substituted for another. The listener, already familiar with the melodic course up to the high A in the first phrase, takes it as a matter of course in the second, even though it is earlier. The original peak of the contour is replaced by a smooth continuation that achieves an even higher peak at the same point in time.

After the B section, or "release," the main melody returns. Again the high A is reached by the third measure, and again the high C seems to be the peak in the fourth. But in his most imaginative and yet logical stroke yet, Kern does not reverse the contour; rather, he continues the upward motion to a high E and makes the final cadence on the high C rather than the low one.

The climactic moment of "Ol' Man River" is generated from within, made possible by the extremely rare, if not unique, motivic consistency within each phrase. In this way Kern overcomes the inherent anti-dramatic nature of the form without doing away with it.

So ends the first scene of *Show Boat*. There are a number of other fine musical moments in the play, but Kern and Hammerstein never again attempt musical-dramatic integration on such a large scale. It is important to note, and characteristic of the American popular stage, that the one tragic moment of the first act, the dismissal of Julie and Steve on a miscegenation charge, has no operatic setting. There is only a response by the black chorus, a brief verse of "Misery," a lament which was cut down during tryouts. It will be a long time before Broadway musicians succeed in setting that sort of serious scene to music.

The remainder of the plot in the first act carries forward the love story, until the finale concludes with the wedding of Ravenal and Magnolia, attended by townspeople with extended musical celebration. The second act, whose story takes place largely away from the *Cotton Blossom,* has been criticized on several counts. The plot concerns Ravenal's gambling problems, his general decline, and his eventual desertion of Magnolia and Kim, their daughter. There is no musical expression for this dissolution. Magnolia goes on to an acting career in her own right. Events bring her back to the *Cotton Blossom* for the finale, to be reunited by a series of coincidences with all her old acquaintances from the first act. Most improbably, Ravenal also appears and the old couple is reconciled at the play's end. Even Miles Kreuger, whose admiration for *Show Boat* produced a monograph study, finds little credibility in this finale:

There is simply no way to rationalize the return of Ravenal. It is clearly an immature concession to musical comedy convention that in days to come Hammerstein himself would help abolish. It is very likely that, had *Show Boat* been adapted for the stage one decade later, Hammerstein would have adhered to Miss Ferber's elimination of the gambler and not permitted him to reappear.[15]

The weakness of the second act is underscored by the lack of new musical material. Only one dramatic number, "Why Do I Love You?," occurs after intermission. The remainder of the music consists of reprises, incidental music, and songs which might be called "prop songs."

A prop song is one which is sung because the character finds himself in a situation which demands or accommodates singing. It might be Don Giovanni serenading a lover, or Adelaide leading the Hot Box Girls at the local club. These songs are part of the scenery, like props, quite distinct from songs which are expressions of a character's emotions, and for which the operatic suspension of disbelief obtains. These appear quite frequently in European operas, and often the composer is at pains to show that the meaning of the character's singing is different. In *The Marriage of Figaro,* Susanna plays a guitar (with pizzicato accompaniment from the pit orchestra) while Cherubino sings his canzonet to the Countess, and Don Giovanni must play a mandolin when singing his second act serenade. Verdi creates a strong-beat, popular orchestral texture for the drinking song in the first act of *Otello*. These devices indicate that the character may no longer be expressing himself, but is performing a song as part of the story.

The best example of the pure prop song in *Show Boat* is "After the Ball," which Magnolia sings as part of a nightclub act in Chicago. There is nothing in the music which further defines her character, emphasizes her emotional state, or brings the action along. She sings because singing is the action. To be sure, the choice of "After the Ball," a tremendously popular song by Charles K. Harris written at the turn of the century, was fortuitous for an audience in 1927, for it was assured of being immediately recognized and yet nostalgic. But these are sentiments of the audience, not of Magnolia.

In other cases, the distinction between what a character sings as a prop song and what he or she really feels is not so clear. In the first act, "Can't Help Lovin' Dat Man" is introduced as Julie's favorite song, purportedly a black folk song. In this sense it is a prop song; it is like a stage prop. However, the lyrics of this "folk song" reflect her own situation quite closely. She loves Steve, an untalented, rather lazy sort, in spite of herself. The same analysis would apply to "Bill" in the second act. This song is performed as part of a nightclub rehearsal, but in another sense Julie, who by this time has been deserted by Steve, is singing about herself in truth.

Despite such subtleties, an act of a musical that contains a high proportion of such prop songs cannot have the dramatic impact that operatic expression is supposed to have. Even in the ambiguous cases such as those mentioned, the dramatic impact of such songs must be weakened, because the audience can never be sure of how much of the sentiment belongs to the character.

Given the wide admiration that *Show Boat* has sustained, not only upon its opening in 1927, but through its first revival in 1932 and in the following decades, it is a wonder that this musical did not effect an instant reform of musical theater practice. Yet the next decade reveals only one work that seems to have learned some of the lessons taught by *Show Boat* well enough to survive—*Porgy and Bess,*—and many would argue that Gershwin's *magnum opus* really stands outside the Broadway tradition. It is more puzzling still considering that the teachers of the lesson, Jerome Kern and Oscar Hammerstein II, continued to work both separately and together and yet did not see such achievement again. There were innovations of the 1930s, to be sure, in the area of musical satire, such as Gershwin's *Of Thee I Sing* (1931), and in Weill and Blitzstein's politically oriented works later in the decade. But in these the political themes dominated, and so did not last beyond the memory of their relevant targets.

One explanation often offered is that the Depression discouraged "serious" musicals because, in view of the conditions, audiences did not want to hear them. The financial constraints in turn discouraged producers from backing innovations and experiments, and it is certainly true that ticket prices were lower and runs shorter than in the 1920s. But the satirical musicals thrived on innovation and were quite successful, and *Porgy and Bess* itself was staged in the depths of the Depression (1935). Lehman Engel, considering what he regards as the pre-history of the mature American musical, has a deeper explanation:

> During these first forty years of *new* musicals in this country, men of enormous and fresh talent composed some of their best music and/or lyrics but, lacking models, what they accomplished, though successful for a time, is unfortunately unreproduceable today.[16]

It took a long time to learn the lessons of *Show Boat* simply because the lessons are so difficult. Remembering that even the most unpretentious types of operas are collaborative efforts, and remembering the failure rates of even the greatest opera composers, it seems less surprising that the fragile though real achievement of *Show Boat* was not repeated for some time, even by Kern and Hammerstein. There are so many things that must fall into place just right, and so many types of mature experience that must be coordinated.

The influence of *Show Boat* was perhaps subliminal or subconscious, but there is no doubt that members of the younger generation of stage composers, especially George Gershwin and Richard Rodgers, were impressed by the play, for it revealed what the Broadway stage could create if given the right materials and appropriate vision. It established a new set of dramatic ideals, ideals only approximated in the 1930s, but realized again and again thereafter.

# CHAPTER 3

# America's
# Folk Opera

*I think the music is so marvelous—I really don't believe I wrote it.*[1]

GEORGE GERSHWIN

By one of those curious coincidences of history, George Gershwin was inspired to compose *Porgy and Bess* at about the same time and in just the same way that Jerome Kern got his idea for *Show Boat*. After a trying rehearsal of his newest musical comedy *Oh, Kay!* in the fall of 1926, Gershwin tried to fall asleep by reading DuBose Heyward's recent novel, *Porgy*. Instead, as Heyward's wife Dorothy recounted later, he "read himself wide awake" and became enthralled with the dramatic prospects of the story. By four o'clock in the morning the composer was writing to Heyward, inquiring if he might be interested in turning *Porgy* into an opera.[2]

DuBose Heyward was an early figure in the Southern Renascence of American literature and the foremost author of the so-called Charleston writers.[3] *Porgy* was his first novel, published in 1925, and ultimately his best-known work. It portrays a black community in Charleston during a summer around the turn of the century. The principal character, Porgy, a crippled beggar who transports himself in a goat-drawn cart, was modeled after a somewhat notorious figure of Heyward's native Charleston known as "Goat Sammy." The plot of the book is extremely loose, "seemingly little more than a series of vignettes in structure."[4] One of its most unusual features is the recurrence of songs and spirituals sung by the community at large. For Heyward, these songs were the most economical means to his end of expressing the collective spirit of the community:

The spiritual said everything for him [the black man] that he could not say in the new language that he found here—awe in the presence of death—his racial terror of being left alone—his escape from bondage into the new heaven—everything.[5]

It could have been these spirituals that attracted Gershwin, or perhaps Heyward's apparent success in getting at the heart of the black community, for Gershwin was already interested in black culture. In 1922, as part of a revue he was writing for *George White's Scandals,* he composed a twenty-minute one-act music drama called *Blue Monday,* with a libretto by G. B. "Buddy" DeSylva. The story, set in Harlem, involves two young men vying for the love of a woman and ends with the woman shooting her lover on suspicion of infidelity. The number was roundly criticized and White withdrew it after a single performance. A revival by Paul Whiteman in 1925 under the title *135th Street* proved no more successful. The critical consensus is that Gerswhin, trying to set a soap-opera libretto, had too little experience in serious dramatic composition.[6]

Despite Gershwin's and Heyward's initial enthusiasm for the new project, there was a hiatus of nine years between Gershwin's first reading of *Porgy* and the premiere of the opera in Boston in September 1935. The first obstacle was Dorothy Heyward, a playwright with several works to her credit, who told her astonished husband that she had already begun to turn the novel into a play, which eventually became a successful production of Broadway's Theatre Guild. This seemed to upset Gershwin not in the least. Dorothy recalls that "It was a great moment when George said there was plenty of room for both play and opera. And plenty of time. He wanted to spend years in study before composing his opera."[7] The last statement reveals no polite assurance on Gershwin's part. His detached estimation of his own talents and of his own music is a characteristic that recurs in almost all Gershwin biographical writing, and in 1926 the failure of *Blue Monday,* his only other attempt at serious music drama so far, could not have been far from his mind.

A second obstacle was Gershwin's own busy career. The late 1920s saw him engaged to write a series of musical comedies for the production team of Alex Aarons and Vinton Freedley, along with his brother Ira as lyricist and Guy Bolton as librettist.

At first, it was the producers' intention to have these shows follow the bright, witty pattern of the old Princess Theatre attractions, only, according to Guy Bolton, on a larger scale. . . . Despite these intentions, the shows soon became star vehicles rather than closely coordinated book-and-music shows.[8]

However, a much more significant series of Gershwin musical plays opened in 1930, in collaboration with librettists George S. Kaufman and Morrie Ryskind, beginning with *Strike Up the Band,* and continuing with *Of Thee I Sing* (1931) and *Let 'Em Eat Cake* (1933). These are often called "satirical operettas" and in these works Gershwin makes a significant advance integrating the music with the story.

The most successful of the three was *Of Thee I Sing*. A story about a fictitious political campaign and presidential administration in which the main issue is "Love," the play successfully lampooned "hush-hush scandals, nonsensical debates, party politics, under-the-counter deals, political campaigns, and ridiculous bids for votes."[9] The play is undoubtedly an important landmark in the history of the American musical, running for 441 performances at the Music Box Theater, winning the 1932 Pulitzer Prize for Drama, becoming the first musical comedy to be published as a book, and attracting praise from all quarters for its musical and dramatic innovations. Despite all this, it has not survived in the repertoire, and critics are equally agreed about the reason, best explained by Lehman Engel:

> In *Of Thee I Sing* (1931) most of the comedy comes out of contemporary political situations. It worked well enough in its own time to win the Pulitzer Prize.
>
> Today it is meaningless, and the show, because it is built squarely on comedy, cannot be revived. It is significant that—and this is surely an important indication of modern-day artistry—the songs, *including* the lyrics, are not dated. The lyrics are universal and therefore enduring. Only the "comic" dialogue is entirely dated, and *Of Thee I Sing*, once funny because of it, is now impossible to revive because of it.[10]

Because of these shows, Gershwin did not begin work on *Porgy and Bess* until 1933. In retrospect, however, the delay must be considered most fortuitous, and the time between the initial inspiration and his actual composition well spent, for surely the satirical operettas constituted the most important part of the "study" he told DuBose Heyward that he wished to make. It should not be forgotten, too, that Gershwin was only twenty-eight years old when he read the novel, and that the gain in artistic maturity in those busy years was probably significant. Indeed, Stanley Green sees Gershwin's compositional *oeuvre* as an uninterrupted progression that, had he not died in 1937 of a brain tumor, was quite unlimited in its promise:

> His entire career had been the most steady, step-by-step advance of any theatre composer. There was some overlapping, but it is remarkable that his rise was so chronologically systematic—from revues (1920–1924), to musical comedies (1924-1930), to satirical comic operas (1931–1933), to an American folk-opera (1935).[11]

Gershwin himself seems to have realized that *Porgy and Bess* was to be his most important composition to date, representing an unprecedented attempt by a Broadway composer to write a serious music drama. As Heyward converted *Porgy* from stage play to opera libretto, along with certain lyric contributions from Ira Gershwin,[12] George spent eleven months composing the music (from February 1934 to January 1935), and nine more laborious months orchestrating it (from January to September 1935), a prodigious length of concentrated effort for any Broadway composer.[13] Because he refused to have the opera done in blackface, black professional singers were recruited from all over the country. There was even a special rehearsal in order to test the orchestrations, an aspect of Gershwin's compositions that had attracted criticism, and still does. Critic Irving Kolodin observed the intense preparations:

> Watching this American folk-opera grow to perfected performance as a theatre work through months of careful rehearsal aimed to unify the drama and the music, the singing and the acting, has been an illuminating experience to a musician accustomed to the perfunctory and uncorrelated rehearsal generally accorded to the productions prepared for the conventional opera.[14]

After a triumphant tryout at the Colonial Theatre in Boston on September 20, 1935, the Theatre Guild presented *Porgy and Bess* to Broadway at the Alvin Theater on October 10, 1935, exactly eight years after the premiere of *Porgy* the stage play.

Except for an intensely symbolic analysis by Wilfrid Mellers,[15] almost all serious dramatic criticism of *Porgy and Bess* has been blunted and forestalled by preoccupation with three other matters.

The first is a concern over exactly what is the "authentic" version of the opera. This is a relatively recent concern, brought about by a history of revival that recorded various cut versions and spurred by a steadily growing appreciation of the opera's value. The first revival, a very successful production for Broadway by Cheryl Crawford in 1942, deleted many of the recitatives. Subsequent revivals in the 1950s restored much of this music, but often altered the order of numbers given in Gershwin's piano-vocal score published in 1935. Thus, when in 1976 Lorin Maazel and the Cleveland Orchestra recorded all the music in Gershwin's original 1935 score, and the Houston opera produced a "complete" stage version, these events were hailed as events that, for the first time, revealed the true greatness of the opera.

As is often the case with matters of authenticity, however, especially in opera, the issue is rarely so simple. Ironically, the original production at the Alvin, under Gershwin's constant and direct supervision, was cut. Rouben Mamoulian, the production's director, wrote three years later that *"Porgy and Bess* as performed in New York was almost forty-five minutes shorter than the original score,"* which was sent to the publisher six months in advance of the premiere.[16] Excluded were the opening piano solo, known as the Jazzbo Brown music, the "Buzzard Song," Maria's denunciation of Sportin' Life in Act II, much of Porgy's solo and the following trio in Act III, and many other snippets from the score.[17]

Why did Gershwin cut music from his original score? Was the opera cut to make it conform to the normal length of a Broadway show, as *Show Boat* was, or were there deeper dramatic reasons? Was Gershwin convinced that they would improve the opera, or simply increase its chances for profit? Ewen writes, unfortunately without citation, that "these cuts hurt Gershwin, who loved every note; but, showman that he was, he accepted them willingly and often insisted on them." [18] But Todd Duncan, the original Porgy, recalls:

> He was upset in Boston. My God, that opening night was killing. I think it was four hours. We performed the whole opera and we didn't get out until one o'clock or something. George didn't want one beautiful blessed note cut. He and [stage director] Mamoulian and [musical director] Smallens walked in the Boston Common all night long, fighting and fussing and talking about it. . . . all that last part that I sang, George Gershwin wrote for my voice. He wrote that after he met me and after he heard me. But it was just too much for one man to sing at the end of an opera. . . .[19]

Charles Hamm's study reveals that cuts were made from the time of the first rehearsals, through the tryout in Boston, up to the New York premiere in October. According to rehearsal scores, they seem to have been the direct result of stage experience, and since Gershin was in constant attendance during rehearsals, they must have had his approval, painful though they may have been to make.[20]

Such a multiplicity of versions places *Porgy and Bess* in the same confusing situation that obtains with a great many classical operas. There is a certain amount of authentic music that was removed or added at one time or another for one reason or another, usually with the composer's consent. One thinks of the cuts Beethoven made in the later versions of *Fidelio* and the extra solo arias Mozart put into his operas at the behest of irate singers. Knowing the precise reasons for such changes might make performance decisions today easier, but will never remove entirely the need to make them. As with these other operas, the "complete" score of *Porgy and Bess* is somewhat of a fiction. Naturally, the critic must be wary of this state of affairs, as it would be embarrassing to analyze some number as the key to the opera, only to find that Gershwin had cut it. On the other hand, the pre-cut score is Gershwin's first attempt to solve the dramatic problems, and as such must be considered a critical resource.

Is it an opera or a musical? This question was the focus of the reviews that followed the premiere and has not yet been dismissed. Olin Downes and Brooks Atkinson, writing for the music and drama columns of the *New York Times* of October 11, 1935, make typical comments:

> The style is at one moment of opera and another of operetta or sheer Broadway entertainment.

> Why commonplace remarks that carry no emotion have to be made in a chanting monotone is a problem [I] cannot fathom. Turning "Porgy" into opera has resulted in a deluge of casual remarks that have to be thoughtfully intoned and that amazingly impede the action.[21]

Generally, the drama critics objected to recitative per se and the music critics to "Summertime," "I Got Plenty o' Nuttin'," and other tunes which seemed "too popular" for opera. Gershwin replied to both in the *New York Times* of October 20, 1935, writing that his recitatives were composed to the natural speech accents of blacks, and that "Nearly all of Verdi's operas contain what are known as 'song hits.' *Carmen* is almost a collection of song hits." [22]

Since it has been shown time and again that dramatic action can be created from any of the various genres subsumed under the various titles of "opera," "music drama," "operetta, "musical," and so forth, the classification of *Porgy and Bess,* as far as its dramatic artistry is concerned, is truly a trivial issue. As Engel so sensibly remarks:

> It has always seemed to me that this annoyance with *Porgy* is far more the product of semantics than of anything Gershwin put into his score. It is as if just calling *Porgy* by the name "Opera" serves to assail the sensibilities of those who believe that such a classification is a slur on the dignity of Wagner, Verdi, and Mozart. [23]

An issue much more serious than the mere classification of *Porgy and Bess,* but related to that matter, has been the quality of its declamatory vocal writing, including accompanied recitative, arioso, and the like. Opinions on this vary wildly, perhaps because there is little theory or consensus about what makes good recitative. At one end of the controversy there is Irving Kolodin, writing in 1935 that the declamatory writing is one of Gershwin's "most impressive accomplishments, for its adherence to the characteristics of the persons in the drama," [24] and at the other end David Hamilton, in review of the 1976 Cleveland recording, insisting that "in much of the scene music, there isn't any consistent idea of how to get from one place to another." [25] Even strident critics admit, however, that some of the most moving and dramatically important passages in the opera—such as Porgy's first speech, his subsequent invocation to the dice, and Bess's final plea to Crown in Act II—are composed in the declamatory style. If there are other awkward moments, if the entire declamatory music is not perfect, it is still absolutely necessary to set up the most striking moments:

> In *La Boheme, Otello, Louise, Die Meistersinger,* and all the others, there are many passages of recitative that in themselves might seem dull to this listener or that; but without the musical texture they create, many lyric passages that are not songs or arias would be impossible because—if there were no musical continuity—they would become small, isolated islands of music, unconnected, rootless, and even silly. [26]

And such passages in *Porgy and Bess* are essential not only for their lyricism and intrinsic beauty but for what music they contribute to the dramatic development.

Lastly, there is the most complex and politically sensitive question of the three: is *Porgy and Bess* a fair representation of black music and black culture?

Generally, the reaction of the black commmunity has not been favorable through the years. [27] "The times are here to debunk Gershwin's lampblack Negroisms," said Duke Ellington after the premiere, and Ralph Matthews seconded this opinion: "The singing, even down to the choral and ensemble numbers, has a conservatory twang."[28] As listeners have become more aware of the sensibilities of racial minorities, the undeniable stereotypical features of the opera have become even more glaring.

It is difficult to fault Gershwin for any conscious misrepresentation of the culture he tried to portray. He stayed for a month on Folly Island off the coast of South Carolina, close to a Gullah community, to hear their music and observe their religious celebrations, and he refused to accept a prestigious contract from the Metropolitan Opera for the premiere of the opera because a black cast would not have been allowed. These are not the actions of a dramatist who is interested in stereotypes. That the opera is in some ways still stereotypical shows not that Gershwin was racist but that he was a child of his time, subject to its cultural prejudice and ignorance.

In the end, Gershwin did what any opera composer must do: he recast raw material into a unified musical-dramatic idiom. Hall Johnson, a black composer writing for *Opportunity* magazine in 1936, realized this even as he described characteristics that bothered him:

> [Gershwin] is an individual artist, as free to write about Negroes in his own way as any other composer to write about anything else. The only thing a really creative artist can be expected to give us is an expression of *his own* reaction to a given stimulus. We are not compelled to agree with it or even like it.[29]

The social and political implications of *Porgy and Bess* for the black community are very real and quite complex, and require discussion, but ultimately they are irrelevant to any dramatic appraisal of the work. This may be difficult to swallow for some, and, indeed, Gershwin's opera has been unjustly criticized on these terms. "Folk-lore subjects recounted by an outsider are only valid as long as the folk in question is unable to speak for itself, which is certainly not true of the American Negro in 1935," wrote Virgil Thomson in that year.[30] "Nor was it true of Spaniards and Spanish gypsies 60 years earlier, but one is grateful that such fine scruples did not keep Bizet from composing *Carmen*," retorted William Youngren.[31] There may not be a single opera that does not distort some social truth held today (one wonders how femininists would receive *The Magic Flute!*), but such defects lie apart from the musical-dramatic issues with which the composer is wrestling, and modern opera lovers forget politics as part of their suspension of disbelief that allows them to enter into the medium in the first place.

Consideration of the ethnic issue brings to the fore, ironically, the central musical-dramatic issue of *Porgy and Bess:* exactly what is a folk opera, and how do its characteristics affect the structure of the drama? By now it should be clear that a folk opera cannot be any sort of ethnomusicological tone poem of some exotic culture, because that kind of portrayal is not in the province of the opera composer and would not be dramatic even if it were. Rather, it must be an opera in which "the folk," taken as a group, acting together, becomes an important, if not central, character in the drama. Certainly it is this feature of *Porgy and Bess* which has impressed listeners perhaps more than any other. The opera has been compared with *Boris Godu..ov, Carmen,*[32] and operas of Janáček.[33] Composer Ned Rorem goes so far as to say that "so familiar are the seventeen arias that we forget they are almost incidental . . . . as against the grand set of numbers of the group that accounts for three quarters of the opera."[34] And director Rouben Mamoulian was sensitive enough to realize how dramatic the chorus was supposed to be as he put the first production together. "Don't stand around like a chorus—break the formality of it all" was the command he reiterated again and again.[35]

The consequence of using "the folk" as an important character is that it can have but little dramatic action, because it is so deep and requires so much time for development. That is why Gershwin's opera and other "folk operas" seem almost undramatic, like a series of tableaux given on stage one after the other. The story of *Porgy and Bess* is studded with little scenes—self-contained "short stories"—that stand on the periphery of the main plot and often develop it not at all. Lawyer Frazier and his fake divorce and the scene of the street peddlers, both in Act II, are only two examples. Some are motivated by a rather obvious irony that is one of the main features of the original novel. Serena begs her husband Robbins in Act I not to play craps; he disdains her advice, and moments later violence erupting from the game kills him. Clara warns Jake not to go fishing during the time of "September storms"; by the end of that second act, a hurricane has killed them both. Episodes such as these might be considered subplots, but a true subplot of an American musical extends throughout the play, and its purpose is to provide a dramatic counterpoint to the main plot and so extend its range. These "vignettes," to use Slavick's term, instead develop the community of Catfish Row as a character. Each one provides a different side of this complex character, and yet maintains and develops certain themes that apply to the community at large: superstition, a tenacious mutual support against the outside white world, and mutual dependence.

This peculiar character of the folk opera derives directly from the original novel. Its loose structure is characteristic of Heyward as "a chronicler or a memorialist,"[36] and the community is placed at the center of the conflicts.[37] The plot is considerably tightened in the stage version of *Porgy* (1927), meaning that the connective love story is brought out, which in turn requires a fuller treatment of Bess. In the novel she is only the most important of many elements in Porgy's struggle; the reader does not even witness the critical seduction by Sportin' Life at the end. The stage version presents the sordid "happy dust" episode in full, except for Bess's surrender. Naturally, the opera required an even more intense focus. The love story is now at the center of the drama in all its details, including her fall at the end.

The result of these transformations is an opera in which the action, while not really tragic, has the exceedingly slow pace of tragedy. Every scene performs two functions. It develops the relationship of Porgy and Bess, and it develops the community as a dramatic character. Sometimes these functions are quite separated in time and action. The saucer burial scene (Act II, scene 2) is constructed as two discrete musical-dramatic sections. The first, organized around the key of G minor and the dirge refrain of "Gone, gone, gone," is a pure "folk scene" and contributes nothing to the Porgy-Bess relationship. Then the music changes to F major, and Bess jumps up to lead the mourners in the "Train" spiritual, and thus the onetime outcast is now accepted in some measure by the community. Other scenes integrate the two functions more fully. The second investigation scene (Act III, scene 2) presents a turning point in the love story when Porgy is taken to identify Crown's body, but includes also a humorous trio in which Serena and her two friends resist yet again the power of whites. Even the last scene, in which the community, now having been explored for three hours, is ready to play its most active dramatic role, even this scene begins with a lengthy and somewhat puzzling introduction in which people simply greet one another ("How are you dis very lovely mornin'?").[38]

The slow pace of the main plot is best revealed by how little actually happens between Porgy and Bess, especially at the beginning of the opera. In the first act, Porgy takes Bess into his room on Catfish Row after she flees the aftermath of her lover Crown's murder of Robbins. Later she is accepted by the community at Robbins's burial service. That is all that happens in the first act. The couple do not express love for one another until well into the second act. With Crown's return, a love triangle is formed and the action picks up. The remainder of this long act includes Bess's seduction by Crown, and her reconciliation with Porgy. The final act has perhaps the most compressed action: Porgy murders Crown, and is hauled off and held in jail for superstitiously refusing to identify the body; Bess yields once again to her drug addiction and leaves with Sportin' Life; and Porgy returns to find her gone.

The treatment of this seemingly tragic story is quite different from that of most tragic operas in that, although the action is slow, the musical setting of the important plot events is not extensive. The murders are brief, though violent, musical interludes; Sportin' Life only needs one round of "There's a Boat Dat's Leavin' Soon for New York" to lure Bess. To insure that such brief moments are convincing is far from easy, and that they succeed so well is another sort of testament to Gershwin's artistry. Sportin' Life's seduction contains in its brassy tune all the allure of the city, while beneath, in its slithering chromatic bass, is barely masked the identity of the seducer. Similarly, "Summertime," the first song of the opera, seems to capture at once the essential spirituality of the community, especially when the chorus joins in harmony, so much so that through its several reprises it becomes their leitmotif. Such musical economy, however admirable, is a necessary constraint of the "folk opera" genre. To portray Catfish Row in depth requires a lot of time, time that cannot be spared for effulgent Wagnerian love duets.

Still, in terms of the music drama, the main plot must remain at the center of the musical action. How indeed does Gershwin's music define, develop, and sustain the Porgy and Bess relationship without losing track of "the folk?"

The inherent conflict in this dual purpose comes to the fore when Porgy is to make his first entrance. The opera has begun with a lengthy scene that introduces the Catfish Row community. Various small scenes are lit on various stage locations. Characters come and go. A crap game begins at center stage. Porgy comes to join it, but how is he to be distinguished as the principal character, and not just another member of the Row? Gershwin chooses a means as simple as it is effective. A command given while the orchestra is quiet,

MARIA: You Scipio! Here come Porgy. Open the gate for him.

a trill, and then the music which began the opera is recapitulated for the first time, signaling that this character brings a new dramatic phase. Then there is a striking new theme, distinguished by the lowered third (G natural) and a powerful accompaniment composed of parallel chromatic chords. This becomes Porgy's leitmotif:

**Ex. 3–1**  Gershwin, *Porgy and Bess,* Act I, Rehearsal 70, mm. 1–3.

With the protagonist established, Gershwin loses no time in moving the action musically. Porgy's first extended solo, a lyric arioso, defines the main dramatic theme:

**Ex. 3–2**  Gershwin, *Porgy and Bess*, Act I, Rh. 80, mm. 3–6, Rh. 81, mm. 1–10.

It is no overstatement to say that the action motivating the entire plot, then, is Porgy's struggle against loneliness. Even the love relationship is portrayed by both words and music to be the cure for this sickness, and is therefore a second-ary dramatic theme. For one thing, while Bess at several points declares her love for Porgy, he never does, at least not in so many words.[39] For another, *Porgy and Bess* owns a leitmotif technique that is Wagnerian in its method and in its intensity—even Sportin' Life's cocaine gets its own leitmotif—and yet Bess is the only one of six major characters that has no distinctive theme. Her music adapts to the material of the man she is with—Crown, Porgy, or Sportin' Life—as if her fickle character is not capable of musical identity, but instead must identify with his.

The effectiveness of this arioso, its success in making the listener cognizant of its dramatic importance, is due to its singular texture. With its sustained polytonal accompaniment, articulating at once both C and A, and slow harmonic rhythm functioning only on the highest level, it is like nothing heard thus far, neither recitative nor song, but a deep and free expression of inner character.

Nothing at all happens between Porgy and Bess until after the murder, when Bess is searching desperately for a room to hide in. No one will take her in until she comes to Porgy. She goes inside and closes the door; not a word is sung or spoken, but the orchestra rises and ends the first scene by quoting the entire "loneliness" arioso (Rhh. 156, 157). Clearly, Bess is to mean the end of Porgy's deepest longing.

The fullest and most explicit unification of Bess with the dramatic theme of Porgy's loneliness, however, comes with the great love duet of Act II, scene 1, "Bess, You Is My Woman Now," (Rhh. 94-106). This, the couple's first real love scene, is set up, through the long preparation and an unusually empty stage, as one of the few dramatic climaxes of the opera. This is where the meaning of the relationship must be explicated by the music, and Gershwin does not fail.

The first connection with what has already transpired is the most obvious. The five-measure introduction to the main melody quotes the "Night time, day time," portion of the arioso (Rhh. 94, mm. 3-5). Then Porgy begins:

you is!  An' you mus' laugh an' sing an' dance for two in-stead of one.

Want    no wrin - kle  on  yo'  brow,    no -

how,    be - cause    de sor - row of  de past is   all  done

**Ex. 3–3** Gershwin, *Porgy and Bess,* Act II, Rh. 95, mm. 1–8, Rh. 96, mm. 1–8, Rh. 97, mm. 1–4.

At this point Bess takes up the same melody in the key of D major for twelve measures before taking a new turn:

**Ex. 3-4**  Gershwin, *Porgy and Bess,* Act II, Rh. 99, mm. 5-8, Rh. 100, mm. 1-6.

The new melody, so different and yet so fitting, is the complete "Night time, day time" melody, very slightly adapted, from the first act arioso. It is then transposed down to lead into the climactic return of the first phrase, now in the key of F-sharp major for the first time. The tune is not quite the same; it refuses the octave syncopations and instead reiterates the gesture to the high A-sharp, amplifying the intensity. For this moment, setting Porgy's name, Gershwin provides a new accompaniment, a rising and falling chromatic figure that recalls the striking harmonization of Porgy's leitmotif (Ex. 3-1). Finally, there is the lovely codetta to the main tune. It is nothing more than an F-sharp arpeggiation, but its "Mornin' time an' ev'nin' time" text amplifies once more the relationship of this duet with the arioso.[40]

How economical these gestures are, and yet how broad their effect! In a brief twelve measures, Gershwin has justified the short introduction, which otherwise might have seemed forced, and made three long-range connections with the most important musical idea in the first act that clarify the relationship of Porgy and Bess even as the piece confirms it.

The place of "Bess, You Is My Woman Now" as the centerpiece of this scene is supported by a seemingly unrelated and much lighter song: Porgy's "I Got Plenty o' Nuttin'," which is heard near the beginning of the scene.

> The song's harmonic pattern is first heard, played softly by the strings, behind Porgy's strangely moving invocation to the dice during the crap game in Act I. The song itself appears fully formed in Act II, as Porgy's carefree response to the fisherman Jake's declaration that he must take his boat out, even in the face of hurricane warnings, if he is to earn the money to give his children a college education. We recall Porgy's luck in the crap game, and his song seems the celebration of the far more significant stroke of the same luck that has, in the interim, brought him Bess. . . .[41]

If such a reading seems far-fetched at first, it becomes less so when the scene ends with Bess departing for the community picnic and Porgy, left alone, singing a reprise of "I Got Plenty o' Nuttin." Now the song acts as a musical frame for the whole scene, and the cause of its underlying emotion by this point has surely been revealed.

Of course, the dramatic climax must depend on the effectiveness of the music on its own terms, no matter how many and how subtle are the leitmotifs. The very first phrase of "Bess, You Is My Woman Now" shows Gershwin at the height of his lyric powers (Ex. 3-3). The first hint of the coming depth of feeling is the lowered seventh step (A-flat) in the second measure; it is only a hint because this chromatic alteration is one of the commonplaces of this opera. But the phrase ending on the long F (Rh. 95, m. 3) is interrupted by the two octave leaps, interrupted because they are emphatic intervals and, more important, because they come on the weak beats. The typical four-measure phrase ending is therefore blurred. The sense of meter in the melody is weakened further by the next measure, in which the repeated groupings of C-sharp and D once more make accents against the meter.[42] Not until the high (m. 7) C is the sense of strong beat restored, but Gershwin now substitutes harmonic and melodic tension for rhythmic, prolonging the tense supertonic with a series of dominant substitutions, harmonic articulations that are quite necessary, that beautifully color Porgy's note before melting into the expected F dominant seventh at the end of the eighth measure, at exactly the place the listener expects.[43] Because Gershwin blurred the sense of periodic phrasing in the fourth measure, its restoration with this long dominant harmony is especially effective and beautiful.

The next phrase is half again as long, a rhapsodic extension based on expressive intervals of the major seventh, then the major ninth, and articulated by a passing modulation through D major and ending in F-sharp major. Since the song began in B-flat, the changes of key reflect the rising intensity of the duet. Bess steps back to the key of D major, but, as noted, returns gloriously to the F-sharp tonality, which Porgy has already prepared, with the climactic gesture of her melody.[44]

And the connection with "the folk"? It is in the musical idiom itself. Gershwin's style has always been associated with American Jazz, and in *Porgy and Bess* there are features of "native" black music as well.[45] The lowered seventh step of "Bess, You Is My Woman Now" (Ex. 3-3) might be described as a blue note, and the octave leaps that follow as typical jazz syncopations. Similarly there are the lowered third step and the bluesy chord progressions of Porgy's leitmotif (Ex. 3-1). And yet, these gestures, in their most important occurrences, have a function far beyond that of a simple jazz or folk flavoring that gives the opera a certain mood. They contribute to dramatic effect and to large-scale musical organization as well.[46] The effect of those octave leaps has already been noted; their syncopation is not just a taste of jazz but blurs the sense of phrase so that a much more climactic phrase ending can occur later. Consider the haunting refrain of the saucer burial.

**Ex. 3–5**  Gershwin, *Porgy and Bess,* Act I, scene 2, mm. 4–7.

The funereal setting prepares the audience to hear spirituals, and so it does, but no authentic spiritual contains such a non-functional chord progression. Its purpose, yes, is to recall the black spiritual, but also to prolong the fundamental key of G minor for this scene, which must last a long time. Notice that the upbeat ("He's a-") continues the preceding G minor harmony (i) and the phrase ends with a D major seventh (V2), leaving the listener with little option but to interpret the entire progression as some exotic passage in G, or, more fundamentally, as a simple i - V progression stretched out. The consequent phrase contains a resolution (V - i) in the same manner:

**Ex. 3–6**   Gershwin, *Porgy and Bess,* Act II, mm. 7–11.

This chromatic harmony succeeds beautifully because of Gershwin's essentially Romantic voice leading, which, as in Wagner, places the weight of organization on continuous melodic lines rather than on harmonic function. This voice leading not only makes for slower harmonic rhythm on the high level but allows Gersh-

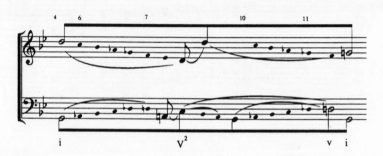

**Fig. 3–1**   Diagram showing high-level harmonic functions (large note heads) and linear voice leading (small note heads) in "Gone, gone, gone" refrain.

win to fashion the local progressions to remind the listener of blues, jazz, or haunting spirituals such as this.

The modulations in "Bess, You Is My Woman Now," while heightening the dramatic expression on stage, are also essentially Romantic in that they delay the strong melodic-harmonic cadence. The first great phrase ends on a half-cadence (Ex. 3-3), and thereafter the music changes key often enough to avoid the inexorable tendency toward the tonic, until the codetta can draw out the final chords over what is the couple's vow of fidelity, combined in counterpoint with all the principal motives and the single full cadence of the song.

**Ex. 3–7**  Gershwin, *Porgy and Bess*, Act II, Rh. 105, mm. 3–7, Rh. 106, mm. 1–6.

The duality of dramatic purpose of this folk opera, then, is accomplished through a musical idiom that has multiple effects at the same time. It colors the opera and develops the community as a character by recalling musical clichés and stereotypes, but uses the idiom in a sophisticated fashion that accomplishes essential dramatic and structural purposes. In this way Gershwin develops the music drama without losing track of "the folk."

Controlling these simultaneous dramatic effects cannot be easy, and they are not always as unified as in the second act duet. In particular, the last scene of the opera—in which Porgy returns from jail laden with gifts for his Bess and other friends on Catfish Row—has been criticized for not meeting the dramatic issues.[47] The aforementioned greeting scene is puzzling enough, but the real problem is the moment of Porgy's reception by the community. It begins confidently enough: they sing a variant of his leitmotif in welcome. But thereafter, Gershwin seems unsure how to set the long period between his arrival and his realization that Bess is gone. Admittedly, the musical expression of simultaneous yet contrary emotions is one of opera's most ticklish problems, but Gershwin simply ignores the issue.

As Porgy recounts his jail experience for the community, and begins to distribute gifts, the various members, of course, are very uncomfortable in the knowledge that the reason for his joyful homecoming has already gone. This is the emotional conflict on stage: his joy, their despair. The music cannot reflect this. The orchestra moves from development of Porgy's leitmotif (Rh. 131, m. 5 – Rh. 134, m. 5), to harmonica chords for Scipio's present of a mouth organ (Rh. 135–Rh. 137, m. 3), to "I Got Plenty o' Nuttin' " (Rhh. 138 –145) as he doles out other presents and tells everyone how he won the money to buy them, to "Bess, You Is My Woman Now," as he prepares to summon Bess. Even if one generously ascribes some sense to the use of "I Got Plenty" while the gift-giving goes on, the use of these themes here is a most superficial substitute for actual music drama, recalling the Broadway practice of calling for a reprise of a show's best song when there was nothing better to do. The tension of the crowd's mood against Porgy's is completely missing, and a significant opportunity for Gershwin is gone.[48]

The conclusion of the opera, containing the most radical transformation of the original story, is much more convincing. The novel ends by cutting out the community and showing only Porgy and Maria in an image as bleak as could be:

> She looked until she could bear the sight no longer; then she stumbled into her shop and closed the door, leaving Porgy and the goat alone in an irony of morning sunlight.[49]

In the stage version, the Heywards, thinking this ending quite undramatic, restore the community and have Porgy strike out for New York in search of Bess, but there is no question that this is a desperate gesture of despair. The departure is retained in the opera, but Gershwin transforms its significance entirely with the spiritual "Oh Lawd, I'm on My Way." Despite its accompanimental syncopated figure, which has been criticized as too casual for such a moment, this song, set in the opera's opening key of E major, is an effective and moving summary of many of its elements. Musically, it contains the jazz vamp, the blues chromaticism, and, of course, the spiritual idiom. In the drama it represents a final unification of the two main strands, the love relationship and the community at large as character, for here the spirit of the community has been changed, from despair to hope, on account of that love relationship. That change of heart and that unification seem to be implied in the construction of the piece, in the way that the emphasis on the tonic note and triad expresses the stalwart hope, and when the chorus joins in with Porgy after only a single phrase of solo. "The folk" at last becomes an active participant in the music drama.

From the vantage point of fifty years of history, it seems that *Porgy and Bess* is one of those rare works, comparable perhaps to the master films of Chaplin, that make the leap from a local popular tradition into world-class art. Since its premiere, which was a financial failure,[50] its appeal to sophisticated opera audiences and popular musicians alike has only increased by leaps and bounds. Having already played in Copenhagen, Zurich, and Stockholm by 1950, and having been added to the regular seasonal repertory of the Zurich Stadttheater,[51] the opera truly arrived on the world stage with a four-year tour sponsored by the U.S. State Department from 1952-56. This included triumphant performances in Berlin, Vienna, the Soviet Union, and at La Scala in Milan.

It is quite clear that just this sort of leap was Gershwin's intention:

> I chose the form I have used for "Porgy and Bess" because I believe that music lives only when it is in serious form. When I wrote the "Rhapsody in Blue," I took "blues"

and put them in a larger and more serious form. That was twelve years ago and the "Rhapsody in Blue" is very much alive whereas if I had taken the same themes and put them in songs they would have been gone years ago.[52]

The longevity Gershwin sought has indeed been achieved, but ironically, its "serious form" has limited *Porgy and Bess* to only superficial influence on subsequent Broadway productions, mostly in the form of musicals boasting black casts: *The Hot Mikado* (1939), *The Swing Mikado* (1939), *Cabin in the Sky* (1940), among others. The high-level harmonic organization and the whole idea of the folk opera has little application in the traditional musical play of Broadway, whose plot is usually much tighter and more directed, and divided into much smaller musical pieces. The long-range interconnections of motive, leitmotif, and dramatic character find no parallel until Leonard Bernstein. They were simply beyond the reach of all other Broadway composers.

Although the opera seems almost to step out of its native tradition, *Porgy and Bess* must be one of Broadway's most luminous moments. Criticisms made here and elsewhere hardly challenge the overall conception of the work, and merely prove once more that there is no perfect opera. The famous opera historian Donald J. Grout is quite right when he writes that "no work has yet risen to challenge the secure place of *Porgy and Bess* in the history of American opera."[53] For how many other works of art can appeal to so many levels of culture, and have done so? Perhaps more important in this age without a commmon musical language, how many have done so in the twentieth century?

# CHAPTER 4

# Second Maturity

*When a show works perfectly, it's because all the individual parts complement each other and fit together. . . . In a great musical, the orchestrations sound the way the costumes look. That's what made* Oklahoma! *work. . . . It was a work created by many that gave the impression of having been created by one.*[1]

RICHARD RODGERS

There are a number of reasons why a particular work of art might be considered a milestone in the history of its genre. It might introduce innovations of technique and style so convincing that they become highly influential. It might attract such wide acclaim that it cannot be ignored by the artists who come after, even if the acclaim eventually fades. It could stand as the first work of an important series, like the First Symphony of Beethoven. Or perhaps, in addition to all of these, it sets a new standard of artistry. All of these reasons can be found in the first musical play of Rodgers and Hammerstein, *Oklahoma!*.

Almost from its first performance at the St. James Theater on March 31, 1943, *Oklahoma!* has been recognized as a new kind of musical play that denied its Broadway audiences many of their most cherished traditions. There was no opening chorus line, no chorus at all until midway throught the first act, in fact. There was a rather serious ballet and other serious overtones, including a killing in the second act. The story, apparently so simple, seemed to engage the audience in a way that went beyond evening diversion. These departures, far from disappointing their viewers, were ratified by a commercial success that was unprecedented in the history of the musical theater. The original production of *Oklahoma!* at the St. James ran 2,248 performances, blasting the previous record for a musical play, 670 for *Irene* (1919).[2] The touring company played contin-

73

ually for ten years, and performed in Berlin, South Africa, Denmark, Australia, and established the performance record at the Drury Lane Theatre in London.

Even if *Oklahoma!* had flopped, it would still be recorded in histories of Broadway as the first collaboration of Richard Rodgers, composer, and Oscar Hammerstein II, lyricist and playwright, who, between the premiere of *Oklahoma!* and Hammerstein's death in 1960, dominated Broadway as no other team has done. When *Oklahoma!* was revived on Broadway in 1953, there were three other Rodgers and Hammerstein musicals playing there already in their opening runs: *South Pacific* (opened 1949), *The King and I* (1951), and *Me and Juliet* (1953). Replace the last with their earlier *Carousel* (1945, revived 1954), and the result is a quartet of the most outstanding achievements of the American musical theater. Their later years produced two more which, while not quite reaching that exalted level, are yet worthy of occasional revival: *Flower Drum Song* (1958) and *The Sound of Music* (1959). The sheer number of their successes places them above any other single composer or lyricist; that this book devotes to them two chapters to everyone else's one is only a constrained reflection of the historical fact: their work is at the center of Broadway's "golden age."

Of course, *Oklahoma!* did not flop. It survives today not because of its supposed innovations, which, real or not, inevitably fade with time, nor because of its original popularity or its historical position, but because of its own integrity. Its solution to the problem of music and drama is quite different from *Show Boat's,* but like the earlier play, *Oklahoma!* took that problem seriously and conjured up a dramatic presentation that has not yet ceased to appeal.

Both Rodgers and Hammerstein had long careers in the musical theater already behind them when they agreed to work together in the early 1940s. Oscar Hammerstein II was born into a theatrical family and in the early 1920s worked with the veteran book writer Otto Harbach. In the middle of the decade he scored successes with Sigmund Romberg and Jerome Kern. After *Show Boat,* he continued to work with Kern intermittently. Their next hit was *Music in the Air* (1933). Hammerstein's career in the theater then entered upon a ten-year drought. He supported himself with lucrative Hollywood film contracts, but he had no commercial or artistic achievements in the theater until *Oklahoma!*.

The years before had been much kinder to Rodgers. Working with the supremely talented but unstable Lorenz Hart from the early 1920s onward, he had composed an impressive number of successful shows including *A Connecticut Yankee* (1927), *On Your Toes* (1938), *The Boys From Syracuse* (1938), and *Pal Joey* (1940). This last play, about a rather dim but good looking nightclub singer who is taken in by a wealthy but bored socialite, has been cited as an example of the musical theater's growing maturity in the late 1930s, and Lehman Engel believes it should be included in the top-drawer canon.[3] Although a large proportion of the score is given over to prop songs, other songs are integrated fairly well into the plot. Rodgers and Hart did not compromise its seamy setting and distasteful characters. The composer commented on the occasion of its successful

1952 revival that "While Joey himself may have been fairly adolescent in his thinking and his morality, the show bearing his name certainly wore long pants and in many respects forced the entire musical-comedy theatre to wear long pants for the first time."[4]

Rodgers would have been quite content to continue his partnership with Hart if the writer's alcoholism had not made working conditions impossible. Even when Rodgers told him that he had been approached by the Theatre Guild to convert Lynn Riggs's *Green Grow the Lilacs* into a musical and that he might approach Oscar Hammerstein, Hart could not reform. Instead, he declined rapidly, and died in November 1943 at the age of forty-eight, eight months after *Oklahoma!* opened.

Lorenz Hart told Rodgers that he did not think the cowboy play would make a good musical, and indeed, in view of Hart's particular talents, he was probably right in sensing that the deep sentimentality of the Riggs play was not for him. Ironically, the very dramatic qualities that put him off were beautifully suited to the subtle talents of Oscar Hammerstein II.

The lyricist's and the librettist's art has always placed a distant second to the composer's in opera criticism, and this book is no exception, even though the words that are sung in a piece are essential to its dramatic expression. Moreover, the phrase structure and rhyme scheme of a lyric influence decisively the important articulations in the music, since they must match if the sense of the words is to be conveyed. Because of this important function of rhyme, the most famous of Broadway's lyricists—Hart, Cole Porter, Alan Jay Lerner, Stephen Sondheim—have been virtuoso wordsmiths, masters of the internal rhyme, the feminine rhyme, the half-phrase. Such devices call attention to themselves and impress the listener with their difficulty. This sensation can be advantageous if the situation is comic. When W. S. Gilbert's pirates of Penzance surprise the unsuspecting maidens and threaten to carry them off immediately to be married, the speech is as funny as the situation is outrageous:

> *Here's a first-rate opportunity*
> *To get married with impunity;*
> *And indulge in the felicity*
> *of unbounded domesticity.*
> *You shall quickly be parsonified,*
> *Conjugally matrimonified,*
> *By a doctor of divinity,*
> *Who resides in this vicinity.*

The audience is regaled not only by the image of twenty pirates threatening to marry twenty maidens at a crack, but by their impudence in their successful attempt to rhyme with "opportunity," "domesticity," "parsonified," and "divinity."

But while comedy, satire, and cynicism may call for such lyrics, romance and other sincerities cannot really abide them. When constructing a situation of serious dramatic intent, the last thing one wants is a lyric that calls attention to its technique rather than to the drama. It is here that Hammerstein separates himself from his virtuoso forbears, Gilbert and Hart:

> While I, on occasion, place a timid, encroaching foot on the territory of these two masters, I never carry my invasion very far. I would not stand a chance with either of them in the field of brilliant light verse. I admire them and envy them their fluidity and humor, but I refuse to compete with them. Aside from my shortcomings as a wit and rhymester—or, perhaps, because of them—my incliniations lead me to a more primitive type of lyric.[5]

This gives the listener an entirely different impression of lyric technique. With Porter or Sondheim the reaction is, "I could never do that." With Hammerstein it is more likely to be, "Anyone could do that." The apparent simplicity of the Hammerstein lyric hides an exceptionally appropriate and often penetrating characterization of the dramatic situation at hand. He is perfectly capable of comedy, and even of wordplay; listen to the comic juxtapositions in "June Is Bustin' Out All Over" from *Carousel*. But most often the comedy in his lyric derives from the comedy of the dramatic situation in the play. That is why the punch line in Ado Annie's verse of "All er Nuthin' " and the the ironic refrain from "Kansas City," both from *Oklahoma!*, work so well.

Hammerstein is best when he describes a complex emotion or experience in the simplest language. In *The King and I*, Anna Leonowens, a middle-aged widow, sings "Hello Young Lovers," in which she assures everyone around that she knows what it is like to be young and in love. The lyric's release section is as follows:

> *I know how it feels to have wings on your heels,*
> *And to fly down the street in a trance.*
> *You fly down a street on the chance that you'll meet,*
> *And you meet—not really by chance.*

There seems nothing complex about this lyric; even the internal rhyme in the first line seems quite plain. And those repeated strong words "street" and "meet" seem to impoverish the song, that is, until it is realized that their repetition creates a most subtle acceleration in articulation that mirrors the action of flying down the street. The second "meet" is indeed a surprise, not only because it is a repetition, but because it occurs so early on in the first foot of the line. But most stunning of all is the last short phrase which completes the overall rhyme, because by insisting on the second "chance" it goes quickly to the heart of young lovers' experience, the pretense of spontaneity and surprise at a chance meeting when chance had nothing to do with it.

This "primitive type" of lyric has the most to gain from a sensitive musical setting. It seems so plain on the page, in contrast to the entertaining verbal gymnastics of the virtuoso lyric, and cries out for a musical expression to mine its hidden worth. In this regard, Hammerstein was immeasurably fortunate to work with Richard Rodgers, who was gifted with just this sort of musical sensibility. He begins the setting of this lyric from "Hello Young Lovers" with a rhythm of even quarters followed by an uneven measure whose eighth notes might suggest a tensed hurrying, and in a foreign key, the subdominant in this case, as he often does in his release sections. This leads the listener to expect a return to the home, or tonic, key sooner or later.

**Ex. 4–1** Rodgers and Hammerstein, *The King and I,* "Hello Young Lovers" (No. 3), mm. 44–60.

With the third line (m. 53), the key becomes more unstable and on the second "meet" the melody moves up climactically to the original tonic note, suggesting with a cadential gesture the sudden meeting that takes place in Anna's mind. But this is no final climax, for Rodgers has harmonized that decisive melodic motion with a deceptive cadence that must move on. The final word, "chance," is given special treatment, harmonized with the minor ii chord over V, a dissonance that seems the perfect expression for Anna'a bittersweet reminiscence, but which then moves into the clear dominant under her sustained note, finally defining the home key of D for which the listener has been waiting. Thus, Hammerstein's imagined meeting is rendered with an equivalent musical metaphor: the cadence in mid-phrase doubles for the unexpected encounter while its deceptive quality mirrors the lovers themselves and allows the phrase its normal period.

Rodgers was one of the most fluent melodists of the American musical theater, composing masterful songs with breathtaking speed. Numerous accounts support this appraisal: "Soliloquy" in two hours, "It Might as Well Be Spring" in one hour, "Oh What a Beautiful Mornin'" in ten minutes. Hammerstein himself wrote:

> This is the annoying part of our collaboration. It takes me a week, and sometimes three weeks, to write the words of a song. After I give them to him, it takes him an hour or two and his work is over.[6]

Despite this remarkable facility, Rodgers' melodies are characterized by an expressive logic of development that seems so calculated and planned. "People Will Say We're in Love," the principal love duet of *Oklahoma!,* has a refrain melody composed almost entirely of fifths and step motion.

**Ex. 4–2** Rodgers and Hammerstein, *Oklahoma!*, "People Will Say We're in Love" (No. 12), mm. 19–34.

As the melody progresses, however, these elements gradually acquire more and more musical tension. The first fifth moves from steps 1 to 5 on the scale; the second from the comparatively more tense leading tone (7) down to 3 (m. 21). The second phrase changes the descending fifth from perfect to diminished (G to C-sharp setting "folks too much"), yet remaining strictly in the key of D major. The third phrase introduces another diminished fifth, now chromatic (D to G-sharp setting "jokes too much"), increasing the tension again. This makes the explicit chromaticism of the next phrase seem well prepared and logical. The next section is identical to the first, except that the end is changed so that it is no less chromatic but more conclusive since it moves up to the tonic (Ex. 4-3, mm. 47–50). The release continues the development by using the more daring lowered fifth step ("Don't start collecting things").

**Ex. 4–3**  Rodgers and Hammerstein, *Oklahoma!*, "People Will Say We're in Love" (No. 12), mm. 47–54.

The final phrase creates a melodic climax by rising to its highest notes yet, but cleverly adapting the chromatic motive once more so that it begins a perfect fifth higher than the original:

**Ex. 4–4** Rodgers and Hammerstein, *Oklahoma!*, ''People Will Say We're in Love'' (No. 12), mm. 63–66.

Rodgers's style is an untainted adaptation of nineteenth-century Romanticism. Chromaticism not only creates expressive effects and emphatic gestures on certain choice lyrics, but by weakening the sense of key it delays the need for a structural cadence. It is true that Rodgers does not always take advantage of this structural chromaticism—''People Will Say,'' for example, has a strong cadence at the end of its second section (Ex. 4-3)—but more often than not his songs are examples of the ''endless melody'' in miniature. What is remarkable in *Oklahoma!* is that he succeeds in retaining a folk-song flavor in many of the numbers while refusing the frequent cadences that such a flavor might suggest.

**Ex. 4–5** Rodgers and Hammerstein, *Oklahoma!*, "Oh What a Beautiful Mornin' (No. 1), mm. 48–64.

In the verse of "Oh What a Beautiful Morning" the melody makes a strong cadence at the end of its consequent phrase (m. 55), just as a real folk song might. Any firm sense of conclusion, however, is dispelled by the harmony and descending bass line; the chord at that point is vi, not I, and the cadence is deceptive. The tension in the song is therefore maintained, and thereafter increased as the bass line becomes chromatic, and as the last phrase sustains a prolonged dominant harmony under the repeated Bs of the melody. There is no strong cadence at all until the very end of the refrain. This sort of melodic tension, created by consistent delay of cadence, is the strategem of the Romantic composer.

Such a technique naturally places great weight on the end of a piece, where strong cadences finally do occur. One of Rodgers's greatest gifts as a songwriter is his gift for ending, perhaps the most treacherous spot in a composition. His endings not only exploit the accumulated tensions beautifully, but often have a way of summing up the content of the song at the same time.

**Ex. 4–6**  Rodgers and Hammerstein, *Oklahoma!*, "The Surrey With the Fringe on Top" (No. 3), mm. 18–25.

There are two salient features of this melody from "The Surrey With the Fringe on Top": the repeated low E and the leap upward, which Rodgers took to represent the flat country road and the scurrying fowl.[7] The successive leaps, however, are not identical and create in themselves a higher level pattern.

**Fig. 4-1**  Diagram of high-level melodic pattern in "Surrey."

The leaps make an overall line of A – B – C-sharp, quite stable. The next note
would be D if the pattern continued, but instead the melody begins again for the
second section of the song. After the release, the tune is heard for third time,
now changed in order to effect one of Rodgers's inimitable conclusions.

**Ex. 4–7**  Rodgers and Hammerstein, *Oklahoma!*, "The Surrey With the Fringe on Top" (No. 3), mm. 42–53.

This time, after the leap to C-sharp the melody progresses smoothly and slowly upward and does give the awaited D, emphasized by its strong position in the measure and the preceding secondary diminished chord (V09/ii). But most deft of all is the little three-measure tag (mm. 50-52), in which the pattering low E and the uninterrupted leap up to the D seem to remind the listener that this was what the melody was about all along, just at the moment when the first strong cadence of the whole refrain arrives.

The essential Romanticism of Rodgers's style and Hammerstein's affinity for the lyrical expression of sentiment were perfectly suited for the task of dramatic characterization. The main purpose of the songs in *Oklahoma!* is to reveal in detail the characters who sing them.

This is why the play's opening has been so often cited as such an effective beginning, revolutionary for its time. With no one but Aunt Eller on stage churning butter, Curly is heard offstage singing the verse to "Oh What a Beautiful Morning," which, unlike the second verse quoted above, is unaccompanied. Upon his appearance, he sings the famous refrain.

**Ex. 4–8**  Rodgers and Hammerstein, *Oklahoma!*, "Oh What a Beautiful Mornin' (No. 1), mm. 29–44.

The melody, once again folklike in its apparent simplicity, hides the deep-seated emotion of the character about his subject. The lowered seventh ("mornin' ") is the first sign of such emotion. When this phrase begins again ("I got a beautiful feelin' "), the expected D is replaced by the D-sharp leading tone in the very same spot, increasing the tension powerfully. The leading tone's resolution is false, harmonized with a diminished seventh (V09/V), yet another expressive delay of cadence. Only at the conclusion of the next phrase is this leading tone resolved, and even that somewhat obliquely, as the lower tonic is substituted for the higher, so that the melody must descend from the leading tone. The last refrain of this number, however, does end on the high E, resolving the melody at last.

Both perceptions of the melody, the impression of folklike simplicity and the impression of something deeper, are essential, and together they establish Curly as a real folk hero in the most economical way. A less often cited but equally important characterization occurs with Jud's song, "Lonely Room." The only song in *Oklahoma!* in the minor mode, it is the necessary explanation of Jud's villainous designs on Laurey, the motivation for all the action in the second act.

**Ex. 4–9**   Rodgers and Hammerstein, *Oklahoma!*, "Lonely Room" (No. 15), mm. 1–12.

The song begins with a quarter-note ostinato sounding an F-sharp/G clash which becomes the most characteristic sonority of the piece. When the voice enters, the accompaniment is filled out, but with a chord that is functionally ambiguous, especially along with the ostinato. The melody that Jud sings for the most part is little more than a recitative-like expansion of the ostinato, mostly F-sharps and Gs. Only with the arrival of the F-sharp major chord (m. 10) does the B minor key become clear. By employing largely non-functional harmony to that point, Rodgers not only highlights the important lyric ("By myself in a lonely room") but establishes a singular musical idiom in this song that is different from all the other music in the play, a musical symbol, in effect, for Jud's isolation from the community.

Jud's melody does not change much as it moves on (mm. 11–12), but the accompaniment begins running notes to effect Jud's "dream." When his dream reaches its climax in his imagination, his melody finally breaks out of the strait-jacket that has confined it.

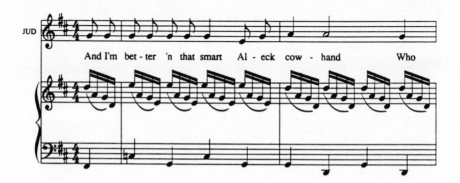

thinks he is bet - ter 'n me! And the

girl that I want ain't a - fraid of my arms And her

own soft arms keep me warm. And her

**Ex. 4–10**   Rodgers and Hammerstein, *Oklahoma!*, "Lonely Room" (No. 15), mm. 22–34.

Given the melody's limited range thus far, the rises up to the tonic B (mm. 31-32) seem dramatic enough, but the subsequent span of a major seventh from D to the triumphant C-sharp (m. 30), harmonized with a major triad, seems a liberation. That chord, however, leads quite logically back to the ostinato and a recapitulation of the opening ten measures. The slow progression to the hymnodic F-sharp chord is heard once again, more painful this time as Jud sings "And the sun flicks my eyes/ It was all a pack o' lies/ I'm awake in a lonely room."

**Ex. 4–11**  Rodgers and Hammerstein, *Oklahoma!*, "Lonely Room" (No. 15), mm. 43–53.

The coda reiterates what Jud has already told the Peddler, that he is through with pictures, that he wants "real things." The identity of the melody setting this resolution with the climax of the dream makes it perfectly clear exactly what things he wants. The final measures, which pit Jud's high C-sharp against the resolving B minor harmony, symbolize Jud's intended liberation and its precise terms more strongly than anything he could say.

"Lonely Room" transforms Jud from a formless villian into a motivated and credible agent of dramatic action.

> Jud is no longer only a sniveling, frightening, hideous, threatening misfit, but a pathetic human being. We recognize his dream, and we pity him even as we fear him.[8]

Rodgers's singular harmonic and melodic idiom in this song is more complex than in any other in the play, for Jud, the psychotic, is the most complex character. The depth of its characterization perhaps explains why this song has had such little popularity, and why it is sometimes—incredibly—omitted in performance. It makes little sense outside its dramatic context, and, like much of Sondheim's music, cannot be popular on the radio.

The "dream" ballet which ends the first act and which is one of the most famous features of *Oklahoma!* is yet another crucial characterization. At this point in the story, Laurey cannot decide whether to go to the box social dance with Jud, whom she fears but promised anyway to spite Curly, or with Curly, whom she really loves. She sniffs some "Elixir of Egypt" which the peddler has sold her to help her think more clearly. She falls into a dream state which the ballet acts out.

The ballet, in brief, runs as follows:

BALLET SEQUENCE

| *Action* | *Music* |
|---|---|
| Laurey and Curly figures dance ecstatically | "Out of My Dreams" |
| "Laurey" and "Curly" continue. Other figures, girls and cowboys, enter and exit. "Curly" kisses "Laurey" and walks off. | "Beautiful Mornin' " |
| Girls arrive and embrace "Laurey" | "Kansas City" |
| Bridal veil floats down and is placed on "Laurey" | "Beautiful Mornin' " |
| "Curly" and cowboys enter, astride horses | "Surrey" |
| A wedding procession is formed | "Surrey" |
| "Jud" enters and removes veil | "Surrey" (chromatic) |
| "French postcard" girls enter | "Pore Jud" and "I Can't Say No" |
| "Postcard" girls dance with "Jud" | "I Cain't Say No" |
| "Curly" fires at "Jud" with pistol | "Pore Jud" |
| Fight | "Lonely Room" |
|  | "Pore Jud" motives |
| "Jud" strangles "Curly" | "Surrey" (chromatic) |
| Jud awakens Laurey and she goes with him | "People" (chromatic) |
| Curly watches them depart with puzzlement |  |

Agnes De Mille, the famous choreographer of ballet, was quite conscious of the particular requirements of dance that was to be incorporated into a musical, and also well aware of what it revealed of Laurey's character:

> The ballet . . . showed what was going on in her mind and heart, her terrors, her fears, her hopes; so in fact the happiness of her life, her life itself, depended on the choice. And the first act, which normally would have ended with a bland and ordinary musical comedy finale, ended starkly with the murder of the hero. The audience was caught on the suspense of the girl's terror.[9]

The ballet is disappointing in only one respect: its music. As indicated in the above plan, the dance is set with only a loose ordering of song reminiscent of a medley overture. The tunes are mostly presented whole, without much adaptation or motivic development, and the relationship between them and the dancing action is tenuous at best. Indeed, there is no apparent reason at all why "Kansas City" is used the way it is, or why "The Surrey With the Fringe on Top" should set a wedding processional. Worse, the original meanings of some songs are distorted when their relationship to the dancing is plausible but superficial. Using "I Cain't Say No" for the pin-up girls is just such a falsification, since the song has nothing to do with promiscuous behavior. Rather, it is a delightful expression of an adolescent girl's first feeble struggles to rein in her own instincts in the face of a universal social code.

Such adaptation of the tunes as does occur consists only of substituting chromatic for conventional harmony, but since the tunes are used whole, and the entire ballet is but a string of them, there is no thoroughgoing rationale behind such development. The musical effect is quite naïve, as is the device itself.

It is difficult to assess Rodgers's role in this design. The music for dance routines in musical plays back then was usually thrown together from existing songs after the routine had been choreographed, often by a talented rehearsal pianist. In any case, a serious ballet demands a serious composition, through-composed, based, perhaps, on motives from earlier songs, but motives that can develop new ideas that might advance the psychological action. The ballet in *Carousel* that occurs when Billy, up in "heaven," watches his daughter being spurned by her community is also weakened by the use of whole themes of questionable choice and by music accompanying her final rejection that has no commensurate weight, but at least in one or two spots there is significant motivic development reflecting the action of the dancers. It is puzzling that Rodgers, who had composed a couple of pure ballet scores before 1943,[10] was not more careful with the dance music for *Oklahoma!*.

Still, the ballet must be performed because it clarifies the most important dramatic issue. "Could anyone give a damn about a story whose burning issue was who takes whom to a box social?" Rodgers asked himself when trying to raise money to produce *Oklahoma!*.[11] Indeed, the audience must. But the issue itself is not the problem; it is one of Eric Bentley's "little dramas," which "to the imagination, are big, and are cast in the likeness of precisely the big dramas described in the newspaper."[12] The problem is making the box social seem big, and this is precisely what the ballet does. It is an expression of Laurey's view of the world at that moment, and in that world the box social means all.

The depth of characterization in song and dance, then, is the outstanding achievement of *Oklahoma!*. Because the music is directed to this end so exclusively, its dramatic quality is static rather than active. In *Show Boat's* "Make Believe," there is dramatic action between the beginning of the song and the end: Magnolia and Ravenal fall in love, or at least, the audience is made aware of it. The songs in *Oklahoma!* tell much more about the characters who sing them, but the dramatic situation is little different after the song than before, unless one considers definition of character itself to be a dramatic act.

To compensate for this Rodgers and Hammerstein developed a method of

integration that, while not really new, revolutionized thinking about the placement of songs in a musical play. It meant actually decreasing the number of
songs, but arranging them within the play more skillfully:

> The score of *Show Boat* contains twenty musical numbers, all different—a feast of
> lovely tunes that punctuate the action without necessarily advancing it. It is almost *too*
> tuneful. The score of *Oklahoma!* comprises just twelve basic musical numbers. But
> these twelve are not just . . . reprised. They are woven in and out of the story,
> sometimes under dialogue, sometimes quoted briefly, at others repeated in various
> guises. . . .[13]

Consider how the play's opening scene, an extraordinarily lengthy one, is designed.

Synopsis—Oklahoma!, Act I, scene 1

"Oh What a Beautiful Mornin' " (Curly)                                      E major
  *Dialogue:* Curly makes clear to Aunt Eller that he has come to ask Laurey to the box
  social.

"Oh, What a Beautiful Mornin' " (Laurey)                                    E major
  *Dialogue:* Laurey enters and exchanges taunts with Curly. She asks how they would
  travel to the social.

"The Surrey With the Fringe on Top" (Curly)                                 A major
  *Melodrama:* Laurey teases him that he has hired the rig without anyone to go with
  him. Curly retorts that he made the whole thing up.

"The Surrey With the Fringe on Top" (Curly)                                 A major
  *Dialogue:* Laurey, thinking she has been tricked, flounces out. Cowboys enter. Will
  Parker intends to marry Ado Annie, now that he has won fifty dollars in Kansas City.

"Kansas City" (Will)                                                        A♭ major
  *Dance:* Cowboys and Aunt Eller
  *Dialogue:* Aunt Eller tells Curly that Jud is infatuated with Laurey. Jud appears and
  tells Aunt Eller that Laurey has agreed to go with him to the social.
  Curly then asks Aunt Eller to go with him in his surrey, which he has indeed hired
  after all.

"The Surrey With the Fringe on Top" (half ref.) (Curly)                     A major
  *Dialogue:* Laurey reveals to Aunt Eller that she is afraid to go with Jud, that she asked
  him merely to spite Curly. Ado Annie enters. When Laurey tells her that Will has
  returned, Ado Annie confesses that she has trouble being faithful to just one "feller."

"I Cain't Say No" (Ado Annie)                                               F major
  *Dialogue:* Peddler enters. Ado Annie asks him if he is serious about marrying her. Will
  enters and woos Annie.

"I Cain't Say No" (trio only) (Will)                                        D major

"Oh What a Beautiful Mornin' " (Crowd, Curley)                              E major
  *Dialogue:* Girls notice that Curly is not paying attention to Laurey.

"Many a New Day" (Laurie, girls)                                        D major
  *Dance:* Laurey, Girls
  *Dialogue:* Ado Annie, Peddler and Annie's father enter. Annie's father forces Peddler
  to become engaged to Annie because of certain indiscretions.

"It's a Scandal" (Peddler, Cowboys)                                     D major
  *Dialogue:* Laurey tells Curly that people are gossiping about them, expecting them to
  be together.

"People Will Say We're in Love" (Curley, Laurie)                       D major
  *Melodrama:* Curly asks Laurey to tell Jud that she would rather go with him. She
  refuses.

"People Will Say" (half ref.) (Laurie)                                 D major
  *Melodrama:* Aunt Eller comforts Laurey.
  Change of scene.

The convention that is completely reformed in this scene is the reprise. Formerly, a song would be introduced into the play and, if it were a crowd-pleaser, would be sung again in the second act, usually for the sake of filler or applause. To hear the songs repeated almost immediately after short dialogue was unknown; even *Porgy and Bess,* which is rich with wonderful reprises, does not repeat them immediately.

The effect of these frequent reprises is to integrate song and spoken word much more closely but, just as important, to create another level of dramatic action. When Laurey enters by singing "Oh What a Beautiful Mornin'," an affinity between her and Curly is established even before she has spoken a single word, an affinity which stands up to the contradictory dialogue that follows. Similarly, Will's ironic reprise of "I Cain't Say No" confirms his match with Ado Annie. Curly's short half refrain of "Surrey" is in effect a most appropriate parting taunt to Laurey, who set herself up for it.

This sort of integration, where it seems as if the dialogue interrupts the song as much as the song interrupts the dialogue, creates the dramatic action that the character songs alone would lack. The dramatic continuity takes place across the numbers, rather than within them. This continuity can have great range. One fine moment in the play occurs in the second act, when Curly and Laurey finally become engaged. After they kiss, "People Will Say We're in Love" begins in the orchestra. The first three phrases are instrumental, over which Curly shouts that Laurey is to marry him. When she warns him that he will be heard "all the way to Catoosie!," he replies:

**Ex. 4–12** Rodgers and Hammerstein, *Oklahoma!*, "People Will Say We're in Love" (No. 24), mm. 13–16.

By a change of a few lyrics, the song, referring far back to the end of the first scene, has been transformed from a pretense of propriety that concealed love into an honest expression of it. The reprise reveals all at once how far the two lovers have come.

This kind of dramaturgy, however, has a distinct disadvantage: because its musical elements are small and dramatically static, the method is quite incapable of expressing in music passages that have rapid dramatic action, even if this action is crucial to the plot. In *Oklahoma!*, the tense moments of the auction scene, the subsequent quarrel between Jud and Laurey, and the killing have no musical setting. Since these events all occur toward the end of the play, it makes the problem especially tricky, and Rodgers seems to have been aware of it. "Let's get to the curtain quickly after the killing," he told Hammerstein during the planning stages. "If we start developing anything new the play will go downhill." [14] This throws the whole conception out of balance in this one respect, since in music drama everything that is sung automatically has greater significance than the spoken parts, and so one would like to have all the most important dramatic acts sung. That they are not is perhaps *Oklahoma!*'s only significant failing.

*Oklahoma!* is one of those art phenomena that seemed revolutionary from the outset. There were enormous difficulties in raising the production money; the usual Broadway backers were wary of investing in a show that broke so many rules. After the premiere, critics praised such daring and were grateful that it "opened new vistas in musical plays." [15] The rush of composers and writers to conform to the new standard after *Oklahoma!* is quite amusing in retrospect. Rodgers recalls:

Everyone suddenly became "integration"-conscious, as if the idea of welding together song, story and dance had never been thought of before. There were also a number of costume musicals, and no self-respecting production dared open without at least one "serious" ballet.[16]

Historian Abe Laufe fills in for Rodgers's discretion:

Ballets were considered so essential that they were injected into musical comedies whether they fit the plot or not. In fact, ballet became so common in the theater that within a few years the same critics who had praised the dance routines in *Oklahoma!* became almost ecstatic when leading players or a chorus line would break into an old, familiar tap routine.[17]

It is easy to see why this happened. The critic of *Dance Magazine* accorded *Oklahoma!*'s dream ballet a historic significance:

These dances are Miss de Mille's greatest contribution to theatre dance; they popularized the ballet and concert idioms of Martha Graham, Doris Humphrey, Charles Weidman, Eugene Loring and Agnes de Mille herself.[18]

Other hindsights suggest that some of the innovations are illusory. It is quite clear, for example, that the creators of *Oklahoma!* did not set out to revolutionize the theater; they were as reluctant to throw out convention as anyone. "Dick and I, for several days, sought ways and means of logically introducing a group of girls into the early action of the play," admits Hammerstein.[19] It was their faithfulness to dramatic logic that forced them to change.

But even the touted changes—the ballet, the setting, the killing—had strong precedents. Rodgers's own *Pal Joey* and *I Married an Angel* have dream ballets, and Hammerstein's *Rose Marie* has a killing, not to mention *Porgy and Bess,* which has two murders and two drownings. No, it is not the introduction of this or that element or technique that gives *Oklahoma!* its historical position and its artistic status among musicals. Explaining why it must be regarded as a milestone of the musical theater, another giant of that theater, Alan Jay Lerner, points to its synthesis of these techniques and elements:

For what "Oklahoma!" had done was to unify and give form to trends that had been growing disparately in the music theater and, in doing so, provide a marker for the next mile into the future.[20]

In other words, *Oklahoma!* stands as a summation as well as a beginning. Its innovation is in its maturity.

# CHAPTER 5

# Morality Play
# as Musical

*One of the most frequent questions I am asked is: "What is your favorite of all your musicals?" My answer is* Carousel.[1]

RICHARD RODGERS

In the fall of 1944, Paul Whiteman, the famous bandleader, convinced the Blue Radio Network (later the American Broadcasting Company) to fund a series of commissions of new instrumental compositions to be played on his radio program. The series, called *Music Out of the Blue,* gave composers advances on royalties in exchange for performance rights for one year. The original thirteen commissioned composers included Aaron Copland, Leonard Bernstein, Igor Stravinsky, and Richard Rodgers, who "worked on a concert waltz called *Tales of Central Park.*"[2] Curiously, Rodgers and Hammerstein's new musical play *Carousel* opened the following April with "The Carousel Waltz" in place of a medley overture, a concert waltz in several sections of roughly the length that Whiteman had been seeking. Are the two waltzes the same piece?

David Ewen believes so. He reports in his biography of Rodgers that although Whiteman commissioned the waltz he never used it, and that "its mood and movement so happily caught the gay and colorful feeling of the opening carousel scene that Hammerstein persuaded Rodgers to use it for the play."[3] Indeed, the Paul Whiteman Archives at Williams College list the title *Tales of Central Park* but contain no recording or arrangement. Rodgers himself, however, refers to no Whiteman commission in his autobiography:

For the overture to *Carousel* I decided not to have an overture. I had become weary—
I still am, in fact—of the sound that comes out of an orchestra pit during an overture.
All that is ever heard is the brass because the orchestra never has a sufficient number
of strings, and the audience must make a concerted effort to pick up any melody that
is not blasted. Instead I tried to avoid this problem by making the audience pay attention, which I did simply by opening on a pantomime scene, with the orchestra playing
a single piece, the "Carousel Waltz," rather than the usual medley. In this way we
also gave the audience an emotional feeling for the characters in the story and helped
to establish the mood for the entire play.[4]

Why all the history? What does it matter? It matters because "The Carousel
Waltz" has an extraordinary relationship with the songs in the musical play.
Like a classical overture, it sets the musical terms of the entire composition and
is the main source of musical material, not tunes so much as basic musical
elements and procedures. If Ewen's story is correct (unfortunately, no reference
is given), then Hammerstein's suggestion is a better testament to his untrained
yet profound musical sensitivity than perhaps any other episode, for the waltz
establishes a musical idiom that belongs to this play alone. But the Whiteman
commission challenges the very idea that Rodgers was a composer concerned
with musical drama, for how could he take a piece composed for a completely
unrelated purpose and stand it at the head of a serious musical play?

As it happens, Rodgers is in quite good company in the matter of adapting
previously composed material for dramatic purposes. Handel's ability to do this
is legendary, of course, but it was also a fairly common practice of early nineteenth century Italians. George Gershwin did it in *Of Thee I Sing*. Furthermore,
this is hardly a case of dredging up some long forgotten movement. The precise
chronology may never be known, but it is certain that Rodgers was deeply involved in *Carousel* when and if he accepted the commission. Even if he originally intended the waltz to be given to Whiteman, it is easy to imagine that
salient musical elements of *Carousel* songs—motives, progressions, harmonic
procedures—would be at the forefront of his composing mind. A strong relationship between those songs and the waltz might be the most natural outcome of
such a situation. Indeed, the coincidence suggests the following chronology: 1)
Rodgers and Hammerstein begin work on *Carousel* in 1944, composing "Soliloquy" first; 2) Rodgers accepts a Whiteman commission to compose a concert
waltz called *Tales of Central Park;* 3) he composes the waltz while continuing
to work on *Carousel;* 4) when the waltz is finished, Rodgers and Hammerstein
see that it would be the perfect accompaniment for the pantomime; 5) Rodgers
decides not to submit the waltz to Whiteman because he would yield performance rights just as the play opened.

In the end, of course, the dramatic effect of the music must stand or fall on
its own terms in the context of the play, not on the facts of its origin. If a
composer can make a successful adaptation, so much the better for him. In this
case, the musical relationships between "The Carousel Waltz" and many of the

other songs in the play are so compelling that it is difficult to believe that the waltz was not composed just for this purpose. Its unique tone, its vocabulary specific to this play, is established on the opening page.

**Ex. 5–1**  Rodgers and Hammerstein, *Carousel,* "The Carousel Waltz" (No. 1), mm. 1–17.

The three most important musical elements are heard in the first long phrase (mm. 1-10). The tonic key of D major is established simply by strumming the chord, but the ear is soon surprised by a motive that seems to be in a different key. Then the short phrase is entirely tranposed down a perfect fourth (mm. 5-6) to make a dominant version of the first. This transposition is reiterated as the upper melody breaks the sequence, articulating the first long phrase (m. 10). So what has been heard? First, a slow and simple harmonic progression in the lower register accompanied by a much faster, chromatic one in the high register: a multi-level texture of harmonic rhythm. Second, chromatic juxtapositions that establish unusual pitch combinations as expressive norms for this play, above all the augmented triad, which is heard in measures 4 (D-F#-A#), 6 (A-C#-E#),

8, and 10 at the peaks of all the short phrases. Third, modal degrees of the scale, F-sharp (sixth degree) and B (third degree), are emphasized by melodic contour and unusual rests that bring out the beginning and ending notes of each fragment. All these elements are strengthened anew in the next long phrase (mm. 11-17). The high-level underlying progression in D is as firm as ever, while the low-level chromatic harmony becomes more biting still, now formed entirely of *parallel augmented chords.*

The power of the multi-level harmonic rhythm is unleashed as Rodgers moves from introduction to waltz proper. The lower-level progressions are easily discerned as four-bar phrases, but under it all is a steady dominant whose tension grows as it is prolonged. In Example 5-2, the high register moves from subdominant to tonic for each phrase, while the dominant A is maintained below.

**Ex. 5-2**  Rodgers and Hammerstein, *Carousel,* "The Carousel Waltz" (No. 1), mm. 27-34.

The prolonged dominant builds to a grand climax, with a final iii chord (F# minor) superimposed onto a V, which leads into the waltz proper.

**Ex. 5–3**   Rodgers and Hammerstein, *Carousel,* "The Carousel Waltz" (No. 1), mm. 47–57.

The waltz tune is a transformation of the opening motive, now reconciled to its key, and yet there is the same harmonic procedure. There are three quick tiny chords for every measure in the upper parts, all subsumed in a slower and more fundamental bass progression. The end of the first phrase shows once again an emphasis on the modal steps, in the F-sharp of the melody and in the Bs which color the tonic and dominant harmony below.

It might seem as though this harmonic procedure would sound too sophisticated or learned for a play that takes place among the simple folk of a New England mill town, but its actual effect is quite the opposite. The slow and simple bass line gives the waltz tune the oom-pah-pah quality of a town band, especially when reinforced by the tuba, which Rodgers insisted on for the pit orchestra. Meanwhile the other benefits of such harmonic control are many. It creates the sense of climax just before the waltz tune because the high-level dominant chord has been stretched out for so long, awaiting resolution. The juxtaposition of two harmonic rhythms generates and justifies unusual chords and harmonic colorings, such as the augmented triad, which would be out of the question in a simpler context. In sum, this two-level harmonic movement, in conjunction with these augmented chords and the emphasis on the modal degrees, is responsible for a tone and ambience so peculiar to *Carousel* that it seems impossible to mistake any of its music for that of another play. As Rodgers himself states, it is "The Carousel Waltz" that establishes this tone, right from the opening bars.

The relationship of the waltz with the rest of the play is made dramatic by the activity that occurs on stage while it is being played: a pantomime in which most of the major characters are introduced in a carnival setting, with a carousel at center stage. It is this scene that establishes the main romantic interest between Billy Bigelow and Julie Jordan, quite abstractly, so that the audience knows almost nothing about them except that they have fallen in love. This is the basis for one of the central dramatic themes; their love has not been explained, and is indeed inexplicable, but remains to be expressed.

Although the motion on stage is not balletic, it is coordinated with the waltz, originally by Rouben Mamoulian. He remarked on the originality of the concept of the mute prologue:

> The highest compliment I could get as a director is that no one has seemed to notice anything very unusual about the prelude, but there it is—seventy people onstage for five and a half minutes, and not a word spoken. In a straight play you couldn't think of getting away with that. But here it is so stylized that within its own framework it is perfectly logical and right.[5]

Mamoulian is quite wrong about its legitimacy in a straight play, for Ferenc Molnar did get away with the very same prologue concept in *Liliom,* the source play for *Carousel.* But it is the successful adaptation of Molnar's prologue idea that is the basis for the transformation of *Liliom,* a complex drama, into a musical play of comparable depth.

The principal source of *Liliom*'s complexity is its cast of characters, and translating these characters into operatic terms was Rodgers and Hammerstein's greatest difficulty and most admirable achievement. Indeed, in comparison with Curly and Laurey, the protagonists in *Liliom* are bundles of subtle contradictions that music could hardly hope to project:

> The dualistic hero, Andreas Zavoczki, is not a villian, only a maladjusted creature who ends up doing the wrong things in spite of all the possible good intentions. This braggart dreamer is an obstinate nonconformist, a primitive person with a vicious temper, yet a noble man full of compassion.
>
> Julie . . . emerges as the eternal female ideal. She loves unselfishly, with undemanding devotion and endurance. With almost supernatural insight and common sense, she grasps the realities of life and the true nature of her man. . . . She is taciturn and inarticulate. . . .[6]

Furthermore, dramatic action occurs not just between characters, as in *Oklahoma!,* but within them, and this action is the more important one. That is why *Carousel* can justifiably be termed a morality play as well as fantasy (as it and *Liliom* are usually called), because the struggle between good and evil that defines a morality play takes place within Billy Bigelow.

Such complexity demands an equivalent complexity of musical expression, and Rodgers and Hammerstein respond to that demand with a number of musical resources. There is much more use of melodrama, which means that characters speak over music from the orchestra. There is also a large amount of sung music which has the freedom of organization, the absence of repetition, and the melodic and rhythmic flexibility of recitative, although the sense of meter never quite disappears. These techniques make transitions from spoken dialogue to song much more gradual and smooth. The musical play therefore seems more serious because one is much less aware of the seams of operatic convention.

The same variety of musical textures allows the construction of extended musical scenes of a type quite different and more sophisticated than those in *Oklahoma!*. In that play, the musical unity of a scene depends on frequent reprises of a central song, but in *Carousel* there is true musical as well as dramatic progression. The first musical number after the prologue begins with dialogue that is rhythmically coordinated with the underplaying of the orchestra: Carrie asks Julie how she feels about Billy Bigelow. As the dialogue continues, it begins to be sung ("You're a Queer One, Julie Jordan"). The texture is close to song; the phrasing is regular and the dialogue rhymed. Next, Carrie describes how strangely her friend has been acting lately, singing monotonic lines to an orchestral accompaniment that represents the whirring of mill machinery. There is a brief return of "You're a Queer One," followed by yet another texture, pure melodrama. This leads into the first real song, "His Name Is Mister Snow," but conventional form does not hold here either, for when Carrie describes Mr. Snow's proposal of marriage, her melody becomes again a *parlando* with chromatic harmony, another pseudo-recitative. It does not conclude, but sets up dominant harmony which leads into the only completely closed song of the scene, "When I Marry Mister Snow."

The musical unity of this scene derives from the consistent key of G major, but also from the consistent usage of musical materials taken from the waltz. The multi-level harmony of "His Name Is Mister Snow" not only provides that song with the same kind of sophisticated yet folk-like harmonic coloring as has the waltz but allows Rodgers to construct the song on a very static alternation of high-level tonic and dominant harmony.

home ev-'ry night in his round bot-tomed boat With a net full of her-ring from the sea.

**Ex. 5–4** Rodgers and Hammerstein, *Carousel,* "Mister Snow" (No. 4), mm. 67–75, with harmonic analysis.

Because the high-level harmony is so static, there is almost no sense of progression until a modulation to B minor (another modal emphasis) which begins the recitative-like proposal sequence. From this point on the listener awaits a clear return to the key of G, but this is delayed by the chromaticism, so that this piece sounds much more like a prelude to "When I Marry Mister Snow" than a song in its own right, and the more active harmony of the latter song is welcome relief to what has gone before.

When I mar-ry Mis-ter Snow, The

**Ex. 5–5** Rodgers and Hammerstein, *Carousel*, "Mister Snow" (No. 4), mm. 115–25.

Here again the musical material for this apparently simple piece is drawn from the waltz. The first phrase begins and ends on modal scale degrees B and E, and the repeated B note in the melody is intensified by the harmony of an augmented tonic triad. The two-level progressions return in the second and third phrases, and include chromatic juxtapositions—the G-sharp against the G, and C proceeding to C-sharp on "churchyard trees"—that recall the beginning of the waltz.

*Carousel* has a number of such scenes that, in their musical continuity and dramatic progression, are much more ambitious than anything in *Oklahoma!*. Their flexibility of design allows the music to speak at length for the laconic New England characters, and the complexity of the musical idiom on all levels meets the demands of the drama.

Lavishing such attention on the likes of Carrie Pipperidge calls into question the nature of the subplot in *Carousel*. Once more *Oklahoma!* provides an instructive contrast because its own usage is so typical. In that play, the triangle of Ado Annie, Will Parker, and the Peddler form a symmetrical and essentially comic counterplot to the triangle of Curly, Laurey, and Jud. Their story is cleverly interwoven into the main story and its purpose is comic relief. The role of

Carrie Pipperidge and Enoch Snow is hardly so simple; the musical setting of "When I Marry Mister Snow" reveals a seriousness that belies the naïve comedy of some of her lines. This is especially apparent at the end, when the main tune returns to be elaborated by Rodgers's favorite device, the extension.

**Ex. 5–6** Rodgers and Hammerstein, *Carousel*, "Mister Snow" (No. 5), mm. 147–66.

The rise to the F natural is the song's climax, a fresh contrast to the chromatic harmony derived from the sharp side of G major that characterizes the song, and the phrase reiterates that F two measures later before moving inconclusively down to the A. Here the augmented triad reappears expressively (m. 157) and quite explicitly in that it does not arise from chromatic voice leading, only to be used again on "bold and darin'." The sentiment overcomes the humorous epithets of the final lyric since the next clear triad and progression in G, as well as the peak of melody, come with "darlin' Mister Snow!"

The depth of feeling in Carrie is brought home only when it is fully realized what she has been singing about. This is no schoolgirl's image of love that is idealized here, but rather a simple and real-life wedding, and married life, certainly very unusual topics for any romantic character, let alone one that is, according to form, supposed to be comic. The song is reprised most appropriately when Carrie announces the engagement to her friends just before the clambake that concludes the first act. Its rendition is identical to the first (except for its key, now F major), until the final section, when Mr. Snow makes his surprise entrance and sings the conclusion in A major. This device shows that Mr. Snow's feelings are as deep as Carrie's, and it also provides a smooth beginning for another extended musical scene between the two of them.

After a short scene, the two are left alone on stage and begin talking about their future together. Like the first scene of the play, it begins with a mélange of arioso and melodrama textures before the song proper, "When the Children Are Asleep," finally arrives, and again, Mr. Snow's participation in a scene of such design makes the audience take him seriously. The new song continues to develop the sentiments of "When I Marry Mister Snow," for its subject is a domestic tranquility that rarely finds expression on any stage.

When the child-ren are a - sleep and lights are low. If I still

love you The way I love you to - day, You'll

par - don my say - ing: "I told you so!"

**Ex. 5–7**  Rodgers and Hammerstein, *Carousel*, "Carrie and Mr. Snow Sequence" (No. 12), mm. 87–114.

The apparently simple melody is given expressive depth by its harmonization. The first phrase (mm. 87-90) is heard three times in the song, and its concluding note is treated differently, with increasing harmonic tension, each time. In measure 89 it is set with a plain tonic chord, with the descending inner voice immediately moving to connect to the next phrase. The second instance (m. 97) finds it the goal of a temporary modulation to D major, an emphasis on the sixth scale degree of F that comes from the waltz. The reference to the waltz is confirmed when the third occurrence (m. 109) is harmonized with an F augmented triad that demands in the strongest terms a continuation on to the conclusion.

The harmonization of this song is not the only agent of its expression, for it also has a subtlety of melodic phrasing that shows yet another advance from *Oklahoma!*, whose tunes are built on clear four-bar phrases through and through. In "When the Children Are Asleep" this easy symmetry is just slightly disturbed even at the beginning: the first phrase barely carries over into the fourth bar while the second phrase is nearly five bars long. The implications of this slight imbalance are shortly realized. The third phrase is identical to the first, clearly setting up a consequent phrase to the original antecedent. Yet, the fourth one does not conclude, but instead breaks up into two sub-phrases ("If I still love you the way / I love you today"), and ends in the wrong key (D minor (m. 102)). The rhythm of the fifth phrase is clearly parallel with the fourth one, as are the lyrics, but this time the two new sub-phrases are bound into a smooth continuous one. This magic transformation occurs in measure 104, where two half notes are substituted for the dotted half and quarter in the parallel spot (m. 100). The evenness of the rhythm, and Hammerstein's lyric, prevent the ear from perceiving a phrase break here where it is now expected. Instead, the smooth restoration of the original phrase length seems the perfect reflection of an up-welling of emotion so strong that the force of its momentum carries through.

The consummation of this love song comes when it is sung as a duet, and Rodgers applies his considerable powers of extension to its conclusion.

**Ex. 5–8**  Rodgers and Hammerstein, *Carousel*, "Carrie and Mr. Snow Sequence" (No. 12), mm. 155–67.

Now that odd emphasis on the offbeats in the accompaniment of the vocal parts ("We'll think what fun we hev had/ And be glad that it all came true") is used to generate a rhapsodic extension of the vocal parts. The climactic power of the moment depends upon the delay of the final cadence for eight more measures beyond its usual place, and upon Rodgers's withholding the texture of the two characters singing in parallel, for the first time, until the last moments.

The enhancement of the subplot that this musical treatment produces is really twofold. Most obviously, it represents a much deeper treatment of subplot characters than in almost any Broadway musical, but it also is an enormous expansion of the original characters in *Liliom*. In that play, Wolf and Marie Beifeld are representatives of conventional society, and therein is the clue to the reason why the roles of Carrie and Enoch Snow had to be different. In Molnar's play, conventional society in the persons of the Beifelds is quite indifferent to Liliom's fate, and therefore the loss of this society after his suicide means nothing to him. In revising the conclusion of *Liliom,* Rodgers and Hammerstein created a ballet which reveals Billy's daughter, Louise, excluded from the New England community because of him. Thus, in order for this exclusion to mean something, in order for it to motivate Billy to descend once again to the world, the community must be important. So we have the loving, and lovable, Carrie and Enoch, who sing in earnest about weddings, married life, and a romance of a quiet evening after the children have been taken care of. Their music does what is quite rare on the stage: it idealizes conventionality, and thereby makes it valuable.

This portrayal of the comic couple causes a dramatic inconsistency in the second act, when Mr. Snow and some of his children, in snubbing Louise, are shown to be not only conventional in their behavior but uncharitable as well. This does not square well with the image of Snow that is constructed through the music of the first act, but by this time, the virtues of the New England community have been pretty well established.

To establish such virtues is the principal justification for adding a chorus to Molnar's *Liliom.* The chorus, of course, was virtually required by the Broadway tradition, and was the principal reason why Rodgers and Hammerstein chose New England as an appropriate setting: the coastal mill town idea offered mill workers and fishermen. Yet the need to make the community itself a value allowed them to integrate the chorus into the dramatic scheme, and it imbues the chorus music with a seriousness of idiom consistent with the rest of the play. Unlike the unseen society of *Liliom,* the community in *Carousel* must have true value, and its ways and traditions become sacred. That is why "This Was a Real Nice Clambake," ostensibly a light chorus number that opens the second act, is really a celebration of a community ritual. The connotation is made quite explicit when the last course of the holy meal, the steamed clams, is recalled.

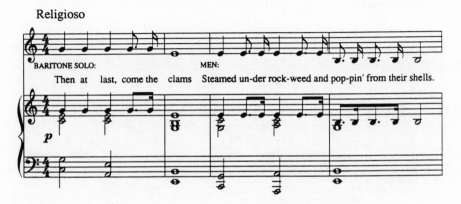

**Ex. 5–9** Rodgers and Hammerstein, *Carousel,* "A Real Nice Clambake" (No. 19), mm. 131–34.

The processional rhythm, the preponderance of minor chords and modal progressions, and Rodgers's tempo mark require no further comment.

The serious tone that is special to the music of *Carousel,* then, dominates the
musical-dramatic techniques of melodrama and quasi-recitative, and pervades the
"comic" subplot characters and the chorus. Its characteristic progressions, harmonies, and subtleties of phrasing are heard everywhere. The result is an intensity of dramatic integration, for all these distinct parts have bearing upon the
central dramatic issue: how Billy Bigelow, the insecure braggart who sees himself as a strong man who can get along without the slightest help or dependency,
will cope with his inexplicable love for Julie.

The struggle between good and evil in this morality play is within Billy himself. It is the struggle to free himself from the evil of his own mostly false self-
image, which will not let him love Julie honestly. Music has little role in painting the dark side of his character, for that is mostly superficial, and music does
not do well with pretense, falseness, and disingenuity. That is the task of the
libretto. Rather, it is the role of music to illuminate Billy's goodness.

This illumination is concentrated in just three numbers which include an extended scene, the famous "Soliloquy," and a brief reprise. The "Bench Scene,"
early in the first act, finds Billy philosophizing about the nature of the world and
his own place in it, responding through Rodgers's pseudo-recitative to the impressive forces of sea and sky. This is the scene that makes explicit the love
match between Billy and Julie so strongly implied in the opening pantomime.
They share the same music in this scene, although they never sing together. The
scene ends with Billy singing the love song which Julie had sung to him moments earlier.

The love song, "If I Loved You," has a lyric that even in its title seems
conditional, but which is prescient in a very specific way and in fact announces
one of the main dramatic themes: the couple's inability to express their love.
The music, as in "People Will Say We're in Love," instantly banishes any
impression that what they say in the lyrics might be true, and through *Carousel*'s
characteristic harmonies, progressions, and phrasing brings the attention to the
dramatic theme.

fraid    and    shy.    I'd    let my gold-en chan-ces pass    me

by.         Soon    you'd    leave me,    Off  you would go  in  the

mist  of  day.    Nev - er,    nev - er    to    know

**Ex. 5–10**   Rodgers and Hammerstein, *Carousel*, "Billy and Julie Scene" (No. 5), mm. 236–71.

The phrasing of the melody is, strictly speaking, in four-bar periods, but is not symmetrical. The last note of the first phrase is not heard until the end of the fourth measure; the second phrase, much more stable, reaches its conclusion on the strong third measure. The first phrase subdivides into two short phrases because of the long note in the second measure and because of the syntax of the lyric; the second phrase changes that rhythm just slightly and so remains a single articulation. The implications of this pattern change are realized in the release (m. 253: "Longin' to tell you . . ."), where the four-bar phrases are now inexorable, emphasizing the all-important lyric by removing a seam where the listener expects one.

The dramatic importance of the release section is brought out in other ways. The modulation to B-flat minor is the first strong chord change since the song's beginning. Indeed, all the others are tonic chords or tonic derivatives, with the exception of the harmonies that begin the second and fourth phrases, and these are in weak inversions that could be considered the result of voice leading from the surrounding tonic chords. The B-flat minor is the first new chord in root position. This harmonic goal is prepared by the opening melodic motive, an outlined B-flat minor triad ("If I loved you"), and its arrival is made inevitable by the introduction of a D-flat *augmented* triad (m. 252), with the A natural moving smoothly to B-flat in the alto voice.

The release itself (mm. 253-60) is characterized by a remarkable harmonization that includes a D dominant seventh under the leading tone C (mm. 255-56, a reference to the key of the waltz?) and an increased harmonic rhythm that sets up the last dominant chord (mm. 259-60) and thereby emphasizes the most crucial lyric with the greatest structural tension.

The musical idiom of the waltz has its greatest impact at this moment of the play. It is the slow high-level harmonic rhythm that sets up the significance of the B-flat minor passage as the only harmonically active section, and thereby justifies the tremendous climax when the music returns to D-flat (m. 261) for the close. It is the augmented triad which initiates this activity. Even the static tonic harmony of the opening section is colored in a way that recalls the waltz. An augmented chord is introduced by the fourth measure, and the long note at the end of the second phrase (mm. 243-44) is harmonized by a I$^6$ that turns into a iii chord for the end of the phrase, an unusual emphasis on a modal degree. This harmonic color is recalled even more decisively when, at the song's end, the melody soars to a high F (mm. 267-68), and the same two harmonies are used again, now alternating twice as fast.

"If I Loved You" is the listener's first insight into the complexity of Billy's character and the course that the relationship will take. It is his first confession of weakness and dependency, a confession given only by the music, not by the words, and therefore not by his conscious self. While this song presages the conflict between self and self-image, the best musical expression of that conflict comes in "Soliloquy," which Billy sings at the very end of Act I when he finds out that he is about to be a father.

"Soliloquy" has long been renowned for its elaborate form, changing textures, and its ability to reflect a number of emotional changes. Actually, this is true of any of the extended scenes in *Carousel*. "Soliloquy" is exceptional only in that it is for a single character. It is constructed on just two passages that could be detached as separate songs, surrounded by a variety of connective pseudorecitative. It is the juxtaposition of the two songs that illustrates the conflict most clearly.

"My Boy, Bill" seems to be missing most of those characteristics peculiar to the sound of *Carousel*.

**Ex. 5–11**   Rodgers and Hammerstein, *Carousel*, "Soliloquy" (No. 15), mm. 37–55.

The harmonic rhythm is fast and takes place on a single structural level. There are no augmented chords and little chromaticism. The rhythm of the melody emphasizes the strong beats and the voice leading is either a rather obvious step motion or an equally pedestrian arpeggiation toward the end. The trumpet fanfares in the blank measures add to the bombast.

The lyrics show why the music is this way:

> *Like a tree he'll grow,*
> *With his head held high*
> *And his feet planted firm on the ground,*
> *And you won't see nobody dare to try*
> *To boss him or toss him around!*
> *No pot-bellied, baggy eyed bully'll boss him around!*

Billy, in describing his imaginary son, is really describing his own image of himself, what he imagines himself to be. The music is just as substantial as the picture that he creates. Moments later, when he considers the sobering prospect of a baby girl who would need his help, he sings in a much different manner.

**Ex. 5–12**  Rodgers and Hammerstein, *Carousel*, "Soliloquy" (No. 15), mm. 205–28.

Now Billy is no longer talking about himself, and so reveals his capacity for sentiment, part of his true self. The setting of this song returns to the *Carousel* sound: an augmented triad in the second measure, chromatic melody and voice leading later on. The tune must be one of Rodgers's most remarkable in all his songs, for its wandering through several keys (mm. 215–20) makes it sound original and new at every moment and yet it is built on just two motivic ideas. The second measure, for example, has exactly the same notes as the first, simply cast in a different rhythmic pattern. The only other motive is heard in the sixth measure (m. 210), where the melody leaps upward by a major seventh, only to fall downward from the leading tone, against its tendency, in an exquisite chromatic decoration. This "chromatic-dotted" motive is then slowed in the next measure to rest on a half cadence. It is no wonder that Rodgers chose this gesture for the end of his song.

The evil side of Billy's inner struggle wins, temporarily, when his admirable resolve to provide for his daughter is perverted into a robbery attempt. Even when, after his suicide, he returns to help Louise, whose unhappiness he has caused, his inability to express love defeats him. He slaps her. But Julie has glimpsed him, and they are left alone as the orchestra plays "If I Loved You" under the action. He breaks in at the release:

> Longing to tell you,
> But afraid and shy,
> I let my golden chances pass me by.
> Now I've lost you;
> Soon I will go in the mist of day,
> And you never will know
> How I loved you,
> How I loved you.

This is one of the greatest and most sentimental reprises of the Broadway stage. It recalls the precise cause and best musical expression of the tragic action at a moment late in the play when the consequences of Billy's character struggle are most evident, and when time is running out. It is a tribute to Oscar Hammerstein's craft to note how little change the lyric requires to create this effect, and that the simplest change—the repetition of the penultimate line, removing all pretense and condition—is the most moving. For Rodgers's part, it shows a fine instinct to have Billy enter mid-song, and the careful harmonic preparation of that middle section has its greatest benefits here.

In his autobiography, Rodgers recounted that this reprise was added during tryouts:

Our New Haven opening in March 1945 went well except for the scene in which we depicted a "Mr. and Mrs. God" as a New England minister and his wife. Oscar rewrote the scene and substituted the Starkeeper. The other major change was to add a reprise of "If I Loved You" in the second act because we felt it needed more music.[7]

If this statement is true, then it is one of the best pieces of evidence that composers create by instinct and not by calculation, often quite unaware of the audible effects of their actions. The reprise, including the orchestral underplaying, is about 60 measures, perhaps two minutes of music. The American musical theater can only be grateful that such a small addition was, somehow, deemed necessary, if not significant. It is difficult to imagine *Carousel* without it.

Rodgers writes in his autobiography that he is often asked which of his musicals is his favorite:

> My answer is *Carousel*. Oscar never wrote more meaningful or more moving lyrics, and to me, my score is more satisfying than any I've ever written. But it's not just the songs; it's the whole play. Beautifully written, tender without being mawkish, it affects me deeply every time I see it performed.[8]

Ironically, it is exactly that charge of being overly sentimental that is occasionally leveled at the play. *Carousel's* first London production was a popular success, but not a critical one; review after review denounced its shallow portrayal of human feeling.

If any single source can be found for such reactions, it must be in the play's ending, the only significant plot change introduced by Rodgers and Hammerstein. The original *Liliom* ends with the title character's final failure to put things right by Julie; the stark conclusion is a logical outcome of the hero's nature. Even though the play had been a hit on Broadway in the 1921 season, the creators of *Carousel* believed that neither the musical audience of the 1940s nor the genre itself was ready for such an overtly unhappy end. So they added the graduation scene, in which Billy, continuing his invisible visit to earth, encourages Louise to believe in herself, as the graduation speech is then advising, and tells Julie at last that he did love her after all. This is accomplished in two brief lines: "Believe him, darling! Believe" and "I loved you, Julie. Know that I loved you!"

For many, this dramatic solution to the moral struggle that the play has portrayed is just too pat, too easy. This impression, however, dawns upon the listener retrospectively, not in the immediate experience of the moment, but only after the play is over. While the scene is played out, the audience is caught up in the power of the musical accompaniment, the graduates singing the hymn about human spirit, "You'll Never Walk Alone." The spiritual dazes the critical sensibilities. But what happens after it is all over? Why has the music lost its power of lasting conviction, a power so evident at so many other points of the play?

Because, for once, the musical idiom is inconsistent, not quite true to itself. The compromises required of Rodgers in his attempt to compose a dramatic piece in the manner of a hymn were simply too great. The simple rhythms and step motion of the melody do indeed recall the hymns with which most Americans would be familiar, but it is not matched with a typical fast harmonic rhythm and simple cadences. Instead, Rodgers engineers a long delay of cadence by chromatic progression, which betrays the simplicity of the melody by making out of it something more than it appears to be. The contrast is most evident in the climactic phrase itself, with the repeated notes C and E reflecting the stead-fastness of resolution while harmonies alter chromatically below.

**Ex. 5–13**  Rodgers and Hammerstein, *Carousel,* "Graduation Scene" (No. 31), mm. 24–37.

And yet, the attempt comes close to success, for the generous use of augmented triads, which in other cases might well be considered an overdose of schmaltz, are here perfectly consistent with the sound of *Carousel.*

The line between true sentiment and sentimentalism can be fine indeed, and perhaps it is crossed in the finale. It is noteworthy, however, that, although the British critics took strong exception to this flavor, the American critics never did, through revival after revival. It might be worth asking whether the unsubtle, unabashed sentiment—not sentimentalism—with which *Carousel* concludes is an Americanism, a characteristic of a number of important American musicals that does not translate well into other languages or cultures. If so, then it was well indeed that *Carousel* was one of two musical plays, along with Leonard Bernstein's *Wonderful Town,* sent to the Brussels World's Fair in 1959 to be part of the American exhibit. Certainly no play other than this musical adaptation of a Hungarian stage classic could better show the finest and most American qualities of its native theater tradition.

# CHAPTER 6

# Shakespeare
# as Musical

*I have no book sense.*[1]

COLE PORTER

The ideal of an integrated musical play that Rodgers and Hammerstein's *Oklahoma!* made so convincing in March 1943 was no boon to the composers who had made successful careers not on the strength of dramatic instincts but simply on the superior quality of their songs as songs. Chief among these composers was Cole Porter, who from the late 1920s through the early 1940s had written show after show that charmed theatergoers with sophisticated and witty lyrics and tunes that have since become standards.

Porter was just not interested in the craft of a libretto, nor in the dramatic issues of characterization and development. His method of composition indicates his real priorities:

> First I think of an idea for a song and then I fit it to a title. Then I go to work on a melody, spotting the title at certain moments in the melody. Then I write the lyric—the end first—that way it has a strong finish. It's terribly important for a song to have a strong finish. I do the lyrics the way I'd do a crossword puzzle. I try to give myself a meter which will make the lyric as easy as possible to write, but without being banal. . . . I try to pick for my rhyme words of which there is a long list with the same ending.[2]

It is telling that the song's creation centers on Porter's own idea, and that of all the ancillary considerations, none is dramatic. There is nothing said about character, how the song will fit into the scene, or how it will lead into the next. The composition of a single song seems a closed process, unrelated to anything else the show might involve. Porter worked with a comprehensive outline of the show, so that he was certainly aware of what type of song was required for a given spot, but he did not have a script, and rarely made suggestions about the book for which he composed. As he once remarked, "I have no book sense."[3]

The result was a series of vacuous plays which cannot stand revival spiced up with songs which have been sung and played as standards the world over. There is perhaps no better example of this curious situation than *Anything Goes* (1934), Porter's most famous and successful musical of the 1930s. It originally contained such hits as "You're the Top," "I Get a Kick Out of You," and the title song, but the book is so weak that the producers of the 1965 revival had to prop it up by ransacking several other Porter shows for "It's Delovely" (from *Red, Hot, and Blue,* 1936), "Friendship" (from *DuBarry Was a Lady,* 1939), and "Take Me Back to Manhattan" (from *The New Yorkers,* 1930). It is no wonder. The original story was written by veteran bookwriters P. G. Wodehouse and Guy Bolton on the subject of a shipwreck. Then the S.S. *Morro Castle* actually sunk off New Jersey with a loss of 125 lives, and producer Vinton Freedley saw the comedy in his plot premise disappear just two months before the scheduled opening. Because Wodehouse and Bolton were in Europe, he quickly hired Howard Lindsay and Russel Crouse to rewrite the story, now set on a very safe ocean liner. But the book was not finished until two days before the Boston opening, and revisions were made even in the last rehearsals.

Such is not the recommended method for composing an integrated musical play, and in performance today *Anything Goes* shows quite plainly its unusual history. Yet it survived over 400 performances in the early '30s, and Porter's successful streak continued well into the next decade, finishing with a series of five shows each of which were box-office smashes: *Du Barry Was a Lady* (1939), 408 performances; *Panama Hattie* (1940), 501 performances; *Let's Face It* (1941), 547 performances; *Something for the Boys* (1942), 422 performances; and *Mexican Hayride* (1943), 481 performances. Then, suddenly, the Porter charm seemed to vanish. There were two flops, *Seven Lively Arts* (1944) and *Around the World in Eighty Days* (1946), film offers declined, and rumor had it that Porter was finished. It is too easy to point to *Oklahoma!* and *Carousel* as the reason, if only because public standards are rarely altered so dramatically, but the integration of those plays was so explicit that it produced an awareness of it amounting to self-consciousness, and even Porter noticed the change wrought by Rodgers and Hammerstein. "The librettos are much better and the scores are much closer to the librettos than they used to be. Those two made it harder for everybody else."[4]

In view of his natural predilection for fusing melody and lyric into closed song forms, his working habits, and his recent history of failure against a background of dramatic reform, it is not surprising that Porter was reluctant to tackle as apparently complex a task as the musical adaptation of *The Taming of the*

*Shrew*. Other factors too seemed to portend failure. Porter's health, never very good since a terrible riding accident in 1937 robbed him of the full use of his legs, was especially poor just when librettist Bella Spewack approached him with the proposal. Spewack, along with her husband Sam, although successful Broadway playwrights, had done only one libretto for a musical, Porter's *Leave It to Me* (1938). The director, John C. Wilson, and producers, Arnold Saint Subber and Lemuel Ayres, were similarly inexperienced in their particular roles, although well familiar with Broadway. The proposed cast included Alfred Drake but no other box-office draws. But it was the idea of translating Shakespeare into a musical play that seemed to scare Porter most of all, despite Rodgers and Hart's popular precedent, *The Boys From Syracuse* (1938).

Once Bella Spewack convinced him, however, the score came from Porter's pen "like an avalanche," [5] and he completed most of the score between February and May 1948. Although he collaborated closely with his librettists, it is fairly clear that he worked as he always had, from an outline, for the Spewacks report that "By the time of the Philadelphia tryout the parts of Lois and Bill contained only the essentials for plot and song cues." [6] What saved the play from the same sort of confusion that sunk *Anything Goes* was the central dramatic conception of a play within a play, and credit for that must go to Bella Spewack. Ironically, she was rather reluctant to adapt *The Taming of the Shrew* herself, but "Then I came up with the story idea and it was exactly the show as it was." [7] It is the idea of a play within a play, and the skillful arrangement of scenes around that idea, that allowed Porter to succeed as a dramatic composer without changing his working methods or song style.

The plot of *Kiss Me, Kate* centers on a theater troupe in Baltimore putting on a musical version of *The Taming of the Shrew*. The whole, then, is an admixture of brilliantly contrasting scenes, some in Baltimore that show the backstage "reality" of the actors' lives and relationships, and others in Padua which portray various scenes from the "unreal" Shakespearean play. One can perhaps imagine why Bella Spewack saw this construction as an inspired solution to the problem of treating Shakespeare in the musical theater. By making *Shrew* the play within the framework of another play, Shakespeare is made into a dramatic object rather than a vehicle. In a sense the issue of adapting Shakespeare is ducked altogether, since whatever of *Shrew* remains is not "the real play." The necessity of translating into music the complex Shakespearian characters and dramatic themes is eliminated, while allowing some of them to come out in correspondences between the two plays. It is just these correspondences that create the one serious dramatic issue and climax of *Kiss Me, Kate*. Fred Graham and his ex-wife Lilli Vanessi, the principals of the acting troupe, are Petruchio and Katherine in the flesh.

The second advantage of the play within a play construction is as a rich source of comic irony for Cole Porter. Porter's lyrics, always dependent upon irony for much of their wit, live off the outrageous yet logical rhyme suited to an unusual situation. The juxtaposition of the two plays, so different in setting and style, provide a number of sources for the irony in the lyrics of *Kiss Me, Kate*.

One such source is the sixteenth-century Italian setting, with all its typical images of learning and courtly manners. Porter condenses Shakespeare's rather involved courting of Bianca by the three suitors into a single quartet that plays on the contrasts, real and apparent, between Padua and Baltimore.

**Ex. 6–1** Porter, *Kiss Me, Kate,* "Tom, Dick or Harry" (No. 6), mm. 4–19.

The humor in the lyric here comes from a collage of American and fake Renaissance idioms, poetic devices, and clever rhymes. The tone is set right from the start with an explicit Americanism, a gangster idiom. This is followed by a line containing another Americanism, an internal rhyming of "which" and "rich," and a triple alliteration, all within the space of three words. "Rip-roaring rich" is one of the cleverest phrases in the show, because it is not only the linchpin of these effects, it also creates a posture of delightful bravado for the suitor. The third line has the one concession to the sixteenth-century setting ("thou woulds't") followed by a reference to the American tax system. What makes it all work, of course, is that, taken all together, this verbal virtuosity presentes a credible, if uproarious, picture of the mythical Renaissance merchant making his suit.

Hortensio's suit continues the contrast of imagery:

> *I come to thee, a thoroughbred patrician,*
> *Still spraying my decaying family tree.*
> *To give a social lift to thy position,*
> *Marry me, marry me, marry me . . .*

Once more, Porter succeeds in evoking a classical flavor at the same time that he makes fun of classical symbols. "Patrician" recalls ancient noble status, but its nobility is immediately undermined by comparison to racehorses, and the metaphor of preventing tree rot is of course as modern as can be.

The musical setting is another source of ironic play between the Renaissance and modern settings, although its effect in this song takes place over whole sections and therefore is less intense, but nevertheless significant. The passage in Example 6-1 has its first phrase in A-flat minor (mm. 4-8), the next in G-flat minor (mm. 8-12), and the last two in A-flat major (mm. 12-20). While the use of parallel modes is an important feature of all the "Shakespeare" songs in *Kiss Me, Kate* save one, the use of G-flat minor, the minor mode on the seventh

degree, is rare in any Western style. Clearly this is Porter's attempt to communicate a vestige, or a stereotype, of a modal Renaissance idiom. This attempt
becomes obvious when Bianca joins the three suitors for the first time.

**Ex. 6–2**  Porter, *Kiss Me, Kate,* "Tom, Dick or Harry" (No. 6), mm. 94–102.

The four-voice a cappella texture here is certainly meant to recall the Italian
madrigal, and the execution of such a characteristic sound in barbershop harmony is yet another example of Porter's ironical imagination at work. Now the
humor comes from a juxtaposition of musical styles.

A subtler exploitation of this musical source of irony occurs in Katherine's
principal number, "I Hate Men."

**Ex. 6–3**  Porter, *Kiss Me, Kate,* "I Hate Men" (No. 9), mm. 1–14.

Its essential character is that of a pattersong, which presents a steady stream of humorous lyrics on a rather monotonous, fast moving melody. But the end of each half verse breaks the patter into a startling melisma on the title (mm. 12-14), accompanied by suddenly faster harmonic rhythm and effecting a most classical modulation to the dominant, and there is the ironic moment. What was

once a song in the most frivolous of styles has been instantly transformed into a
hymn. The craft of this transformation takes its root from the song's beginning.
The listener first hears a solemn, somewhat impressionistic progression by the
harp which establishes a rather solemn air. This solemnity is confirmed, if somewhat humorously, by Katherine, who presents the title in long notes. The next
phrase (mm. 4-6) is nothing more than a variation of Katherine's first three
notes, but it establishes the rhythm of the patter, so that the transition from
introduction to pattersong is seamless. The near religious quotation of the refrain
in measure thirteen simply realizes the implications of the beginning, the same
process reversed.

The Shakespearean motif of *Kiss Me, Kate,* of course, is itself a rich source
of ironic amusement. The melismatic singing in "I Hate Men" makes ironic
sense in the context of a pattersong because, after all, this is a Shakespearean
character. In other words, Porter and the Spewacks take full advantage of the
snob appeal of Shakespeare, a fully American sentiment to be sure. Nowhere is
this clearer than in the hilarious exit number for the two gangsters who are forced
to take tacit parts of their own design in the musical *Shrew.*

Porter added "Brush Up Your Shakespeare" at the last moment because he
felt that the gangsters deserved an exit song. If one can forgive the rather obvious contrivance of its presentation, there is a wealth of comic juxtaposition to
be savored. First there is the spectacle of two criminal ignoramuses quoting
various Shakespearean titles and terms, an improbability made credible by a
number of scenes like the following:

FRED: Quiet, dammit!
HOWELL: Look here, Graham!
FIRST GUNMAN: He said quiet, dammit.
SECOND GUNMAN: Shhh . . .
FIRST GUNMAN: (softly) Ain't you got no appreciation of the finer things of life?
SECOND GUNMAN: (softly) Man cannot live by bread alone.
HOWELL: What?
FRED: (to GUNMEN, very quietly) Be tolerant, gentlemen. Remember Mr. Howell didn't
    have your advantages—eight years in the prison library in Atlanta!

So they are not quite ignoramuses after all. That they propose in their singing
that familiarity with Shakespeare will help any man with his love life is clearly
a contrivance, but the irony remains.

Next there is the "Bowery Waltz tempo" which Porter chooses for his gangsters. This is a texture common to popular songs from Tin Pan Alley around the
turn of the century, and Porter clearly intends it to conjure up images of middle-
class gentility and sentiment.

**Ex. 6–4** Porter, *Kiss Me, Kate,* "Brush Up Your Shakespeare" (No. 20), mm. 61–83.

The perfection of the imitation of the old waltz style turns small harmonic details into humorous gestures. Every time a typical secondary dominant (mm. 62, 63, 73, etc.) comes along, the sense of the genteel style is reinforced and one cannot help but smile to see gangsters singing it.[8]

The most obvious source of ironic humor, however, is in the outrageous rhyming and increasingly bawdy imagery that Porter derives from Shakespeare's titles. The Porter trademark of the forced rhyme works here better than ever, because it is yet another play on the ignorant gangsters singing about Shakespeare.

The play within a play construction is what allows all these many sorts of juxtapositions, far more than a more straightforward adaptation of *The Taming of the Shrew* would have afforded. And yet since the playing of *Shrew* within the framework of the larger play does occupy a large portion of the stage time, it cannot simply be the butt of all the jokes. There must be a deeper dramatic reason for devoting as much music to it, for playing out as much of the Shakespearean dialogue as is presented. Because both plays receive equal emphasis, there must be a unification of their two sets of action.

Once source of this unity is in the arrangement of scenes and especially in the ordering of the musical numbers. This ordering in the first act results in two separate blocks of music which, in effect, are two small "sub-acts" (see figure). The first block, the "Baltimore songs" are those sung in the context of the larger framework play, and the second block, the "Padua songs," are those sung as part of the musical *Shrew* that the troupe is presenting.

The two plays become distinct through their music as well as through the deployment of songs in the first act. The "Padua" songs all have a characteristic alternation of the parallel mode. The excerpt from "Tom, Dick or Harry" (Ex. 6-1, mm. 3-6) is as good an example as any. It begins in A-flat minor, then moves to the rather unusual G-flat minor, using that key as a substitute dominant. But the setting of the third phrase in A-flat major makes an obvious and startling contrast to the second phrase, since so many flats have now been removed. This special flavor, moving from a minor mode to the parallel major, is heard in all the Padua songs of the first act with the exception of "I've Come to Wive It Wealthily in Padua," in which the alternation is reversed. Clearly this contrast of modes is Porter's stratagem for imbuing those songs with a "Renaissance spirit," and the variety of ways in which this simple idea is put to use is remarkable: in "Tom, Dick or Harry" the contrast is within individual phrases; in "I Hate Men" only the introduction to each verse is in minor (Ex. 6-3, mm. 3–6); and "Were Thine That Special Face" is entirely in minor except for the last climactic phrase. To be sure, Porter takes advantage of a number of other musical stereotypes of early music—the pavane rhythm in "I've Come to Wive It Wealthily in Padua," the madrigal texture in "Tom, Dick or Harry"—but the alternation of minor and major modes is by far his most consistent and subtle means of distinguishing the *Shrew* part of *Kiss Me, Kate* from its frame.

The Baltimore songs have no such structural consistency, and show instead Porter's vaunted and bewildering eclecticism. The four songs in the first act are examples of four different stylistic effects: an old-fashioned musical chorus number, a blues song, a parody of a Viennese waltz song, and a very serious, almost operatic, soliloquy. Among the songs of comic intention, which means all of

Order of Music in *Kiss Me, Kate,* Act I

Action in Baltimore                    *The Taming of the Shrew*

Overture

1. "Another Op'nin, Another Show"
   (Hattie and company)

2. "Why Can't You Behave"
   (Lois and Bill)

3. "Wunderbar"
   (Fred and Lilli)

4. "So in Love"
   (Lilli)

        5. "We Open in Venice"
   (Ensemble)

        6. "Tom, Dick or Harry"
   (Gremio, Lucentio, Hortensio, Bianca)

        7. "Rose Dance"

        8. "I've Come to Wive It Wealthily in Padua"
   (Petruchio and ensemble)

        9. "I Hate Men"
   (Katherine)

       10. "Were Thine That Special Face"
   (Petruchio)

       11. (Change of Scene—"I Hate Men)"

       12. "I Sing of Love"
   (Chorus)

       13. Finale - Act I
   (Petruchio, Katherine, Company)

    14. Entr'acte

them except "So in Love" and "I Am Ashamed That Women Are So Simple," the only common characteristic is Porter's virtuoso lyric.

In *Kiss Me, Kate* there is an effortless merger of high and low cultural references. Having had the advantage of a classical education with its emphasis on Latin and Greek—to say nothing of his later mastery of French, German, Italian and Spanish—Cole produced metaphors of a unique nature in popular music. Equally unexpected are the allusions to chemistry and biology which blend (seemingly with ease, but actually through hard work) with fashionable personalities, fads and foibles of modern society, in the larger sense.[9]

Indeed, catching all the inside jokes of *Kiss Me, Kate* poses quite a stiff challenge to the listener's erudition. One needs at least a smattering of Italian, German, and French, and passing familiarity with Italian cities and landmarks, Shakespearean titles and expressions, classical poets, the Kinsey report, the Theatre Guild, the "Jungfrau," the "Back bay," L. B. Mayer, and Lassie.

Once the first act, in its ordering and use of stylistic references, has given the two plays palpable identities, the second act can begin to unite them.

Order of Musical Numbers in *Kiss Me, Kate,* Act II

| Action in Baltimore | *The Taming of the Shrew* |
|---|---|
| 15. "Too Darn Hot"<br>(Paul and Boys) | |
| | 16. "Where Is the Life That Late I Led?"<br>(Petruchio) |
| 17. "Always True to You in My Fashion"<br>(Lois) | |
| 18. "Bianca"<br>(Bill) | |
| 19. "So In Love"<br>(Fred) | |
| 20. "Brush Up Your Shakespeare"<br>(Gunmen) | |
| | 21. "Pavana ("Why Can't You Behave") |
| | 22. "I Am Ashamed That Women Are So Simple"<br>(Katherine) |
| | 23. Finale - Act II<br>(Petruchio, Katherine, and Company) |

The distinctions made in the first act begin to blur in the second, as the two sets of action begin to merge. Gone is the blocklike arrangement of numbers for Baltimore and Padua; they are now intermingled. In addition, there are curious cross references within the songs that are supposed to be contained in one play or the other. Bill Calhoun's romantic trifle to his lover Lois uses her character name, "Bianca," and the music for the pavane in the last scene of *The Taming of the Shrew* is a stately version of "Why Can't You Behave."

A second unifying device of *Kiss Me, Kate* is the perhaps more obvious one of constructing a parallel plot between the two plays. Fred Graham, the rather overbearing leading actor and director, and Lilli Vanessi, the leading lady, are Petruchio and Katherine. Or are they? Their conflict and reconciliation at the play's end clearly mirrors that of their Shakespearean counterparts, but this is certainly a superficial parallel. Do the complex motivations of Petruchio and Katherine bear upon the actions of Fred and Lilli?

> On the stage . . . Petruchio comes over far less as an aggressive male out to bully a refractory wife into total submission than he does as a man who genuinely prizes Katherina and, by exploiting an age-old and basic antagonism between the sexes, manoeuvres her into an understanding of his nature and also her own.[10]

There is no such subtlety in Fred's actions, not in the least. He is still in love with Lilli, and wants her, and that is that. A cynical listener might not be so generous: he wants her so that his play can continue its run. The parallel of Lilli and Katherine is not really much closer.

> Heartily sick of a single life . . . she is really more than ready to give herself to a man but, imprisoned within a set of aggressive attitudes which have become habitual, has not the faintest idea how to do so.[11]

Lilli's aggressions are not habitual; each one has a perfectly obvious cause, usually some attention paid by Fred to Lois. There is a faint echo of boredom with life, but not with the single life she currently leads, but ironically with the married life she intends to begin with her new suitor Harrison, a married life which, according to Fred's malicious depiction, would in effect be single.

In short, any effort to make a parallel plot between the principals must be considered a partial success. However, there is a stronger parallel between the plays in terms of dramatic focus, their concentration on a single romantic relationship:

> Alone of the comedies, and virtually alone in the canon, *The Taming of the Shrew* concerns itself with such relationship. If we set aside *Antony and Cleopatra* and perhaps *Romeo and Juliet,* no other play of Shakespeare's concentrates on a single relationship. This play is about Katherina and Petruchio, and the rest of the dramatis personae compose the backdrop to their relationship.[12]

The comic couple of Bill Calhoun and Lois Lane seem to fill the Broadway form of the secondary plot, but there is really nothing to give substance to the form. There is no progression to their story, no resolution, and not a single serious musical number is sung by them. There is but one dramatic theme of *Kiss Me, Kate* and that is the reconciliation of Fred and Lilli.

The remarkable aspect of the treatment of this theme is that it is so simple and yet so long-range, occupying the entire stage time. The simplicity lies in its singularity of action. The causes of the conflict and divorce are never shown, only alluded to, so that the whole play could be described as an action of reconciliation. The range of this apparently simple action is brought about, again, by the ordering of scenes and musical numbers within the two-play scheme. The action begins when Lilli and Fred, alone in her dressing room, reminisce about the old days in the song "Wunderbar." This song has attracted a good deal of notice because of its brilliant parody of the sentimental Viennese waltz, but the important point about it is that by the end, it is clear that Fred and Lilli are still in love. This perception is utterly confirmed on Lilli's part when she sings "So in Love" upon Fred's departure.

Now the action is interrupted, first by the large block of music devoted to *Shrew,* then by some comic numbers that begin the second act, not to be resumed until late in the second act when Lilli walks out on the troupe for the last time. Fred sings "So in Love," and this reprise has an unusual double function, for it not only confirms that Fred loves as well as Lilli, but makes a structural link with the main action begun early in the first act. Porter seems to have appreciated the dramatic weight this song would have to bear, for it is one of only two serious songs of the show, and its melody shows all the learning of his remarkable musical training.

The first two phrases present the two most salient aspects of the melody, the half-step motion and the upward leap of a perfect fifth.

**Ex. 6–5** Porter, *Kiss Me, Kate,* "So in Love" (No. 4), mm. 5–12.

The rising half-step ("Strange, dear" and "true dear") seems startling at first because the D makes a dissonant minor ninth over the bass, but because the key is F-sharp minor, the melody is diatonic. The next phrases reach a peak and then descend.

**Ex. 6–6** Porter, *Kiss Me, Kate,* "So in Love" (No. 4), mm. 12–20.

The upward leap to the high point is not the expected fifth, but only a minor third (mm. 13-14). When Porter begins the tune again and reaches the corresponding peak the second time, he stretches the leap to a fourth (Ex. 6-7, mm. 29-30) before descending to a cadence in A major.

**Ex. 6–7**  Porter, *Kiss Me, Kate,* "So in Love" (No. 4), mm. 28–36.

This high E becomes the focal point of the release melody.

**Ex. 6–8**   Porter, *Kiss Me, Kate*, "So in Love" (No. 4), mm. 36–51.

The third phrase of the release melody, moving smoothly by step up the A scale as did the first phrase, suddenly skips the E and climaxes on F natural, which shocks the ear because it is foreign to the key and especially since the previous phrase had ended on a low F-sharp, recalling the original key. And yet, the shock is quickly apprehended as a deeply expressive but eminently logical gesture, a new realization of the half-step motion so emphasized at the beginning. Despite this effect, the most expressive peak is yet to come. The return to the main melody is once again a literal repetition of the beginning, but the third and fourth phrases develop still more Porter's opening motives.

**Ex. 6–9**   Porter, *Kiss Me, Kate*, "So in Love" (No. 4), mm. 60–73.

The great leap to the high F-sharp at once restores the perfect fifth interval, and completes the high-level half-step motion implied when the high E changed to high F natural (Fig. 6-1).[13]

**Fig. 6–3**  An implication-realization graph of "So in Love," main melody.

But the exploitation of expressive semitones is not over, for the last phrase is extended from its original four and one-half measure length to ten and one-half measures by interpolating every chromatic half-step from D down to A. This is of course the typical Romantic device of delaying the cadence for expressive purposes, but in this case the chromatic extension has particular justification and musical logic.

In the context of the whole of *Kiss Me, Kate*, "So in Love" is the chief dramatic number. It confirms the love of both Fred and Lilli and establishes them as the only two serious characters. Further, the depth of its craft and musical expression qualify it as the only number with sufficient dramatic weight to resume by its reprise late in the second act the serious action that was suspended in the first.

The masterstroke of unifying the play within a play construction is the combination of both plot resolutions, and therefore the dual structure, in a single number, "I Am Ashamed That Women Are So Simple." When Fred sings his reprise of "So in Love," it is in reaction to Lilli's decision to walk out on the production, and on him. Because *Shrew* is now without a Katherine, Fred tries to improvise the wager scene:

PETRUCHIO: I know she will not come. The fouler fortune mine and there an end.
    (Enter KATHERINE. *Startled sighs from guests, also relief.*)
KATHERINE: (*going right into part as if she'd never quit the show*) What is your will, sir?
PETRUCHIO: (*really moved, forgetting Shakespeare*) Darling—(*Then, as actor, picking up play again*) Katherine, that cap of yours becomes you not; Off with that bauble, throw it underfoot. (*She does so.*)
BIANCA: Fie! What foolish duty call you this?
PETRUCHIO: Kate, I charge thee, tell these headstrong women what duty they do owe their lords and husbands.[14]

The musical setting of Shakespeare's text that follows must be considered to be not only a resolution of the Shrew story but also as a lasting reconciliation between Fred and Lilli. The Spewacks' clever device of having Lilli quit only to return with her entrance on stage makes this interpretation inevitable; it remains for Porter to make it credible.

He does so by drawing once more on his immense musical experience and

composes a brief arietta in eighteenth-century style, a style that because of its
revered status in Western culture has the necessary weight for the dramatic purpose at hand, and at the same time because of its anachronism recalls again a
flavor of the past appropriate, to Porter's mind, for Shakespeare.

are our bod-ies soft and weak and smooth,       Un - apt to toil and trou- ble in the

world.       But       that our soft con-di-tions and our   hearts       Should well a-

gree with our ex-ter - nal  parts?       So       wife, hold your tem-per and

(Broader, with great emphasis)

**Ex. 6–10** Porter, *Kiss Me, Kate,* ''I Am Ashamed That Women Are So Simple'' (No. 22).

The elements of the classical style are not only in the clear and periodic phrasing and fast harmonic rhythm but in the overall form of the song. It is really a tiny sonata form. The first two phrases firmly establish the key of E-flat major with a melody and accompaniment that makes two small cadences (m. 3 and m. 5). The third phrase makes a clear modulation to the dominant key,

B-flat major, but an important point is not that Porter uses the same key relationships as are found in Mozart arias, but that the modulation is so authentically classical in method. The end of the first phrase in measure 3 is accompanied by a moving plagal bass line; the end of the second is accompanied by the same bass line, but accelerated so that the fast harmonic rhythm seems to propel the modulation.

The development part of the song begins in G-flat major, a subdominant key which along with the delicate orchestration and high register of the accompaniment reflects the words at that point. Another reason for choosing that key becomes apparent at the end of the sixth phrase, when its relative E-flat minor is touched upon (mm. 12-13), a last reminiscence of the contrast of parallel modes that has characterized all the Shakespearean numbers. Another two phrases that move through B-flat major set up the recapitulation, with the key of B-flat acting as a prolonged dominant chord here. This makes the recapitulation ("So wife, hold your temper . . .") as emphatic as the style demands, and it is again a credit to Porter as a lyricist that he is able to coordinate this essential musical gesture of the sonata style with the definitive answer to Katherine's rhetorical queries. After that, the mimicry of the style falters—with the chromatic chord in measure 23, and in the asymmetrical delay of the last cadence—in favor of a more intuitive expression. In the main, however, it is apparent that Porter understood not only the form of the eighteenth-century aria but also its structural procedure.

The text for "I Am Ashamed," of course, is a direct adaptation, almost word for word, of about one-third of Katherine's long climactic speech in the last act of The Taming of the Shrew. One literary interpretation of this speech claims that Katherine is not saying what she means:

> In this most recent reading of the play, Petruchio, far from "taming" or subtly having a beneficent influence on a woman, is in reality tamed by her. While having the illusion of conquering, he is conquered by her; when she says what he wants to hear, she is being ironic, and undermining him with a show of acquiescence and virtually a wink to the audience.[15]

Because Porter makes such a near-perfect imitation of eighteenth-century classicism in the music, however, any such ambiguity is blasted, simply because the seriousness of the effort and the effect cannot admit of irony here. Porter, finally the dramatist, has clarified his text through his music.

It is ironic that the dramatically satisfying and musically logical conclusion which is missing from Show Boat, Porgy and Bess, Oklahoma!, and perhaps even from Carousel is the glory of Kiss Me, Kate, if only because the bulk of the show seems such lightweight stuff. There is so much that reminds the audience of the old Broadway shenanigans, such as the collapse of the madrigal singing into a silly foxtrot in "Tom, Dick or Harry" or the entertaining but dramatically vapid "Too Darn Hot" which begins the second act. And if it is too harsh to criticize the lack of any substantial deep parallelism between Fred-

Lilli and Petruchio-Katherine, it can certainly be termed a missed opportunity. Yet, by focusing his most sophisticated and expressive musical resources on a single couple, on a simple dramatic action, Porter has managed to succeed where many have failed, in the end.

The irony points up the vexing problem of how to approach this musical among its contemporaries. Its popular success was enormous, both here and abroad, and it holds a secure place in the repertoire of the American musical theater and other popular theaters around the globe, and yet Brooks Atkinson was forced to ask himself:

> Does it rank with the immortal trio of "Show Boat," "Porgy and Bess," and "Oklahoma!," as some of its idolaters believe, or with "Annie Get Your Gun," which is perfection in the more modest field of book-and-song entertainment? In my opinion that is where it belongs.

The matter of evaluating artistic success in terms of artistic aspiration comes again to the fore. *Kiss Me, Kate* is no *Carousel,* either in its characterizations, its portrayal of action through music, or in its consistency of musical idiom, but Cole Porter is not Rodgers and Hammerstein, and there is certainly no discernible attempt to make *Kiss Me, Kate* like *Carousel.* It does not aim so high, but it does hit its own more modest mark. "Its only profundity is its skill, which is enormous"[17] is a remark that may be too stern in view of Porter's marvelous finale, but it is essentially true. *Kiss Me, Kate* is a musical which takes a complex production idea, the Shakespeare play within a play, and with it tells a simple story, and the skill required to turn that trick is quite enough to admire.

# CHAPTER 7

# The Pure
# Love Story

*I can never forget a man who says:*
*"I saw a girl and I love her."* [1]

FRANK LOESSER

If any distinction can be made between the musical plays of Broadway's golden age of the 1940s and '50s and those of recent years, it is that the traditional musicals are always love stories of one sort or another. After the cynicism of *Evita* and *A Chorus Line,* after the bleak humor of *Sweeney Todd,* a popular nostalgia for the simpler stories might be understandable. Yet, the old formula was never quite as simple as it seemed. While most traditional musicals have the romantic love of a leading couple as its central musical-dramatic construct, it is almost always elaborated and complicated by other elements of the plot. In *Oklahoma!* the listener is never allowed to forget the ominous threat of Jud; in *Kiss Me, Kate* it is a pair of comic gangsters, an utterly improbable beau, and the pressure of making a successful play that divert the action; and in *Brigadoon* there is the mysterious miracle. Furthermore, these plays and most others like them have important comic subplots, which add another measure of romantic interest, to be sure, but which divert attention from the main dramatic action yet again. The truth is that, despite appearances, falling in love is not the action of a traditional musical; indeed, the fact that the leading couple are in love is never seriously in doubt. Rather, the action is concerned with surmounting obstacles to their living happily ever after, in the tradition of classic comedy.

Such a formula offers a clear design of dramatic conflict and resolution. With the attraction of the lovers taken for granted, their separation becomes the source of dramatic tension, and getting them together becomes the generating action. The obstacles may take a variety of forms, of course: another person, such as Jud, or Crown in *Porgy and Bess;* a peculiar situation, such as the ethos of tradition in *Fiddler on the Roof,* or the distinction in social rank in *The King and I;* or, perhaps best of all, flaws in the characters themselves, as in *Carousel's* Billy. Why then the complications, the subplots? They lend necessary articulation to what is essentially a very simple action. The comic scenes and surprise twists in the story articulate the immediate stage activity so that the main tension can be prolonged for two acts. In addition, each turn of the elaborated story allows the principal characters to express their feelings for one another in a variety of ways.

None of this is very easy, of course, and that is why only a comparatively small number of musicals succeed. What seems to be simple in theory turns out to be murderously difficult to execute, perhaps because in art it is the small details that become as essential as the form, that distinguish perfection from run-of-the-mill. A musical play that coordinates the complexities of plot so that the essential action, so simple in form, is extended but not obscured, and all the while convincingly carried by music, is an impressive thing. How much more impressive, then, is a musical which succeeds without all the necessary complications, without the elaborate form! Such a work is *The Most Happy Fella* of Frank Loesser.

The difference in *The Most Happy Fella* is that the love story is not just the essential action, it is the only action. There is really no other plot, and nothing else of significance happens. There are other events and even dramatic themes which affect the course of the love story, but these do not complicate the plot by diversion, but rather by enrichment. How is that possible? Why doesn't the audience fall asleep? Loesser, who is composer, lyricist, and librettist for this, his most ambitious work, accomplishes it by taking away one of the fundamental assumptions of the traditional musical, the love of the leading couple. By making the question of whether Rosabella will fall in love with Tony a real question, Loesser creates a new source of dramatic tension. In effect, the plot allows the audience a rare chance to watch a romance grow slowly and beautifully over the course of two acts.

When one recalls that a number of expert Broadway teams, including Rodgers and Hammerstein, and Lerner and Loewe on the first go round, gave up the idea of setting Shaw's *Pygmalion* simply because there was no subplot, the difficulties of composing *The Most Happy Fella,* which seems to have hardly any plot at all, can be appreciated. Without diversions from the main plot, Loesser somehow had to slow down the action without loss of interest. He had to develop the traditional sort of conflict and resolution, without overshadowing the main action of this play, the action of falling in love. It is extraordinary then, but not surprising, that Loesser took four years to finish the project. He first considered the idea of setting Sidney Howard's *They Knew What They Wanted* in 1952, and *The Most Happy Fella* opened on May 3, 1956, at the Imperial Theater.

Well may Loesser have taken the time. His previous effort, *Guys and Dolls,* had opened in November 1950 and would run 1200 performances, a tremendous popular and critical success in the mature strain of musical comedies descending directly from *Oklahoma!,* including *Kiss Me, Kate,* and continuing into the 1950s. It is mature in the sense that the techniques of musical-dramatic integration, so new and almost mysterious in *Oklahoma!,* are by now completely mastered and seem almost easy.

*Guys and Dolls* is a typical example of the embellished love story tradition against which *The Most Happy Fella* stands out so clearly. The libretto of Abe Burrows makes a double plot of "The Idylls of Sarah Brown," a short story of Damon Runyon, by adding a number of characters from Runyon's other stories.[2] That Nathan Detroit and Adelaide are in love, as are Sky Masterson and Sarah Brown, is an accepted fact from early on in the play. The audience does witness the capitulation of Sarah, but it is not a slow process, and not a dramatic issue. At issue are the obstacles to true happiness. Nathan has a compulsion to run a floating dice game, and the unpredictable exigencies of this profession interrupt his relationship with Adelaide: their wedding has been postponed for fourteen years. On the other side, Sarah, a Salvation Army mission officer, is put off by Masterson's principal activity of high-stakes betting.

There is no question that *Guys and Dolls* is a consummate example of the comic love-story formula at its best. Perhaps its greatest virtue is the translation of Runyon's highly ironic language, with its curious insistence on the present tense and sophisticated vocabulary in the mouths of gangsters and gamblers, into musical numbers. At the very outset, after a brief medley overture, three gamblers on a busy New York street give conflicting advice on which horse to back in "Fugue for Tinhorns." The ironic tone of this piece comes from its juxtaposition of musical rightness and dramatic absurdity: the strict imitation is a perfect setting for three different opinions on the same subject, with each character trying to outtalk the other, but to have gamblers sing a musical texture reminiscent of Bach is a typically outrageous translation of the Runyon *personae.* A larger ensemble of gamblers later on sings "The Oldest Established," a paean to Nathan's floating dice game. With its close chromatic harmony and concluding ornamental suspensions, this song is part alma mater and part hymn, an irony which is amplified in the second act when these same gamblers are forced to attend a real prayer meeting. Finally there is "Adelaide's Lament," an amusing spoof of modern psychoanalysis, replete with jargon, but sung by a nightclub dancer, another absurd contrast which maintains the Runyon flavor of the whole work.

The high standards of musical integration are set in the opening scene when, after the "Fugue for Tinhorns," the Salvation Army troop marches onstage singing "Follow the Fold" to round up sinners, concluding a musical sequence which begins with the overture and manages to introduce the opposed groups of gamblers and city missionaries, who will dominate the play. The dramatic integrity is flawed only where most musical plays are flawed, at the end. Although the conversion of Sky Masterson is subtly implied from the beginning by his humorous familiarity with the Gideon Bible, there is no explanation for the reformation of Nathan Detroit. The musical finale, a reprise of the title song by the full company, is completely without dramatic motivation.

For all its typical features, *Guys and Dolls* contains the seeds of things essential to the much more innovative and ambitious play *The Most Happy Fella*. The latter is heavily dependent upon various types of recitative texture, which attracted some critical fire. No one complained of such textures in *Guys and Dolls*, but what is one to make of Masterson's "My Time of Day"?

**Ex. 7–1**  Frank Loesser, *Guys and Dolls*, "My Time of Day" (No. 17), mm. 8–17.

This is no *secco* recitative, of course, but the sense of meter is so obscured as
to make it into something akin to an arioso. The first clue is in Loesser's tempo
marking, "Slowly and freely." Then there are changes of time signature and
irregular subdivisions of the beat, both greatly weakening the sense of downbeat.
Chromaticism in both the main melody and underlying harmony obscures the
sense of key as well, so it is difficult for the ear to assign any important rhythmic
status to a tonic note. What sort of piece this might be becomes clear at the end.

**Ex. 7–2** Frank Loesser, *Guys and Dolls*, "My Time of Day" (No. 17), mm. 27–34, and "I've Never Been in Love Before" (No. 17a), mm. 1–8.

Clearly, the function of "My Time of Day," musically and dramatically, is to lead into the much more stable music and consistent emotion of "I've Never Been in Love Before." Just as many opera composers precede set pieces with accompanied recitatives to clarify the dramatic situation and to give the set piece a greater musical weight by virtue of a significant prelude, so has Loesser done here. It is curious that, although the rhythm of the second piece is now quite regular, the chromaticism has not disappeared from the accompaniment. This harmonic coloring will become a regular feature of *The Most Happy Fella* and make possible more distant harmonic relationships than would be likely in more conventional material.

The musical eclecticism of *Guys and Dolls* is another aspect that carries over into the later show. The strict counterpoint of the "Fugue for Tinhorns" and the college-song style in "The Oldest Established" have already been mentioned, but the show also offers traditional hymnody in "Follow the Fold," blues in "Adelaide's Lament," and gospel music in "Sit Down, You're Rockin' the

Boat.'' This variety derives from the superb sense of integration that character-izes most of the play: each style is called forth by the dramatic situation in which it occurs. For Loesser, the coordination of such various styles is an essential aspect of his dramatic art: ''If a song sounds like Verdi, Berlin, or Scarlatti, it's entitled to. I don't invent languages. I make use of them.''[3]

The eclecticism in *The Most Happy Fella* is once again suggested by an American setting which appears to bring out quite naturally a number of ethnic types. The main character Tony is an Italian immigrant, and his ethnic devotion to family, particularly his mother, becomes an important dramatic issue that allows for a number of Italian song textures, but Loesser is able to bring in other musical associations drawn from the American characters as well. That these borrowings seem drawn from the associations of the characters themselves rather than the plot situation is especially fitting, since critics have generally agreed that, in the case of Sidney Howard,

> Undoubtedly his forte is character portrayal. His finest creations along this line are the simpler types—sterling, vivid, individual, and solidly human—which people our het-erogenous American scene. Be they immigrants, like Tony in *They Knew What They Wanted,* or deeply rooted national stock . . . they have a raciness, a quality of forth-rightness, independence, and integrity which epitomizes what is best and most typical in our American tradition.[4]

The play tells the story of Tony, a California bootleg vintner of middle age, who at the curtain's rise is awaiting the arrival by train of a San Francisco waitress who is to be his bride. He had fallen in love with her at first sight while on a trip, but, nervous about his age and appearance, he chose not to introduce himself but to court her by mail. Worse still, he has sent her a picture of his handsome foreman, letting her believe it is his own. He is now so upset over this deception that he leaves for the station late, has an accident, and breaks both legs. Meanwhile Amy arrives and finds Joe, the foreman, at the ranch. She is stunned, first in finding out that her fiancé is not whom she expected, and then by Tony's serious injury. In urgency and confusion she decides to go through with the marriage to Tony. In the second act, Amy goes along with the celebra-tions but feels utterly abandoned and even mocked by the turn of events. She turns to Joe, and in comforting her he kisses her. He chases after her as the curtain falls. The third act reveals that Amy has indeed grown to love Tony, but carries Joe's baby. In the last scene, she bravely tells Tony, and he, through great struggle, forgives her and decides to adopt the child as his own.

The play also concerns itself with themes of workers' rights and religious conflicts, but to Loesser these ideas were only so much chaff.[5] ''I figured take out all this political talk, the labor talk, and the religious talk. Get rid of all that stuff and you have a good love story.''[6] By concentrating on the love story, and only that, Loesser solved the principal dramatic problem of *They Knew What They Wanted,* the conflict aroused by Amy's pregnancy:

Because this revelation is placed so late in the play, and in the act itself, the dramatist is obliged to crowd the principal problem of his drama—the effect of Joe's and Amy's casual and fortuitous affair upon a lasting relationship between Amy and Tony—into one tightly written scene. A situation rich in implications and dramatic possibilities is broached, discussed, and resolved in one scene. The dramatic action of *They Knew What They Wanted* is confined to the first act, one scene in the second, and one in the third. The rest is padding.[7]

This problem disappears from *The Most Happy Fella* because the affair and its effects are no longer the central dramatic action. Rather, they merely test and temper and clarify the main action, that of Rosabella's falling in love with Tony.

The simplicity of the plot is compensated by the complexity and variety of musical idiom. The paucity of spoken dialogue and frequency of recitative texture have encouraged critics to call *The Most Happy Fella* an opera, but that term does not do justice to the diversity of styles, from the most serious aria to the lightest American dance number, from the deceptively simple "Somebody, Somewhere" in the first act to the ensemble quartet "How Beautiful the Days" in the second. Of course, a style is never evoked for the sake of variety alone; there are always dramatic reasons, usually deriving from the characters involved, for using it, reasons that go beyond the simple formula of having the comic characters always sing light music and the romantic leads serious music. When Tony's three servants sing "Benvenuta"—recalling the cavatina-cabaletta tradition of Italian opera while parodying it—the music is not light, or even simple, and yet the effect is comic. However, such variety does allow Loesser to save the most sublime effects for the principal characters alone, without having the whole seem so ponderous.

Above all, it is the recitatives which allow the musical-dramatic focus on the love story. There are fourteen solo roles in the musical, but only the six most important characters—Rosabella and Tony, his sister Marie, Joe, and the added comic couple Herman and Cleo—may sing recitative. And, with a single exception in the third act, they sing it only in connection with the main love story. Its most important function is to act as a supporting prelude to an important lyric number, just as "My Time of Day" precedes "I've Never Been in Love Before" in *Guys and Dolls*.

The central musical-dramatic problem of *The Most Happy Fella* remains how to portray in music the action of falling in love in stages, as a dramatic progression. Loesser's first strategy is to compose a series of duets for Tony and Rosabella that create such a progression by withholding love's ultimate and irrepressible expression until the last.

Rosabella's first lyric arioso ("I don no noting about you") arises when she reads to herself the love letter that Tony has left in the San Francisco restaurant where she waits on table.

**Ex. 7–3** Frank Loesser, *The Most Happy Fella*, Act I, scene 1, "Ooh! My Feet," mm. 115–27.

The emphatic parallel fifths in the accompaniment, almost a cultural symbol of some mysterious power, lend this piece a sound unique to itself, and express the depth of Tony's feeling. The chromaticism is now functional; it effects the modulation from F major to G major (mm. 119-20), heightening the expression of the repeated lyric, and is responsible for the wistfully inconclusive marriage proposal (mm. 126-27). The little piece may be called a kind of "separate duet" because Tony sings the same music minutes later in answer to his sister's skepticism about his romance. In any case, the piece beautifully accomplishes its purpose: the establishment of a powerful, but one-sided, love interest.

The next song Tony and Rosabella sing together occurs just after the wedding, when he is just beginning to recover from his injury. He apologizes for sending the wrong picture, and says that they must "start all over." So he introduces himself, and "Happy to Make Your Acquaintance" is nothing more than Rosabella's instruction in the proper English phrases of a polite introduction. It reveals an essential compatibility of spirit and the possibility of true friendship, but stops short of love. The teacher-pupil role is reversed for "How Beautiful the Days," which follows upon a lesson in the Italian names for the days of the week. Its expression of happiness is deeper, but it does not articulate the cause.

The climax of this slow progression begins with a passionate *accompagnato* for both characters (Act II, scene 5) in which Rosabella makes it clear that she indeed loves Tony and needs him "like a woman needs a man." He is overjoyed, for such a speech is the fulfillment of his dreams, and the recitative leads directly into the great "My Heart Is So Full of You." Here the recitative passage is absolutely required, both musically and dramatically. The duet proper begins with a solo voice and the simplest of rhythmic textures; its power would be utterly lost if not preceded by the unstable *accompagnato,* to which the song is a resolution. At the same time, the sentiments expressed in the preceding justify those in the duet.

Just as the progression of duets mirrors the growing relationship, so does the construction of the individual duets. "How Beautiful the Days" begins with Rosabella echoing fragments of Tony's melody as she repeats the Italian names for the days of the week.

**Ex. 7–4**  Frank Loesser, *The Most Happy Fella*, Act II, scene 2, "How Beautiful the Days," mm. 4–18.

The echo is regular for four bars (mm. 10-13). By simply moving Rosabella's reponse ahead by two beats in measure 14, however, Loesser brings the voices into closer proximity and creates a high-level rhythmic acceleration which hurries the end of the next phrase so that it arrives after only two measures. In this way, joining of the two voices in parallel thirds in the concluding phrase seems to arise naturally from the previous texture.

''Happy to Make Your Acquaintance'' is a more sophisticated example of the same idea. Once again, a contrapuntal duet is justified dramatically because she is teaching him lines, and he repeats after her.

**Ex. 7–5** Frank Loesser, *The Most Happy Fella*, "Happy to Make Your Acquaintance," mm. 17–32.

Although the phrase pattern is a typical one of four bars, Tony's mimicry blurs the ends of her phrases by extending over the beginning of her next one. This effect, rather like a syncopation at the rhythmic level of the phrase, maintains a clear structural distinction in the music of the two singers, even though their words are the same. With the onset of the third and fourth phrases (mm. 25-32), however, Loesser begins to alter this delicate rhythmic balance. Tony's interjections become much shorter, so that they no longer make up a phrase system on their own. At the same time, Rosabella adds an extended anacrusis ("And let me say the . . .") to the beginning of the fourth phrase, so that her own separate system is less apparent. Both changes blur the structural distinction so clear at the beginning, so that for the first time, the two singers can agree on the end of their phrase (m. 32).

The transformation of separate melodies into a more unified texture becomes more forceful and conclusive as the song begins its melody again.

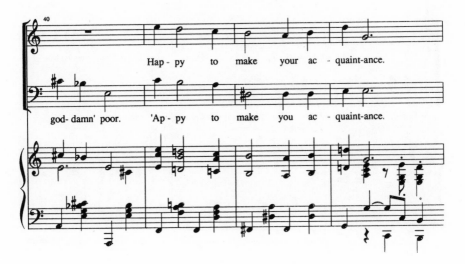

**Ex. 7–6** Frank Loesser, *The Most Happy Fella,* "Happy to Make Your Acquaintance," mm. 33–43.

Now the entire third phrase is sung together; the transformation comes sooner in the song and lasts longer than before. The same musical logic applies to the fourth phrase, extending it into a humorous coda.

**Ex. 7–7**   Frank Loesser, *The Most Happy Fella,* "Happy to Make Your Acquaintance," mm. 44–52.

Just as in "How Beautiful the Days," Loesser begins with a regular imitation, and by simply decreasing the amount of time for the third answer (m. 49), he creates a rhythmic acceleration that both drives to the cadence and expresses the lack of hesitation that accompanies Tony's mastering the pronunciation. The cadence, which expresses the pleasure of the achievement, is the only authentic one in the piece, and the singers make it together.

The song is reprised twice almost immediately, after two short dialogues. The arrival of Rosabella's friend Cleo occasions the first reprise, an opportunity for Tony to practice his new etiquette. The second, however, comes after Rosabella confesses that she really isn't so lonesome on the farm because Tony is such a "nice kind man." In this reprise, Tony and Rosabella sing every phrase in unison (octaves, actually) until the little coda, which is as before. This is a complete reversal of the normal handling of musical texture in an operatic ensemble, where tension and intensity of emotion are created by complicating the texture. Here the most intense emotion is caused by what is signified in simplifying the texture into the unison. Exactly the same effect is heard in "My Heart Is So Full of You," when the harmonically and texturally complex middle section is followed by the couple singing in unison.

So it is not merely in the lyrics and in the placement of these duets that Loesser paces his action, it is the construction of the individual numbers themselves that reflects, in miniature, the direction and outcome of that action.

When Tony and Rosabella sing "My Heart Is So Full of You" near the end of Act II, that action is essentially complete. Loesser now has the pretty problem of how to work in the conflict and resolution of Rosabella'a pregnancy. How does the third act attach to an action that is over?

Loesser's entirely original solution is to make the conflict appear to be the result of flaws in the principal characters, flaws which remain understated and inarticulate in the first two acts, but whose effects become explosive in the third. Rosabella's sensuality, portrayed as sympathetically as anyone could imagine in a musical play by her prelude to "My Heart Is So Full of You," is yet the cause of her downfall, a source of weakness in a time of great stress. But her affair with Joe can be no great surprise, because of what Loesser has given her to say in the very first scene of the opera, in response to the advances of her employer:

> ROSABELLA: . . . I guess I've helped a few fellows prove they were fellows, but they were guys I liked and they thought I was something special . . .

Tony's defect is much more serious: a lack of faith in himself. This, the reason for the photograph deception, is developed by Loesser into a full-blown dramatic theme ancillary to the main action, supported by Tony's sister, who time and again reminds him of his age, his lack of wit, and what his mother might think. The resolution of this theme, which has its own set of musical numbers[8] and musical development, comes at the close of the second act, when Tony sings what must be one of the great baritone arias of the Broadway tradition, "Mamma, Mamma." The full power of this piece can only be touched on here, as any detailed analysis would require discussing all the related pieces, but some sense of the relief that Rosabella has given him might be heard in the following.

**Ex. 7–8**  Frank Loesser, *The Most Happy Fella*, "Mamma, Mamma," mm. 45–55.

The accompaniment to this exultant lyric is a metaphor for Tony's character. Its meter and phrase rubato are unabashedly Italian, and its characteristic rocking motive (mm. 50, 52, 54) accompanying Tony's long notes is related to motives from his song "Rosabella" in Act I and to the leitmotif for his mother. This relationship is made most explicit when the mother leitmotif is exactly quoted by the strings during Tony's long B-flat in the tremendous final cadence, the only one in this Romantic-style piece.

**Ex. 7–9**  Frank Loesser, *The Most Happy Fella,* "Mamma, Mamma," mm. 55–69.

The placement of this song at the curtain of the second act gives it a bittersweet irony to go with its triumph. Rosabella, and the audience, have just learned of her pregnancy. In this way, the moment when Tony's greatest wishes have been granted is tied into the impending blow of the third act.

As a consequence of these aspects of character, the action of the second act can be seen not only in terms of Rosabella's growing to love Tony, but also in terms of her forgiving him his shallow deception. This forgiveness is never made explicit; it is left for the listener to construe through songs and actions. In Act III, the tables are turned: now it is Tony who must forgive.

There are indeed a number of criticisms one might make about the final sequence of *The Most Happy Fella*. Loesser feels that he must reconcile Cleo and Herman in classic Broadway fashion, and the comic number "I Made a Fist" interrupts the continuity of the much more serious events that surround it. Tony's discovery of his ability to forgive and his realization that his love for Rosabella outweighs his own pride are expressed by a recitative and aria ("She gonna come home wit' me") that seem to lack the length and weight commensurate with such a dramatic moment. But at the very end, when Tony has to convince Rosabella that he really has forgiven her—and her greatest fear is that he cannot, ever—that is when Loesser shows his best dramatic imagination. It begins with Tony's longest and most important speech.

> ROSABELLA: (Guiltily, apprehensively) You'll know . . . you'll know and you'll hate me, and you'll hate the baby. I'm . . . scared.
> TONY: (Very gently) Nunja be scared, Carissima. It's-a bad to be scared. Me, Tony, I was-a scared one night last springtime. Omma scared to drive down da station to meet my Rosabella. Omma scared omma too old, an' omma talk funny. So omma drive da truck too fast an' have accidente. Maybe dat same night . . . dat same night last springtime you was-a be scared too an' you was have accidente. An' before dat, I was all da time scared. I was-a so scared omma send you wrong fella's pitch, pitch young handsome fella. First time omma see you in da ristorante in Frisco, I should-a no left a sneaky li'l note onna bill o' fare. I should-a knew what I want an' say what I want. Now, tonight, we start all over.[9]

And so the two replay the first scene in the restaurant. Tony's speech reveals a symmetry in the character flaws that were the dark side of the love story. His proposition that her affair was an "accidente" analogous to his own is not merely a comforting line to make her feel better, for in it he realizes that his own lack of faith in himself was the direct cause not only of the car accident but of Rosabella's unspoken infatuation with the image of Joe. In fact, his leg injury has become a symbol of this deeper infirmity: that is why Tony rises to his feet from his wheelchair when he sings "My Heart Is So Full of You" in the second act and at the end of the finale. His cure is Rosabella herself.

The first music after the speech, Tony's reprise of "I don know not'ing about you/ Where you ever go/ What you ever done" is moving not because it is reminiscent of his powerful first sight and feeling of her in the restaurant, but because it expresses that, after all that has happened, he recognizes the cost of loving blindly, and accepts it anyway. This is all Rosabella needs to hear. The symmetry of fault yields to a symmetry of forgiveness.

As a confirmation of the happy ending to this pure love story there are the middle and final sections of "My Heart Is So Full of You." Because it represents both the consummation of Rosabella's love of Tony in Act II and the reconciliation of this love in Act III, this song perhaps carries the greatest expressive weight of any number in the opera, and there is no better example of Loesser's handling of chromatic harmony, texture, and form.

An asymmetrical phrase design at the very beginning of the song generates its most expressive features.

**Ex. 7–10**  Frank Loesser, *The Most Happy Fella*, "My Heart Is So Full of You," mm. 1–11.

The first phrase (mm. 1-6) is characterized by a sequence in the vocal melody, but because it creates the sequence by adopting only measures three and four as the pattern (transposed down one step to yield measures five and six), the whole phrase is asymmetrical. Instead of two balanced sub-phrases of four bars each, measures three and four complete the first sub-phrase and begin the second one, made articulate by the sequence, at the same time. It need not have been this way; Loesser could easily have composed a symmetrical eight-measure phrase by making a sequence out of the whole.

Ex. 7–11  Alternative opening phrase to "My Heart Is So Full of You."

Indeed, he did something quite close to this in "I've Never Been in Love Before" from Guys and Dolls.

Ex. 7–12  Frank Loesser, *Guys and Dolls,* "I've Never Been in Love Before" (No. 17a), mm. 1–8.

Here, the sense of phrase is complete and balanced, or, to use a more technical term, closed. In "My Heart," Loesser wants some sense of something missing. Its first phrase has, by virtue of its V-I cadence in D-flat, a closed harmony, but the asymmetry of the sequence and an ambiguity of the high-level meter argue for continuity.[10] The result of this conflict is that the six-measure phrase, somewhat unusual in popular style, is taken by the listener to be real while requiring some sort of structural resolution.

This structural ambiguity justifies the surprising A dominant seventh chord in the next measure: perhaps the tension arising from this harmony being foreign to the key as well as its dissonant structure will carry the phrase to a new, balanced resolution in the eighth measure. Instead, its tension generates the next phrase, and Loesser's particular usage of this chord here determines important effects later on. The beautifully expressive high F-flat that Tony sings in measure ten seems to grow out of that earlier sound, for three of the five pitches (G, $F\flat = E$, $D\flat = C\sharp$), two of them chromatic, were introduced in the A dominant seventh. Curiously, the melody leading up to this F-flat contains the pattern that was "missing" from Loesser's sequence in the first phrase (see Ex. 7-11). The second phrase therefore responds to some aspect of the structural ambiguity of the first. However, in doing so it adds another, stronger, higher-level structural asymmetry, pitting a five-measure phrase (mm. 7-11) against the original six.

The resolution of that A dominant seventh is quite irregular, slipping right back into the key of D-flat with a half-step descent. Such progressions, deriving from the music of Tony's love letter (see Ex. 7-3, mm. 123-24), power the release section of the song.

**Ex. 7-13**  Frank Loesser, *The Most Happy Fella*, "My Heart Is So Full of You," mm. 23–31.

The modulation from A-flat major to G-flat major (mm. 23-27) is made through a G dominant seventh which demands a resolution in the same manner as above. This is at first denied (m. 25), then completed. Later on the bass line moves from D-flat to C, then E natural to E-flat. The harmonic ambiguity of these progressions transforms the release into a tiny development section. Rosabella'a melody, clearly the prominent one, consists of a two-measure phrase repeated twice. The second repetition increases the tension by transposing it so that it is now the dissonant seventh factor of the chord instead of the third (m. 27). Her highest note of the whole song, the G-flat, is reserved for the precise moment when harmonic functions begin to be clarified and the strong progression ii - V - I in D-flat begins the return to the opening theme, turning it into a recapitulation in the classical sense.

As recapitulations are designed to resolve high-level tension, so is the last phrase of the song changed to resolve the asymmetry of the opening.

**Ex. 7–14**  Frank Loesser, *The Most Happy Fella,* "My Heart Is So Full of You," mm. 30–43.

By extending the F-flat, Loesser restores the symmetry of balanced six-measure phrases which seemed missing from the beginning.

The duet is the most ambitious and successful piece in the opera. It integrates a number of expressive features—the C-flat chord of the fourth measure, the chromatic A dominant seventh, the high F-flat, and the whole midsection—into a short piece into which these features are introduced with impeccable skill. Each seems to grow from music which precedes it, proceeding from the design of the very first phrase. As the central number, "My Heart Is So Full of You" deserves its place as the climax of the love story. Indeed, that its full version appears in the second act, with only its last two sections used as the reprise in the third act, shows that the dramatic climax of the opera is in the second act. The conflict of the third is an affirmation of this central action.

The rarity of making a pure love story the central action of a musical play may have caused the confusion and disagreement that has characterized the critical history of *The Most Happy Fella*. A sample of the critical problems noted:

> [The actors] don't really have flesh-and-blood characters to create, nor much of a plot to embody.[11]

> Having established the foreman as the third party in this combustible romantic triangle, Loesser simply forgets about him in the second act.[12]

> The rather tatty recitatives in "The Most Happy Fella," for example, gain nothing by being sung, except a certain grand pretense. . . .[13]

In each case the critic has missed the central dramatic issue. To say that the recitatives in *The Most Happy Fella* gain nothing is to be unaware of how carefully the recitatives are reserved for certain characters in certain situations, how they can slow down the musical action while creating a varied musical texture. Loesser has not forgotten part of the romantic triangle because there is no triangle. And naturally, if one cannot appreciate the simple action of falling in love, then there will seem to be no plot and no characters.

Of course, there are the ecstatic defenders as well:

> Egad! the nerve of it! One may write *lots of music,* including some that narrates plot! One may compose duets, trios, *quartets,* that express individual intents within group agreements, or even a *conflict!* One may try using music to shift the level of reality, to voice private thoughts in a public milieu! One may create vocal settings that demand voices of professional range and quality, and allow them to sing damn near as long as in, say, *Madama Butterfly!* [14]

In a sense, even this deeply felt indignation misses the point. Yes, Loesser's work has all these things, but its great achievement is not in them but rather in their coordination into a sure dramatic vision. The irony is that the usual plan for an American musical invariably calls for a complicated love story, but Loesser, in stripping the old love story to its simplest essentials, required all the complexities of the operatic tradition. The pity is that, because this complexity makes it so difficult to sing, *The Most Happy Fella* is not better known, for it is a fine example of how far the American theater tradition can reach.

# CHAPTER 8

# Myth as Musical

*What Shaw wanted us to know about Higgins was that he was passionate about the English language . . . and that he was a misogynist. Because they are the outstanding aspects of his character, it seemed to us they should be dramatized in music and lyrics.*[1]

ALAN JAY LERNER

From time to time composers, lyricists, and writers of the American theater have borrowed stories from mythology for the main plots of musical plays. Rodgers and Hart's *A Connecticut Yankee* (1927) translated Twain's Arthurian tale, and *By Jupiter* (1942), their last original collaboration, retells Hercules's quest for the magic girdle of Hippolyta. Cole Porter based his *Out of This World* (1950) on the story of Amphitryon. E. Y. Harburg adapted music of Jacques Offenbach to transform the plot of Aristophanes's *Lysistrata* into *The Happiest Girl in the World* (1961). And the operatic score and libretto by Jerome Moross and John Latouche presenting the return of Ulysses in *The Golden Apple* (1953) was deemed so clever that it captured the Drama Critics Award for best musical of the season. However, in the great majority of these musicals and others based on mythology, the borrowing ceases with the outline of the plot. There is little attempt to translate other, deeper mythic elements into dramatic terms.

The treatment of mythic elements in modern literature seems to be an enormously complex subject that sees little agreement about the purpose or effect of such borrowing in novels, poetry, and drama. For some, the myth is merely a commonly understood point of departure:

You display your originality by exercising ingenuity in discovering new ways of writing about old myths. Operating within a network of shared allusions among educated readers, you can by-pass the explicit in order to explore the tacit and ironic.[2]

For others, the relationship of the new work to the old can be quite beside the point:

> Yet one must ask to what extent the design once seen gives an associative enrichment to the work as a whole. Do we look back to the Telemacheia and understand Joyce better? In one sense we obviously do in that we see a dimension of Joyce's intention expressed. But the actual light thrown on Joyce's novel by the associative echoes from the Homeric original seems academic and thin, and to think too closely on it is to look away from the richness of what Joyce has created.[3]

Neither of these viewpoints is very useful for musical theater. They assume a detailed knowledge of classical mythology which is almost sure to be lacking in the popular audience. Much more appropriate is the approach of Eric Gould, who believes that the essence of myth in modern culture is that it is a familiar story or lesson the meaning of which is never quite fixed:

> . . . myth is both hypothesis and compromise. Its meaning is perpetually open and universal only because once the absence of a final meaning is recognized, the gap itself demands interpretation which, in turn, must go on and on, for language is nothing if it is not a system of open meaning.[4]

Closing the gap, fixing the interpretation is the moment on which a drama can turn.

The attempt to fix an interpretation of a myth through music is what sets the work of Alan Jay Lerner and Frederick Loewe apart from most other Broadway adaptations. *My Fair Lady* (1956) and *Camelot* (1960) are based on mythological plots, of course, but they are also explorations of mythic elements carried in those plots across the ages. No small part of these stories' power comes from their legendary status, their age-old themes and associations as a common property of Western culture. That is why the interpretation of Gould's mythic gap in a given work can be such an important event, and in a drama, perhaps the most important moment. That is also why Lerner and Loewe's earlier and excellent musical, *Brigadoon* (1947), is not germane to a discussion of myth, for although its premise of a Scottish village that materializes but one day in a century seems mythical, the story is original with Lerner and cannot claim the cultural associations so essential to myth.[5]

*My Fair Lady* is a musical adaptation of George Bernard Shaw's *Pygmalion* (1912), which in turn is a dramatic adaptation of the classical myth about the sculptor who brings his own statue of a woman to life. One version of the story is told in Ovid's *Metamorphoses 10,* beginning with Pygmalion's disgust for the first prostitutes of Cyprus:

> Pygmalion saw these women leading a life of sin and was repelled by the many vices that nature had implanted in the feminine mind. And so he lived alone without a wife for a long time, doing without a woman to share his bed. Meanwhile he fashioned

happily a statue of ivory, white as snow, and gave it a beauty surpassing that of any woman born; and he fell in love with what he had made. It looked like a real maiden who you would believe was alive and willing to move, had not modesty prevented her. To such an extent art concealed art; Pygmalion wondered at the body he had fashioned and the flames of passion burned in his breast. He often ran his hands over the creation to test whether it was real flesh and blood or ivory. And he would not go so far as to admit that it was ivory. He gave it kisses and thought that they were returned; he spoke to it and held it and believed that his fingers sank into the limbs that he touched and was afraid that a bruise might appear as he pressed her close. . . .

The most celebrated feast day of Venus in the whole of Cyprus arrived; heifers, their crooked horns adorned with gold, were slaughtered by the blow of the axe on their snowy necks and incense smoked. When he had made his offering at the altar, Pygmalion stood and timidly prayed: "If you gods are able to grant everything, I desire for my wife . . ." He did not dare to say "my ivory maiden." Golden Venus herself was present at her festival and understood what his prayers meant. As an omen of her kindly will a tongue of flame burned bright and flared up in the air. When he returned home Pygmalion grasped the image of his girl and lay beside her on the bed and showered her with kisses. She seemed to be warm. He touched her with his lips again and felt her breasts with his hands. At his touch the ivory grew soft, and its rigidity gave way to the pressure of his fingers; it yielded just as Hymettan wax when melted in the sun is fashioned into many shapes by the working of the hands and made pliable. He is stunned but dubious of his joy and fearful he is wrong. In his love he touches this answer to his prayers. It was a body; the veins throbbed as he felt them with his thumb. Then in truth Pygmalion was full of prayers in which he gave thanks to Venus. At last he presses his lips on lips that are real and the maiden feels the kisses she is given and as she raises her eyes to meet his she sees both her lover and the sky.[6]

Shaw turns Pygmalion into Henry Higgins, a dialectician and phonetics expert, who on a dare from a colleague takes a common girl, Eliza Doolittle, into his home, teaches her proper English, and turns her into a gentlewoman in all respects but birth. The interpretation of the myth fixed in the play, however, emphasizes Pygmalion's initial misogyny and eliminates the infatuation for his creation so prominent in Ovid. Although Higgins has strong feelings about Eliza, the true nature of these is quite unclear, as is the ultimate destiny of the couple even at the play's conclusion:

That famous unresolved ending of the play, teasing us forever with the question of whether Eliza will come back to Higgins after she has walked out on him, is of course far more than an effective theatrical finale. It reflects, as do the finest plots, aspects of character and theme. The ambiguity of the ending transposes into structure the ambiguities of feeling between Higgins and Eliza which date from their first encounter. . . .[7]

Shaw added a prose postscript to the published play two years after its opening which explained why, contrary to popular will, Eliza had really married someone

else. In his study of Shaw, Arnold Silver attributes this postscript to Shaw's
upset over actress Stella Campbell, for whom he had written the lead part and
who had married just prior to the opening. Arguing that the ambiguous ending
is truer to the themes of the play, Silver believes that the characters of Eliza and
Higgins are completely spoiled in the postscript.[8] In any case, the ending has
left a mythic gap to be closed by the musical drama in *My Fair Lady*.

> What Shaw wanted us to know about Higgins was that he was passionate about the
> English language, believed it to be the principal barrier separating class from class,
> and that he was a misogynist. Because they are the outstanding aspects of his charac-
> ter, it seemed to us they should be dramatized in music and lyrics.[9]

So recalls Alan Jay Lerner. Outstanding aspects they are, but only the misogyny
is mythic, and so while "Why Can't the English" is an important initial statement for Higgins, his second song, "I'm an Ordinary Man," is the one that
establishes his character in a way that begins to interpret the myth.

The song is built on two contrasting sections which alternate for three hearings each. In the first (A) section Higgins describes himself.

**Ex. 8–1**   Lerner and Loewe, *My Fair Lady*, "I'm an Ordinary Man" (No. 5), mm. 1–7.

In the second (B) section Higgins describes what would happen to this sterling character if he ever allowed himself to become involved with a woman.

**Ex. 8–2**   Lerner and Loewe, *My Fair Lady,* "I'm an Ordinary Man" (No. 5), mm. 13–33.

The lyrics of all the B sections obviously establish Higgins as a misogynist, but equally important, the A sections reveal that he lives with a much idealized and warped image of himself. Though he has been on stage but a few minutes, it is quite clear to the audience that Higgins is far from "ordinary," "average," or "of no eccentric whim." Subsequent action will give the lie to his further claims that he is "a very gentle man" or "a quiet living man." The accompanying music seems ill-matched to these weighty confessions; its quick dotted rhythms trip along more in the manner of the lightest intermezzo than of a soliloquy. But if this setting can be understood to suggest that all is not what Higgins claims it is, should not the music of the B section be similarly considered? For here the increased tempo, pattersong rhythms, absolutely periodic phrasing, and brassy orchestration give over a vaudevillian superficiality. Funny, yes, but is it real? This is the first hint of Loewe's reinterpretation of the Pygmalion myth: if Higgins's self-image must be questioned, then so must his misogyny.

Eliza's opening song reveals a character that sharply contrasts with that of Higgins.

Ex. 8–3  Lerner and Loewe, *My Fair Lady,* "Wouldn't It Be Loverly?" (No. 3), mm. 20–27.

Like Higgins, she fantasizes, but instead of imagining the worst that could happen to herself, she imagines the best. And the images of that best are simple images, not Higgins's high-minded contemplation of Keats and Milton. The music, again, is composed in a light Broadway texture, but its phrasing lends an impression of sincerity quite absent in Higgins's music. Chord changes establish a clear two-bar period at the beginning with strong metric accents on every downbeat. The third phrase, however, begins in measure 24 by eliminating the downbeat altogether, and this disruption of the established pattern, together with a chromatic intensification that makes every chord act like an upbeat, cause the next accent to be delayed until the highest note of the melody in measure 26. The coordination of the refrain lyric with this melodic climax makes the wistful sentiment credible.

By far the most important interpolation Lerner introduces into Shaw's script, which otherwise is followed quite faithfully, is the latter half of Act I, scene 5, which shows Pygmalion sculpting his statue. It is a succession of vignettes, made distinct by stage lighting, showing the tedious, repetitious drilling Eliza has to endure under the watchful eye of her indefatigable taskmaster, a succession which develops Higgins's sardonic character rapidly and makes it quite clear that he does not really think of Eliza as a human person. Eliza makes no progress, and yet the torture continues, the atmosphere charged by looming defeat.

> ELIZA: I can't. I'm so tired. I'm so tired.
>
> PICKERING: *(Half asleep)* Oh, for God's sake, Higgins. It must be three o'clock in the morning. Do be reasonable.
>
> HIGGINS: *(Rising)* I am always reasonable. Eliza, if I can go on with a blistering headache, you can.
>
> ELIZA: I have a headache, too.
>
> HIGGINS: Here. *(He plops the ice-bag on her head. She takes it off her head and buries her face in her hands, exhausted to the point of tears)*
> *(With sudden gentleness)* Eliza, I know you're tired. I know your head aches. I know your nerves are as raw as meat in a butcher's window. But think what you're trying to accomplish. *(He sits next to her on the sofa)* Think what you're dealing with. The majesty and grandeur of the English language. It's the greatest possession we have. The noblest sentiments that ever flowed in the hearts of men are contained in its extraordinary, imaginative and musical mixtures of sounds. That's what you've set yourself to conquer, Eliza. And conquer it you will. *(He rises, goes to the chair behind his desk and seats himself heavily)* Now, try it again.
>
> ELIZA: *(Slowly)* The rain in Spain stays mainly in the plain.[10]

The brilliant flash of insight is possible not because of the appeal to the language of Shakespeare and Milton, but because in the opening lines of the speech lie the first indications that Higgins recognizes the person in Eliza, and therein perhaps she catches the first glimpse of common humanity in Higgins himself.

The famous tango that follows Eliza's triumph is in the mold of the classic operatic set piece. "The Rain in Spain" has not a speck of dramatic intuition. Its sole function is to heighten the emotion far beyond the level of any speech, and to give the three main characters a chance to revel in the amazing turn of events. Yet, the song is so beautifully placed, just after the peak tension of the drilling scene, understated, comic, and yet deep, and just before listeners have had a chance to realize that victory has been won, that it can hardly fail to move despite its simplicity. It caps the joy of creation.

The creation scene ends with Eliza singing "I Could Have Danced All Night." This song has commonly been taken to express, through its lyric, Eliza's joy in her own achievement. That it well may do, but the music conveys another meaning. The melody of the refrain is sequential in typical Romantic style: the second phrase (mm. 22-30) is little more than a transposition of the first phrase (mm. 14-22) upward by one step.

**Ex. 8–4** Lerner and Loewe, *My Fair Lady,* "I Could Have Danced All Night" (No. 10), mm. 13–28.

The release has two short phrases based on a variant of the main motive (contained in mm. 13-14), and then the climactic A section of the song arrives.

**Ex. 8–5** Lerner and Loewe, *My Fair Lady,* "I Could Have Danced All Night" (No. 10), mm. 37–45.

The climax is produced not so much by the *tenuto* upbeat chords of measure 37 but rather by the melodic structure of the last phrase, for it is an accelerated combination of the first two phrases: the essential notes C and B ("know when he") are then transposed up to become D and C ("dance with me"). This musical emphasis on a key lyric brings out the first hint of Eliza's almost paradoxical attraction to Higgins and makes it the song's primary statement.

In Act III of Shaw's *Pygmalion,* Mrs. Higgins, Henry's mother, points out to Higgins and Pickering that, in taking in Eliza, they have taken on a big problem:

PICKERING: Oh, I see. The problem of how to pass her off as a lady.

HIGGINS: I'll solve that problem. I've half solved it already.

MRS. HIGGINS: No, you two infinitely stupid male creatures: the problem of what is to be done with her afterwards.[11]

In the original myth, the obstacle is the creation itself. In Shaw, it becomes the consequences of creation, and although *My Fair Lady* touches on both, it is the latter that dominates the drama of the second act. The second act therefore bears an unusual distinction among American musical plays: it is more serious than the first.

The tone changes abruptly with the shouting match between Higgins and Eliza that occurs just after their victory at the ball. Eliza, ignored and hurt by Higgins, realizes that now that the ball is over, her sabbatical is indeed through. A series of four musical numbers follows, with remarkably little dialogue separating them.

**Ex. 8–6**  Lerner and Loewe, *My Fair Lady,* "Reprise: Just You Wait" (No. 20), mm. 5–12.

This is a reprise of Eliza's escape fantasy that she permitted herself in the beginning of her language training. At that point, the song, although funny, had the intensity and weight of a two-year-old's tantrum. How changed in effect it is here! The difference is that the lyrics no longer convey fantasy: Eliza now has the power to do what she says.

The next two numbers, a reprise of "On the Street Where You Live" and "Show Me," introduce Freddy Eynesford-Hill as a half comic, half serious suitor. Then there is a reprise of Eliza's very first song, "Wouldn't It Be Loverly," as she attempts to return to her home environment at the flower market. The cockneys who sing it, her old friends, believe her to be a gentlewoman and do not recognize her, and in response to her growing isolation, Eliza picks up this strain.

**Ex. 8-7** Lerner and Loewe, *My Fair Lady*, "Loverly" (No. 21), mm. 68-76.

Once again the point of this emphasis on a particular phrase of lyric is unmistakable, though understated. It is remarkable how little altered are these two reprises and yet how much the new dramatic context alters their effect.

At the end, the nature and meaning of the mythic relationship between Eliza and Higgins, a relationship which has been tormenting Eliza since her "creation" while leaving Higgins apparently untouched, is crystallized in a single number.

Moderato con tenerezza *(tenderly)*

HIGGINS

Damn!! I've grown accustomed to her face!     She al-most

makes the     day be-gin.          I've grown ac - cus-tomed to the tune     She

whis-tles night and noon.     Her smiles, her frowns,     her ups,     her downs Are sec-ond

na - ture to me now; Like breath-ing out and breath-ing in.

I was se - rene-ly in - de-pend-ent and con - tent be-fore we met;

Sure-ly I could al-ways be that way a- gain and yet I've grown ac- cus-tomed to her looks; Ac-

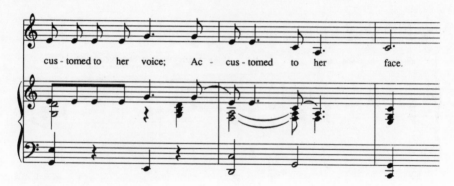

**Ex. 8–8** Lerner and Loewe, *My Fair Lady,* "I've Grown Accustomed to Her Face" (No. 26), mm. 19–39.

What is immediately arresting about this piece is how outstanding is its character in the context of the whole show. The lyric is still of a pattering sort, as all the lyrics for Higgins are, but for once the language is simple, direct, and honest, as a confession should be. The music is by far the most serious of the play. The harmonic functions of the accompaniment are often weakened by lack of clear identity—is the last chord of the second phrase (mm. 23-24) a dominant, subdominant, or tonic?—which gives the melody an impressionistic vagueness that seems curiously appropriate for the overt nostalgia that has engulfed Higgins. The rhythm within each phrase, a few quick notes ending with a very long note, adds to this musing quality by making each one appear to be spontaneous and independent, almost like talking to oneself, and yet the overall phrase structure is clearly designed for motion. The long notes all occur on the weak beat of the measure, so that the cadence of each phrase is effectively canceled, and so demands yet another phrase. Only at the end, when the third hearing of "accustomed" is accompanied by a deft slowing of rhythm (m. 38), is there a strong cadence on the downbeat. The accumulated power of this delayed cadence, with the lyric in the last phrase emphasizing "her looks," "her voice," "her face," underlines the cause of Higgins's new wonder at himself.

Even if this song were set off by itself, alone, barely twenty measures long, it would command attention, but when it is set amid other musical sections that clarify its dramatic function, "I've Grown Accumstomed to Her Face" becomes the capstone of the play.

The song is introduced with Higgins stomping across the stage in a great rage, accompanied by what must be considered his leitmotif.

**Ex. 8–9** Lerner and Loewe, *My Fair Lady,* "I've Grown Accustomed to Her Face" (No. 26), mm. 1–7.

The quotation is actually a parody of the original because some beats are missing (see Ex. 8-2), which is just as well, since the intention of the introduction is ironical. Higgins is furious because he at last has let a woman into his life, as "I've Grown Accustomed" is about to make clear.

The first rendition of the main song (Ex. 8-8) is followed by an interlude in which Higgins imagines the consequences of Eliza's threat to marry Freddy. When this interlude turns to the minor mode, it takes on a curious but indubitable resemblance to an earlier song.

**Ex. 8–10**  Lerner and Loewe, *My Fair Lady,* "I've Grown Accustomed to Her Face" (No. 26), (mm. 72–88).

The melody is a transformation of "Just You Wait," another fantasy song.

**Fig. 8–1**  Comparison of melodies from "Just You Wait" and "I've Grown Accustomed to Her Face," *Meno mosso.*

Does this turnabout on the revenge motive imply a mutual affinity between the two protagonists, who have been portrayed so differently throughout, or merely that Higgins's emotional maturity is at a stage comparable to Eliza's at the beginning of the play?

The course of Higgins's fantasy takes him to an image of Eliza coming to him in tears and begging to be taken in once again. His reaction calls for another reprise.

**Ex. 8–11** Lerner and Loewe, *My Fair Lady,* "I've Grown Accustomed to Her Face" (No. 26), mm. 119–33.

At last, through the contradiction of his imagined rejection and his self-described nature, all the pretense of the original "I'm an Ordinary Man" is revealed, and by Higgins himself. What had once been only hinted at in the music becomes undeniable. But the most revealing moment is still to come, for the motives of "Let a women in my life" lead directly to the second and final rendition of "I've Grown Accustomed to Her Face."

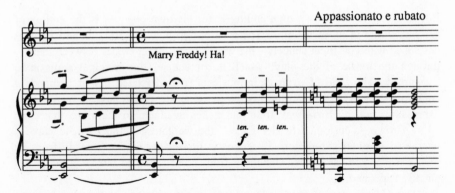

Ex. 8–12  Lerner and Loewe, *My Fair Lady*, "I've Grown Accustomed to Her Face" (No. 26), mm. 141–48.

Now, because one leads directly into the other, it is clear that the principal motive of "Accustomed" is a dramatic transformation of the motive of "Let a woman . . . ."

Fig. 8–2  Comparison of motives setting "Let a woman in my life" and "I've grown accustomed to her face."

The anacrusis beats and the entire melodic shape make the relationship quite audible. The wonderfully ironic transformation of the motive mirrors the transformation of Higgins, from a self-imagined misogynist to someone who has become accustomed to love a woman.

Eric Bentley, somewhat predictably, objects to what he calls the "utter sentimentalizing" of Shaw's ending:

In *My Fair Lady*, what had been a hint stuck on at the end [of *Pygmalion*] becomes the main theme of the second half of the show and involves having Higgins turn into the standard leading man of musical comedy and at that as cornily love-lorn as they come.[12]

But as effective as Shaw's own ending is for his own play, so is the ending of *My Fair Lady* in its own terms. The relationship between Higgins and Eliza is developed with consistent subtlety—the word "love" never comes between them—through the music of the play, which is, of course, the principal addition to *Pygmalion.* The tone of even their music is so understated that it demands a compromise of style: Lerner and Loewe forswear all serious devices of romantic expression that the Broadway tradition makes available to them, so that even "I've Grown Accustomed to Her Face," the weightiest number of the play, is restrained in overt expression. Its dramatic impact derives only partly from its own musical and resources, and more from how its music interprets what has already happened.

"I've Grown Accustomed to Her Face" is the capstone of the play because it is in that moment that the mythic elements are fixed, and not just the love relationship, but its specific character. For the transformation of the principal motives in the song reveals that the principal characters have reversed roles. Eliza is the sculptor, after all, and Higgins the block. Such a theme is discernible in Shaw:

> Eliza, in the role reversal that occurs during the play, becomes the teacher and sculptor, and we want her to finish the job by bringing her wooden man to life. We want this particularly because the phonetics professor contains bits of ourselves, for who has not at times been more wooden than he would wish to admit?[13]

Lerner himself seems to have been aware of this interpretation:

> In a far less tangible way, Higgins goes through as much of a transformation as Eliza, the only difference being that Shaw would never allow the transformation to run its natural course.[14]

But the achievement of *My Fair Lady* lies not in that it chose this particular interpretation of the myth, but in that it crystallized the mythic elements in its music with such subtlety.

How different is the case of *Camelot.* To point out that the adaptation of T. H. White's Arthurian tetralogy, *The Once and Future King,* for the musical stage was a much more imposing task than the adaptation of *Pygmalion* does not tarnish in the least the shining achievement of *My Fair Lady;* it simply underscores some rather obvious facts. First, there is enormous difference in the breadth of the two myths. The *Pygmalion* legend is a short story of a sculptor, a statue, and a goddess, requiring of Ovid only 54 lines for the telling. The legend of King Arthur is a vast tapestry of tales contributed by a variety of sources spanning several centuries. There are a good number of subplots set into the main story, and there are dozens of important characters. Second, George Bernard Shaw did Lerner and Loewe the enormous favor of translating Pygmalion directly to the stage, with a plot so ingenious and dialogue so witty that there was little to add but music. That, of course, is no trivial task, but it is a limited one. To fashion *Camelot*, Lerner had to boil down over six hundred pages of dense novel into a workable libretto that would play under three hours and still allow for music.

He helped himself by eliminating from consideration the book of Arthur's youth, *The Sword in the Stone*, and concentrating on material from the third book, *The Ill-Made Knight*, while working in some background from the second, *The Queen of Air and Darkness*, and the denouement from the fourth, *The Candle in the Wind*. Even so, he was still left with a tremendous saga filled with elements of satire, playful anachronism, and complex motivations and characters. Even the story of the love triangle among Arthur, Guenevere, and Lancelot is far from simple, as John K. Crane notes in his study of White:

> . . . it is a wonderful study of three human beings who are in conflict and in love with one another. More than this, White investigates three human beings who are in conflict with themselves when their developed noble ideals fight furiously to overcome their inbred selfishness and inadequacies.[15]

The causes of the final tragedy in the tetralogy are many, and its course occupies hundreds of pages as Arthur tries heroically, but in vain, to keep his dream alive by initiating quests and inventing legal systems that subvert the inclinations of his knights to war:

> White is careful to avoid taxing the adultery of Lancelot and Guinevere with responsiblity for the failure of Arthur and the fall of Camelot. He blames the tragedy on the greed and selfishness and violence in the heart of man.[16]

Making the fall of Camelot dependent upon the adultery, however, is precisely Lerner's strategy. In this way he strips the Arthurian legend down to two mythic elements upon which the drama should hang: the love triangle and the fate of the Round Table, which to Lerner seemed the "universal dream."[17] The resolution of Lancelot's and Guenevere's affair therefore takes on a mythical significance well beyond that of the typical love story.

Despite such a promising version of this vast legend, *Camelot* fails to dramatize the mythic elements set in relief so clearly.

The book is fatally defective in several ways. Much of the dialogue, though inspiring in theme, is badly overwritten. Consider Arthur's soliloquy which concludes the first act:

> ARTHUR: Proposition: If I could choose, from every woman who breathes on this earth, the face I would most love, the smile, the touch, the voice, the heart, the laugh, the soul itself, every detail and feature to the smallest strand of hair—they would all be Jenny's.

Proposition: If I could choose from every man who breathes on this earth a man for my brother and a man for my son, a man for my friend, they would all be Lance.

*(His bitterness mounts)*

Yes, I love them. I love them, and they answer me with pain and torment. Be it sin or not sin, they betray me in their hearts, and that's far sin enough. I see it in their eyes and feel it when they speak, and they must pay for it and be punished. I shan't be wounded and not return it in kind. I'm done with feeble hoping. I demand a man's vengeance!

*(He moves violently, then tries to control himself)*

Proposition: I'm a king, not a man. And a civilized king. Could it possibly be civilized to destroy what I love? Could it possibly be civilized to love myself above all? What of their pain and their torment? Did they ask for this calamity? Can passion be selected?

*(His voice rising)*

Is there any doubt of their devotion . . . to me, or to our Table?

*(He raises high the sword in his hand)*

By God, Excalibur, I shall be a King! This is the time of King Arthur, and we reach for the stars! This is the time of King Arthur, and violence is not strength and compassion is not weakness. We are civilized! Resolved: We shall live through this together, Excalibur: They, you and I! And God have mercy on us all.[18]

It is a fair summary of the mythic elements of the play, but an academic, not a dramatic one. Why the formal propositions and resolutions, which clash sharply with Arthur's usual good humor and easy dismissal of court formality, and which lend the whole scene more an air of parliamentary debate than of an internal agony? And why the rehearsal of Arthurian ideals, by now well familiar to the audience, which turn the moment into an uncomfortable sermon?

A casualty of this kind of writing is the character of Lancelot, who is portrayed as a pretentious boor at best, a buffoon at worst. There is no precedence whatsoever for this kind of Lancelot in White. Indeed, it is difficult to account for such a transformation, for it threatens the very credibility of the triangle on which the drama is based. "Why was Guenevere disenchanted with Arthur, a kind, loving and attractive husband, and so carried away by Lancelot, a second-rate romantic superman?" asks Lehman Engel, and quite rightly.[19]

Then, too, much of the plot seems undermotivated. The tragic element of Arthur's soliloquy is hard to grasp because it is not yet clear that, if Guenevere is unfaithful, the very existence of the Table is threatened. Evidence of Lerner's struggle with the sheer complexity of the original story shows through now and again. "Many of the crucial events—the invention of the Round Table, Guenevere's sudden infatuation with Lancelot, the appearance of the villianous Mordred—spring up almost arbitrarily."[20]

This is because these crucial events find hardly any musical expression, which must be the primary agent of motivation in a music drama. The moment right after Lancelot's miracle of the tournament, when he and Guenevere look at one another in love for the first time, has no song to express this love. There is only an orchestral underscoring of "C'est Moi," which has only the most banal leitmotivic association with Lancelot and certainly adds nothing to the drama of the scene. Underscoring is again the best that Loewe can do for the finale of the first act, which contains Arthur's soliloquy quoted above; this time it is "How to Handle a Woman" for the first part (until "I demand a man's vengeance") and then, incredibly, "I Wonder What the King Is Doing Tonight," Arthur's self-mocking comedy song, for the second. The rescue of Guenevere, set as a sort of oratorio sung by the company of ladies and knights, has been universally condemned, and Lerner himself recognized the flaw in the very design of the scene:

> The one scene in the play that I knew was a breach in style was the penultimate scene involving the song "Guinevere" in which the story of Lancelot's rescue is told. . . . It was not only a stylistic change, but it was breaking a second major theatrical law: it was describing events that took place offstage.[21]

Strangely enough, the saving grace of *Camelot* occurs just where most shows are weakest, at the very end. The second act finale at last brings into dim focus one of the mythic elements with which composer and lyricist grappled:

> For me, the raison d'etre of *Camelot* was the end of the journey when Arthur has lost his love, his friend, and his Round Table and believes his life has been a failure. Then a small boy appears from behind a tent who doesn't know the Round Table is dead and who wishes to become a knight. Arthur realizes that as long as his vision is alive in some small heart he has not failed. Men die but an idea does not.[22]

The reality of the dream is expressed in one of those reprises characteristic of *My Fair Lady,* which dramatically changes the meaning of a song by a new context, and not by significant changes in the song itself. The last scene shows Arthur almost chanting the title song, which at the play's beginning was a whimsical account of Camelot's meteorological perfection, but whose whimsy has now become legend. The name "Camelot" is now synonymous with the dream, and it is the last word sung in the play, by Arthur and his full court, accompanied by the triadic fanfare which is its musical symbol.

Lerner's recognition of this central mythic element came to him during *Camelot*'s Boston tryout, after the Toronto opening, and too late for extensive rewriting that might have provided the focus that this stage version of the myth so desperately needed.[23] Yet, although it is a truism that the plot and book form the cornerstone of any traditional musical play, it is too easy to blame *Camelot*'s critical failure on the quality of the libretto alone. Why composer and lyricist did not provide original music for some of the play's most significant events remains a great mystery, for it amounts to an abdication on their part. Perhaps these moments were the victims of Broadway's three-hour rule, which in the case of *The Once and Future King* made a Herculean task of adaptation quite impossible. The limitations of time and space that help to define the American musical play did not allow the music its proper dramatic role.

That is indeed a pity, because the music composed for *Camelot,* taken as music alone, is perhaps Loewe's best score. The songs are more serious than those of *My Fair Lady,* and have more ambitious designs. "Fie on Goodness," a choral number for the knights which was unfortunately cut early in the New York run, is a masterful synthesis of sardonic humor and chivalrous frustration that rises to an impressive musical climax and expresses an important mythic element of White's novel. The triadic "Camelot" motive is pervasive, so that its accumulated meaning is not lost on listeners in the finale. Indeed, *Camelot* is one of those sad cases where one enjoys listening to the original cast recording more than to a performance of the play itself.

It is curious that *Camelot* remains in the "repertoire" of the American musical theater; its unusual place is probably due to its unusual performance history. The opening of *Camelot* on December 3, 1960, at the Majestic Theater marked one of the very few times that critical disdain did not doom a show's commercial success, for *Camelot* had already sold two years' worth of tickets on the strength of Lerner and Loewe's reputation as the creators of *Brigadoon,* the musical film *Gigi,* and above all, *My Fair Lady.* Meanwhile, its cast recording was vigorously promoted by the exploding recording industry, so that the show was nationally famous, in a sense, before being seen. It created its own legend.[24]

It could be argued that such status is not entirely undeserved, that *Camelot,* in undertaking to interpret such a vast mythical tale, had aimed very high and just missed. It is the opposite number to *Kiss Me, Kate.* Yet, to dwell on the dimension of the original myth is to miss part of the point of a myth's adaptation. How comparatively simple is the legend of Pygmalion, and how powerful are the several revelations of "I've Grown Accustomed to Her Face." The musical interpretation of this simple and small mythical gap is found again and again to be more wonderful than what might have been with the manifold myth of Camelot.

# CHAPTER 9

# Tragedy as Musical

*Street brawls, double death . . . it's all much less important than the bigger idea of making a musical that tells a tragic story in musical-comedy terms. . . . Can it succeed?*[1]

LEONARD BERNSTEIN

Tragedy has been the most elusive dramatic expression for the Broadway tradition. Though a number of its best plots have offered opportunities for tragic composition, Broadway music has generally failed those moments that come closest to tragedy. Gershwin could not find the means to set the despair of either Porgy or his beloved community after Bess's final departure. Jerry Bock's "Anatevka," more nostalgic than tragic, falls far short of conveying the shattered lives and the death of an ethnic tradition at the end of *Fiddler on the Roof*. And Sweeney Todd is given the tragic situation but not the music that would express his comprehension of his own destruction. At other times, composers have simply given up the attempt, and avoided the necessity of tragic music by leaving the matter in the hands of the librettist or by changing the plot. Thus, Gershwin composes the uplifting "O Lawd, I'm on My Way" to transform the end of *Porgy and Bess*. Thus, Rodgers and Hammerstein rewrite the end of Molnar's *Liliom* for their *Carousel,* and leave no music at all for Julie's grief over Billy's suicide, only a song of consolation. The missed chances and unanswered challenges have ironically made tragic drama in the American musical theater into an Olympus, beckoning beyond reach. Indeed, that the Broadway tradition is seen as a lightweight music drama is due in no small measure to its little success with the most serious genres: epic myth, sacred history, and tragedy.

To comprehend the brilliant creation of a tragic music drama within this tradition in Leonard Bernstein's *West Side Story* is to appreciate a beneficent set of circumstances that brought together four men who were or who would be major Broadway talents—Bernstein, director and choreographer Jerome Robbins, playwright Arthur Laurents, and lyricist Stephen Sondheim—at a time when gang wars in New York City encouraged faith in Robbins's original conception. But it is also to comprehend what tragedy demands.

It demands first of all a tragic plot. That means much more than a story in which the hero dies some terrible death at the end. "The tragic writer has generally been concerned with last things, with death, with the meaning of life as a whole, with 'destiny' or 'fate.' . . ."[2] The tragic circumstances are ordered so that they not only portray but make sense of good and evil in characters. "Observing that human beings suffer, go to pieces, or die prematurely, the tragic vision . . . will not permit these things to happen meaninglessly."[3] Rather, they are seen to occur as part of a higher order that in many plays is a moral order. So "tragedy, like many societies, decrees that a terrible death is evidence of terrible sin, and by this alchemy which is not the logic of philosophy or history as we know it, some meaning is drawn from human calamity."[4]

In its purest form, the sin or "tragic flaw" resides in the character around which the tragedy evolves: Oedipus the King or Macbeth. But in Shakespeare's *Romeo and Juliet,* the model upon which playwright Arthur Laurents based the libretto for *West Side Story,* the sin is far removed from the principals. Indeed, there is not the slightest suggestion of malice in them. One could stretch the theory by arguing that the tragic flaw lies in Romeo's lack of self-control, so that he kills Tybalt in a frenzy after seeing him run Mercutio through, just as Tony stabs Bernardo after Riff's death, and so precipitates the banishment and all the rest, but such a view forgets the baseless hatred of the two families, which certainly must be considered to be the greater sin. Otherwise, what sense can be made of Prince Escalus's awful remonstrance to them?

> *See what a scourge is laid upon your hate,*
> *That heaven finds means to kill your joys with love.*
>
> (V, iii, 192-93)

Not for its missing "terrible sin," but for some lack of "tragic necessity" has *Romeo and Juliet* been criticized. Because Friar John is prevented by a suspicion of plague from delivering to Romeo the message that Juliet is just asleep, not dead, in the Capulet tomb, critics have contended that Shakespeare "offends against his own criteria for tragedy by allowing mere chance to determine the destiny of the hero and heroine." For this, the play "has been admired for its pathetic rather than for its tragic power."[5]

*West Side Story* follows the plot of *Romeo and Juliet* even down to the transmutation of particular lines in spots, but Laurents introduces two changes toward the end, the first of which answers this very criticism and, in a tragic sense, improves the plot. After Anita, Maria's confidante and friend, reluctantly agrees to take Tony the message that will ensure the lovers' escape, she is prevented from delivering it by the Jets, who mock her story and begin to abuse her maliciously. They are stopped just short of rape by the appearance of Doc, the drugstore owner. Anita, livid, cries out that Maria has been killed by her former fiancé. "Chance, which Shakespeare uses to bring about the final disaster, is eliminated by Laurents. Instead, the social prejudice, the mutual suspicion and hate that motivate the gang warfare become, in Act II Scene 4, the causes for Anita's lie about Maria's death and thus of the disaster that follows."[6] This projects the tragic flaw much more directly onto society and makes *West Side Story* more of a social tragedy than *Romeo and Juliet*.

Laurents's other change is that Maria, unlike Juliet, lives at the end. Otherwise the story is much the same. The parallels of the lovers' meeting, the famous balcony scene, the wedding, the duel, were all noticed even in the first reviews. The parallels run deeper than plot, however. *West Side Story* has the same sense of fatefulness, of inevitability, that marks *Romeo and Juliet* from its opening chorus. Before entering the Capulet ball Romeo remarks

> *for my mind misgives*
> *Some consequence, yet hanging in the stars,*
> *Shall bitterly begin his fearful date*
> *With this night's revels, and expire the term*
> *Of a despised life closed in my breast,*
> *By some vile forfeit of untimely death.*

> (I, iv, 106-11)

Likewise, Tony sings "Something's Coming" just before the dance at the gym where he will meet Maria.

For Bernstein, the tragic plot was a new challenge. Completely sympathetic to the Broadway tradition despite his status as a world-class conductor of Western art music, he had three successful Broadway shows already behind him in 1957, but none of them serious. *On the Town* (1944) was adapted from his own ballet *Fancy Free* about three sailors on a wild shore leave in New York City. *Wonderful Town* (1953) set a popular comic play, *My Sister Eileen*. Neither of these has a single moment of gravity comparable even to, say, any of the Sky Masterson and Sarah Brown scenes in *Guys and Dolls*. Ironically, his ambitious *Candide* (1956) does have such moments, but they work at cross-purposes to the overall theme of Voltaire's classic satire and Lillian Hellman's libretto. The music for all of these shows was much acclaimed, and it deserves to be, but Bernstein seemed not to be very fussy about the sort of librettos he set. His talent was waiting for an idea and a libretto such as *West Side Story* to come along.

For what tragedy demands of a music drama, besides the tragic plot, is a music that is capable of the darker emotions, even of evil, that can yet relate them to utterly opposite human aspirations. That is because tragedy is itself a twofold dramatic expression:

Tragedy cannot be extreme optimism, for that would be to underestimate the problem; it cannot be extreme pessimism, for that would be to lose faith in man. At the heart of tragedy is a tough dialectical struggle in which the victory of either side is credible.[7]

*West Side Story* demanded an accessible musical integration the like of which Broadway had never heard, and that is the challenge for which Bernstein's compositional imagination, with its peculiar brand of popular eclecticism and its thorough acquaintance with the Western art tradition, was ready.

Critics have occasionally noted clear motivic relationships in the music of *West Side Story*. In his essay for a recent recording conducted by Bernstein himself, David Stearns describes how the interval that Tony sings to begin "Something's Coming" is inverted to become the first interval in the main tune of "Maria," in effect a resolution of his feeling of expectancy.[8]

**Ex. 9–1** Bernstein and Sondheim, *West Side Story*, "Something's Coming" (No. 3), mm. 8–9, and "Maria" (No. 5), mm. 8–9.

This is but the most famous example of a motivic and thematic integration so thorough that by it alone is *West Side Story* set apart from any preceding Broadway musical. The interval above is the tritone, a traditional dissonance of three whole steps, a favorite interval of Bernstein in his whole corpus. Its prominence in "Something's Coming" and "Maria" is important, but only the tip of the iceberg, for it is heard in every other musical number of the play. But even that understates the variety of dramatic and musical uses to which this very characteristic sound is put. Between Tony's two songs, for instance, comes "The Dance at the Gym" which begins this way.

Allegro moderato

**Ex. 9–2** Bernstein and Sondheim, *West Side Story*, "The Dance at the Gym" (No. 4), m. 1.

The scoring and orchestration of the octaves is such that the E natural, the raised fourth step that makes the tritone, seems approached from above and below at the same time. So the inversion of Example 9-1 is not abrupt, but mediated just before the meeting that prompts Tony to sing "Maria."

The tritone is just the beginning. There are at least four other important elements of structure which characterize the music of *West Side Story* and, as in *Carousel* and *Porgy and Bess,* lend it a sound so particular that it seems impossible to mistake any of its songs for those of another play. One of these is the chromatically lowered seventh step of the scale.

**Ex. 9–3**  Bernstein and Sondheim, *West Side Story,* "Jet Song" (No. 2), mm. 28–43.

The A-flat in measure 32 of the "Jet Song" is a lowered seventh in the local context of B-flat major. The D-flat in measure 40 is a lowered seventh in the local context of E-flat major. In "Something's Coming" the lowered seventh is introduced in Tony's melody at the end of the second phrase (mm. 17-18), gradually becoming so prominent that it ends the whole song, even though it is a dissonance.

**Ex. 9–4**  Bernstein and Sondheim, *West Side Story*, "Something's Coming" (No. 3), mm. 138–48. The last sung note is a lowered seventh in the key of this song, D major.

A third characteristic element is a tone cluster made up of a triad with both major and minor third factors. Many of the chords harmonizing the "Jet Song" are constructed in this way (Ex. 9-3, e.g. the first two chords). Such a sound has a double effect for *West Side Story*. It stamps the music with an American flavor appropriate to the story's setting, since the simultaneous major/minor third approximates pitch shadings in jazz, particularly the blue third. The association is reinforced by the typical rhythmic texture of a solidly metric bass line against which the upper parts are syncopated. The other effect concerns structure. Along with the tritone, the half-step juxtapositions of this cluster soon accustom the ear to an idiom of chromatic progressions and modulations that are so important to the latter part of the play.

Indeed, the chromatic half-step develops into another element in its own right. By establishing the tritone as a structural interval at the outset, Bernstein makes easy a vocabulary of chromatic modulations that would otherwise be distant.

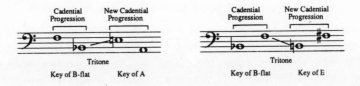

**Fig. 9–1**  Modulation possibilities using the tritone.

To the Western ear, the leap of the perfect fifth can establish a key, since it signals a cadence. By combining that interval with the chromatic tritone, tonal centers one half-step above and one half-step below the original tonic become accessible. Theory becomes practice in the interludes between the verses of "To-night."

**Ex. 9–5** Bernstein and Sondheim, *West Side Story*, "Balcony Scene" (No. 6), mm. 81–90.

Finally, there is the hemiola, a characteristic rhythm that juxtaposes a division of a beat (or a measure, itself a big beat) into three parts against a division into two. The most famous example from *West Side Story* is the alternation of 3/4 and 6/8 meters in the refrain of "America," famous perhaps because it is such a classic case, but there are many variants of the hemiola idea throughout the score. In the "Jet Song" (Ex. 9-3), the contrasting division of the measure by the vocal melody against that by the bass melody has the same effect, but it is complicated further because the accompaniment repeats its pattern every two bars, and its principal motive is a two-beat cell (one beat being a dotted quarter). One level of triple meter given by the singer competes with several levels of duple in the orchestra. Similarly, the bass line of "Something's Coming" (Ex. 9-4) pits a clear triple pattern against a duple division in the upper parts. This gentle sort of syncopation is what lends this song its effect of anticipation, almost breathlessness.

How striking these elements are, striking in the sense of being on the fringe of the Western tonal language. The normal procedure is to organize the rhythm with a steady simple meter and clear rhythmic groupings, not with complex hemiolas. The tritone, for centuries strictly controlled or avoided altogether, can be found in the diatonic scale, but not in the way Bernstein usually uses it, as an augmented fourth above the tonic. And the clash of third factors, regardless of any appeal to jazz idioms, is a very strong semitonal dissonance. Yet, these sounds emerge so naturally from the "Prologue" of the work that in the end the listener notices not how weird or unusual they are, but how well they work together.

Like *Carousel, West Side Story* dispenses with the medley overture and begins the play with a "Prologue" that accompanies silent action on stage. The scene is given as "The months before" and as the "Prologue" is played, the Jets and Sharks dance and mime their growing rivalry, until the Sharks leader Bernardo cuts the ear of one of the Jets in ritual fashion as the police whistle sounds. As the action on stage is the premise for the rest of the drama, so is the music of the "Prologue" the source of all Bernstein's important musical elements.

**Ex. 9–6**    Leonard Bernstein, *West Side Story,* "Prologue" (No. 1), mm. 1–18.

The very first chord introduces the first important element, the major/minor triad. Again, its rhythmic disposition and the cultural setting justify this dissonance as "blues" sound. It quickly becomes a norm, since every chord is built the same way, save for alterations needed when the fifth is diminished (mm. 4, 8).[9] The first cadence comes at the end of measure eight, defined by the first simple pitch formation, the unison C.

Next, the tritone is heard, from the A to D-sharp in measure 12, arising from a theme that seems to be in the key of A. Then, when that theme repeats three bars later, its C-sharp clashes with a C natural in the following measure (m. 17). Yet, what should be a salient chromaticism develops easily from the earlier material. The sustained D-sharp is a pitch that has already been heard, in the very first chord. In fact, all the notes of that A major theme have already been in the listener's ear from the first two bars. The relationship is made explicit when Bernstein sounds the opening chord progression to accompany the long D-sharp (mm. 13-15). Similarly, the theme which juxtaposes C-sharp/C natural later on is nothing more than an arpeggiation of Bernstein's chord on the downbeat of measure three (A–B-sharp–C-sharp–E) with the added D-sharp.

After the second cadence in C (m. 18), the "Prologue" begins again with a fresh motive.

**Ex. 9–7**  Leonard Bernstein, *West Side Story,* "Prologue" (No. 1), mm. 19–40.

It sounds fresh because the prominent pitches, F in the high melody and F-sharp in the bass, are the only two of the complete twelve-tone collection which have not been sounded. The upper melody is clearly derived from the opening bars both in rhythm and in contour. The bass, however, introduces the hemiola idea, since it is an ostinato of three chords that moves across the duple measures; the upper melody counterpoises its two measure periods, as in the "Jet Song." The bass also raises the tritone to higher structural significance: it is in the key of

F-sharp, a tritone distance from the original key of C, in which the upper melody can still be heard at the same time.

When this melody is heard again two pages later, it is recomposed to "fit in" with the harmony of this bass line.

**Ex. 9–8**  Leonard Bernstein, *West Side Story,* "Prologue" (No. 1), mm. 101–9.

The important feature here is that what should be the key-defining leading tone, E-sharp, is missing. Finally, the melody rises to a peak and culminates with an E natural, so that the sound of the modal lowered seventh, perhaps the least striking of all these elements, is made explicit (mm. 105-106).

The more anomalous and dissonant harmonization of the "swing" melody is heard first, not second, because it is consistent with a harmonic procedure heard from the beginning. The music has polytonal aspects; that is, more than one key can be simultaneously implied, or actually sounded. The opening phrase, for example (Ex. 9-6), begins with a colored C triad and a colored A triad, and ends on a G-sharp triad, also colored. Is the real key C, as the first bass note would suggest, or A, as the second and last would suggest? The issue is resolved by the first cadence, the unambiguous unison in measure eight, but meanwhile Bernstein has founded an important high-level feature, a harmonic polarity between C and A. It is immediately strengthened as the first theme is sounded in A major (mm. 11-13, 15-17), yet harmonized with exactly the same chords as began the piece, and rounded off with the same C cadence (m. 18). The next passage expands the idea yet again (Ex. 9-7). The C/A polarity continues in the upper melody, while the bass part moves in the key of F-sharp, which of course is the relative minor of A. Once more the structural predominance of C is emphasized as the section ends with the unison cadence (m. 40).

So the "Prologue" establishes not only the significant melodic and rhythmic elements for the play, but also significant harmonic procedures and pitches, C, A, and F-sharp, which will unify the musical numbers in a way that no other Broadway composer has attempted. *West Side Story* is the first American musical play to be organized around a central pitch.[10]

Such a deep and multi-faceted musical integration is wholly admirable, but should not be so astonishing, coming as it does from a composer who by 1957 had composed two full-length symphonies and several other important instrumental works, for such integration in instrumental music is essential. The easy alliance of jazz idioms and symphonic textures are as nothing to one who was a practicing jazzman and Koussevitsky protégé at the same time. To attribute the high achievement of *West Side Story* to its symphonic organization, however, is to underrate it seriously and miss its singular drama. Indeed, many of the same elements that characterize this play are also heard in abundance in *Candide,* particularly the tritone, the lowered seventh, and the hemiola.[11] Once the scheme of musical integration is apparent, what becomes important is its power to project tragic drama.

From the dramatic perspective, there is no surprise in Bernstein's choice of materials: they are dissonant, chromatic, syncopated, in other words, filled with musical tension, a roughness that matches the story and its setting. But if Bentley's tragic dialectic is to be translated into music, these same materials must also project the other side. That is the basis for the tragedy within the music: not the collection of motives, keys, and musical ideas alone, but these together with their transformation. Consider the main tune of the famous balcony scene, "Tonight."

**Ex. 9–9**  Bernstein and Sondheim, *West Side Story*, "Balcony Scene" (No. 6), mm. 51–60.

There in the middle-voice accompaniment is the tone cluster as before, but the half-step dissonance has been exchanged in favor of the less dissonant whole-step so that the whole chord sounds like a mild tonic ninth. There is the E natural sounding the tritone against the tonic B-flat, but now its harmonic context transforms it into an old-fashioned secondary dominant. There is the chromatic half-step in the bass moving from A natural to A-flat (mm. 58-59) and in the vocal melody right after, but since the voice leading in all the other voices produces a concomitant change of chord, the effect is no more startling than in Wagner. More explicit chromaticism is limited to the modulation passages that separate each verse. Tragedy is made possible through Bernstein's design of a musical idiom capable of both sorts of expression, pessimism and optimism, evil and aspiration, which are thus related in musical terms. The motivic unity of the idiom is, of course, essential, but so is its capacity for expressive range through transformations.

Thematic correspondences among the musical numbers are also resources for dramatic transformations, although by and large their role has more to do with structure and musical continuity. Bernstein does not use leitmotifs in the Wagnerian sense of symbolizing characters or emotions, but rather as a means to connect the musical parts in long chains. This is most evident in the opening scenes of the play. The music of the "Prologue" is so similar to the "Jet Song" that one leads directly into the other without any noticeable break. In the middle of the song (m. 100 ff.), the Jets sing the tune that will become the opening stage band melody in "The Dance at the Gym." Later in the gym sequence comes the delicate "Cha-Cha," which is a dance arrangement of "Maria." That song in turn is quoted to begin the "Balcony Scene." Such relationships create a high-level continuity among the numbers that allows Bernstein to slow the action around Tony and Maria's meeting to a pace suitable for tragedy.

It is also possible, although difficult to demonstrate convincingly, that Bernstein's use of tonal centers has a dramatic symbolism attached. There is the central pitch of the musical, C. Certain keys on the sharp side seem reserved for the expressions of the lovers: "Something's Coming" in D, "Cha-Cha" in G, the wedding vows music in G, C, and E, "Somewhere" in E. Flat keys are related to themes of violence and hate: the chase music of the "Prologue" in B-flat, the first "Jet Song" in B-flat, "Cool" in C minor, "A Boy Like That" in B-flat minor. E-flat is the last pitch heard in the first act, sustained in tremolo as the curtain covers the dead bodies of Riff and Bernardo. That E-flat and E natural create the first dissonance of the musical may have some connection with the choice of E-flat for the latter "Rumble" music and the reservation of E major for "Somewhere." The one gross inconsistency is the setting of "Maria" in E-flat major, but a comment by Larry Kert, who created the part of Tony, indicates that Bernstein's original key may have been different:

> At the audition I sang "Maria" in the original key. I cracked on the high note. Still they saw something they liked and had me do it again one note lower.[12]

Restoring the transposition would put "Maria" in E major, and since the introduction is set in the key a major third down, that would be C, which connects very nicely with the C of the last dance of the previous scene, the "Jump." Again, since "Maria" moves right into the "Balcony Scene," perhaps its original keys were B, B-flat, and A major.

To build his tragic idiom into the higher structural levels of *West Side Story*, Bernstein depends on two techniques which, although not new to Broadway, are in this play exploited as never before: the continuity of several musical numbers in succession, and the drama of dance.

Three times in the course of the play musical numbers follow in succession without appreciable break for dialogue, and each such succession occurs at a crucial point in the tragic plot. The first extends from the "Mambo" of the dance scene through the following "Cha-Cha" and "Jump" into "Maria," and finally ends with the "Balcony Scene." There are short conversations but music plays under all of them, and various musical connections leave no doubt that continuity is intended.

This music, of course, accompanies the dance scene where Tony and Maria meet, and the most immediate effect of the continuous sequence is to portray in music how their love arises miraculously from a battleground. The "Mambo" is a barely disguised show of force between the two gangs. After the lovers catch sight of one another, the lights dim and the crowd moves offstage as the music in the key of A begins to sound a sequence of I-VII progressions, using the major triad of the lowered seventh step to shift the key in a subdominant direction. Then the "Cha-Cha" begins in G, and Tony and Maria become lost in their intimate dance.

That they fall in love at first sight is a necessary economy of Shakespeare's plot. The circumstances and aftermath are so complex that no time is left to develop a love relationship; it must happen at once. And the audience must be fully convinced of the profundity of their love and their utter helplessness in giving themselves to it. Shakespeare carries it off with his great love poetry. "Did he wonder for a moment," asks Granville-Barker, "how to make this stand out from everything else in the play? They [the lovers] share a sonnet between them, and it is a charming device." [13] Bernstein relies on his music, its particular character and the succession of numbers that slow the action. The "Cha-Cha," for example, has such a different texture and orchestration from the preceding dances that the separate world in which Tony and Maria find themselves is immediately apparent. The many long rests which articulate phrase endings and the feminine cadences make it easy for Bernstein to fashion a transition into the "Meeting Scene" melodrama.

The first full expression of sentiment comes in Tony's song "Maria," a piece with an astonishing number of wonderful features for its short length. Bernstein captures Tony's dazed amazement with an introduction that is sung, beginning with a monotone on D-sharp. The sense of bewilderment comes from the insecurity of key, nominally in B major but without any confirming cadence or rhythm.

**Ex. 9–10**  Bernstein and Sondheim, *West Side Story*, "Maria" (No. 5), mm. 1–11.

Only when the rhythm accelerates and the music erupts into the key of E-flat does the listener realize that Tony's monotone was the tonic after all. The "Cha-Cha" melody returns in full-blown lyricism over a bass line tango of mild Spanish character which at the same time recalls the jazz idiom through its tied notes in mid-measure. The high point comes with what should be the onset of the second verse, and instead becomes a great rhapsodic singing counterpoint to the main tune in the orchestra, as if to suggest that Tony's sudden happiness is so boundless that he can do nothing but name its cause.

**Ex. 9–11**  Bernstein and Sondheim, *West Side Story,* "Maria" (No. 5), mm. 27–33.

The famous tritone setting Maria's name is already muted in its dissonant effect, since Bernstein allows the raised fourth step in the third bar of the melody (m. 11) to fulfill its traditional function as a secondary leading tone. As regards the tragic development, the downbeat upward appoggiatura associated with "Maria" becomes more important than its tritone setting, although the connections which that interval makes with previous numbers, especially the dance numbers, cannot be gainsaid. The coda of the song, whose harmony recalls the mysterious introduction, leaves this "Maria" motive as the last gesture in the listener's ear just before it is significantly developed in the following "Balcony Scene."

**Ex. 9–12**  Bernstein and Sondheim, *West Side Story,* "Maria" (No. 5), mm. 46–53.

The dramatic function of the main tune "Tonight" from the "Balcony Scene" is to allow Maria the chance to express her own feelings as a balance to Tony's previous song, and then to deepen and make credible the relationship itself, as does Shakespeare's balcony scene. It is significant, therefore, that she sings the first verse alone. Otherwise, little more need be said, except that it is a beautiful song which makes its effect in traditional Romantic manner: every phrase is in a different key, so that the return to the original in the last phrase resolves a high-level tension in its single cadence. However, the melodrama surrounding the verses contains dialogue which begins to describe the particular quality of this love. As Juliet warns Romeo of the dangers her kinsmen pose, and he replies,

> *Alack there lies more peril in thine eye*
> *Than twenty of their swords; look thou but sweet,*
> *And I am proof against their enmity*

> (II, ii, 71-73)

so does Maria warn Tony, who says, simply, ''I'm not afraid.'' Their love is a
fearless love, and this fearlessness will lead to Tony's hopeless attempt to stop
the rumble. This first glimpse of looming tragedy, ironic in that such a disaster
could spring from such a love, is turned into music at the very end of the scene.

**Ex. 9–13**  Bernstein and Sondheim, *West Side Story,* ''Balcony Scene'' (No. 6), mm. 144–54.

For the first time, the singers do not sustain the fifth scale degree on the last
''Tonight,'' as they have done in every verse till now, but rise to the tonic,
making the strongest cadence of the whole piece. As they sing this high A-flat,

a striking melody in the 'cellos decorates a plagal cadence, the first phrase from
the song "Somewhere," a song not to be heard until well into the second act.
The final gesture is the upward appoggiatura "Maria" motive less the chromatic
half-step, now allied to another song to which it already belongs so well, since
it will set the very word "Somewhere."

This curious practice of giving the listener advance notice of very important
melodies to come, first in the "Cha-Cha" and now at the end of "Tonight,"
can have only a dramatic explanation. Of course the gestures must work on their
own musical terms, whether one recognizes their connections or not; the "Cha-
Cha" is a perfectly fine little dance whose different character makes its point
immediately, and the last cadence of "Tonight" has a very nice bit of part
writing which amplifies the cadential effect so that it can convincingly finish the
scene. For the listener who already knows the musical, however, the forward
direction of such references builds a sense of destiny that is so much a part of
the original *Romeo and Juliet*. Who can fail to sense the implication of the
"Somewhere" quotation at the very moment when Tony and Maria are celebrating their fearless love?

The second continuous musical sequence ends the first act and includes "One
Hand, One Heart," the quintet "Tonight," and "The Rumble." Its purpose is
quite different from the first one, for the depth and character of the love relationship are no longer at issue. The second sequence, coming at the end of the
act, operates much more in the manner of a traditional classical finale, juxtapos-
ing various dramatic themes and characters in order to accelerate the pace before
the curtain falls. The order of the numbers makes this intention quite clear: the
first song continues the love theme, the last presents the violence of hatred, and
the middle number contrasts both at once in climactic fashion.

It is unfortunate that the bridal shop scene is often described as a "mock"
wedding just because Tony and Maria playfully banter about wedding plans and
surround themselves with a wedding party of mannequins. This view neglects
the profound change of mood brought about by the "Somewhere" motive, heard
just before they take their vows. It also neglects the Catholic teaching, to which
Tony, the Polish-American, and Maria, the Puerto Rican immigrant, would pre-
sumably be sympathetic, that the sacrament of marriage is conferred not by a
priest but by the man and woman on one another. For the tragedy to have its
greatest pathos, the love sacrificed at the end must be the greatest love possible,
love for a lifetime. Thus Shakespeare includes the brief sixth scene of the second
act in which it is made clear that Romeo and Juliet do marry. Even though it is
rare for a Broadway musical play to show a wedding, mostly because that is the
presumed end of the plot, here it is the subject of very moving music.

Barely have the final *pianissimo* chords of "One Hand, One Heart" died
away when the ear is jarred by the opening of the great ensemble "Tonight."

Ex. 9–14   Bernstein and Sondheim, *West Side Story,* "Tonight" (No. 10), mm. 1–13.

Here all the important elements that have been continually transformed since their first occurrence in the "Prologue" return in their harshest, most dissonant form. Most obvious is the hemiola rhythm, the bass line proceeding in groups of three quarter notes against duple meter in the upper parts. The texture is polytonal, not in the sense of the key being ambiguous, but in the sense of two keys pitted against one another, and the two keys are C and A, the two harmonic poles established on the opening page of the play. The rising bass line E–F-sharp–G-sharp, heard against the upper part, gives the impression of A while the insistent G natural in the middle voice (mm. 2-3) allows the upper parts to be heard in C. This harmonic design allows other important motives to be embedded in the texture: the E major/minor triad resulting from the simultaneous G natural and G-sharp, and G natural acting as a lowered seventh in the context of A.

**Ex. 9–15**  Bernstein and Sondheim, *West Side Story*, "Tonight" (No. 10), mm. 14–20.

The tritone is used more circumspectly, in the contour of the melody which emphasizes B and F (mm. 11-13) and F-sharp and C (mm. 15-18), but nevertheless colors the music.

So much for the symbols of tragedy. The dramatic purpose of the quintet is to present the five principal characters anticipating the coming evening in a way that summarizes their fated courses in the drama. The construction is quite traditional: each principal gets a solo in the first half (except Maria, who has the same music and lyrics as Tony) in order to present both words and music clearly, and then the intensifying counterpoint on two musical themes can begin. Bernstein is bitterly ironic when he gives the Jets and Sharks the same music to sing (although its use for Anita's part must be considered a musical economy). For the lovers' side, he reprises the "Tonight" song from the "Balcony Scene." The transition from the violent to the sublime is prepared when the gangs anticipate the modulation to A major.

Ex. 9–16   Bernstein and Sondheim, *West Side Story*, "Tonight" (No. 10), mm. 33–40.

The G naturals in the vocal melody and the F naturals in the bass part maintain a certain connection to the key of C, yet the sense of tonal center is much closer to a real A than it was before. Anita's solo returns the music to C/A, but the preceding interlude for Jets and Sharks effectively prepares Tony's change to an unambiguous A major.

Ex. 9–17  Bernstein and Sondheim, *West Side Story,* "Tonight" (No. 10), mm. 63–71.

The reprise of "Tonight" supports the polytonal design of the beginning beautifully, since the modulation plan of the tune moves the music from A major to C major with the second phrase. The danger in incorporating such a lyrical piece into the quintet is a loss of tension after the dissonance of the opening. To avert it, Bernstein has the violins double Tony's singing in the second phrase. Then, for the third phrase, they continue to play his melody, but one measure later than his singing, as a canon.

**Ex. 9–18** Bernstein and Sondheim, *West Side Story*, "Tonight" (No. 10), mm. 83–93.

This solution is so breathtakingly simple that it is hard to believe the original tune was not designed for it, for it gives up none of the lyricism that the situation demands while the counterpoint intensifies the texture without extreme dissonance.

Tony's song finishes without a firm cadence, and now the first music returns briefly in the key of E-flat/C. The reason for this transposition is purely structural, so that the second reprise of "Tonight" will occur in C major, not A major, and so end the quintet in C. It is important, though, that the return to the first Jet/Shark theme be brief, so that the immediate onset of Maria singing "Tonight" may quicken the pace. Thereafter the five parts are severally introduced, the chromatic notes of the first theme coloring the predominant second theme, the structure of which governs the rest of the course. The greatest intensity of contrast occurs in its third phrase, where the key of C minor expresses at once the lovers' longing and the gangs' raging.

**Ex. 9-19** Bernstein and Sondheim, *West Side Story*, "Tonight" (No. 10), mm. 133–40.

Even here, the tonal idiom is so flexible that the Jets can sing "They began it" on an E-flat minor triad (mm. 138-39), a considerable harmonic distance from C, without losing the continuity of the overall key. The end of the quintet, in one sense, has been built up from the beginning, since there have been no strong cadences, and none at all since Anita's first solo. The moment when the five parts come together, the topmost hitting the high C, is the most climactic musical moment in the play.

**Ex. 9–20** Bernstein and Sondheim, *West Side Story,* "Tonight" (No. 10), mm. 143–51.

The last measures of the ensemble, filling out the powerful cadence, contain the E natural/E-flat conflict and the F-sharp, all of which, in the context of C, recall the musical premises of the "Prologue." That, in short, is the secret of the entire ensemble. By dramatizing this inextricable intertwining of love and hate in consistent musical motives and symbols, the quintet summarizes the progress of the tragedy just before the fatal moment. It is the musical-dramatic climax of the first act and the greatest operatic ensemble ever composed for the Broadway stage.

A short dialogue precedes the rumble. Tony tries in vain to prevent the fight from starting. He endures Bernardo's insults, but his best friend Riff cannot, and when he hits Bernardo with his fist, "The Rumble" music begins.

The opening measures continue the development of explicit "Prologue" material. The first chord in the bass is C–F-sharp–C, answered by an A major/minor cluster. Later on the keys of E-flat major and minor become important (the last note of the act is E-flat), having been prepared by the closing bars of the quintet, and connected to the other material by the common G-flat/F-sharp of the minor mode. Much music from the "Prologue" is recapitulated with little change. The music surrounding the moment when Tony kills Bernardo is the same as that setting Bernardo's knifing the Jet A-Rab, a plausible symmetry.

A stronger element of symmetry between the "Prologue" and "The Rumble" is their choreography. They are dances. Dance, of course, has always been an essential part of the Broadway tradition, but West Side Story used it to such an extent that many critics named it the most outstanding element of the show, one calling the piece a "ballet-opera." [14] There are twelve choreographed pieces in the play. That Jerome Robbins, the original choreographer, was not only the show's director but the one who came up with the original conception for the play in the late 1940s certainly influenced the show's final shape. By that time, his extremely fortunate match with Bernstein was years old, for it was Robbins who helped launch the composer's career when he asked Bernstein to compose a ballet in 1943, before the famous conducting debut with the New York Philharmonic. This turned out to be Fancy Free, which was so popular in New York that the collaborators persuaded Betty Comden and Adolph Green to help them turn it into a Broadway musical, On the Town, which was also a hit.

So many dance numbers in a single musical play would be intolerable had they not a significant dramatic purpose. That is why West Side Story is the first musical for which the composer himself created significant and separate pieces of music for the dance sequences, rather than leave them for an arranger to patch together out of the song material. Serious music drama with serious dancing demands serious music.

The most important dance sequences—"Prologue," "Cha-Cha," "The Rumble," "Ballet Sequence," "Taunting Scene," "Finale"—narrate the story while abstracting it. They narrate in that they convey facts which need to be known. "There's hardly a divertissement. We tell everything, the dance hall incident, the killing of the men, the taunting of the girl in the drugstore, through dance." [15]

The "Prologue" tells that the Jets and Sharks have been warring for months. "The Rumble" shows who is killed and how. The "Taunting Scene" reveals what happens to Anita when she tries to give Tony Maria's message. But narration alone is insufficient for the drama of dance; the dances must abstract the events that they portray. That allows the integration of the events themselves with accompanying emotional reactions carried in the accompanying music. But more than that, abstraction can make the event more frightening, triumphant, powerful than if it were seen true to life, because it allows the viewer's imagination to become an active participant, to blow what it has seen out of all proportion. Just as an actress's gesture or movement in cinema, sufficiently subtle, can be more erotic than a full-length love scene, so can the choreographed violence of a gang fight seem more horrible than any attempt at staging the real thing with fake punches and pratfalls.

The third continuous music sequence of *West Side Story,* the "Ballet Sequence," is dominated by such dancing. When Tony and Maria are together after the rumble, he sings the arioso "I'll Take You Away." The bass motives are developed into transition material based on the "Somewhere" motive. The dream ballet begins:

> . . . the two lovers begin to run, battering against the walls of the city, beginning to break through as chaotic figures of the gangs, of violence, flail around them. But they do break through, and suddenly—they are in a world of space and air and sun. They stop, looking at it, pleased, startled, as boys and girls from both sides come on. . . . They begin to dance, to play: no sides, no hostility; just joy and pleasure and warmth.[16]

During this sequence, an offstage voice sings "Somewhere." The dancers on stage join in a brief reprise in the "Procession" before the "Nightmare" recalls both the music and events of the rumble.

It is unfortunate that both choreography and stage directions paint the lovers' dream as a sort of paradise, for this is quite untrue to the tragic plot and denigrates the pathetic loss at the end. There is no reason why the lovers deserve such a paradise, and no audience would feel pity at their failure to find one. The pity is rather that they are denied the simplest joy, to be left alone in their love. The spirit of that longing is caught by Shakespeare when Romeo bemoans his banishment:

> *heaven is here*
> *Where Juliet lives; and every cat and dog,*
> *And little mouse, every unworthy thing,*
> *Live here in heaven and may look on her,*
> *But Romeo may not.*
>
> (III, iii, 29-33)

Tony's dying words, "They won't let us be," express as a negative the source of the pathos much better than the utopia of the ballet. And yet, to express somehow in dance this simpler freedom for Tony and Maria would also be insufficient, for that would leave the cause of this social tragedy unchecked. It would mean an escape, not a resolution. The gang characters must be included as an expiation of the tragic flaw, but including them falsifies the lovers' role in the story. It truly is a dramatic dilemma, which is perhaps why the ballet has not been well received by critics. Even Robbins himself, reflecting on the ballet in 1980, doubted its purpose.[17]

Despite such problems on stage, the music of the ballet is quite faithful to the tragic plot and so requires the performance of the whole sequence. The central piece, the song "Somewhere," speaks nothing of harmony between races or the perfect society but only "peace and quiet and open air," "time together" to be left alone. It is the musical expression for Tony and Maria's simpler dream. It is woven into the tragic plot by its use of all the important musical elements that characterize the whole play, although, as in the other lyric numbers for the lovers, their tensions are softened. The song begins with an upward leap of a minor seventh which, when imitated at the fourth, introduces the lowered seventh step.

**Ex. 9–21** Bernstein and Sondheim, *West Side Story*, "Somewhere" (No. 13d), mm. 1–8.

The gentle triplet in measure five becomes a more explicit, although still gentle, hemiola effect later on when the harmony changes against it (mm. 19, 21). Other elements arise out of the harmonic design. The principal key of the song is E major, but the triumphant central section modulates to C, the central tone of the whole play.

**Ex. 9–22** Bernstein and Sondheim, *West Side Story*, "Somewhere" (No. 13d), mm. 13–24.

It is no coincidence that the highest note of that phrase is an F-sharp, nor that the tritone relationship is further enhanced by a modulation to that key (m. 23). But again, it is the motivic development that carries tragedy forward. The choice of setting for ''Someday! Somewhere . . .'' seems so suited to the accent pattern of the words that the listener overlooks its clear derivation with the ''Maria'' motive that became an omen in the ''Balcony Scene.'' Now the upward appoggiatura has become a complete harmony, but the identity of its rhythm and essential dissonance is unmistakable. The lovers' longing for peace has become inseparable from love itself, for indeed, one causes the other.

Even though this passage is set in C major, Bernstein, because of his consistency of motivic technique, is able to recall this essential moment at the end of the song, which of course is in E.

**Ex. 9–23** Bernstein and Sondheim, *West Side Story,* "Somewhere" (No. 13d), mm. 25–37.

The melody moves as before, toward C major, but the last measures interpret the D natural as a lowered seventh in E, a melodic and harmonic progression which by now is so much a part of the musical idiom of the play that the final cadence (VII-I, m. 35) is as convincing as any.

The "Procession" makes a march, a dirge really, out of this motive, until it is cut off by a recapitulation of "The Rumble" music. The rather too obvious message is that there can be no paradise, not even escape. Curiously, this does not spoil the final moment of the dream sequence, when a sustained note in the oboe leaps up a seventh to begin the "Somewhere" melody again, soon joined by the flute, a nice touch of orchestration. When Tony picks up with "Hold my hand and we're halfway there," the fearless love triumphs again, and the lovers' faith in it, however naïve, is nonetheless moving.

The power of love against all odds must be considered one of the important subthemes of *West Side Story*. Certainly it characterizes the high-level articulations of its music. The harsh music of the "Prologue" and "The Dance at the Gym" becomes transmuted into the "Cha-Cha," "Maria," and the "Balcony Scene." Here the memory of "The Rumble" is subverted and soothed by a brief reprise of "Somewhere." The denouement of the tragedy will present a bleak reversal of this order, but not before that contrast is prepared and heightened by one last fleeting triumph of love over mindless hate.

"A Boy Like That," Anita's bitter rebuke of Maria for her relationship with Tony, brings back in its opening measures the "Prologue" material in its harshest form yet.

Ex. 9–24   Bernstein and Sondheim, *West Side Story*, "A Boy Like That" (No. 15), mm. 1–8.

The texture is full of tone clusters, tritones, and halting weak beat accents that all contribute to Anita's venom. Most striking of all is how the D natural D-flat semitone which makes the difference between major and minor is emphasized by putting it right in the vocal melody, on "brother" (m. 4) and "find another" (m. 6). The more dissonant harmonic minor ninths and major sevenths, introduced early in the "Prologue" when Bernstein wanted F naturals against F-sharps and E naturals (see Ex. 9-7) return here with both musical and textual accents: *"One* of your own *kind, stick* to your own *kind."* The conversion of Anita's reproach to some kind of understanding of Maria's plight is reflected in Bernstein's handling of theme and motive (discussed in Chapter 1), yet another instance of a consistent musical-dramatic conception that forms the whole play.

**Ex. 9–25** Bernstein and Sondheim, *West Side Story,* "A Boy Like That" (No. 15), mm. 68–73.

Once again the tone clusters in measure 68, the tritone in measure 69 which, as in "Somewhere," prepares a modulation to the tritone key (here, D-flat major, m. 90), the semitone progressions, and the hemiola in measure 72 are all cut from the same material as Anita's singing, yet muted in their tensions. When Bernstein pulls out the old trick of having the two sing in parallel to show Anita's complete capitulation to Maria's conviction (mm. 105-116), it works beautifully, indeed it is a tremendous moment, because it confirms what the listener has already understood on a more fundamental level of musical discourse.

The most immediate apprehension of the tragic moment in *West Side Story,* as in *Romeo and Juliet,* is as a deeply pathetic one. "Somewhere," since it represents the lovers' simple hope, becomes the central piece of the play's denouement, which reveals the ultimate denial of that hope. But its reprise at the end is no simple quotation.

**Ex. 9–26**  Bernstein and Sondheim, *West Side Story*, "Finale" (No. 17), mm. 1–14.

After Tony's last spoken words, Maria begins, without any accompaniment, to sing the end of the song, picking it up at the precise spot where Tony did to rally her courage at the end of the nightmare sequence. Now it is for her to brace his failing faith, even if she cannot save his failing life. Bernstein's melody loses little of its power for the missing orchestra; the essential modulation from E to C is implied in its very notes. That Tony dies at its climax summarizes the awful juxtaposition of hope and hate that the play is about. The significance for the Broadway tradition is that he dies while he is singing. Tragedy is within reach at last.

And what of Maria? She cannot complete the melody, for she is broken by her loss; the orchestra must do it for her, and in so doing returns the music to E major, as before. But now comes Bernstein's greatest touch of imagination. That plagal cadence, which ended the "Balcony Scene" and the ballet, which has always been based on "Somewhere" 's opening phrase, now uses that phrase to begin the piece again in the subdominant key. The renewal is absolutely stunning, but nothing could be more appropriate musically or dramatically. This is Maria's moment of grief, when her intense sorrow is translated into musical terms of pathos, however brief.

To move from the pathetic to the truly tragic demands something beyond the loss of a couple in love, some meaning, some renewal of the wider world. Shakespeare has been criticized for making this movement a rather awkward conclusion:

> The story of a young and idealistic love thwarted is not enough to make it a great tragedy; but Shakespeare, trying to place it within a grander conception, has not been able to achieve a larger unity. . . . The awe that we should feel as well is not inherent in their story but is indicated (rather than effected) in what seems to us like an epilogue; it is something explained to us at the end rather than rendered immediately dramatic and compelling as the heart of the design.[18]

The epilogue, Friar Lawrence's recitation of the series of mischances, is necessary since "the action of the tragedy is not complete until the survivors have been influenced by the events, and the explanations are necessary that we may witness their effect,"[19] especially in *Romeo and Juliet* where the sin of tragedy lies outside the dead ones.

Arthur Laurents's design has two remedies that go far to achieve such larger unity. The first is that the gang members witness the disaster and the loss; the stage is full while "Somewhere" is sung. The second, more important remedy is that Maria survives, and cries out in anguish during a pause in the "Finale," confronting the sinners with the result: "WE ALL KILLED HIM; and my brother and Riff. I, too. I CAN KILL NOW BECAUSE *I* HATE NOW." Bernstein was disappointed that he could not find music to set this speech:

> My first thought was that this was to be her biggest aria. I can't tell you how many tries I made on that aria. I tried once to make it cynical and swift. Another time like

a recitative. Another time like a Puccini aria. In every case, after five or six bars, I gave up. It was phony. . . .[20]

His confession emphasizes once again the supreme difficulty of tragic music drama, but the speech on its own terms does bring the tragic meaning in close proximity to the pathetic loss:

> . . . her act of *not* killing herself or any of the gang members whom she threatens in the final scene, underlines the basic difference between this play and Shakespeare's: *West Side Story* is conceived as a social document, *Romeo and Juliet* as a *Liebestod*. Consequently, it becomes important to the contemporary play's message that a resolution of the gang warfare be effected, not as a postscript, so to speak, but by the hand of one of the play's protagonists.[21]

Her speech ended, her last farewell to Tony spoken, Maria silently begs various members of both gangs to carry the body away. The "Procession" music has no words, but perhaps that is most appropriate in a play in which dance has become so much a part of the drama, at a moment when the players are moving to the world's most solemn dance.

**Ex. 9–27** Bernstein and Sondheim, *West Side Story,* "Finale" (No. 17), mm. 15–28.

The dirge is more than a funeral march. Composed as it is of the "I Have a Love" melody in the top voice, the "Somewhere" motive in the middle voice, and a last reminiscence of its opening phrase toward the end, the dirge is a summary of the meaning of the tragic loss. How fitting that the last sound is a high C major triad over the doleful F-sharp in the bass. The larger unity has been glimpsed with musical means.

Whether *West Side Story* is tragic music drama depends to an extent on one's conception of tragedy. Although one could complain with some justice that the plot, stolen from Shakespeare, must share the flaws of *Romeo and Juliet,* or that Maria's last speech should indeed have been her biggest aria, somehow such complaints seem petty in view of what has been achieved, especially given the constraints of the Broadway tradition. Certainly they have been overlooked in the universal acclaim the work has inspired, from its initial Broadway run of 732 performances at the Winter Garden Theater, to its wild receptions in London and inhospitable Paris, to its incorporation into the permanent repertory of the Vienna *Volksoper*. And the achievement is not only in the creation of a musical play whose numbers are all motivically related or that fits some grand theory of tragedy. The most precise understanding of tragedy and the most thorough musical integration will be for nothing if the individual pieces are not wonderful music besides. In art the details are as important as the design. When one realizes that "I Feel Pretty," which has little function in the tragic scheme other than to offer a comic relief at the opening of the second act, would have been hailed as a top song in almost any other show, the true excellence of the score is approached. There are no dull numbers, and there is the sense of something grand among all of them. On this account, as on many others, *West Side Story* may be called not only tragedy but masterpiece.

# CHAPTER 10

# The Ethnic Musical

*I felt a sense of quiet confidence in being able to write this score . . .
because I was able to draw on my own background, my own memories
of music I grew up with. I never felt the urge to research the score; I
felt it was inside me.*[1]

JERRY BOCK

When librettist Joseph Stein was asked in 1967 to explain the stunning and rather
unexpected commercial success of his *Fiddler on the Roof,* he remarked, "This
isn't a play about Jewish people, it's a play about people who happen to be
Jewish."[2] The comment points up the apparent paradox in the best musical plays
based on an ethnic setting: the particular choice of ethnic quality is not supposed
to matter, but it nevertheless seems essential.

Perhaps the exotic is an intrinsically attractive element in music drama. Certainly a large number of operas have settings foreign to the composer's home
culture: *The Abduction from the Seraglio* (Mozart in Turkey), *Aïda* (Verdi in
Egypt), and *Turandot* (Puccini in China) come to mind immediately, and perhaps
the entire Baroque tradition of *opera seria,* preoccupied with antiquity and myth,
could be compared with these, although it does not use the foreign elements in
the same way. In the American tradition, the melodramatic operettas of the 1910s
and 1920s were so dominated by the exotic that it became the main attraction,
at the expense of dramatic interest (see Chapter 2). A much more restrained and
wise handling of the ethnic setting came about with the maturing of the American musical theater. Exotic places were just as common, if not more so, in the
1940s and 1950s as in the 1920s, but they ceased to be the play's dominating
theme and instead formed a rather highly flavored background against which the
real action was played out.

A typical example of this more mature ethnic setting is Lerner and Loewe's *Brigadoon*. The story is about two American hillwalkers on vacation in Scotland who lose their way and come upon a strange village that appears in the Highlands for one day each century. The songs are therefore filled with jig rhythms and melodies that emphasize the sixth step of the major scale in order to sound Scottish. The principal drama, however, has little to do with this setting, but instead asks whether the main character can give up everything he knows for a love that must be bound to this mysterious village. Such a theme could be set anywhere. A different locale would require different music, to be sure, but perhaps not as different as one might expect.

George Gershwin's *Porgy and Bess* is a more complicated case owing to its intensity of ethnic setting and expression. *Brigadoon* can offer an occasional "Almost Like Being in Love," which does not sound Scottish in the least, even in context, but Gershwin's effort to compose a folk opera that develops the community at large as a character required that the ethnic idiom permeate every moment. That he succeeded in cutting the whole out of one such piece without being overbearing or tiresome is indeed one of the opera's triumphs. The stature of the community is so important to the essence and impact of the opera that here the ethnic element very nearly becomes an inextricable part of the drama, and in fact does become part if one considers the formation of the community character as a legitimate dramatic issue. Otherwise, the main dramas of Porgy's loneliness and Bess's weakness are bigger than the Charleston setting in which they are framed, and so *Porgy and Bess* remains an extreme but typical case of ethnic usage.

The work of Richard Rodgers and Oscar Hammerstein depends more on ethnic settings than perhaps that of any other composer or librettist from the mature period. *Oklahoma!*, the "cowboy musical," and *South Pacific* are examples of fine shows in which the foreign setting remains in the background. The characters who sing in *South Pacific* have much more say about the varied style characteristics of the songs than do Polynesian islands. Thereafter, however, Rodgers and Hammerstein learned to take advantage of ethnic elements to give sharper articulation to dramatic problems, if not to actually form them. The clash of Western and Asian values in *The King And I*, for example, arises quite naturally from the story of a Welsh school teacher who goes to work in the palace of the King of Siam. So Rodgers uses his "Siamese" music to help define the sides of the conflict. The King's "A Puzzlement," the slave lovers' two songs, and all the incidental music for marching and ceremony have the open fifth chords, parallel fifth progressions, and pentatonic scales that create Rodgers' "Siamese" idiom, but Anna's music—"I Whistle a Happy Tune," "Hello Young Lovers," "Getting to Know You," and "Shall We Dance"—concedes nothing to the setting, dominated instead by Western dance rhythms and harmony. Flower *Drum Song*, a musical of San Francisco's Chinatown, portrays two young Chinese couples who at first are confused about who is really the object of their mutual desires, but their true intentions are matched in the styles of the songs they sing even before the characters themselves realize them. So Wang Ta, the traditional dutiful son who thinks he loves a nightclub dancer, and Mei Li, the immigrant mail-order bride who is supposedly intended for the older nightclub owner, sing only "Chinese" songs: "You Are Beautiful," "Like a God," and "I Am Going to Like It Here." Meanwhile, the dancer Linda Low and the owner Sammy Fong, both quite acculturated to their new country, sing numbers that are nothing but American Broadway: "I Enjoy Being a Girl," "Don't Marry Me," and "Sunday."

But what are the musical sources of these ethnic idioms, however they are disposed in the play? How is the ethos of the setting carried in the music?

History has shown that composers have consistently paid scant attention to any ethnomusicology that might bear upon the musical setting of their ethnic operas. In the American tradition, Rodgers himself is not in the least apologetic about his refusal to be accurate in the ethnomusicological sense:

> If my melodies [in *Oklahoma!*] were going to be authentic, they'd have to be authentic in my own terms.
>
> This is the way I have always worked, no matter what the setting of the story. It was true of my "Chinese" music for *Chee-Chee*, of my "French" music for *Love me Tonight*, and later of my "Siamese" music for *The King and I*. Had I attempted to duplicate the real thing, it would never have sounded genuine, for the obvious reason that I am neither Chinese, French, Siamese, nor from the Southwest. All a composer—any composer—can do is to make an audience believe it is hearing an authentic sound without losing his own musical identity.[3]

Such an attitude does not preclude familiarity with the real thing, of course, but suggests that it is seldom required and that, in any case, authenticity will be subordinated to the needs of drama.

In short, projection of ethnic idioms in music drama depends on musical stereotypes, sets of musical commonplaces which the audience associates with the culture in which the play is set. The composer selects, by instinct or reason, some characteristics that will work together to conjure an idiom that for the American audience seems to be typically Chinese, Scottish, or French without ever giving up the fundamental musical grammar of the West. More often than not, the results have some connection with the real thing: some authentic Asian music does have pentatonic scales and open fifths; the modes typical of Scottish folk music often emphasize the sixth degree. George Gershwin took the trouble to spend some hot summer weeks on Folly Island to immerse himself in Gullah culture there, and the folk idiom of *Porgy and Bess* seemed so close to the real thing that he got into trouble over the ethnic issue (see Chapter 3). Fabricated idioms of the musical theater are stereotypical not as much in their inaccuracy as in their incompleteness. The line is fine but nevertheless real. There can be no excuse for musical stereotypes that are demeaning, yet an incomplete but otherwise sympathetic ethnic portrayal may be defended on the grounds of dramatic art itself. Musical plays and operas are dramatic works, and they must communicate with their audiences. The medium of such communication is the musical language of the culture viewing the drama. If intelligibility is compromised in the interest of ethnic authenticity, communication breaks down and so does the drama.

When composers think that they have no conception at all of a particular setting or style, they either refuse the project or take extraordinary measures. Even Rodgers felt compelled to do research when composing the "Catholic" chant for the opening scene of *The Sound Of Music:*

> Writing "Western" songs for *Oklahoma!* or "Oriental" songs for *The King and I* had never fazed me, but the idea of composing a Catholic prayer made me apprehensive. Given my lack of familiarity with liturgical music, as well as the fact that I was of a different faith, I had to make sure that what I wrote would sound as authentic as possible.[4]

His apprehensiveness may have been rooted in the certainty that a significant number of viewers in an American audience would be quite familiar with real Catholic polyphony and chant compared with the number familiar with authentic Asian music. Hammerstein, too, occasionally drew on authentic ethnic forms, never for the sake of cultural accuracy, but only when he thought it would help him achieve some necessary dramatic effect. Thus he borrows a Malaysian poetic form, the pantoum, for the lyric of "I Am Going to Like It Here," sung by Mei Li, a Chinese character in *Flower Drum Song.*

In any case, the theater composer, writing for his audience, depends upon his own sensitivity to the musical preconceptions of his own culture to choose the proper set of musical characteristics for an ethnic suggestion. Curiously, a particular commonplace may be used for remarkably differing and distant ethnic purposes. Stephen Sondheim discovered this when he tried to invent a texture that would approximate the flexibility of the Japanese scales for his *Pacific Overtures:*

> I was searching for a Western equivalent, and one day I hit on the correlation between the Japanese scale and the music of Manuel de Falla, a composer whose work I admire a lot. So I just started to imitate him. I took the pentatonic scale and bunched the chords together until they resembled that terrific guitar sound. And I was able to relate to it because suddenly it had a Spanish Western feeling and at the same time an Eastern feeling.[5]

Both *Brigadoon* and *Flower Drum Song* have melodies which emphasize the sixth scale step, sometimes as a false tonic. In the former case this is a significant aspect of the show's Scottish flavor; in the latter, it makes the music sound Chinese. Similarly, *Show Boat* uses the "gapped" pentatonic scale to characterize the black people in its opening scene, while *The King and I* uses it to portray the Siamese. What matters is not the presence or absence of a particular motive, but coordination in the whole set that constructs the idiom.

Specifying the idiom precisely depends on essential dramatic context, defined by the scenery, the time and place, and the foreknowledge that the audience brings with it to the theater. "People want to believe what they see on a stage, and they will gladly go along with whatever is done to achieve the desired effect. Ask them to accept Ezio Pinza as a Frenchman, Yul Brynner as a Siamese or a heterogeneous group of actors as Chinese, and they are prepared to meet you nine tenths of the way even before the curtain goes up."[6] In other words, the suspension of disbelief accounts for much of the effect of ethnic commonplaces in the music. A repeated emphasis on the sixth degree in the overture and opening song sounds a bit strange, but the stage setting is Asian and the singer Chinese, so that must be Chinese music. A different stage and a few men dressed in kilts will transform the same emphasis into something quite different.

Of all ethnic sources, perhaps Jewish folk music is most apt to adaptation since that tradition itself has borrowed from a great number of other ethnic traditions encountered during the period of worldwide wanderings of the Jewish people.

> The stylistic basis of hasidic tunes, as of eastern Jewish song in general, is a mixture of a variety of styles, including ancient formulae of oriental chanting and prayers; Russian, Ukranian, Romanian, Hungarian and German songs, instrumental pieces adapted to devotional vocalizing; and even marches and vaudevilles. All these elements are however to some extent unified by means of a tonal basis, mainly variants of the minor mode.[7]

This variety of characteristics, combined with the willingness of a theater audience to hear what it expects to hear, gives composer Jerry Bock a free hand to establish a pervasive and original ethnic idiom for *Fiddler On The Roof* without giving up the resources of Western functional harmony.

Bock had known success with such idioms in his previous work. *She Loves Me* (1963), which opened the year before *Fiddler on the Roof,* has a number of waltzes and gypsy songs to go along with its East European setting. His Pulitzer Prize-winning *Fiorello!* (1959) has one scene in which the main character, politician Fiorello LaGuardia, campaigns for Congress in a number of ethnic neighborhoods of New York. Bock dresses each verse of "The Name's LaGuardia" in music aimed at the group he addresses. Curiously, the last verse is addressed to Hasidic Jews, and ends with a lively hora that could have been found just as easily in the wedding scene of his best-known musical play, *Fiddler On The Roof.*

In that musical, Bock concentrates the greatest number of "Jewish" commonplaces in "If I Were a Rich Man." That the song offers such a strong dose of idiom early in the show is good for the overall unity, of course, but it also has an important dramatic function, for it introduces in music the character of Tevye, the rock on which *Fiddler On The Roof* is built.

**Ex. 10–1**  Bock and Harnick, *Fiddler on the Roof,* "If I Were a Rich Man" (No. 4), mm. 4–19.

The first suggestion of mode rather than major scale comes early on at an emphatic point in the melody, the high C-flat in measure six. The second phrase builds on this suggestion, slipping easily into a chromaticized version of the minor mode. The alternation of parallel major and minor modes within songs, sometimes within phrases, is an extremely important and very audible characteristic of the show as a whole, informing almost every song, and Bock's technique differs essentially from Cole Porter's in *Kiss Me, Kate* (see Chapter 6). In that play, Porter alternates modes to suggest a Renaissance flavor for the "Shakespeare" scenes by changing the third scale step, usually after an intervening dominant chord. In *Fiddler on the Roof,* the modal change is almost always routed through the subdominant. It is the sixth degree (the B-double flat in measure 8) that announces the change, and the third simply follows suit. It is on such technical minutiae that ethnic idioms succeed or fail.

Thus, the final cadence of the section (m. 19) is a major triad, but that introduces the next section, composed in the subdominant minor already well prepared by the earlier phrases.

**Ex. 10–2**　Bock and Harnick, *Fiddler on the Roof,* "If I Were a Rich Man" (No. 4), mm. 19–26.

By now, the mix of minor subdominant (mm. 20, 21, 24), minor tonic (m. 22, 23) and major tonic (m. 26) has been well established. How surprising it is, then, when the same tune is immediately repeated with the subdominant major chord substituted on its first downbeat.

**Ex. 10–3** Bock and Harnick, *Fiddler on the Roof*, "If I Were a Rich Man" (No. 4), mm. 35–42.

This harmony is actually closer to the original key of D-flat major than the more prominent minor subdominant, but Bock has saved it until after it has been distanced by the idiom that he is trying to create. Perhaps that accounts for the perfectly appropriate wistful effect of the change.

After the half cadence of this section, the song goes back to the beginning strain and once again has the section based on the subdominant (like Ex. 10-2). This time, however, it is interrupted.

Ex. 10–4   Bock and Harnick, *Fiddler on the Roof,* "If I Were a Rich Man" (No. 4), mm. 83–92.

This passage, entirely in the subdominant minor key of G-flat, suggests chant with its unison texture, then moves unabashedly into a chant texture where Bock marks the music "Freely." Another important characteristic occurs in the measure introducing this section: the lowered second degree (E-double flat), an unusual but unmistakably modal reference suggesting the oriental roots of much Jewish music.[8] This altered scale step is so important to the sound of *Fiddler on the Roof* that it is introduced in the first music the audience hears, the famous "fiddler" tune.

Moderato (in 2)

**Ex. 10–5**   Bock and Harnick, *Fiddler on the Roof,* "Prologue—Tradition" (No. 1), mm. 1–9.

When this lowered tone is conjoined with the normal third of the major scale, the melody takes on more Jewish flavor through the resulting augmented second interval. In "If I Were a Rich Man," this interval is the basis for the expressive ending of the chant section (m. 90).

To dwell on the harmonic and melodic constructions does not necessarily mean that the more local effects—the nonsense syllables used throughout, the dance rhythms and instrumental ornaments in the accompaniment, even the pronounced use of the accordian as an ethnic sign—contribute but little to the ethnic character of the music. But chords and intervals must be the pre-eminent ethnic ingredients of *Fiddler On The Roof* because they can be integrated into a system which Bock can use to construct and unify the music of the whole play. The augmented second interval, for example, is very familiar to Western listeners through its prominent usage in compositions composed in the minor. In such pieces it occurs as the space between the lowered sixth step and raised seventh step (leading tone), and is therefore an important cue for the perception of key. Now when Bock introduces the same interval between steps 2 and 3, the same associations between the augmented second and the tonal center create in the Western listener a bias toward the subdominant.

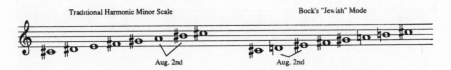

**Fig. 10–1**   The melodic augmented second interval in traditional minor scales and in Bock's modal scale for *Fiddler on the Roof.*

The third degree becomes a false leading tone, identified by the augmented second interval below it. The penchant to alternate major and minor modes through the subdominant chord, acting as a tiny key, is therefore justified by the characteristic intervals with which Bock constructs his "Jewish" idiom.

Despite this ingenuity of integration, the expressive qualities of the songs come not from these particular "Jewish" commonplaces but from Bock's manipulation of song forms. The chant section (Ex. 10-4) of "If I Were a Rich Man" interrupts the second section, which originally contained four phrases: two phrases based on the subdominant minor (Ex. 10-2), one on the subdominant major (Ex. 10-3), and a final one back in the minor which leads to a half cadence. Consistency of form would lead the listener to expect a return of the major form after the interruption, but the chant section instead moves into the minor form (Ex. 10-4, m. 92). Only after the next half cadence does the expected phrase in major arrive.

**Ex. 10–6**  Bock and Harnick, *Fiddler on the Roof,* "If I Were a Rich Man" (No. 4), mm. 99–115.

The recall of this formally delayed harmony at this point, with Harnick's telling lyric, completely reforms the dramatic function of the song. No longer the typical comic character piece, it quickly reveals Tevye's deep and traditional religious side, without which much of the later action would be incomprehensible. Even when the harmony returns to the minor mode, in an extension of Bock's pattern, the high melody in the string parts accompanying the contemplation of Talmudic scholarship (mm. 110-14) maintains the delicate force of this moment.

   The credibility of the ethos in *Fiddler on the Roof* is most in debt to the source of the play itself. Most Broadway musicals take ethnic models written by authors who are not themselves members of the ethnic communities they attempt to describe. Gershwin depended on a white Southerner's image of the Gullah community for *Porgy and Bess,* and Richard Rodgers chose stories by James Michener for *South Pacific* and British novelist Margaret Landon for *The King and I.* But Sholem Aleichem is renowned the world over for his tragicomic portrayals of the Yiddish *shtetls* of the Ukraine, and there is no denying his authority to write about them, since he grew up among them. The plot of *Fiddler on the Roof* is drawn from Sholem Aleichem's eight stories about Tevye the

Dairyman, which appeared separately between 1895 and 1914. Four of those stories—"Modern Children" (1899), "Hodel" (1904), "Chava" (1905) and "Get Thee Out" (1914)—supply the main plot for the play, but inspiration is not limited to them. Here is a brief paragraph in "The Bubble Bursts" (1899) that describes one of Tevye's many daydreams:

> God in Heaven! If I had only a tenth of what all of this is worth! What more could I ask of God and who would be my equal? First of all, I would marry off my oldest daughter, give her a suitable dowry and still have enough left over for wedding expenses, gifts, and clothing for the bride. Then I would sell my horse and wagon and my cows and move into town. I would buy myself a Synagogue seat by the Eastern Wall, hang strings of pearls around my wife's neck, and hand out charity like the richest householders.[9]

Surely this was the beginning of "If I Were a Rich Man." Reforming the four separate stories into a continuous book was the task of librettist Joseph Stein, who was singularly equipped for the job. He could speak Yiddish and read the almost untranslatable Sholem Aleichem in the original. Even though he refrained from using even one word of Yiddish, he believed that "through the quality of the talk, the construction of sentences, there is a kind of ethnic rhythm without any Yiddishisms."[10]

The title of the musical, however, does not originate in Sholem Aleichem. That was inspired by an entirely different source, but one that shared the same time and culture with the Yiddish author: the Russian painter Marc Chagall. His large oil painting "The Green Violinist" of 1923-24, "an oval-eyed violinist seemingly dangling in space over the roofs of a peasant village—inspired the title . . . as well as the whole decor of the production," according to assistant director Richard Altman.[11] "The title was absolutely suggested by the Chagall picture," concurs producer Harold Prince. "I think Chagall hovered over the look of the show for a long time."[12] This was literally true, since set designer Boris Aronson was told "to capture the flavor and special essence of Chagall."[13] The Chagall connection goes beyond the coincidence of one picture and the painter's personal history, however. In another, "The Dead Man," which depicts a mourning or funeral scene, the figure of a fiddler is shown actually sitting on the roof of a nearby house while playing. Indeed, many Chagall pictures have fiddlers in them.

> Certainly the fiddler had always been in Chagall's mind. Ever since 1908 he had constantly appeared in a variety of scenes. He was a central figure in the festivities of the Jewish community in the Russian suburb, and his tune accompanied the basic events of life—birth, marriage, and the funeral. By making his appearance at these important moments in life, he became an almost legendary figure—the attendant of human destiny—in the life pattern of the community. He appears as such in Chagall's pictures of births, weddings, and funerals.[14]

Marc Chagall. *Green Violinist*. 1923–24. (Courtesy, Solomon R. Guggenheim Museum, New York. Photo by David Heald.)

Thus, when the collaborators hit upon the image of a fiddler on the roof, they not only discovered a suitable title but borrowed an authentically ethnic metaphor that would symbolize the most ambitious and dramatic theme of the play.

For what distinguishes *Fiddler on the Roof* from other ethnic musicals is its attempt to place the ethnic identity of the play not in the background but at the center of its dramatic theme. The mute fiddler figure who appears to Tevye at various important junctures is made into a symbol in the opening speech:

> TEVYE: A fiddler on the roof. Sounds crazy, no? But in our little village of Anatevka, you might say every one of us is a fiddler on the roof, trying to scratch out a pleasant, simple tune without breaking his neck. It isn't easy. You may ask, why do we stay up here if it's so dangerous? We stay because Anatevka is our home. And how do we keep our balance? That I can tell you in a word—tradition![15]

Rarely is a dramatic action so explicitly defined. Preserving tradition is the key to the community's existence, and the fiddler who represents it in the play takes on the same symbolic value as he does in Chagall: he is "the attendant of human destiny."

Such a theme puts ethnic identity in the center of the drama because tradition is where ethnic identity resides. The music accompanying this exposition then quite rightly establishes the principal commonplaces of the Jewish musical idiom. The solo violin tune (Ex. 10-5) is heard even before Tevye begins to speak, reaffirming the symbol and introducing the modal scales so important to the sound of this play. The first singing then elevates into music what Tevye has just said.

Moderato (in 2)

**Ex. 10–7**   Bock and Harnick, *Fiddler on the Roof*, "Prologue—Tradition" (No. 1), mm. 35–47.

Now the lowered second step first heard in the violin tune is expanded into a full harmonic progression, so that the C major chord (mm. 35-37) moves to the exotic D-flat major (m. 38). In measure 44 the D-flat is used in a new motive, which repeats incessantly under the forthcoming explanations of the various community traditions, becoming associated with them. Meanwhile, the traditional roles of "the papas," "the mamas," "the sons," and "the daughters" are told to the audience with four different tunes, which are then combined in a rather raucous counterpoint. Perhaps it is not coincidental that "the daughters" tune is that of the opening fiddler tune.

**Ex. 10–8** Bock and Harnick, *Fiddler on the Roof,* "Prologue—Tradition" (No. 1), mm. 119–27.

Since it is Tevye's daughters, in *Fiddler on the Roof* as in Sholem Aleichem, who cause him to upset the balance of tradition that he has just proclaimed, how appropriate it is that the original fiddler tune is now allied with a lyric emphasizing the tradition of arranged marriages. The tune ends the entire lengthy prologue in grand fashion as Tevye recapitulates the fiddler metaphor one more time.

**Ex. 10–9** Bock and Harnick, *Fiddler on the Roof,* "Prologue—Tradition" (No. 1), mm. 232–40.

The dramatic focus on tradition does not come from Sholem Aleichem's stories. Tevye's Jewishness is essential, but it does not derive from blind adherence to tradition, nor does tradition bind him to a community of Jews. In Sholem Aleichem's stories Tevye's is the only Jewish family in the immediate locale; he lives not in Anatevka but some miles distant. When the poor tailor Motel Kamzoil informs him that he and his daughter Tzeitel have pledged themselves to be married, Tevye does not agonize over a broken tradition. He is hurt at being left out, but he quickly recovers. "He talked me into it," says Tevye simply.[16] No, the tradition theme is a transformation wrought by Joseph Stein, perhaps as a response to director Jerome Robbins's constantly pestering question: "What is the show about?"[17] For their part, Bock and lyricist Sheldon Harnick created the "Prologue—Tradition" at Robbins's behest to make the dramatic theme crystal clear.[18]

Having been so boldly asserted, tradition then becomes the bone of contention in each of the crises brought about by Tevye's daughters. Each crisis concerns the marriage traditions. Yente, the comic matchmaker (completely invented by Stein), has arranged a match for Tevye's oldest daughter Tzeitel with a rich butcher, but she has long ago fallen for Motel. She begs Tevye to give her permission to marry him instead, leaving Yente without her accustomed role, and her fee. Next, his second daughter Hodel loves Perchik, a visiting revolutionary student. When he is called away, they inform Tevye that they would like his blessing, but will marry in any case. Finally, his third daughter Chava runs off to marry a Christian boy, and she tearfully begs Tevye to accept them. With each crisis, Tevye goes into a recitative-like soliloquy while the action freezes.

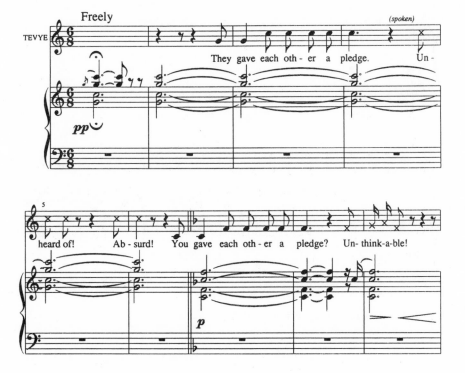

**Ex. 10–10**  Bock and Harnick, *Fiddler on the Roof,* "Tevye's Monologue" (No. 9), mm. 1–9.

Tevye's rising fourth is the same interval, in the same metric pattern, that set the chorus singing "Tradition" in the prologue. Later that tune is recalled explicitly, along with the accompanying instrumental motive.

**Ex. 10–11**   Bock and Harnick, *Fiddler on the Roof*, "Tevye's Monologue" (No. 9), mm. 31–41.

And so Tevye weighs, with much struggle, the costs of holding fast against the costs of "pulling out a prop."

But after all, aren't the preservation of tradition and the struggle with changing times, even the loss of homeland, experiences common to people everywhere? Why is this an ethnic issue? There can be no doubt of the theme's universal appeal. The history of foreign productions of *Fiddler on the Roof* is full of stories about well-intentioned advice that any play about small-town Jews in Russia would not work in Amsterdam, in London, in Paris.[19] All were proven wrong. Joseph Stein, attending the Tokyo production, is reported to have been approached by a young admirer who was astonished that the musical had done well in New York, because "it is so Japanese."[20] But that is precisely the point. As Stein himself has said, it is not the Jewishness of the play that is essential; that is only the particular vehicle chosen for ethnic expression, but what is expressed—the struggle to maintain an ethnic way of life—is a truly ethnic issue that evokes universal response. That is why the dramatic premise of *Fiddler on the Roof* is so special.

Despite a premise of such profundity, despite such a sure-footed opening, the musical fails to play out the tradition theme on the highest level of dramatic action.

Tevye's three monologues, which should be among the most dramatically powerful moments in the play, are colossal disappointments. Here, when he ponders aloud the consequences of sacrificing tradition to his daughters' wishes, the principal drama of the play is brought to the fore, and yet very little happens. The fault is not in the libretto or lyrics; it is a musical failure, a gross awkwardness in the handling of recitative texture. The transformation of the "tradition" motive makes a fair beginning, but Bock can do nothing but repeat the same idea in different keys, winding his way around the circle of fifths, and to the flat side at that, which in classical tradition is associated with declining, not rising musical tension. There is not the slightest change to convey the moment when Tevye begins to see the other side; the music that vainly expresses his outrage must also express his tenderness. Even when he recognizes the depth of his daughters' love, nothing.

When the release of emotion contained in these struggles does come, there is little use of the "Jewish" idiom Bock has labored to create, and so there can be little connection to the dramatic dissolution of tradition. "Matchmaker," sung by the three older daughters in naïve anticipation of their arranged marriages, "Miracle of Miracles," sung by Motel in celebration of his victory, and "Now I Have Everything," Perchik's own song of triumph, were singled out by critics as "catering to Broadway taste."[21] In fact, each of these songs does have some reminiscence of the ethnic setting. "Matchmaker" has a gypsy dance in the middle of it when Tzeitel parodies the machinations of Yente; the citation of Biblical miracles in Motel's song is accompanied by a modulation to the subdominant minor with appropriate suspensions in the cadences; and "Now I Have Everything" also has a section in the subdominant minor. But the Jewish characteristics are not integrated in such a way as to signify a victory over an oppressive tradition, and so they do not make musical-dramatic sense.

At the end of *Fiddler on the Roof,* the Jews are thrown out of Anatevka by an edict from "the authorities." They sing a nostalgic song, "Anatevka," and leave. The final scene shows Tevye dragging his wagon with what is left of his family on to America, accompanied by a halting tonic-dominant ostinato and disjointed fragments of the various tradition tunes from the prologue played in various keys. What is one to make of this? Do the fragments mean that the tradition that has held the community together is now but a fleeting memory? Then why was the same fragmentation technique used in "Prologue—Tradition?" Are Tevye and his family taking tradition with them as they take their last leave of friends and loved ones? Then how can the play be about tradition as the essence of a community?

There is little sense to be made of tradition here because tradition has no part in the end of the play. It is true that the edict is not totally unexpected, since such treatment of Jewish communities in Russia is part of history and was introduced by the "unofficial demonstration" that spoils the wedding celebration at the end of the first act. But as regards its relationship with the play's dramatic theme, the edict might as well have been a hurricane or a plague. There is simply no connection between the gradual breakdown of community tradition and the action of the authorities, not in the play at any rate. Such a criticism appeals first of all to the old-fashioned notion that a tragic result should be contained in the premises of the drama, but even if that standard is judged too severe, how can one justify the complete absence of the dramatic premise at the play's final curtain?

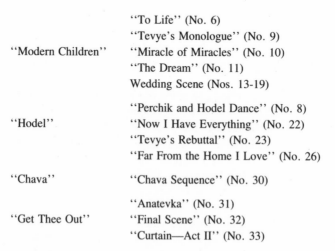

|                     |                                      |
| ------------------- | ------------------------------------ |
|                     | "To Life" (No. 6)                    |
|                     | "Tevye's Monologue" (No. 9)          |
| "Modern Children"   | "Miracle of Miracles" (No. 10)       |
|                     | "The Dream" (No. 11)                 |
|                     | Wedding Scene (Nos. 13-19)           |
|                     |                                      |
|                     | "Perchik and Hodel Dance" (No. 8)    |
| "Hodel"             | "Now I Have Everything" (No. 22)     |
|                     | "Tevye's Rebuttal" (No. 23)          |
|                     | "Far From the Home I Love" (No. 26)  |
|                     |                                      |
| "Chava"             | "Chava Sequence" (No. 30)            |
|                     |                                      |
|                     | "Anatevka" (No. 31)                  |
| "Get Thee Out"      | "Final Scene" (No. 32)               |
|                     | "Curtain—Act II" (No. 33)            |

**Fig. 10–2** Comparison of Sholem Aleichem's stories with the order of numbers in *Fiddler on the Roof.*

The show succeeds much better in Sholem Aleichem's original form, on the level of the short story. Although the four stories on which the play is based were knit together quite convincingly by Joseph Stein, the plan of the numbers clearly reveals that the integrity of each individual story survives (see Fig. 10–2). Only the placement of the "Perchik and Hodel Dance" interrupts the continuity of each individual story. Under the arch of the tradition theme, then, *Fiddler on the Roof* presents three well defined love stories on a lower level of dramatic structure, each with its familiar pattern of conflict and resolution.

The high achievement in all of these little dramas is the railway station scene (Act II, scene 3), when Hodel takes leave of her family and all that she knows to join Perchik at his Siberian camp. This is one of the most poignant scenes in Sholem Aleichem, with Tevye assuring the reader throughout that he is "no woman," only to break down at the end. He cannot comprehend the sort of love that draws his beloved daughter away from him, and that gulf between father and daughter is the subject of Bock and Harnick's best song of the play.

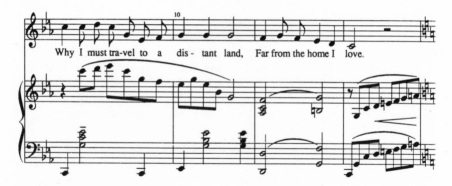

**Ex. 10–12**  Bock and Harnick, *Fiddler on the Roof*, "Far From the Home I Love" (No. 26), mm. 1–12.

The harmonic progression and high melody played by the accordion immediately define the melancholy of the moment, and yet by using the emphatic ethnic motive of the lowered second (in the harmony in measure three, in the melody in measures three and four), the melancholy begins to be related to the loss of community. Hodel's melody is heard against the accordion melody, a counterpoint that is rhythmically equivalent until measure six. Here sorrow is surpassed by her inexplicable steadfast devotion, expressed by the repeated Gs, insistent even when they no longer fit the harmony below them.

**Ex. 10–13**  Bock and Harnick, *Fiddler on the Roof,* "Far From the Home I Love" (No. 26), mm. 13–20.

The two phrases in minor are balanced by a repetition of the same, now converted to major. The change is consistent, of course, with the idiom of the play, but here it is also expressive of the lyric that reflects on Hodel's past life. The change of mood here is effected not only by the change of mode but in Don Walker's orchestration. The accordion is missing. Bock's penchant for expression through form shows up at the end, just as in "If I Were a Rich Man."

**Ex. 10–14** Bock and Harnick, *Fiddler on the Roof,* "Far From the Home I Love" (No. 26), mm. 29–46.

Again, two phrases in the minor. At measure 37, the major version begins. But just as the listener expects a second phrase, as before, the accordion enters and its high E-flat, converting the music prematurely to minor, confirms with great emotion how quickly her former life dies away. Hodel's last cadence is the most expressive, as she sings for the first time the D-flat that has colored her accompaniment throughout. In that instant, the music comes closer to uniting the ethnic idiom with the action of the drama than at any point in the play.

The failure to follow through with ethnic tradition as the focus of the drama is disappointing not only on its own terms, but also in that there is no lack of other potential dramas in Sholem Aleichem. Critics have pointed to the Tevye stories as a deep "psychological analysis of a father's unhappy love for his daughters."[22] The song "Chavaleh" deals with this point in a nostalgic sort of way, but such analysis might have been the central focus. Another focus an ethnic play about Jews might have chosen would be the messianic. "Messianic thinking, with its peculiar blend of pessimism and hope, is the spiritual base for most of Sholem Aleichem's comic monologues. The most sustained example of hope that survives disaster and even seems to derive from it is the series of stories devoted to *Tevye der Milkhiger*."[23] Finally, there is the relationship between Tevye and God, which in *Fiddler on the Roof* is turned to comic effect, but which is capable of more serious and lengthy treatment:

> Other religions may have their folktales about men who debate with and even rebuke God, but only in Jewish tradition, I believe, are such stories taken with high seriousness, the behavior in question being regarded . . . as the highest form of religious service.[24]

Any of these would have maintained, or even insisted upon, the Jewish ethnic identity and made it even more essential. Of course, in the limited format of a musical play one is foolish to expect the thematic range of literature, but it is still regrettable that, especially in the second act, the collaborators of *Fiddler on the Roof* chose sentiment at the expense of consistent dramatic action. "Do You Love Me?," sung by Tevye and his wife Golde to console one another after Hodel's announcement, rarely fails to make the handkerchiefs appear, but it is music of strong emotion unrelated to the higher purposes on stage. It is not that sentiment itself is always undesirable or false. As Isaac Bashevis Singer points out, Sholem Aleichem himself is a genius who writes with sentiment, "but his sentimentality is redeemed by its utter genuineness, which shows no trace of artifice and is therefore never vulgar."[25] When the action on stage is not genuinely dramatic, the traces of artifice show up.

There is yet much of value here, otherwise how can one explain its apparently immortal popularity all over the world? The libretto is skillfully crafted and very funny, and the whole pacing of the show, with its mixture of monologue, dialogue, dancing, dreams, and crowd scenes, proclaims the domineering vision of Jerome Robbins. And the songs, if not always dramatically centered, are in themselves meticulous compositions for the most part. Sheldon Harick's lyrics are simple and natural expressions in the mold of Oscar Hammerstein, and the comic ones derive their humor from situation and character, not from verbal

trickery. The little dramas of the short stories look forward to dramatic constructions in musicals of the next decade. The vignettes of the play can indeed be
cherished; it is only the shape of the whole that is flawed. That has hardly
diminished the world's affection for the play, only the claims of *Fiddler on the
Roof* to dramatic art.

# CHAPTER 11

# Religious Experience as Musical

*. . . to weave God's spell over the audience . . .*[1]

JOHN-MICHAEL TEBELAK

In the early spring of 1970, a young drama student named John-Michael Tebelak was losing interest in his graduate work. Then, on March 29, Easter Eve, he happened to go to church.

> I had been working on my masters thesis for Carnegie Tech's School of Drama, but put it aside. Then I went to the Easter Vigil service at the Anglican Cathedral in Pittsburgh. It was snowing, and I was aware of the proper setting for a tremendous religious experience. But the people in the church seemed bored, and the clergymen seemed to be hurrying to get it over with. I left with the feeling that, rather than rolling the rock away from the tomb, they were piling more on. I went home, took out my manuscript and worked it to completion in a non-stop frenzy.[2]

Such a frenzy, born of a disappointment in what should be the most triumphant moment of the Christian liturgical year, produced that most unlikely of events in theater history: a significant debut for both playwright and composer. *Godspell* indeed has been a most unorthodox success story.

It is no coincidence that nearly all the significant works of the Broadway tradition were preceded in their history by a vast amount of experience in every department. It should be no surprise that the early works of Kern, Gershwin, Rodgers, Porter, and Bernstein form no part of this repertoire, that their highest achievements come much later in their careers, and that those achievements are supported over and over by the same names in production and direction: George

Abbott, Rouben Mamoulian, Jerome Robbins, Moss Hart, Harold Prince. History has shown that experience provides the fine tuning of the collaboration that even the most mature dramatic vision requires.[3]

*Godspell* was dominated by amateurs from the beginning. Tebelak formed a cast of friends and acquaintances from the Carnegie Tech School of Drama, had them set some old Episocopal hymn texts to original music, and mounted some trial performances at the school. The show eventually moved to Cafe LaMama in New York City. The response there convinced producers Edgar Lansbury and Joseph Beruh that the show might be a commercial success if a new score were composed. In March of 1971, they called another schoolmate of Tebelak's, Stephen Schwartz, who at the time was in New York trying to interest producers in his own *Pippin*. "To this day, I don't know why they called me about the score. . . . I can hardly believe, given my inexperience, that I was anyone's first choice."[4] Schwartz finished the score in five weeks, and *Godspell* opened formally at the small Cherry Lane Theater, off-Broadway, on May 17, 1971, less than fourteen months after the snowy Easter of 1970. There were no name producers or directors, certainly no stars, and for all its subsequent success, including a move uptown in 1976, the play seems not to have launched any careers on Broadway with the important exception of its composer-lyricist. Stephen Schwartz was enlisted by Leonard Bernstein to help write lyrics for his *Mass* in July following *Godspell*'s opening. In 1974 he won wide acclaim for his *Pippin,* and followed that with the somewhat less well known *Magic Show* and *Working.*

Upon reflection, it seems that this contravention of all Broadway's sacred ways, taking the million-to-one chance in a small off-Broadway theater, may have been *Godspell*'s only chance. Clearly, Tebelak tried to create the religious experience he expected but missed at the Easter Vigil, to "weave God's spell over the audience," as he put it.[5] Would any savvy producer have underwritten such an idea? Would any seasoned director have agreed to do it? The very idea of putting religious experience on a stage and trying to communicate its essence to an audience seems, if anything, anti-dramatic, but frequent local revivals over the last twenty years and a major one on Broadway in 1988 argue to the contrary. It is not too late to wonder at *Godspell*'s most unusual conception, how it is that religious experience can be dramatized.

Dramatizing religious experience can be immediately distinguished from setting a religious story. Sacred histories such as are found in the oratorios of Handel use plot in an entirely conventional way. Even an agnostic can sympathize with the plights of Saul or Jephtha. He regards the divine element in Old Testament stories just as he would the pantheon of Greek mythology; it requires a suspension of disbelief, nothing more. The distinction is subtler with the passions of J. S. Bach. Here, faith and spirituality are premises taken for granted by the composer, and so certain events of the plot take on significance that they would not otherwise have, which is why extraordinarily lyrical recitative is reserved for a simple meal called the Last Supper. Those ignorant of these significances must ignore an entire level of dramatic meaning and fall back to admiring the musical ideas and construction for their own sake. But even the passions do not dramatize pure religious experience in any direct sense because they assume such experience on the part of the faithful listeners. "Everything takes place in the mind of the Christian, or in Bach's mind, or in the mind of the communal singer," writes Joseph Kerman.[6] The drama may draw on that assumption in such a way that deepens and invigorates it sublimely, but it does not communicate the fundamental experience, since it is already there. A true dramatization of religious experience would demand that the audience be taken along in a progressive action that is analogous to the experience itself. How can such an experience be expressed in a way that does not just preach to the converted?

The central problem is that there seems to be no such progression inherent in spiritual experience. Nothing can happen; spirituality just is. "Plain spirit in the popular arts can last just about four and a half minutes, and after that it has to start explaining itself. In drama, particularly, we expect the issue to be defined in human terms as soon as possible."[7] But there is one crucial sort of religious experience which is itself an action, which requires no explanation even for the agnostic because it is at base inexplicable, and which has no specific religious content or doctrine: the conversion.

The "Prologue" of *Godspell* makes it clear that this is a play about the experience of conversion, the "turning toward" the divine. When the cast first appears on stage, each member wears a sweatshirt bearing the name of a famous Western thinker: Socrates, Aquinas, Luther, Da Vinci, Gibbon, Nietzsche, Sartre, and Fuller. Each person pronounces his philosophical sentence to the music of the "Prologue," after which all sing them simultaneously in an "ivory tower of Babel." They are silenced by a note from the shofar, the traditional ram's horn of Jewish ritual, and by the appearance of John the Baptist who sings the famous verse from Matthew (3:3, quoting Isaiah 40:3): "Prepare ye the way of the Lord!" The others are amazed. Shortly after they join in his singing, shed their sweatshirts, don clown costumes, and receive his baptism. They are converted.

The contrast in the music of the first two numbers, no less than the action, attempts to express the essence of this conversion. For the construction of the "Prologue" Schwartz chooses one of the most learned of devices, the chaconne, or repeating chord progression.

E: I-V2/V

C#: IV2-ii7-V-I-V2/V

Bb: IV2-ii7-V

G: VII-I-I7-IV7-VII

E: N6-V2/V-iv-V-I

**Fig. 11–1** Repeating chord pattern of "Prologue" from *Godspell*, showing principal keys used and progressions within each.

Now it is true that the popular rock style lives on repeating chord progressions, mostly very brief and simple ones, but this example truly deserves to be called a chaconne because of its length and multi-level harmonic design, and because over it the singing of each philosopher makes a set of continuous variations on the harmonic pattern. The device makes it possible to babble all the pronouncements simultaneously at the end without essential dissonance.

This ancient demonstration of musical learning is replaced by a piece of the most simple design and lyric. There are but two phrases to "Prepare Ye," an antecedent and a consequent, over a bass that repeats many times with the lyric, but which despite its repetition is as far from the spirit of the chaconne as can be. In the juxtaposition of musical forms is dramatized the conversion of the philosopher, who replaces his vain and ostentatious wisdom with simple assent.

The clown costumes, particularly on the person of Jesus, create a startling stage presence that has elicited a variety of explanations from critics: "a metaphor for Christian grace";[8] a means of "making high theater from the immediate emotions of the child";[9] a rainbow of "ethnic suggestions" that universalizes the themes of the play.[10] Tebelak himself, however, points much more directly to *The Feast of Fools,* a theological essay by Harvey Cox published in 1969, which argues that humanity must recover its lost capacity for festivity and fantasy if civilization is to survive.[11] Cox saw signs of such a recovery in the vigorous political movements, youth culture, and rock music festivals of the late 1960s, but any lasting effect would require a complete renovation of stale church traditions, including a new theological image of Christ himself:

> Christ has come to previous generations in various guises, as teacher, as judge, as healer. In today's world these traditional images of Christ have lost much of their power. Now in a new, or really an old but recaptured guise, Christ has made an unexpected entrance onto the stage of modern secular life. Enter Christ the harlequin: the personification of festivity and fantasy in an age that had almost lost both. Coming now in greasepaint and halo, this Christ is able to touch our jaded modern consciousness as other images of Christ cannot.[12]

Such an image supplies for *Godspell* the stage premise for all the high-jinks, the infectious quality of playing that impresses even the skeptic. Playing is nothing less than Cox's prescription for church reform:

> Only by assuming a playful attitude toward our religious tradition can we possibly make any sense of it. Only by learning to laugh at the hopelessness around us can we touch the hem of hope. Christ the clown signifies our playful appreciation of the past and our comic refusal to accept the spectre of inevitability in the future. He is the incarnation of festivity and fantasy.[13]

The essay also gives the nod to the often outrageous juxtapositions of what is spoken in parable or sung in lyric and what is portrayed in the acting, such as when one of the female characters sings the traditional hymn text "Turn Back,

O Man" to brothel music with stage gestures and humorous ad libs between the lines to fit. Such juxtapositions for Cox make up a necessary ingredient of festivity.

But whatever theological cues from *The Feast of Fools* have turned up in *Godspell,* the most decisive dramatic effect of donning the clown suits is to symbolize a profound inner change in those who wear them. For what can be more opposite to a philosopher than a clown? In such an image, Tebelak has dramatized the Pauline proclamation that God has made "foolish the wisdom of this world" (1 Corinthians 1:20).

But is not conversion an instant's event, a blinding flash in the desert? What is left for the dramatist thereafter? To dramatize its effects in individual lives, especially in a religious tradition that exalts rather than subsumes the individual person. That is why it is important in *Godspell* that the characters other than Jesus are drawn with much more anonymity than is usual in a musical play. They do not have stage names; rather, they carry their own real names, but only first names, so as not to specify their characters too much: they could be anybody. But each gets his own solo music, his own response to conversion. Listeners recalling the play remember the individuals not by who they are but by what they have sung. "The performers are or create the illusion of being ordinary people sublimating their erstwhile secular talents," [14] or rather turning those talents to the divine call.

The music of the first act, then, expresses the range of religious experience that comes from conversion. Such expressions are prayers, but in so being they do not give up the spirit of festivity and play that is the premise for *Godspell.* Cox maintains that "in several ways prayer and play are strikingly similar. Both are acts of disciplined fantasy. . . . There are four traditional forms of prayer: supplication, intercession, thanksgiving, and penitence. Each can be understood as a form of play." [15] All of these forms are represented in the musical: intercession in "Save the People," thanksgiving in "Bless the Lord" and "All Good Gifts," penitence in "We Beseech Thee," and supplication in "Day by Day."

The music of "Day by Day," in particular, concerns the deeper form of religious experience known as contemplation. The text is medieval, attributed in the Episcopal Hymnal 1940 to St. Richard of Chichester. The music, like all the music in *Godspell,* in written in one of several popular styles, but its specific construction is unlike that of any other song.

**Ex. 11–1**   Stephen Schwartz, *Godspell*, "Day by Day" (No. 4), mm. 1–16.

What is the key of this song? There is no simple answer to this innocent question, as it turns out. Initially one hears F major as the most likely tonal center, but beginning with the F major seventh chord introduces an ambiguous dissonance immediately, and the ambiguity is heightened by the unusual device of having the singer enter on the seventh factor E and then prolonging the modal D. The initial impression of F seems to be confirmed with the B-flat major seventh (which would be IV7) at the beginning of the second phrase, but the confirmation is soon shattered when the B-flat is replaced two bars later (m. 7) with a B natural. The key now seems to be G major, but again it is compromised with the major seventh chord. The third phrase (mm. 9-12) sounds the first clear triad, so that the progression acts like a strong ii7-V in yet another new key, D major. The fourth phrase (mm. 13-16) does not yield the expected cadence, however, but translates the third phrase down one step as a modulating sequence, and the ii7-V progression now directed toward C does make a cadence, but with a C major seventh. This harmony not only withholds the sense of firm conclusion, but progresses naturally as a substitute dominant back to the F major seventh to begin the next verse.

On the lower level of structure, then, there is a succession of weak tonal centers or keys, and on the higher there is really none. The song is held together by a tight, motivically consistent melody that ends on the same note with which it began, and by an intelligent use of seventh chords which, in addition to giving the song its popular flavor, makes each tonal center just credible without the harmonic commitment of a cadence.

The lack of high-level tension and resolution recalls impressionism. The structure almost seems to have no beginning and no end, and the constrained range of the melody (from C to A only) also contributes to the sense of a devotion that is effortless and yet ecstatic. And how else can the endlessly repeating text be understood, except as the contemplative's centering prayer or mantra?

For a play that in 1971 seemed so innovative in its portrait of Christian religious experience, the extent to which *Godspell* depends on traditional Christian
materials and forms is striking. Almost all of the book is taken directly from the
Gospel of Matthew, as are some of the lyrics to the songs. As is shown below,
many of the remainder come from traditional hymn texts selected by John-
Michael Tebelak. Even the form of the whole show is traditional, comparable to
the Service of the Word of the very same Easter Vigil rite that inspired Tebelak
in the first place. In that part of the rite, choice readings from the Old Testament
are alternated with responsorial Psalms sung by the congregation. In *Godspell*,
the readings are replaced by the book, which is little more than readings from
Matthew, and the Psalm responses are replaced by the songs, two of which are
Psalm adaptations.

|  | *Song Title* | *Source* |
|---|---|---|
| No. 1 | "Prologue" | Various philosopical and historical sources, adapted by Tebelak |
| No. 2 | "Prepare Ye" | Matthew 3:3 (Isaiah 40:3) |
| No. 3 | "Save the People" | Episcopal Hymnal 1940, No. 496; text by Ebenezer Elliott, 1850 |
| No. 4 | "Day by Day" | Episcopal Hymnal 1940, No. 429; text by St. Richard of Chichester, 1197–1253 |
| No. 5 | "Learn Your Lessons Well" | Original lyric by Stephen Schwartz |
| No. 6 | "Bless the Lord" | Episcopal Hymnal 1940, No. 293; text by James Montgomery, 1819; adaptation of Psalm 103 |
| No. 7 | "All for the Best" | Original lyric by Stephen Schwartz |
| No. 8 | "All Good Gifts" | Episcopal Hymnal 1940, No. 138; text by Matthias Claudius, 1782 |
| No. 9 | "Light of the World" | Adaptation of Matthew 5:13–16 |
| No. 10 | "Turn Back, O Man" | Episcopal Hymnal 1940, No. 536; text by Clifford Bax, 1919 |
| No. 11 | "Alas for You" | Adaptation of Matthew 23:13–37 |
| No. 12 | "By My Side" | Original lyric by Jay Hamburger |
| No. 13 | "We Beseech Thee" | Episcopal Hymnal 1940, No. 229; text by T. B. Pollock, 1871 |
| No. 14 | "Day by Day" (reprise) |  |
| No. 15 | "On the Willows" | Adaptation of Psalm 137 |
| No. 16 | "Finale" | Original lyric by Stephen Schwartz; reprise of Matthew 3:3 |

The theatrical conception could not do without these traditional texts, forms,
and symbols. Tradition adds a cultural weight to the proceedings that insures
that the antics of these converted clowns cannot be dismissed out of hand. The
language of the texts themselves, replete with "Thee" and "Thou" and other
anachronisms of the King James usage, affirm the gravity of what they express

at the same time they act in juxtaposition to the popular styles of music to which they are set. The wonder is that it all works so smoothly.

At least part of the reason must be the extent to which Schwartz's music captures some essence of these texts and translates it into a popular idiom. "Day by Day" is a fine example. Another more sophisticated one is his setting of Psalm 103, "Bless the Lord."

Although the text for "Bless The Lord" is taken directly from James Montgomery's adaptation in the Episcopal Hymnal, Schwartz's setting accentuates certain aspects of the text in a way that brings it closer in spirit to the original Psalm. Consider first the following comparison of Psalm 103 (King James version) with its paraphrase as it appears in the song. (Numerals refer to traditional verses of the psalm or to the order of the quatrains in "Bless the Lord." Brackets indicate lyrics by Montgomery having no direct parallel in the psalm. "R" shows refrains interpolated by Schwartz.)

| Psalm 103 | | "Bless the Lord" | |
|---|---|---|---|
| 1 | Bless the LORD, O my soul! | 1 | O, bless the Lord, my soul! |
|   |   |   | [His grace to thee proclaim!] |
|   | And all that is within me, | | And all that is within me, joins, |
|   | bless his holy name. | | To bless His holy name. |
| 2 | Bless the LORD, O my soul! | 2 | O, bless the Lord, my soul! |
|   |   |   | [His mercies bear in mind!] |
|   | And forget not all his benefits: | | Forget not all His benefits, |
|   |   |   | [The Lord to thee is kind.] |
| 3 | Who forgiveth all thine iniquities; | 4 | He pardons all thy sins, |
|   |   |   | [Prolongs thy feeble breath;] |
|   | Who healeth all thy diseases; | | He healeth thy infirmities, |
| 4 | Who redeemeth thy life from destruction; | | And ransoms thee from death, |
|   |   | R | O, bless the Lord, my soul! |
|   | Who crowneth thee with lovingkindness and tender mercies; | 5 | He clothes thee with His love |
|   |   |   | [Upholds thee with His truth] |
| 5 | Who satisfieth thine advancing age with good; | | And like the eagle, He renews |
|   | Thy youth is renewed like the eagle's. | | The vigor of thy youth. |
|   | . . . | | |
| 9 | He will not always chide: | 3 | He will not always chide; |
|   | Neither will he keep his anger for for ever. | | [He will with patience wait;] |
|   |   |   | His wrath is ever slow to rise. |
|   |   |   | [And ready to abate.] |
|   | . . . | | |
| 20 | Bless the LORD, ye his angels, | 6 | Then bless His holy name, |
|   | Who excel in strength, who do his commandments, | | [Whose grace hath made thee whole;] |
|   | Hearkening unto the voice of his word. | | Whose love and kindness crowns thy days. |

Psalm 103                                    "Bless the Lord"

21   Bless ye the LORD, all ye his hosts;
     Ye ministers of his, who do his plea-
        sure.
22   Bless the LORD, all his works
     In all places of his dominion:
     Bless the LORD, O my soul.               O, bless the Lord, my soul.

Psalm 103 belongs to the class of psalms known as hymns (as distinguished from the laments or penitential psalms, thanksgivings, blessings, curses, and didactic psalms) and shares its form with others in the group. There is the laudatory invocation at the beginning, a recitation of reasons for praising, then a closing that uses the same formula as the beginning. Psalm 103 is special, however, in that its praise formulas are repeated so often, suggesting that the psalmist can barely contain his joy. "Few psalms are better known or more beloved. All the evangelical theology is here, for here is present the evangelical experience in all its fullness."[16] Indeed, there is a natural progression at the end from the description of human frailty to the hope of the Lord's grace, which is "from everlasting to everlasting." The refrain "Bless the Lord" returns four times, accelerating the pace of the verses until the last recalls the first.

It is just this sense of acceleration that Schwartz restores to Montgomery's adaptation, on several levels. The song begins with a typical repeating rock bass line in a dorian version of A minor.

Rock with a solid bass (a la Laura Lyro)

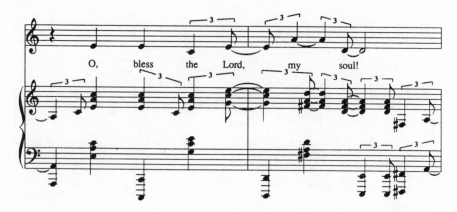

**Ex. 11–2**  Stephen Schwartz, *Godspell,* "Bless the Lord" (No. 6), mm. 1–14.

The second verse begins with the same line as the first (mm. 13-14), as per the Montgomery adaptation. That verse, however, is followed by a new section of music, faster and in the parallel major, which begins to use that text as a refrain.

Brighter tempo

**Ex. 11-3** Stephen Schwartz, *Godspell,* "Bless the Lord" (No. 6), mm. 21–39.

The faster tempo and major mode begin here to reflect the joyful tone of the psalm, but no less an important aspect toward this end is the integration of the refrain with the harmonic construction. Barely two chords, a prolonged tonic (mm. 21-28) and a prolonged dominant (mm. 30-38), make up this faster section. The great tension of the dominant is prepared by a single measure of very fast harmonic rhythm with a metric syncopation (m. 29). The dominant then arrives along with the first use of imitative counterpoint among the voices, with ever decreasing time intervals between entrances to increase the pace, and the refrain "O, bless the Lord" finally bound to this acceleration.

The long dominant resolves quite classically back into A minor to begin the third verse (m. 39), and the whole pattern repeats. When the faster section arrives for the second time, it ends with all voices singing "O, bless the Lord, my soul" in the accelerating counterpoint (mm. 72-80). This leads into the coda.

**Brighter tempo**

**Ex. 11–4**  Stephen Schwartz, *Godspell*, "Bless the Lord" (No. 6), mm. 85–92.

The tempo of the coda is faster still. There is only one text, the refrain. And Schwartz here shows his sense of form by alternating the major and minor modes within the coda as more voices are layered on, emphasizing the change by placing the C-sharp or C natural in the top melody, thus summarizing an important premise of the composition. The pace is increased again by doubling this alternation and cutting the text down to "Bless the Lord."

**Ex. 11–5**  Stephen Schwartz, *Godspell*, "Bless the Lord" (No. 6), mm. 101–2.

The refrain is restored for the last cadences, and the "tag" sung by the soloist after the last structural cadence has already sounded (m. 115) embodies once more the burst of emotion at the end of Psalm 103, an unceasing urge to praise. Yet Schwartz has made the small gesture almost necessary for the music too, since the previous phrase included as its melodic high note the C natural of the A minor mode, while the harmonic destiny of the piece is clearly A major. The last call to praise brings a most classical ending to a great piece of poetry.

**Ex. 11–6** Stephen Schwartz, *Godspell,* ''Bless the Lord'' (No. 6), mm. 111–18.

The drama of conversion and its various manifestations dominate the first act of *Godspell*. The major dramatic problem with this musical arrives with the second act which, with the exception of the very beginning and the singing of ''We Beseech Thee,'' takes the form of a traditional passion play. This transformation is uncomfortable at best.

> The first act is located in non-linear theatrical time, the time of the revue, or more precisely, the artistic time of the clown, the time of not telling a story but of enacting an identity. But halfway through the second act, we career into an arbitrary shift of gears, suddenly crammed into narrative sequence to accommodate the Passion and Crucifixion.[17]

The shift is from the personal to the historical, from who Jesus and his believers are to what happened to him. It seems arbitrary because the virtues of the first act now become vices, severing all connections. The subtle anonymity of stage people about whom nothing is known except their first names makes no sense in a traditional narrative that must depend on clearly drawn characters who motivate the action. Schwartz's setting of Matthew's castigation of the Pharisees, ''Alas for You,'' is rhythmically and harmonically imaginative and appropriate for its rather harsh text, but can such passion come from a clown?

A musical passion play demands a much tighter relationship between songs and specific actions. Schwartz comments that Psalm 137 was chosen for the Last Supper ''because it was about 'believers' isolated and persecuted by a hostile society,'' [18] but such subtleties are in the domain of the Biblical exegete, not the musical theater audience. Unfortunately, when the crucifixion music in the "Finale" tries to be explicit, it falls far short of expressing anything of the complexity of what should be the central event in the narrative. The use of rapid harmonic rhythm seems no different than in other, happier songs, and the jamming of the electric instruments is but a superficial substitute for dramatic expressions drawn from more essential musical elements. The lyrics here too are absurdly simplistic. There is some saving grace in the reprise of "Prepare Ye" which ends the show, for it at least rounds its form, but otherwise the end of *Godspell* is fodder for the cannons of those who claim that rock is essentially undramatic music.

Of course, *Godspell* is not really a "rock musical," as some have claimed, for its diversity of popular styles is far too broad for that label to do it justice. The vacuity of the passion sequence and the various light touches of the first act have led some to charge that the musical presents an image of Christianity without teeth. "One wonders if a true religion does not call for a certain moral toughness and spiritual fiber as well as a sense of humor?"[19] But the teachings from Matthew heard before and after every song are not soft ones. It is true that in musicals, music speaks louder than words, but the cumulative weight of the Lazarus parable, the unjust servant, the Sermon on the Mount, and the Last Judgment must have their sobering effect.

It is the deliberate inclusion of such crazy ideas about throwing away one's hand or one's eye that shows *Godspell* to be a theater of the festive religious spirit. It is curious that it does not appear so to its composer:

> I never saw *Godspell* as a "Christian" show, or indeed, as a show about "religion." To me, the basic dramatic event of the show has to do with the formation of a community. . . . The idea of community and the need for people to understand and support one another seems to me to transcend any specific religion or creed.[20]

*Godspell*'s peculiar genesis should perhaps be remembered here, the most unusual feature of which is that Schwartz was called in after the show had already attained its form. His role in shaping the drama is as essential as any theater composer's, but limited to the extent that he was able to reconcile Tebelak's conception of a clown Christianity with the traditional texts given him. In most respects he did that admirably. If he sees *Godspell* only in the most general terms of community formation, he does admit of "the idea of community" and "the need for people to understand." Even that idea and that need demand some sort of conversion, and the dramatization of that spiritual action remains the play's best achievement.

# CHAPTER 12

# History as Musical

*We tried to put over what we think might have happened.*[1]

ANDREW LLOYD WEBBER

A drama with a particular historical setting need be no different than one using any other kind of fictitious plot. The setting may strike a tone, conjure a period atmosphere, or simply provide a certain convenience in designing the background of the plot. Like a historical novel, it may take advantage of what the setting has to offer while refusing any and all associations that frustrate its artistic purpose. But when history itself is dramatized, when events of the past step out from merely coloring the action to be the action itself in a way that involves historical personages, then the dramatist is challenged in peculiar ways. The principal events that articulate the action are now beyond control; contradiction of well known facts and episodes cannot be admitted, otherwise what is the use of history at all? It would be better, certainly simpler, to make a plot from scratch. So the history must be carefully chosen, so that the potential for drama is there in the foggy patches of a character's biography or in the ambiguities of recorded events. Despite such peculiarities, the history has attracted dramatists from time to time, for there are compensatory advantages. The plot is ready-made, credible, and often fascinating. In the most famous episodes, the plot premises and even small details of action need no explanation. Most important, the stakes of the story, what motivates the characters, are abundantly clear from the beginning.

The Broadway musical tradition has occasionally tried its hand with history. Jule Styne's *Gypsy* (1959) and Jerry Bock's *Fiorello!* (1959) are biographies that create dramatic interest by filling in the flat public images of Gypsy Rose Lee and Mayor Fiorello LaGuardia. Sherman Edwards managed a humorous, visually striking, and occasionally moving retelling of the Continental Congress in his *1776* (1969). But no composer has incited such controversy while making the dramatization of history the foundation of his young career as has Andrew Lloyd Webber, who with lyricist Tim Rice took the world of popular music by storm in 1969 with his recorded opera *Jesus Christ Superstar,* and again seven years later with another, *Evita.*

Although far removed from one another in time and place, the two operas share some principal themes. One would expect operas about Jesus and Eva Peron to be about religion and politics, but as director Robert Brustein remarks, these seem to be secondary concerns:

> But the political implications of *Evita* are the least convincing aspect of the work, just as religion was the one thing missing from *Jesus Christ Superstar*. What apparently attracts [the authors] to Eva Peron is her surefire blend of sex, show biz, and ambition; she is, in short, another superstar who experiences a similar rise from poor beginnings to great influence. I suspect that the real subject of Rice and Webber is success, its rewards and human cost, and that has about as much political, religious, or intellectual significance as one finds in *Aïda* or *Madame Butterfly*.[2]

It is no coincidence that the crowd or mob plays an important role in both operas, and that they call both Jesus and Eva Peron "saviour."

To refer to *Jesus Christ Superstar* as a historical drama rather than a religious one might appear to miss the obvious, but the authors' own comments prove without doubt that they were interested in Jesus as a historical personage who happened to be a religious leader, not as a God-figure who intervened at a certain point in history. Consider how librettist Tim Rice prepared for his assignment:

> I used the King James and Catholic versions—whichever was handier—interchangeably. They're quite similar, actually. My biggest aid was Fulton Sheen's *Life of Christ,* in which Bishop Sheen calibrates and compares the Gospels. Andrew and I examined the books of the Bible—Matthew, Mark, Luke, and John—to write the libretto. Each book differs on their accounts. Matthew, Mark, and Luke seem more dependable, even though John is supposed to have been present most often. He tends, however, to lean more on the supernatural and visions. I only wanted to work from one established perspective, and the Bible and Bishop Sheen are about as established as you can get.[3]

His complete ignorance of the modern Scripture scholar's view of what the Gospels represent and his concern for "dependability" and "one established perspective" can only mean that he read them as biographical documents, not as spiritual tracts. The interpretations of religious traditions were purposefully excluded. "We read the gospels very carefully and that was it. What we did not read was eighty-three other people's interpretations of Christ. . . ."[4] Indeed, the principal complaint of picketers who protested the Broadway opening was that Jesus was not portrayed as a divine figure.

The form of both *Evita* and *Jesus Christ Superstar* is explicitly operatic, with the libretto entirely sung, and borrowing heavily on the traditional devices of aria and recitative. This departure from the norm of the partly spoken, partly sung musical play owes something to Webber's preferences for continuous music[5] but also to the curious history of the two works. Both were introduced to the listening public as record albums, produced entirely in the London recording studios of Decca and MCA. Only after their enormous commercial success as albums were they put into stage production. *Jesus Christ Superstar* opened officially at the Broadway theater on October 12, 1971. *Evita* was presented first at the King Edward Theatre in London on June 21, 1978; an American production, including a number of revisions by the authors, premiered on May 8, 1979, at the Dorothy Chandler Pavilion in Los Angeles.

Thus the conventional procedure of putting a dramatic work on stage and letting its popularity justify a cast recording was completely reversed. Such a change might have been predicted on the basis of a number of shows in the 1960s whose record albums earned more than the Broadway productions that generated them, but in any case the record album is no less legitimate a source for a staged opera than a novel or previously written spoken play. The album, however, does create an unusual problem for the critic. Is it to be evaluated, more than the subsequent staged version, as the "original" conception?

Generally not, except that the Broadway production of *Jesus Christ Superstar* was by most accounts so outlandish that it might be unsound to relate the music to any of the stage activity. Frank Corsaro of the City Center Opera was the original director-apparent, consulting with Webber and Rice even before he had a contract. "Corsaro envisioned Christ's last seven days as a series of vignettes, strong on dramatic experience with little emphasis on theatrical titillation. He stressed that it should be a very human play."[6] When Corsaro was hospitalized by an auto accident, still without contract, he was summarily replaced by Tom O'Horgan, who had produced *Hair* in 1967. Apparently he turned Corsaro's vision of the opera on its head, and asked little advice of the authors, who were virtually excluded from production decisions. When the opera opened, the audience saw Jesus rise from the floor in a giant silver chalice, and that was only the beginning. "There were too many purely decorative effects, artistic excrescences dreamed up by the director and his designers . . . that seemed to make us gasp and our blood run cold," wrote Clive Barnes.[7] "Let's just say that we don't think this production is the definitive one," remarked Webber politely.

One new song, "Could We Start Again Please?," sung by Mary Magdalene and Peter just before the trial scene, was added for the stage production and would need to be included in any detailed study, but, considering the circumstances, the impression given by the original recording alone may be at least as reliable as that of the staged version. There is also a certain validity in thinking that, if the authors' views are important, the recordings of *Jesus Christ Superstar* and *Evita* represent the best evidence of them, since Webber was involved in every stage of the recording and editing process and was rather fussy about the results. The original recording of *Jesus Christ Superstar* required 60 sessions and 400 hours of studio time at an extraordinary cost of $65,000.

To attribute the operatic form of these works to their origins in recording alone, however, is to underestimate Webber's own preparation for them. His father directed the London College of Music, and Andrew himself was trained on the piano, violin, and horn. Opera and theater interested him from his childhood. His first successful collaboration with Tim Rice was a children's cantata on another Biblical theme called *Joseph and His Amazing Technicolored Dreamcoat* (1966), which was eventually staged in New York. If he and Rice had been given the backing for a staged production of their drama about Jesus in 1969, there is no reason to think it would have been altogether different in form.

In dramatic histories the focus is on character more than on action. That is why four of the best-known musical histories of the Broadway tradition are biographical. In a story that involves someone famous, the interest is naturally in the person more than in the events of his or her life, which are already familiar. The audience wants to know not what happened to Ben Franklin, but what he was like. The desire squares well with the constraints of factual history, since character is the part of a history most easily given to the dramatist's extrapolation beyond what is known. In this way Judas, Mary Magdalene, Pilate, and Caiaphas, barely sketched in the Gospels, can be fully drawn. Says Tim Rice: "It's all complete fiction—the way it might have been. I used the information available and took certain liberties."[8] In one of the few scholarly essays on *Jesus Christ Superstar*, Ulrich Prinz rightly claims that the various characterizations are the best aspect of that opera, and that they derive from an often cited feature: its musical eclecticism.[9] Although the work is commonly termed a "rock opera," only a fraction of its songs are thoroughly composed in a rock style, though certain characteristic elements of rock may be found throughout. Webber avails himself of a number of popular and serious styles, choosing one or another to express best a particular situation or, most often, the nature of a particular character. So Mary Magdalene sings in the gentler popular folk style ("Everything's Alright" and "I Don't Know How to Love Him") and the ostentatious King Herod is given a music-hall rag ("King Herod's Song"). The song of the Apostles, "The Last Supper," a critical scene, "is like a caricature of a Gregorian chant sung by a troop of tired and self-satisfied monks,"[10] with its simple quarter-note rhythms and melodic contour. The crucifixion scene abandons popular idioms altogether and relies for its wordless acerbity on tone clusters reminiscent of Ligeti and Penderecki.[11]

The diversity of styles does wonders for the art of characterization, but since style is the principal means by which an opera is made to sound all of a piece, the aural mediation between the action in one song and another, the introduction of various styles in *Jesus Christ Superstar* makes an issue of the high level structure. How is any kind of musical-dramatic continuity to be maintained in the opera as a whole?

Webber must have been aware of the problem, at least subconsciously, for he arrived at a solution unique to the Broadway theater tradition. Although styles may differ within the opera, he creates musical points of reference by using compositions over and over again, not as reprises, but in the manner of what the musicologists of early music call *contrafactum*. This term refers to a piece of vocal music whose text has been replaced by an entirely new one, usually unrelated to the original. In the Renaissance, when stylistic distinctions between sacred and secular music began to crumble, it was common to convert one sort of piece into another simply by according it a new set of words.

"This Jesus Must Die," from *Jesus Christ Superstar,* is first heard when the high priests, including Caiaphas and Annas, are plotting to arrest Jesus. Later, after Judas explains to them why he is betraying Jesus ("Damned for All Time"), they reply to him in the music of "This Jesus Must Die" with completely new words and a different dramatic situation. Later still, when Judas is horrified at what they have done to Jesus ("Judas' Death") the music returns again to set their replies to him, and his line about being dragged through slime and mud. The same music returns one last time at the beginning of "Trial Before Pilate," when Caiaphas asks for the sentence of crucifixion.

The following schematic shows how thoroughgoing is this technique of contrafactum. The first eight songs are new; thereafter the pace of borrowing increases as the opera progresses.

Melodic Material in

| *Number in Opera* | *Source of Melodic Material* |
|---|---|
| 1. Overture | |
| 2. Heaven on Their Minds | |
| 3. What's the Buzz | |
| 4. Strange Thing Mystifying | |
| 5. Everything's Alright | |
| 6. This Jesus Must Die | |
| 7. Hosanna | |
| 8. Simon Zealotes | |
| 9. Poor Jerusalem | Simon Zealotes (lines 1–7) |
| 10. Pilate's Dream | Poor Jerusalem |
| 11. The Temple | |
|     Moneylenders | |
|     Jesus | I Only Want to Say (fragment) |
|     Crowd of Sick | Moneylenders |
| 12. Everything's Alright | (brief reprise) |
| 13. I Don't Know How to Love Him | |
| 14. Damned for All Time | |
| 15. Blood Money | This Jesus Must Die |
| 16. The Last Supper | |
|     Jesus' speech | Everything's Alright (minor verse) |

Melodic Material in *Jesus Christ Superstar*  (*continued*)

| Number in Opera | Source of Melodic Material |
|---|---|
| 17. I Only Want to Say | |
| 18. The Arrest | What's the Buzz |
| | Moneylenders |
| | Strange Thing Mystifying (fragment) |
| 19. Peter's Denial | Strange Thing Mystifying |
| 20. Pilate and Christ | Hosanna (including reprise) |
| 21. King Herod's Song | |
| 22. Judas' Death | Damned for All Time (fragment) |
| | This Jesus Must Die |
| | I Don't Know How to Love Him (reprise) |
| 23. Trial Before Pilate | This Jesus Must Die (fragment) |
| 39 Lashes | ostinato from Heaven on Their Minds |
| 24. Superstar | |
| 25. Crucifixion | |
| 26. John Nineteen Forty-one | I Only Want to Say |

There is no doubt that the method helps to unify the opera. By restricting the amount of melodic material, there is simply less music to unify. But there are dramatic connections to be perceived as well. The example of "This Jesus Must Die" is consistent in that the music is always associated with the high priests. The music which sets the dramatic exchange between Jesus and Judas in "Everything's Alright" early in the opera returns to set a similar confrontation during "The Last Supper." The connections can be ironic, as when the music of the moneylenders and merchants in the temple is used for the pleading of the sick and poor for miraculous cure, suggesting perhaps some shallowness in their common appeal. At other times, the relationship between contrafacta seems far-fetched. Why should "Peter's Denial" have the same music as Judas's reproach of Jesus for befriending Mary Magdalene ("Strange Thing Mystifying")?

Webber's contrafactum method expands and in some ways replaces the time-honored device of reprise. While reprise operates, in the best instances, by re-vealing the dramatic relevance of an earlier expression to a new dramatic con-text, the contrafactum, in changing the lyrics, actually changes the expression, and therein is the price paid for its use. The leitmotif idea, from which both reprise and this operatic contrafactum ultimately derive, depends on a consistent association of music with some kind of dramatic expression, be it words or some physical action. When Webber drastically alters the lyric to a certain melody, there is less dramatic association between the melody and action, and he risks a fatal weakening of the melody's dramatic function.

When compared to *Jesus Christ Superstar*, *Evita* seems much more unified in its use of musical style. It depends on just two styles. One is an easy soft-rock, often tinged with Spanish effects, such as the tango bass in "Don't Cry for Me, Argentina." This style is used by all the major characters, but is reserved for occasions that call for some kind of dissembling or pretense, which are many in this cynical opera. Public speeches, small talk, political slogans, and all the music relating to Eva Peron's love affairs are set to this style. The expression of real feeling is given to the second, rather modernistic style. After Eva and Juan Peron have told one another of their mutual attraction, they face away and sing this curious waltz to themselves, which states that every lover, regardless of gender, has used his partner for ulterior purposes.

**Ex. 12–1** Webber and Rice, *Evita,* "There Is No One" (from No. 7, "Charity Concert/I'd Be Surprisingly Good for You").

The heavy syncopations, accentuated by notes that are dissonant not only with one another but with a strong tonal background, remind one of Stravinsky.

The distinction in styles in *Evita* has nothing to do with characterization, but instead governs two domains of expression for all characters: pretense and cynicism. One might expect, then, that Webber's contrafactum method would no longer be necessary, since the problem of musical unity for the whole opera is taken care of by a singularity of dramatic purpose for each style. It is shocking to discover that not only is the method very much a part of *Evita,* it is more prevalent than in *Jesus Christ Superstar.*

Melodic Material in *Evita*

| *Opera Number* | *Source of Melodic Material* |
|---|---|
| ACT I | |
| 1. Cinema | |
| 2. Requiem for Evita | |
| Oh What a Circus | |
| Sing You Fools! | |
| 3. On This Night of a Thousand Stars | |
| Eva and Magaldi | |
| Eva Beware | |
| 4. Buenos Aires | |
| And If I Ever Go | |
| 5. Goodnight and Thank You | Eva Beware |
| There Is No One | |
| 6. The Art of the Possible | |
| Eva on the Air | |
| 7. Charity Concert | On This Night of a Thousand (reprise) |
| I'd Be Good for You | |
| There Is No One | (reprise) |

| *Opera Number* | *Source of Melodic Material* |
|---|---|
| ACT I | |
| 8. Another Suitcase in Another Hall | |
| 9. Peron's Latest Flame | And If I Ever |
| Army Theme | |
| Aristocrat Theme | |
| 10. A New Argentina | I'd Be Good for You |
| | Eva on the Air |
| | Eva and Magaldi (fragment) |
| | |
| ACT II | |
| 11. Don't Cry for Me | Oh What a Circus |
| 12. High Flying Adored | |
| 13. Rainbow High | Eva and Magaldi (fragment) |
| 14. Rainbow Tour | |
| 15. The Actress Hasn't Learned | Aristocrat Theme |
| | Another Suitcase in Another Hall |
| 16. And the Money Kept Rolling In | |
| 17. Santa Evita | Oh What a Circus |
| 18. Waltz for Eva and Che | There Is No One |
| | And If I Ever Go |
| 19. She Is a Diamond | Army Theme |
| 20. Dice Are Rolling | I'd Be Good for You |
| | There Is No One |
| 21. Eva's Final Broadcast | Oh What a Circus |
| 22. Montage | Oh What a Circus |
| | Eva Beware |
| | A New Argentina |
| | High Flying, Adored |
| | Sing You Fools! |
| 23. Lament | Requiem for Evita |

Not only are contrafacta more prevalent, they are much more baffling. Why should Che, when dismissing Eva's lovers one by one like so many hired hands in "Goodnight and Thank You," sing the same music as Magaldi used when he warned her not to go to Buenos Aires ("Eva Beware of the City")? Why is the lovely song of Peron's mistress, "Another Suitcase in Another Hall," converted to become Eva's subversion of the aristocracy's society charity ("The Actress Hasn't Learned")? And what is the audience to understand when it hears the tune known by the world as "Don't Cry for Me, Argentina" sung at the opera's beginning by the leftist Che to the cynical lines "Oh, What a Circus, Oh, What a Show!"? The contrafactum method in *Evita* has become a rather careless infatuation with Webber's not inconsiderable powers of melody.

It is possible that the contrafactum technique in the two operas resulted quite naturally from the authors' working methods. Tim Rice remembers that, with *Jesus Christ Superstar,*

> the music came before the lyrics. We would discuss the scene, and I'd say, "Right, this number will be Judas saying so-and-so," and Andrew would say, "Right, therefore, we want this kind of music, we want an agitated kind of song, or a ballad, or a love song, or vaudeville, or whatever." So Andrew would write his tunes, and I would be given a tune that was obviously sympathetic to what I wanted to say.[12]

If the authors truly operated with the naïve belief that a kind of music is analogous to a kind of dramatic action, it is all too easy to see how they could decide that one dramatic situation might be similar in character to another, so why not use the same music again, with different words? In *Evita,* which depends on just two styles, the repetition has no justification save the sort of dramatic connections and ironies that music can make. Whatever sensible connections are in the opera, however, have their impact diffused by other absurd contrafacta which have none.

*Jesus Christ Superstar* works better because its principal action depends almost totally on its characterization, which the stylistic diversity creates and the musical repetitions in the contrafacta help to reinforce. The juxtaposition of conflicting characters singing contrasting music has its own dramatic interest that is especially effective when subsumed within a single, often symmetrical musical form. "Everything's Alright," which Mary Magdalene sings as she annoints Jesus with the precious ointment, has such a form: A B A B A. The beginning section of the song brings a clear and simple action: she is trying to calm his indignation after Judas questioned the political wisdom of his associating with "women of her kind."

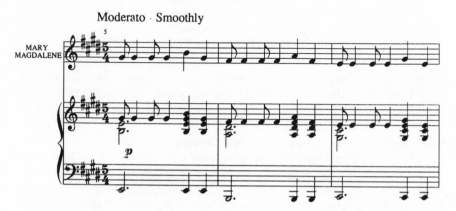

**Ex. 12–2**  Webber and Rice, *Jesus Christ Superstar,* "Everything's Alright," mm. 5–7.

Her lyric, to the effect that Jesus should try not to become anxious about the day's troubles, makes the intention explicit, but the music makes it credible in the constrained melodic range, easy sequential patterns (mm. 5-8), and above all in its 5/7 meter, which by obliterating the strong sense of regular strong beats and divisible rhythmic groupings gives the melody an almost chant-like flow.

In the B section Judas charges that Mary's attention has been wasteful, that the valuable ointment could have been sold for the benefit of the poor.

**Ex. 12–3**   Webber and Rice, *Jesus Christ Superstar,* "Everything's Alright," mm. 19–22.

The musical contrast is made in the change of mode, from E major to E minor, the more active bass line and faster harmonic rhythm. Rhythmic accents are stronger. Nevertheless, the meter remains in 5/4, and Judas's melody, though different enough to articulate his character, is based on the same rhythmic motive as Mary Magdalene's melody, thus justifying the continuity of form underlying the contrast. The second B section, with Jesus' reply to Judas, has the same contentious music. Between them is Mary's more gentle insistence to calm down. The rondo-like return to her verses is well prepared by Webber's harmonic scheme for the B sections. Both Judas and Jesus rise to climaxes of passion, expressed by the strongest syncopations of the song and a sustained dominant harmony.

**Ex. 12–4**  Webber and Rice, *Jesus Christ Superstar*, "Everything's Alright," mm. 41–49.

The resolution of the dominant prolongation into Mary's music at one stroke makes the form more continuous and makes more palpable her insistence that calm is needed in the time of greatest tension, for that is what this moment portrays in its musical progression. The only disappointing feature of the form is its ending. Here Webber resorts to the recording industry's all-purpose answer for composers who cannot end their songs properly: the fade-out. Unfortunately several of the principal numbers in *Jesus Christ Superstar* drift off in this fashion, including "Heaven on Their Minds" and "Superstar," and in this regard the compositional technique of *Evita* shows a certain maturity, for the fade-out is not used once in that opera.

A similar rondo arrangement is made out of "The Last Supper" with the Apostles' song serving as the returning section. Between the repetitions are more loosely ordered, but more dramatic sections containing Jesus' predictions of denial and betrayal and the last face-to-face confrontation with Judas, set once again to the minor mode music from "Everything's Alright." Again, the rondo usage of the Apostles' song functions not just as a structural device but as a means of symbolizing their utter obliviousness to the significance of the action within the scene.

This juxtaposition of characters within single musical forms is complemented in the opera by a longer range development of two characters, Jesus and Judas. All other personages in the opera are static; these two undergo dramatic changes. The changes are brought about in a flash, although neither is unprepared. Jesus has an indignant tone of righteousness until he sings "I Only Want to Say," Webber's dramatization of the Gethsemane scene. The portrayal of indecision, near failure of nerve, and almost childish pout is so stark that this piece single-handedly created the image of an abased Jesus that the listening public took away, forgetting his earlier remonstrance of Judas ("Strange Thing Mystifying"), bracing of his disciples ("What's the Buzz"), and castigation of the temple merchants ("The Temple"). But there is a hint of this weakness earlier, when he cannot endure the crowd of sick who press him. The transformation of Judas is easier to take since it follows the expected course, but it traverses a greater distance. His opening words, the first words of the opera, "My mind is clearer now," are ironically recalled in his last words while still alive, sung to the same music: "My mind is darkness now." This number, "Judas' Death," is a patchwork quilt of contrafacta, but it also includes the most important reprise of the opera. When Judas sings one verse of "I Don't Know How to Love Him," the audience recognizes that even though Jesus has brought him, in his mind, down a torturous path to the brink of insanity, Judas cannot help feeling something mysterious for this man he has betrayed.

*Evita* fails to create any similar character action. In an opera in which the most beautiful music is given to pretended emotion and a modernist style can express only the cynical, all becomes passionless. There is no character action because there is no room given for development. Eva and Juan Peron are cold opportunists from beginning to end. Che is a cynical leftist commentator from beginning to end. The opera fairly starves for emotional expression, which is perhaps why Webber lavishes one of the best songs, "Another Suitcase in Another Hall," on Peron's teenage mistress, a nameless character who is on stage for five minutes. The authors make no use of historical evidence suggesting that

Peron and Eva had more than a marriage of convenience, which at least might have lended some contrast between the public and private characters.[13]

Another opportunity for character action was provided by the authors' insertion of Che as a commentator, or one-man chorus. He might have been someone who was initially enthusiastic about Peronism, only to be disillusioned, or someone whose liberal inclinations were revolted by the political methods of the First Lady but who at the same time could not deny her effectiveness in raising living standards of certain segments of the working classes, in ridding Argentina's railroad and principal industries of foreign ownership, and in enfranchising women for the first time in Argentine history. But the opportunity is missed. Instead he is Che Guevara, the Argentine-born aide to Fidel Castro, who in the final version comes off as a negative image of Eva, nothing more. The attempt to conflict these images at the opera's end in "Waltz for Eva and Che" fails utterly. They snipe at one another with clever and cynical words, but they sing the same pretty music, so nothing substantial comes of the contrast.

This woodenness of character, which reduced the opera into little more than a political editorial, may have been exacerbated by certain changes made when it was brought to Broadway. The London premiere was greeted by a number of notices and letters complaining that the opera glorified fascism, and American producers hesitated to carry the project further. "I had qualms when I saw the show in London," said one, "but when I learned how Hal Prince was going to reshape it, I was pleased and thrilled. Hal persuaded the authors to change four minutes of dialogue and develop the character of Che Guevara as a counterpoint to Evita, so that now Evita's critic and opponent is just as important as she is."[14] The London Che cannot be as clearly identified with Guevara, for he is actually an inventor with capitalist designs through much of the opera, and makes only intermittent political comments. The new Che is clearly in the image of Guevara, and plays in virtually every scene. Webber, stung by the London criticism, went so far as to say of the new version that "The basic point of Evita is that it's very anti-Eva."[15] The politically sensitive held their peace on Broadway, but not so the critics. "The purpose of the rewrites, obviously, was to take the appeal out of Evita. In this they have absolutely succeeded. The evening is now emotionally icy, psychologically chromatic, a cut-and-dried sermon. . . ."[16] The revisions do not materially change the opera's statement—Eva and Peron, for example, are virtually the same in both versions—but they do remove even what little remained of the ambiguity on which the dramatist of history thrives.

To be sure, the history of the Perons is more problematic than the Christ story. The nature of Eva Peron's demise, which of course is quite out of the authors' hands, is undramatic. The crucifixion in Jesus Christ Superstar arises from the action of the characters, but the cancer that kills Eva Peron comes from nowhere and has no explanation. One almost wishes that the authors had defied the historical fact and fabricated their own ending that would somehow clarify what preceded it. As it stands, the plug is suddenly pulled on Eva's career, and on the opera, too.

But the crucial difference is simply that the Peronist history is so much less well known. In *Jesus Christ Superstar,* the authors had the luxury of simply sketching a rather obscure episode such as Mary's annointing of Jesus in the song "Everything's Alright" without having to explain it. The assumption of a certain historical literacy in the audience is clearly on their side in that opera, but it could not be with *Evita.* When she was First Lady of Argentina from 1946 to 1953, Eva Peron was world famous, but the younger generations of the 1970s had never heard of her, and the details of her story were the preserve of Latin American historians. So it would not do to try to interpret what had happened; first it had to be explained, and in some detail. This required that a substantial portion of the music be given over to an expository function, and historical events that took place in distant places or over a considerable period of time, such as Eva's "Rainbow Tour" to Europe, had to be narrated without actually being shown. Critics complained about the violation of the offstage action rule, and labeled *Evita* a secular oratorio.[17] That it might be an oratorio has little to do with its success or failure, for many of Handel's finest choral numbers describe offstage action too, but they never fail to reflect on that action even as they describe it, or else they are immediately followed by such reflection. This is really the root problem: in an opera which trivializes all emotion as mere means to an end, there is no possibility of dramatic reflection.

The failure to move beyond exposition is what distinguishes *Evita* from Rice and Webber's earlier, though partial, success in *Jesus Christ Superstar.* "No one expects a musical to be a political handbook. . . . But when Rice and Webber chose this subject, they assumed some obligation to make the Perons' rise to power credible in the theater, rather than relying on the extrinsic fact that they *did* rise to power, just as they had some obligation to shape the materials into a cumulative and discerning drama rather than relying on the fact that the actual lives were dramatic."[18] Even as a study of power, *Evita* does not work well because Eva is only shown singing about, never moving among, her *descamisados,* her people, the source of her power, something that she did in fact do very well. Jesus, on the other hand, is effectively shown as the object of the crowd's adoration in the elegant "Hosanna," and later as the object of their derision, made ironic through the use of the same music, in the Pilate scenes.

The portrayal, in both lyric and music, of Eva, Peron, and Che as political symbols rather than as human characters eliminates the ambiguous aspects, the hidden dimensions which can make drama out of history. The contrast with *Jesus Christ Superstar* is quite instructive. In that opera, it is the authors' unorthodox images of Judas and Jesus that move that drama forward, that reinterpret the famous events that follow in a fairly consistent way. What the Gospels have only sketched is clarified for a dramatic moment. History is not left on its own.

# CHAPTER 13

# Frame Story
# As Musical

*I wanted to do a show with dancers.*[1]

MICHAEL BENNETT

The dramatic conceptions that underlie musical plays or operas may be adapted from most any source that has some potential for dramatic action. Legitimate plays are perhaps the most common source in the Broadway tradition, simply because their adaptation is so much more straightforward than other sources, but even this limited survey has encountered inspirations in many other forms: novels, legends, short story collections, the New Testament, historical biography, and sound recordings. The translation of these latter forms onto the stage has always resulted in some difficulty, even as the resulting musicals realize some, even extraordinary success. The luxurious length and detail which are the very fiber of novels and legends proved too overwhelming for *Show Boat* and *Camelot*. The thematic consistency of Sholem Aleichem eluded *Fiddler on the Roof*. The dichotomy of religious experience and religious narrative melded so well in St. Matthew's Gospel was the undoing of *Godspell*. Is it any wonder that the majority of the most critically acclaimed American musicals—which might include, but not be limited to, *Porgy and Bess, Carousel, My Fair Lady, The Most Happy Fella,* and *West Side Story*—sprang from conceptions already staged?

Imagine, then, the prospects of staging a musical play whose only source is an extended conversation:

It all began at midnight in a dance studio on January 18, 1974, when I met with 22 dancers, including me, and we danced for an hour and then just talked, one at a time,

309

about why we had started dancing. The subtext of that evening became the play. We did it twice, and I had thirty hours of tape.[2]

That is how Michael Bennett recalled the birth of *A Chorus Line*.

In retrospect it seems that the spark for such an experiment could only have come from Bennett, or someone very much like him. His career epitomized the meteoric rise to fame in the theater world. He broke in on Broadway at age seventeen as a chorus dancer and was designing dances for shows in his mid-twenties. These included *Promises, Promises* (1968), *Coco* (1969), and two important Sondheim musicals, *Company* (1970) and *Follies* (1971). He wished to present a show that captured the experience of dancers on Broadway, not in starring roles, but as everyday chorus dancers, as "gypsies." His own experience both as chorus dancer and director made him sympathetic to the very idea and see its dramatic possibilities. It is no surprise that his own personality is stamped on *A Chorus Line*'s Zach, the unseen director whose voice booms from the back of the theater, and Bennet admitted that Zach was modeled on himself. "He's cut off, dehumanized in a sense. That's a period I went through."[3]

Bennett organized the tape sessions out of conviction that the typical routines of composing a Broadway show would not permit him to realize his conception. In his view of the norm, "The director sits in a room with the composer and lyricist for a year. The costumes and sets are designed. Orchestrations are done." After auditions and hurried rehearsals, "You cross your fingers and hope it comes together."[4] Bennett brought in James Kirkwood, an actor and playwright with one off-Broadway show to his credit *(P.S. Your Cat Is Dead)*, and Nicholas Dante, one of his midnight dancers, to convert the raw tape into a script. Joseph Papp, director of the New York Shakespeare Festival, generously granted Bennett a place to run a workshop to refine the idea, including funds to pay participating dancers $100 per week. Only then were the composer Marvin Hamlisch and lyricist Ed Kleban hired on. Bennett had turned the normal procedure on its head, taking a cue from experiments in modern legitimate theater:

> The book, the songs and the dances were worked out as they went along, from materials that came out of rehearsals, including the lives of all the participants. This is clearly the appropriation by Broadway musical people of a method that has been developed, not by Off Broadway but by Off Off Broadway—in "matrix" groups, such as Joseph Chaikin's now disbanded Open Theater, which evolved their productions out of the contributions in rehearsal of all the participants, with writers and composers (if used at all) as collaborators in the evolution. In fact one moment near the beginning of *A Chorus Line*—when a dance ends with the line of dancers holding up their photographs in front of their faces—is strongly reminiscent of a similar device in the Open Theater's *Mutation Show* (1973).[5]

How could a source material such as the taped conversations—extremely honest in expression, without artifice, very loose, totally unrelated except by the theme of dancing—be converted into a script without spoiling its nature?

Bennett's solution was to stage an audition, a competition for eight places in the chorus line of an unnamed Broadway musical. Because the chorus dancers would be required to act small parts in this show, the director Zach asks each of the seventeen finalists to step out of line and talk about himself, so that Zach might make judgments about the characters he is hiring. They resist at first, but soon begin to open up through a series of musical numbers. The "autobiographies" are drawn from the original tapes. "It is their lives, although they are not necessarily telling their own stories," said Bennett about the actors in *A Chorus Line*.[6] "It is a psychological striptease," wrote Clive Barnes in review of the opening on May 21, 1975, "and slowly the kids undress in a series of sad if funny vignettes."[7]

Bennett's conception is the frame story, a literary form with a long history, whose most conspicuous example in English is Geoffrey Chaucer's *Canterbury Tales*, "a single narrative within whose framework are placed other and distinct narratives."[8] As the pilgrimage to the shrine of St. Thomas à Becket of Canterbury is the occasion, or excuse really, for the telling of stories of exceptional variety in both genre and content, so are the audition and Zach's extraordinary request the excuse for the autobiographical revelations of the dancers. It is a curious coincidence that, although there is no evidence that Michael Bennett thought of the *Canterbury Tales* while creating *A Chorus Line,* the pilgrims' tales are encouraged and orchestrated by the Host, "the director of the proceedings, firm, commanding, and gracious,"[9] who makes the storytelling into a competition.

The conception of *A Chorus Line* as a frame story enabled Bennett and his writers to preserve the individuality and honesty of the original autobiographies without having to weave them into some plausible plot line, probably an impossible task. *A Chorus Line* is a frame story because its stories are neither episodes of a high-level plot nor subplots, which abound in more traditional musicals as a means of articulating the main action. Such episodes and subplots relate directly to the main plot and affect it in important ways. Without the bantering relationship of Bernardo and Anita in *West Side Story,* the action of the final scenes cannot be understood. If Mary Magdalene does not sing "I Don't Know How to Love Him," then the listener has much less sense of Jesus' mysterious and powerful attraction in *Jesus Christ Superstar.* But the various autobiographies in *A Chorus Line* could be altered significantly, have their order of presentation changed, or be replaced by new ones without the slightest effect on the show as a whole. That is because the high-level plot, the competitive audition, the excuse, is divorced from the low-level events which fill up the stage time.

Indeed, the dramatic structure of a frame story emphasizes the low-level events, that is, the individual stories, at the expense of overall plot. The frame story sacrifices high-level tension and resolution, and puts in its place a series of small dramas, little waves of tension and resolution. Now, Helen Cooper, in her overview of frame-story practice,[10] points out that in some examples the frame functions as the focus of attention, and this is perhaps the case in *Company* (1970), the show that begins the mature period of Stephen Sondheim, which at least one critic cited as *A Chorus Line*'s natural model.[11]

*Company* dramatizes the situation of Bobby, a thirty-five-year old handsome bachelor, and five couples, his friends, who are in various states of matrimony. Each scene involves Bobby with one or more of these couples and amounts to some comment on marriage. There is very little directed plot; Sondheim called it "non-linear." Some of the individual scenes could probably be re-ordered without much effect, as in *A Chorus Line*. But the overall theme of how Bobby will deal with his unmarried state is still dominant in the play. In fact, the last song, "Being Alive," forms a real dramatic climax as Bobby admits that being alone in life isn't enough. Sondheim, who was persuaded to replace a more satirical piece, "Happily Ever After," with this song, never thought that it worked dramatically—"When Bobby suddenly realizes that he shouldn't be alone at the end of the scene, it's too small a moment and you don't believe it"[12]—but nevertheless it insures that the frame is the primary dramatic focus.

That is surely not the case in *A Chorus Line*. If the audition were the real plot, then who wins would matter very much at the end of the play. But anyone who has seen it will not be able to name the winners, except for one or two personal favorites perhaps. The fact is that the audience never learns the reasons for Zach's particular selections at the end, and it doesn't matter who wins the audition. Where is the development of the theme of competition, the plotting of strategy, the dreams of victory? There is none because that is not the true subject of the play. And the weightiest evidence of all is that there is no musical expression for the drama as competition after the opening number, "I Hope I Get It," which functions mostly as a curtain raiser that establishes the frame. Harold Clurman's characterization of the play is therefore most apt: "There is hardly any 'story' except for the stories of the young people on the line."[13]

Paradoxically, the retreat of the frame into the background of the drama does not mean that the choice of frame was unimportant. If one could imagine *A Chorus Line* as a bunch of interviews taken by some feature magazine writer in a crowded dressing room, for example, it becomes immediately clear how much the frame influences the character and effect of the stories without affecting their contents. "When you see the sixteen [sic] boys and girls competing for eight jobs, there's something so naked about it," recalls James Kirkwood, who collaborated on the book. "You want everyone to get the job, but you know only half can. And that's the pull."[14] Certainly, knowing what is at stake in the personal confessions colors the confessions themselves. Nevertheless, the competition can affect only the tension in the little dramas that are the autobiographies; it is not a vehicle for high-level dramatic action.

The frame story changes the nature and purpose of the songs in the play. Rather than contribute to a developing action by defining character or dramatic movement through music, Marvin Hamlisch and Ed Kleban had to create entire dramas in miniature. It is not that the songs had to be complete narratives in themselves, but they had to have a dramatic role in the storytelling. This role might be as simple as a character definition, as in the comical "Sing." Very much in the mold of *Oklahoma!*'s "I Cain't Say No," "Sing" supplies an answer to Zach's question—Val dances because she can't sing—and closes her story. Generally the pieces have more ambitious dramatic functions and therefore have more complex structures. It was a demanding assignment, and although there are a number of clever moments in the score, even the best attempts of Hamlisch and Kleban are flawed.

In "At the Ballet" three of the women—Sheila, Bebe, and Maggie—explain that they began dancing to escape from troubled home lives, as a way to be beautiful. The verse and refrain form of each section contrasts music that stands for the reality against music that expresses the fantasy life offered by the ballet school. The opening melody is an admirable image of the loveless home Sheila is trying to recall. An insistent, monotonic A, very fast, clashes with a prevailing G minor harmony, creating a subdued but ever present tension (m. 1).[15] Metrical asymmetry in the phrasing increases the bitterness (m. 2). After another verse on the same music, there is a transition to the refrain, which expresses how beautiful everything is "at the ballet." Here Hamlisch resorts to an imitation of a classical waltz, which, especially in the accompaniment, suits well the fantasy world of the ballet (mm. 20-36). Yet, the anachronistic texture can still be expressive, as when the vocal melody becomes chromatic (mm. 29-32), seeming to modulate out of A major, only to return forcefully on the word "Hey" (m. 33), with its sudden yet appropriate emphasis on the tonic just before the cadence. The second part of the refrain is composed in the parallel minor, which prepares the next verse.

The form of the entire song is more ambitious than a simple verse-refrain alternation for each character.

### "At the Ballet"

| | | |
|---|---|---|
| Verse 1 | (Sheila) | G minor |
| Verse 2 | (Sheila) | G minor |
| Refrain—part 1 | (Sheila) | A major |
| —part 2 | (Sheila and Bebe) | A minor |
| Verse 3 | (Bebe) | A minor |
| Verse 4 | (Bebe) | A minor |
| Refrain—part 1 | (Bebe and Maggie) | D major |
| —part 2 | (all) | D minor |
| —interlude | (spoken dialogue) | G major |
| Development | (all) | C# minor |
| Refrain—part 1 | (Maggie) | D major |
| —extension | (all) | D major |

The development is a rendition of the refrain tune in C-sharp minor, over which fragments of the verses are sung intermittently by the three women. The section is important, for it makes clear how much the three women love their ballet for the same reason, and since its texture is less continuous it creates a higher-level tension. This tension sets up the most expressive moment: when the key and melodic continuity are stable again, Maggie extends a chromatic passage, singing three times the key words of the title (mm. 134-43).

This peak moment of the song is made possible by the varied pattern within the form, the development and interlude sections which make the return to the familiar refrain more dramatic than it would have been otherwise. Yet, for all its ambition and imagination, the structure of "At the Ballet" is a puzzling one. Why does Hamlisch forgo the powerful tensions and unity that a central key can provide? The use of various keys for both expressive variety and structural articulation is of course a necessary component of tonal form, but their deployment in "At the Ballet" seems just haphazard.[16] The form lacks the tonal unity, and therefore the expressive power, it might have had.

Defects in the details, too, detract and distract from the song's dramatic function. The change from duple to triple meter and from minor to major mode at the end of the first verse (mm. 8-10) might serve as some preparation for the waltz to come, which is in triple and in major. But the tonal preparation is lost when, at the same point in the second verse (mm. 20-21), the music remains in the original G minor. That makes the modulation to A major incomparably more distant and, since there seems to be no call in the material for such a modulation, grating. Indeed, most of the changes of key in the piece strike the listener as ill-conceived and clumsy. The lyrics for these important measures do not match up well with the the musical content, an intermittent problem characteristic of the entire play. Why should the music change to major when Sheila recalls her mother's marriage (mm. 8-10)? After an entire verse in minor, the change of mode romanticizes the marriage, when just the opposite is intended.

The tonal unity missing from "At the Ballet" finds its place in "Montage," the most ambitious structure in *A Chorus Line*. It is a rondo-like form using the refrain "Hello twelve, hello thirteen, hello love" as its recurring theme. "Montage" involves the entire cast of seventeen, many having solo bits which describe their own teenage years. The piece is therefore a frame within a frame, for within the entire confessional scheme of *A Chorus Line*, "Montage" constructs yet another artifice in which a considerable number of the dancers can reveal themselves.

Plan of "Montage"

| Part I | | | |
|---|---|---|---|
| Refrain | ("Hello Twelve") | (all) | E major |
| | "Gonorrhea" | (Mark) | F#-A major |
| | "Four foot, ten" | (Connie) | C major |
| Refrain | ("Goodbye Twelve") | (all) | E major |
| | "Four foot, ten" | (Connie) | C major |
| Part II | | | |
| | "Nothing" (verse 1, 2) | (Diana) | Eb major |
| | "Nothing" (verse 3, coda) | | E major |

Part III

| | "The summer I turned" | (Don) | E major |
|---|---|---|---|
| Refrain | ("Goodbye Twelve") | (all) | E major |
| | "Please take this" | (Maggie) | B major |

Part IV

| | "First time I'd ever" | (Judy) | ——— |
|---|---|---|---|
| Refrain | ("Goodbye Twelve") | (all) | E major |
| | "Gimme the ball" | (Ritchie) | E minor |
| Refrain | ("Goodbye Twelve") | (all) | E major |

The plan given here shows only the lengthy solos. There are innumerable short interjections, both sung and spoken, throughout the sections between the refrains, and the refrains themselves are often overlaid with other words and melodies. But it makes clear how the key of E major acts as the principal tonal center and, in conjunction with the refrain, organizes this sequence of twenty minutes.

The security of the overall form cannot insure success in the composition of details, however, and defects in handling the musical continuity from section to section and once again in the match of music and lyrics undermine the potential of such an ambitious piece.

The lyric begins with a promise that is never fulfilled. The refrain line "Hello twelve, hello thirteen, hello love" introduces the theme of adolescence, it is true, but there is nothing in the song about love. All of the lyrics, save perhaps Maggie's message to her mother, are directed back at those who sing them. They are too busy talking about themselves to consider love. It makes a clever refrain, nothing more. At other places in "Montage" the lyrics simply do not fit the music, which is a failure not of imagination but of craft.

A striking example of this failure is Diana's song about her acting class in high school, "Nothing," which is Part II of "Montage." The tune, one of the best in the play, has as its most identifiable feature the leap of the chromatic major seventh, from B-flat to A on the words "to feel" (m. 22-23), introducing a sequential motive in the following bars. The word "feel" in measures 23 and 25 receives a great musical emphasis because of the leap and the length of the note and the prominence of the melody given by the meter. That is fine, because in this context, "feel" is the active word of the line, and the chromatic leap seems to express the kind of intense, longing effort required of the budding actors. But this rather positive association is soon subverted. The same music in the second verse emphasizes "be," a much less active and emotional word. But the worst comes in the next phrase, when the melodic peaks bring out "ex*cept*" and "try" as Diana tells how her teacher singled her out of the class with a plea to try harder, while actually ridiculing her. The first case is simply poor, but the second actually distorts the whole dramatic premise of the song. By emphasizing "try" in the same way it emphasized "feel," the music paints the teacher, Mr. Karp, in rather sympathetic, not villainous tones as Diana intends. The third verse crowns the effort with an egregious dangling modifier that Oscar Hammerstein could never have condoned. The phrase pattern of the earlier verses only makes it stand out.

The problems in musical discontinuity perhaps derive from the ambitiousness of "Montage." It covers a great deal of verbal and emotional ground, perhaps more than it should. The sections between the refrains are filled with extended solos, short vocal interjections, and spoken dialogue. There is no attempt to treat the melodic lines or accompaniment with any motivic consistency, so the entire burden of organization is put on the refrain, and the continuity between refrains is therefore carried entirely by the text. Hamlisch and Kleban might have succeeded had they used recitative exclusively, but when that texture is used intermittently with spoken dialogue, there must be some dramatic justification for the inherently greater emphasis and expressive weight that music gives to a text. In the following lines from "Montage—Part 3"

> Well, she really took to me. I mean, we did share the only dressing room and she did a lot of dressing . . .
>
> Anyway, she used to come and pick me up and drive me to work nights.

why should the text up to "a lot of dressing . . ." be spoken and the rest sung? Recitative in the right hands can be an expressive resource of great profundity, but in "Montage" its use, once again, seems haphazard.

A Chorus Line is performed without intermission, probably because the fragile continuity of the frame story could not tolerate a lengthy break, but there is a kind of visual intermission when Zach lets the dancers have a break out in the hall. The stage is now empty except for one dancer, Cassie. As Zach speaks with her, it becomes clear that they were once lovers, and that although she was once a star dancer, she now needs "a job." When she joins with the others in a unison dance number ("One"), Zach criticizes her dancing as too special, and the argument soon turns into an old-fashioned lovers' quarrel.

It is difficult to understand why Bennett wanted this scene, except perhaps as some autobiographical expiation of his own, because it has no dramatic premise and does grave injury to the device of the frame. Zach, who instigates all the storytelling from the beginning, is really the personification of the frame. When he enters into this little "plot," the distinction between the frame and the stories is critically blurred. It is an attempt to create a high-level dramatic tension where none should exist. To confound the inconsistency, Cassie's song, "The Music and the Mirror," has nothing to do with the past love affair; it reverts to the self-portrait, like the others. It is no wonder that a number of critics objected to this scene and to the knee injury scene which follows.[17]

Perhaps the greatest difficulty of the frame story is finishing it in a way that brings the stories together in some sort of artistic whole, a difficulty Chaucer neatly avoided by leaving his *Canterbury Tales* unfinished. The composer of the variation set faces the same structural issue: after having linked a number of small, essentially closed forms, how does one compose the last in a way that seems not to simply break off in stride but to conclude in a summary way?

As the dancers are rehearsing the big ensemble number, "One," which in dramatic terms is a prop song since it belongs to the show for which they are auditioning, one of them, Paul, falls on a turn and hurts his knee.[18] After he has been taken to the hospital, Zach faces the rest and asks the summary question: "What do you do when you can't dance anymore?" The question is intended to evoke responses from the dancers about dancing, and isn't this a musical play about dancing? Their reaction is the show's most popular song, "What I Did for Love," sung at first as a solo by Diana but then by the whole chorus. The undeniable impression is that the song, and the whole episode, is forced, an impression which producer Joseph Papp had from the beginning.

> In Mr. Papp's judgment, Marvin Hamlisch's song "What I Did for Love" did not belong in the musical. Mr. Papp recalled having "a little go-round" with the composer and to this day he can hear Mr. Hamlisch's insistent plea: "Joe, listen, I've got to get something on the charts!"[19]

Hamlisch concurs: "Joe Papp didn't want it. . . . It was written to be a hit. . . . It doesn't fit in as well as the other ones."[20] But why doesn't it? Because, once again, it is inconsistent with the dramatic premise and form of the play, the frame story. Contrary to the opinion of many, *A Chorus Line* is not a show about dancing, but a show about individual characters who happen to dance. If Zach's last question had been asked at the beginning, then the frame would have been constrained in such a way as to dramatize the role of dancing, but there is no such constraint. The stories, and the songs, touch on a great variety of themes and personal experiences, many of which have nothing to do with dance.

The effort to end the frame story drama suitably goes beyond "What I Did for Love" and the final selection into the curtain call. After the stage empties to the applause of the audience, the entire cast reappears after a quick change into opulent gold top hats and coats, dancing the ensemble number to "One." This elaborate curtain call has occasioned a variety of critical comment, an amazing token of the effectiveness of the trick.[21] Is it a stunning revelation to the audience of the great dream of the chorus-line dancer, symbolized by the utter contrast of audition rags and show costume? Then why is the whole cast included, even the losers, whose dreams have been shattered once again? Does it show the audience, in Bennett's words, that "the transformation of people it has come to know as individuals into a mechanical unit is the sad truth of the matter"?[22] Or is it something much simpler, much more traditional, the reprise of a prop song to bring the curtain down, to send the audience home with, to quote Bennett again, "the kind of happy show-biz number they've been waiting for all evening"?[23]

The controversy provokes an important question. Perhaps criticism of the shortcomings of the music in *A Chorus Line,* or more precisely the music drama, is misdirected. Perhaps this musical, coming at the end of three decades in which the role of dancing in the Broadway tradition has grown steadily more significant, from the dream ballets of Rodgers and Hammerstein to Jerome Robbins' dance episodes in *West Side Story,* is the one in which dance succeeds music as the conduit of dramatic meaning. Bennett himself seems to have sought this power in his dancers: "The really good dancers are dramatic dancers. They're not just watching their bodies. Something is going on in their heads."[24] He believed, too, that dance had not only the potential but the duty to be expressive in a dramatic way:

> Choreography is not about steps, just steps, in terms of shows. I like to think I make the best dances I can, but I'm also interested in dancing being right for a character. Most importantly, dancing has to continue the story line. And it's got to have a point of view. It's got to be about something.[25]

But it is one thing to maintain that dance can be expressive of a particular moment or of a particular part of the dramatic action—few who have seen *West Side Story* would argue with that—and quite another to say that dance can carry dramatic action over the course of a two- or three-hour play. Can physical gesture take on character identification or dramatic meaning as easily, and develop them as flexibly, as a musical theme or harmonic progression?

In building *A Chorus Line* as a frame story, Bennett greatly simplified the theoretical problem for himself, since in that form there is little need to carry the action for a long time, only as long as an individual story. Cassie's universally acclaimed solo dance, certainly, is a fine demonstration of how dance might fulfill the drama of an individual story within the frame, as are some of the pantomimic routines in "Montage." And yet, there seem to be few other moments when dance acquires that importance. "For a show built around dancers, 'A Chorus Line' is loath to release any of its meaning through dance," reflects Arlene Croce, the *New Yorker*'s articulate dance critic.[26] It is possible that the premise of the play actually compromises the meaning of individual dances, because it is characters as dancers who perform them. The line between the expressive dance and the "prop dance" runs thin; is what they are doing a dramatic expression of themselves, or are they showing off for Zach?

The dances of *A Chorus Line* provide a spectacular visual element, no doubt, but spectacle by itself is not drama, and in the absence of a consistently dramatic dance, the play must fall back on its songs and lyrics, its music. For its composer and lyricist, the brilliant originality of *A Chorus Line*'s conception proves too great a challenge. Their music, however inventive and memorable at times, fails to make convincing drama out of the frame story.

# CHAPTER 14

# Thriller as Musical

*I've never been conscious of trying to further the theatrical language. It comes from a feeling of not wanting to cover the same material twice or to bore yourself.*[1]

STEPHEN SONDHEIM

When Stephen Sondheim was awarded the Tony for Best Musical of the season in 1988 for *Into the Woods,* Broadway more or less officially recognized a domination of the American musical theater over the last two decades reminiscent of an earlier reign during the 1940s and '50s by Rodgers and Hammerstein. In retrospect, Sondheim seems to have been bred, like an heir apparent, for such a crown. Beginning at age fifteen, he composed a number of "studies" in musical drama under the tutelage of his friend and neighbor in Pennsylvania, Oscar Hammerstein II. His debut on Broadway was the most auspicious imaginable, as the somewhat reluctant lyricist (he wished to be a composer-lyricist from the beginning) for Leonard Bernstein's *West Side Story* (1957) and Jule Styne's *Gypsy* (1959). His first offering as the complete songwriter was a commercial if not artistic success, an adaptation of Plautus called *A Funny Thing Happened on the Way to the Forum* (1962). Yet his domination of the Broadway stage from 1970 onward is difficult to characterize, best described, perhaps, as a triumph of integrity over commercial interest, marked by an unflagging seriousness of purpose and an astounding dramatic range:

In his 13 shows . . . Sondheim has staked out a turf as big as the emotional landscape of post-World War II America. Even when the shows have been set abroad or in the past, their themes have addressed contemporary topics—or universal ones, Sondheim might aver—by way of metaphor. This is particularly true of the Sondheim shows

since 1970. He has treated the travails of modern marriage in "Company," the cor-
rosion of American optimism in "Follies," injustice and revenge in "Sweeney Todd,"
idealism and compromise in "Merrily We Roll Along," and Western imperialism in
"Pacific Overtures."[2]

It is the range that makes choosing a representative work of Sondheim's quite
impossible, much more difficult than choosing one of Rodgers and Hammerstein's. No one would say that the older men wrote the same show many times,
of course, but there are common elements that unite all their great ones, principally the dramatic organization around a resolution of conflict in a romantic
couple along with a contrasting subplot. There is nothing so consistent in Sondheim's plays. "He doesn't duplicate himself, does he?" mused Michael Bennett.
"He'll tackle things no one else would think of. You can't think of any Sondheim show that's like any other."[3] The choice of *Sweeney Todd,* however, is
not entirely capricious. Because it is virtually through-composed, it is the most
ambitious of Sondheim's scores, and it is the only show whose composition and
production he initiated.[4] And while all Sondheim's mature musicals offer severe
challenges in dramaturgy, those inherent in the adaptation of a thriller are particularly formidable, as are the composer's attempts to meet them.

Sondheim's domination of the musical theater differs further from his predecessors' in that it has not been accomplished by overwhelming public success or
critical acclamation. His commercial successes are few, and the critical reception
for each show is invariably divided and controversial. The reaction of Walter
Kerr to *Company* (1970) seems typical of the critical frustration. After describing
a multitude of virtues, he writes:

> Now ask me if I liked the show. I didn't like the show. I admired it, or admired vast
> portions of it, but that is another matter. Admiration stirs in the head; liking sends out
> its signals somewhere lower in the anatomy, the pit of the stomach maybe, and grad-
> ually lets you know that you are happy to have been born, or to have been lucky
> enough to have come tonight.[5]

There has never been any dispute over Sondheim's powers as a lyricist. He is
routinely compared with Lorenz Hart and Cole Porter for sheer virtuosity of
rhyme and construction. The statement of playwright Arthur Laurents, with whom
Sondheim worked closely in *West Side Story, Gypsy,* and the early failure *Anyone Can Whistle* (1964), contends that he surpassed even those masters in his
deeper understanding of the lyric's dramatic responsibilities:

> Without question, Steve is the best Broadway lyricist, past and present. Any lyric he
> has written can be quoted to illustrate this contention. Steve is the only lyricist who
> writes a lyric that could only be sung by the character for which it was designed,
> who never pads with unnecessary fillers, who never sacrifices meaning or intention
> for a clever rhyme, and who knows that a lyric is the shortest of one-act plays, with
> a beginning, a middle and an end. Moreover, he knows how the words must sit on a

musical phrase. His approach to writing for the musical theater is nothing less than remarkable.[6]

Yet the same voice pronounces a devastating sentence upon the first Sondheim works directed by Hal Prince, which include *Company, Follies* (1971), and *A Little Night Music* (1973), award winners all:

> I can only point to the shows that Steve and Hal have done together and say that they are all cold . . . which may be their aim. But I've never liked the theory of alienation. I think it's an intellectual conceit. The gloss and technical excellence of those shows should have made you care.[7]

Most of the criticism has been directed at Sondheim the composer. The charge: a general lack of feeling, a "salon music that revels in an Old World sophistication, with hardly a trace of jazz that excited Gershwin, Weill, and Bernstein."[8] One occasionally hears that Sondheim's melodies are "unhummable," a characterization which incenses the composer.

> I don't understand it entirely. Quite often the stuff I write is not simple. I think I'm getting more and more accepted, but sometimes my work is too unexpected to sustain itself very firmly in the commercial theater. The only shows of mine since *West Side Story* and *Gypsy* that paid back their investments and went into profits on Broadway were *A Funny Thing Happened on the Way to the Forum, Company,* and *A Little Night Music.* It would be nice to have a smash.[9]

Sondheim's vocal melodies are neither "unhummable" nor unmemorable in the perjorative sense, but they can be difficult to remember on just a few hearings. The cause is not extreme chromaticism in the melodic line, nor his much vaunted dissonance, but rather an asymmetrical phrasing, and most of all a harmonic style that is essentially non-functional.

Until quite recently, the harmonic idioms of all American popular styles have been firmly based on functional harmony, the harmonic language that has dominated Western music since the seventeenth century. Chords are chosen not only to harmonize with the prevalent melodic note but also to construct relationships with the chords preceding and following them. Progressions have a syntax, an expected order. Such an idiom is known as "functional" because the various chords within a key have assigned "tasks" or "functions" in the construction of harmonic "sentences" or progressions. Functional progressions have an integrity all their own, quite distinct from the melody which they set or the rhythm with which they are imbued. For that reason functional harmony has great power to create the articulations so necessary to music, and when joined to a melody, these articulations offer powerful memory cues for the listener. The chords themselves seem to direct the melody to its predestined goal.

It is no accident that Sondheim counts Ravel, Prokofiev, Copland, and Britten among his most important models,[10] for his harmonic language derives from the

non-functional progressions of early twentieth-century impressionism and its derivatives. In *Sweeney Todd,* except in the parody numbers, there is an almost
complete absence of harmonic syntax, conventionally ordered progression, on
the low level of structure.

**Ex. 14–1** Stephen Sondheim, *Sweeney Todd,* "The Ballad of Sweeney Todd" (No. 1), mm. 1–25.

Here in the opening number of the opera,[11] the tonal center of F-sharp minor is clearly established, not by any harmonic progression but rather by a sustained pedal in the bass. The first change of chord (m. 4) makes little sense in a functional idiom. The E natural, stressed in the upper voice, is dissonant against the

D in the bass, and does not act as a leading tone to F-sharp because it is the lowered seventh step. The vocal melody is completely diatonic, yet receives no accompanying harmonic articulations, not even in measure six where some form of authentic cadence might be expected. In a structural sense, the notes of the melody are simply ignored by the harmony.

On the higher levels of structure, the chords may form a functional progression. In the "Ballad," for example (Ex. 14-1), the long F-sharp in the bass moves to D (m. 15), then to C-sharp, then to F-sharp, sketching the conventional progression of i-VI-V-i. But the harmonic rhythm is so slow that the syntactic relationships are strained, and the progression still does not coordinate with the vocal melody; the return to the tonic occurs at the beginning of the last phrase (m. 24), even though the sung notes do not imply the F-sharp harmony that arrives there. Elsewhere in the opera, even the high-level progressions in *Sweeney Todd* are non-functional, and harmonic organization and coherence are accomplished with sustained pedal tones and inconspicuous ostinato figures. These alternative methods of musical organization were perhaps the focus of Sondheim's compositional studies with Milton Babbitt, undertaken after he graduated from Williams College. "I learned from Milton the means of holding an ear over a period of time, how you keep someone listening for 45 minutes so that at the end they feel they've heard a piece." [12]

The great advantage of such an idiom is the enlarged harmonic vocabulary and wealth of fresh harmonic progressions so familiar from Debussy and Ravel. Non-functional harmony is the true source of Sondheim's free dissonances so often noticed by listeners and critics, for the rigid coordination of melodic and harmonic articulations is no longer necessary. Traditional rules of harmony control dissonance to maintain the clarity of functional progressions. When those progressions are absent, dissonant intervals can become the norm, the stable terms of a composition. Notice that the first verse melody of "The Ballad of Sweeney Todd" (Ex. 14-1, m. 25) ends on the second scale step, G-sharp dissonant against the F-sharp tonic in the bass. This can make aural sense only when it is heard as the same ninth that opened the opera (see m. 1), established then and there as a relatively stable sound.

The non-functional idiom encourages Sondheim's penchant for modal melodies, founded on scales other than the traditional major and minor. The traditional scales have "tendency tones" built in to reinforce the syntax of the supporting functional harmony. But if there is little harmonic syntax to sustain, the tendency tones can be altered or dispensed with entirely. The opening phrase of "The Ballad of Sweeney Todd" (Ex. 14-1) has a tune clearly centered on F-sharp, yet the lowered seventh, E natural, is used in place of the more functional E-sharp. Modal tunes are particularly appropriate for *Sweeney Todd*, set in nineteenth-century London, since they can be reminiscent of old-fashioned English folk music, and lend a musical substance to the fiction that the tale is some hoary legend.

Of course, in abandoning traditional functional harmony Sondheim gives up a great deal, particularly its power to create and sustain the harmonic tensions and resolutions which have been so important to musical expression in the Western art. On the highest levels of structure, it means that in Sondheim the motion away from a tonal center and back may be a colorful event, but does not generally produce, by itself, a significant tension. The lovely "Green Finch and Linnet Bird" of Act I, for example, contains several modulations away from its main tonal center of F. Each return is marked by the main motive, but this motive is used in the other keys as well, and none of the returns has any trace of the high-level resolution or arrival heard in, say, "Tonight" of *West Side Story*. The absence of high-level harmonic functions may explain why Sondheim, after taking care to organize the opening scenes of *Sweeney Todd* around the tonal center of F-sharp, does not mind ending the opera in G, even though the same "Ballad" is the final piece. The penultimate piece is also in G. Apparently the lower-level connections are more important to him than any overall tonal organization.[13]

Without functional harmony, the onus of musical tension falls on other elements. The middle section of the opening "Ballad" begins as follows.

**Ex. 14–2** Stephen Sondheim, *Sweeney Todd*, "The Ballad of Sweeney Todd" (No. 1), mm. 102–9.

Although this music changes the tonal center from F-sharp to E, the bass register is entirely forgotten, so that the change can hardly assume structural significance. The important element is the phrase rhythm. The first measures establish a four-bar period, which is carried on in the second phrase (mm. 106-9). But the rhythm of ''Back of his smile, under his word'' already suggests a potential foreshortening of the phrase, an acceleration of the rhythm. This suggestion shortly erupts into the climactic entrance of the title character.

**Ex. 14–3** Stephen Sondheim, *Sweeney Todd*, "The Ballad of Sweeney Todd" (No. 1), mm. 128–43.

The F-sharp harmony returns well in advance of the true arrival of the climax (m. 136), and has little to do with it. It eases the transition, nothing more. But Sondheim has drawn almost every other element into play: texture, in the slow adding of the choral voices and in the withholding of the bass register; harmonic dissonance, not in the functional sense but in the purer sense of dissonant intervals in the choral writing, particularly in the sustained final chord (mm. 132-35); rhythm, in the use of the short periods predicted earlier (mm. 128-29); and dynamics and orchestration. In a traditional harmonic idiom, such marshaling of forces might sound grossly out of proportion, even histrionic. Without the idiom, they are just sufficient, and make a very satisfying musical climax.

When Sondheim restricts himself to only a few of these musical forces, the effects are much more understated. Sweeney Todd's first aria, ''There Was a Barber,'' one of the dramatic linchpins of the opera, depends entirely on phrase rhythm and melodic contour for its effects. The song is in two sections. The first describes an unknown barber married to a beautiful, virtuous woman. Todd is, of course, describing his own past. It is fairly even in tension and ends inconclusively. The second begins as the first, then expands its melody.

**Ex. 14–4** Stephen Sondheim, *Sweeney Todd*, ''There Was a Barber'' (No. 2), mm. 229–44.

There is no question about the sense of climax at the end of this passage, but what produces it? Certainly not the chord beneath. The high D on the last ''beautiful'' is the highest note Todd sings, but that alone would not be sufficient. It is rather the preparation for that upward contour by the phrase rhythm.

How are phrases even articulated without a syntactic harmony to indicate beginnings and endings? Sondheim relies on characteristic rhythms consistently placed. The three eighth notes that begin the vocal melody are made into a clear anacrusis (upbeats), for example, by the onset of the accompaniment in measure 230. That must be the downbeat, the beginning of a phrase event. Then the harmony changes on the 6/8 measure, "beautiful." A return to the G harmony (m. 233) along with the same motive in the melody indicates the second phrase. So the listener has one rhythmic figure associated with phrase beginnings, another, the dotted figure, with endings. In effect, Sondheim has defined his "phrasing grammar" for this particular song.[14] Yet no sooner is it defined than it becomes purposefully ambiguous. What should be the ending of the second phrase is in precisely the same rhythmic position as the 6/8 measure, and has the same pitches and harmonic change underneath, but the note rhythm of the melody has been altered to accommodate more syllables, and now sounds suspiciously like a phrase beginning. This is the justfication for a most subtle acceleration in the phrase rhythm, the shortening lengths of the phrases. The third has no "ending" at all. Instead, the fourth anticipates itself by augmenting the three pick-up eighth notes into quarters ("Then there was") which lead into the downbeat of four eighths.[15]

| First | "There was another man" | (mm. 229-32) | 26 |
| Second | "A pious vulture" | (mm. 232-35) | 23 |
| Third | "Removed the barber" | (mm. 235-36) | 12 |
| Fourth | "Then there was nothing" | (mm. 237-42) | 31 |

**Fig. 14–1** Phrase diagram of "There Was a Barber," second verse. Numerals in the right column count the number of eighth note beats in each phrase.

The fourth phrase goes on for what seems an excruciatingly long time, because it denies the ending rhythm as Sondheim has defined it, denies it against the insistent pattern of ever shortening phrases, until the peak of the melody, "beautiful" once again, makes it resound with feeling.[16] The acceleration of the phrase rhythm, free and gentle because of the lack of strong meter and Sondheim's ingenious preparation, has created Todd's slow but dangerous fire.

The use of harmony in "There Was a Barber" shows that changes of chord in a non-functional idiom are neither unimportant nor haphazard. Indeed, the clarity of the most musically dramatic moment in the whole opera depends on a chord change (see Ex. 14-15). In "There Was a Barber" the harmonic changes help to define the phrase grammar. But in a syntactic harmonic accompaniment, there would have been no need to define one, for its functions are already defined by the culture. Paradoxically, when non-functional harmony must articulate structure, the harmonic changes often must be more carefully deployed than if they were functional.

Such a harmonic idiom lends itself to certain types of expression and not others. "Mood" and "atmosphere" are likely strengths that come to mind first, and it is no surprise that such powers would attract Sondheim, for his ability to fashion a musical ethos of a stage work is perhaps unsurpassed in the Broadway tradition. "Once you have a musical atmosphere—which could be anything from a running figure to a chord change—you have a way to start some melodic ideas. They're not related to a conscious lyrical phrase, but it gives you a basic melodic rhythm and that can spring into other things."[17] The highly extroverted dissonances which the idiom allows contribute mightily to the acerbic cynicism that pervades *Company*, the sense of contrivance in *A Little Night Music*, and foreboding, mysterious evil in *Sweeney Todd*.

"Atmosphere" is, in this sense, opposite to dramatic action, and perhaps it is this preference for atmosphere, with a coherent musical style to support it, that makes Sondheim's mature shows seem like tableaux, an impression that becomes explicit with *Sunday in the Park With George*, in which tableau merges with drama. But there is a corresponding lack of overall tension that makes one scene demand the next. The music is intent upon atmosphere, feeling, idea, but not action. When Joseph Kerman writes, "Each of the short scenes gets something done, but their effect is of a 'slice of life' with a drabness and incoherence characteristic enough of ordinary living,"[18] could he not be describing *Company* instead of Debussy's *Pelleas et Melisande?*

The exception is *Sweeney Todd*. This tale of an honest barber who returns to take revenge on a corrupt judge and, failing that, madly turns his razor on anyone who happens along, this horrific thriller would not seem to be a likely choice for a composer whose style seems ill-tuned to complicated action. Yet, Sondheim chose this story on his own.

He was in London in 1973 when *Gypsy* was revived with Angela Lansbury. On a free evening he went to see a melodrama called *Sweeney Todd*. "I'd always been interested in Grand Guignol and had heard about this play . . . I went to see it, thought it was terrific and bought all the published versions—which were all terrible."[19] They all derive from a play by a popular Victorian dramatist, one George Dibdin Pitt, written in the 1840s but never published. The source of the story is unknown. Montague Slater, editor of a 1928 printed version, suspects that it was a popular legend, since "Pitt usually borrowed the plots of his plays, and this one seems too good for him to have invented."[20] Others cite a novel by Thomas Preskett Prest,[21] and playwright Christopher Bond claims that Pitt "based it on a 'penny dreadful,' a newssheet containing sensational descriptions of depravity, violence and grotesque murder with a few lines of pious editorial humbug at the end . . . ."[22]

The play has enjoyed a curious popularity over the years. Brian J. Burton added music and lyrics to it in 1962, and a film version was directed by Herb Roland and produced by the Canadian Broadcasting Corporation in 1972. The version that Sondheim enjoyed so much, however, was written by Bond. It is a play that not only transmits the core plot from Pitt but borrows heavily from other melodramatic sources to make a better play.

I have "borrowed" from, amongst others, *The Count of Monte Cristo, The Revenger's Tragedy, The Spanish Tragedy,* the family green-grocer, and Shakespeare, as well as Dibdin-Pitt's original melodrama. My object has been to add to the chair and the pies an exciting story, characters that are large but real, and situations that, given a mad world not unlike our own, are believable.[23]

He succeeds fairly well. In the mostly Pitt versions,[24] Sweeney Todd is simply a madman who kills his customers to enrich himself—a pure villain. Even as such he is incredibly overdrawn by standards of modern taste; here the too-often used critical phrase "cartoon character" really fits, for, as he points his pistol at his accomplice, Mrs. Lovett, he actually gloats, "Now say your prayers,"[25] anticipating Yosemite Sam and Bugs Bunny by a century.

In Bond, there is something of a dramatic motivation. Todd first appears just having been returned to London by the sailor Anthony. After an encounter with a crazed beggar women who seems to know him, he meets Mrs. Lovett in her pie shop under his old establishment. She recounts how the former tenant, a handsome barber, was transported for life by a judge who desired his wife. Then, feigning repentence, the judge lured the wife, Lucy, to his house where he raped her as part of the fun at a masked ball. She took poison, leaving her daughter Johanna to become the judge's ward. Todd now reveals himself to Mrs. Lovett as the barber and together they plan his revenge on the judge and his beadle who aided him. Meanwhile, the sailor Anthony tells Todd that he has fallen in love with a beautiful ward of a certain Judge Turpin, who of course is Johanna, Todd's daughter, but the judge intends to marry Johanna himself. An early opportunity for revenge presents itself to Todd when the judge himself arrives for a shave, but as he is about to slash his throat, Anthony barges in to announce that Johanna has agreed to elope with him. The judge leaves indignantly, swearing to lock his ward away. Todd, his chance lost, now swears revenge on all comers until a second opportunity arrives. Mrs. Lovett, privy to this confession, sees a new sort of filling for her failing pie business and the curtain falls on the mad laughter of them both.

The second act opens upon a prosperous pie business. Mrs. Lovett has even taken on a hired boy, Tobias Ragg. When Anthony finds Johanna imprisoned in an asylum, Todd sends him off disguised as a wigmaker in search of hair to free her. At the same time he lures the judge back to his tonsorial parlor with a letter telling about Anthony's rescue. Then the beadle comes around to inspect the bakeshop because of complaints about the curious stench. Todd tricks him into sitting in his special chair, and down the chute he goes. But as Todd waits for the judge to arrive, the mad beggar woman enters. Fearing to be caught with questionable company once again, he slashes her throat just before the judge arrives. After he kills the judge, Mrs. Lovett's screams summon him to the bakeshop, where he discovers that the old beggar woman was his wife Lucy. Enraged, he throws Mrs. Lovett into the oven. As he mourns his error, the boy Tobias, now half-mad with discovery of what has been going on in the shop, appears from the shadows, picks up Todd's razor, and slashes Todd's throat as Anthony, Johanna, and the rest of the company run on.

When Sondheim inquired into the rights, he found that Richard Barr and Charles Woodward were already negotiating to put on the play in New York. After Sondheim proposed a musical version, they agreed to wait until he had finished up his commitment to *Pacific Overtures,* which opened in 1976. Hugh Wheeler adapted the Bond version quite faithfully into a book from which Sondheim could work. The premiere of *Sweeney Todd* was March 1, 1979, at the Uris Theater.

The decision to set such a thriller brought with it at least two pervading problems. First, how to manage a story of such pacing and complexity without having it bog down in hours of music? Music dramas with plots of comparable complexity do exist, of course, but they are mostly comedies, where the quick pacing is essential to comic effect. The comic elements in *Sweeney Todd* are very important, but it is clear that Sondheim wanted to preserve the dark tone and atmosphere of the original, and he recognized the pacing difficulty: "It is highly plotted. You can't spend a lot of time saying, 'It's a lovely day today.' "[26] Second, how does one prevent the story from overwhelming the musical commentary that accompanies it? There is no question that the increased pace toward the end of the second act and the surprise conclusion are stunning when first encountered, but what happens the second time around, when the listener knows the end?

The plot complexity demands a musical construction that can accommodate the large number of significant events without sacrificing either clarity or pacing. In short, it demands a unified musical continuity.

**Ex. 14–5** Stephen Sondheim, *Sweeney Todd,* "No Place Like London" (No. 2), mm. 6–30.

This excerpt from the first number of the opera after the "Prologue" is brief, and yet it contains three characterizations and two important events. At the beginning, Anthony sings happily of his return to his most wondrous city, his melody and its accompaniment of altered chords echoing the bells of London. When Sweeney Todd interrupts him, his bitter mockery of Anthony's sentiment is immediately felt in his substitution of the G-flat for Anthony's G natural, changing the mode of the tune from major to minor, and in the mysterious chromatic accompaniment that will come to stand for his obsession. Then, in the underscoring, the opening motive of "There Was a Barber" is heard (m. 22), although its significance is yet undefined. This music is suddenly interrupted by the appearance of the Beggar Woman (m. 26), her depravity and her insanity both imaged by her descending, chromatic motive beginning at a tritone over the bass. All this in 25 measures, with no stop in the musical flow.

This dexterity in handling extended musical forms, which Sondheim traces back to his work with Bernstein on *West Side Story*,[27] allows the composer to include many events into each number, rather than one or two. Thus there are not too many little pieces to be organized for the listener, and fewer higher-level structures than there might have been.[28] The intermittent snips from "The Ballad of Sweeney Todd" not only offer chorus-like comments on the action, but set the musical boundaries of each scene, as well as of the opera as a whole.

Essential to this continuity are leitmotifs for each character and important dramatic theme. "The notion of using motifs is to pique the audience's memory, to remind them that this theme represents that idea or emotion. They're guideposts along the way. In a sustained piece you have to do that. . . ."[29] In other words, Sondheim's use of leitmotifs is purely Wagnerian: they contribute to the musical-dramatic expression at the same time they build a thematic unity into the musical texture.

The heavy reliance on a texture of leitmotifs means that the accompaniment of the singer may well be as important at times as the music that he sings. Counterpoint is therefore an essential aspect of this musical thriller. The ostinato figure that underlies "There Was a Barber," for example, is responsible for the particular tone and subliminal unease of that statement.

**Ex. 14–6**  Stephen Sondheim, *Sweeney Todd*, "There Was a Barber" (No. 2), mm. 215–17.

That is because it derives from the source of mystery, the ostinato in "The Ballad of Sweeney Todd."[30]

Fig. 14–2 Comparison of accompanimental figures from "The Ballad of Sweeney Todd" and "There Was a Barber."

It is equally important that this figure, and the end of Todd's song, merge with the "obsession" leitmotif which accompanied his very first words after the prologue.

Ex. 14–7 Stephen Sondheim, *Sweeney Todd,* "There Was a Barber" (No. 2), mm. 241–44.

This, too, is formed from "The Ballad," from the brassy interpolation that occurs between each of Todd's phrases as he sings after rising from the grave, the musical climax of the prologue (see Ex. 14-3, mm. 142-43).

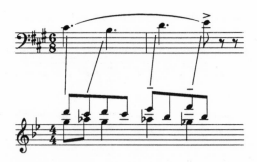

**Fig. 14–3** Transformation of "obsession" motive from "The Ballad of Sweeney Todd" to the conclusion of "There Was a Barber."

Counterpoint, then, is the chief means of developing the musical-dramatic action in a manner sufficiently economical for the pace of the plot. Because leitmotifs may be used as accompaniment, they have great power to color what is sung in words around them. When Mrs. Lovett begins to recount the tale of Todd's misfortune, she reprises, logically enough, "There Was a Barber."

**Ex. 14–8** Stephen Sondheim, *Sweeney Todd,* "There Was a Barber" (No. 4), mm. 5–7.

How quickly essential information is conveyed in these three measures. Sondheim's clever alteration of "And he was beautiful" immediately hints at Mrs. Lovett's longstanding attraction to Todd, which is made more explicit later. At the same time, even though she sings Todd's earlier melody, it is missing its haunting effect, because the crucial ostinato figure is gone, replaced by sustained chords.

Counterpoint also quickens the pace of certain ensembles for comic effect. The comedy of the opera is of many kinds and has many sources, and greatly helps to justify the unflagging pace of action. There is the grisly sort, of course, which brings the curtain down on the first act in "A Little Priest," but Sondheim's humor appeals more often to the intellect. He sets the title line from "The Worst Pies in London," Mrs. Lovett's first song, to a romantic waltz melody. He parodies the venerable British ballad when the beadle, about to inspect the bakeshop, sits at a harmonium and sings, "I am a lass who alas loves a lad who alas has a lass in Canterbury." At other times, however, the comic effect derives from clever use of contrapuntal texture. The comments of the bystanders and customers in "Pirelli's Miracle Elixir" and "Mrs. Lovett's Meat Pies" (the second a contrafactum of the first), are set in counterpoint against the sales pitch of Tobias Ragg, making the construction itself funny.

There is one other ensemble which actually compresses the action in a way that finds virtue in the inherent pace difficulties of the thriller. The one significant change introduced by Sondheim and Wheeler into Bond's play is to bring on stage the early encounters between Anthony and Johanna. The first of these elicits the purest love song Sondheim has written for the theater, Anthony's "Johanna."[31] The second shows them secretly meeting in her room, planning what to do next.

**Ex. 14–9**  Stephen Sondheim, *Sweeney Todd*, "Kiss Me" (No. 13), mm. 1–9.

Here it is the counterpoint between the vocal parts that increases the pace of the action. The opening music, especially Johanna's, is comic in effect, like a patter-song, but the expression changes abruptly at measure eight, a change which comes naturally out of Anthony's exasperation at getting her to listen to him. At the same time the suddenness of it, and the chromatic C natural in the vocal parts for the first time, shows some real feeling in what appears to be comic relief. Then Johanna resumes her fretting and the music recapitulates until this point:

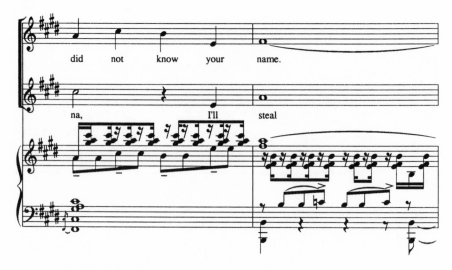

**Ex. 14–10**   Stephen Sondheim, *Sweeney Todd*, "Kiss Me" (No. 13), mm. 18–27.

Now the pace of musical events picks up. Johanna, comprehending at last, responds to Anthony's melody, filling up beats that were vacant or sustained before. By measure twenty there is motion on every eighth note before "Kiss Me" resumes. The rhythmic acceleration is played out again, intensifying its effect. Much more important, however—and here Sondheim teaches another advantage of his harmonic idiom—is how the chords begin to move after sustaining a single harmony, E major, since the beginning. All this reaches a musical climax at measure 23, just when Anthony begins a reprise of his love theme. This is a moment of true contrapuntal art, a coordination of rhythmic preparation, of the two singing together for the first time, and of the ineffable rightness of Anthony's sustained theme which cancels all memory of pattersong, all concentrated on a single point of time. It all builds, of course, the dramatic image of the besieged couple who are so much in love that they cannot take their own danger seriously enough. Curiously, it is the duet's compression of several dramatic necessities, information, and feeling in a brief number that creates its effect, one of the most enduring of the opera.

There seems little to complain about and much to admire in *Sweeney Todd*'s first act. There is no piece without its dramatic function and the thrilling plot loses none of its power to absorb. The second act is disturbed by some puzzling problems of pacing just opposite to what one might expect from the plot: the music appears to run out of episodes; at least, the "Johanna" ensemble and Mrs. Lovett's music-hall number "By the Sea" add little to the story. On the whole, however the musical construction of *Sweeney Todd* is a triumph of counterpoint and imagination.

But the craft and continuity of Sondheim's music insures only that it is able to carry the plot of the thriller. Does it make of the story something it could not be on its own? Does the music allow, even reward, a second and third hearing of the opera?

Sondheim needs to go beyond his intellectual cues such as the old "Dies Irae" sequence in "The Ballad of Sweeney Todd" and other places, and the theme linking the Beggar Woman to her true identity. Music needs to be made the substance of a dramatic issue. For Sondheim, that issue is obsession.

> I was using the story as a metaphor for any kind of obsession. Todd is a tragic hero in the classic sense that Oedipus is. He dies in the end because of a certain kind of fatal knowledge: he realizes what he has been doing.[32]

Obsession takes on the musical identity of a leitmotif, drawn from the opening ballad, and first given clear identity in the confession song "There Was a Barber." But Todd's horrific progress from an obsession with revenge on the judge and his beadle to an obsession with revenge on all humanity, at any cost, must be made palpable in musical terms. That is the reason for "Epiphany."

"Epiphany" is perhaps Sondheim's best improvement on Bond's melodrama. In Bond, this progress of Todd is without motivation. When Judge Turpin escapes Todd's razor in Act I, the barber simply says: "A second chance may come. It must, it shall! Until it does, I'll pass the time on less honored throats."[33] Compare how the sudden entrances of the bass under the "obsession motive" convey Todd's inexpressible rage in the Sondheim version.

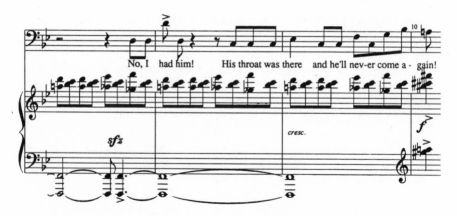

**Ex. 14–11** Stephen Sondheim, *Sweeney Todd,* "Epiphany" (No. 17), mm. 4–10.

Then his resolution follows, and his mad explanation of why all deserve to die has yet a musical rationale.

**Ex. 14–12**  Stephen Sondheim, *Sweeney Todd*, "Epiphany" (No. 17), mm. 27–32.

For the first time, Todd sings his obsession. The A, B-flat, and C setting "all of the whole human race" are the notes and intervals of the obsession leitmotif, amplified by the accompaniment. The progress is shown in musical terms. It is also given depth by a new theme growing out of the lyricism which sets his oath.

**Ex. 14–13**  Stephen Sondheim, *Sweeney Todd,* "Epiphany" (No. 17), mm. 38–44.

It is odd that the theme invoking Johanna sets a variety of lyrics, invoking Lucy, invoking vengeance in general. At the end it crowns Todd's insane proclamation of himself.

**Ex. 14–14** Stephen Sondheim, *Sweeney Todd,* "Epiphany" (No. 17), mm. 75–83.

The last chords show once again the peculiarly expressive powers of Sondheim's dissonant harmonic idiom. The fortissimo B-flat chord in measure 82 has no dissonance in it. For that reason, it stands out against the whole composition, interpreting Todd's last high F, "joy," with a terrifying clarity, only to give way once again to the diminished octave (m. 83) characteristic of the obsession motive.

"Epiphany" is the central moment of the music drama. After this, all is really denouement. The corresponding event in the second act is the revelation to Todd of what Sondheim calls the "fatal knowledge."

**Ex. 14–15** Stephen Sondheim, *Sweeney Todd,* "Final Scene" (No. 29), mm. B, 1–4.

The Beggar Woman's leitmotif and the lyrical theme from "Epiphany" have
always been related, both derived from long descending half-steps, but only here
is the relationship made explicit. The inner voice counterpoint is maintained as
Sondheim succeeds one motive with the other, but, ironically, this dramatic moment is revealed most clearly by the harmony. The beggar woman's motive has
always begun with a tritone over the bass, while the lyric theme began as a
consonant third factor. When the chord changes from a harmony based on C in
measure one to one on D-sharp in measure three, the melodic F-sharp is brilliantly reinterpreted and identified, matching the horrible realization in Todd's
mind. The only thing missing: he is not singing.

**Ex. 14–16** Stephen Sondheim, *Sweeney Todd,* "Final Scene" (No. 29), mm. 5–8e.

Sondheim's idea of having Todd sing at last by choking on the lyrical theme in halting fashion is a beautiful one, but it is defeated by the counterpoint, of all things. First, the complex inner part writing, and then Mrs. Lovett's babbling at much faster speed steal the listener's attention and obscure what should be the paramount expression. Even in the purely instrumental rendition (mm. 1-4), the effect of the essential chord change is almost too subtle. The impact is also diffused because the dramatic associations with the lyrical theme are not clear. What exactly does it mean? Is it the price of revenge, or the sorrow at the loss of another loved one?

The opera ends with Todd's reprise of the first section of "There Was a Barber," followed by his death at the hands of Tobias and a recapitulation of the opening ballad by the cast. Todd's death seems necessary in some vague sense of tragic justice, but to use Tobias as the instrument is unconvincing. It is clear that the boy has a maternal affection for Mrs. Lovett, best expressed in the lovely "Not While I'm Around" in the second act, but by that time it seems too late, contrived. If he had given some sign of his deep gratitude when she fed his ravenous hunger with pies in the first act, that thread might have held.

The reprise of "There Was a Barber" also falls short of its intention. Since it is immediately followed by "The Ballad of Sweeney Todd," the reprise creates a structural symmetry with the beginning of the opera, but what does it offer besides elegance of form? What does it do for the moment? It recalls what the opera was about, of course, but such a reminder seems hardly necessary just after the disaster, and there is no transformation or alteration in the music suggesting that Todd has been changed, or that he has learned anything since then. One wonders whether Todd cared more for his wife or his justice. If the former, then the reprise is lacking in grief; if the latter, the scene of horrible recognition loses its power. The instructive comparison with this moment is the reprise of "Somewhere" in *West Side Story*. That song communicates what Tony and Maria have lost—their love, their hope for a life together—in musical terms that show how that loss grows from the tragic story. The transformation in setting and the extension at the end differentiate the new context of the song without losing its accumulated meaning. When Sondheim's finale fades, the question of what Todd has lost still lingers.

A number of writers criticized *Sweeney Todd* for a lack of dramatic focus. "The horrors are not entirely Grand Guignol jokes. They are not entirely tragic statements about the human condition, or protests of social rottenness, or studies of abnormal psychology. They attach themselves at one point or another to all of those things, but without a real hold on them."[34] Director Harold Prince fairly admitted as much: "I suppose people who are collaborating should be after the same thing, but Steven and I were obviously not with respect to *Sweeney*. I think it's also about impotence. . . . The reason that the ensemble is used the way it is, the unifying emotion for the entire company, is shared impotence. Obviously, Sweeney's is the most dramatic, to justify all those murders."[35] The disjunction may have had its effect on the New York production as a whole, but when the music and libretto are considered alone, the opera is admirably consistent in its musical dramatic point. Sondheim's idea of Sweeney obsessed is there in the notes for all to hear, but presented so subtly that it is too easily missed or overpowered by other aspects of stage production. A more sympathetic production would surely make this theme more powerful.

Within the purview of Sondheim's career it is surprising that *Sweeney Todd*, surely one of his most brilliant musical creations, is the one show that ignores all his most cherished principles of musical theater. Take the notion of converting a legitimate play:

> Now lots of things can be a challenge—such as making a musical out of "Pygmalion." But personally, as much as I enjoyed "My Fair Lady," I don't think the challenge was really worth it. If I'd been asked to do it, I'd have said no. It was a fine play, so why mess around with it?[36]

*Sweeney Todd*, of course, comes from a play which the composer thought was "terrific." Next, the uses of rhyming in lyric:

> One function of rhyme is that it shows intelligence and a controlled state of mind. . . . For the songs for the character of Fredrik, the lawyer in *A Little Night Music* . . . I used heavy rhyming because he is a man who rationalizes everything and does a lot of thinking.[37]

By this standard, Tobias Ragg merits a doctorate in literature for his masterful "Pirelli's Miracle Elixir," and yet even the stage directions describe him as a "simple-minded assistant." On the musical reprise:

I find the notion that the same lyric can apply in the first and the second act *very* suspect. Most of the time the character has moved beyond, particularly if you're telling a story of any weight or density.[38]

Yet *Sweeney Todd,* with leitmotifs as the basis for its musical continuity, is a study in reprises. Finally, in a discussion of *West Side Story,* Sondheim's view of the theater's dependence on character:

. . . the show isn't very good . . . because the characters are necessarily one-dimensional. They're not people. What lasts in the theater is character, and there are no characters in *West Side,* nor can there be.[39]

How many "types" are there in *The Demon Barber of Fleet Street?*

Now it is not really fair to put Sondheim on trial as drama theorist, for his calling is a much higher one, and if these comments dating mostly from the early 1970s sound extraordinarily doctrinaire, perhaps it is because they come on the heels of three award-winning shows—*Company, Follies,* and *A Little Night Music*—that reflect very well that atmospheric, static sort of drama that Sondheim's impressionistic style serves so well. But how remarkable it is that the composer could adapt such a style and predilection to the packed action of a thriller!

It seems more remarkable that he would go after such a project himself, without prodding from writers or producers who could not have realized the enormity of the musical task. But then, Sondheim has been accused of being intentionally and outlandishly innovative, of tackling "things no one else would think of," and all of his mature works contain a dramatic problem that appeared insoluble from the start: the end of *Company,* the central theme of personal histories in *Follies,* the reverse chronology in *Merrily We Roll Along,* the great chasm of time and mood between the acts of *Sunday in the Park with George.*

To every innovation, Sondheim can bring to bear the formidable power of his lyrics, which at their best go beyond the cleverness and jocularity of a Hart or Porter. Alan Rich described the experience of listening to an evening of Sondheim's music: ". . . you constantly found yourself *thinking*—about words, about music, about great singers singing great songs. It's not such a bad thing, now, is it—being treated in the theater as if you just might be a grownup with a grownup's intelligence?"[40] But can the musical theater consist of thinking alone, without feeling? The matter of Sondheim's music is brought round once again, for in the end, the vitality of the work depends on its music, the language of feeling, even more than its lyrics.

Specifically, the fate of Sondheim's works rests on their vocal melodies, what the singers have to sing, and of all musical aspects simple melody is the deepest mystery. No one understands it. There is no theory that accounts for melodic invention, that distinguishes the profoundly great from the mundane. "Sondheim, side by side or upside down or rightside up, is simply defective in invention. He can supply the necessary changes for numbers like the opening chorus or the patter songs, which are really only matters of mild rhythmic acuteness, music which need not be—and isn't—memorable in itself. But when melody is absolutely required, as in the love songs, Sondheim just spins series of notes, which could just as easily be other notes."[41] A great deal of Stanley Kauffmann's impression derives from the harmonic idiom, whose lack of syntax makes the tunes at times seem equally undirected. But he touches on a severe critical question, whether Sondheim's music is capable of the deep emotions certain dramatic situations require. The paucity of popular hits, compared to, say, Rodgers and Hammerstein, could be a symptom, and the excuse that the songs are too closely wed to the situation for them to stand on their own will not do, not for the whole corpus. The music and lyrics of "I Got Plenty o' Nuttin'," "To Life," even "Non più andrai," for that matter, relate specifically to their situations, yet as separate songs and tunes they have done all right. Does so singular a harmonic idiom require a period of acculturation, perhaps, or is it fundamentally inappropriate?

If any show could make apology for Sondheim's emotional power, it would be *Sweeney Todd*. The love music for Anthony seems undeniably right, and even if the audience is never sure whether Todd feels more for his vengeful obsession than for his wife, the melodic climax in the first-act version of "There Was a Barber" shows what is in the style's capablilty.

All operas are flawed, of course, and Sondheim's shows, because they reach higher than any other current Broadway composer's, seem to ask for more severe critical standards. Thus their faults eclipse their virtues, but their virtues are nevertheless formidable. They all have a dramatic integrity unsurpassed in the American musical theater, untainted by gimmicks or star vehicles.[42] They never insult the listener's intelligence, and give back much for the effort the listener contributes, rewards, perhaps, other than emotional ones. Sondheim may well be Broadway's answer to Eric Bentley, who criticized the tradition in particular and opera in general as an unthinking medium. His place in American musical culture is indeed special, if not unique. One test of the vitality of contemporary music is to wonder who are the composers to whom the listening public eagerly looks for a new composition. Who else but Stephen Sondheim?

# CHAPTER 15

# Epilogue

A statistician might well be uncomfortable with conclusions drawn from a sample of sixteen about a population of more than a thousand. Musical plays, however, like other art works, are not like voters, and the power and character of an artistic tradition can hardly be judged by methods of random sampling. Most plays will have barely closed before they are forgotten, but some out of the thousand will make a more lasting impression and bear upon subsequent productions. A very few will become pillars of the tradition, to be heard and studied by everyone who thereafter participates in it; some of them have been the concern of this book. Since their influence on the tradition is out of all proportion to their number, it is fair to make a few observations about this select group of musical plays. What does it say about the tradition of American musical theater?

Any tradition of art is first of all a collection of artists with a common purpose. That purpose, to make music drama, is found in the Broadway tradition again and again, but beyond that there is in this group of two dozen composers, lyricists, and librettists a homogeneity so remarkable that it nearly suggests a predestination for their appointed achievements. To begin with, all are Caucasian males, and all grew up in rather advantageous surroundings. In some cases this simply meant money—Kern, Gershwin, Rodgers, and Bernstein were the sons of successful businessmen—and in others it meant an early appreciation of serious learning and music in particular. Frank Loesser's father and brother were classical pianists of note; Frederic Loewe's father was a world-class opera singer in Vienna; Andrew Lloyd Webber's was the director of the Royal College of Music in London; Stephen Sondheim spent his teen years living next door to Oscar Hammerstein II.

Almost all were American immigrants or sons of immigrants, and the group is completely dominated by Jewish-Americans. Now it is well to remember that the Broadway musical tradition has a geographical center in New York City, which has been home for many Jewish-Americans and Jewish immigrants throughout the twentieth century, but the singular influence of this particular ethnic group is nonetheless astonishing. Of the eighteen composers and lyricists studied here, Jewish-Americans are in the vast majority; only Cole Porter, Andrew Lloyd Webber, and his partner Tim Rice (both British) may be counted out with certainty.

Perhaps it is this similarity of family background and experience that allowed the many significant partnerships to work so well. Musical composition is not by nature a collaborative enterprise, but in the theater it must be, and the best Broadway composers seem to have thrived on such collaboration. Indeed, it would be fair to say that several of Broadway's most notable names—Richard Rodgers, Leonard Bernstein, and Stephen Sondheim among them—might not have survived as popular songwriters without the theater. The requirements of drama were a most necessary stimulus.

Collaboration in the musical theater meant that a composer might work with not only a lyricist and a librettist but also a director, an orchestrator, a choreographer, a set designer, and all the other technicians of the stage, to say nothing of actors and actresses. It is remarkable that this survey, which has sought a broad selection of composers, has repeatedly turned up the same names in all the other posts: Rouben Mamoulian, Moss Hart, Jerome Robbins, Agnes De Mille, Michael Bennett, Harold Prince, Boris Aronson, and Robert Russell Bennett. How necessary their contributions are to the enduring qualities of the best plays is difficult to say, since dance routines, sets, and subtleties of direction are much more fragile and less easily transferred than music and lyrics, but the list suggests an intricate network of acquaintances that underlay the great variety of musical productions.

One focal point of the network might be Oscar Hammerstein II, who with Jerome Kern wrote *Show Boat*. His most famous and fruitful association was with Richard Rodgers, of course, but he also worked with Moss Hart, who much later directed Lerner and Loewe's *My Fair Lady*. The choreographer for that show, Hanya Holm, also did Cole Porter's *Kiss Me, Kate*. Rodgers and Hammerstein wanted Rouben Mamoulian to direct both *Oklahoma!* and *Carousel* after having seen what he had accomplished with Gershwin's *Porgy and Bess*. Another focal point would be Stephen Sondheim, who began his career working with Leonard Bernstein and Jerome Robbins. Robbins later directed Bock and Harnick's *Fiddler on the Roof*. Sondheim's landmark *Company* involved the talents of director-producer Harold Prince, later the director of Webber and Rice's *Evita*, and choreographer Michael Bennett, the creator with Marvin Hamlisch of *A Chorus Line*. The most improbable line of all, in retrospect, is that which connects the two centers, Sondheim and Hammerstein, since they would appear to represent opposite poles within the limited aesthetic of the Broadway theater. Sondheim once asked Hammerstein to sit in on a run-through of *West Side Story*. Hammerstein, who could never have written such a piece himself, nevertheless admired it, but suggested that the fire escape scene needed a song that "soared."[1] His pupil and Leonard Bernstein turned that suggestion into "Tonight," the central melody of that scene and the great quintet. The connection, however improbable, was real.

The artists of Broadway built a network of collaboration, tutelage, and friendship that is the musical theater. To refer to such a community as a "tradition" is certainly justified; one might even call it an artistic "school."

A clever person might look at the history of the mature tradition and note some curious parallels with the history of European opera. Broadway has had its founding father in Jerome Kern, its boy genius who died young in George Gershwin, its long-lived and expert practitioner of inherited forms in Richard Rodgers, and its reformer in Stephen Sondheim. But the dependence of the musical tradition on the techniques and prevailing style of nineteenth-century opera goes far beyond coincidence, to the heart of the tradition.

Simplified though they may be, operatic techniques show up throughout the best musical plays. The ancient recitative-aria scheme survives in the verse-refrain song form in which the verse presents a musical passage lacking in marked periodic phrasing, clear harmonic direction, and occasionally in clear meter. All these produce the introductory texture that mimics the function, if not always the sound, of recitative, the function of preparing the musical and emotional ground for the stability of the refrain to follow, and also the transition from spoken dialogue to song. The refrain, often composed in the modified, miniature *da capo* of A A B A, expresses unmistakable feelings in articulated phrases and directed harmonic progressions. Operatic ensembles more involved than a duet are rare early in the period, but the later shows of the survey include them regularly. The best of them operate in purely classical, almost Mozartean fashion, by allowing each character a solo to explain himself before giving way to contrapuntal invention. Finales, of course, hold sway throughout the tradition, and if they often fail to measure up to their forbears in musical sophistication and dramatic content, their essential character and function of bringing down the curtain remains unchanged.

The cantankerous distinctions, therefore, made between musicals and musical plays on one hand and operettas and operas on the other hand, in the words of Professor Higgins, "by now should be antique." How many times in the annals of criticism has the dirty word "opera" been used to snub a Broadway production? *Porgy and Bess, The Most Happy Fella,* and *Sweeney Todd* are but a few that have suffered such nonsense. The fact is that one critic or another in one place or another has used "opera" or "operetta" to describe nearly every work in this survey. The challenge remains to write a definition of opera that includes *The Magic Flute* but not *West Side Story.* That the New York City Opera and other less famous opera companies mount fully-staged productions of these musical plays, that world-class opera singers are rushing to record them, shows how silly the whole terminological business is. The matter at hand is music drama.

The seriousness of the matter among the composers selected here can be heard not only in their adaptation of operatic vocal forms but in their distinct preference for orchestral "prologues" over medley overtures, despite the overwhelming predominance of medleys in the tradition taken as a whole. Of the sixteen musical plays discussed here, only *Oklahoma!*, *Kiss Me, Kate*, *My Fair Lady*, *Camelot*, and *Jesus Christ Superstar* follow common practice.[2] The prologue allows the serious musical dramatist to replace a loose collection of tunes, which at that point have no significance other than that they will be heard later in the play, with a succinct summary of the most important terms of the musical drama. The summary may simply contain principal motives, as does the prologue to *The Most Happy Fella*, but it may be more ambitious, establishing an unusual harmonic progression, as in "The Carousel Waltz," or even establishing a harmonic structure for the whole play, as does the prologue to *West Side Story*. The things that are important in prologues are often tiny things—motives, single phrases, harmonic progressions—but they become the structural underpinnings for whole songs and other forms later on. It is curious that almost all the prologues are played with the curtain up and some kind of activity on stage: pantomime, dance, or later, singing. The only exceptions are *Show Boat* and *The Most Happy Fella*, whose prologues are very short and come closest in construction to the medley overtures. It is as if composers were unwilling to let the musical statement be as abstract as cultural associations would allow; they preferred some setting, some immediate and specific interpretation. Thus, the community background of *Porgy and Bess* and the violent dancing of *West Side Story*, while retaining a certain abstraction, yet become essential components of the drama. The insecurity seems greater in the newer plays, for the prologues of *Fiddler on the Roof*, *Godspell*, *Sweeney Todd*, and *Evita* narrow the interpretative possibilities further by having their casts explicitly define the dramatic themes in song.

The most signal link of the Broadway tradition with European Romantic opera is its dependence on the reprise for incisive dramatic effect. The reprise, of course, is Broadway's answer to the leitmotif, and just as many of Wagner's and Verdi's greatest dramatic statements depend upon a carefully developed leitmotif scheme, so do Broadway's more limited achievements. And how successful the sensitive and timely reprise has been! Stephen Sondheim's argument (quoted in Chapter 14) that to recapitulate a particular song and lyric at a later point in the play is to betray its original dramatic intent assumes that the transfer of meaning between music and drama goes one way only. Music can inform the drama, but drama cannot inform the music. But that is to argue that the dramatic context of a song is irrelevant to it, that the definition of what is going on comes entirely from the music. If the many examples from the Broadway repertoire quoted in this survey have shown anything, it is that the transfer of dramatic meaning is circular: the dramatic context of the play and cultural background of the audience condition and narrow the possible meanings of a piece of music, which in turn specifies the dramatic context and action.

The most effective reprises, therefore, make their point not through changes in the music or lyrics, although such changes may contribute, but because the dramatic situation which calls for their reprise is different from the original. The reprise juxtaposes for the audience both the original context and the new, and thereby gives rise to a host of possible ironies and dramatic meanings. When Billy Bigelow sings "If I Loved You" in the second act of *Carousel*, when Maria helps Tony through "Somewhere" at the end of *West Side Story*, the musical and lyrical alterations are quite minor. The power of these moments derives from the accumulated meanings of these pieces, which at the point of reprise must be reassessed against the new situations Billy, Tony, and Maria face and against all the action that has happened since they were first sung. These particular examples are two of the best reprises of the Broadway stage because they express in their accumulated meaning the very essence of the actions of their respective plays in a way that is marvelously appropriate for those moments. That is perhaps why the reprise of "There Was a Barber" in *Sweeney Todd* falls short, because its musical focus on Todd's obsession seems at cross-purposes with what he must be feeling.

Such summations may be accomplished without reprises. "O, Lawd, I'm on My Way" at the end of *Porgy and Bess* and "I Am Ashamed That Women Are So Simple," the finale of *Kiss Me, Kate,* are examples of songs that affect the audience's sense of dramatic action superbly, and yet they are completely new. They are the exceptions to the general rule, in works which have important reprises elsewhere. In this book only *Godspell* and *A Chorus Line* have no dramatic use of reprise (they occur as "bow music"), and that is because they have what Sondheim called "non-linear" plots.

The survey indicates a disjunction in the historical tradition in the mid-1960s, a reading which would agree with the opinion of many critics. The shows after *Fiddler on the Roof* part company with their forbears in several respects. The romantically involved couple, which had been the central source of dramatic conflict till then, is gone. Neither *Godspell, Jesus Christ Superstar, A Chorus Line, Sweeney Todd,* nor *Evita* have people in love at the center of their dramas. The significance caught the attention of Lehman Engel in 1972:

It should be clear that—to date—no musical without principal romantic involvement has worked. Romance is the fuel that ignites the music and lyrics. But romance has not been a prerequisite for the most significant non-musical plays of almost a century. I think the simplest explanation is to be found in the difference between words (drama) and music (feeling). Shakespeare alone combined both with a grandeur and magnificence that is still unique. And his methods of employing romance are echoed in today's best musicals.[3]

The loss of romance has required plays to dramatize other values, and so they have done: power, revenge, religious experience, and, most prosaic of all, getting "a job" in *A Chorus Line*.

There is much less dependence, in these shows, on the high-level, sequential plot and the tension that can be derived from it, with the exception of *Sweeney Todd,* which is also exceptional in Sondheim's works. The emphasis on lower-level "stories" and on idea as opposed to action can be glimpsed even in *Fiddler on The Roof.*

Finally, the later shows, in their creation, feature the director more prominently than ever before, with a complementary decrease in the importance of the composer and lyricist. When Rodgers and Hammerstein composed *Oklahoma!*, they did it virtually by themselves. When they finished, they set about raising money, contracting a director, choreographer, stars, and so on, but it was their show. *West Side Story* was billed as "a conception of Jerome Robbins," who became its choreographer-director and a significant influence. That influence increased substantially when he directed *Fiddler on the Roof,* to the point where Robbins defined the dramatic themes for Bock and Harnick and even fiddled with orchestrations. In the case of *A Chorus Line,* it is safe to say that the director, Michael Bennett, is the essential creator. Indeed, Hamlisch was called in only toward the end of the process.

There is nothing intrinsically wrong with a director doing these things, but it does change the nature of the art. If the composer is not in control of the essential dramatic materials from the beginning—music, certainly, but also lyrics, plot, how much dancing and when—then it is hard to see how he can be the essential dramatist. The musical theater loses its link to opera, and becomes something else.

Whether this change in command has contributed to the declining fortunes and critical reception of musicals in the last two decades is difficult to say. Certainly there must be other factors. As everyone knows, the 1960s saw the rise of rock music as the dominant popular style of American culture. The music of Broadway has in its history withstood the assault of various popular currents by absorbing the most useful of their characteristics within its central style of simplified nineteenth-century Romanticism. Thus the blues and bop influences permeate the scores of *Porgy and Bess* and *West Side Story* without changing their essential Romantic structures. Such a strategy succeeded dramatically because composers did not have to yield the powerful resources of the Romantic style, and it succeeded commercially because the popular culture at large never abandoned that style for anything else. Rock music, however, opened a chasm between the popular culture and the musical theater by replacing the predominant popular style with another that resisted dramatic adaptation. For the first time in Broadway's mature history, there is a significant disjunction between the principal expressive tools of the theater and the most popular musical style of the surrounding culture.

If there can be any credence at all in the notion that an artistic tradition, especially a popular one, reflects in some essentials its parent culture, then any fundamental change in the culture must be accompanied by either the reform or death of the tradition. Artistic traditions do have a life cycle; they are founded in obscurity, grow to maturity, flower, and pass away. "In 1929, there were about eighty new musicals on Broadway; in 1978 there were fewer than fifteen."[4] And that meager offering, over the past few years, has been choked with revivals, revues, and tremendous stage spectacles such as *Cats* that entertain without dramatizing. Sondheim, virtually alone, insists on dramatic integrity.

Perhaps the real and ironic burden of theater composers since the 1960s has been the oppression of their own heritage. It is worth noting in the history of music that whenever a tradition of compositional practice is consciously noticed, defined, analyzed, and admired, it is often already dead. The celebrated legacy of Gershwin, Rodgers, Loesser, and the rest could be, in this most individualistic of all centuries, not a source of inspiration but of despair. The consciousness of a tradition, that vital, flexible system of conventions and artistic goals, renders it forfeit to those who contemplate it, for how can one compose within it without slavish imitation? The only solution is an equally slavish innovation.

Whether the decline is terminal or not, the sixty years of the Broadway tradition since *Show Boat* have been a good run. The best reasons for celebrating the tradition are those rare and brief bursts of creativity marked by musical-dramatic integrity. Each of these is an attempt to respond to a particular dramatic problem, and the artistry and invention of that response allows the play to endure. That is why all of the great Rodgers and Hammerstein shows may be admired even though some stage formula may be clearly discerned. Each has its own dramatic difficulty, and therefore its own unique musical solution. Perhaps the greatest moments of the tradition are those in which the dramatic integrity and musical imagination are sufficient to achieve a musical unity that can be heard, musical plays such as *Porgy and Bess, Carousel,* or *West Side Story* which create and maintain their own characteristic sound that is one with the action. Such integrity assures a life for these plays regardless of the fate of the Broadway theaters in the twenty-first century. They will take their place among the national musical theater traditions of the world as the one that imitates an action through music in its distinctively American way.

# Notes

## Chapter 1.  Introduction

1. Joseph Kerman, *Opera as Drama* (New York: Vintage Books, 1956).

2. Eric Bentley, *The Playwright as Thinker* (New York: Reynal & Hitchcock, 1946), 284.

3. Francis Fergusson, *The Idea of a Theater* (Princeton, N.J.: Princeton University Press, 1949), 8.

4. Kerman, *Opera as Drama*, 12–13.

5. Eric Bentley, *The Life of the Drama* (New York: Atheneum, 1964), 15.

6. For example, in another activity in which humans extract meaning, listening to spoken language, the mechanism of perception is clearly circuitous. The incoming sounds are at once verified by subsequent ones and at the same time form the basis for the evaluation of the following words.

7. Bentley, *The Playwright as Thinker*, 6–7.

8. Kerman, *Opera as Drama*, 269.

9. See Richard Rodgers, *Musical Stages* (New York: Random House, 1976), 202.

10. One of the applicants for this job was George Gershwin, but Berlin told him that he should be spending his time writing his own music. See Michael Freedland, *Jerome Kern* (New York: Stein and Day, 1978), 57.

11. Bentley, *The Playwright as Thinker*, 6.

12. Ibid., 281.

13. *Poetics of Music*, Lesson Three (Cambridge: Harvard University Press, 1956).

14. Freedland, *Jerome Kern*, 31.

15. "Some Remarks on Value and Greatness in Music," in *Music, the Arts, and Ideas* (Chicago: University of Chicago Press, 1967), 37.

16. "Music: A View from Delft," *Musical Quarterly* LXVII (1961), 439–53.

17. Fergusson, *The Idea of a Theater*, 2.

18. The exception to this rule is Webber's *Evita*, which is discussed along with *Jesus Christ Superstar* in Chapter 12, "History as Musical." It opened in London in 1977 and in New York in 1979. However, the producer was the American Harold Prince in both places, and since a Broadway run was undoubtedly planned, contingent on the London success, and since the two cities shared by the 1970s all their musical successes, the opera may be regarded as a product of the Broadway tradition.

19. For a discussion of some of the problems, see Stephen Holden, " 'Show Boat' Makes New Waves," *New York Times*, September 25, 1988, pp. 1, 27.

## Chapter 2. First Maturity

1. Stanley Green, *The World of Musical Comedy* (New York: Ziff-Davis, 1960), 71.

2. "Out of Thin Air," *New Yorker* 30 (April 17, 1954), 116.

3. Miles Kreuger, *Showboat: The Story of a Classic American Musical* (New York: Oxford University Press, 1977), 49.

4. This is obviously a simplified view of the situation, but a more detailed description would not be clearer nor likely more accurate. Edith Boroff summarizes 28 different viewpoints about the origin of the American musical theater in "Origin of Species: Conflicting Views of American Musical Theater History," *American Music* 2, No. 4 (Winter 1984), 101–8.

5. Review of *Show Boat, New York Times,* December 28, 1927, p. 26.

6. Ethan C. Mordden, *Better Foot Forward* (New York: Grossman, 1976), 75.

7. *The Life of the Drama* (New York: Atheneum, 1964), 259.

8. These are the original lyrics of the 1927 version. In deference to black sensitivity to racial slurs, the first two lines were changed to "Colored folks work on de Mississippi, colored folks work while de white folks play" for the 1946 revival, and these appear in the vocal score published by Welk. In the 1966 revival, the lyrics were further toned down to read "Here we all work on de Mississippi, here we all work while de white folks play."

9. Bordman traces this tune back to the entrance music of Act I, One, scene 2 of Kern's *The Beauty Prize*. He also notes several other themes in *Show Boat* that were adapted from earlier works. See Gerald Bordman, *Jerome Kern: His Life and Music* (New York: Oxford University Press, 1980), 291.

10. Oscar Hammerstein II, *Show Boat,* complete libretto (New York: Rodgers & Hammerstein Theatre Library, n.d.), 9.

11. Ibid., 15–16.

12. The choice of keys for the various pieces in the opening scene of *Show Boat* indicates some organization, but it is a very loose one based on absolute pitch rather than some hierarchical relationship. The opening choral sequence is based on E, the parade sequence on B-flat, Ravenal's first song on D. The 1928 vocal score has "Make Believe" also begin in D and eventually move to E-flat, but the 1946 revision places the beginning in C, which matches the key of "Ol' Man River" in both scores. Clearly the semitone transpositions are supposed to create a limited increase in intensity and have no structural importance. The loose quality of these connections is revealed in the decision to sing "Ol' Man River" in B-flat in the London engagement of 1928 in order to suit Paul Robeson's lower range.

13. The 1946 version of the score contains some equivocation about whether Magnolia and Ravenal are supposed to sing together in that the last phrase is given in small notation in Magnolia's part. The 1928 vocal score (T. B. Harms), however, indicates clearly that they should sing together until the cadence in m. 113. In my view this makes more dramatic sense.

14. Hammerstein, *Show Boat,* 19.

15. Kreuger, *Showboat,* 50.

16. Lehman Engel, *Words With Music* (New York: Macmillan, 1972), 7.

## Chapter 3. America's Folk Opera

1. Edward Jablonski, *Gershwin* (New York: Doubleday, 1987), 287.

2. This story is recounted in Dorothy Heyward, "Porgy's Goat," *Harper's* 215 (December 1957), 37–41, and in Stanley Green, *The World of Musical Comedy* (New York: Ziff-Davis, 1960), 120.

3. William H. Slavick, *DuBose Heyward* (Boston: Twayne, 1981), 9.

4. Ibid., 57.

5. Letter from DuBose Heyward to Kathryn Bourne, December 21, 1931. Cited from Frank Durham, "DuBose Heyward's Use of Folklore in His Negro Fiction," *The Citadel: Monograph Series No. 2* (Charleston, S.C.: The Citadel, 1961), 18–19.

6. See Charles Schwartz, *Gershwin: His Life and Music* (Indianapolis and New York: Da Capo, 1973), 60–61, for more details on this piece.

7. Heyward, "Porgy's Goat," 37.

8. Green, *The World of Musical Comedy*, 111.

9. Abe Laufe, *Broadway's Greatest Musicals* (New York: Funk & Wagnalls, 1969), 32.

10. *The American Musical Theatre: A Consideration* (distrib. by Macmillan, 1967), 112. For similar assessments, see Laufe, *Broadway's Greatest Musicals*, 33, and Schwartz, *Gershwin*, 219–20.

11. Green, *The World of Musical Comedy*, 123.

12. It is very difficult to know precisely what Ira contributed to the whole text of *Porgy and Bess*. See Schwartz, *Gershwin*, 261–62, and Slavick, *DuBose Heyward*, 81.

13. See Schwartz, *Gershwin*, 258 ff., for a detailed chronology of the composition.

14. *"Porgy and Bess;* American Opera in the Theatre," *Theatre Arts Monthly* (November 1935), 853.

15. *Music in a New Found Land* (New York: Hillstone, 1964), 392–413.

16. "I Remember," in Merle Armitage, *George Gershwin* (New York, London: Longmans, Green, 1938), 52.

17. For a complete list and discussion of cuts, see Charles Hamm's recent "The Theatre Guild Production of *Porgy and Bess,*" *Journal of the American Musicological Society* XL, No. 3 (Fall 1987) 495–532.

18. David Ewen, *A Journey to Greatness* (New York: Henry Holt, 1956), 266.

19. "Todd Duncan," in Robert Kimball, Alfred Simon, and Bea Feitler, *The Gershwins* (New York: Atheneum, 1973), 181.

20. Hamm, "The Theatre Guild Production," 505–7, 514–21.

21. *New York Times*, October 11, 1935, p. 30.

22. *New York Times*, October 20, 1935, Sec. X, p. 1.

23. Engel, *The American Musical Theatre*, 143.

24. Kolodin, *"Porgy and Bess,"* 858.

25. Quoted in Andrew Porter, "Musical Events," *New Yorker* 61 (February 25, 1985), 93.

26. Engel, *The American Musical Theatre*, 144–45.

27. For a fine introduction to this complex issue, see Richard Crawford, "It Ain't Necessarily Soul: Gershwin's *Porgy and Bess* as a Symbol," *Yearbook for Inter-American Musical Research* VIII (1972), 17–38.

28. Robert Garland, "Negroes Are Critical of 'Porgy and Bess,' " *New York World-Telegram*, January 16, 1934, p. 14.

29. "Porgy and Bess—A Folk Opera," *Opportunity* (January 1936), 26.

30. "George Gershwin," *Modern Music* (November–December 1935), 13.

31. "Gershwin, Part IV," *New Republic* 176 (May 14, 1977), 25.

32. Kolodin, *"Porgy and Bess,"* 861, and Ewen, *A Journey to Greatness,* 273.

33. Clive Barnes, "Porgy and Bess," *New York Times*, September 27, 1976, p. 40.

34. "Living With Gershwin," *Opera News* 49 (March 16, 1985), 14.

35. Kolodin, *"Porgy and Bess,"* 856.

36. Slavick, *DuBose Heyward,* 10.

37. Ibid., 59.

38. This was cut for the New York production. See Hamm, "The Theatre Guild Production," 530.

39. In "Bess, You Is My Woman Now," Bess sings "Porgy, I's yo' woman, now," and "I's yours for ever," and Porgy sings "you loves yo' Porgy." In the second duet of Act II, Bess sings "I loves you, Porgy." The most explicit statements of Porgy's feelings occur in the same duet when he sings "You got a home now, Honey, an' you got love," and in the "Buzzard Song" of Act II: "Sharin' grief an' sharin' laughter, an' love like Augus' sun." It should be noted however, that the first occurrence is quite difficult for the listener to catch because Bess is singing the main tune with an different text.

40. Mellers also notes this textual connection, although not the motivic one. See *Music in a New Found Land,* 404.

41. Youngren, "Gershwin, Part IV," 24.

42. The sense of meter derives from regular accents, which in turn may be produced by melodic groupings. Here the C-sharp to D motion, because it recurs insistently, is heard as the beginning of a melodic group, and thus becomes accented. Because each of the groups has only three eighth notes, however, this new accent pattern is heard as a disruption of the prevailing meter, since three eighths cannot divide eight evenly.

43. Lawrence Starr notes that relationship of the particular harmonies used here to the chromatic notes of Porgy's melody. "In measures 7 and 8, the blue notes A-flat and D-flat infiltrate the bass line and are given complete harmonic status as the roots of chords. The result is an intense and colorful precadential progression which also provides a summary of the events related to the blue notes thus far. . . . ." See "Gershwin's 'Bess, You Is My Woman Now': The Sophistication and Subtlety of a Great Tune," *Musical Quarterly* LXXII, No. 4 (1986), 434.

44. Lawrence Starr also notes this relationship. See "Toward a Reevaluation of Gershwin's *Porgy and Bess,"* *American Music* 2, No. 2 (Summer 1984), 35–36.

45. For an extended discussion of jazz influences in *Porgy and Bess,* see David R. Baskerville, "Jazz Influence of Art Music to Mid-Century," Ph.D. Diss., University of California, Los Angeles, 1965, pp. 486–503.

46. Lawrence Starr also notes this relationship. See Starr, "Gershwin's, 'Bess, You Is My Woman Now,' " 441, 443.

47. In particular, Ronald Duncan, *"Porgy and Bess:* The Work and Its Conception," *Opera* (December 1952), 711–13.

48. Hamm notes that much of this passage was cut from the New York production (see Hamm, "The Theatre Guild Production," 531), but that version still leaves a critical moment in the drama without musical expression.

49. DuBose Heyward, *Porgy* (George H. Doran, 1925), 196.

50. This means that the production failed to recover its investment. It still played 124 performances before closing, many more times than it would have played had the Metropolitan Opera produced it.

51. Ewen, *A Journey to Greatness,* 281.

52. George Gershwin, "Rhapsody on Catfish Row," *New York Times,* October 20, 1935, Sec. X, p. 1.

53. *A Short History of Opera,* second edition (New York: Columbia University Press, 1965), 545.

## Chapter 4. Second Maturity

1. Richard Rodgers, *Musical Stages* (New York: Random House, 1976), 227.

2. There were several revues produced during the period 1919–43 which had significant runs, but none so long as *Oklahoma!: Hellzapoppin* (1938, 1,404 performances); *Pins and Needles* (1937, 1,108 performances); *Stars on Ice* (1942, 830 performances); and *Sons o' Fun* (1941, 742 performances).

3. See his discussion throughout *The American Musical Theater: A Consideration* (New York: Macmillan, 1967).

4. Rodgers, *Musical Stages,* 202.

5. Oscar Hammerstein II, *Lyrics* (Milwaukee, Wis.: Hal Leonard, 1985; rpt. 1949), 20.

6. Ibid., 17.

7. Rodgers, *Musical Stages,* 219.

8. Engel, *The American Musical Theater,* 105.

9. Agnes De Mille, *America Dances* (New York: Macmillan, 1980), 188.

10. They are the *Nursery Ballet* (1938) an *Ghost Town* (1939).

11. Rodgers, *Musical Stages,* 223.

12. Eric Bentley, *The Life of the Drama* (New York: Atheneum, 1964), 7.

13. Deems Taylor, *Some Enchanted Evenings* (New York: Harper, 1953), 172–73.

14. Oscar Hammerstein, "On Writing 'Oklahoma!,' " *New York Times,* May 23, 1943, Sec. X, p. 2.

15. William Beyer, *School and Society* 67 (June 26, 1948), 475.

16. Rodgers, *Musical Stages,* 229.

17. *Broadway's Greatest Musicals* (New York: Funk & Wagnalls, 1969), 68.

18. Leo Lerman, *Dance Magazine* 32 (May 1958), 17.

19. Hammerstein, *Lyrics,* 8.

20. *New York Times,* May 12, 1963, Sec. VI, p. 30.

## Chapter 5. Morality Play As Musical

1. Richard Rodgers, *Musical Stages* (New York: Random House, 1976), 243.

2. Thomas DeLong, *Pops: Paul Whiteman, King of Jazz* (Piscataway, N.J.: New Century, 1983), 269.

3. *Richard Rodgers* (New York: Holt, 1957), 239.

4. Rodgers, *Musical Stages,* 238.

5. John Hutchens, "About a Man on a Tightrope," *New York Times,* May 6, 1945, Sec. II, p. 1.

6. Clara Gyorgyey, *Ferenc Molnar* (Boston: Twayne, 1980), 152–53.

7. Rodgers, *Musical Stages,* 241.

8. Ibid., 243.

## Chapter 6. Shakespeare As Musical

1. Howard Taubman, "Cole Porter Is 'The Top' Again," *New York Times,* January 16, 1949, Sec. VI, p. 20.

2. David Ewen, *The Cole Porter Story* (New York: Holt, Rinehart and Winston, 1965), 114–15.

3. Taubman, "Cole Porter Is 'The Top' Again."

4. Quote in Stanley Green, *The World of Musical Comedy* (New York: A. S. Barnes, 1974), 177.

5. George Eels, *The Life That Late He Led* (New York: G. P. Putnam's Sons, 1967), 241.

6. Sam and Bella Spewack, "Much Ado About 'Kate,' " *Saturday Review* 36 (October 31, 1953), 55.

7. Eels, *The Life That Late He Led*, 238.

8. Lynn Siebert traces some of the motives in "Brush Up Your Shakespeare" to particular songs. See Lynn Laitman Siebert, "Cole Porter: An Analysis of Five Musical Comedies and a Thematic Catalogue of the Complete Works," Ph.D. Diss., City University of New York, 1975, pp. 310–14.

9. Eels, *The Life That Late He Led*, 254.

10. Anne Barton, "The Taming of the Shrew," in *The Riverside Shakespeare*, textual ed. G. Blakemore Evans (Boston: Houghton Mifflin, 1974), 106.

11. Ibid., 107.

12. Ralph Berry, *Shakespeare's Comedies: Explorations in Form* (Princeton, N.J.: Princeton University Press, 1972), 54–55.

13. Some aspects of this high-level use of half-step motion are also noted in Siebert, "Cole Porter," 265.

14. Sam and Bella Spewack, *Kiss Me, Kate* in *Theatre Arts* 39, No. 32 (January 1955), 57.

15. Robert B. Heilman, "The Taming of the Shrew," in *The Complete Signet Classic Shakespeare*, General Ed. Sylvan Barnet (New York: Harcourt Brace Jovanovich, 1972), 323.

16. *New York Times*, January 16, 1949, Sec. II, p. 1.

17. John Mason Brown, "Kiss Me, Kate," *Saturday Review of Literature* 32 (January 22, 1949), 35.

## Chapter 7.   The Pure Love Story

1. Quoted by Murray Schumach in *New York Times*, April 27, 1956, Sec. II, p. 1.

2. Burrows was not the first to be asked by the producers Cy Feuer and Ernest Martin to adapt the Runyon stories, but he is the sole author. Jo Swerling's name appears on programs and scores because of contractual arrangements. See Stanley Green, *The World of Musical Comedy* (New York: Ziff-Davis, 1960), 296.

3. Gilbert Millstein, "Greater Loesser," *New York Times*, May 20, 1956, Sec. VI, pp. 20, 22.

4. Eleanor Flexner, *American Playwrights 1918–1938* (New York: Simon and Schuster, 1938), 30.

5. For a discussion of these themes, see Walter J. Meserve, "Sidney Howard and the Social Drama of the Twenties," *Modern Drama* 6 (1963), 256–66.

6. Green, *The World of Musical Comedy*, 298.

7. Flexner, *American Playwrights*, 33.

8. These would include Marie's advice in "The Most Happy Fella" (mm. 232–47), Tony's song "Rosabella," Marie's conversation with Cleo at the end of "Happy to Make Your Acquaintance" (mm. 126–82), "Young People," "Mamma, Mamma," and the trio of Act III, scene 2 (mm. 133 ff.)

9. Frank Loesser, *The Most Happy Fella* (New York: Frank Music, 1957), 262.

10. The metrical ambiguity is addressed by the notion of "hyper-measure," or which measures seem strong and weak in the same sense that beats within measures seem strong and weak. The normal

pattern would be to alternate measures strong-weak, as beats might be alternated downbeat-upbeat. This is what happens at the beginning of the phrase. The stable tonic harmony of the first measure establishes a strong measure; the unstable augmented triad of the next brings the sense of weak measure. This works fine until measure four, in which the chromatic harmony of C-flat can be heard as a resolution of the previous G-flat. Does this then become a strong measure? In addition, measure five, which should be strong, has dominant harmony (A-flat), and measure six, which should be weak, has tonic (D-flat). Thus, there is a conflict between the harmony of those measures and the pattern that was established at the beginning, and this conflict causes unresolved tension. For a theoretical discussion of high-level meter, see Fred Lerdahl and Ray Jackendoff, *A Generative Theory of Tonal Music* (Cambridge, Mass.: MIT Press, 1983), Chapter 2.

11. Catherine Hughes, "The Most Happy Fella," *America* 141 (November 10, 1979), 281.

12. David Ansen, "The Most Happy Fella," *Newsweek* 94 (October 22, 1979), 130.

13. Richard Hayes, "The Most Happy Fella," *Commonweal* 64 (June 1, 1956), 226.

14. Conrad L. Osborne, "The Most Happy Fella," *High Fidelity/Musical America* (February 1980), 37.

# Chapter 8.   Myth As Musical

1. Alan Jay Lerner, *The Street Where I Live* (New York: Norton, 1978), 44.

2. K. K. Ruthven, *Myth* (London: Methuen, 1976), 44.

3. William Righter, *Myth and Literature.* (London and Boston: Routledge & Kegan Paul, 1975), 34.

4. Eric Gould, *Mythical Intentions in Modern Literature,* (Princeton, N.J.: Princeton University Press, 1981), 6.

5. Abe Laufe points out the similarity of Lerner's *Brigadoon* story to "Germelshausen," a nineteenth-century German story by Wilhelm Friedrick Gerstacker. See *Broadway's Greatest Musicals* (New York: Funk & Wagnalls, 1969), 101.

6. This translation appears in Mark P. O. Morford and Robert J. Lenardan, *Classical Mythology* (New York and London: Longman, 1985), 117–18.

7. Arnold Silver, *Bernard Shaw: The Darker Side* (Stanford, Calif.: Stanford University Press, 1982), 181–82.

8. Ibid., 254.

9. Lerner, *The Street Where I Live,* 44.

10. Alan Jay Lerner, *My Fair Lady* (New York: Coward-McCann, 1956), 85–86.

11. George Bernard Shaw, *Pygmalion,* Act III.

12. "A Directly Sensuous Pleasure," *New Republic* 134 (April 9, 1956), 29.

13. Silver, *Bernard Shaw,* 196–97.

14. "Shavian Musical Notes," *New York Times,* March 11, 1956, Sec. II, p. 3.

15. *T. H. White* (New York: Twayne, 1974), 99.

16. J. R. Cameron, "T. H. White in Camelot: The Matter of Britain Revitalized," *The Humanities Association Bulletin* XVI (1), 45.

17. See William K. Zinsser, "Camelot," *Horizon* 3 (May 1961), 104.

18. Alan Jay Lerner, *Camelot* (New York: Chappell Music, 1962), 130–33.

19. *Words With Music* (New York: Macmillan, 1972), 87.

20. Frank Rich, "Stage: Burton Stars in Revival of 'Camelot,' " *New York Times*, July 9, 1980, Sec. III, p. 15.

21. Lerner, *The Street Where I Live*, 232.

22. Ibid., 228.

23. See ibid., 227.

24. Another factor may be *Camelot*'s association with the administration of President John F. Kennedy. See Lerner, *The Street Where I Live*, 250–52.

## Chapter 9. Tragedy As Musical

1. "Excerpts from a *West Side Story* Log," *Findings* (New York: Simon and Schuster, 1982), 144. Quotation dated "New York, Jan. 6, 1949."

2. Eric Bentley, *The Playwright as Thinker* (New York: Reynal and Hitchcock, 1946), 160.

3. J. Leeds Barroll, *Shakespearean Tragedy* (New Jersey, London, and Canada: Associated University Presses, 1984), 15–16.

4. Ibid., 16.

5. Frank Kermode, "Romeo and Juliet," in *The Riverside Shakespeare*, ed. G. Blakemore Evans (Boston: Houghton Mifflin, 1974), 1055. Harley Granville-Barker shares this opinion, although he remarks that Shakespeare "set out, we see, in the shaping of his characters, to give all likelihood to the outcome. It is by pure ill-luck that Friar John's speed to Mantua is stayed while Balthasar reaches Romeo with the news of Juliet's death; but it is Romeo's headlong recklessness that leaves Friar Laurence no time to retrieve the mistake. It is, by a more subtle turn, Juliet's overacted repentance of her 'disobedient opposition,' which prompts the delighted Capulet to '. . . have this knot knit up to-morrow morning.' " *Prefaces to Shakespeare*, Second Series, "Romeo and Juliet" (London: Sidgwick & Jackson, 1948), 17.

6. Norris Houghton, *"Romeo and Juliet* and *West Side Story:* An Appreciation," in *Romeo and Juliet/West Side Story* (New York: Dell, 1965), 10–11.

7. Bentley, *The Playwright as Thinker*, 55–56.

8. David Stearns, " 'West Side Story': Between Broadway and the Opera House." Liner notes to recording of *West Side Story*, Deutsche Gramophon Gesellschaft 415 254–2, pp. 13.

9. The idea of an unusual musical procedure becoming a norm for a particular composition can be defended with data from the cognitive sciences which show how humans can learn and accept patterns for a particular situation. See Joseph P. Swain, "The Need for Limits in Hierarchical Theories of Music," *Music Perception* 4 (1) (Fall 1986), 121–48.

10. The recent Deutsch Gramophon recording conducted by Bernstein himself begins as the vocal score given in Example 9–5 does. The original Broadway cast recording produced by Columbia, however, begins with the Jets "whistle motive" which in the "Prologue" does not occur until measure 89:

This is certainly a more arresting gesture with which to begin the musical. However, by beginning with the tritone so brazenly, Bernstein's careful motivic development is pre-empted. In addition, by startling with a G-sharp to C-sharp leap, followed by the turn ending on B, the C/A polarity so subtly established and so important to the unity of the whole play is threatened.

11. The consistency of Bernstein's idiom in all his work may be seen in that the melody to "Somewhere" was composed some dozen years before the show as a whole. See Joan Peyser, *Bernstein: A Biography* (New York: William Morrow, 1987), 267.

12. Ibid., 267.

13. Granville-Barker, *Prefaces,* 7–8.

14. Henry Hewes, *Saturday Review* 40 (October 5, 1957), 22.

15. See interview with Jerome Robbins by Moira Hodgson, *New York Times,* February 10, 1980, Sec. II, p. 4.

16. From *West Side Story* libretto, printed in *Romeo and Juliet/West Side Story* (New York: Dell, 1965), 201.

17. See interview of Jerome Robbins by Moira Hodgson.

18. Harold S. Wilson, *On the Design of Shakespearean Tragedy* (Toronto: University of Toronto Press, 1957), 30.

19. Ibid., 25.

20. Stearns, " 'West Side Story,' " 13.

21. Houghton, *"Romeo and Juliet* and *West Side Story,"* 11.

## Chapter 10. The Ethnic Musical

1. Quoted in Richard Altman with Mervyn Kaufman, *The Making of a Musical: Fiddler on the Roof* (New York: Crown, 1971), 34–35.

2. Dan Sullivan, "A Robust 'Fiddler' Approaches Its 3rd Birthday," *New York Times,* September 14, 1968, p. 25.

3. Richard Rodgers, *Musical Stages* (New York: Random House, 1975), 220.

4. Ibid., 301.

5. Craig Zadan, *Sondheim & Co.,* second ed. (New York: Macmillan, 1986), 211.

6. Rodgers, *Musical Stages,* 295.

7. Eric Werner et al., "Jewish Music," *The New Grove,* ed. Stanley Sadie (London: Macmillan, 1980), Vol. IX, p. 642.

8. See ibid., 642.

9. Sholem Aleichem, *The Tevye Stories and Others,* transl. Julius and Frances Butwin (New York: Pocket Books, 1965; rpt. Crown, 1946).

10. Altman, *The Making of a Musical,* 39.

11. Ibid., 40.

12. Ibid.

13. Ibid., 46.

14. Werner Haftmann, *Marc Chagall,* trans. Heinrich Baumann and Alexis Brown (New York: Harry N. Abrams, 1984), 70.

15. Joseph Stein, *Fiddler on the Roof* (New York: Crown, 1964), 1.

16. Butwin, *The Tevye Stories,* 28.

17. See Altman, *The Making of a Musical,* 31.

18. Ibid.

19. See Ibid., Chapter 9.

20. Ibid., 156.

21. Abe Laufe, *Broadway's Greatest Musicals* (New York: Funk & Wagnalls, 1969), 377.

22. Hillel Halkin, introduction to Sholem Aleichem, *Tevye the Dairyman* and *The Railroad Stories,* trans. Hillel Halkin (New York: Schocken Books, 1987), xxiv.

23. Butwin, *The Tevye Stories,* 84.

24. Halkin, "Introduction," xxv.

25. *New York Times,* September 20, 1964, Sec. II, p. 1.

## Chapter 11.   Religious Experience As Musical

1. Joseph Barton, S. J., "The Godspell Story," *America,* 125 (December 11, 1971), 517.

2. Ibid., 517.

3. The career of Stephen Sondheim, which began so auspiciously with *West Side Story, Gypsy,* and *A Funny Thing Happened on the Way to the Forum,* might be mentioned as an obvious exception. In the first two cases, however, he was working with quite a large team of much more experienced men.

4. Stephen Schwartz, personal communication, September 10, 1988.

5. Barton, "The Godspell Story," 517.

6. *Opera as Drama* (New York: Vintage, 1956), 65.

7. Michael Murray, "The Stage," *Commonweal* 95 (February 11, 1972), 447.

8. Tom Prideaux, "On This Rock, a Little Miracle," *Life* 73 (August 4, 1972), 20.

9. Stephen Koch, "God on Stage," *World* 1 (September 12, 1972), 61.

10. Robert P. Ellis, " 'Godspell' as Medieval Drama," *America* 127 (December 23, 1972), 543.

11. See H. Elliot Wright, "Jesus on Stage: A Reappraisal," *Christian Century* 89 (July 19, 1972), 786 for details of Tebelak's acquaintance with the Cox book.

12. Harvey Cox, *The Feast of Fools* (Cambridge, Mass.: Harvard University Press, 1969), 139.

13. Ibid., 142.

14. Ellis, " 'Godspell,' " 543.

15. Cox, *The Feast of Fools,* 147.

16. John Paterson, *The Praises of Israel* (New York: Charles Scribner's Sons, 1950), 59.

17. Koch, "God on Stage," 61.

18. Schwartz, personal communication.

19. Edwin Wilson, "Taking the Long Route to Broadway," *Wall Street Journal,* June 24, 1976, p. 16.

20. Schwartz, personal communication.

## Chapter 12.   History As Musical

1. Ellis Nassour and Richard Broderick, *Rock Opera* (New York: Hawthorn, 1973), 41.

2. "Sex and Power in the New York Theater," *New Republic* 181 (November 10, 1979), 26.

3. Nassour and Broderick, *Rock Opera,* 37.

4. Ibid.

5. "I have always felt that is the key to musicals, to make them a continuous musical event like

opera.'' Michael Owen, ''A London Hit Arrives—With a Controversial Heroine,'' *New York Times,* September 23, 1979, Sec. II, p. 26.

6. Nassour and Broderick, *Rock Opera,* 99–100.

7. Quoted in ibid., 174.

8. Ibid., 41.

9. ''Jesus Christ Superstar—eine Passion in Rock,'' *Musik und Bildung* 4 (April 1972), 194–99.

10. Ibid., 198. ''. . . so wirkt ihr Gesang wäahrend des 'letzten Abendmahls' eher wie die Karikatur selbstzufriedenen Monchsschar vorgetragen wird.''

11. Ibid., 199.

12. Nassour and Broderick, *Rock Opera,* 46.

13. See the latter chapters of John Barnes, *Evita, First Lady* (New York: Grove, 1978).

14. Owen, ''A London Hit Arrives,'' 1.

15. Ibid., 26.

16. Walter Kerr, '' 'Evita'—A Bold Step Backward,'' *New York Times,* October 7, 1979, Sec. II, p. 1.

17. See Brendan Gill, ''The Theatre: Crying for Eva,'' *New Yorker* 55 (October 8, 1979), 100; T. E. Kalem, ''Vogue of the Age: Carrion Chic,'' *Time* 114 (October 8, 1979), 84; Stanley Kauffmann, ''Theater: Down Argentine Way,'' *Saturday Review* 6 (November 24, 1979), 49–50; and Kerr, '' 'Evita.' ''

18. Kauffmann, ''Theater,'' 50.

## Chapter 13. Frame Story As Musical

1. Mel Gussow, ''The Director Who Listened to Chorus Line,'' *New York Times,* May 23, 1975, p. 22.

2. Jack Kroll and Constance Guthrie, ''Gotta Dance . . . Gotta Dance,'' *Newsweek* 85 (June 9, 1975), 85.

3. Gussow, ''The Director Who Listened''; Barbara Gelb, ''Producing and Reproducing 'A Chorus Line,' '' *New York Times,* May 2, 1976, Sec. VI, p. 20.

4. Gussow, ''The Director Who Listened.''

5. Stanley Kauffmann, ''A Chorus Line,'' *New Republic* 172 (June 21, 1975), 20.

6. Gussow, ''The Director Who Listened.''

7. ''A Tremendous 'Chorus Line' Arrives,'' *New York Times,* May 22, 1975, p. 32.

8. Daniel Cook, eds., *The Canterbury Tales of Geoffrey Chaucer* (New York: Anchor Books, Doubleday, 1961), xvii.

9. Ibid., xviii.

10. *The Structure of the Canterbury Tales* (Athens, Ga.: University of Georgia Press, 1984), 25.

11. Clive Barnes does so in his review, ''A Tremendous 'Chorus Line' Arrives.''

12. Craig Zadan, *Sondheim & Co.,* second ed. (New York: Macmillan 1986), 125.

13. ''Theatre,'' *Nation* 220 (June 14, 1975), 734.

14. Samuel G. Freedman, ''332 Dance on a Record 3389th 'Chorus Line,' '' *New York Times,* September 30, 1983, Sec. III, p. 5.

15. Measure numbers refer to the published vocal score, *A Chorus Line,* music by Marvin Hamlisch, lyrics by Ed Kleban (n.p.: E. H. Morris, 1977). Unfortunately, Wren Music Co., the print agent for

this music, would not permit excerpts to be reprinted here, due to the critical nature of the commentary.

16. Gelb, "Producing and Reproducing 'A Chorus Line,' " notes (p. 28) that keys of individual songs were changed in rehearsal to accommodate vocal ranges. It is possible that the individual sections of "At the Ballet" fell victim to such conditions, even though the vocal ranges demanded of the three singers are not extreme.

17. See, for example, Frank Rich, "At the Age of 5, 'Chorus Line' Has Lots of Offspring," *New York Times,* July 20, 1980, Sec. II, p. 4.

18. The removal of one dancer makes possible the rather manipulative "surprise ending," whereby when Zach comes to make the final selection, he asks eight to step forward, leaving eight on the line. Naturally everyone, including the characters, thinks that the eight coming forward are the winners, until he thanks and dismisses them. If Paul had not been hurt, he would have had to call nine forward, and the trick would have been exposed.

19. Carol Lawson, "Broadway," *New York Times,* August 26, 1983, Sec. III, p. 2.

20. "Larry King Live," Cable News Network, August 19, 1988.

21. This effectiveness was enhanced exponentially when all past cast members were invited to dance for the performance of *A Chorus Line* which broke the record for longest-running musical play on Broadway on September 29, 1983. For a description, see Frank Rich, *New York Times,* October 1, 1983, Sec. I, p. 13.

22. Henry Hewes, "Broadway's Bountiful Season," *Saturday Review* 2 (July 26, 1975), 19.

23. Ibid.

24. Gelb, "Producing and Reproducing 'A Chorus Line,' " 26.

25. Richard Philip, "Michael Bennett and the Making of 'A Chorus Line,' " *Dance Magazine* 49 (June 1975), 65.

26. Arlene Croce, "A Chorus Line," *New Yorker* 51 (August 25, 1975), 78.


## Chapter 14.   Thriller As Musical

1. Samuel G. Freedman, "The Words and Music of Stephen Sondheim," *New York Times,* April 1, 1984, Sec. VI, p. 28.

2. Ibid., 25.

3. Ibid., 28.

4. At least through *Sunday in the Park With George.* See ibid., 22.

5. *New York Times,* May 3, 1970, Sec. II, p. 1.

6. Quoted in Craig Zadan, *Sondheim & Co.,* second ed. (New York: Harper & Row, 1986), 230.

7. Ibid., 360.

8. Stephen Holden, "The Passion of Stephen Sondheim," *Atlantic* 254 (December 1984), 121.

9. Zadan, *Sondheim & Co.,* 367. Although this quotation dates from 1973, the statement about the profits is still true through 1988, as long as the profits are regarded as those deriving from the initial Broadway runs of the plays.

10. Freedman, "The Words and Music of Stephen Sondheim," 26.

11. The Broadway production actually began with an organ prelude, reminiscent of the Gothic horror theater. The prelude is built on various important motives of the opera in rather tortured versions. However, the vocal score states that the performance of the prelude is "optional," so that it must not be an important contributor to the opera's scheme, at least for the composer.

12. Freedman, "The Words and Music of Stephen Sondheim," 26.

13. In most of Sondheim's shows, the keys of individual songs were determined at the time of orchestration, when the singer had been contracted. See ibid., 60.

14. The ability of the perceiving mind of the listener to learn such definitions quickly from context is described at length in Joseph P. Swain, "The Need for Limits in Hierarchical Theories of Music," *Music Perception* 4 (Fall 1986), 121–48.

15. The lyrics here also indicate the beginning of a new phrase. "Then" is a strong beginning of a new sentence.

16. The four eighths on "lost and oh, so" (m. 241) are not four eighths in the same grouping that has obtained up to that point. The first two ("So lost") are clearly another occurrence of the motives in the previous measure, leaving the last three eighths to carry out the anacrusis. The beaming in the notation should really be two and three.

17. Freedman, "The Words and Music of Stephen Sondheim," 30.

18. *Opera as Drama* (New York: Vintage, 1956), 177.

19. Robert Berkvist, "Stephen Sondheim Takes a Stab at Grand Guignol," *New York Times,* February 25, 1979, Sec. D, p. 5.

20. Montague Slater, Introduction to George Dibdin Pitt, *Sweeney Todd: The Demon Barber of Fleet Street* (London: Gerald Howe, 1928).

21. Stanley Kauffmann, "Slay It With Music," *New Republic* 180 (March 24, 1979), 24. Kauffmann gives no source for this information. Joanne Leslie Gordon, in her dissertation, "The American Musical Stops Singing and Finds Its Voice: A Study of the Works of Stephen Sondheim" (UCLA, 1984), writes: "Pitt apparently based his play on the blood-chilling reports of Thomas Peckett Prest. His serial, 'A String of Pearls,' had been published earlier in *The People's Periodical,* a Victorian penny dreadful which titillated and edified its readers with a combination of pious homilies and tales of gore."

22. *Sweeney Todd: The Demon Barber of Fleet Street* (London: Samuel French, 1974), v.

23. Ibid., 5.

24. There is no single version of the Pitt original play because it was never published, but rather transmitted through numerous pirated versions.

25. Act II, scene 4. See Slater, ed., *Sweeney Todd,* 135.

26. Mel Gussow, " 'Sweeney Todd': A Little Nightmare Music," *New York Times,* February 1, 1979, Sec. C, p. 15.

27. Berkvist, "Stephen Sondheim Takes a Stab," 5.

28. See Swain, "The Need for Limits," for the relationship between musical structure and the listener's limited ability to perceive musical events.

29. Zadan, *Sondheim & Co.,* 250.

30. The term "ostinato" is used rather loosely here, denoting not an exactly repeating bass line, but a seemingly incessant melodic-rhythmic pattern, in the vein of Stravinsky.

31. Even this moment, however, is not allowed for sustained expression. It is broken into parts, between which the judge and beadle arrive and find the two lovers engrossed in one another. Johanna is taken away and Anthony sings the lyric, "I'll steal you, Johanna." All in the interests of pacing.

32. Zadan, Sondheim & Co., 245.

33. Bond, *Sweeney Todd,* Act I, scene 8.

34. Richard Eder, "Critic's Notebook: 'Sweeney' 's Dark Side," *New York Times,* March 29, 1979, Sec. III, p. 16.

35. Zadan, *Sondheim & Co.,* 245.

36. Clive Hirschhorn, "Will Sondheim Succeed in Being Genuinely Japanese?," *New York Times,* January 4, 1976, Sec. II, p. 5.

37. Zadan, *Sondheim & Co.,* 233.

38. Ibid., 234.

39. Ibid., 28.

40. Ibid., 207.

41. Kauffmann, "Slay It With Music," 25.

42. Angela Lansbury, who created the role of Mrs. Lovett, is certainly a star, but there is no evidence that Sondheim made any concessions to her in composing the opera, and the opera is certainly no vehicle in the sense that star qualities are high-lighted at the expense of dramatic integrity.

## Chapter 15.   Epilogue

1. Joan Peyser, *Bernstein: A Biography* (New York: William Morrow, 1987), 267.

2. The early versions of Jerome Kern's *Show Boat* also begin with a prologue. It was not until the 1946 revival that producer Billy Rose insisted on a medley overture to replace it. This is still the one most used today.

3. *Words With Music* (New York: Macmillan, 1972), 88.

4. John Lahr, "Sondheim's Little Deaths," *Harper's* 258 (April 1979), 71.

# Index

# Asian Americans

AN INTERPRETIVE HISTORY

Forthcoming titles in

*Twayne's Immigrant Heritage of America Series*

---

*Chinese Immigration to the United States*
*Cuban Americans*
*Japanese Americans*

# Twayne's Immigrant Heritage of America Series

Thomas J. Archdeacon, General Editor

# Asian Americans

## AN INTERPRETIVE HISTORY

## Sucheng Chan

*Twayne Publishers* ✶ Boston
*A Division of G. K. Hall & Co.*

Published by Twayne Publishers
A division of G. K. Hall & Co.
70 Lincoln Street
Boston, Massachusetts 02111

Jacket photograph by Fred Mancao, courtesy of Fred Cordova, *Filipinos: The Forgotten Asian Americans* (Seattle: Demonstration Project for Asian Americans, 1983).

Maps courtesy of Materials for Today's Learning, Inc. Reproduced from ASIAN CALIFORNIANS by Sucheng Chan (Materials for Today's Learning, 1990).

Copyediting supervised by Barbara Sutton.
Book design and production by Gabrielle B. McDonald.
Typeset in Meridien with Novarese display type
by Huron Valley Graphics Inc. of Ann Arbor, Michigan.

The paper used in this publication meets the minimum requirements of American National Standard for Information Sciences—Permanence of Paper for Printed Library Materials, ANSI Z39.48-1984. ∞

Printed and bound in the United States of America.

**Library of Congress Cataloging-in-Publication Data**

Chan, Sucheng.
    Asian Americans : an interpretive history / Sucheng Chan.
        p.      cm.—(Twayne's immigrant heritage of America series)
    Includes bibliographical references and index.
    ISBN 0-8057-8426-8.—ISBN 0-8057-8437-3 (pbk.)
    1. Asian Americans—History.      I. Title.   II. Series.
E184.O6C47   1991
973'.0495—dc20                                              90-44174
                                                                 CIP

0-8057-8426-8 (alk. paper) 10 9 8 7 6 5 4 3 2
0-8057-8437-3 (pbk.: alk. paper) 10 9 8 7 6 5 4 3

*For my students and colleagues in*
*Asian American Studies*

# Contents

# Foreword

As the United States begins a new decade, it seems a most appropriate time for Twayne Publishers to revive its Immigrant Heritage of America Series. The 1980s set a record in terms of the number of people added permanently to the population of the United States through some form of immigration. During the decade approximately nine million people entered the United States—some under the nation's standard immigration and refugee policies and others without such authorization. That total was approximately three-quarters of a million larger than the number of aliens who arrived on these shores from 1900 to 1909, the decade that formerly held the record.

Today's immigrants to the United States come from places far removed from those that sent the large majority of earlier immigrants. Between 1981 and 1985, only 11 percent of documented immigrants to the United States were of European origin; approximately half came from Asia and the Middle East, and more than a fifth from Latin America. Because the fertility rate of native residents of the United States is low, especially in comparison with that of recent arrivals, a continuation of current immigration and reproductive patterns will bring important change in the ethnic composition of the United States over the next 30 years. Demographers have estimated that, between 1990 and 2020, the percentage of non-Hispanic whites in the population will fall from 75.6 to 64.9. According to the same set of projections, Latinos will rise from 8.7 percent to 15.4 percent of the population and Asians from 3.3 percent to 6.5 percent.

The goal of this revived series is to present the stories behind these modern developments and to place them in the proper historical context. The focus will be on those immigrant peoples most numerous among recent arrivals, whether or not they were a visible part of American society prior to 1965. The series will also have room for volumes on European groups for which up-to-date treatments are needed.

Sucheng Chan's *Asian Americans* gets the series off to a strong start. Professor Chan's comprehensive study tells the story of Asians and Asian Americans in the United States from the gold rush to the space age. It is a gracefully written, comprehensive history and an acute, social-scientific analysis. Professor Chan deftly demonstrates the similarities among the experiences of the several groups examined but is equally careful to point out the differences among them as well. Perhaps most important, Professor Chan has portrayed the women and men who are her subjects, despite the hardships and discrimination they often faced, as shapers of their own fates and full participants in the making of America.

THOMAS J. ARCHDEACON, GENERAL EDITOR
*University of Wisconsin–Madison*

# Preface

A good work of synthesis can be produced only when there is a sufficient number of sound monographs to serve as its foundation. Given the strong anti-Asian bias in some of the older works, the uneven quality of the current scholarship on Asian Americans, and the fact that more has been published on Chinese and Japanese Americans than on other groups of Asian Americans, it is perhaps premature to attempt a comparative history that gives each of the major subgroups its due. As Asian Americans increase in numbers and in visibility, however, and as college students in many parts of the country press their faculty for a more ethnically diverse curriculum, the need for a succinct history of Asian Americans becomes more urgent by the year.

This study is an interim effort to meet such a need. It offers a quick overview of important aspects of Asian American history within a framework that emphasizes the commonalities in the experiences of the Chinese, Japanese, Korean, Asian Indian, and Filipino immigrants who have been in this country since the nineteenth century and, in a much more abbreviated way, of the refugees and immigrants from Vietnam, Laos, and Kampuchea, who have come only since 1975. Though it is often thought that these various groups are lumped together as "Asian Americans" because they or their ancestors have all come from Asia, there is a more important reason for treating them as a collective entity: for the most part, the host society has treated them all alike, regardless of what differences might have existed in their cultures, religions, and languages, or in the status of their homelands in the family of nations.

Broadly speaking, scholars have studied Asian Americans and other minority groups in the United States from at least four different perspectives. The oldest approach, popular before the 1960s, implies that members of minority groups are deviant or deficient. To become "normal," they must shed their "dysfunctional" cultures in order to assimilate into the majority Anglo-American one. The second stance is celebratory and emphasizes the colorful cultural contributions that various immigrant groups or the indigenous peoples of the Americas have made. Though heartwarming, this perspective often fails to question why the different components of America's multiethnic mosaic have not been treated equally. The third viewpoint depicts minority groups as victims, exploited in myriad ways as a result of their low placement within the institutional structure of the United States. It focuses primarily on collective behavior and the organization of society—especially the economy—and not on individual aspirations or achievements. The fourth angle of vision sees members of minority groups as agents of history—men and women who make choices that shape their lives, even when these may be severely limited by conditions beyond their control.

In this book, I tell the story of Asian Americans mainly from the third and fourth perspectives. In a short volume such as this, however, I cannot include lengthy life histories, even though they may be the most effective way of demonstrating "agency" on the part of the protagonists. I can depict Asian immigrants and their descendants as agents in the making of their own history only implicitly, by framing the story in a manner that assumes they made conscious calculations about their life chances as they pondered whether or not to come to the United States in the first place and, after experiencing great hardship here, whether to leave or to remain—all within the limits set by the socioeconomic and political environments in which they found themselves.

Those who stayed had to fashion mechanisms to ensure their own survival. One such means was standing up and fighting for their rights. Recounting this history of struggle is one way to tell the story from an Asian American point of view. Therefore, even though more has been written about the anti-Chinese, anti-Japanese, and anti-Filipino movements than about any other topic in Asian American studies, I allot relatively little space here to explicating the causes of anti-Asian sentiments and actions. I focus, rather, on how Asian immigrants themselves have fought against the discrimination they faced, as they tried to claim a rightful place for themselves in American society.

Two other consequences follow from my choice of framework. First, I do not accord the assimilationist approach the central importance that many older studies of European immigration have given it. This is so not because Asians refused to assimilate—that is, to discard their own heritage in order to adopt Anglo-American beliefs and behavior, as their detractors have claimed repeatedly—but because assimilation does not depend solely on the predilections of the newcomers. It can occur only when members of the host society give immigrants a chance to become equal partners in the world they share and mutually shape. As this book will reveal, Asian immigrants were never given that chance until quite recently.

Second, instead of discussing Asian cultures in general and how they have been preserved in the United States, I look only at those aspects that have been selectively used by Asian immigrants to cope with life in the New World. Culture is dynamic and is constantly molded by its carriers—including humble men, women, and children who may not even be able to articulate its norms and values with clarity. As immigrants confront a new environment, they inevitably take on some of its characteristics, in the process creating a new synthesis that goes beyond a simple "blending" of two different legacies. For that reason, Asian immigrant communities are not, and cannot be, exact replicas of those in Asia, either sociologically or culturally, nor are they carbon copies of other communities in mainstream American society. Rather, they are components of an increasingly multiethnic American landscape and can best be understood and appreciated as such.

I call this an interpretive history because the topics I choose to emphasize and the manner in which I have linked them together reflect how I have come to understand Asian American history, after taking into consideration the best scholarship available to date. I shall no doubt revise my analysis as new research becomes available. Moreover, other scholars would have told the story in other ways.

Finally, given the brevity of my account, I could not discuss four important concerns that a fuller history would have to include: 1) an analysis of the changing social, economic, and political environment in the United States—particularly in the American West—that have influenced how Asian immigrants were and are being received; 2) theories that social scientists have advanced for understanding the relationship between majority and minority groups in the United States and elsewhere in the world; 3) a historiographical essay that examines the assumptions—often hidden—of various authors and how their works reflect the temper of the times; and

4) a fuller treatment of Asian American women's history from a feminist perspective, which would force us to reconceptualize many aspects of Asian American history. These analytical, rather than narrative, aspects of the story will have to be dealt with in a future work.

# Terminology and Transliterations

To create a conceptual parallel between Americans of European and Asian ancestry, I call the former Euro-Americans. I use the term "white" only when I discuss anti-Asian laws and activities: the distinction between white and nonwhite peoples was one that those involved in the anti-Asian movements chose to draw. Such dichotomies, codified into state and federal laws, bedeviled the lives of Asians in America for a century.

I call Asians who lived and worked in the United States before the 1960s immigrants. I refer to their children who grew up during the first half of the twentieth century as the American-born or the second generation. For the years after the mid-1960s, I use the term *Asian American*, regardless of where the individual referred to was born, because most Asians now come to settle and to acquire citizenship.

The term *Asian American* has political and bureaucratic origins. Young activists in the 1960s popularized it in order to emphasize the commonality among the different groups of Asian Americans, while government agencies adopted it because they found it convenient to lump together the various Asian groups and people from the Pacific Islands as *Asian Pacific Americans*.

I call people from the Indian subcontinent Asian Indians because it is the nomenclature most widely used at present, having received official sanction in the 1980 U.S. census of population. But people from India have also been known as East Indians, Hindus, and Hindustanis.

I refer to people from the Philippines as Filipinos, and not Pilipinos, even though in the 1960s and 1970s community activists and leftist academics in Hawaii and the Pacific Coast chose to spell the word with a *p* as a way to honor the old immigrants, many of whom were laborers without much education. There is no *f* sound in most of the languages and dialects spoken in the Philippines, so some Filipinos pronounce words beginning with an *f* as though they begin with a *p*. Today's highly educated immigrants consider it an insult to imply they cannot pronounce the *f* sound, so *Filipino* is now more acceptable.

I use *Cambodia* and *Cambodians* when I write about the pre-1975 period and *Kampuchea* and *Kampucheans* for the period following the establishment of Democratic Kampuchea in 1975.

Rendering personal and place names in Chinese American history is especially vexatious because most of the early immigrants were Cantonese-speakers, and Cantonese pronunciation is quite different from *putonghua* (Mandarin), the official dialect that is usually transliterated in English-language writings on China. There is a standard transliteration for Cantonese designed by scholars at Yale University, but I choose to use the forms found in the available writings on Chinese Americans, inconsistent though they be, so that readers can identify the proper names in this book with those found in the existing literature. When a name first appears, I give the pinyin transliteration, then in parenthesis either the Wade-Giles transliteration for Mandarin names and words, or the old Post Office spellings commonly used before 1949, or the nonstandard (but accepted) transliteration for Cantonese ones.

When writing about Asians in their homelands, I generally give the names in the Asian order, with an individual's surname (family name or "last" name) first, followed by his or her given name(s). Exceptions occur when a particular individual (e.g., Syngman Rhee) chose to reverse the order to conform to Western usage. The names of Asian immigrants in the United States are given in the form they themselves used (in English), whether they be the Asian or Western order. The names of American-born persons of Asian ancestry are given in the Western order: first name, middle name, and family name. All foreign words are italicized only at their first appearance in the text.

# Acknowledgments

Gary Y. Okihiro and Michael A. Omi offered detailed, incisive, and copious comments that greatly improved this book. Thomas J. Archdeacon, General Editor of this series, asked me to clarify various points that made the narrative more cogent. Wendy Lee Ng and Amado Y. Cabezas each read one chapter, while Spencer C. Olin and K. Scott Wong reviewed most of the chapters to assess how students might react to the text. Carrie L. Waara helped with proofreading and Donna Wilke prepared the index. I am grateful to all of them, as well as to Athenaide Dallett, John Martin, Barbara Sutton, Gabrielle McDonald, Katherine Cronin Connors, Deborah Azerrad, and Larry Hamberlin of Twayne Publishers who guided the manuscript through the publication process. Since a work of synthesis by its very nature is built on the intellectual foundation laid by other scholars in the field, I am indebted to all the authors whose works I cite in the Notes and References and Bibliographic Essay.

I also thank Adrienne Morgan who drew the maps, which are reprinted with the permission of Jack Taylor of Boyd and Fraser Publishing Co., publisher of another work of mine, *Asian Californians*. I am grateful to Daniel S. Lev, who gave me the information used to design the map on the refugee outflow from Vietnam, Laos, and Kampuchea, and to the University of Hawaii Press for permission to reproduce the map of Korea showing the locations where David Deshler set up his recruitment offices.

Janice Mirikitani has kindly granted permission to reprint lines from her poem "Breaking Silence," originally published in her book *Shedding Silence* (Berkeley: Celestial Arts, 1987).

The photographs are reproduced with the permission of the Bishop Museum, Honolulu; the Public Archives Canada; the Bancroft Library at the University of California, Berkeley; Visual Communications, Los Angeles; the Demonstration Project for Asian Americans, Seattle; U.S. National Archives; the U.S. Navy; the San Joaquin County Recorder's Office, Stockton, California; the Educational Opportunity Program at the University of California, Santa Barbara; Mary Paik Lee; Katsuji Uranaga; Kats Nakamura; and Shulee Ong.

The several thousand students who have taken my courses over the last two decades at Sonoma State University and at the Berkeley, Santa Cruz, San Diego, and Santa Barbara campuses of the University of California also deserve my thanks. Without their always probing and sometimes troubled questions—to which I was forced to find answers—my understanding of the Asian American experience would be considerably shallower.

Finally, I wish to express my appreciation to Mark, who left me alone, and to sweet Cotufa, who refrained from mischief, while I produced this book under great pressure of time.

# Asian Americans

AN INTERPRETIVE HISTORY

*Japanese contract laborers assigned numbers in a Hawaiian sugarcane plantation, ca. 1890.*
Courtesy Gilman Collection, the Bishop Museum

# chapter one

# The International Context of Asian Emigration

D uring the second half of the nineteenth century and the early decades of the twentieth, almost a million people from China, Japan, Korea, the Philippines, and India emigrated to the United States and to Hawaii. (The latter was an independent kingdom from 1810 to 1893, a republic between 1894 and 1900, and a territory of the United States from 1900 to 1959.) Customs officials recorded approximately 370,000 Chinese arrivals in Hawaii and California between the late 1840s and early 1880s. In the next three decades, immigration authorities counted about 400,000 Japanese landings at Honolulu and at ports of entry along the Pacific Coast. During the first third of the present century, they processed some 7,000 Korean, 7,000 Asian Indian, and 180,000 Filipino entries in the islands and the mainland. In each instance, the actual number of individuals involved was smaller, because reentries were combined with new arrivals in the extant statistics. In comparison, approximately 35 million European immigrants set foot on American soil between 1850 and 1930.

The five groups of Asian immigrants came under three different sets of circumstances. The Chinese, the first to arrive, were pushed out by powerful forces at home as well as attracted by the discovery of gold in California, the Pacific Northwest, and British Columbia and by jobs that became available as the American West developed. Opponents of Chinese immigration charged that those who came to North America were part of the coolie trade that brought indentured laborers from southern China to Latin America between 1847 and 1874. But in fact, most of the men who came to North America bought their tickets on credit and were not contract laborers per se. Once they repaid their debts from the wages they earned, they were free to do as they pleased.

Initial Japanese, Korean, and Filipino immigration followed a second pattern: it was induced by Hawaiian sugar plantation owners who sent agents to recruit workers by the thousands as sugar cultivation expanded. Before Hawaii was annexed by the United States, contract laborers could enter the islands legally. Japanese, Korean, and Filipino immigration into the continental United States was initially a spillover of the traffic to Hawaii, although a small number of diplomats, students, and merchants from each country had preceded the masses of their compatriots to the mainland. Once transoceanic migration had been set in motion, it acquired a momentum of its own. By the time contract labor was outlawed in Hawaii, recruitment was no longer necessary to continue the flow.

Asian Indian immigration was far smaller in scale and formed a third pattern. Most of the pioneers were adherents of the Sikh faith from the Punjab region of northwestern India. They paid their own passage to Canada and the Pacific Coast and came in small groups of three to five persons, relying on their own social networks—particularly their temples, which served as hostels—to facilitate their journey. They came in search of work, but Hawaii was not one of their way stations; neither did any gold rush lure them to North America. Furthermore, they were not part of the traffic that shipped several million Indians to different parts of the British Empire to work in plantations, mines, or construction projects during the nineteenth and early twentieth centuries.

Despite differences in detail, however, Asian international migration was part of a larger, global phenomenon: the movement of workers, capital, and technology across national boundaries to enable entrepreneurs to exploit natural resources in more and more parts of the world. The capitalist form of production, under which goods are produced for sale in order to make the largest profit possible and workers receive wages for selling their labor, first appeared in England. As industries were established in that country and in other parts of western Europe, and as more and more of their arable land was used to grow cash crops for the world market, peasants who had formerly grown food mainly for subsistence were dislocated from the land. Some of them moved to urban centers within their own countries to work in factories and construction projects, while others journeyed across the seas in search of better economic opportunities, including a chance to buy farmland of their own.

Places with a temperate climate—particularly Canada, the United States, Australia, New Zealand, and South Africa—became major destinations for millions of European colonists, settlers, and immigrants. In comparison, relatively few Europeans went to the more tropical lands of Asia, Africa, and Latin America, even though their homeland governments had colonized parts of those continents in order to extract precious metals and minerals and to cultivate tropical and semitropical crops. The workers needed for these new enterprises came from different sources. Where the indigenous population did not provide a large enough labor supply, the European colonizers shipped hands from other lands. Until the beginning of the nineteenth century, enslaved Africans provided much of the imported work force in the warmer regions of the Americas. But after Great Britain stopped participating in the African slave trade in 1807 and especially after slavery was abolished in the British Empire in 1833, Indians and Chinese became the two main groups of nonwhite international migrant workers. Indians went to what were then and what became British colonies: Malaya, Singapore, and Burma in Southeast Asia; Kenya, Uganda, Zanzibar, Rhodesia, and South Africa in Africa; British Guiana in South America; Trinidad and Jamaica in the Caribbean; Mauritius Island in the Indian Ocean; and the Fiji Islands in the Pacific Ocean. Large numbers of Chinese were recruited to work in some of those places and in Peru and Cuba as well.

In the United States, due to regional differences in its economy, labor needs were filled by different groups. European immigrants tilled the land taken from the continent's native peoples and worked in the industries that developed along the Atlantic Coast and in the Midwest. In the southern United States, enslaved Africans and, in the early years, European indentured servants cultivated the farms and plantations owned by Euro-Americans. In the southwestern part of the country, acquired from Mexico in 1848, racially mixed descendants of Spanish conquerors and Native Americans met the demand for manual labor. Along the Pacific Coast and in Hawaii, Asians provided most of the backbending labor in mining, commercial agriculture, public works, and domestic service.

Chinese emigration had begun, however, centuries before Europeans and Americans became interested in Chinese labor. In the seventh century, people from Fujian (Fukien) province in southeastern China started crossing the narrow Taiwan Straits to fish and to settle in the small Penghu Islands and the larger island of Taiwan. They were joined the following century by people from the neighboring province of Guangdong (Kwangtung). Soon, inhabitants of these two provinces were sailing on a regular basis in ships called *junks* to various localities in Southeast Asia. Their trading season and shipping routes were dictated by the monsoons. Junks left southeastern Chinese ports in January and February, when the northeast monsoon blew across the South China Sea, and returned in August during the southwest monsoon. On the heels of traders came more permanent settlers. Chinese maritime activity reached its zenith in the early fifteenth century when the Chinese government financed several expeditions that reached the east coast of Africa.

But China's interest in maritime expansion did not continue for long. In the seventeenth century, officials of the Qing (Ch'ing) dynasty (1644–1911), which had succeeded the Ming dynasty (1368–1644), promulgated a series of edicts to prohibit emigration. Following the Manchu conquest of China (which established the Qing dynasty), thousands of Ming loyalists had fled abroad. Fearing that such dissidents might foment anti-Qing activities, the new government forbade individuals to leave; those who did so would return to China on pain of death. The decrees remained on the books until the end of the nineteenth century, but they were not enforced effectively. Throughout this period, people from Fujian and Guangdong continued to emigrate.

Virtually all the Chinese who went abroad came from only five small regions in the two provinces of Fujian and Guangdong and the island of Hainan.[1] Three of the groups settled mainly in Southeast Asia. The other two went also to Hawaii and the Americas. A vast majority of those who landed in California during the nineteenth century came from Guangdong province.

The Guangdong natives in North America can in turn be divided into three subgroups, each of which spoke its own dialect. Sanyi (Sam Yup) people came from three districts immediately west and north of the city of Guangzhou (Canton) in the Pearl River Delta; Siyi (Sze Yup) inhabitants hailed from four districts to the southwest of Sanyi; while Xiangshan (Heungsan) natives originated from a district located between Canton and the Portuguese colony of Macao, some 40 miles west of Xianggang (Hong Kong). This district was later renamed Zhongshan (Chungsan).

The fact that the Chinese who came to the United States originated from such a geographically concentrated area requires explanation; to fathom the causes of Cantonese emigration, it is not enough to point to such factors as

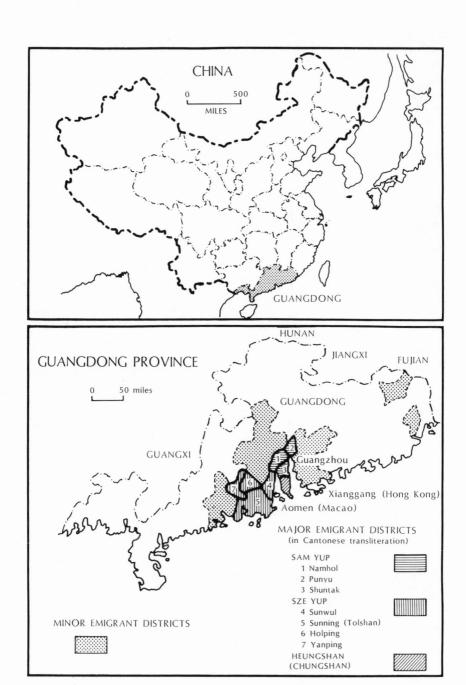

Map 1. *Major emigrant districts in the province of Guangdong, China, nineteenth century.*

population pressure, economic change, political upheaval, religious persecution, or natural disaster, which students of emigration and immigration usually rely on for explanation. That so many Chinese emigrants to the Western hemisphere should have flowed out of Canton and its vicinity is explicable only in terms of the special role that city has played in Chinese history, especially vis-à-vis China's interaction with the outside world.[2]

During the late Tang (T'ang) and Northern Song (Sung) dynasties (618–907 and 960–1127, respectively), China's maritime trade was centered at Canton, where thousands of foreign merchants congregated. But beginning in the Southern Song dynasty (1127–1279) and lasting until the first half of the eighteenth century, shipowners and merchants in the lower Yangzi (Yangtze) valley and along the southern coast also became active in international commerce. During these centuries, the central government favored Quanzhou (Ch'uanchou) in Fujian province, in particular, as its chief port for foreign commerce, because it was closer than was Canton to Hangzhou (Hangchow), the center of silk production—silk being one of China's most sought-after exports. Canton regained its monopoly in foreign trade, however, in 1760. For the next eight decades, foreigners interacted there with licensed Chinese merchants known as *cohong*. As more and more Europeans became active in the China trade, Canton became a funnel through which Western influence penetrated the country.

Great Britain led the Western powers in "opening" China to trade and Christian proselytizing. Initially, the trade balance between Britain and China was in the latter's favor. The chief item that the British purhased was tea, but the amount they bought far exceeded in value the woolens and other merchandise they offered the Chinese, who demanded payment in silver bullion. In an attempt to reverse the trade balance, the British imported increasing amounts of opium into China. As more and more Chinese became addicts, the balance of trade reversed. To pay for the rising volume of opium imports, silver started flowing out of China into British coffers. In the late 1830s, to curb the influx of this drug—grown in India, by then the "crown jewel of the British Empire"—Lin Zexu (Lin Tse-hsü), a Chinese official, confiscated and destroyed thousands of chests of opium stored in the English merchants' warehouses in Canton. To avenge England's honor, London sent a naval squadron to China. The war that ensued is known as the first Opium War (1839–42), which China lost.

The Treaty of Nanjing (Nanking), which ended the war, forced the Chinese to open five ports to foreign commerce, abolish the cohong system, sharply limit the amount of customs duty they could charge, pay an indemnity of 21 million silver dollars, cede the island of Hong Kong to Great Britain, allow Christian missionaries to preach in various localities, get rid of certain diplomatic protocol that had irked the Europeans, and most damaging of all, grant not only Great Britain, but also its allies, extraterritoriality, which made Westerners immune to Chinese law.

These terms affected the common people adversely. Porters and dockhands lost their jobs as Canton lost its trade monopoly. Cottage industries, unable to compete against the imported factory-manufactured piece goods, declined, depriving many peasant households of an important source of supplementary income. Taxes soared as the government tried to raise sufficient funds to pay the indemnity. And as opium continued to pour into the country, the number of addicts multiplied.

To make matters worse, the Treaty of Tianjin (Tientsin), which ended the Anglo-Chinese War (1856–60), wrung further concessions from China. The conflict had begun after Chinese soldiers arrested some pirates on a Chinese-owned boat that flew the British flag and had an English captain. The alleged affront to Britain's honor provided England with a pretext to attack China. The war was fought in two phases, with French troops joining the English ones during the latter. When the Chinese lost this war also, they had to open more ports to trade, legalize opium, pay an additional indemnity, cede Jiulong (Kowloon)—territory on the Chinese mainland opposite Hong Kong—to Britain, and allow missionaries to proselytize in the interior of China. Moreover, English and French soldiers occupied Canton between 1858 and 1861. Their presence made it far easier for labor recruiters to lure peasant boys aboard foreign ships, thus circumventing the central government's ban on emigration.

Along with the widespread social, economic, and political dislocations caused by the presence of Westerners, domestic developments also created pressures for emigration. Hong Xiuchuan (Hung Hsiu-ch'uan), a native of Guangxi (Kwangsi), the province west of Guangdong, who had been exposed to Christian teachings, concluded he was the younger brother of Jesus Christ and led an uprising—the Taiping Rebellion—that swept through much of South and Central China, lasted more than a decade (1850–64), and resulted in an estimated 10 million deaths. Though the fiercest fighting did not take place in South China, the Taiping armies did trample fields, sack dwellings, and conscript villagers as they marched through some of the emigrant districts of Guangdong. Further destruction was caused during the same years by a series of bitter interethnic feuds between two dialect groups, the Cantonese and the Kejia (Hakka). At the same time, members of a secret society, dubbed the Red Turbans because of their headgear, rose in revolt in five of the major emigrant districts. Imperial troops burned large areas to deny them cover. Both types of local warfare devastated the Pearl River Delta, making life extremely precarious for the inhabitants in the region. Emigration therefore became not just a means to a better life, but a lifeline. Although aspiring emigrants had many destinations to choose from, places where gold had been discovered—most notably California, Australia, and the Fraser River valley in British Columbia—were the most alluring. Had Western ships not called at Canton, Hong Kong, or Aomen (Macao) to take them to these far-off destinations, however, they very likely would have simply traveled by junk to Southeast Asia.

Western incursion was less violent but no less profound in Japan. During the Tokugawa period (1600–1868), when military rulers known as the shogun held sway over lesser feudal lords, the only outsiders the Japanese interacted with were Chinese merchants they allowed at Nagasaki and on the Ryukyu Islands (Okinawa) and a handful of Koreans and Dutch they permitted on the Tsushima islands and Deshima, respectively. Situated off the coast of mainland Asia, Japan had throughout its history been relatively protected from external infringement. Before the nineteenth century, the island-nation suffered from invasions only twice, when Khubilai Khan tried unsuccessfully in 1274 and 1281 to take Japan. The Japanese first encountered Europeans when the Portuguese landed in 1543 on a small island off the southern tip of Kyushu Island in southwestern Japan. Christian proselytizing began in 1549 with the arrival of the Jesuit Francis Xavier. The Catholic missionaries were quite effective: it is estimated that by the end of the sixteenth century, there were perhaps 300,000 converts in Japan. To counter the missionaries' visible success, the first Tokugawa shogun, Ieyasu, started issuing anti-Christian decrees in 1606. The persecution of Japanese Christians culminated in 1637–38, when some 20,000 of them revolted and were brutally suppressed on the Shimabara peninsula. Thereafter, Japan withdrew unto itself, enjoying almost two and a half centuries of peace, with minimal foreign influence.

Japan's policy of seclusion was rudely interrupted in 1853, when the American naval officer Matthew Perry sailed into Edo (later Tokyo) Bay. He had been dispatched to East Asian waters to "open" Japan to Western—particularly American—navigation, trade, and diplomatic relations. After considerable debate, and with the recent example of the British subjugation of China in mind, some of the Tokugawa leaders reluctantly decided to negotiate. The United States and Japan signed a treaty in 1854 that wrested privileges from Japan similar to those acquired by European nations in China. In the next few years, Japan signed additional "unequal" treaties with several of the imperialist powers, which periodically reminded the Japanese of the potential disaster that could befall their country should it refuse to abide by these treaties. British ships bombarded the city of Kagoshima in 1863 in retaliation for the death of an Englishman; the following year, joint Western naval forces destroyed the cannons the Japanese had used to block the passage of ships through the Straits of Shimonoseki.

Such an external show of force led to a severe domestic political crisis, one result of which was the Meiji Restoration of 1868. New leaders, who favored learning the ways of the West in order to cope with its might, came into power in the name of "restoring" the emperor—for centuries a titular leader but an important symbol—to paramount status. They reformed virtually every aspect of national life, but the burden of their country's dazzling ascent as an international power was borne by those least able to afford it.

To finance their program of rapid industrialization, the Meiji oligarchs imposed a new system of land taxation, whereby farmers had to pay taxes based on the assessed value of their land rather than on the size of their harvest—as they had done in earlier days. This meant that landowners, tenant farmers, and agricultural laborers no longer had a built-in safeguard against crop failures. This land tax was absolutely crucial in Japan's modernization efforts: it provided 90 percent of all tax revenues and 70 percent of all fiscal revenues during the first year it was in effect; by the end of the century, it still constituted more than half of the government's total income. When the feudal domains were abolished, the government paid "stipends" to ex-samurai who had been deprived of the privileges they formerly enjoyed. The common people also bore the brunt of this expenditure. Putting down the 1877 Satsuma Rebellion further drained the national treasury. To curb rising inflation, the finance minister introduced deflationary measures that exacerbated hardships as the price of rice—the chief source of income for the agricultural population—plummeted. During the 1880s some 367,000 farmers were dispossessed of their land for failure to pay taxes. By 1890 some 40 percent of the cultivators had become tenants. That figure rose to 45 percent the following decade.

HIROSHIMA

YAMAGUCHI

OKAYAMA

FUKUOKA

JAPAN

NAGASAKI

WAKAYAMA

KUMAMOTO

Map 2. *Major emigrant prefectures in Japan, late nineteenth and early twentieth centuries.*

In addition to the negative impact of the economic changes on the common people, another reform undertaken during the Meiji era helped to make emigration attractive. A national conscription law was enacted in 1873, as a warrior class obligated to bear arms—the samurai—no longer existed. A series of amendments to the original law allowed students studying abroad and emigrants to be exempted from military service, first until the age of 26 and, later, until age 32. Until 1908, when the government decided to exercise stricter control over individuals trying to evade their national obligation, Japanese men who remained abroad past their thirty-third birthdays could escape conscription.

These political, social, and economic changes created some necessary preconditions for emigration, but they do not by themselves account for the pattern of departures from Japan.[3] Like the Chinese, the bulk of the Japanese emigrants who left from 1885 onward originated from only a relatively small area—a region in southwestern Japan that was by no means the country's poorest. In fact, the relatively mild weather there allowed two crops to be grown a year, and the area was home to some of Japan's most profitable commercial crops. Hiroshima, Yamaguchi, Okayama, and Wakayama prefectures on Honshu Island, and Fukuoka, Kumamoto, Nagasaki, Saga, and Kagoshima prefectures on Kyushu Island sent the most emigrants to the Western hemisphere but not because they suffered the worst disasters or were the most overpopulated or most barren parts of the country. Rather, these prefectures became emigrant communities because, as Hilary Conroy has discovered, an American, Robert Walker Irwin, had developed a relationship with Inoue Kaoru, the Japanese foreign minister, and Masuda Takashi, the president of Mitsui Bussan, an import-export company.[4] Such a friendship took on significance because of the misfortune that had befallen three small groups of Japanese taken to the Western hemisphere a decade and a half earlier.

Aside from a few shipwrecked sailors and members of a diplomatic mission, the first Japanese to set foot in the Americas did so in 1868 and 1869, when the American Eugene Van Reed, a German company, and the Dutchman Edward Schnell illegally spirited several hundred individuals out of Japan to work in Hawaii, Guam, and California, respectively.[5] The 149 persons sent to Hawaii were treated so poorly that in late 1869 the Japanese government, greatly annoyed, dispatched two representatives to bring 40 of them home. As a result of this misadventure, officials decided to ban all emigration. Amicable relations between Japan and Hawaii were restored in 1871 by a treaty. Ten years later, Hawaii's King Kalakaua visited Japan during his world tour and tried, among other things, to persuade Japan to allow its subjects to emigrate to Hawaii, but to no avail. Two different Hawaiian envoys visited Japan in 1882 and 1883 for the same purpose. They likewise failed in their mission. Meanwhile, several other countries also requested Japanese workers, but the government did not lift the prohibition until 1885, when the first shipload of legally sanctioned Japanese contract laborers sailed for Hawaii. The men and women departed under the terms of an agreement worked out between Irwin—who, though an American, was then serving as consul general and special agent of the Board of Immigration for the Kingdom of Hawaii, while simultaneously acting as a foreign advisor to Mitsui Bussan—and the Japanese government.[6] Tokyo had decided to allow its subjects to go abroad only if they could do so under strict

supervision. Under the Irwin Convention, which remained in force until 1894 and over which both the Hawaiian and Japanese governments provided oversight, some 29,000 Japanese went to work in sugar plantations on three-year contracts. Men were initially paid 9 dollars and women 6 dollars a month. Later, their wages were raised to 15 and 9 dollars, respectively. The workers labored for 10 hours a day in the fields or 12 hours a day in the sugar mills for 26 days a month. Passage to Hawaii, lodging, fuel, medical care, and interpreter service were supposed to be provided free of charge, but from time to time, the plantation owners passed these expenses onto the workers.

Irwin himself took charge of the initial recruitment. He went to southwestern Japan because that was where his friends, Inoue Kaoru and Masuda Takashi, both natives of Yamaguchi, had suggested he go. Masuda even sent employees from his company into the countryside to assist Irwin's paid agents, who traveled from one village to the next, signing up prospective emigrants, some three-quarters of whom were farmers. The sugar plantation owners desired only able-bodied young men with farming experience. Moreover, they specified that no batch of workers could contain more than 25 percent women. The recruiters encountered no problems in finding people willing to go. Not only did the Japanese have a long tradition of *dekasegi* (leaving home temporarily in search of employment in neighboring villages or even prefectures), but the monthly wage in Hawaii was approximately twice the earnings of skilled artisans in Japan and six times what farmers made.[7] Of those who went to Hawaii between 1885 and 1894, 44 percent settled there, 46 percent returned to Japan, 3 percent went to the continental United States, and 7 percent died.

After 10 years, Irwin and the Japanese government both tired of the emigration business, so it was turned over to private companies. Alan Moriyama has shown how these firms operated under a strict set of regulations. They charged aspiring emigrants various fees to help them process applications, obtain passports, purchase tickets, and prepare for their medical examinations. Some of the companies also ran boardinghouses near the docks where they housed the emigrants until they set sail. Between 1894 and 1908 about 125,000 Japanese—approximately 15 percent of them female and more than half of them from Hiroshima, Yamaguchi, Fukuoka, and Kumamoto—went to Hawaii through these companies. During the same period, an additional 17,000 persons traveled to the islands independently.[8]

While conditions in Japan made it relatively easy for recruiters to lure Japanese first to Hawaii and then to the mainland, the exodus from Korea depended less on general social dislocations than on the willingness of an American diplomat to aid Hawaii's sugar planters. He succeeded in his efforts because of his friendship with the Korean king. However, though royal intervention made emigration possible, had international politics not brought Americans to Korea in the 1880s, Korean emigration probably would not have occurred when it did.

After being ravaged by Japanese invasions in 1592 and 1597 and by Manchu invasions in the 1630s, Korea sealed itself off from the outside world for almost two and a half centuries until the 1860s, when Western ships began to appear in Korean waters. Korean shore batteries drove off seven French ships in 1866, five American vessels in 1871, and a Japanese ship in 1875. The following year, Japan demanded reparations for the damage. Korea was forced

to sign the Treaty of Kanghwa with Japan—a document modeled after the unequal treaties that both China and Japan had entered into earlier with Western imperialist nations. In addition to granting the Japanese the right to trade at three ports, virtually complete control over the country's foreign trade, the right to operate pawn shops and to lend money, and the right of extraterritoriality, at Japan's insistence Korea also had to declare itself an independent state, in order to undermine the suzerainty that China had enjoyed over the so-called Hermit Kingdom for centuries.

In 1882 the United States, acting through Adm. Robert W. Shufeldt, became the second nation to secure a treaty with Korea. Treaties with Great Britain, Germany, Russia, Italy, and France followed in short order. As was the case in China and Japan, the entry of foreigners and the concessions they wrested led to intense factional struggles within the Korean court and among the *yangban*, the country's ruling class. Meanwhile, a syncretist religious group known as the Tonghak ("Eastern learning," in contrast to Sohak, "Western learning"), which had first appeared in the early 1860s with visions of an earthly paradise, gained many followers in the late 1880s, when poverty became widespread. Though the movement counted many scions of fallen yangban families among its adherents, an increasing number of disgruntled farmers now joined its ranks. Between 1892 and 1894 Tonghak believers staged demonstrations to demand the posthumous rehabilitation of their founder (who had been put to death in 1864) and an end to their own persecution. When the government rebuffed their efforts, a full-scale rebellion broke out, sweeping the countryside like wildfire. The government finally quelled the revolt with the help of Chinese troops.

Japan reacted to the arrival of Chinese soldiers by sending an even larger contingent of its own to the peninsula. The presence of these foreign troops turned Korea into a battleground where its neighbors vied for political and military supremacy. The Sino-Japanese War of 1894–95 was fought on Korean soil. So was the Russo-Japanese War of 1904–05. Japan won both contests and declared Korea its protectorate. Then in 1910 it annexed the peninsula outright and enacted harsh measures to exploit its new colony's natural resources and people.

During those years of turmoil, an American medical missionary, Horace N. Allen, who had arrived in Korea in 1884, managed to win King Kojong's confidence because he had saved the life of an important relative of the queen.[9] Allen's friendly relationship with the royal couple enabled American Protestant missionaries who came after him to work with relative freedom, quite in contrast to the persecution that French Catholic missionaries had encountered in earlier years. Dozens of American Methodists and Presbyterians soon came bearing the gospels and doing good works.

Allen himself did not remain a missionary long. In 1890 he became secretary of the American legation in Seoul, a post he occupied for seven years until he was appointed as the American minister to Korea. He served in the latter capacity until 1905. Throughout those years, he acted as an intermediary between the United States and Korean governments, as well as between private American citizens and the Korean authorities. He succeeded in gaining for his friends several lucrative concessions and franchises, including the Unsan gold mines, the richest mines ever worked in Korea.

In 1902, on his way back to Korea after a visit to the United States, Allen

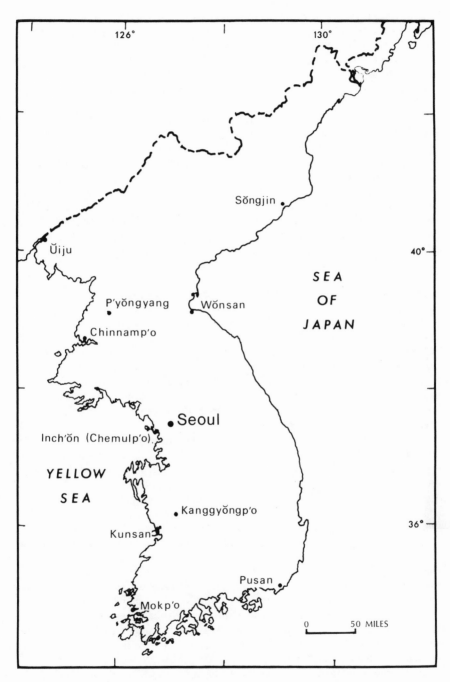

Map 3. Cities where David Deshler set up recruiting offices, Korea, early twentieth century.

stopped in Honolulu, where, as Wayne Patterson has chronicled, he met with representatives of the Hawaiian Sugar Planters' Association (HSPA) at their request. The HSPA was interested in recruiting Koreans in order to counter the growing militance of Japanese plantation workers, who now comprised two-thirds of the entire plantation work force in the islands. Upon his return to Seoul, Allen talked to the king and persuaded him to allow his subjects to emigrate.

Actually, at the turn of the century thousands of Koreans were already living abroad, the majority of them in the Russian maritime provinces and in Manchuria, China, and Japan. Those who settled in the Asian mainland had simply drifted across Korea's northern border without government approval. King Kojong accepted Allen's suggestion to allow his subjects to go to Hawaii partly because famine had stalked several northern provinces the year before, but more important, because he liked the American minister's logic: according to Allen, the Hawaiian plantation owners' desire for Koreans, when they no longer welcomed Japanese, would boost Korea's international standing. The monarch granted the emigration franchise to one of Allen's friends, David W. Deshler, a businessman with enterprises in Japan and Korea.

Deshler set up an office, hired a number of interpreters and recruiters, and opened a bank, in which the HSPA was the sole depositor. By this time the United States had annexed Hawaii, and after the Organic Act was promulgated in 1900, American laws against contract labor became applicable to the islands. This meant that unlike the pioneer Japanese emigrants, Koreans could not be shipped to the islands under contract with prepaid fares. Furthermore, before aspiring immigrants—regardless of whence they came—could land in American territory, they had to prove they were not about to become public charges. It was precisely to deal with these obstacles that Deshler had established his bank. This institution lent money to Koreans for their passage and for the "show money" they had to have in their possession upon arrival.

Few Koreans responded to the recruitment efforts, however, until a number of missionaries persuaded members of their congregations to go to Hawaii, a Christian land. As a result of the active role that missionaries played, an estimated 40 percent of the 7,000 emigrants who left the country between December 1902 and May 1905 were converts. Moreover, unlike the Chinese and Japanese who came from geographically confined areas, Korean emigrants originated from many places, especially seaports and their vicinities, where Deshler's agents were hard at work. Furthermore, fewer of the Korean emigrants than Chinese or Japanese came from agricultural backgrounds: the extant (though skimpy) sources suggest that a large percentage of them were laborers, former soldiers, and artisans.[10] Of the seven thousand Koreans taken to Hawaii, about 1,000 eventually returned home, while another 1,000 proceeded to the mainland.

Korean emigration lasted only two and half years for several reasons. A shipload of about 1,000 Koreans who had been taken to Mexico were so maltreated that the Korean government halted emigration not only to that country but also to Hawaii. Then, as the Russo-Japanese War drew to a close, Japan pressured Kojong to close the emigration bureau he had established. Japan was concerned about its subjects in Hawaii, who had begun to engage in spontaneous work stoppages to demand improvements in their working condi-

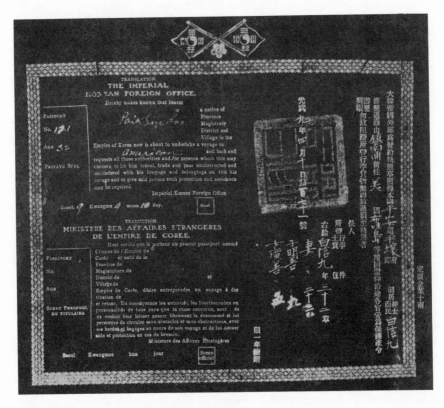

Korean passport issued to Paik Sin Koo and his family, 1905.
Courtesy Mary Paik Lee, Sucheng Chan collection

tions. The planters countered such efforts by hiring scabs of other nationalities, including Koreans.

After Korean emigration ended in 1905 and especially after the Japanese government agreed in 1907 to stop issuing passports to laborers in accordance with the Gentlemen's Agreement it had reached with the United States government, Hawaii's sugar growers focused their efforts on recruiting Filipinos. At the same time, to prevent any single ethnic group from dominating the plantation labor supply, they continued to seek potential pools of workers from other countries, including European ones. American officials strongly encouraged the planters to recruit Europeans, in order to "Americanize" the islands' population.

Filipino emigration had some unique features because of the special relationship between the Philippines, a Spanish colony for more than three centuries, and the United States, which had acquired the archipelago in 1898 as part of the peace settlement following the Spanish-American War. The Spaniards had set up their first permanent settlement in the Philippine Islands (named after King Philip II of Spain) in the 1560s. A decade later, they had gained nominal control over the entire island chain. Catholic priests played a key role in Spain's subjugation of its Asian colony. During the latter half of the nine-

teenth century, members of an educated mestizo elite, called *ilustrados*, organized what became known as the Propaganda Movement, in order to voice
their desire for representation in Spain's government, more freedom of speech
and assembly, less onerous taxes, and more clergy of Filipino ancestry. In
particular, they attacked the large landholdings of the church and the friars.
Jose Rizal, the leader of the reform movement, was arrested and executed for
an uprising that took place in 1896, even though that revolt was the doing of a
more radical group, the Katipunan. A year later, the Spanish colonial authorities routed the forces of Emilio Aguinaldo, one of the Katipunan's leaders, and
sent him into exile.

Meanwhile, as the United States and Spain fought over the future of the
Cuban revolution half a world away, the American commander of the Pacific
fleet, Adm. George Dewey, steamed into Manila Bay and destroyed the Spanish
squadron anchored there. Dewey also arranged to bring Aguinaldo back to
Manila. The latter declared independence for the Philippines in June 1898, set
up a government, and began taking control over the rural areas of Luzon, the
largest island in the Philippines, on which Manila, the capital, is located. When
the war ended between the United States and Spain, however, the defeated
Spanish troops surrendered not to the Filipinos but to the Americans. The
Filipino forces that had been blockading Manila were not even allowed to enter
the city.

After intense debate, Congress finally decided to retain the Philippines as an
American possession. Several years of guerrilla warfare ensued, as Filipino
nationalists fought to oust their new overlords. But a series of bloody pacifica-
tion campaigns finally subdued them. Estimates of the death toll from fighting,
disease, and starvation range in the several hundred thousands. To this day,
very little information about the Philippine-American War can be found in
American textbooks, although some aspects of this "hidden" war can be reconstructed from information in congressional documents.[11]

Aguinaldo was captured in 1901, and the fighting wound down somewhat,
although mopping up campaigns continued for several more years. As a civilian
government replaced military rule, along with bureaucrats came hundreds of
idealistic American teachers. Their mission was to impart Western civilization to
Filipinos under a policy of "benevolent assimilation" and political tutelage.[12]

One group of Americans who seemed quite aware of events in the Philippines were Hawaii's plantation owners. According to Mary Dorita, as early as
1901 William Haywood, former consul general of the United States in Hawaii,
went to Washington, D.C. on behalf of the HSPA to meet with the secretary of
war and the chief of the Bureau of Insular Affairs in an effort to obtain permission to bring Filipino laborers to Hawaii. But nothing came of his trip. Five
years later, concerned about the competition that Philippine-grown sugar
posed to Hawaiian sugar, the HSPA sent a Honolulu attorney to the nation's
capital to ask that a tariff be imposed on Philippine sugar. Then the association
sent another attorney, Albert F. Judd, to Manila with the assignment to recruit
300 Filipino families for Hawaii's plantations. Judd succeeded in obtaining
permission from the Philippine Commission—the body that governed the Philippines between 1901 and 1907—to carry out his task, but after six months of
work he managed to find only 15 individuals willing to embark for Hawaii. He
did somewhat better in 1907, sending 150 Filipinos there. Given the poor

results, recruiting was halted the following year, but it began anew in earnest in 1909 after it became apparent that the Gentlemen's Agreement did have a deleterious effect on the supply of Japanese laborers.[13] More important, a long strike that year by Japanese plantation workers made the growers realize that it was imperative to find a more reliable source of labor.

Filipinos were particularly attractive because of their unusual legal status. As U.S. "nationals" they traveled with American passports, so that the existing immigration laws and the Gentlemen's Agreement, which barred other Asians, were not applicable to them. Recognizing this fact, Hawaii's Territorial Board of Immigration proclaimed them "the only hope of the future under the existing laws." By the end of 1910, more than 4,000 Filipinos had sailed to Hawaii. Total Filipino arrivals in Hawaii numbered 28,500 between 1907 and 1919, 29,200 during 1920–24, 44,400 during 1925–29, and almost 20,000 during 1930-35. The "bulge" during the second half of the 1920s clearly reflects the termination of Japanese immigration in 1924.[14]

Obstacles had to be overcome to create this emigrant stream. Sugar interests in the Philippines, fearful of losing workers they themselves needed, criticized the HSPA's recruitment efforts. Townspeople in some places attacked recruiters with sticks and clubs. In 1915 the Philippine legislature passed a bill imposing a tax of 6,000 pesos on any agent engaged in recruiting individuals for employment outside of the islands, with an additional tax of 500 pesos for every province where recruitment took place. Problems also surfaced in Honolulu, where the territory's Board of Immigration discovered it could not turn back Filipino arrivals with contagious diseases because they were not aliens and were therefore not under its jurisdiction. But the HSPA was determined to get the laborers that plantation owners needed. In 1915 it promptly paid the sums needed to enable its agents to recruit in the provinces of Ilocos Norte, Ilocos Sur, La Union, Cebu, Romblon, and Capiz, and the city of Manila. Once people from those provinces became familiar with emigration, recruitment efforts abated, as chain migration kept the outflow steady.

The HSPA's choice of where to seek workers explains in part why 60 percent of the Filipino emigrants to Hawaii came from the Ilocano-speaking provinces of Ilocos Norte, Ilocos Sur, La Union, Abra, and Pangasinan, while about 30 percent originated from the Cebuano-speaking provinces of Cebu, Bohol, and Negros Oriental.[15] The Ilocano provinces in mountainous northwestern Luzon were among the country's most densely populated. Since their narrow coastal plains are not suitable for the large-scale cultivation of export crops, their hardworking people, who long ago developed a tradition of outmigration in search of work, have been the main natural resource the region has relied on for survival. The Cebuano provinces in the center section of the Philippine archipelago, on the other hand, were where the Spanish and the Americans established sugar plantations, so their inhabitants were familiar with sugar cultivation. When Filipinos realized that work could be had not only in Hawaii but also on the mainland, more than 50,000—a third of them reemigrants from Hawaii—headed for the latter destination in the 1920s and 1930s.

Contrary to conditions in the Philippine emigrant regions, the Punjab region of northwestern India, where the bulk of the Indian emigrants to North America came from, had served as one of the subcontinent's

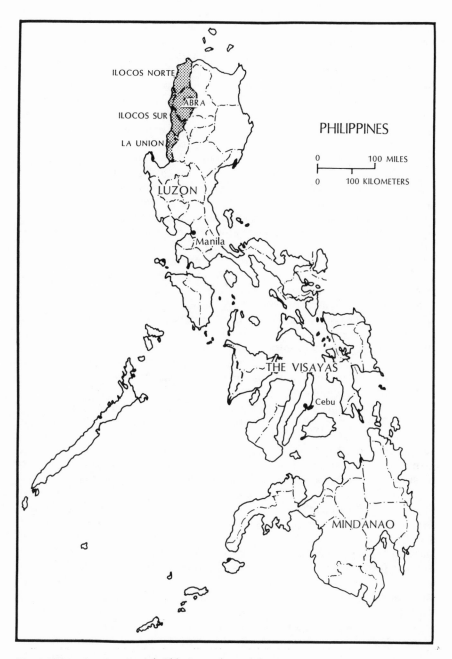

Map 4. *Major emigrant provinces, the Philippines, early twentieth century.*

breadbaskets during certain periods of its history. However, changes following the British annexation of the area in 1849—achieved only after the British subdued the fierce resistance put up by the Punjabis—created conditions conducive to emigration.[16]

An 1862 report noted that "the Punjab is not half cultivated; there are immense waste tracts almost unpopulated; the communications are incomplete; and the resources generally but partially developed."[17] So the new colonial administrators set about building roads, railways, and irrigation canals, thereby opening up many areas to cultivation, especially of cash crops. However, their decision to collect land revenue in cash in place of the old system of payment in kind affected many farmers negatively. Although the stated policy was to "assess low," the total amount collected in the Punjab increased from £820,000 in 1847–48 (just before annexation) to £1.06 million three years later. When colonial officials realized the dire effect of the new system, they reduced the tax from one-third to one-quarter of the average gross product during the 1850s and early 1860s, and later to one-sixth.

Nevertheless, because taxes were now fixed and had to be paid with money, the burden on many cultivators increased, even though the Tenant Bill of 1868 and the Punjab Land Revenue Act of 1871 attempted to protect the traditional rights of tenants. An increasing number of people mortgaged their plots to secure the cash for their tax obligations, but in time many lost their property. The result was a greater concentration of landownership, rising tenancy, and a higher rate of land dispossession. Large numbers became migrant workers; others found employment in the British colonial army and police force. Since the British Empire at its zenith stretched around the globe, these soldiers and policemen were often sent to other parts of the empire to keep law and order. In this manner, many Punjabis became worldly travelers, unafraid to try their fortunes in far-flung places.

The vast majority of the Punjabi Sikh emigrants to North America—and indeed, to most other parts of the world—came from the districts of Jullundur, Hoshiarpur, Gurdaspur, Ludhiana, Ferozepur, and Amritsar. No in-depth research on why this was so has yet been done. Until the relevant findings are available, several interrelated hypotheses regarding transportation routes, social networks, access to credit, and recruitment efforts may be offered.

Aside from those who were already abroad by virtue of service to the British, villagers from the Punjab could also find their way overseas without undue difficulty. By the turn of the century, when Punjabi Sikhs began their worldwide diaspora, modern transportation was available to take them to the port city of Calcutta in Bengal, along the northeastern coast of India. Both the Grand Trunk Road and the British-built railway, which link Amritsar, the religious center of the Sikhs, with New Delhi, India's capital after 1912, run through the towns of Jullunder and Ludhiana, the seats of districts with the same names. People from Hoshiarpur, Gurdaspur, and Ferozepur could make their way to these transportation lines fairly easily. From New Delhi, aspiring emigrants could take the train to Calcutta, whence they could board steamers for Hong Kong. From that British colony, they could then secure passage to many parts of the world, including Manila, Singapore, Shanghai, Yokohama, Vancouver, San Francisco, and even ports in Australia, New Zealand, and the South Pacific.

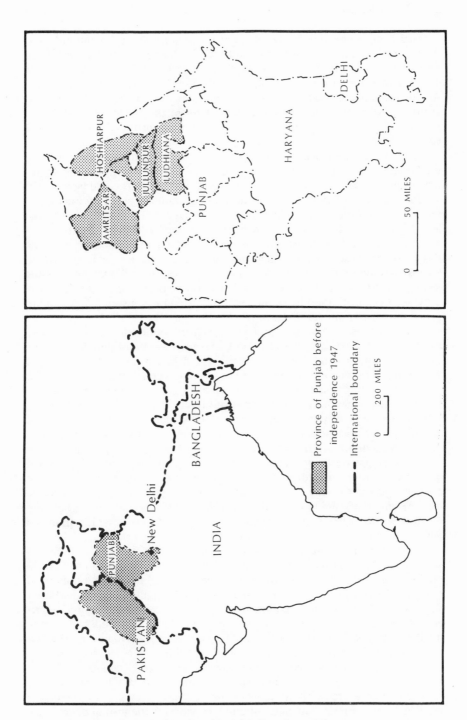

Map 5. *Major emigrant districts in the province of Punjab, India, early twentieth century.*

That Hong Kong very likely served as a key link in their migration is partially corroborated by information collected by Rajani Kanta Das, an Asian Indian employee of the United States Bureau of Labor Statistics in the early 1920s. According to Das, who interviewed some 200 Indians and 200 Euro-Americans and Canadians individually and talked to another 400 Indians in groups up and down the Pacific Coast, many of them had worked for the British in "Hong Kong, Shanghai, and other parts of the Far East" before coming to America.[18]

Such work experience was possible because the British, after they pacified the Punjab, recruited large numbers of the region's hefty men into their colonial army and police force. Within India itself, Sikh soldiers could be found in virtually every place with a British cantonment (military post). By the turn of the century, not only Sikh soldiers and policemen but also privately employed guards and nightwatchmen—all with their distinctive turbans and beards—were a common sight in British possessions outside of India, such as Hong Kong. In that island city the men built a temple, called a *gurdwara*, which served both their religious and social needs. Because any Sikh traveler passing through was entitled to temporary lodging and board in the gurdwara, it became a crucial institution in Sikh emigration, as individuals sometimes had to wait a month or more for their ships.

Not only was the journey from India to North America longer and more complicated, but passage was also more expensive —almost double what the Chinese, Japanese, and Korean emigrants had to pay from their points of departure. Consequently, access to credit was an even more critical factor for Punjabi Sikh emigrants than for the other groups. There is only episodic evidence on how they acquired the requisite funds: according to Joan Jensen, some had savings, others mortgaged their family's land to moneylenders, and yet others borrowed from relatives. In a later period, those already abroad might have sent prepaid tickets to their brothers and cousins. That such means were representative can be adduced from the fact that many Punjabi Sikhs had been wage earners and consequently knew how to handle cash and savings. Moreover, given the widespread practice of mortgaging land to pay taxes, the aspiring emigrants and their families probably felt less hesitant about borrowing against their property for their fare. After all, unlike taxes, which drained a family's income, emigration was an investment.

As was true in the other four countries, emigration agents were also hard at work in the Punjab. According to a report that a royal commission in Canada published in 1908, three types of people were actively encouraging Indians to emigrate.[19] Agents of steamship companies wanted to fill the steerage of their ships with passengers; labor contractors for railroad companies desired workers; and Indian pioneers themselves saw a chance to make a profit by bringing their countrymen to North America and hiring them out to employers. The first two distributed leaflets in the villages, while the third wrote letters home. It is not surprising, therefore, that Punjabi Sikhs, with their considerable experience in overseas travel, work, and residence, were among those who most readily responded to the siren songs of these agents. Canada became a destination for Punjabi Sikhs because Canadian railroad companies at the turn of the century were among the enterprises most actively looking for section hands. The companies stepped up their advertisements for immigrants from 1904 onward after the Canadian government imposed a head tax of $500 on each incoming Chinese, thereby greatly reducing the number of Chinese arrivals and causing employers to turn their attention to attracting workers from Japan and India.

As a result of the glowing propaganda spread about economic opportunities in Canada, the number of Indians—almost all of them Punjabi Sikhs—entering British Columbia increased from 258 in 1904 to some 1,500 in 1906 to more than 2,000 in 1907. But Indian immigration into Canada was short-lived. As alarm spread about the "turban tide," the Canadian government sought ways to stop the influx. The fact that India and Canada were both part of the British Empire posed a problem, however, because people from one part of the empire were supposed to be able to travel freely to another. The solution found was contained in two Orders-in-Council passed in 1908: one required incoming immigrants to possess $200 in place of the $25 formerly required; the other forbade individuals who had not come by "continuous journey" from their homeland to enter. Since there was no direct steamship service between India and any Canadian port in those days, this law effectively reduced the influx of Indians. Compared to the more than 2,000 Indians who entered in 1907, only about a tenth of that number did so in 1908.

After Canada's new regulations went into effect, Indians began coming directly to the United States, even though the reception they received was less than friendly: in September 1907, 600 Euro-American workers drove some 200 "Hindus" out of Bellingham, Washington, where they had found employment in the lumbermills.[20] The hostility they encountered in the Pacific Northwest pushed them further south into California. The peak years of Indian immigration into the United States were 1907–10; exclusion was formally imposed in 1917.

Asian immigration into Hawaii and the United States was but one aspect of a larger historical process that has sometimes been called the "expansion of Europe." For several centuries, colonists, capitalists, soldiers, and missionaries from Europe roamed the earth in search of land, profits, power, and souls. When Americans joined this venture, they justified it as part of their manifest destiny. But in many places, white men could not accomplish their goals without the sinews of nonwhite men. Where the local population did not supply the needed labor, the Europeans or Americans brought workers from other countries.

British actions in China and India indirectly started the emigrant stream from those countries to California and British Columbia, while American schemes facilitated the outflow of people from Japan, Korea, and the Philippines to Hawaii and the Pacific Coast. Because what Euro-Americans desired was muscle power, the vast majority of the Asians they enticed to the other side of the Pacific were young men in their prime working years, most of whom came without their wives, parents, or children. Abused and maligned, their deeds unsung, these men were an indispensabale work force that helped to build the American West.

*Chinese workers on a sugarcane plantation in Hawaii, 1895.*
Courtesy Bishop Museum

# chapter two

# Immigration and Livelihood, 1840s to 1930s

Asian immigrants came to the United States primarily to earn a living. Work was available because the entrepreneurs who operated within America's capitalist economy wanted the cheapest labor they could find, so that they could maximize their profits. However, Euro-American workers who felt threatened by the Asian competition and nativists from all classes who felt hostile toward them for racist reasons agitated to stop their coming. With the exception of Koreans, members of each immigrant group managed to enter without restriction for only two or three decades before they were excluded.

Though there were many similarities in the occupational history of the five major Asian immigrant groups, differences also existed. Hawaii and California were frontiers in the early 1850s, when the Chinese came; they were undergoing rapid economic transformation in the 1880s, when the Japanese entered; and were becoming mature capitalist economies by the early twentieth century, when Asian Indians, Koreans, and Filipinos arrived. Given the shortage of Euro-American workers in California during the 1850s and 1860s, the Chinese there found work in a wide range of occupations. But as more and more Euro-Americans settled along the Pacific Coast after the first transcontinental railroad was completed in 1869, they wanted the better jobs for themselves. Through a variety of means—including discriminatory legislation and taxes, boycotts, and barring nonwhites from unions and consequently unionized jobs—they increasingly confined the Chinese and the other Asians who came after them to low-status menial work.

The first Asians to set foot in the New World came with the Manila galleon trade. Filipino and Chinese sailors and stewards were employed in the specially constructed ships that carried cargoes of Chinese luxury goods between Manila and Acapulco from 1565 to 1815. A number of Filipinos apparently had settled in Acapulco by the late sixteenth century, while some Chinese merchants had set up shop in Mexico City by the seventeenth. Marina E. Espina and Fred Cordova have surmised that the Filipinos known as Manilamen found in the marshlands of Louisiana's Barataria Bay (about thirty miles south of New Orleans) in the 1760s were descendants of sailors who had worked on the Manila galleons.[1]

The historical record is clearer with regard to the earliest Chinese arrival in Hawaii. Several Chinese artisans being taken by a British sea captain to build ships in Nootka Sound in British Columbia touched shore at the mid-Pacific islands in 1789—only 11 years after Captain James Cook first landed there and named them the Sandwich Islands. Ships engaged in the China trade soon began calling at Hawaiian ports and took sandalwood, which grew abundantly in the islands, to sell in China. For that reason, Chinese have called the Hawaiian islands Tanxiangshan (Tanheungsan, "the Sandalwood Mountains") from the time they learned of their existence.

The first Chinese to reside in Hawaii for any length of time were men skilled at sugar making. According to Tin-Yuke Char, long before the first sugar plantation was established in 1835, a Chinese "sugar master" had reportedly reached Hawaii by 1802 on a ship engaged in the sandalwood trade, bringing with him boiling pans and other paraphernalia for sugar making.[2] That he should have done so is not surprising, as Guangdong province is one of China's major sugar-producing areas. By the 1830s several Chinese sugar companies were in operation on the islands of Maui and Hawaii. At least half a dozen Chinese sugar masters and their mills were at work in the 1840s. The first sizable batch of Chinese—195 contract laborers recruited from the city of Amoy in Fujian province—arrived in 1852, imported into Hawaii in response to fundamental changes occurring in the kingdom.

When plantations were first organized, their managers relied on Hawaiian labor, but since many of the local people still had subsistence plots to depend on for survival, they did not take readily to the harsh work regime that sugarcane cultivation required. More important, the indigenous population was declining rapidly: its size in 1860 was at most a fifth of what it had been in 1778 when Captain Cook appeared. This sharp decline had multiple causes. Many Hawaiians with no immunity to the diseases brought by Americans and Europeans died from them, while others succumbed to cold and exposure as they went up the mountains to cut sandalwood. The commercialization of the islands' economy—in particular, a new system of land tenure urged upon the king by his American advisers—also deprived an increasing number of commoners of their traditional means of livelihood.

The alienation of land occurred very rapidly, as Edward D. Beechert has documented.[3] In the 1840s the king first made informal grants to Westerners, then signed formal leases with them, and finally allowed them to buy land outright. The changes culminated in the Great Mahele or land redistribution of 1848. Land that hitherto had been communally held could thenceforth be sold. This enabled more and more missionary-entrepreneurs to acquire large tracts for sugar plantations.

Because sugarcane cultivation is so labor-intensive, however, before plantations could materialize a sufficient and dependable labor supply had to be secured. Several pieces of legislation were passed in 1850 toward this end. In that year, because Hawaiians, like other people from around the world, were joining the California gold rush, a law was enacted to forbid them to leave the islands without permission. Another law made it illegal for them to sign on as sailors on outbound ships. Finally, "An Act for the Governance of Masters and Servants" specified how apprentices and contract laborers were to be treated, while a judicial and administrative apparatus with penal sanctions was set up to implement it. In 1850 also, the Royal Hawaiian Agricultural Society came into being for the purpose of obtaining labor needed for land development. It was succeeded by the Planters' Society and a Bureau of Immigration in 1864.

As cane acreage expanded—albeit slowly at first—and as the Hawaiian population dwindled, an attempt was made to import Chinese laborers. The group that came in 1852 had five-year contracts. Each man received free passage and three dollars a month, including food and lodging. No more Chinese were brought in under contract again until 1865, but a handful of free immigrants entered every year in the interim. The renewed attempt to import contract laborers was a reflection of the fact that sugar production had increased greatly during the American Civil War, when sharply rising prices boosted Hawaii's output from under 600 to almost 9,000 tons. The 1865 arrivals were paid eight dollars a month; each man was supplied with two suits of clothing, a warm jacket, a pair of shoes, a bamboo hat, a mat, a pillow, and a blanket. A greater leap in numbers occurred after 1876, following the signing of the Reciprocity Treaty, which allowed Hawaiian-grown sugar to enter the United States duty-free. According to figures compiled by Ronald Takaki, sugar tonnage rose to 32,000 in 1880, 130,000 in 1890, 300,000 in 1900, and more than 500,000 in 1910.[4] Whereas only 151 Chinese had entered in 1875, 1,283 did so in 1876. Arrivals averaged more than 2,000 a year for the next decade. A very large percentage came in under contract, but there were also some who paid their own way. Altogether, around 50,000 Chinese set foot on Hawaiian soil between 1852 and the end of the nineteenth century.

As the number of Chinese increased, different groups of people began to find fault with them. Though the plantation owners considered the Chinese satisfactory workers, the fact that most of them declined to sign on for a second term after their contracts expired posed a problem. The Chinese left the sugar plantations as soon as they could because the luna (overseers) were abusive and the working conditions extremely unpleasant. Some became peddlers and merchants in towns such as Honolulu and Hilo, while others went into independent rice farming (some as owner-operators, others as tenants) and truck gardening. For several decades, rice was the second most important source of income in the Hawaiian economy, and Chinese were its main cultivators.[5] Rice acreage rose from about 1,000 acres in 1875 to almost 7,500 in 1890 to over 9,000 by 1900. A good portion of the crop grown in Hawaii was shipped to California to help feed the Chinese there.

Meanwhile, as Edward C. Lydon has recounted, the native Hawaiians, as well as missionaries and politicians who claimed to champion their welfare, thought that the increasing Chinese presence endangered the survival of the Hawaiian population. The Chinese were accused of introducing dreaded diseases, such as leprosy and smallpox, and immoral habits, such as opium smoking and gambling. Though some Chinese men had married or cohabited with Hawaiian women, their critics did not consider them a desirable vehicle for replenishing the islands' declining population. When Walter Murray Gibson, a Mormon missionary-turned-politician and an opponent of Chinese immigration, became simultaneously minister of foreign affairs and premier under King Kalakaua in 1882, he issued one regulation after another to restrict the Chinese influx, which finally ended in 1886. The planters did not protest because before stopping the flow of Chinese, Gibson had made sure a supply of Japanese would be forthcoming.[6] The Hawaiians also welcomed the change, as they considered the Japanese a more compatible "cognate" race for the purpose of repopulating the kingdom.

Far more Chinese landed in California than did in Hawaii because of the gold rush. In 1852—the same year that the first 200 or so Chinese contract laborers set foot in Hawaii—more than 20,000 Chinese passed through the San Francisco Customs House enroute to the gold fields in the Sierra Nevada foothills. Fewer than 5,000 stepped ashore in 1853, partly because California had imposed a Foreign Miners' Tax, which greatly reduced the income of non-American prospectors, but also because news of the gold discovery in Australia had by then reached Guangdong province, causing thousands to rush southward instead of eastward. However, more than 16,000 came in 1854. For the next decade, arrivals in California fluctuated between 2,000 and 9,000 a year. Then between 1867 and 1870, partly in response to recruitment efforts by the Central Pacific Railroad Company, which was building the western section of the first transcontinental railroad, some 40,000 Chinese poured into the country.

The singular importance of gold to the early immigrants in California is reflected in the folk memory of many Chinese around the world to this day: until quite recently, they called San Francisco Jiujinshan (Gaogamsan, "the Old Gold Mountain"), while Australia is known as Xinjinshan (Sungamsan, "the New Gold Mountain"). A few statistics will also illustrate the significance of gold in Chinese American history. The 1860 census takers found that virtually 100 percent of the Chinese in the continental United States were still living in California. The state continued to hold a majority of the nation's Chinese population until the turn of the century: 78, 71, 67, and 51 percent of them lived in California in 1870, 1880, 1890, and 1900, respectively. Within the state itself, 84, 45, 32, 13, and 12 percent of them were found in the mining counties in 1860, 1870, 1880, 1890, and 1900, respectively.[7] Unlike the independent white prospectors, most of whom had left the mining regions by the late 1850s, sizable numbers of Chinese remained there until the 1880s.

In terms of occupational distribution, in 1860, when surface deposits had already been depleted, fully 85 percent of the Chinese in the mining counties were still panning or digging for gold. A decade later, 65 percent of them were doing so, while in 1880, 59 percent persisted in prospecting. Since the manuscript schedules of the 1890 census were lost in a fire, no computation can be made with regard to how many Chinese miners were still at work that year, but census takers counted over 2,000 Chinese miners in California in 1900—a year when the overall Chinese population was 45,753 in the state and 89,863 in the nation.

Three principal methods were used for obtaining the precious metal: placer, hydraulic, and deep-shaft or quartz mining. The vast majority of the Chinese worked only placer claims. In the early years, when surface deposits were abundant, many miners, including Chinese, used nothing more complicated than a pan, into which they placed a small amount of gold-bearing dirt, swirling it to wash the lighter earth off the rim while letting the gold settle at the bottom. A more efficient contraption was the rocker or cradle—a wooden box with cleats (called riffles) nailed across the bottom and mounted on rockers. "Pay dirt" was placed with water into the box, which was then rocked back and forth. Such motion separated the heavier gold dust and nuggets from the rest of the dirt; as water flowed over the mixture, the gold was caught by the cleats at the bottom, while the nonauriferous dirt flowed out the open end. Another device, the long-tom, was a longer rocker that remained stationary.

Mounted at an angle with a continuous stream of water flowing through it, it could handle a large volume of dirt with a minimal amount of human labor. Sluices—a series of open troughs with cleats—evolved from long-toms, requiring large volumes of water for their proper functioning.

Chinese miners used all of the above devices and also introduced some implements of their own. The most notable was the waterwheel, similar to those used by farmers in China. Mounted with buckets to scoop water from a stream or river, the wheel, as it turned slowly, emptied the buckets of water into a trough that carried the water to where it was needed. Chinese were also skilled at building wing dams that diverted water either from a small tributary or one section of a river, in order to expose the riverbed for mining. Perhaps they resorted to such ingenious contrivances because, as J. D. Borthwick observed in the early 1850s, they did not seem to like standing in water for long periods. Borthwick thought that the way Chinese mined resembled "scratching": instead of pushing their shovels forcefully into the ground as Euro-American miners did, they scraped its surface to loosen the gravel.[8]

Only a small number of Chinese attempted hydraulic mining. The most likely reason is that this method, which shot powerful jets of water against ore-bearing hillsides to wash down the dirt, required considerable capital. Since Chinese miners were periodically subjected to violence, investing a lot of money in heavy equipment was simply too risky. Those who did engage in hydraulic mining did so in rather remote areas, largely in the Siskiyou and Trinity mountains of northwestern California.

Documentation regarding Chinese participation in quartz mining—digging tunnels into the mountains that contained veins of ore—is conflicting. Some accounts suggest that no Chinese could be hired by the mining companies extracting gold this way because unionized Euro-American miners—particularly imported ones from Cornwall, who were the world's most skillful deep-shaft operators—stopped any attempts by the companies to employ Chinese. Other sources claim that a large number of Chinese miners worked for companies from the late 1860s on, and although their authors do not indicate the mining methods these companies used, they could not have been exploiting placer claims, which had been completely depleted by then.

The presence of so many miners among the Chinese influenced what other Chinese did for a living. Wherever groups of miners congregated, merchants opened stores to provision them and to serve their social and recreational needs.[9] Merchants imported a variety of ingredients needed for Chinese cooking. Invoices of Chinese import-export firms found at San Francisco's Custom House in the early 1850s list rice, noodles, beans, yams, sugar, tea, vinegar, peanut oil, dried vegetables, bamboo shoots, dried mushrooms, ginger, cured eggs, sweetmeats, sausages, salted fish, dried shrimp and oysters, dried bean curd, and dried as well as fresh fruits. The immigrants' diet was supplemented with vegetables grown by local Chinese truck gardeners, with meat from pigs, ducks, and chickens raised by Chinese farmers, and with fish caught by Chinese fishermen. Once in a while, they also ate American canned sardines and ham, as well as fresh beef purchased from Euro-American butchers.

In addition, merchants brought in Chinese textiles and clothing, although the Chinese miners early learned to wear American leather boots. In time, some workers grew to favor durable blue jeans over baggy Chinese cotton pants. As shown in many photographs taken of them, another item of American apparel they seemed to fancy was felt hats, although men working in the countryside continued to depend on imported conical bamboo hats.

Merchants made it possible for Chinese immigrants to be surrounded by all the essential and familiar items of their material culture. Even rice paper and Chinese ink and brushes found their way across the Pacific, as did matches, firecrackers, joss sticks (made from Hawaiian sandalwood), washbasins, pots and pans, Chinese-style weights and measures, and a large array of herbs. Opium entered without restriction during the early years, but it was not the only recreational drug the Chinese used: most Chinese stores, even those in remote mountain areas, also stocked American cigarettes and whiskey.

Merchants played such a critical role that they became the wealthiest members and most important leaders of the community, even though in the rural areas and small towns they usually comprised only about 3 percent of the population. The larger the urban center, however, the more numerous they were. In San Francisco, not counting the gamblers, brothel owners, and other underworld entrepreneurs, merchants hovered around 10 percent of the gainfully employed.

One development that affected both Chinese miners and merchants was the building of the western half of the first transcontinental railroad—a project that employed more than 10,000 Chinese workers at its peak, many of whom were former miners.[10] In fact, the railroad company's effort to recruit Chinese laborers provided the impetus that finally took large numbers of Chinese away from the mines. Meanwhile, Chinese merchants profited from the construction project, since they served as labor contractors who gathered the men into gangs, charged each one a commission for finding him work, and provisioned the whole lot.

Proposals for a transcontinental railroad had been made since the 1840s, but it took the Civil War to spur Congress finally to pass a bill that made the construction possible. To enable private entrepreneurs to finance such a momentous undertaking, the federal government issued bonds on behalf of and granted public land to the railroad companies—land they were supposed to sell to raise the capital needed. The amount of land granted depended on the miles of tracks laid and on the difficulty of the terrain traversed. The Union Pacific Railroad Company got the contract to build westward from the Missouri River, while the Central Pacific Railroad Company, formed by four Sacramento merchants, was to build eastward from that city. Unlike the Union Pacific, which could lay one mile of track a day across open plains using cheap Irish immigrant labor, the Central Pacific had to traverse several ranges of high mountains and had, moreover, to deal with the fact that California had the nation's highest wages.

First hired as an experiment to do grading in 1865, Chinese workers numbered 3,000 by the end of the year. Despite the skepticism that was expressed about their physical strength, Chinese soon became the backbone of the company's construction crews, providing the bulk of the labor not only for unskilled tasks but for highly demanding and dangerous ones as well. Regardless of the nature of the work they did, however, all Chinese were paid the same wage, which was considerably lower than what Euro-American skilled workers received.

The first true test the Chinese faced was a huge rock outcrop called Cape Horn, around which no detour was possible. To carve a ledge on the rim of this granite bulk, Chinese were lowered by rope in wicker baskets from the top of cliffs. While thus dangled, they chiseled holes in the granite into which they stuffed black powder. Fellow workers pulled them up as the powder exploded. Those who did not make it up in time died in the explosions.

As the road ascended into the high Sierras, it often took 300 men a month to clear and grub a bare three miles. Grading the way thus cleared took even more effort. As the crew neared the crest of the mountain range, they began the almost impossible task of drilling a tunnel through solid granite. Before they got very far, winter came and snow fell. Nevertheless, the company decided to press on, conscious that its rival was racing across the plains and getting the larger share of the land grants. Thousands of Chinese worked underground in snow tunnels around the clock through the winter of 1866. It took all summer and fall to grade the route thus created, but before tracks could be laid, winter descended again with even heavier snowfalls. As one of the Central Pacific's engineers admitted years later, "a good many men" (i.e., Chinese) were lost during the terrible winter of 1867.[11] The bodies of those buried by avalanches could not even be dug out until the following spring. Once the tracks descended the eastern slopes of the Sierras, the Chinese crews sped across the hot, dry plateaus of Nevada and Utah until the two ends of the railroad joined at Promontory Point, Utah in 1869. Despite their heroic feat, the Chinese were not invited to the jubilant ceremonies that marked the completion of America's first transcontinental railroad, hailed as one of the most remarkable engineering feats of its time.

But the railroad was more than a technological wonder: it transformed the American West, especially California. Before its completion, California was geographically isolated from the rest of the country. Immigrants had to come by wagon train, while manufactured goods from the eastern United States arrived by ship around the tip of South America. The state's exports—primarily wheat from the 1860s through the 1880s—traveled by the same long route to Atlantic seaboard and British ports. The railroad's full effect was not felt for more than a decade after its completion because high passenger and freight rates limited its usage. In the mid-1880s, after a second transcontinental railroad was built, the two engaged in a cutthroat rate war. The fares they charged became so cheap that hordes of people rode the trains to California—if not to settle, then at least to sightsee.

The manner in which railroad construction was financed also affected California's development. The railroad company was supposed to have sold most of the land the federal government granted it—some 9 to 11 million acres, depending on how one counts—but it never did so, keeping the land, instead, for speculation. Because prices were so high, few settlers in California could afford to buy land. They blamed the railroad, on the one hand, and the Chinese, on the other, for their plight. As Varden Fuller has argued, in their eyes, were it not for the availability of Chinese "cheap labor," owners of large tracts would have been forced to subdivide and sell the plots at affordable prices.[12] But there was little that angry citizens could do to break the railroad company's power: with its enormous economic assets, it controlled state politics for decades.

Ironically for the Chinese, the completion of the railroad affected them negatively. The company retained several hundred of them for maintenance work, but discharged the rest, thereby instantaneously rendering almost 10,000 Chinese jobless. These former employees were not even allowed to ride the trains free of charge back to California. Instead, they straggled on foot westward in small groups, finding work wherever they could, mostly as common laborers and migrant farmworkers. But as more and more Euro-Americans appeared in California, they began to compete with the Chinese for jobs. Their resentment helped to fan the flames of the anti-Chinese movement.

Discharged Chinese railroad workers could find work in agriculture because California in the 1870s was one of the world's leading producers of wheat, a large percentage of which was shipped to Liverpool, headquarters of the world wheat market. The long and rainless California summers proved to be a real advantage: because the wheat could be thoroughly dried before being loaded in the holds of ships, it did not mold during the long voyage down the South American coast, around Cape Horn through the Straits of Magellan, and across the South and North Atlantic Ocean to Liverpool, where it brought premium prices due to its superior quality. Chinese helped to harvest the wheat but also found employment cultivating, harvesting, and packing a wide variety of other crops.

Farm owners welcomed Chinese workers when they discovered that employing them was convenient: instead of having to deal with individual seasonal laborers, they could simply arrange with a Chinese crew leader or labor contractor to have so many men at a given place on a given date, paying the contractor a lump sum for a specified job. Moreover, the Chinese boarded themselves and even provided their own tents or slept under the stars. Each group of men either chose one of their own to do the cooking or jointly paid the wages of a cook. Some of the contractors were local merchants, who charged each man a small commission for finding him a job and earned sizable profits by selling the crews their provisions.

But harvest labor was not the only kind of agricultural work the Chinese performed. In California's great Central Valley as well as smaller coastal valleys and plains, in Washington's Yakima Valley, Oregon's Hood River Valley, and in arable areas in other states west of the Rocky Mountains, Chinese leased land to become tenant farmers. For the most part, they specialized in labor-intensive vegetables, strawberries and other small fruits, deciduous tree fruits, and nuts. In the Sacramento-San Joaquin Delta, a reclaimed marshland that is one of the most fertile agricultural areas of California, Chinese tenant farmers grew potatoes, onions, and asparagus—leasing large plots, many of which they had earlier helped to drain, dike, and put under the plow. Other Chinese became commission merchants, selling the crops that their fellow countrymen as well as Euro-American farmers produced. Yet others worked as farm cooks, feeding the farm owners' families as well as the workers the latter employed.

Life was quite different for the Chinese in San Francisco, the metropolis of the Pacific Coast, where thousands of Chinese artisans and factory workers lived. Manufacturing occupied some two-fifths of the gainfully employed Chinese in the city in the 1870s and early 1880s. In crowded, poorly lit and ventilated sweatshops and factories, they made shoes, boots, slippers, overalls, shirts, underwear, woolen blankets, cigars, gunny sacks, brooms, and many other items. In other towns along the Pacific Coast, Chinese also worked in a few nascent manufacturing industries, but they did so only in very small numbers: before such places as Sacramento, Stockton, Marysville, Portland, or Seattle could develop into industrial centers, Chinese had already been driven out of light manufacturing as a result of anti-Chinese sentiment and activities. Boycotts against Chinese-made goods in the second half of the 1880s effectively eliminated them from the market.

One occupation that acquired a special significance in Chinese American history is laundering.[13] Large numbers of Chinese eventually became laundrymen, not because washing clothes was a traditional male occupation in China, but because there were very few women—and consequently virtually no washerwomen of any ethnic origin—in gold-rush California. The shortage was so acute that shirts were sent all the way from San Francisco to Honolulu to be washed and ironed at exorbitant prices in the early 1850s.

According to one anecdotal account related by Paul C. P. Siu, the first Chinese laundryman to appear in San Francisco was Wah Lee, who hung a sign, "Wash'ng and Iron'ng," over his premises at the corner of Dupont Street (now Grant Avenue) and Washington Street in 1851.[14] By 1860 there were 890 Chinese laundrymen in California, comprising 2.6 percent of the total employed Chinese in the state. By 1870 almost 3,000 Chinese in California (6 percent of the gainfully employed) were washing and ironing clothes for a living. A decade later, the number had increased to more than 5,000, representing 7.3 percent of the working Chinese in the state. There were still almost 4,800 laundrymen (11 percent of the gainfully employed Chinese) in California at the turn of the century, even though the overall Chinese population had declined drastically from the peak it had reached in the early 1880s.

Important as they were in California, laundries were even more significant in other parts of the United States, for laundering was one of four "pioneer" occupations that enabled Chinese to move eastward across the continent. Just as mining drew Chinese to the Pacific Northwest and the northern tier of the states in the Rocky Mountains and Great Plains, and railroad construction introduced Chinese first to Nevada and Utah and then to Arizona, New Mexico, and Texas, so operating laundries and restaurants allowed them to find an economic niche for themselves in towns and cities of the Midwest and along the Atlantic seaboard. By rendering a much needed service, Chinese laundrymen found a way to survive wherever they settled.

Siu's detailed study of laundries in Chicago gives an idea of how they grew. The first Chinese laundry in the city opened in 1872. Eight years later, there were 67; in 1883, 199; and ten years later, 313. The peak was reached in 1918 with 523; after that, the numbers declined. More interesting than the numerical increase was the spatial spread and the kind of people who made use of Chinese laundries. At first, the laundries were confined to the periphery of the central business district, but they soon became established in more outlying residential neighborhoods. Young married couples with both spouses employed in white-collar salaried jobs and single men and women living in rooming houses were the laundries' two main groups of customers. Relatively few laundries existed in neighborhoods with single-family dwellings; an even smaller number was found in industrial areas occupied by recent European immigrants.

Laundries both sustained and entrapped those who relied on them for survival. On the one hand, washing and ironing clothes was one of the few occupations the host society allowed the Chinese to follow after the 1880s. On the other hand, as one person interviewed by Siu observed: "white customers were prepared to patronize him as a laundryman because as such his status was low and constituted no competitive threat. If you stop to think about it, there's a very real difference between the person who washes your soiled clothing and the one who fills your prescription. As a laundryman he occupied a status which was in accordance with the social definition of the place in the economic hierarchy suitable for a member of an 'inferior race.' "[15]

Precisely because laundering was deemed an "inferior" occupation, those who relied on it for a living were isolated from and subservient to the larger community. Though Chinese laundries were located primarily in white neighborhoods, their occupants lived in a self-contained world. A great deal of both their business and social needs were met by people who came to their doors. Agents of laundry supply companies visited them regularly to take and deliver their orders; drivers of "food wagons" brought them cooked food, fresh produce, and staples; tailors came to take their measurements for custom-tailored suits that they could pay for by installment; jewelers tried to sell them gold watches and diamond rings (two of the conspicuous-consumption items that Chinese laundrymen seemed to fancy); and, on occasion, prostitutes dropped by to see if they felt in need of sex. Most laundrymen left their stores only on Sunday afternoons to eat, gamble, or visit friends in Chinatown.

Restaurants likewise enabled Chinese to settle and survive in communities with few of their fellow countrymen, for their business did not depend solely on a Chinese clientele. In gold-rush California, which was filled with men but had few women, men of any nationality willing to cook and feed others found it relatively easy to earn a living. A few observant Chinese quickly realized that cooking could provide a more steady income than many other occupations. In time, thousands of Chinese worked as cooks—in private homes, on farms, in hotels and restaurants—all over the American West. In the late nineteenth century, Chinese started moving to other parts of the country to open restaurants. Establishments in the larger towns and cities generally served only Chinese food and used only fellow Chinese as waiters and busboys, but those in the smaller communities dished up large plates of American-style beef stew, pork chops, or fried chicken as well as Chinese spare ribs, sweet and sour pork, fried rice, or chow mein, and relied on Euro-American waitresses for help.

One feature common to Chinese enterprises—be they mining claims, groceries, laundries, or restaurants—was that a large number of the people who worked in them owned shares in the business, and were thus partners, albeit often unequal ones. This practice, together with the fact that the men were often bound by kinship ties and lived in the same premises, modulated whatever conflicts might have arisen between the "bosses" and the "workers." The ability to get along with each other in close quarters was crucial: given the inhospitability of the larger society in which they found themselves, "ethnic confinement" was an important survival mechanism.

Chinese—and the other Asian immigrant groups who came after them—could find economic niches that sheltered them because of the nature of American capitalism. In the late nineteenth century, as firms became bigger and more oligopolistic through mergers and the growth of new industrial sectors, independent artisans found it more and more difficult to survive. This development was by no means universal, however: there has always been considerable room in the less-developed parts of the economy for small businesses to operate. Chinese laundries persisted until the 1950s and restaurants to this day because they fill needs unmet by the corporate structure.

At the turn of the century, the emerging capitalist structure affected not only industries but also agriculture. In the development of the large-scale cultivation and marketing of specialty crops for the export market, Hawaii and California led the nation. By the 1880s neither region was a frontier any longer, and immigration into each was dictated in large part by the needs of the agribusiness that became the very foundation of both their economies. But Hawaii and California did differ in one important way: Hawaii's economy has been based on one crop, sugar, and has been dominated by five big companies, while that in California has been more diverse, in terms of what crops are grown as well as the pattern of landownership and the marketing of crops. The capital to develop both places, however, came initially from the eastern United States and, to a smaller extent, from Great Britain.

Sugar production increased rapidly in Hawaii between 1876, when the Reciprocity Treaty was signed, and 1891, when the McKinley tariff eliminated the duty-free status of Hawaiian sugar and restored protection to American producers on the mainland. Important as the Reciprocity Treaty was, the Hawaiian sugar boom could not have occurred without the importation of a new group of Asian laborers, the Japanese.[16] The newcomers soon outnumbered Hawaiians and Chinese, up to that time the mainstays of the plantation labor force. Although Hawaiians and part-Hawaiians still comprised a majority of the workers, their numbers were declining. Chinese, meanwhile, were coming both from China and the Pacific Coast, but these arrivals were barely sufficient to replace the Chinese leaving the plantations after their contracts expired. Thus, new labor supplies had to be found if the Hawaiian sugar industry was to take advantage of the preferential treatment conferred by the Reciprocity Treaty.

By the time Japanese started coming, commercial sugar production was concentrated in what historians of Hawaii have called "industrial plantations"—a more efficient, large-scale system that enabled the yield per acre to increase from just under 6,500 pounds in 1895 to almost 8,700 pounds in 1900. The importation of Japanese laborers for these plantations was much more organized than it had been for the Chinese. Under the Irwin Convention, before each Japanese worker left home, he or she signed a contract that specified which plantation he or she would be assigned to. With the exception of the first two shipments, all the emigrants sailed to Hawaii on Japanese ships. Family groupings were kept intact, and more often than not, people from the same villages ended up in the same plantations.

After Irwin stopped supervising labor emigration, private companies took over. They operated under close government supervision between 1894 and 1908. Their representatives negotiated with plantation owners for the number of workers the latter desired, the terms of the contracts, as well as the amount ($30 in the 1890s) the companies would receive for each worker brought to the islands. After the 1900 Organic Law made Hawaii a formal U.S. territory, the entry of contract laborers became illegal. Thereafter, arriving passengers had to prove they were free immigrants, each with a minimum of $50 in his or her pocket.

Furthermore, Japanese ships no longer monopolized the Yokohama-Honolulu traffic. Japan's fleet was tied up during the Sino-Japanese War (1894–95), which gave American lines such as the Pacific Mail Steamship Company (the major carrier of Chinese passengers to the United States) and the Occidental and Oriental Steamship Company a chance to enter the Japanese steerage-passenger business. From the late 1890s on, American vessels dominated the Japanese passenger traffic to both Hawaii and the mainland. The emigration companies' agents, along with representatives of the Planters' Labor and Supply Company (which became the Hawaiian Sugar Planters' Association in 1895) and officials of the Bureau of Immigration (and after 1900, federal immigration officers), met each incoming shipload. Inspectors, doctors, and interpreters all participated in the landing process. Before the workers could be distributed to the plantations, each of them had to register with the Japanese consulate in Honolulu. Japanese destined for plantations in Oahu were transported there without further ado, while those intended for the other islands had to reboard inter-island steamers for the final leg of their journey.

Living conditions on the plantations were primitive. On most plantations, workers of various national origins were segregated in different camps. Single men slept in bunkhouses on wooden shelves several feet above the ground, while families were assigned cottages where these were available. On plantations without such separate dwellings, families were crammed into rooms created in bunkhouses with partitions that went up only to the rafters, thus offering no auditory privacy. Sometimes women with crying babies were told to leave the bunkhouse; they had to spend the night in the cane fields so others could sleep. Campsites in general, and the water supply in particular, were frequently unsanitary. Neither cooking nor recreational facilities were available in the early years. These were built only after laborers repeatedly engaged in work stoppages and strikes to demand improved working conditions, and after rising desertion rates alarmed the planters.

Plantation work was both regimented and unpleasant. A 5 A.M. whistle roused the camps each morning. After a quick breakfast, laborers divided into gangs, each led by a luna, and set off for the fields at 5:30. These luna supervised each step in the production process, frequently on horseback. Some were infamous for their cruelty: they not only verbally abused the laborers but on occasion hit and kicked them to maintain discipline and to keep up the pace of production. They did not allow the workers to talk in the fields or even to stand up to stretch while hoeing weeds.

During different stages of the cane's growth cycle, workers performed different tasks in the fields and mills: plowing and cultivating the fields in preparation for planting; planting, watering, and otherwise caring for the growing cane; hoeing the earth between the rows of cane to get rid of weeds; digging ditches for irrigation and maintaining them; stripping dead leaves from the stalks before the 12-foot-tall cane was cut and harvested; loading the stalks onto carts or trams running on movable single-gauge tracks; transporting the loads to the mills and unloading them; placing the cane into crushers to extract the juice; boiling the liquid to make molasses; and desiccating the thick syrup into coarse brown sugar. The final process of turning the moist, brown lumps into dry, white granules was usually carried out somewhere else, often in refineries on the mainland. Because cane leaves have tiny, sharp bristles, the field workers wore several layers of clothing to protect their hands and bodies, despite the humid heat under which they labored. The dust during harvesting was also awful, clogging nostrils and windpipes. Given such harsh working conditions, it is little wonder, then, that plantation laborers were not eager to renew their contracts or to stay on the plantations if they had saved up sufficient funds to leave.

When the 1900 Organic Law made all contracts null and void in Hawaii, labor recruiters from the mainland, working in conjunction with Japanese boardinghouse owners in both the ports of departure and arrival, descended on Hawaii to lure Japanese workers away with the prospect of higher wages. Railroad companies, lumber mills, and farmers in the Pacific Northwest and in California all desired Japanese labor. (The recruiters did not try to entice Chinese because Chinese exclusion, as chapter 3 recounts, had been in effect in the United States since 1882.) Between the beginning of 1902 and the end of 1906, almost 34,000 Japanese left the islands for Pacific Coast ports. To plug this leakage, plantation owners successfully urged the territorial government to pass a law in 1905 requiring each recruiter to pay a $500 license. Two years later, President Theodore Roosevelt signed an executive order to prohibit Japanese holding passports for Hawaii, Mexico, or Canada from remigrating to the continental United States. As a result, the Japanese exodus to the continental United States soon became a mere trickle. By the 1910s a vast majority of the Japanese departing from Hawaii was headed for Japan, and not the mainland United States.

The lives of Korean and Filipino plantation workers were no different from those of Japanese. By the late 1920s Filipinos had become the largest ethnic group in the plantation labor force, working in plantations whose average size had grown steadily from an average of slightly over 400 acres in 1880 to almost 2,500 acres in 1900 to over 5,300 acres by 1930. Along with the size increase came improvements in housing, recreational facilities, and sanitation conditions. Plantation owners and managers had learned by then that they could better control and keep workers by small acts of kindness than by harsh treatment.

Japanese, Korean, Asian Indian, and Filipino immigrants along the Pacific Coast likewise performed farm work, but because Hawaiian plantations and mainland agribusiness are organized differently, the lives of Asian farm workers in the islands and on the mainland were dissimilar in one fundamental way: plantation workers remained in one place, while mainland farm workers moved with the crops. Given the great variety of crops grown along the Pacific Coast, something is being harvested virtually every month of the year, but each harvest lasts only two to six weeks. Once it is over, the farm workers must move on, a migrant labor force constantly in search of work. Nevertheless, despite the fact that a migratory existence was, in many ways, even harsher than plantation life, the mainland offered a better chance for climbing up the so-called agricultural ladder, whereby laborers save up enough money to lease land as tenant farmers and eventually to buy land as farm owner-operators. The Japanese, in particular, had a penchant to use this channel of advancement.[17]

The fact that Japanese immigrants were able to benefit from the rapid growth in the production of specialty crops in the western United States is reflected in immigration statistics. Before 1908 only 55,000 Japanese had come to the mainland, compared to the more than 150,000 landing in Hawaii. But between 1908 and 1924 more than 120,000 arrived at Pacific Coast ports, in contrast to the 48,000 entering the islands. Japanese first entered the California migrant farm labor force in 1888, when several dozen students harvested crops during their summer vacation in the Vaca Valley of Solano County, located to the northeast of San Francisco. Two years later, several hundred Japanese appeared as grape pickers in the Fresno area of the San Joaquin Valley. From this modest beginning, Japanese farm workers eventually found their way to all the other major agricultural regions up and down the Pacific Coast and into the Southwest and the intermountain states. During the first years of the twentieth century, fully two-thirds of the Japanese in California (about 16,000 individuals) earned a living as farm laborers.[18] That number remained stable for the next decade as a result of a change in the pattern of immigration: although the Gentlemen's Agreement cut off any further influx of male laborers, immigrants found a loophole by sending for brides and younger relatives known as *yobiyose* (those "called" abroad by kinsmen), who worked for their husbands or elder relatives after arrival.

By saving their wages and by pooling resources, many immigrants scraped together the funds needed to lease small plots usually to grow strawberries, medium-size tracts to plant tomatoes, celery, onions, and a wide variety of other vegetables and fruits, or even rather large acreages to cultivate row and field crops. By 1913, when California passed its first alien land law, more than 6,000 Japanese had become tenant farmers. This number increased to 8,000 four years later. The growth of Japanese tenant farming was likewise highly visible in Oregon and Washington and to a lesser degree in the other western states. In Utah and Colorado many Japanese produced and harvested beets on contract. Those farmers who purchased land in California tended to specialize in grapes—a fact that caused them considerable financial hardship when Prohibition went into effect in 1919.

The agricultural productivity of Japanese immigrants in the western United States reached its zenith in 1917, when the United States finally entered World War I, greatly increasing the country's need for food while simultaneously removing male citizens from their farms for military service. In that year Japanese in California produced almost 90 percent of the state's output of celery, asparagus, onions, tomatoes, berries, and cantaloupes; more than 70 percent of the floricultural products; 50 percent of the seeds; 45 percent of the sugar beets; 40 percent of the leafy vegetables; and 35 percent of the grapes.[19]

The achievements of Korean and Asian Indian tenant farmers were less spectacular simply because there were far fewer of them.[20] Unlike Japanese farmers, who were found virtually everywhere, Korean tenant farmers worked largely in the San Joaquin Valley around the towns of Reedley and Dinuba, where they specialized in deciduous fruit; in the Sacramento-San Joaquin Delta, where they grew row crops; and in the upper Sacramento Valley, where they cultivated rice. A handful of Koreans also grew sugar beets on contract in Colorado and Utah. Small numbers of Asian Indian tenant farmers were found in scattered locations, but the bulk of them congregated in the Imperial and

Coachella valleys in southern California, where they raised cotton, cantaloupes, and winter lettuce, after irrigation works made the desertlike land there
arable.

Filipinos became the largest group of Asian farm laborers along the Pacific
Coast in the 1920s, but they never managed to climb the agricultural ladder for
reasons related to the timing of their arrival.[21] First, various anti-alien land
laws had been passed by the time they came in large numbers. Whereas the
Chinese, Japanese, Koreans, and Asian Indians—either by virtue of having
American-born children in whom alien parents could vest title to whatever
land they owned, or by relying on relationships they had formed earlier with
landowners who continued to lease to them—found ways to continue farming,
the newly arrived Filipinos could use no such loopholes. Second, farm prices
were falling drastically in the early 1920s, following the prosperity agriculture
had enjoyed during World War I. So, even if there had been no legal obstacles,
Filipinos would have found it difficult to become tenant farmers or independent owner-operators in those years. Finally, by the time Filipinos came, the
defenders of Euro-American supremacy had had more than half a century to
refine and perfect mechanisms for keeping nonwhites in their place. In short,
by the 1920s economic niches such as those the Chinese and Japanese had
carved out for themselves were much harder to find.

Two other outdoor occupations that had sustained tens of thousands of
Chinese—gold mining and railroad construction—provided a living to only a
few of the later-arriving Asian immigrant groups, again because the latter
entered an economy that was considerably more mature than the one that had
greeted the Chinese. By the late 1880s and early 1890s, when Japanese started
coming, the gold rush in California, the Pacific Northwest, and the Dakotas was
over. However, several thousand Japanese and dozens of Koreans did work as
wage laborers in mining companies.[22] As for the railroads, their trunk lines had
been completed. Workers were now needed not so much for laying track as for
maintaining what had been built. Accordingly, more than 12,000 Japanese and
smaller numbers of Koreans and Asian Indians labored as section hands.[23]

Unlike mining, fishing is an extractive industry whose resource is less easily
depleted. Following the footsteps of the Chinese, who had been among the
pioneer fishermen of the Pacific Coast—catching not only fish but also shrimp
and abalone, which they dried and exported to China—many Japanese operated their own small fleets all the way from Baja California in the south to
Alaska in the north. Meanwhile, thousands of Japanese and Filipinos (alongside some Chinese) worked in the salmon canneries of Oregon, Washington,
British Columbia, and Alaska every summer.[24]

In towns and cities, similarities and differences also existed in the occupational history of the various Asian immigrant groups. Large numbers of Japanese entered the labor market as domestic servants, just as the Chinese had
done. In fact, Japanese first competed successfully against the Chinese by accepting lower wages. There were three kinds of Japanese domestics. "School
boys"—young men from poor families who worked as live-in servants while
attending school part-time—usually received free room and board plus a token
weekly or monthly salary. Day workers cleaned houses, washed windows,
prepared meals, washed and ironed clothes, or tended yards and gardens for a
daily wage, while living in Japanese-operated boardinghouses. The third kind

Asian Indian workers in a lumber camp, Canada, ca. 1903.
Courtesy Public Archives Canada

of domestic workers found long-term employment in restaurants and Japanese-owned companies, performing whatever tasks their employers desired. By the end of the first decade of the twentieth century, the U.S. Immigration Commission estimated that 12,000 to 15,000 Japanese in the western United States earned a living in domestic service.[25]

Filipino boys and men were also readily hired as household servants, as janitors in office buildings and other institutional facilities, as bellhops and doormen in hotels, and as waiters and cooks in restaurants and other eating facilities. Few Koreans or Asian Indians, however, relied on domestic service for their livelihood, for reasons that have not yet been studied.

Unlike the Chinese who actively pursued manufacturing for a quarter century in San Francisco, only a few Japanese immigrants and an even smaller handful of Koreans, Asian Indians, or Filipinos did so. In 1886 Euro-Americans launched a boycott of merchandise made by Chinese, which drove the latter out of producing merchandise for the wider market. Thereafter, Asian entrepreneurs were confined to manufacturing ethnic foodstuffs. Chinese and Japanese made soy sauce and tofu (soybean cake) and germinated bean sprouts; Japanese made miso (bean paste for seasoning broth and other dishes) and *kamaboko* (fish cake); and Koreans made *kimchi* (hot pickled vegetables).

Like the Chinese, many Japanese became merchants, importing cooking ingredients for fellow immigrants, and curios and art goods such as lac-querware, china, parasols, fans, scrolls, tea, and silk goods for Euro-American customers. One special group of Japanese merchants were silk importers in New York, who worked hard over several decades to capture a share of the silk trade between Japan and the United States. According to Scott Miyakawa, the pioneers in this venture landed in New York in 1876, only four years after a Japanese consulate had been established in that city. At that time, all silk from Japan that entered the United States came via Europe, Japanese silk export being entirely in the hands of Western merchants. When the Japanese merchants showed samples of the silk threads spun in Japan that they had brought with them to some of New York's largest silk importers, they were told that their threads were neither strong enough nor uniform enough in size for the fast machinery then in use in America. Only after years of effort, as well as a vast improvement in the quality of their merchandise, did these Japanese silk merchants succeed in setting up direct shipments of silk from Japan to the United States. In time, silk became the most valuable item in the trade between the two countries.[26]

Very few Koreans and almost no Asian Indians or Filipinos became merchants in the United States for a variety of reasons. Though the earliest Koreans to enter the continental United States were ginseng (a medicinal root) merchants, few persons with a business background came during the brief period of Korean mass emigration to Hawaii. Then after Japan declared Korea its protectorate in 1905, and especially after it colonized the country in 1910, Japanese officials prohibited Koreans from engaging in the import-export trade. Moreover, given the small size of the immigrant community, there was no ready-made ethnic market to speak of. Koreans in Hawaii who went into business kept boardinghouses and bathhouses or ran used furniture and clothing stores.

No study has yet been done to discover why Asian Indian immigrants did not become merchants. One likely reason is that most of them were *jats*, members of a farming caste. The Indian caste system prescribed what occupations various groups could follow, so people rarely took up work that was not traditional among their ancestors. Even though Sikhs, as members of a separate religion, did not subscribe to Hindu beliefs and were theoretically outside of the caste system, they nevertheless adhered to certain broad cultural norms, which, though based on the tenets of Hinduism, affected Hindus and non-Hindus alike.

In the case of Filipinos, history provides an answer to why so few of them entered business in the United States. Since Spanish colonial days, retail trade in the Philippines had been in the hands of immigrant Chinese merchants, so relatively few of the indigenous people acquired experience in trade. Those who did so tended to be Filipinas, and not Filipinos. In the United States, Filipinos ran only very small operations: cigar stalls, candy stands, and barbershops. In Hawaii, they were barbers, tailors, grocers, and importers of Philippine consumer goods.

Quite apart from the cultural baggage that various groups of immigrants brought with them, and the different timing of their entry, differences in the regional economies of the United States have also affected the manner in which each has been incorporated into American society. During the late nineteenth and early twentieth centuries, while millions of European immigrants found jobs in the growing metallurgical, chemical, and electrical industries of eastern and midwestern cities, hundreds of thousands of incoming Asians worked in the fields, orchards, households, laundries, and restaurants of the American West. Each new group of European immigrant industrial workers initially experienced economic exploitation, but in time, most of them managed to secure a measure of protection through unionization. In contrast, wage earners in agriculture and in the service sector, regardless of their ethnic origins, have been extremely difficult to organize, as their work is seasonal, migratory, or part-time. To this day, farm and service workers, the vast majority of whom are either nonwhite or female, remain trapped in nonunionized, dead-end jobs. Ironically, as will be seen in chapter 5, even when Asian immigrant workers did try to organize, their petitions for affiliation with national unions were rejected.

Economic factors alone, however, do not account fully for the obstacles the early Asian immigrants encountered. Social, political, and legal barriers, which became increasingly clearly defined vis-à-vis Asians as the nineteenth century progressed, have also played a significant role in delimiting the world in which they lived. That is why, although Chinese initially found work in many sectors of the economy and over a wide geographic area, they eventually had to retreat to urban enclaves. Most members of the later-arriving groups likewise found themselves relegated to the lowest echelons of the labor market. Briefly put, racial discrimination is what separates the historical experience of Asian immigrants from that of Europeans, on the one hand, and makes it resemble that of enslaved Africans and dispossessed Native Americans and Mexican Americans, on the other hand.

*An anti-Japanese poster used in the 1920 elections in California.*
Courtesy Bancroft Library

# chapter three

# Hostility and Conflict

The presence of Asians on American soil highlighted some fundamental cleavages in American society. This fact makes Asian immigration history more important than the small number of Asians in the United States might otherwise warrant. During the first period of their immigration, vested interests that stood to gain by their labor promoted their influx, while other groups threatened by their coming strove to exclude them. But both those who wanted them and those who did not agreed on one point: like the indigenous populations of Hawaii, Alaska, and the continental United States pushed aside by Euro-Americans who desired their land, like Africans enslaved and condemned to hard labor in the New World, like Mexicans conquered and subjugated, Asians were deemed members of "inferior races." Negative perceptions of nonwhite peoples have a long history in the Western world. Color prejudice had become such a habit of heart and mind among Euro-Americans by the time Asians started coming that the former had no difficulty justifying hostile actions against the latter—actions that culminated in efforts to expel Asians from some parts of the United States as well as to prevent them from entering the country altogether.

Hostility against Asian immigrants may be divided into seven categories: prejudice, economic discrimination, political disenfranchisement, physical violence, immigration exclusion, social segregation, and incarceration.[1] The first six are dealt with in this chapter, while the World War II incarceration of 112,000 persons of Japanese ancestry is covered in chapter 7.

As the Chinese were the first to arrive, prejudice toward them has been most clearly delineated and long-lived. Unfavorable views of the Chinese predated the first landing of Chinese on American soil. Most Americans during the nineteenth century acknowledged that China had once had a magnificent civilization, but they also agreed that by then the country had reached an advanced state of decay. In their eyes, China's people were nothing more than starving masses, beasts of burden, depraved heathens, and opium addicts. As Stuart Creighton Miller has revealed, three groups of Americans who had experienced frustrations in China helped to spread adverse images of the Chinese in the United States: diplomats who resented the elaborate protocols of the Chinese court, merchants who bridled against the limitations placed on their freedom to trade, and missionaries who wrung their hands over the slow rate of Chinese conversion to Christianity. Through private letters and reports, published articles, and public speeches, these men and women disseminated their negative or at best ambivalent views of the Chinese to the American public.[2]

Chinese inferiority soon came to serve as a foil for Euro-American superiority in the minds of many. But interestingly, the fear and loathing that developed over the presence of the Chinese paradoxically became the very "exotica" that titillated many an Euro-American. The exotic image of Chinese was based in part on their unusual appearance. But their looks aroused more than curiosity—they also led to penalties. An ordinance passed in 1870 in San Francisco, for example, authorized prison wardens to cut off the queues worn by Chinese men, even though these pigtails were required by their Manchu rulers and did no one any harm. Fortunately for the Chinese, the ordinance was never implemented because the mayor vetoed it.

Of the other Asian immigrant groups, the Japanese seemed to be most conscious of the controversy that their Chinese predecessors' visage had caused, so they tried hard to give an opposite impression. Japanese men walked down gangplanks in Western-style suits; picture brides who arrived wearing kimonos and wooden clogs were whisked off upon landing by their husbands to dressmakers and shoemakers to be outfitted with Victorian clothing and shoes. Unlike Japanese, who could doff their traditional garb without disapproval, Punjabi Sikhs had no alternative except to retain a part of theirs for religious reasons: Sikh men had to wear turbans because not cutting their hair was one of the five requirements of their faith. As a result, they had to endure the opprobrium of being called "ragheads."

Far more serious than such personal harassment were laws that cut into the immigrants' earnings.[3] A Foreign Miners' Tax first passed in 1850 and reenacted in 1852 was enforced primarily against Chinese, even though in theory it applied to all foreigners. More problematic than the tax itself was the manner in which it was collected. Since the collectors received a percentage of the take, they were not above extorting hapless Chinese miners, who were often intimidated into paying more than once for the same piece of ground. Imposters also preyed on them. Worse, once Euro-American miners realized that the Chinese had no protection of any sort, they showed no qualms in driving them off good claims. Attacks against and robbery of Chinese became so common that one reporter for the *Placerville American* was moved to declare in 1857, "There ought to be a protection against his having to pay the onerous foreign miners' tax over three or four times; against sham licenses being given out and taken away from him, and his money extorted; and against being gagged, whipped and robbed whenever a worthless white rowdy chooses to abuse him thus, for pleasure or profit."[4]

In urban centers, Chinese laundrymen seemed to have been singled out for discrimination. The San Francisco Board of Supervisors decided in 1870 that every three months, laundries using one horse for their delivery wagons had to pay $2, those using two horses owed $4, while those using no horses were liable for $15. Since it was Chinese who did not use horses, the spirit of the law discriminated against them, even though its letter ostensibly did not. Between 1873 and 1884 the Board of Supervisors passed 14 separate ordinances to curb the spread of Chinese laundries. (Chinese efforts to challenge them are discussed in chapter 5.)

The ability of Chinese, Japanese, Korean, and Asian Indian immigrants to earn a living in agricultural areas was affected by alien land laws, the first of which was passed in California in 1913. Under it, they could no longer buy agricultural land or lease it for more than three years. The law had little effect, however, because district attorneys did not try to enforce it strenuously during World War I, given the nation's need for maximum food production. But once the war was over, anti-Japanese groups mounted a new campaign to close the loopholes in the 1913 law. California's voters supported an initiative on the 1920 state ballot that ended the ability of Asian aliens to lease farm land altogether. It also forbade them to purchase land through corporations in which they held more than 50 percent of the stocks or in the names of their American-born (hence citizen) minor children. A 1923 amendment made cropping contracts—agreements between landowners and alien farmers under which the latter planted and harvested crops for wages—illegal, even though such arrangements technically conferred no legal interest in the land itself.[5]

Following California's example, Arizona enacted a similar law in 1917, Washington and Louisiana in 1921, New Mexico in 1922, Idaho, Montana, and Oregon in 1923, and Kansas in 1925, as detailed by Dudley McGovney.[6] (There being few Asians in Kansas, the law in that state very likely was a response to the widespread presence of foreign-born Scottish landlords and creditors in the Great Plains.) Then, during World War II, while most Pacific Coast Japanese were in concentration camps, Utah, Wyoming, and Arkansas also passed alien land laws, probably as preventive measures. The legislatures of those states apparently did not want any Japanese to get the idea they could easily settle there after the war was over.

These various economic sanctions were possible because Asian immigrants, being denied the right of naturalization, could not vote and consequently had no political power. Unlike their European counterparts, who could participate in the electoral process after they acquired citizenship, Asian immigrants were unable to influence politicians to heed their needs. Asians, who could cast neither individual nor bloc votes, had no political voice whatsoever. Denial of the right of naturalization to anyone other than "free, white persons" was first written into the Constitution. Then in 1870, as part of the reforms during Reconstruction, new legislation extended the right to "persons of African nativity or descent." The question of naturalization for Chinese had been debated when a Civil Rights bill was first introduced in 1866. Senator Charles Sumner of Massachusetts had declared that "the right to vote shall not be abridged on account of color,"[7] but the opposition to franchise for the Chinese was so strong that in the end they were not included.

However, since petitions for naturalization during the 1870s were reviewed by local courts, the rule was not applied uniformly across the nation. Fifteen Chinese in New York gained citizenship in 1878, for example, and the newspaper reporter who interviewed them noted that one of their friends had become a citizen as early as 1873 and had "served as a juryman . . . the first Chinaman who ever acted in the capacity in Europe or America."[8] Several dozen others may have been similarly successful before the U.S. circuit court in California declared Chinese ineligible in *In re Ah Yup* (1878). A handful of Japanese and Asian Indian immigrants likewise managed to become naturalized before the U.S. Supreme Court ruled unequivocally in *Ozawa* v. *United States* (1922) and *United States* v. *Bhagat Singh Thind* (1923), respectively, to disqualify them.

An equally severe political handicap the Chinese suffered from was that California, where the vast majority of them lived, during the first dozen years of its statehood disallowed court testimony from blacks, mulattos, and (native American) Indians. The prohibition was originally enunciated in the 1850 Criminal Proceedings Act; it was extended the following year to civil proceedings as well. In late 1853 one George Hall was convicted for the murder of a Chinese, but in 1854 the California Supreme Court reversed his conviction on the grounds that it had been based on evidence given by Chinese witnesses. The chief justice ruled that since native American Indians had originally crossed the Bering Straits from the Asian continent into Alaska, they were in reality "Asiatics"! Hence, the 1850 act that barred Indian testimony applied to "the whole of the Mongolian race." Though the state's Civil Procedure Code was amended in 1863 to permit Negro testimony, the prohibition against Chinese testimony was written into the statute books that same year. Only in 1872 was reference to them quietly dropped from the Civil Procedure Code, as the state legislature revised its statutes to conform to the Fourteenth Amendment. Even after this change, evidence offered by Chinese was virtually never accepted except in cases involving other Chinese, as Hudson Janisch has chronicled.[9]

Deprived of political rights and legal protection, the Chinese were subjected to repeated acts of violence.[10] Violence against Asian immigrants falls into three patterns: the maiming and wanton murder of individuals, spontaneous attacks against and the destruction (usually by fire) of Chinatowns, and organized efforts to drive Asians out of certain towns and cities. (Not all expulsions were violent, though.)

Violence against Asians surfaced in the early 1850s and was directed at Chinese miners. Although there is no accurate record of all the Chinese miners who were injured and killed, in 1862 a committee of the California State Legislature stated that it had received a list of 88 Chinese known to have been murdered by Euro-Americans, eleven of them by collectors of the Foreign Miners' Tax. The committee concluded in its report, "It is a well known fact that there has been a wholesale system of wrong and outrage practised upon the Chinese population of this state, which would disgrace the most barbarous nation upon earth."[11]

The first documented instance of a spontaneous outbreak against a Chinese community took place in Los Angeles in 1871.[12] According to William Locklear, troubles began when two factions within Chinatown, then located in so-called Nigger Alley, fought with each other over possession of a Chinese woman. In the early evening of 24 October, a police officer in the vicinity heard shooting and went to investigate. As he neared the Chinese quarters, a shot was fired at him, whereupon he called for help. A large crowd soon gathered. The Chinese, meanwhile, scurried for safety inside their dwellings. One man in the crowd, brandishing a six-shooter and followed by several others, climbed to the roof of an adobe building in which a number of Chinese were hiding. They cut holes through the walls and started firing inside. Chinese attempting to flee were shot down in cold blood. Others were dragged along the street, then hanged. The mob battered down buildings, hauled out the terrified Chinese, beat and kicked each one before lynching him, and looted the Chinese houses in search of gold and other valuables. A number of impatient men cut off the fingers of a Chinese herbalist in order to take the rings he wore. By the time the sheriff arrived with 25 deputized volunteers at 9:30 P.M. to quell the riot, the mob had begun to disperse. The sheriff found 15 Chinese hanged, 4 shot, and 2 wounded. Though 8 men were convicted and sent to jail for the crimes, all were released a year later.

In early 1877 there was an outbreak of anti-Chinese violence in Chico, a small town in the Sacramento Valley, and a number of its surrounding communities. First, a soap factory owned by John Bidwell, a pioneer landowner and employer of Chinese, was burned. Next, arsonists set fire to the barn of a widow who had leased part of her farm to Chinese, killing 6 of her horses. Flames also consumed the shack in which the Chinese tenants lived. Several weeks later, the home of some Chinese in the neighboring town of Nord and a Chinese laundry in Chico Creek were set aflame. Arsonists also attempted unsuccessfully to burn Chico's entire Chinatown. This spate of violence culminated in the murder of four Chinese (whom the Euro-American intruders tied up, doused with kerosene, and set on fire) and the wounding of two others who managed to escape. During the trial of the suspects arrested for the crime, it was revealed that the perpetrators were members of a Laborers' Union, an offshoot of the Order of Caucasians, a white supremacist organization. Though the suspects were convicted and sentenced, all were released on parole long before their sentences were up.[13]

Violent outbreaks against the Chinese became more organized in the 1880s. The two best-known incidents—well publicized because they involved the intervention of federal troops—took place at Rock Springs in Wyoming Territory in September 1885 and at Seattle in Washington Territory from October 1885 through February 1886. According to studies by Paul Crane, Alfred Larson, and Shih-shan H. Tsai, in Rock Springs, more than 600 Chinese employed by a coal mining company worked peaceably side by side with Euro-American laborers for some time.[14] When the Chinese declined to join the latter in their proposed strike for higher wages, however, they became objects of white animosity. On 2 September a mob gathered, marched toward the Chinese workers, guarded all escape routes, and fired at the unarmed and defenseless Chinese. As the latter fled pell-mell, some Euro-Americans shot them down, others searched their persons for valuables before wounding them, while still others put their shacks to the torch. By nightfall the houses owned by the coal company and all 79 huts belonging to the Chinese had been destroyed by fire. Meanwhile, the mob threw the bodies of some dead Chinese as well as those of live but wounded ones into the flames. In all 28 Chinese were killed, and 15 wounded. Some of the latter eventually died from their wounds.

More than 550 Chinese succeeded in fleeing to safety only because a nearby railroad company telegraphed its conductors to pick up the stragglers making their way to the town of Green River. The survivors had gathered by 5 September in Evanston, where federal troops arrived to protect them. Four days later, the soldiers escorted the Chinese back to Rock Springs, where the coal company lent them clothing and provisions, gave them a number of wagons for shelter, and put them back on the payroll.

Chinese suffered losses totalling more than $147,000. Certain that no local justice could be obtained, Chinese diplomats investigated and strenuously protested this outrage, but the U.S. secretary of state denied that the federal government could be held responsible for action that had occurred in a territory.

*The massacre of Chinese miners at Rock Springs, Wyoming Territory, 1886. Drawing by T. de Thelstrup from photographs by Lt. C. A. Booth, 7th U.S. Infantry.*
Courtesy Bancroft Library

Nevertheless, "solely from a sentiment of generosity and pity," President Grover Cleveland did ask Congress to allocate $150,000 to indemnify the Chinese. Congress complied, but declared that its action should not be construed as a precedent for future compensation.

The anti-Chinese activities in Washington Territory stretched out over a longer period, but caused less bloodshed, as documented by Jules Karlin.[15] In the fall of 1885, in response to the arrest of several men accused of killing some Chinese hop pickers while they were asleep in their tents in Issaquah Valley, an Anti-Chinese Congress convened in Seattle, issued a manifesto demanding that all Chinese leave Tacoma and Seattle by 1 November, and formed two committees, whose members visited the Chinese house-to-house to inform them of the impending deadline.

That deadline came, but nothing happened. The Chinese remained in both Tacoma and Seattle. But on 3 November, during a heavy rainstorm, about 500 of Tacoma's residents forcibly expelled 600 or so Chinese from their town, took them to Lake View, a station on the Northern Pacific Railroad, and dumped them in the open, with no shelter for the night. Two men died from exposure, and one woman eventually went insane as a result of her ordeal. The refugees were rescued by the railroad, which transported them to Portland. Two days later, a fire razed Tacoma's Chinatown.

Meanwhile, certain citizens in Seattle who were concerned about the potential outbreak of violence in their own city formed a Home Guards unit of about 80 men. After being informed of events in the Pacific Northwest, President

Cleveland issued a proclamation asking people to respect the treaty rights of the Chinese. He also sent a part of the Fourteenth Infantry Division to Seattle, but those troops left when no incidents occurred.

It was not until Sunday, 7 February, of the following year that an anti-Chinese mob gathered, marched into Chinatown, loaded about 350 Chinese into wagons, and took them to the docks, with the intention of shipping them off on the *Queen*, a steamer that was due to arrive in Seattle from San Francisco that day. The captain of the *Queen*, however, prevented anyone from boarding his ship until fare was paid. The anti-Chinese group thereupon took up a collection among themselves and gathered enough money to pay the passage of about 100 persons. Still the ship could not depart, because a local judge had issued a writ of habeas corpus requiring each Chinese to appear at the court-house the following morning to be informed of his or her rights and to tell him whether he or she indeed wished to leave.

While all this was happening, Washington's territorial governor issued a proclamation ordering people to desist from violence and to disperse. He also telegraphed the U.S. secretary of war. Throughout that tense Sunday, the Home Guards, aided by small contingents of the Seattle Rifles and the University Cadets, stood off the much larger mob. They succeeded in marching the Chinese (whom they flanked on four sides) back to Chinatown. The next day, after the Chinese were done with their court appearance, the Home Guards escorted those who wished to leave on the *Queen* back to the docks and the rest home to Chinatown. As crowds continued to mill around, the governor declared martial law, imposing a curfew between 7 P.M. and 6 A.M. Federal troops finally arrived on 10 February, but the situation continued to be tense for several months after that, though no further outbreaks of violence occurred.

Though not as well documented, dozens of other anti-Chinese outbreaks occurred in the mid-1880s all over the American West. Incidents outside of California include the murder or expulsion of Chinese at Snake River Canyon in Idaho; Denver, Colorado; Portland, Oregon; and Squaw Valley, Coal Creek, Black Diamond, Tacoma, and Puyallup in Washington. In California in 1885, local residents drove the Chinese out of Humboldt County in February, and set fire to some buildings and killed thirteen Chinese in San Francisco's China-town in November. Newspaper accounts reveal that the following year Chinese were forcibly removed from Redding and Red Bluff in January; Sheridan, Wheatland, Marysville, San Jose, Gold Run, and Arroyo Grande in February; and Sonora, San Pablo, Dutch Flat, Lincoln, and Nicolaus in March. In 1886 also, arsonists set fire to the Chinatowns in Placerville in January; Redding and Chico in February; Yreka, Sawyer's Bar, and Folsom in March; Truckee in June; Red Bluff in August; and Los Angeles and North San Juan in October.[16] A second wave of expulsions took place in 1893, driving the Chinese from Selma, Visalia, Fresno, and Bakersfield in the San Joaquin Valley and from Pasadena, Redlands, Riverside, and San Bernardino in southern California.[17]

Asians who came after the Chinese likewise suffered from violence. Assaults against Japanese began when boys stoned a number of Japanese scientists—including a famous seismologist from Tokyo Imperial University—inspecting the ruins of the 1906 San Francisco earthquake and fire. Later that summer, 19 Japanese immigrants filed complaints to an investigator sent by President Theodore Roosevelt claiming they had been physically attacked.

Then in October, demonstrators smashed the windows of several Japanese restaurants in the city.[18]

Most of the Asian victims of expulsions during the early twentieth century were farm laborers. At the beginning of 1908 a mob drove approximately one hundred Asian Indian farm workers at Live Oak, some 30 miles south of Chico, out of their camp and set it afire. The attackers also robbed the Asian Indians of $2,500. When the local district attorney was asked by California's governor to investigate the incident, he claimed that the fault lay with the Asian Indians because they had allegedly stolen some chickens and had exposed themselves indecently.[19]

Even the very small number of Korean farmworkers on the mainland encountered hostility. Small incidents began in 1909, but one that occurred in 1913 is especially noteworthy. According to Hyung June Moon, in June 1913 an orchard owner in Hemet, some 100 miles southeast of Los Angeles in Riverside County, arranged with a Riverside Korean labor contracting agency to hire fifteen Korean fruit pickers. When the latter disembarked from the train, they were met by several hundred unemployed Euro-Americans, who quickly surrounded them. A spokesperson for the crowd threatened the Koreans with physical harm if they did not leave immediately. Terrified by such an unexpected reception, the Koreans boarded the next train out of town.

This incident was widely reported in the press. When the Japanese ambassador in Washington, D.C. received news of it, he lodged a protest with the U.S. State Department, whereupon the secretary of state asked the Justice Department to investigate the matter. But the Japanese ambassador's action angered the Koreans, who refused to be treated as Japanese subjects, even though their country had been colonized by Japan three years earlier. The Korean National Association wired the State Department, declaring that Koreans were "responsible for" themselves and did not "look to Japan for redress." Not wishing to offend Japan, the secretary of state did not respond directly to the Koreans' message. Instead, he issued a statement to the Associated Press, announcing that the investigation would be "discontinued." He also noted that the Koreans had informed him that they were "not Japanese subjects, . . . [having] left their native land before it was annexed by Japan."[20]

Some years later, Japanese farmworkers themselves became victims of eviction. As Yuji Ichioka has documented, during the summer of 1921 the Chamber of Commerce and the local post of the American Legion in Turlock, a town in the San Joaquin Valley, passed resolutions at the behest of Euro-American workers censuring landowners who employed Japanese. One night, 50 to 60 armed individuals surrounded a Japanese store, forced their way in, and roused the 18 Japanese farmworkers sleeping inside. They put the men into trucks, drove them to the railroad tracks, and unloaded them in the dark of night. The Japanese were told that should they ever dare to return, they would be lynched. Later that same evening, the mob raided a bunkhouse and three Japanese-operated farms, roused 40 more Japanese laborers, and likewise forced them to leave town.

As soon as the Japanese consul general in San Francisco found out about what had happened, he demanded that California's governor investigate the incident. Meanwhile, he sent two representatives of the Japanese Association of America to carry out an independent inquiry. They discovered that right after

the intruders had barged into the store, one of the farm laborers had tele-
phoned the head of the local Japanese Association, who then called the police.
However, no one at the police station answered his call, even though two
policemen were supposed to be on duty that night. This led the investigators to
suspect that the police had been tipped off ahead of time and had deliberately
absented themselves at the crucial hour. Six men were eventually arrested, but
they did not come to trial until April of the following year. By then, Japanese
migrant farm laborers who might have served as witnesses had all left the area.
All six defendants were acquitted.[21]

The last major round of violence against Asians was directed against
Filipinos—activities that Emory Bogardus and Howard De Witt have studied.[22]
The first attempt to drive out Filipinos occurred in the Yakima Valley in Washington in 1928, but the most publicized incident took place in the summer of
1930, when 500 restless Euro-American youths picketed a new taxi-dance hall
in Palm Beach that had just opened to cater to Filipino clients. This facility was
located a few miles down the road from Watsonville, an important apple-
growing area along the central California coast, where thousands of Filipino
and Mexican farm workers gathered every harvest. Several days later, a mob of
400 attacked the Northern Monterey Filipino Club, beating up dozens of Filipinos and killing one. A second Filipino, a 22-year-old lettuce picker, was shot to
death as he hid in a bunkhouse outside of town. The sheriff, along with dozens
of deputized citizens, finally ended the rioting. Seven suspects were arrested,
but none of them was indicted.

Several factors help to account for the violence that Asian immigrants experienced. Quite apart from the racism and nativism that fueled such attacks, the
outbreaks were efforts by Euro-American workers to find scapegoats for their
problems. It is no coincidence that the incidents tended to occur during years of
economic crisis. The string of arson in California in 1877 took place at a time
when the effects of the depression of 1873 finally reached California. Likewise,
the almost ubiquitous outbreaks between late 1885 and the end of 1886 can be
seen as the Western American manifestations of the industrial upheavals that
racked the nation in 1886. The 1893 outbursts in southern California also took
place during a national economic downturn, and of course the 1930 Watsonville riot occurred during the depths of the Great Depression.

It would be a mistake, however, to assume that these violent episodes were
merely spontaneous eruptions. They were, in fact, an integral part of what
historian Alexander Saxton has called the "growth sequence" of the anti-
Chinese movement—and, by extension, movements against other Asian
groups. First, a seemingly spontaneous attack against the pariah group would
occur, followed by the formation of a legal defense committee to support the
arrested perpetrators of the violence while they were on trial. After that came
mass meetings to protest whatever punishment might be meted out to the
criminals. Riding on the crest of the emotions whipped up by the mass meetings would emerge organized political groups to work for the ultimate goal of
ridding the country of whichever Asian group was under attack. This pattern
first congealed in San Francisco in 1867, but its basic dynamics remained intact
thereafter, even though the target of Euro-American hostility changed with the
appearance of each new group.[23]

More law-abiding citizens sometimes criticized the violent means used, but they ultimately sympathized with and condoned the actions because they supported the ends espoused by the most vociferous elements. Elaborate "scientific" explanations of nonwhite "inferiority" and the belief that minorities should be kept in their place were widely accepted by the late nineteenth century and provided an ideological justification for treating not only Asians, but other people of color, in a discriminatory and exploitative manner. To preserve Anglo-Saxon purity, it was argued, no interracial mixing should be allowed. The outbreaks of violence, therefore, served two functions: they were at once intimidation tactics to drive out Asians and expressions of frustration over the fact that, even after exclusionary laws had been passed, sizable numbers of the "undesirable" aliens remained.

Attempts to exclude Asians began in 1855 in California, when the state legislature levied a capitation tax of $50 on "the immigration to this state of persons who cannot become citizens thereof." An act passed three years later explicitly named "persons of Chinese or Mongolian races," who would thenceforth be barred. In 1862 another act designed to "protect free white labor against competition with Chinese coolie labor" provided for a $2.50 monthly "police tax" on every Chinese. Two acts passed in 1870 were directed against the importation of "Mongolian, Chinese, and Japanese females for criminal or demoralizing purposes" and of "coolie slavery." None of these laws had an impact, for they were all declared unconstitutional when tested in the higher courts.

One reason that a state such as California could not control immigration was that the U.S. Supreme Court had decided that immigration was a form of international commerce—something that only the federal government could regulate. Realizing the handicap that states operated under, anti-Chinese forces turned their attention to getting a federal exclusion law enacted. One obstacle in their path was the 1868 Burlingame Treaty, which recognized the right of citizens from the treaty's two signatory nations, China and the United States, to change their domiciles—that is, to emigrate.

But in 1875 Congress passed the Page Law to forbid the entry of Chinese, Japanese, and Mongolian contract laborers, women for the purpose of prostitution, and felons. As George Peffer has argued, this law reduced the influx of Chinese women but not of men.[24] So the United States negotiated a new treaty with China in 1880 that gave it the unilateral right to limit, though not absolutely to prohibit, Chinese immigration. This opened the way for Congress to enact the 1882 Chinese Exclusion Law, which suspended the entry of Chinese laborers for ten years but exempted merchants, students and teachers, diplomats, and travelers from its provisions.[25] The exempted classes could enter either by showing a certificate issued by the Chinese government and countersigned by an American consul in China or on the basis of oral testimony. Parole evidence, however, created innumerable problems, so an 1884 amendment to the 1882 act made certificates the "sole permissible" evidence for all Chinese nonlaborers who wished to land on American soil.

The screws were further tightened in September 1888, when Congress approved an act that allowed Chinese laborers who left the country to return only if they owned at least $1,000 in property or had a wife in the United States. Even this last loophole was closed a scant three weeks later when Congress, acting on a rumor that China would probably not ratify a treaty negotiated earlier that year, passed the Scott Act, under which it became impossible for Chinese laborers to return at all once they left the United States. The Scott Act, which went into effect immediately, abrogated the reentry right of an estimated 20,000 Chinese laborers with certificates in their possession, including 600 who were enroute across the Pacific. These individuals were denied landing when they reached American shores. Chinese exclusion was extended in 1892 and again in 1902. Finally, in 1904 it was made indefinite. Chinese were also barred from the newly acquired territories of Hawaii, the Philippines, and Puerto Rico.

Efforts to exclude Japanese took a different form, because the United States was careful not to antagonize Japan, a rising military power in the Pacific Basin.[26] None of the laws affecting Japanese immigration named them explicitly—a face-saving device. Thus, the Japanese government in 1907 consented to a Gentlemen's Agreement whereby it would stop issuing passports to laborers. Furthermore, it did not protest Executive Order 589, signed by President Theodore Roosevelt to prohibit Japanese laborers holding passports for Hawaii, Mexico, or Canada from remigrating to the continental United States. Then in 1920 it once again acquiesced by denying passports to picture brides, whose coming had by then become controversial. The Immigration Act of 1924, which barred the entry of "aliens ineligible to citizenship," virtually ended Japanese immigration.

The American government did not have to do anything to exclude Koreans, because emigration from Korea had already been curbed by the Japanese colonial administration. Nonetheless, according to Bong-Youn Choy, an estimated 500 Korean nationalists who had managed to slip out of their country ended up in the United States between 1910 and 1924. Many of them had first gone to Russia, Manchuria, China, or Europe before showing up at American ports, where they petitioned to enter as political refugees without passports.[27] This trickle of expatriates ended after 1924, however, as the immigration act passed that year was extremely strict.

An unusual geographic criterion had to be used to exclude Asian Indians because their racial or ethnographic status was unclear. Anthropologists classified some of the inhabitants of the Indian subcontinent as "Aryans," but no one was sure whether Aryans were Caucasians and whether the latter referred only to whites. Between 1910 and 1917, immigration officials tried to minimize the number of Asian Indians coming in by using administrative regulations, but a clause in the 1917 Immigration Act finally enabled them to stop the influx. An imaginary line was drawn from the Red to the Mediterranean, Aegean, and Black seas, through the Caucasus Mountains and the Caspian Sea, along the Ural River, and then through the Ural Mountains. All people living in areas east of the line—which came to be called the "Barred Zone"—were denied entry from then on. Asian Indians were of course among those excluded.[28]

Restricting Filipino immigration took greater ingenuity. Since Filipinos were "wards" of the United States and were called "nationals," they were neither aliens nor citizens. To exclude them required a change in their status. Accordingly, in the early 1930s, after an unsuccessful attempt to repatriate Filipinos at government expense, those favoring Filipino exclusion joined forces with others who supported independence for the islands. The result was the Tydings-McDuffie Act of 1934. The major clauses of the act spelled out the conditions under which the Philippines would receive its independence, while one small section cut Filipino immigration to fifty persons a year.[29]

Much to the chagrin of the exclusionists, sizable numbers of Chinese, Japanese, and Filipinos, small but visible clusters of Asian Indians, and scattered handfuls of Koreans remained in the country even after the exclusionary laws went into effect. The anti-Asian forces therefore had to find ways to confine those immigrants who doggedly refused to disappear, so that the social "contamination" engendered by their presence could be minimized and their presence made invisible. They did so by social segregation of various sorts.

Chinese prostitutes in San Francisco were the first Asians whom the host society tried to remove to a confined geographic locality outside of municipal limits. The city took official notice of their presence in 1854. By the end of that year, a grand jury had indicted and the Court of Sessions had convicted several Chinese madames for keeping Chinese "houses." After imposing a fine of $1,000 on each of the women, however, the judge expressed the hope that "the prisoners might elect the alternative of removing outside certain limits which the Court would hereafter prescribe."[30]

Extant documents do not indicate whether the women chose that option. But the idea of removing Chinese brothels to a less visible location did not die. In 1861 the city's chief of police first arrested and then released fourteen Chinese prostitutes, after giving them a "translated admonition to seek other quarters, which they promised to do . . . in [a] . . . more secluded locality than Washington Alley."[31] This effort succeeded, at least temporarily. But because landlords found renting their property to brothel operators lucrative, the prostitutes soon returned. A new board of health appointed in 1866 once again recommended that Chinese prostitutes be removed outside the city limits. Apparently, the women agreed thereafter to occupy only those buildings and localities approved by the board of health and the police commissioners. Confinement, if not complete removal, had thus been achieved.

The efforts to isolate Chinese prostitutes soon became generalized to a desire to segregate all Chinese persons. A chance to legalize such segregation came in 1879, when the California State Legislature passed a law obligating all incorporated towns and cities to remove Chinese from their territories. Fortunately for the Chinese, the U.S. circuit court in California, while ruling on the constitutionality of another discriminatory law, referred to the one mandating segregation as equally unconstitutional, since it denied Chinese the equal protection guaranteed by the Fourteenth Amendment and violated the terms of the Burlingame Treaty besides. A second attempt in 1890 to remove San Francisco's Chinatown outside city limits also failed for constitutional reasons.

Constitutional obstacles notwithstanding, San Francisco officials did not give up their efforts to confine or remove the Chinese. An unexpected chance came at the turn of the century when deaths from bubonic plague were reported in the city. As Joan Trauner and Charles McClain have shown, bubonic plague had been found in Canton and Hong Kong in 1894.[32] At the end of 1896 the San Francisco board of health decided that all arriving passengers had to be medically inspected. Chinese and Japanese, however, were singled out for detention in quarantine because the ports of Shanghai, Hong Kong, Yokohama, and Kobe, according to the medical officials in San Francisco, were "infected." Their fears were exacerbated when two cases of the dreaded disease were discovered in Honolulu's Chinatown and the Hawaiian board of health ordered 4,500 Chinese removed to a quarantine camp and burned Chinatown to the ground. Such drastic measures might not have been taken were it not for the fact that strong anti-Chinese sentiments had existed in Hawaii for years.

In San Francisco, an autopsy of a Chinese corpse in early March of 1900 revealed that the deceased had enlarged lymph nodes; the coroner suspected the man had died of plague. City officials immediately cordoned off China-town, placed guards to control traffic into and out of the area, and carried out a house-to-house inspection. Chinese and Japanese were forbidden to travel outside of California without certificates issued by the surgeon general of the U.S. Marine Hospital Service, the federal agency responsible for quarantine. Due to the population density of the Chinese quarters and the inability to control any fires that might be set, the solution used in Honolulu could not be applied to San Francisco. Instead, every house in Chinatown was washed from garret to basement with lime, while gutters and sewers were disinfected with sulfur dioxide and mercury bichloride. The cordon around Chinatown was lifted only after a court order declared it discriminatory.

The bubonic plague episode represented the last official attempt to remove Asians from within San Francisco's city limits. However, though residential segregation never became legal, Euro-Americans nevertheless succeeded in confining Asian immigrants by threatening them with violence should they dare to step outside clearly understood (though not visibly demarcated) bound-aries. More important, landlords refused to rent any premises outside of the ghetto areas to them, while realtors declined to sell them property anywhere except in the most "undesirable" neighborhoods. This pattern of segregation had become so prevalent that by the time Japanese, Koreans, Asian Indians, and Filipinos arrived in numbers, there was no need for state, county, or municipal officials to pass any laws to specify where they could live.

Those who wished to segregate Asian immigrants and their children socially had more success within the public school system. According to Charles Wollenberg, black Americans in California, as elsewhere, led the fight against school segregation.[33] A "colored school" was established in San Francisco for 45 black children in 1854, but in the 1860s black parents decided to challenge school segregation. They took their case to the California Supreme Court, which ruled in 1874 that though Negroes had the right to an education, there was no reason it had to take place in an integrated setting. Black children could attend schools for whites only in those places where no separate facilities were available.

In line with how blacks were treated, as Victor Low has documented, a separate school for Chinese children was opened in the city in 1859, but due to low enrollment, it was made into an evening school a year later. Then in 1871 the school superintendent terminated even the evening classes. Henceforth, the only education available to children of Chinese ancestry, regardless of where they had been born, would be from private tutors hired by their parents or in a few English and Bible classes taught by Protestant missionaries working in Chinatown.

This situation continued until 1884, when Joseph and Mary Tape went to court to challenge the school board's denial of the right of their daughter, Mamie, to a public education. Unwilling to budge, the school superintendent requested funds from the state legislature to build a new "Oriental School," which opened its doors in 1885.[34] San Francisco and the four Sacramento-San Joaquin Delta communities of Rio Vista, Isleton, Walnut Grove, and Courtland, kept Chinese children in segregated schools until well into the 1930s.

California was not the only state where the battle for integrated schooling for Chinese children was fought. In the Mississippi Delta, where several hundred Chinese lived by the early twentieth century, public education for nonwhite children was virtually nonexistent in the rural areas and very poor in the larger urban centers. As James Loewen has found, Chinese children who wished to attend public schools had to go to those set up for black children.[35] In a few small towns, however, where there were only one or two Chinese families, the handful of Chinese children were sometimes allowed to enroll in the schools for whites. In 1924 the school superintendent of Rosedale told Lum Gong, a well-known Chinese merchant in that town, that his elder daughter, Martha, who had been quietly attending the white school, could no longer do so. In response, her father hired white lawyers who argued successfully before the U.S. Circuit Court for the First Judicial District that since no school had been established for Chinese children, she was being denied an equal education. The school officials appealed the decision to the Mississippi Supreme Court, which reversed it. In the opinion of the court, since Chinese were not white, they must be "colored." Martha Lum, the court declared, was not being denied an education because she *could* attend the schools for "colored" children.

Lum's lawyers then took the case to the U.S. Supreme Court, which upheld the Mississippi Supreme Court's ruling and affirmed that "[i]t has been at all times the policy of the lawmakers of Mississippi to preserve the white schools for members of the Caucasian race alone."[36] But perhaps recognizing that such a practice violated the Fourteenth Amendment, the Chief Justice referred to *Plessy* v. *Ferguson* and explained that "[a] child of Chinese blood, born in, and a citizen of, the United States, is not denied the equal protection of the laws by being classed by the State among the colored races who are assigned to public schools separate from those provided for the whites, when equal facilities for education are afforded to both classes."[37] Chinese children were not admitted into white schools in Mississippi until 1950. And of course, a few more years passed before de jure school segregation in the South was ended, although de facto segregation continues in various forms there and elsewhere.

The experience of Japanese students proved to be quite different from that of the Chinese. For one thing, many of the earliest Japanese students were not children but young men. As part of its effort to modernize the country after the Meiji Restoration, the Japanese government sent hundreds of its brightest youth to Europe and the United States on scholarship to study Western science, military technology, business and public administration, and other modern subjects. In the United States, such Japanese government-sponsored students attended some of the most prestigious universities in New England and the middle Atlantic states.

Less fortunate students without government stipends still could hope for an American education: they came as "school boys" to earn their way through school by working, mainly as domestic servants. Most of the poorer students, who ranged in age from 15 to 25, found their way not to the Atlantic but the

Pacific Coast. As early as 1885 an estimated 300 of them were living in San Francisco, according to Yuji Ichioka.[38] Until the turn of the century, when sugar plantation workers from Hawaii came to the mainland in large numbers, students composed a majority of the Japanese population in California and Washington, their two favorite destinations on the mainland. Between 1882 and 1890 the Japanese government issued more than 1,500 passports to students— almost 44 percent of the total number of passports issued for travel to the United States.

The presence of Japanese students eventually caught the eye of San Francisco's officials, as Roger Daniels has shown.[39] In 1905 the city's Board of Education ordered Japanese and Korean students in the public schools to transfer to the "Oriental School" serving the Chinese. News of this decision caused a great outcry in Tokyo. Wary of offending Japan, whose new military prowess—as demonstrated during the Russo-Japanese War—had impressed him greatly, President Theodore Roosevelt sent his secretary of commerce and labor to San Francisco to investigate the situation. The secretary discovered that there were only 93 students scattered in some two dozen public schools, and fewer of them were overage than the school board had alleged. He tried to persuade the board to rescind its decision, but the latter refused, whereupon Roosevelt asked the U.S. attorney general to initiate court action against the San Francisco board of education.

Meanwhile, however, recognizing that what San Franciscans were concerned about was not education per se, but rather immigration, Roosevelt invited some of the city's officials to Washington, D.C., for a conference. Eventually they reached a compromise: in exchange for the school board's willingness to let Japanese students attend public schools reserved for white children, the federal government would persuade Japan to stop issuing passports to laborers.

Compared to the Chinese and Japanese pupils, there were relatively few Korean and Filipino children in the period before World War II, so their school attendance never became a political issue. (Or more accurately, no scholar has yet investigated whether it was a problem.) As for Asian Indians, virtually no Asian Indian women immigrated before World War II, so they had few progeny on American soil. The only group of Asian Indian men to form families did so in the Imperial Valley: they wed Mexican women and sired mixed-ancestry children who attended schools set aside for Mexican children.

Regardless of whether they attended integrated or segregated schools, children of Asian ancestry on the mainland were taught by white teachers and learned from textbooks that contained no information about their own cultural legacy. Some teachers of Asian ancestry were employed by the schools in Hawaii, but there, too, the teachers' main concern was to inculcate Anglo-American values, behavioral patterns, and speech patterns. Students who spoke pidgin English at home and in the playgrounds had to master standard English if they wished to pursue higher education. The message they received everywhere was that their own origins were inferior and their people powerless. Only by "Americanizing" could they hope for a better life.

Another form of social segregation imposed on Asian immigrants was the prohibition against interracial marriage. The colony of Maryland passed the first antimiscegenation law in U.S. history in 1661 to prohibit black-white marriages. In time, 38 states in the union had such laws in their statute books. The question of the legality of Chinese-white marriages came up during California's second constitution convention. A bill to prohibit the "intermarriage of white persons with Chinese, negroes, mulattoes, or persons of mixed blood, descended from a Chinaman or negro from the third generation, inclusive" took final form in 1880 as Section 69 of the Civil Code, which regulated the issuance of marriage licenses, with the word Mongolian substituted for the word Chinese. But Section 60 of the Civil Code, which dealt with antimiscegenation, was not changed to make it applicable to Chinese. These two contradictory sections existed side by side until 1905. In that year, fearful of a new "yellow peril"—the Japanese—California's lawmakers finally amended Section 60 to forbid marriages between whites and "Mongolians."

In those days, Chinese, Japanese, or Koreans were not particularly inclined to marry whites, so while these statutes did pose obstacles, they affected relatively few individuals. The Asian immigrants most inconvenienced by antimiscegenation laws were Filipinos, many of whom were and are of mixed origins—primarily Melayo-Polynesian, Spanish, and Chinese. Concern over a new type of "hybridization" became increasingly hysterical in the late 1920s as anti-Filipino spokespersons called public attention to the tendency of Filipino men to seek the company of white and Mexican women at taxi-dance halls. At these clubs, patrons bought strings of tickets, which the hostesses tore off one at a time as they danced with the men, giving rise to the phrase "ten cents a dance."

Some couples who got acquainted this way desired to marry. Since the precise racial classification of Filipinos was open to question, some county clerks issued marriage licenses to Filipino men and white women, while others refused to do so. Megumi Dick Osumi has found that Los Angeles recognized such marriages because its county council had decided in 1921 that Filipinos were not Mongolians.[40] Anti-Filipino groups and individuals, including California's attorney general, eventually sued Los Angeles County to compel it to end this practice. In 1930 a superior court judge prohibited the Los Angeles county clerk from issuing a marriage license to Tony Moreno, a Filipino man, and Ruby Robinson, a white woman. Thus chastised, the county clerk thereafter stopped issuing licenses to Filipino-white couples.

But Filipinos refused to abide by such a decision. Four cases they filed reached the county superior court in 1931. There the judge decided that Filipino-white marriages did not violate Sections 60 and 69 of the Civil Code because, in his view, Filipinos were not Mongolians. The county, backed by anti-Filipino organizations, appealed one of these cases, *Salvador Roldan* v. *L. A. County*. The majority opinion handed down in 1933 by the appellate court, based on an exhaustive reading of the works of nineteenth-century ethnologists, declared that since the most influential writer of the day divided *homo sapiens* into five racial groups—Caucasian (white), Mongolian (yellow), Ethiopian (black), American (red), and Malay (brown, the category to which Filipinos belonged)—Mongolians and Malays were obviously not synonymous. Thus couples like Salvador Roldan and Marjorie Rogers could wed.

Undaunted by their failure in the courts, the anti-Filipino forces sought remedy through the legislature, which unanimously passed two bills to amend Sections 60 and 69 to allow antimiscegenation laws to include Filipino-white marriages. Only in 1948 were California's antimiscegenation statutes declared unconstitutional, and it was not until 1967 that all such statutes in the United States were removed from the books or lapsed from disuse.

In terms of their reception by the host society, Asian immigrants shared many experiences with both European immigrants and with oppressed racial minority groups. Because ethnocentrism is a worldwide phenomenon, Asian immigrants, as foreigners and newcomers, were looked upon with disdain and curiosity by earlier arrivals. Like most European immigrants, they started at the bottom of the economic ladder. Unlike their European counterparts, however, their upward climb was impeded not only by a poor knowledge of the English language, a lack of familiarity with the American way of doing things, limited education, and the absence of relevant job skills, but also by laws that severely limited—on racial grounds—the opportunities they could pursue. Like other people of color, they were victims of legally sanctioned color prejudice.

Asian immigrants found it difficult to fight such prejudice because, again like other nonwhite minorities, they lacked political power. They could not vote, because the right of naturalization was denied them. Consequently, they could neither enjoy the rights nor bear the responsibilities of citizenship. Thus the Asian American historical experience has been an ironic one: in a country that prides itself in being a democracy with a government of laws and not of men, those very political and legal structures institutionalized and helped to perpetuate their inferior status for a century. But despite such institutional racism, a sufficient number of each group remained in the United States to become small but important parts of the American multiethnic mosaic. They were able to do so because almost as soon as each new group arrived, its members set up mechanisms to ensure their own survival.

*Directors of the Chinese Consolidated Benevolent Association, also known as the Chinese Six Companies, San Francisco, ca. 1890.*
Courtesy Bancroft Library

*chapter four*

---

# The Social Organization of
# Asian Immigrant Communities

The communities that Asian immigrants established in North America have
been quite different from the ones they left behind, the image that Asians
tend to "cling" to their ancestral cultures notwithstanding. These communities were not "normal," demographically speaking, in at least two ways.
First, most of their inhabitants were men in their prime working years, many of
whom led a migratory existence. With few women, children, or older folks
around, the young male immigrants relied on a complex network of organizations to maintain social cohesion among themselves. Second, due to the need
to survive in a new setting, individuals who had learned to deal with a host
society that had a different culture and used a different language, rather than
members of the traditional elite or elders, provided leadership. Such a social
configuration characterized non-Asian immigrant communities during their
early years as well, but it lasted far longer in Asian ones because exclusionary
laws prevented women from coming just at that point in each group's immigration history when they might have done so.

The ability to form associations, along with their repeated efforts to resist
oppression, enabled Asians to carve a place for themselves in a host society that
did not welcome them. Doing so became especially important for those who
chose to raise families on American soil. Associations formed by Asian immigrants, like those created by immigrants of other origins, provided mutual aid
to their members and served as settings where coethnics could partake of
warmth and conviviality. At the same time, they functioned as instruments of
social control over the masses of immigrants and as legitimizers of the status
accorded particular immigrant leaders. The latter exercised power and acquired
prestige not only by virtue of being officers of community organizations but
also by serving as communication links—and consequently, as power
brokers—between their compatriots and the external world. Broadly speaking,
Asian immigrants organized themselves on two kinds of basis: primordial ties,
such as common locality or dialect, kinship bonds, and religious affinity; and
pragmatic interests, such as the desire to secure economic advantages or
achieve political ends.

Of the five major Asian immigrant groups who came before 1975, the
Chinese established the widest array of community organizations.[1] Associations made up of people from the same districts, called *huiguan*, were the most
important in American Chinatowns. The first two district associations, the

Sanyi Huiguan (Sam Yup Association, sometimes called the Canton Company in English) and the Siyi Huiguan (Sze Yup Association), came into existence in 1851 in San Francisco. In subsequent years additional associations were formed. The bonds that held their members together extended beyond common locality to shared dialects, residence, and occupations. Villages and districts in nineteenth-century China were quite autonomous, given the poor state of transportation, so different dialects were often spoken by inhabitants of neighboring areas. People who shared a dialect identified strongly with one another. Members of dialect groups who went abroad tended to settle in the same neighborhoods, towns, or counties and took up similar occupations. Heungsan people and Hakka-speakers headed for Hawaii; Sze Yup people flocked to California, where they constituted an estimated three-quarters of the Chinese population until the middle of the present century; Sam Yup people went to both the islands and the mainland. The more urbanized Sam Yup people became import-export merchants, grocers, butchers, tailors, and other kinds of entrepreneurs; most of the poorer Sze Yup folks got their start in America as laborers; while Heungsan natives in California specialized in tenant farming in the Sacramento-San Joaquin Delta or earned a living as nurserymen in the Santa Clara Valley.

Almost as important as the district associations were the family or clan associations. In traditional China, people with the same surnames assumed they shared a common (or at least a putative) ancestor and observed exogamy. In the New World, each clan with a large number of members created a family association of its own, while those with only a handful of members combined into coalitions. Just as people from the same districts had a tendency to settle together, so those with similar surnames often congregated in the same places and tended to specialize in particular occupations.

Both the district and family associations provided multiple kinds of mutual aid. Their officers met incoming steamers, offered temporary lodging in the buildings owned by the associations, outfitted aspiring miners headed for the gold fields or laborers about to set off to harvest crops or work on construction projects, settled quarrels, formed rotating credit associations, sent letters and remitted money back to China for individuals, cared for the sick and indigent, built altars or even temples, maintained cemeteries, and shipped the exhumed bones of the deceased to their home villages for final burial. In short, these organizations performed all the crucial functions that in China were carried out by extended families, clans, or lineages.

Given the strong value placed on ancestral ties among the Chinese, those in America were especially concerned about rites of passage, which in the early years meant mainly funerals, as there were relatively few marriages or births. It was possible for the district and family associations to serve religious or quasi-religious needs because popular Chinese religion is a syncretist amalgamation of Confucian, Taoist, Buddhist, and animist beliefs. All that a believer requires is an altar with a deity and a metal pot for holding sticks of incense. There are no regularly scheduled worship services—although there are many festivals of religious significance—or much of an organized priesthood. Individuals can simply go to temples or pray in front of altars as their spiritual needs or particular occasions demand. Each district and family association that owned a building usually set aside a room with one or more altars, so that members who desired to do so could make use of the facilities.

Another significant form of mutual aid was the rotating credit association, which enabled individuals or groups to start businesses. Such an association is formed when individuals agree to pool funds on a regular basis and to allow each member of the group to use the total sum contributed each month (or some other specified length of time) on a rotating basis until everyone has had a chance at the money. This practice was most prevalent in urban areas. Asian immigrants who became tenant farmers relied on it less, because landowners, commission merchants, and even banks were quite willing to extend credit to them.

One of the more interesting contrasts between the history of Asian immigrants in the continental United States and those in Hawaii is that, unlike the mainlanders, who formed organizations almost as soon as they stepped off the boat, Hawaii's Asians took longer to do so. According to Clarence Glick, Chinese in Hawaii created a funeral society in 1854—the first organization they established in the islands—but no family association was formed until 1889 and no huiguan until 1890.[2] One probable reason for their delayed appearance may be that the regimented rhythm of plantation life precluded as well as rendered unnecessary such institutions. A second possible explanation could be that, given the smaller Chinese population in the islands, there were not enough people from each district or clan to support an association of its own. A third cause very likely is the fact that the early plantations were extremely isolated, making it very difficult for people living in different plantations to communicate and interact with each other. Besides, as contract laborers, neither the Chinese nor the groups who came after them enjoyed freedom of travel, even if transportation had been better. Asians in the American West, in contrast, were quite mobile. But the very fact that so many of them led a migratory existence made organizations a necessity.

To adjudicate quarrels among members of the different associations, officers of the six existing huiguan in California in 1862 formed a loose federation called a *gongsuo* (public hall), composed of representatives from each huiguan. Euro-Americans referred to this organ as the "Six Chinese Companies." Twenty years later, as the 1882 Chinese Exclusion Law went into effect, community leaders, at the behest of the Chinese consul general in San Francisco and feeling the need to present a united front to a hostile outside world, established a formal umbrella association called the Zhonghua Huiguan (Chinese Consolidated Benevolent Association), the history of which Him Mark Lai has chronicled.[3] This new confederation soon acquired a variant of the old nickname and in English became known as the Chinese Six Companies.

One of the main functions of the Chinese Six Companies was to fight against anti-Chinese legislation. For this purpose, it hired a bevy of Euro-American lawyers over the course of the next half century to defend the rights of its members. Another important service it provided was a Chinese language school (set up in 1884) for the children of immigrants. Its activities were supported by membership dues, by special assessments, and by fees collected for issuing "exit permits" to all Chinese desiring to return to China. No one could get one of these permits unless the Chinese Six Companies or one of its component associations had cleared him or her of debt. Since the Chinese Six Companies managed to persuade steamship companies not to sell tickets to those without exit permits, it exercised a degree of control over Chinese immigrants that some scholars have called despotic.

To take care of Chinese in other parts of the Western hemisphere, Consolidated Chinese Benevolent Associations were formed in New York in 1883, in Honolulu and Vancouver in 1884, Lima in 1885, Portland around 1886, and Seattle a few years after that. The one in Honolulu went by the English name United Chinese Society. Until recent years, the organizations outside of California looked to the San Francisco one for leadership in all matters affecting Chinese in America. From the late 1920s—when the Guomindang (Kuomintang or Chinese Nationalist Party) began to rule China and, after 1949, to govern Taiwan—to the present, Chinese consuls have tried to use the Chinese Consolidated Benevolent Associations to influence affairs in American Chinatowns.

Merchants occupied almost all the available positions of leadership in the district and family associations and especially the Chinese Six Companies. They dominated the presidencies, vice presidencies, boards of directors, and committee chairs. And because these associations touched so many facets of the lives of Chinese immigrants, merchants became the power elite in Chinese immigrant communities.

The elite status of merchants is what most clearly differentiates Chinese immigrant communities from those in China. There the top stratum of the social structure was made up of scholar-gentry. China under the dynasties was governed by men who had passed a series of imperial examinations. There being no system of free compulsory public education, it meant that the scions of well-to-do landowning families had the best chance for acquiring the learning that would enable them to pass these examinations in order to become officials. Once in office, myriad opportunities existed for them to obtain greater wealth and more land. According to the teachings of Confucius, peasants ranked below the scholar-gentry as the next most valuable class in society because they produced the material goods that enabled people to survive. Then came artisans who made useful things. Merchants, who earned a living by buying cheap and selling dear without themselves creating any new material goods, were at the bottom of the social hierarchy. In reality, of course, merchants with money could hire tutors to prepare their sons for the imperial examinations or could, on occasion, purchase degrees as well as land. But whatever status they acquired was always tenuous.

Few sons from scholar-gentry families emigrated. But many merchants did, because they found opportunities overseas that traditional Chinese society denied them. All over Southeast Asia, Chinese merchants large and small thrived in business. The Cantonese merchants who emigrated to the Western hemisphere also did rather well: having dealt with foreigners for centuries, they were quite urbane and had little trouble taking charge of things. By the time that masses of peasant-laborers arrived in 1852, the several hundred Chinese merchants already in San Francisco had formed associations, rented or purchased buildings, set up stores, and established ties to the Euro-American community. By aiding their fellow countrymen, they also quickly gained control over them. The dominance they enjoyed lasted for more than a century.

The fact that American immigration laws favored them after 1882 also allowed them to consolidate their social, economic, and political power.

Chinese immigrants also grouped together on the basis of common interests, forming sworn brotherhoods, trade guilds, and political parties. One of the most important associations that cut across common geographic origins or kinship was the *tang* (tong). Tong simply means "hall," but in the Americas, the term referred to fraternal organizations that bound its members together through secret initiation rites and sworn brotherhood. The best known fraternal order among Chinese in the Americas was the Zhigongtang (Chee Kung Tong), an outgrowth of secret societies in China that were formed originally to espouse the overthrow of the (Manchu) Qing dynasty and the restoration of the (Han Chinese) Ming dynasty. These secret societies went by a variety of names; Western scholars generally call them Triads. Some Triad members participated in the Taiping Rebellion. When that movement was finally subdued in 1864, quite a number escaped to Southeast Asia, Hawaii, and the Pacific Coast, bringing with them their beliefs, rituals, and long years of organizational experience.

The Chee Kung Tong, which Euro-Americans sometimes called the "Chinese Freemasons," was by no means the only fraternal organization among the Chinese in North America. More than a dozen existed in different parts of the Americas, including Hawaii, where the first one appeared in 1869. Many of the early tongs in Hawaii were dominated by Hakka-speakers, but in time, other dialect groups also formed their own. Tongs were popular because they provided alternative, antiestablishment social organizations with which people, especially the déclassé within the immigrant population, could affiliate.

In time, tongs became notorious as "fighting tongs," which employed "highbinders" or "hatchetmen" to kill off their rivals. Their aim was to control the Chinese immigrant underworld by staking out territory and monopolizing the profits from gambling, opium smoking, and prostitution, as well as from smuggling in Chinese after immigration exclusion was imposed. Because of the profits to be made, some erstwhile respectable merchants became tong members. In contrast to the bloody feuds on the mainland, there is no record of tongs in Hawaii being involved in criminal activities, nor did "tong wars" break out in the islands.

Guilds were another kind of organization found in American Chinatowns that were based on mutual interests rather than common origins. Craft as well as labor guilds had existed in China for centuries. They trained apprentices, upheld standards of workmanship, set prices for the merchandise they produced and sold, and enforced territorial rights. In the old country, masters and apprentices or employers and employees in the same trades often belonged to a single guild. However, there were also instances where employers formed guilds called *dongjia* (east houses), while workers formed *xijia* (west houses).

Given this tradition, it is not surprising that Chinese in the United States set up guilds to protect their economic interests. Guilds for laundrymen, shoemakers, and cigarmakers had come into existence in San Francisco by the late 1860s. The laundrymen's guild, the Tongxingtang (Tung Hing Tong) was especially effective. It set uniform prices for different items washed (in order to eliminate cutthroat competition), divided up neighborhoods among its members (so that each laundry had a fair chance at survival), and collected funds and hired lawyers to fight against anti-Chinese laundry ordinances.

Among Japanese immigrants in the continental United States, the most common organization was the *kenjinkai* (prefectural association).[4] Unlike the huiguan, which predated Chinese immigration into the United States, kenjinkai assumed importance mainly after Japanese arrived in North America. Common prefectural origin became a basis for association because there were not enough people from smaller geographic units—cities, villages, or neighborhoods—to form viable organizations. Although kenjinkai were also formed in Hawaii—the first was a joint venture between Hiroshima and Yamaguchi *kenjin* (prefecture mates)—they apparently did not become as important as they did on the mainland. Again, the nature of plantation life may have made such organizations less necessary. Research on the history of Okinawans in Hawaii shows that locality organizations among them did not develop until people started moving away from plantations to urban areas.[5] The same was very likely true of Japanese from other prefectures.

Kenjinkai furnished mutual aid and enriched the social life of their members, but they did not exercise as much control over their members as did the Chinese huiguan and family associations, because Japanese newcomers were not as dependent on them for temporary shelter and food as were arriving Chinese on their district and family associations. Japanese-operated hotels and boardinghouses in every major port of entry in North America catered to their owners' or managers' kenjin, while labor contractors set up employment agencies on the premises of these lodging houses to help greenhorns find jobs.

Just as the Chinese consul general in San Francisco had urged Chinese immigrant leaders to form a community-wide association in 1882 when the anti-Chinese movement was at its height, so the Japanese consul general played an instrumental role in establishing the most important institution in pre-World War II Japanese American communities—the Japanese Association of America, of which Yuji Ichioka has written.[6] Formed in 1908, when strong anti-Japanese sentiment existed in California, the association in time consisted of a national headquarters in San Francisco, several branches called "central bodies," and dozens of local associations. The jurisdiction of the "central bodies" coincided with the territorial boundaries of the various Japanese consulates. The Northwest American Japanese Association, established in Seattle in 1913, dealt with Japanese in Washington and Montana. The Japanese Association of Oregon, formed in Portland in 1911, presided over residents in Oregon and Idaho. The San Francisco national headquarters (and later, a separate San Francisco branch) took care of business in northern and central California and in Nevada. The Central Japanese Association of Southern California, established in Los Angeles in 1915, looked after affairs in southern California, New Mexico, and Arizona. In addition, branches existed in Colorado, Utah, Texas, Illinois, and New York. For reasons that have not yet been studied, the system did not include Hawaii.

The Japanese Association of America acquired the power that it did partly because of the unusual regulations governing Japanese immigration and the travel of Japanese living in the United States. Under the Gentlemen's Agreement, Japanese who hoped to return to the United States after visits to their homeland were required to obtain certificates before departure that attested to the fact they were bona fide residents eligible for reentry. The Japanese Foreign Ministry, through its consulates, authorized the various Japanese Associations to issue these certificates and allowed them to keep half of the fees collected for this service—a practice that not only made the associations financially solvent, but also gave them great control over the Japanese immigrant population. This fact led critics of the Japanese Association of America to declare it a tool of the Tokyo government, just as detractors of the Chinese Six Companies had labeled it a "secret tribunal."

Another similarity between the Japanese Association of America and the Chinese Six Companies is that both hired Euro-American lawyers to challenge discriminatory laws. Whereas the Chinese focused on the exclusion laws, the Japanese tried strenuously to invalidate the alien land laws. In addition, the association published and distributed a number of pamphlets in English with the hope of swaying American public opinion in a positive direction.

Visible as it was, and despite the control it exercised over the movement of Japanese immigrants, the Japanese Association of America and its various branches never enrolled more than a third of the adult Japanese male population. There was a limit to how much an immigrant could spend on membership fees. Those with limited resources probably chose to support organizations that had a more direct bearing on their livelihood. Such organizations were numerous, for Japanese immigrants showed an extraordinary penchant for setting up trade associations.

According to *Zaibei nihonjinshi* (A history of the Japanese in America), a comprehensive history published in Japanese in 1940, the first trade association appeared in 1893, when 20 or so Japanese shoemakers organized a Shoemakers' League with the aid of the vice president of the Tokyo Shoemakers' Alliance during his visit to San Francisco. The league soon formed a cooperative purchasing and marketing union to benefit its members. By 1903 so many import-export merchants had opened Japanese art goods stores in the city that they were undercutting each other's prices savagely. To deal with the situation, they founded the Art Goods and Notions Commercial Association (renamed the San Francisco Art Goods and Notions Commercial Association the following year) to minimize harmful competition. Those who owned dye shops banded into the San Francisco Japanese Cloth Dye Trade Association in 1908. Sellers of Japanese books and magazines formed the American Magazines and Books Commercial Association in 1915. Dry goods store owners, grocers, hotelkeepers, restaurant owners, bathhouse operators, dry cleaners, laundrymen, barbers, confectioners, flower shop proprietors, doctors—all organized trade associations, making it possible for a Japanese Chamber of Commerce to emerge around 1915.[7]

Despite the proliferation of urban businesses and professions, agriculture remained the foundation of the Japanese immigrant economy. Therefore the trade associations that affected the largest number of Japanese were those concerned with the production, processing, distribution, and marketing of farm products. As Noritake Yagasaki has shown, Japanese immigrants started setting up numerous local agricultural cooperatives, central agricultural associations, and farm labor contractors' organizations early in the present century.[8] Flower growers in the San Francisco Bay Area formed the California Flower Growers Association in 1906 and six years later opened the California Flower Market, which they incorporated under the laws of California. Flower growers in the Los Angeles area followed suit with the Southern California Flower Market in

1913. Lettuce and potato cultivators in the Salinas Valley started the Salinas Valley Japanese Agricultural Contractors' Association in 1908. The same year, farmers in the Sacramento-San Joaquin Delta established the Delta Agricultural Association with headquarters in Walnut Grove "to promote fraternity, improve mutual communication, . . . do away with conventional abuses and unrestricted competition . . . and to promote farming by unity and cooperation."[9] In the mid-1910s producers of vegetables, strawberries, celery, cantaloupes, and scores of other crops also formed cooperatives of their own. Meanwhile, the Central Japanese Agricultural Association of California served as an umbrella organization for farmers in northern and central California, while the Southern California Central Agricultural Association functioned as the overarching body in the southern part of the state.

By far, the two most important agricultural associations in which Japanese were involved were the Ninth Street Market (also known as the Los Angeles City Market) and the Seventh Street Market in Los Angeles. Neither was a purely Japanese undertaking. Rather, both were multiethnic enterprises with a significant number of Japanese and Chinese participants. Following the San Francisco earthquake, Japanese were among the thousands of people who moved to Los Angeles. Many of them became produce growers and sellers. In late 1907 a group of them met to discuss the possibility of opening a new produce market, even though a small one already existed on Third Street. Their plans materialized in 1909, when the Los Angeles City Market at Ninth and San Pedro streets was established in cooperation with Chinese, Italians, and other ethnic groups. The Japanese owned 18 percent of the stock, the Chinese 41 percent, and Euro-Americans 41 percent. The market's officers were of American, Italian, Russian, Chinese, and Japanese ancestry. But the Japanese were the market's main users: they rented two-thirds of the stalls inside and more than half of the wagon spaces in the yard. In contrast to the grassroots origins of the Ninth Street Market, the Seventh Street Market was established in 1918 by the Southern Pacific Railroad. Although Japanese immigrants had no say in its management, they were among its prime users.

These various agricultural associations served multiple functions. They enabled immigrants to gain vertical control over their own sector of California's agribusiness: Japanese growers out in the countryside or suburbs sold their produce to Japanese commission merchants, who in turn sold it to wholesalers, who then supplied the numerous Japanese retail fruit and produce stores in the city. Furthermore, in each step of the production process, pooling their resources enabled them to share important information among themselves, translate and disseminate new research findings, plug into a nationwide network of marketing cooperatives (which California growers had taken the lead to establish), buy supplies in bulk, and show newcomers how to get started in various branches of the business. Finally, these associations were more than economic entities: they served social needs as well, holding annual picnics, celebrating important festivals, organizing fairs, recognizing the achievements of their members, awarding scholarships, and giving birth to myriad subsidiary organizations, including youth groups.

Until the 1930s meetings of these associations were always conducted in Japanese; their records were also kept in Japanese. But as the immigrants' children came of age and began one after another to participate in the associations' affairs, English translations were introduced.[10] As might be expected, men who served as officers of these associations became the elite members of their communities. Thus farmers who owned their own land as well as large tenant farmers shared elite membership with urban merchants. George Shima, the potato king, was president of the Japanese Association of America for many years.

Just as merchants in China did not belong to the elite stratum in China, so merchants and ordinary farmers did not occupy positions of wealth, status, and power in Japan. However, the social structure of Japan in the years when large numbers of Japanese emigrated to North America was a rapidly changing one. The Meiji government had abolished the Tokugawa social system, but members of the old feudal houses continued to enjoy considerable prestige—and power, if they held office in the Meiji government. Only a relatively small number of the new bureaucratic elite emigrated; those who traveled to America came mainly to study at institutions of higher learning, but a few of them ended up in Texas, where they grew rice. Leadership in the immigrant communities, therefore, fell largely into the hands of self-made men who, after a period of hard work and frugality, had managed to become independent entrepreneurs.

In addition to the successful merchants and farmers, underworld entrepreneurs also existed in Japanese immigrant communities, but their activities have not been as widely or as luridly sensationalized by Euro-American journalists as those of Chinese tong members. The Japanese government, ever concerned about its international image, early tried to stop the emigration of women intended for prostitution, while immigrant religious leaders, together with the help of journalists, officers of the Japanese associations, and local police tried to stamp out gambling. Japanese community leaders tried to stop the immigrants from gambling not only for moral reasons but also because they thought too much of the latter's hard-earned money was being lost to Chinese gambling joints, which Japanese, Koreans, Filipinos, and Euro-Americans, as well as Chinese, all frequented. As Yuji Ichioka has noted, a Japanese Protestant clergyman in Fresno claimed, for example, that Japanese grape pickers lost $200,000 to 19 Chinese gambling houses in the summer of 1907.[11] This was a sizable sum: the daily wage of a farmworker in those days was only one dollar. In response to the community leaders' efforts to crack down on gambling, a few owners of Japanese gambling syndicates cynically encouraged their countrymen to patronize *their* premises—for nationalistic reasons!

Quite apart from the dizzy excitement of gaming and the ever present possibility of striking it rich, many indigent Asian immigrants spent whatever spare time they had in Chinese gambling houses because the owners often served free food or at least pots of hot tea. These premises were among the few places—others being dingy poolhalls and cheap restaurants—where overworked, persecuted, and homeless Asian men, young and old, felt more or less welcome.

In contrast to those who hung around gambling houses and poolhalls, immigrants who desired more "wholesome" fellowship turned to religious institutions. A large percentage of the Japanese immigrants were Buddhists. Louise Hunter and Tetsuden Kashima have observed that five of the more than fifty divisions within Japanese Buddhism were represented in the United States.[12] Since the Jodo (Pure Land)—and especially the Jodo Shinshu (True

Pure Land)—branches of Amida Buddhism were prevalent in the southwestern prefectures of Japan where so many immigrants came from, an estimated three-quarters to nine-tenths of those immigrants belonged to the Nishi Hongwanji (also called the Honpa Hongwanji, meaning the West School of the Temple of the Original Vow), a sect of Jodo Shinshu. Amida is the Buddha of Infinite Light and Love, through whose compassion, it is believed, individuals can gradually purify themselves and transform their character. Jodo, "pure land," refers to the land where the faithful are reborn. Adherents of the Jodo sect believe they can reach the "pure land" through faith and by continually reciting the *nembutsu* (a chant of homage to the Amida Buddha), whereas those who follow the Jodo Shinshu sect do not think it is necessary to recite the verses on a routine basis. The Jodo Shinshu itself split into two sects—East and West—when a dispute broke out over who should succeed to the abbotship of the mother temple in Kyoto in the late sixteenth century. There are also followers of the Higashi (East School) Hongwanji in Hawaii and the continental United States, but they are in the minority.

According to Hunter, the first Nishi Hongwanji priest arrived in Hawaii in 1889. He stayed seven months and collected enough money from plantation workers on the island of Hawaii to build a small temple in Hilo. He then returned to Japan to solicit support from the abbot to set up a mission in Hawaii. He failed to persuade him, but two young priests did sail to Hawaii in late 1889 and early 1890 to cater to the spiritual needs of their compatriots.[13] For the next few years, however, a number of imposters preyed upon Japanese plantation workers, collecting donations from them with the alleged intention of building temples but absconding with the funds. Finally, in 1897, in response to a poignant appeal from Japanese believers in the islands, the Nishi Hongwanji decided to incorporate Hawaii into its foreign missions program. A veteran missionary, who had served Japanese emigrants in Russia and Taiwan, was appointed superior general of the Hawaiian mission, but failing health soon forced him to return to Japan. He was succeeded by an energetic and dedicated priest, Imamura Yemyo, who organized a Young Men's Buddhist Association (YMBA), started a night school to teach English to the workers, and published a newsletter. Japanese residents contributed funds to build a bigger and better temple in Hilo in 1898 as well as a two-story temple in Honolulu in 1900.

The first two Nishi Hongwanji missionaries to the mainland arrived in San Francisco in 1899, as Kashima has discovered.[14] They came because three years earlier, two Japanese who had spent time in California returned to Japan and asked that a priest be sent to serve their countrymen there. In response, the abbot dispatched two representatives to investigate the situation. While in San Francisco, these men met with several dozen followers and helped them to set up a YMBA in 1898. They then moved on to visit the faithful in Sacramento, Seattle, Vancouver, and other towns and cities with sizable numbers of Japanese. When two missionaries subsequently arrived, they founded the North American Buddhist Mission, which was incorporated under the laws of California. One of the priests conducted services for the Japanese in their native tongue, while the other held services for Euro-Americans in English. The two also set up YMBAs in Sacramento and Fresno, organized a Buddhist Women's Association, and published a newsletter. The organization changed its English name several times: to the Buddhist Church of San Francisco in 1905, then the Buddhist Mission in 1906, and finally the Buddhist Churches of America in 1944. Use of the word "church" was one way in which Japanese Buddhism adapted itself to the American setting; other modifications include the installation of pews and the use of hymnals.

Protestant denominations competed with the Chinese and Japanese religious institutions for adherents. As studied by Wesley Woo, they began their proselytizing efforts among Asians in California in 1851, when the Presbyterians started holding Bible classes for Chinese in San Francisco.[15] William Speer, a missionary who had served in China and who spoke Cantonese, arrived in 1852 and opened a mission. Because he spoke their language and understood their ways, everywhere Speer traveled in California, the Chinese welcomed him. Still, he made few converts before he left California because of ill health. The presbytery closed the mission in 1857, reopening it only when Augustus Loomis, another missionary who had worked in China, came in 1859. Loomis catered to the needs of the Chinese and Japanese until his death in 1891. Besides the Presbyterians, the Baptists, Methodists, and Congregationalists worked most actively among Asian immigrants.

Whereas the denominations hired mainland Chinese only as colporteurs and assistants, Asian Christians in Hawaii played a more prominent role. A year after Samuel Damon opened a Sunday school for the Chinese in the islands in 1868, S. P. Aheong, an eloquent Chinese Christian, came to Hawaii to work among his countrymen. Sit Moon, another convert who arrived in 1875, became the first Chinese pastor of a church in Hawaii in 1881, even though at that time there were fewer than 300 Chinese Christians in the kingdom. Japanese converts, likewise, were served mainly by Japanese pastors, among whom Miyama Kanichi, a Methodist-Episcopal evangelist who worked in Honolulu; Sokabe Shiro, who became pastor of the Honomu Church on the island of Hawaii; and Okumura Takie, an indefatigable foe of Buddhism, were the best known. Neither on the mainland nor in the islands, however, did the Christian missionaries—whether Asian or Euro-American—win large numbers of Chinese and Japanese converts. Nevertheless, the immigrants who were Christians had a significance far beyond their numbers, for, as the most acculturated members of their communities, they sometimes served as bridges between two cultures. Euro-Americans, who preferred to deal with them, conferred on them a mantle of legitimacy that helped to underpin the leadership positions they occupied in the immigrant communities.

The situation was quite different among Koreans immigrants, for whom Christian churches became the most important community institutions, since many of them had already converted to Christianity before they left their homeland. After their arrival, the Christians worked hard to convert others. According to Hyung-chan Kim, Korean immigrants held their first church service and organized a Korean Evangelical Society only half a year after their arrival in Hawaii. They formed a Korean Episcopal Church in 1905 and an independent Korean Christian Church in 1917.[16] By 1918 there was a total of 39 Korean Protestant churches and an estimated 3,000 Korean Christians in Hawaii. On the mainland, Koreans held their first church service in Los Angeles in 1904, established the Korean Methodist Church a year later, and started the Korean Presbyterian Church the year after that. Even though there were only about 1,000 Koreans along the Pacific Coast during the first two decades of the present century, they set up more than a dozen churches. The Methodist and Episcopal churches had the most members in Hawaii, while on the mainland Methodists and Presbyterians predominated.

Churches not only met the religious needs of Korean immigrants but their social and political ones as well. More so than the Chinese or Japanese, Korean immigrants were deeply involved in politics, because they felt responsible for fighting against the Japanese colonization of their homeland. Churches became vehicles through which they could raise funds, discuss politics, and organize for action. Because of the importance of religion and politics, neither merchants nor farmers became the elite among Korean immigrants; rather, Protestant ministers and expatriate political leaders—often the same persons—most clearly voiced their collective aspirations.

Perhaps out of necessity, Korean immigrants were very adept at governing themselves. According to Bong-Youn Choy, as soon as they arrived, they created *tong-hoe* (village councils) on each plantation with ten or more Korean families.[17] Every year the adult males chose a *tong-jang* (council chief) from among themselves, a sergeant at arms, and a few policemen to enforce the rules the councils set down. They formed a Sinmin-hoe (New People Society) in 1903, the chief function of which was to protest Japanese interference in their homeland. Four years later, the tong-hoe on the different plantations combined into the Hanin Hapsong Hyop-hoe (United Korean Society), with headquarters in Honolulu and branch offices throughout the islands.

On the mainland, the first organization to come into being was the Chinmok-hoe (Friendship Society), established in 1903 by an expatriate intellectual, Ahn Chang-ho, who had arrived in San Francisco in 1899. The Kongnip Hyop-hoe (Mutual Assistance Society) appeared in 1905 and soon began publishing the first Korean-language newspaper. In 1909 Hawaii's United Korean Society and California's Mutual Assistance Society merged to form the Taehan Kookmin-hoe (Korean National Association, commonly known as the KNA). The KNA claimed to be the official voice of all Koreans working and living in the Western hemisphere. Every Korean immigrant was encouraged to join, paying annual membership dues of three to five dollars. Seventy-eight branches of the KNA were formed in Hawaii alone.

The KNA not only played a major role in the struggle for Korean independence but also did welfare work among its members, set up schools for their children, and published textbooks for the Korean language schools as well as a newsletter. Its stated objectives were to promote the intellectual and economic development of Korean immigrant communities, to work for the restoration of national independence for Korea, and to promote the welfare of Koreans in America.[18]

Compared with the information available on Chinese, Japanese, and Korean community organizations, much less is known about the social structure of Asian Indian and Filipino immigrant communities. Since such a large percentage of the Asian Indians were Sikhs, their common religion was naturally the social glue that held them together. A nontheistic faith, Sikhism relies for doctrinal authority on the *granth sahib*, a collection of the sayings and writings of its first 10 gurus. The first gurdwara or Sikh temple in the United States was built in Stockton in 1912. For years, it served as the spiritual and social center for Sikhs up and down the Pacific Coast. People came from hundreds of miles to worship in it.[19]

Another important institution among Punjabi Sikhs on the Pacific Coast was the Khalsa Diwan, organized in 1912 near Holt, a small town in the Sacramento-San Joaquin Delta, shortly before the Stockton gurdwara was built. The founders filed incorporation papers for the organization, so it was a legal corporation under the laws of California. Its stated purpose was to provide a hostel for and aid to newcomers, especially laborers and indigent students, but it also became a place where the more politically minded Sikhs gathered for discussions, read newspapers, and planned fund raising efforts for the Indian independence movement. Sikhs in Oregon and Washington started a Hindustan Association in 1913 with centers in Portland and Astoria. A rich labor contractor for the lumber mills in the Pacific Northwest supplied most of the organization's operational funds.[20]

There were also a small number of Muslims and Hindus among the Asian Indian immigrants. Even though Hindus comprise a majority in the Indian subcontinent, very few of them emigrated. For that reason, the derogatory term "Hindoo," by which Euro-American nativists referred to Punjabi Sikhs, was a misnomer. To transcend sectarian differences, Asian Indians of the three faiths established the Hindustani Welfare Reform Society in 1918 in the Imperial Valley, where many of them farmed. (Unlike the word *Hindu*, which refers to a believer of Hinduism, *Hindustani* is an adjective for things Indian.) Finally, the immigrants also organized a political party, the Ghadar (also spelled Gadar or Ghadr) party, to fight for Indian independence. As was the case among Koreans, revolutionary intellectuals enjoyed the most prestige in the Asian Indian immigrant community. But since they could not accomplish much without material support, which came mostly from the more well-to-do tenant farmers, some of the latter played a leadership role among their fellow immigrants.

Intellectuals likewise stood at the apex of Filipino immigrant society. In contrast to Hawaii, the first Filipinos to come to the United States mainland were students on government scholarships. Called *pensionados*, several hundred of them were sent to study in American colleges and universities during the first decade of this century. Their coming was part of the American effort to acculturate Filipinos and to train selected ones to staff the lower echelons of the colonial administration. Many *pensionados* returned home after their studies and later emerged as national leaders. Some who failed to complete their courses, too ashamed to return home, remained in America to make a living as best they could.

One reflection of the influence that American culture had on Filipinos was the existence of many American-style fraternal organizations within the Filipino immigrant communities. The three most popular and important were the Caballeros de Dimas Alang, Inc. (Dimas Alang being the nom de plume of Jose Rizal, the martyred nationalist leader); the Legionarios del Trabajo, Inc.; and the Gran Oriente Filipino, Inc., which Mario P. Ave has described.[21]

The Dimas Alang was originally founded in Manila in 1906 to further Philippine independence from the United States. It set up a branch in San Francisco in 1921. Its goal was to disseminate the ideals of nationalist heroes Jose Rizal and Apolinario Mabini, but these were expressed in very general terms: members were to strive to achieve "human brotherhood under the

*Caballeros de Dimas Alang convention, Seattle, 1928.*
Mary Arca Inosanto collection, courtesy Fred Cordova, *Filipinos: Forgotten Asian Americans*
(Seattle: Demonstration Project for Asian Americans, 1983).

Fatherhood of God" through a love of country, justice, dignity, decency, freedom, and equality. Membership was strictly reserved for men, although
women could organize auxiliary units. Individuals of all occupational backgrounds and provincial origins could join, so long as they led a "clean life" and
their character was deemed acceptable by the existing members. The fraternal
organization had lodges all over the Pacific Coast that were sustained by initiation fees, monthly and annual dues, and special assessments. Its funds were
used to hold dances, banquets, and other social functions, as well as to provide
emergency aid to its members. It also maintained a mortuary fund to buy
coffins for and meet the other funeral expenses of deceased members.

The Legionarios del Trabajo also had its roots in Manila. It came into being
in the wake of a strike at the Manila Electric Company in 1916. A branch was
established in Hawaii in 1921 and one in San Francisco in 1924, from whence
it spread all over California, Oregon, and Washington. Permeated by Masonic
theology, the Legionarios eschewed commercial gain and politics. The Gran
Oriente Filipino was likewise a Masonic fraternal order, very similar in structure and purpose to the other two. It first appeared in the early 1920s.

Several nonfraternal associations were also heavily infused with Christian
overtones. The Filipino Federation of America, Inc., was founded in 1925 in
Los Angeles by Hilario Moncado, a conservative community leader. Its purpose
was to promote friendly relations between Filipinos and Euro-Americans by
urging Filipinos to uphold the Constitution of the United States, to respect the
flag, and to develop Christian fellowship by fostering high moral standards
among its members. In Hawaii, where Filipino plantation laborers became
some of the most militant workers in the islands, the Filipino Federation of
America strongly opposed their unionization efforts.

Another association, the Filipino-American Christian Fellowship, has been studied by Severino F. Corpus.[22] It was established in 1928 through the joint effort of a former woman missionary and a Filipino evangelist, Sylvestre Morales. The organization conducted separate Bible classes for men, women, and children and held worship services every Sunday morning. It also opened a Filipino center in Los Angeles, with enough room to house 40 to 50 young men dedicated to the Christian way of life. Several auxiliary organizations, including a women's club, a debating club, and a chapter of the Filipino Student Christian Movement, which had its headquarters in New York City, were offshoots of the Fellowship. Morales started a Filipino Christian Church and became its first pastor, but he did not remain long. Another Filipino, a graduate of the California Christian College, succeeded him.

These various organizations did a great deal to meet the spiritual needs of Filipino immigrants, a large majority of whom were Catholics. But Catholicism in the Philippines had developed some unique features, and Filipino Catholic immigrants did not feel at home nor were they really welcome in Catholic churches in the United States. These were served mainly by priests of northwestern, central, and eastern European—but not Iberian, much less Filipino—origins. Two parishes, however, were established specifically to serve Filipino Catholics in the United States: Our Lady Queen of Martyrs Church in Seattle, staffed by Maryknoll fathers with Filipino assistants, and St. Columban's Church in Los Angeles, founded by the Columban fathers. Filipinos in Hawaii frequented the Our Lady of Peace Cathedral in Honolulu.

Smaller numbers of Filipinos were Protestants. In Stockton, one of the most important centers of Filipino immigrant life, three Protestant institutions—the Lighthouse Mission, the Filipino Christian Fellowship, and the House of Friendship—opened their doors to the thousands of migrant farm workers who passed through the town. In Hawaii, Protestant Filipinos were under the care of "Filipino departments" within the Hawaii Board of Missions and the Methodist Board. In addition, a sizable number of Filipino immigrants both in Hawaii and on the mainland belonged to the schismatic, independent Alipayan Church, founded at the end of the nineteenth century by Gregorio Alipay, a former Roman Catholic priest who developed a large following in the Philippines, particularly among Ilocano speakers.

Associations based on common locality existed in Filipino immigrant communities, but almost nothing has been written about their history. Some examples of such groups are the Narvacan Association, which brought together people from the town of that name to support the educational advancement of its members, to provide mutual aid, and to promote social intercourse, and the Pangasinan Association of Southern California, whose members tried to perpetuate the traditions and folkways of their home province.

Finally, in the aftermath of the 1930 Watsonville riot, Filipino immigrants established community-wide organizations to better protect themselves. The Filipino Community of Stockton and Vicinity, Inc., was created in 1930; a Filipino Community Center appeared in New York City in 1934; the Filipino Community of Seattle, Inc., was formally established in 1935; the Filipino Community of Salinas Valley, Inc. in 1936, and the Filipino Community of Yakima Valley in 1937.[23] Similar groups sprang up in smaller towns on the mainland. Meanwhile, the Filipino Federated Organizations became the first coordinating council in Hawaii in 1935, taking under its wing nineteen different groups.

Without the extraordinary panoply of organizations in each of the immigrant communities, the pioneer generation of Asians would have found it much more difficult to survive in a host society that needed their labor but tolerated them only so long as they "kept their place" at the bottom of the socioeconomic ladder. Denied access to the social and political life of the larger society, Asian migrant laborers and immigrants created a world of their own. Belonging to clubs was definitely not a habit they brought from the homeland, where kinship formed the basis of virtually all aspects of social life, but they readily became joiners in the New World out of necessity.

Parochial villagers when they left home, they initially felt at ease only among others who most resembled themselves, but as immigration exclusion cut off new blood, those who remained learned to form larger groupings in order to defend themselves. Slowly, ever so slowly, they became Chinese, instead of Toisanese or Heungsanese; Japanese, instead of Hiroshima or Kumamoto kenjin; Koreans, instead of Pyongyang or Inchon residents; Indians, instead of Punjabis or Gujeratis; and Filipinos, instead of Ilocanos or Cebuanos. Perhaps even more important, they soon realized that while the organizations they formed offered them occasional respite from the harsh realities they daily confronted in their workaday lives, only by fighting back on the job, in the courts, and on behalf of their countries of origin in a world shaped by imperialism could they, as individuals and as peoples, enjoy a measure of dignity and hope.

*Koreans marching to Independence Hall, Philadelphia, 1919, in support of Korean independence after the Mansei Uprising in Korea.*
Courtesy Sucheng Chan collection

*chapter five*

# Resistance to Oppression

S tereotypes of Asian immigrants as plodding, degraded, and servile people—indeed, virtual slaves—notwithstanding, members of every Asian immigrant group did stand up for their rights and fought oppression in myriad ways. Historians and sociologists of the Asian American experience have often argued among themselves whether Asian immigrants have been discriminated against as a class, a race, or a nationality. Marxists claim that Asian Americans have suffered because they were and are part of the proletariat; scholars and activists who consider racism as the most fundamental issue employ race as a central category of analysis; while those with an international perspective emphasize the link between the national subjugation of certain Asian countries and the maltreatment of their emigrants abroad.

To argue that class, or racial, or national subordination can subsume the other two is too simplistic, for Asian immigrants have experienced all three forms of inequality. Looking at the principal ways they have used to fight against their lowly status—strikes, litigation, and involvement in efforts to liberate their homelands—it is clear that the immigrants themselves realized their suffering had multiple causes. As workers they struck for higher wages and better working conditions; as nonwhite minorities "ineligible to citizenship" they challenged laws that denied them civil rights on account of their race; and as proud sons and daughters of their countries of origin, they supported political movements to free those lands from foreign encroachment.

Asian immigrant workers began their struggle for equality quite early in their history. Despite the fact that the Chinese have been widely depicted as docile, there is considerable evidence to show that when their sense of justice was violated, they rose up in revolt. The largest strike undertaken by Chinese in the nineteenth century occurred in June 1867 during the building of the transcontinental railroad. At that time, Chinese workers, regardless of what tasks they performed, were paid $30 a month without board, compared to unskilled Euro-American workers who received $30 a month with board. (Board was worth 75 cents to a dollar a day.) A few skilled ones among the latter even got as much as $3 to $5 a day. Six days a week, the Chinese toiled from sunrise to sundown, while subject to whipping by overseers and forbidden by the company to quit their jobs. Unhappy with their lot, 2,000 men digging tunnels in the high Sierras went on strike, demanding $40 a month, 10 hours of work a day for those laboring outdoors and eight hours for those inside the tunnels, an end to corporal punishment, and the freedom to leave whenever they desired. Their strike lasted a week—until their food ran out. The railroad company simply stopped bringing them rations, thus starving them back to work. The company also took the precaution of asking employment agencies to stand ready to supply it with black workers should the Chinese strike again.[1]

Chinese elsewhere likewise protested unequal treatment. As shown in Lucy Cohen's study, after the Civil War ended, Southern plantation owners searched for a work force they could control.[2] One scheme some of them tried was to import Chinese both directly from China and from the Pacific Coast. Railroad companies laying tracks in the region also turned to Chinese labor. As a result, almost 2,000 Chinese entered the South in 1869 and 1870 to work for wages ranging from $13 to $18 a month, plus free return passage and room and board. The first batch of 250 men hired by the Houston and Texas Central Railroad arrived in Calvert, Texas, in December 1869. They were followed in 1870 by four shipments totalling over 600 persons, who were distributed among several cotton and sugar plantations in Arkansas, Mississippi, and Louisiana. The largest contingent, almost 1000, came to work in August 1870 for the Alabama and Chattanooga Railroad Company.

All the laborers came to the South under contract. Before they started their recruitment, the Southern employers had written the U.S. State Department to inquire about the legality of contract labor. In his reply, the assistant secretary of state stated that whereas the Chinese coolie trade to Latin America had been condemned by a joint resolution of Congress, "[t]he fact that an emigrant embarks under a contract by which he is to reimburse the expenses of his transportation by personal services for a period agreed upon does not deprive him of the character of a free and voluntary emigrant, if the contract is not vitiated by force or fraud."[3]

That no coercion was used can be adduced from the fact that the Southerners had considerable difficulty recruiting workers from California, where Chinese could earn an average monthly wage of $26. Moreover, those Chinese workers who did come expected their employers to adhere strictly to the terms spelled out in the agreements. Southern employers, however, were used to exercising complete autocratic control over their workers and did not always live up to the conditions they had promised. Much to their surprise, the Chinese reacted vehemently to such breaches of faith.

Trouble first brewed among the railroad workers when in September 1870 all the Chinese employed by the Houston and Texas Central Railroad ceased work and filed suit against the company for "wages and for a failure of compliance with contract." Unfortunately, the available sources do not indicate what became of this dispute. Then during the summer of 1871 the Alabama and Chattanooga Railroad Company declared bankruptcy. When U.S. marshals appeared to take possession of the trains, angry workers, including several hundred Chinese, who had not been paid for six months, seized the cars to prevent them from running. But they never did receive the wages owed them.

Chinese sent to work on the plantations, meanwhile, had grievances of their own. Those in a Louisiana plantation became upset when they discovered that black freedmen could stop work at noon on Saturdays, whereas they were required to keep laboring until sunset. They were pacified only after their interpreter won for them the right to cease work at noon every other Saturday.

On another plantation, a Chinese worker who struck back at an overseer who had shoved at him was fatally shot. The rest of the Chinese immediately armed themselves with sticks and knives and marched to the home of the owner, demanding that the overseer be turned over to them. The owner stalled for time by talking to the group, thus enabling the overseer to escape.

That these protests were not merely expressions of interracial antagonism is shown by the fact that Chinese workers also rebelled against Chinese proprietors or labor contractors. Garment workers (at that time virtually all male) struck a Chinese sweatshop owner in San Francisco for higher wages in 1875. Ronald Takaki has found that 300 plantation workers in Hawaii in 1891 quit work and marched to the courthouse to demand the arrest of a Chinese labor contractor whom they claimed had cheated them. To disperse the marchers, the police arrested and imprisoned 55 of them on charges of assault.[4]

Japanese immigrant workers also have a long history of militance. The boatload illegally shipped to Hawaii in 1868 complained and protested so much that the Japanese government brought some of them home. Soon after legal immigration began in 1885, as Edward Beechert, Alan Moriyama, and Ronald Takaki have revealed, spontaneous work stoppages recurred throughout the 1880s and 1890s, usually to protest beatings or shootings by lunas or to complain about the lack of water and fuel.[5] On one occasion, three men representing disgruntled workers in a plantation on Oahu walked almost ten miles to Honolulu to lodge complaints with the director of the Japanese Section of the Immigration Bureau. To their disappointment, this man, who was supposed to look after their welfare, showed them no sympathy whatsoever.

Only after the contract labor system ended in 1900 did the plantation workers' struggles begin to bear fruit. In the year and a half after the Organic Act went into effect, 39 cases of labor strife occurred, though none of these was organized. The first organized strike undertaken by Japanese plantation workers took place in 1904 in Waialua, when cane cutters and loaders demanded higher wages. When their request was not granted, the cutters continued working, but the loaders stood idle. This was a conscious strategy on the workers' part: they knew that if cut cane is not immediately processed, it loses a good deal of its juice. The stalks lying on the ground thus threatened the owners with severe loss. Despite the fact that the plantation manager sent for the sheriff and a squad of police, the workers refused to return to work until several of their more important nonwage demands were met. All the Japanese employees-— field workers, millhands, stable boys, and carpenters-—participated in the week-long strike: a total of almost 1,200 men.

The second large-scale organized strike by Japanese took place in Lahaina on the island of Maui several months later. It started as a protest by some 900 laborers against a sentence imposed by a judge, who had fined a luna only $25 for blinding a Japanese worker. They considered this sum much too small in light of the permanent damage done to their fellow worker. Police and militia called to the scene fired into a milling crowd, killing one person and wounding several others. The strike ended when the luna in question was fired and better housing was promised. However, the strikers did not receive the higher wages they demanded.

Like the Chinese workers who did not hesitate to strike against Chinese employers, Japanese workers also sometimes struck against oppressors from their own ethnic group. In Waipahu in 1906 workers demanded that a Japanese luna who had forced them to buy lotteries from him periodically—lotteries that offered only old watches or other worthless prizes—be dismissed. The Japanese consul general intervened and proposed that the luna be transferred to a Korean crew, but the more than 1,600 striking Japanese workers rejected this suggestion. The strike finally ended when the luna resigned and several lesser field bosses were discharged. But again, the strikers failed to get a pay increase.

Having tested their mettle, 7,000 Japanese workers struck the major plantations on Oahu for four long months in 1909. It all began when several Japanese newspapermen and professionals set up a Higher Wages Association in late 1908. They pointed out that Japanese workers deserved to earn more than the $18 a month they were getting. They suggested that $22.50 would be a more equitable wage, since that was what Portuguese and Puerto Rican workers received. On behalf of the laborers, the officers of the Higher Wages Association requested a meeting with the HSPA, but received no response.

Despite efforts by the Japanese consul general and the well-known Protestant minister Okumura Takie to stop the strike, it quickly spread from one plantation to the next on Oahu during the latter part of May. Workers on the other islands continued working, in order to send contributions to Honolulu to support the strikers. Important associations in the Japanese community such as the Carpenters' Association, the Public Bath Operators Association, the Japanese Hotel and Inn Association, the Honolulu Retail Merchants Association, and the Barbers Association also backed the strikers. Even Chinese merchants provided food on credit. But some Japanese newspapers and other urban groups bitterly opposed the militant action.

Because the Japanese community was divided, the HSPA was able to use the tactic of divide and conquer to defeat the strike. It coopted a number of Japanese and used them to spy on their fellows. Using evidence seized without a search warrant, the HSPA succeeded in placing the four leaders of the Higher Wages Association and a number of newspaper staff in jail. Plantation owners also evicted the strikers and their families from plantation housing, forcing them to march into Honolulu, where thousands camped out in tents and dilapidated buildings. The plantations kept production going by hiring scabs. The HSPA further decreed that all its member plantations should share the losses suffered by the ones that were struck. Finally, the English-language press charged that the strike was in reality an effort by the Japanese to take over the sugar industry and, indeed, Hawaii itself.

The strike fizzled out in August when the participants ran out of all resources to keep themselves going. Three months after it was over, the planters agreed to end the practice of paying workers of different national backgrounds unequal wages, but they never fully carried out their promise. They also instituted a bonus system based on the price of sugar and the number of days worked. This modest adjustment, however, was insufficient to enable plantation workers to make ends meet, especially after World War I when inflation kept spiraling.

Japanese and Filipino workers therefore started organizing in 1919 to do something about the situation. The Japanese formed a Federation of Japanese Labor in Hawaii to coordinate the efforts of Japanese labor organizations on the different islands. The association worked out a long list of demands, including a daily wage of $1.25, a revised bonus system that would allow men working only 15 days and women 10 days a month to qualify, 8-hour workdays, double pay for overtime, and 8 weeks of paid maternity leave for women. Filipinos, meanwhile, formed a Higher Wages Association under the leadership of Pablo Manlapit, who had founded the Filipino Federation of Labor in 1911 and the Filipino Unemployed Association in 1913.

Although the Japanese and Filipinos had agreed initially to act jointly, Manlapit unilaterally decided to begin the strike on 19 January 1920, even though the Japanese were still trying to negotiate with the HSPA in the hope of forestalling a strike. Furthermore, the Japanese thought it would be best to strike in the late spring or early summer at the height of the harvest in order to cripple the sugar industry. They also wanted to give themselves more time to build up a war chest. So they pressured Manlapit to call off the action by the Filipinos. He agreed to do so on 17 January, but discovered that he had no means of communicating with the workers, 2,600 of whom, along with 300 Spaniards and Puerto Ricans, walked off the job as planned. Left with no choice, the Japanese joined them on 1 February, pushing the total number of strikers above the 8,000 mark.

Eight days later, the mercurial Manlapit once again tried to call off the strike, but the militant Filipino workers refused to follow his orders. To save face, he announced the strike was on again. The planters responded by evicting 12,000 people (more than 4,000 of them children) from plantation housing in mid-February. Since the Filipinos had not accumulated a strike fund, those Japanese supporting the strike housed and fed them in addition to the 10,500 evicted Japanese. To make matters worse, an influenza epidemic that was spreading around the world at that time hit Hawaii, causing more than 2,000 of the strikers to fall ill and more than 100 to die. Despite these extraordinary hardships, all but 166 of the Japanese plantation workers on Oahu remained on strike. The planters hired more than 2,000 scabs to keep their operations going.

Several days after the eviction, the Reverend Albert W. Palmer of the Central Union Church stepped in to mediate. He proposed that the unions disband themselves and that interracial labor-management committees be set up on each plantation to deal with all issues related to wages, work conditions, and living conditions. Many community leaders in Honolulu—Japanese as well as Euro-Americans—supported the Palmer plan. After heated debate, the Japanese strike leaders also decided to accept it if the HSPA would likewise do so, but the latter said it would not deal with the Federation of Japanese Laborers. Thus the stalemate continued. In mid-April, because of rising anti-Japanese sentiment, the Federation of Japanese Labor changed its name to the Hawaii Laborers' Association and applied for membership in the American Federation of Labor (AFL). The Central Labor Council recommended that the renamed organization be accepted for membership as a multiracial industrial union of plantation workers, but the American Federation of Labor never took up the matter.

After the failed attempt at mediation, some 3,000 Japanese and Filipino strikers and their families staged the huge 77 Cents Parade—77 cents being their average daily base wage—to counter the charges of anti-Americanism and radicalism. They marched through the streets of Honolulu carrying American flags and pictures of Abraham Lincoln. Their signs contained slogans such as "We Are Not Reds, God Forbid, But Are Brown Workers Who Produce White Sugar," "We Want to Live Like Americans," and "How Can We Live Like Americans on 77 Cents?"

The HSPA held firm, despite its estimated $12 million loss. The real issue for the planters was not wages but collective bargaining, to which they absolutely refused to accede. By the beginning of July, the weary and starving strikers decided to end the six month-long strike, but not all of them returned to work. The Japanese plantation work force in Oahu fell by over 2,000, and though the number of Filipinos increased, a large percentage of them were in fact new recruits from the Philippines.

After the workers resumed production, the plantation owners made significant improvements in housing, sanitation, and recreational facilities, raised wages, and started distributing bonuses on a monthly basis. The strike had important long-term consequences as well: the HSPA increased its centralized control over the sugar industry; the Hawaiian territorial government passed a series of laws that made it virtually impossible for labor organizers to function legally; local plantation unions declined in numbers; and the Hawaii Laborers' Association faded from the scene.

Historians also deem the 1920 strike significant because it was the first major strike in which workers of different national origins participated. In fact, however, it was not the first such action involving Asian immigrant workers. Back in 1903 Japanese and Mexican farmworkers struck jointly to demand higher wages in the beet-growing Oxnard area of Ventura County, California, after they formed a Japanese-Mexican Labor Association (JMLA) and elected a Japanese president, a Japanese vice president, and a Mexican secretary. Baba Kozaburo, the president, was actually not a laborer but a labor contractor, but he got involved because he opposed the monopoly enjoyed by the Western Agricultural Contracting Company (WACC), which had a "Japanese department" responsible for recruiting Japanese workers. The JMLA accused the WACC of paying lower wages than it promised, of charging workers a double commission by forcing independent contractors to act as its subcontractors, and of forcing workers to shop at designated stores with inflated prices. In March, 1,200 members of the JMLA went on strike over these issues—an event that has been studied by Karl Yoneda and Tomas Almaguer.[6]

When scabs were brought in from San Francisco, the strikers held a demonstration in front of the labor camp where the scabs were housed. A shooting took place; one Mexican worker was killed, while two were wounded, as were two Japanese. The local police then arrested the JMLA officials. At this point, the American Federation of Labor sent one of its representatives to the scene to mediate. The growers, the WACC, and the JMLA sat down to negotiate. The JMLA demanded the right to bargain directly with all the growers. Eventually, the WACC agreed to cancel all but one of the contracts it had with growers, who in turn promised to raise wages. The AFL representative also managed to get those who had been arrested released.

After the strike ended, J. M. Larraras, the secretary of JMLA, applied for a charter from the American Federation of Labor, but AFL President Samuel

Gompers replied that a charter would be granted only if no Chinese or Japanese were admitted into the local. In response, Larraras wrote:

> Our Japanese here were the first to recognize the importance of cooperating and uniting in demanding a fair wage scale . . . We have fought and lived on very short rations with our Japanese brothers, and toiled with them in the fields . . . We would be false to them and to ourselves and to the cause of unionism if we now accepted privileges for ourselves which are not accorded to them.[7]

But Gompers—long a foe of Asian immigration who had once declared, "Every incoming coolie means the displacement of an American, and the lowering of the American standard of living"—was not moved. JMLA never became part of the AFL.

By the middle of the mid-1920s, relatively few Japanese remained in the plantations of Hawaii or in the fields of California. Instead, Filipinos provided most of the agricultural labor force in the islands and all along the Pacific Coast. Not surprisingly, they became the main Asian immigrant group to engage in labor militancy. Moreover, as Beechert has noted, they did so in politically repressive environments with criminal syndicalist laws.[8]

In April 1924 Pablo Manlapit once again called a strike, demanding wages of $2 for eight hours of work a day, an end to the bonus system, and better housing. The HSPA sent out a bulletin indicating that Manlapit should not be allowed to speak on the premises of any plantation. Over an eight-month period some 2,000 workers on twenty-three plantations participated in the rather disorganized strike, which probably would not have spread beyond Oahu had the police not arrested Manlapit while he was in Hilo. The arrest brought Filipino workers on the Big Island out on strike. Then on 9 September the most violent incident in the history of Asian American trade unionism occurred in the Hanapepe plantation on Kauai. During a fight between two factions of Filipinos, the camp police summoned special deputies who fired their rifles into the crowd, killing 16 and wounding many others. Four policemen also died. The deputies arrested 161 strikers, 76 of whom were subsequently indicted for rioting. Another 58 pleaded guilty to assault and battery.

Manlapit himself was tried, convicted, and sentenced to two to ten years at hard labor. The parole board freed him in 1927 on the condition that he leave Hawaii and never return. He departed for California, where he immediately plunged into labor organizing. There he met Manuel Fagel, another Filipino labor leader. The two slipped back into Hawaii in 1932 and revived the Filipino Federation of Labor with the help of Epifanio Taok. Both Taok and Manlapit were arrested when they were caught organizing. This time Manlapit was banished to the Philippines. Fagel then took the Filipino labor movement in Hawaii underground, forming an innocuous-sounding organization called the Vibora Luviminda as a front.

Fagel worked mainly on Maui, where two Euro-American organizers from the American Communist party came to assist him. Their efforts culminated in a strike at Puunene in 1937 that involved 1,500 Filipinos—the last "ethnic"

*Filipino union members on strike, 1930s.*
Courtesy Visual Communications

strike in Hawaii's history. The Congress of Industrial Organizations set a historical precedent when it filed a complaint with the National Labor Relations
Board office in San Francisco after a plantation guard beat up Fagel. The
International Labor Defense set another precedent when it sent a lawyer to
defend the strikers on Maui. The strike leaders, however, were convicted.

On the mainland, organized labor eventually also had to take note of the
militant Filipinos. As Howard De Witt and Fred Cordova have shown, in the
Salinas Valley of California in 1933, lettuce pickers, in cooperation with several
labor contractors, formed a Filipino Labor Union (FLU) after the AFL turned
down their request that it organize a union on their behalf.[9] Seven hundred
Filipino workers staged a one-day walkout in August. It failed, but the following year, when the union had some 2,000 members, it joined the Vegetable
Packers Association (an AFL affiliate) in a strike in Monterey County.

The FLU wanted growers to recognize it as a legitimate union—so it could
bargain with them, as the National Industrial Recovery Act required employers
to do with recognized unions—and to double the wages of Filipino farm workers from 20 to 40 cents or higher per hour. During the strike, the growers shot
two of the Filipinos. To avert further violence, the California Department of
Industrial Relations offered to mediate through binding arbitration. The Vegetable Packers Association accepted the offer, but the Filipinos decided to continue

the walkout. Meanwhile, the growers kept bringing in Mexican strike breakers to harvest the crop.

The determined strikers held on in the face of mounting hostility from every side. Newspapers in the surrounding community criticized them severely. The Vegetable Packers Association severed its ties with the FLU. The Associated Farmers of California branded the FLU a communist front group. The Salinas Grower-Shipper Association distributed pamphlets denunciating the dangers posed by Filipino militancy. Local law enforcement officers, with the help of the California Highway Patrol, arrested a number of the labor leaders for vagrancy. And because Hilario Moncado, the leader of the Filipino Federation of America in Los Angeles, strongly opposed the strike, most of the Filipino fraternal organizations in the Salinas Valley dared not support it, either. Other internal schisms developed: strikers beat up other Filipinos who crossed their picket lines. Finally, the strike ended when local vigilantes burned to the ground a camp where hundreds of Filipino farm workers were housed.

But Filipino labor activism eventually received recognition from organized labor, however grudging it may have been. In 1936, Filipino and Mexican farm workers succeeded in persuading the AFL to grant a charter to the Field Workers Union, Local 30326, a dual-ethnic Mexican-Filipino union. Then in 1940 the AFL chartered the Federated Agricultural Laborers Association, a Filipino union, after it successfully represented thousands of asparagus cutters, Brussels sprouts pickers, celery cutters, and garlic harvesters in a series of strikes in central California.

Farm workers among Filipinos were not the only active unionists. Those working in the salmon-canning industry in Alaska likewise participated in the labor movement, usually as officers and as members of mainstream unions. In 1938 the Filipino salmon cannery workers finally got rid of the labor contractors—often individuals from their own ethnic group—who had severely exploited them. From then on, workers were hired through the union hall. But the road to success was paved with blood: the union's president and its secretary were gunned down by assassins in late 1936.

On the other side of the continent, in New York, another group of Asian workers—Chinese sailors—eventually also entered an integrated union, the National Maritime Union, as Peter Kwong has recorded. Though little has been written about them, tens of thousands of Chinese worked in American and British ships in the late nineteenth and early twentieth centuries.[10] Even though Chinese could no longer be employed in the U.S. Marine Service after the Seamen's Act of 1915 was passed, thousands continued to work in privately owned ships. A major port, New York became a temporary home to large numbers of Chinese sailors on shore leave or in between jobs.

During the Great Depression, U.S. shipping companies, in efforts to cut costs, hired an increasing number of nonunionized foreign sailors, stewards, and cooks. The Chinese were subjected to especially harsh treatment: each individual had to sign a contract that allowed the companies to withhold 50 percent of his wages until he was discharged and post a $500 bond. Moreover, unlike other foreign sailors, all of whom could go ashore while their ships were anchored at American ports, Chinese alien sailors could not. Immigration officials charged that if Chinese were permitted such a privilege, countless numbers would slip into the country illegally. As more and more Chinese found employment on U.S. ships, the Seamen's International Union, an AFL affiliate, asked immigration officials to search for, arrest, and deport Chinese sailors, especially those who had allegedly jumped ship, and pressured Congress to pass an act to bar foreign sailors from working on U.S. ships.

Certain members of the Seamen's International Union did not approve of its stance. In 1933 they formed a new organization, the National Maritime Union (NMU), which soon became the largest maritime union in the United States. Because the NMU's constitution forbade discrimination on the basis of race, color, national origin, creed, religion, or political affiliation, many black sailors joined it. When the NMU called a strike in 1936, it invited Chinese sailors to participate. The Chinese said they would do so if the NMU would take up their special concerns: equal treatment of and a uniform wage scale for everyone, and the right of alien Chinese sailors to shore leave. When the NMU agreed to support these ends, some 3,000 Chinese participated in the strike.

In contrast to strikes where a majority of the participants (though not all of the leaders) were workers, legal action—the second method Asian immigrants used to defend their rights—was generally undertaken by more well-to-do and educated individuals. The umbrella organizations within the Chinese and Japanese immigrant communities—the Chinese Six Companies and the Japanese Association of America, respectively—usually took responsibility for retaining the Euro-American lawyers who argued their cases in court. There were also individuals, however, who filed suit without any organizational backing. Asian Indians and Filipinos likewise took their grievances to court, but it is not known what community organizations, if any, were behind their efforts.

The volume of litigation that Asian immigrants undertook is truly astonishing. Between 1882 and 1943, when Chinese exclusion was in effect, more than 1,100 cases (according to my count) involving Chinese plaintiffs or defendants were published in the *Federal Reporter*, which contains all the reported cases in the nation's lower federal courts. In addition, some 170 cases showed up in *U.S. Reports*—the compilation of published U.S. Supreme Court cases—though most of the post-1900 ones have no written opinions. More than 80 Japanese cases can be found in the *Federal Reporter* and 15 in *U. S. Reports* in the pre-World War II years. Asian Indian cases, meanwhile, number almost 40. Since these reported cases comprised less than a tenth of the total number filed and heard, tens of thousands of Asians sought justice through legal action.[11]

The three issues that concerned Asian immigrant litigants the most were immigration exclusion, the right of naturalization, and economic discrimination. Chinese tried hardest to fight exclusion: more than 90 percent of their reported cases arose from efforts to gain entry into the United States. Japanese, Asian Indians, and Koreans were most concerned about acquiring citizenship through naturalization, while Chinese and Japanese were determined to remove impediments to their right to earn a living.

The encounter between Asian immigrants and the American legal system began in 1852, when Chinese went to court to recover gold dust that had been stolen from them or money that was owed them, according to Hudson Janisch.[12] Apparently, though Chinese were well known for their tendency to take care of their own problems, they did not hesitate to use the American judicial system when necessary, as Charles McClain and other scholars have demonstrated.[13] And, of course, when they were charged with violating a law, or with failure to pay the Foreign Miners' Tax or some other levy, or when non-Chinese sued them, they had to appear before the judges. Between 1854 and 1882, more than 100 Chinese cases were heard in the supreme courts of California and some of the territories in the western United States.[14] Thus, by the time the 1882 exclusion law was passed, they had become experienced and sophisticated litigators.

During the first few years after Chinese exclusion went into effect, aspiring immigrants were surprisingly successful in challenging the laws, as Christian Fritz and Lucy Salyer have shown.[15] The federal officer responsible for implementing them was the collector of customs. Even though the San Francisco collector, who inspected the vast majority of the Chinese coming into the country until the turn of the century, announced that he would be as strict as possible, the Chinese he detained kept filing writs of habeas corpus, which enabled them to receive a hearing by a judge or a commissioner appointed by the court. During the first decade of exclusion, the judges allowed more than 85 percent of those whom the collector had tried to prevent from landing to enter the country—a fact that caused a public outcry. Newspapers and anti-Chinese groups castigated the judges for their decisions, but the latter, out of a firm commitment to due process, insisted that all individuals, regardless of their color or race, had the right to seek liberty through a habeas corpus proceeding.

Both the 1882 exclusion act and its 1884 amendment allowed Chinese laborers who had resided in the United States before November 1880—the date of the last treaty with China—to reenter the United States after visits to China, so long as they had the evidence required by the laws. On 1 October 1888, however, Congress unilaterally and abruptly abrogated this right, thereby denying reentry to some 20,000 laborers with the requisite certificates who were out of the country at the time.

Chae Chan Ping, a laborer who had lived in San Francisco from 1875 to 1887 and who had obtained a return certificate before departing to China for a visit, was enroute to California when the new law went into effect. He arrived on 7 October and was denied landing. The two judges in the U.S. circuit court who heard his case decided to uphold the 1888 law, even though they had earlier repeatedly defended the right of Chinese to be admitted under the 1882 and 1884 acts. Chae then took his case to the U.S. Supreme Court, arguing that the 1882 law contravened both the 1868 Burlingame Treaty and the 1880 Treaty between China and the United States. In an 1889 landmark decision, *Chae Chan Ping* v. *United States* (sometimes known as the *Chinese Exclusion Case*), a unanimous court decided that whereas the 1888 law and the treaties indeed seemed to be in conflict, the later document superseded the earlier ones. Moreover, whatever right Chinese laborers had to reenter the United States was "held at the will of the government, revocable at any time, at its pleasure."

When the 1882 law expired in 1892, a new and more stringent one took its place. Known as the Geary Act, it required all Chinese in the United States to register. Thereafter, any Chinese in the country caught without a registration certificate was subject to immediate deportation. Three Chinese about to be deported took their case to the U.S. Supreme Court. In *Fong Yue Ting* v. *United*

*States* (1892), the high court held that since deportation is part of immigration and a sovereign nation has the right to decide who to let within its borders, it can rightfully compel aliens to register.

Despite these unfavorable rulings, the Chinese persevered. After an 1894 amendment gave executive officers the final say over the admission of Chinese—permitting the latter a court appearance only if they had not received a "fair hearing"—Chinese repeatedly charged that the hearings given them by the immigration officials were unfair. To put a stop to this, the U.S. Supreme Court ruled in *Lem Moon Sing* v. *United States* (1895) that district courts could no longer review Chinese habeas corpus petitions. But the exclusionists went further: they wanted to deny the courts any say over Chinese immigration altogether. In 1903 the commissioner general of immigration, acting under the secretary of commerce and labor, assumed full control over the matter. The U.S. Supreme Court affirmed this change in *United States* v. *Ju Toy* (1905), declaring that the secretary of commerce and labor had final jurisdiction over not only the entry of Chinese immigrants but that of American citizens of Chinese ancestry as well. But there was one privilege the high court refused to deny persons of Chinese ancestry: in *Wong Kim Ark* v. *United States* (1898), the court held that anyone born in the United States was a citizen and could not be stripped of the right thereof.

Recognizing the value of citizenship, Asian immigrants fought hard to gain the right of naturalization. The legal history of their struggles with regard to this issue reveals more clearly than does anything else the ambiguities, inconsistencies, and irrationality of racial exclusion. The Constitution stated that only "free white persons" could be naturalized. In 1870 the privilege was extended to "aliens of African nativity and to persons of African descent." As noted in chapter 3, though Senator Charles Sumner tried during the congressional debates over this question to strike the word "white" from the proposed statute, he failed. However, the compiler of the 1873 U.S. Revised Statutes somehow omitted the reference to "whites" in Section 2169 of Title 30, the section on naturalization. This error was corrected by an amendatory act in early 1875. Between 31 December 1873 and 18 February 1875, therefore, no racial or color restriction existed with regard to citizenship, and a number of Chinese in New York were naturalized. A court decision, *In re Ah Yup* (1878), and the 1882 Chinese exclusion law, which expressly denied the right to Chinese, closed this loophole.

As Japanese began coming, a number of them who desired naturalization challenged Section 2169, as Frank Chuman has found.[16] When a Japanese in Massachusetts contested the statute, the U.S. circuit court, after reviewing a large body of pseudoscientific literature on ethnographic and racial classifications, declared in *In re Saito* (1894) that Japanese were not eligible because they were Mongolians. Fifteen years later, *In re Knight* (1909) held that an individual born of an English father and a mother who was half Chinese and half Japanese was insufficiently "white" to be granted citizenship.

In the following decade, federal courts in various parts of the country handed down conflicting opinions with regard to the naturalization petitions of individuals from different parts of Asia. In general, persons from the western part of the Asian continent—that is, the Middle East—with more Caucasoid features received favorable rulings; those who looked neither European nor

"Oriental," such as Asian Indians and Filipinos, elicited contradictory responses; while petitioners from eastern Asia more often than not were barred. Syrians were found to be eligible; Armenians likewise qualified, as did Parsees (individuals of Persian origins residing in India). A Washington court admitted an Indian Muslim, while California and Oregon courts granted citizenship to two Sikhs. However, a court in Pennsylvania denied the petition of a Sikh. Filipinos were denied naturalization in Pennsylvania, New York, and Massachusetts, but surprisingly, one received citizenship in southern California. Koreans had no luck at all: courts in Missouri and California declared them ineligible.[17]

A few Japanese were naturalized, the first being Shinsei Kaneko of Riverside, California, who became a citizen in 1896 and later served as a juror and traveled abroad with an American passport. Among the others were Takuji Yamashita and Charles Hio Kono of Seattle, Washington. But these two eventually lost their citizenship when they attempted to set up a corporation—something that only citizens could do in the state of Washington. Upon reviewing their application, the secretary of state of Washington decided that the superior court that had admitted them to citizenship had erred, and he refused to grant them the incorporation papers they sought. The petitioners took their case to the U.S. Supreme Court, which held off a decision until after it had ruled on the landmark *Takao Ozawa* v. *United States* (1922) case. The justices then rescinded the citizenship granted earlier to Yamashita and Kino on the basis of the *Ozawa* decision.

The long history of the *Ozawa* case, one of the most drawn-out suits that an Asian has ever filed in the United States, has been studied by Yuji Ichioka.[18] Takao Ozawa was born in Japan, came to the United States as a "school boy," graduated from Berkeley High School, and attended the University of California for three years before moving to Honolulu in 1906. He spoke good English, was familiar with American institutions, married a woman brought up in the United States, sent his children to Sunday school, spoke English at home with them, reported neither his marriage nor the birth of his two children to the Japanese consulate in Honolulu, and worked for an American company. Moreover, said he, "I neither drink liquor of any kind, nor smoke, nor play cards, nor gamble, nor associate with any improper persons."

Ozawa first submitted a petition of intent in 1902 but did not follow with a petition for naturalization until 1914. When the U.S. district court in northern California denied the latter application, he tried to file in Hawaii, where he was likewise rebuffed. Undiscouraged, he appealed. Up to this point, Ozawa had acted alone, but after his case was referred to the U.S. Supreme Court in 1917, the Japanese immigrant community as well as the Japanese government became involved. The Deliberative Council of the Pacific Coast Japanese Association—the coordinating body for the Japanese Association of America and its counterpart in Canada—decided to support Ozawa's effort, but the Foreign Ministry in Tokyo opposed it. The latter did not want a negative decision to foreclose its chance for reaching a diplomatic settlement on the issue. After delays related to international power politics, the U.S. Supreme Court finally ruled on the case in 1922. It decided that Ozawa could not be naturalized because, all his qualifications notwithstanding, he was neither a free white person nor someone of African descent. In the eyes of the court, racial origins, rather than skin color, was what mattered.

The justices reversed themselves a few months later, however, in *United States* v. *Bhagat Singh Thind* (1923), a case that has been studied by Harold Jacoby and Joan Jensen.[19] Thind had lived in the United States since 1913, had served in the U.S. armed forces during World War I, and had received his citizenship papers from the U. S. district court in Oregon in 1920. But Thind was known for advocating independence for India—something that the federal government found embarrassing, given the close relationship between the United States and Great Britain—and immigration officials looked for a pretext to deport him. The bureau of immigration took him to court in an attempt to "denaturalize" him. The U.S. Supreme Court upheld the federal agency, arguing that whereas Thind, as a native of India, might indeed be an Aryan ethnographically, he was nonetheless not "white." In this instance, skin color took precedence over racial classification. Following the *Thind* decision, immigration officials successfully canceled the naturalization certificates of several dozen other Asian Indians.

Though defeated in their efforts to become citizens, those Asian immigrants still in the country fought hard to defend their right to earn a living. Chinese import-export merchants and laundrymen and Japanese tenant farmers used the courts most frequently for this purpose. I have found almost 20 reported cases in the *Federal Reporter* involving Chinese firms that went to court to insist on their right to import ingredients such as soy sauce, salted duck's eggs, dried duck meat, dried mushrooms, Chinese sausages, olives, almonds, edible roots, edible fungus, and salted cabbage. Even relatively innocuous things like embroidered fans and ornamental swords encountered difficulties. What merchandise could be imported was not the only issue: the firms also fought with officials over whether or not a particular item was dutiable.[20]

The harassment Chinese importers experienced was nothing compared to what laundrymen went through, especially in San Francisco, where the board of supervisors passed 14 ordinances between 1873 and 1884 to restrict the 300 or so Chinese laundries (staffed by some 3,000 washers and ironers) in the city. One ordinance required washhouses in wooden buildings to be licensed or be subject to a fine of $1,000 or six months in jail for their owners. All the Chinese laundries were in wooden buildings. In 1885 the board rejected every Chinese license application, but granted all but one of the 80 licenses sought by non-Chinese, according to John Gioai and Charles and Laurene Wu McClain.[21]

In defiance, about 200 Chinese laundrymen decided to keep their premises open for business. Among them was Yick Wo. (Yick Wo was actually the name of a laundry, not a man, but it was common in those days for owners of Chinese businesses to be known by their firms' names.) He arrived in San Francisco in 1861, opened a laundry two years later, and had been in business ever since. When he applied for his license in June 1885, he already had in hand permits from the city's board of fire wardens and its health officer certifying that the building housing his laundry met the city's fire and sanitation standards. The board of supervisors nevertheless denied his application. And though Yick Wo's license would not expire until October, the police filed a complaint against him and arrested him in August.

The Chinese laundry guild, the Tung Hing Tong, hired one of the most famous trial lawyers of the day to defend the entire group of laundrymen in a class action suit. Yick Wo filed a writ of habeas corpus and was released from prison, but the city appealed, the California Supreme Court upheld the ordinance, and he once again landed in jail. Then the U.S. Court of Appeals for the Ninth Circuit granted him a second habeas corpus, but would not restrain the city from enforcing the laundry ordinance. When the case went to the U.S. Supreme Court, Yick Wo argued that the ordinance was arbitrary and discriminated against persons like himself who were consequently denied due process of law.

The city responded that regulating laundries was part of its police power. Furthermore, the ordinance in question was not discriminatory, since the non-Chinese laundries did not have scaffolds on their roofs for drying clothes (which the city considered to be fire hazards), whereas the Chinese ones did. The high court ruled in *Yick Wo v. Hopkins* (1886) that to divide laundries arbitrarily into two classes was a denial of equal protection under the law as guaranteed by the Fourteenth Amendment, which covered not only all citizens but all *persons*, including Chinese aliens. In the court's view, a law that could be applied in a discriminatory manner, even though it might be neutral on its face, was unconstitutional.

Several decades later, as shown by Peter Kwong, Chinese laundrymen in New York had to fight against not only discriminatory ordinances but also New York Chinatown's power elite—the Chinese Consolidated Benevolent Association (CCBA).[22] In the early 1930s there were approximately 3,500 Chinese laundries in New York, which enabled almost 10,000 men to eke out a living. Because they charged very low prices and offered services such as mending and pickup and delivery free of charge, Euro-American laundries considered them a threat. At the height of the Great Depression, when all businesses had trouble staying open, the Euro-American laundry owners convinced the city's board of aldermen to pass an ordinance to require one-person laundries (most of them operated by Chinese) to pay an annual registration fee of $25 and to post a $1,000 bond.

Instead of coming to the aid of the laundrymen, the CCBA asked each one to pay a fee before it would investigate the matter. Outraged, the laundrymen banded together into the Chinese Hand Laundry Alliance (CHLA). The CCBA tried repeatedly but unsuccessfully to sabotage the new organization. Meanwhile, the CHLA hired two lawyers who persuaded the aldermen to reduce the registration fee to $10 and the bond to $100. Heartened by this victory, the CHLA remained for years a staunch opponent of the conservative CCBA and a supporter of progressive political activities.

Just as Chinese fought to keep their import-export stores and laundries—two of their most important means of livelihood—open, so Japanese defended time after time their right to farm. In this they were less lucky than Yick Wo had been: four landmark cases heard by the U.S. Supreme Court in 1923 cumulatively stripped away whatever rights they had enjoyed. As detailed by Frank Chuman, in *Terrace v. Thompson* a unanimous court upheld the 1921 Alien Land Law of the state of Washington and denied the plaintiff the right to lease his land to a Japanese alien. The court also upheld the constitutionality of the 1920 California alien land law in *Porterfield v. Webb*. Sharecropping agreements were ruled illegal in *Webb v. O'Brien*, concerning a Californian landowner who wanted to sign a contract with a Japanese to plant, cultivate, and harvest crops, arguing that this was a contract for the performance of labor. But California's attorney general considered such an agreement a ruse that allowed Japanese aliens to possess and use land—an interpretation with which the high court concurred. Finally, *Frick* v. *Webb* forbade aliens ineligible to citizenship from owning stocks in corporations formed for the purpose of farming. According to the justices, owning such stocks would give the aliens an interest in land also.[23]

The only positive decision Japanese tenant farmers won was *Estate of Tetsubumi Yano* (1922), in which the California Supreme Court held that the parents of two-year-old American-born Tetsubumi Yano, to whose name they had transferred 14 acres, were allowed to serve as her guardians. But their victory was short-lived. A year later, California amended Section 175(a) of its Code of Civil Procedures to prohibit aliens ineligible for citizenship from being appointed as guardians of any estate consisting in whole or in part of real property, though they could otherwise still serve as guardians to minors.[24]

As Asian immigrants went on strike and went to court, some of them increasingly realized that the host society found it easy to discriminate against them because their countries of origin were weak. Even Japan, the strongest among them, frequently had to compromise the welfare of its emigrants for the sake of international power politics. Chinese, Asian Indians, and Koreans, in particular, understood the connection between their homelands' subjugated status and their own maltreatment abroad. As this insight deepened, they threw their support behind efforts to liberate their countries of origin from foreign domination.

At the turn of the century, a number of important Chinese political leaders—broadly divided into two groups, reformers and revolutionaries—visited North America, looking for supporters and funds for their causes. Their travels have been studied by Eve Armentrout Ma, Robert Worden, and Him Mark Lai.[25] Sun Yat-sen, whose vision was to overthrow the Qing dynasty and establish a republic in China, founded the Xingzhonghui (Revive China Society) in Hawaii in 1894. Eleven years later in Tokyo, he established another organization, the Tongmenghui (Revolutionary Alliance), most of whose members were also overseas Chinese. Meanwhile, reformers Kang Youwei (K'ang Yu-wei) and Liang Qichao (Liang Ch'i-ch'ao) organized the Baohuanghui (Protect the Emperor Society, also known as the Chinese Empire Reform Association) in Canada in 1899. Its purpose was to restore the Guangxu emperor (in China) to power vis-à-vis the empress dowager. Kang and Liang believed that China could strengthen itself through various reform measures. Their message fell on receptive ears, and Baohuanghui branches immediately sprang up in Hawaii and the continental United States, attracting many more members than did Sun's more radical group. Both the revolutionary and reformist parties espoused nationalism. Chinese in the United States who became members got their first taste of modern politics through participating in these parties' activities.

One of the most explosive manifestations of the new Chinese nationalism was the 1905 boycott of American goods—a movement to protest the maltreatment of Chinese in the United States. According to Shih-shan Tsai, what irked the Chinese was not just that laborers were barred but that immigration officials abused even merchants and temporary visitors, who were technically "exempt" from the workings of the exclusion laws.[26] Most of the existing studies of the boycott assume that its genesis lay in China, but research by

Delber McKee indicates that Chinese in Hawaii and the United States also played significant roles in it. The timing of the outbreak, especially, was a direct result of several developments in the United States.[27]

In April 1904 Congress quietly attached a rider to an appropriations bill to extend the existing Chinese exclusion laws indefinitely and to make them applicable to all American insular territories. The Chinese government, meanwhile, announced that it would not renew the 1894 Gresham-Yang Treaty, which was due to expire at the end of 1904, because its existence had allowed Americans to treat Chinese in ever-harsher ways. Between August 1904 and May 1905 the Chinese ambassador tried to work out a new compromise treaty with the U.S. secretary of state, but negotiations stalemated. Another blow came on 8 May 1905, when the U.S. Supreme Court upheld the right of the bureau of immigration to deport Chinese in the *Ju Toy* decision. Right after the ruling was announced, Chinese in the United States, Hawaii, and the Philippines sent more than twenty telegrams to the Chinese Foreign Ministry opposing the proposed new treaty. They also called for a boycott of American goods as a means to compel the federal government to retrench its draconian measures.

In response to these developments, merchants, students, and other patriotic individuals in port cities along the central and south China coast launched the proposed boycott at the beginning of August. Chinese firms in Shanghai, Canton, and elsewhere canceled orders they had previously given American companies and made no new ones. Individuals stopped smoking American cigarettes and refrained from purchasing American consumer goods. After two months, however, the movement fizzled as a result of official action. The Chinese central government, under strong pressure from the United States, sent out a proclamation to provincial officials asking them to crack down on boycott demonstrations, while Yuan Shikai (Yuan Shih-k'ai), the governor general of Zhili (Chihli) province, opened Tianjin to American imports. The boycott persisted longest in the Canton area, where remittances from the Chinese in North America helped sustain it. But these funds dried up abruptly after San Francisco's Chinatown was demolished by the 1906 earthquake.

The boycott had only a negligible impact on America's trade with China, but it had a salutary effect on the Chinese in the United States. Even before it began officially, President Theodore Roosevelt had asked his secretary of commerce and labor (who oversaw the bureau of immigration) to instruct immigration officials to treat arriving Chinese more courteously and to be more liberal in their interpretation of who could enter. The bureau dropped its proposal for a new round of registration, shortened delays in processing arriving Chinese, ceased arbitrary deportations, and stopped raiding Chinatowns without search warrants. Equally important, Chinese immigrants themselves developed a new political consciousness. During the boycott, the Chinese Six Companies, the tongs, the Baohuanghui branches, Sun Yat-sen's supporters, Chinese Christians, and various newspapers had all worked together for a common end.

Asian Indians in North America likewise learned to transcend sectarian divisions as they worked for Indian independence, as Mark Juergensmeyer, Joan Jensen, and Harish Puri have argued.[28] In 1913 members of the Hindustan Association of the Pacific Coast decided to publish a newspaper, *Ghadar* (also transliterated as *Gadar* and *Ghadr*, meaning "revolution" or "mutiny" in

Urdu). Its first editor was Har Dayal, a Hindu intellectual who had refused a scholarship at Oxford University to protest British educational policies in India. After coming to the United States in 1911, he taught briefly (without salary) at Stanford University, became secretary of the San Francisco Radical Club, and founded the Bakunin Institute and the Ghadar party. Whereas the Radical Club and Bakunin Institute had mostly Euro-American members, the Ghadar party was an entirely Asian Indian enterprise. It was a secular organization that aimed to overthrow British colonial rule and establish a republic in India.

Dayal's radical rhetoric alarmed immigration officials, who arrested him in 1914. But before they could deport him, he jumped bail and went to Europe. After his departure, Ram Chandra (like Dayal, a Hindu), became the editor of *Ghadar*, which was printed in Urdu as well as Grumulki and several other languages. Though the newspaper was widely distributed—in the United States, Canada, Hong Kong, Japan, the Philippines, Malaya, Singapore, British Guiana, Trinidad, Honduras, South Africa, East Africa, and India itself—the party never became a disciplined organization, relying instead on spontaneous uprisings to achieve its goals.

The Ghadar party's appeal reached its zenith following an incident in Vancouver harbor. As recounted by Hugh Johnston and Joan Jensen, several hundred Asian Indians arrived there in late May 1914 on a chartered Japanese ship, the *Komagata Maru*, in an attempt to bypass Canada's "continuous journey" regulation that had hindered Asian Indian immigration, but they were not allowed to land.[29] As their food and water ran out, Vancouver Sikhs sent telegrams to the British king, the viceroy of India, and other leaders, entreating their help, but all to no avail. Two months to the day after it arrived, the ship sailed away after a show of force by Canadian authorities. The poor aspiring immigrants had lost $70,000 in this misadventure. Their fate aroused the sympathy of Asian Indians all along the Pacific Coast and awakened them to the connection between their powerlessness as a people and their mistreatment as immigrants.

In the months following the *Komagata Maru* incident, small bands of Ghadarites from North America and elsewhere returned to India to foment revolution. By this time, World War I had broken out and Indian nationalists looked to Germany as a possible source of support against Great Britain. Some Ghadarites received arms from the Germans, but in the end they accomplished little, for British intelligence agents arrested and disarmed them as soon as they touched shore. Quite a number of them were court-martialed and executed. What was left of the party in the United States fell into disarray after 1915, a development partly spurred by infiltrators and informers paid by the British government. The party's American branch fell apart in 1917 with the assassination of Ram Chandra, when he and others were on trial for conspiracy.

Of the different efforts made by Asian immigrants to support their homelands, the fight by Koreans in America for Korean independence persisted the longest. In fact, the Korean provisional government-in-exile set up by expatriate leaders in Shanghai in 1919 could not have sustained itself without the funds remitted to it by Koreans in Hawaii and the United States over the course of three decades. The Korean independence movement, however, was often torn by interpersonal rivalry among its key leaders, Ahn Chang-ho, Park Yongman, and Syngman Rhee, the American phases of whose lives Bong-Youn Choy and Kinsley Lyu have recorded.[30]

Ahn believed in salvation through cultural renewal. Towards this end, in 1903 he established the Chinmok-hoe, the first organization among Koreans on the mainland, and founded the Hung Sa Dang (Young Koreans Academy) a decade later. The goals of the academy were to promote truth, loyalty, and courage through knowledge, virtue, and good health. Though the Hung Sa Dan itself was nonpolitical, many of its members were active in the Korean National Association, through which they wielded power. After the Korean provisional government came into existence in Shanghai, Ahn went there to serve as its secretary of the interior and later as secretary of labor. Japanese police arrested him in 1935. He died three years later, shortly after being released from jail, but the Hung Sa Dan continued to attract members for a decade after his death.

In contrast to Ahn's views on self-regeneration, Park Yong-man thought Korean independence could best be achieved through military means. After he graduated from the University of Nebraska in 1909, he set up five different military academies in Nebraska, California, Kansas, and Wyoming to train Korean cadets. Park went to Hawaii in 1912 to take charge of the military training centers supported by the Korean National Association. He consolidated the different groups into a single Korean National Brigade with 300 members. Park, too, went to Shanghai in 1919 to become minister of foreign affairs, but he left soon afterward when Syngman Rhee (with whom he had long-standing differences) arrived to become the head of the provisional government. He then went to Manchuria, where he trained Korean youth until he was assassinated in 1928.

Syngman Rhee, the first Korean to receive a Ph.D. from an American university (Princeton), advocated using diplomacy to further Korean independence. He went to Hawaii in 1913 to become principal of the Korean Community School. As the conflict between him and Park Yong-man became increasingly acrimonious, he started a church, a newspaper, and a community organization—the Tongji-hoe (Comrade Society)—to create a power base for himself. Though he was chosen as the president of the provisional government, he did not live in Shanghai long. Instead, he returned to the United States and divided his time between Hawaii and Washington, D.C., where he lobbied for Korean independence. After World War II ended, he was invited by American occupation forces back to Korea to serve as an advisor. In 1948 he became the first president of the Republic of Korea and remained in power until he was ousted by student demonstrators in 1960. He died in Hawaii in 1965.

Korean immigrants faithfully donated their savings to support the organizations led by Ahn, Park, and Rhee, as well as to the provisional government in Shanghai and independence armies in Manchuria. They willingly contributed what they could, for they yearned to see their homeland freed from Japanese rule. The fire of nationalism burned so fiercely in their breasts that whenever representatives of the Japanese government in the United States claimed them as subjects, they objected vehemently. They were so intent on overthrowing Japanese colonialism that in the 1930s they joined forces with Chinese—both in China and in the United States—to protest Japan's conquest of the Asian mainland.

Efforts to defeat Japanese militarism also drew different factions within America's Chinatowns together. Patriotic organizations emerged to raise funds, to disseminate information to the American public about developments in

China, and to lobby the federal government to give up its neutralist stand. In New York, according to Peter Kwong, the Chinese Hand Laundry Alliance became an active leader within the Anti-Imperialist Alliance formed to support the "resist Japan, save China" movement. However, because Chiang Kai-shek, leader of China's ruling party, the KMT, showed no inclination to resist Japan's encroachment, the KMT-controlled Chinese Consolidated Benevolent Association initially branded the CHLA a "Communist" organization. But after the KMT and the Chinese Communist party formed a united front in China to resist further Japanese aggression, rightist and leftist community groups in America's Chinatowns likewise put aside their political differences to establish an All-Chinatown Anti-Japanese Patriotic Association.[31] When Chinese picketed docks where ships were being loaded with scrap iron for Japan's war industries, Koreans participated enthusiastically in the demonstrations.

Almost from the day they first set foot on American soil, Asian immigrants and migrant workers have been exploited and abused, but they have fought back in whatever ways they could. They seldom received higher wages as a result of their strikes, but their militance often forced employers to improve their living and working conditions. They lost most of the cases they took to court, but they did win a few notable victories. Their participation in political efforts to liberate their homelands brought few results, but in the process they acquired a new consciousness that transcended parochial boundaries. Through these myriad activities, they sank deeper roots into American soil while simultaneously maintaining ties to their homelands. They struggled not only to enable themselves to live, but also for the sake of their children, who had become quite visible and numerous by the late 1920s and early 1930s.

*A marriage certificate issued to Lew Wing Chew and Koo Shee in San Joaquin County, California, 1908.*
Courtesy San Joaquin County Recorder's office, Sucheng Chan collection

*chapter six*
_____

# Women, Families, and
# the "Second-Generation Dilemma"

In the existing literature on Asian Americans, the years between the end of
World War I and the beginning of World War II are often depicted as an
interregnum about which little is known. Whatever news there was about
Asian immigrants in the late 1910s and early 1920s focused on the fierce "tong
wars" being fought in the Chinatowns of North America. These feuds subsided
after 1925, when a truce was declared by all parties concerned; thereafter, all
seemed quiet in the Asian immigrant ghettos. The following decade, in the
midst of the Great Depression, labor conflicts erupted in the fields and orchards
of the Pacific Coast. Since Filipino farm laborers were among the most militant
strikers, they received some press coverage for their activities.

Aside from the tong wars and the strikes, not much has been recorded
about other developments in the Asian immigrant communities during the
interwar years. The most important change taking place went almost unno-
ticed: a sizable American-born generation finally appeared. American-born
children of Chinese and Japanese ancestry were the most numerous, but a
handful of Korean American and Filipino American children were also born,
while in the isolated Imperial Valley of southern California dozens of children
of Asian Indian fathers and Mexican mothers came into the world.

These children affected not only the families into which they were born but
also the Asian immigrant communities at large, because the fathers of the
children often were the communities' leaders, while their mothers made up the
bulk of the Asian women in the United States. Bringing youngsters up in a
world in which the parents themselves were pariahs was a difficult task; being
parents forced many immigrants to assess where they stood vis-à-vis their
homelands as well as America. This question of belonging became especially
vexing for Japanese residing in the United States in the late 1930s, as militarists
in their homeland conquered and occupied Manchuria and northern China.
The American government and press did not look kindly upon Japan's actions,
which consequently threw an unfavorable light on the Japanese in the United
States.

Though second-generation Asian Americans date back to the early 1850s,
they composed a very small subpopulation until the 1920s. Children were few in
number because very few Asian women came. Scholars such as Lucie Cheng,
Judy Yung, Yuji Ichioka, and Eun Sik Yang have attributed the virtual absence of
Asian female emigrants to the patriarchal, patrilineal, and patrilocal nature of

Chinese, Japanese, and Korean societies.[1] (Filipino kinship was bilateral.) In societies where girls were reared to serve men and to procreate, respectable women did not travel far from home. The only females who left their ancestral villages were girls from destitute families sold as servants or as prostitutes to work in the larger towns and cities of China, Japan, or in foreign countries.

But quite apart from traditional attitudes toward women, there were other reasons that limited the number of female immigrants. One was that labor recruiters initially wanted mainly unattached male workers able to survive under rough conditions. In time, however, plantation managers in Hawaii who wanted a stable labor force began to request a small number of women because they thought a feminine presence would have a salutory effect on the men. In California, on the other hand, where a migratory labor force best suited the growers' needs, no similar desire for women developed. From the Asian workers' point of view, it was less costly to sustain their families in their homelands than to feed them in the United States. Furthermore, given the hostility that they encountered in the American West, many considered conditions on this side of the Pacific too unsafe for women and children.

Among the Chinese, just because the number of female emigrants was small did not mean that the majority of male emigrants were single: many men married shortly before they went abroad. Most waited until they were sure their wives were pregnant before departing. Thereafter, whenever they could afford to do so, they would return to spend a few months with their families, with the hope of fathering additional children during their visits. Parents of emigrant sons believed that keeping the latter's wives in China ensured that they would faithfully remit money home to support their extended families. In the households of some emigrants, when sons born in China of fathers residing and working in America became teenagers, they joined their fathers, brothers, uncles, or grandfathers across the Pacific. Some of these boys attended public school or classes run by Protestant missionaries in order to learn enough English to help their older relatives in business. Others went to work almost immediately upon arrival. Most of the wives and daughters, however, remained in the villages of China.

Relatively fewer of the Japanese male emigrants were married, but a good number of those who were likewise left their wives and children behind. Once they found a settled occupation, however, many sent for their families. Bachelors, meanwhile, asked their parents to find them brides. Among Koreans, about 10 percent of the early emigrants to Hawaii were women and another 10 percent children. One likely reason that more Korean women and girls accompanied their husbands and fathers to Hawaii was that the Christians among them intended to settle in what they had been told was a Christian land. Among Filipinos, too, far more women went to Hawaii than to the Pacific Coast—a reflection of the difference between the two labor systems. Virtually no Asian Indian women came before World War II, for reasons that have not yet been studied.

During the three decades of unrestricted Chinese immigration, only about 9,000 Chinese women arrived in the continental United States. Throughout the latter half of the nineteenth century, according to my analysis of population census records, no more than 5,000 Chinese women were found on the entire

U.S. mainland at any one time. There are no statistics on the number of Chinese women entering Hawaii each year, but the first visible batch of 52 arrived in 1865. As late as 1884 there were under 900 foreign-born Chinese females in the islands. That number rose to a little over 1,400 in 1896. But given the smaller number of Chinese males in Hawaii, the sex ratio was actually less skewed there than on the mainland.

A large majority of the pioneer Chinese female immigrants were poor girls who had been sold into prostitution.[2] This fact had a profound impact on the subsequent history of Chinese female immigration, for beginning in 1875, federal laws forbade most Chinese women—all of whom the government suspected of being prostitutes—from entering. The existence of such restrictive laws is one important factor that differentiates the settlement history of the Chinese from that of Europeans. Among most immigrant groups, working-age men tend to precede women, children, or older people to a new land, but in the case of the Chinese, exclusion was imposed just at that point in the immigrant community's development when men might have sent for their wives and children. Exclusion therefore truncated the natural development of the community.

Attempts to bar Chinese women began just a few years after they first set foot on American soil, as I have discussed elsewhere.[3] San Francisco's municipal officials tried repeatedly in the 1850s and 1860s to close down brothels staffed by Chinese women. When it became apparent that their efforts were a failure, the California legislature passed a law in 1870 to "prevent the kidnapping and importation of Mongolian, Chinese and Japanese females for criminal or demoralizing purposes." But four years later, because the law was vaguely worded and could easily be abused by the state commissioner of immigration charged with enforcing it, the California Supreme Court struck it down when Chinese in San Francisco went to court on behalf of 22 women denied entry by the commissioner. After the Chinese won their case at the state supreme court level, they sought a U.S. Supreme Court judgment regarding the law's constitutionality. In *Chy Lung* v. *Freeman* (1876), the high court did rule the law unconstitutional because it interfered with the federal government's control over the regulation of foreign commerce—immigration being considered an aspect of foreign intercourse.

Meanwhile, Congress itself passed an act—commonly called the Page Law, after the California congressman who introduced the bill—to prohibit the entry of Chinese, Japanese, and "Mongolian" contract laborers, women intended for prostitution, and felons. The Page Law was not particularly effective in restricting Chinese men: more than 100,000 came into the United States between 1876 and 1882. But it proved to be an effective curb against Chinese women—at least those alleged to be prostitutes. Only some 1,340 Chinese women were admitted between 1875 and 1882. The figures for males and females are especially telling for the years 1881 and 1882. After a new treaty was signed between China and the United States in 1880—which gave the latter the right to regulate, but not absolutely prohibit, Chinese immigration—aspiring Chinese emigrants realized it would soon become very difficult to enter the country. Accordingly, more than 50,000 rushed in before exclusion was imposed, but women numbered only 219—a clear indication that the Page Law was being enforced. Later, clauses in the general immigration laws of 1907 and

1917 provided additional bases not only for barring Chinese women suspected of being prostitutes but also allowed commissioners to arrest and deport those already in the country.

The successive Chinese exclusion laws passed between 1882 and 1904, being aimed primarily at Chinese male laborers, contained no specific clauses on women. It was thus left to the courts to interpret how these laws affected females. Chinese women became plaintiffs when immigration officials denied them admission: their sponsors hired lawyers to file writs of habeas corpus to set them at liberty until the U.S. district and circuit courts could hear their cases.

In general, the courts treated Chinese females in a manner parallel to males. Because the original 1882 exclusion law barred Chinese laborers, the courts decided that the wives of laborers also could not be admitted. The status of merchants' wives was likewise derivative: because their husbands were among the "exempted classes," they were allowed to land. Until all the Chinese exclusion laws were rescinded by Congress in 1943, the wives of merchants received more favorable treatment than any other group of Chinese women, although in some instances the legality of their marriage was called into question. Chinese wives of U.S. citizens encountered greater difficulty than did merchants' wives—they could not enter at all after the 1924 Immigration Act went into effect. Only after Chinese American men and their Euro-American supporters strenuously protested this fact did Congress pass an amendment to allow Chinese women who had married U.S. citizens before 1924 to come into the country. Girls of Chinese ancestry born in the United States (who were by birth American citizens) seeking reentry after visits to China had to show conclusive evidence of their American citizenship, while daughters of Chinese men who were citizens had to prove their relationship to their fathers beyond a reasonable doubt. The fathers, on their part, had to convince immigration officials that they were bona fide U.S.-born citizens.

Under such strict conditions, the number of Chinese females entering the country each year during the six decades when Chinese exclusion was in effect numbered in the hundreds rather than the thousands. Not only could few women enter, but the 1922 Cable Act made it a real liability for American-born women of Asian ancestry to marry immigrant men. The clause in the Cable Act that affected Asians negatively stipulated that female U.S. citizens who married aliens ineligible to citizenship would lose their own citizenship. Women of European or African ancestry, who were eligible for naturalization, could regain their citizenship should they divorce or if their alien husbands died, but women of Asian ancestry could not since they themselves were racially ineligible for naturalization. This invidious clause in the Cable Act remained in effect for 10 years until an amendment passed in 1931 declared that "any woman who was a citizen of the United States at birth shall not be denied naturalization . . . on account of her race." The entire Cable Act was repealed in 1936.

Given these myriad attempts to restrict the number of Chinese women in the country and to place hurdles in the way of family formation, little wonder, then, that the sex ratio in the Chinese immigrant community was extremely skewed. The nadir was reached in 1890, after the exclusion of Chinese women had been in effect for fifteen years, when the sex ratio stood at an appalling 27:1. As a result, the number of Chinese American children was very small:

about 500 in 1870 and only 9,000 as late as 1900—half a century after Chinese immigration began. Only in 1940, after nine decades of settlement, did the 40,000 or so American-born individuals of Chinese ancestry (comprising 52 percent of the population) outnumber the foreign-born.

Since relatively more Japanese women came, more resident families were established in Japanese immigrant communities. The first Japanese women to arrive were also prostitutes, but in time they were vastly outnumbered by wives. The history of Chinese and Japanese family formation in the United States differed not because of any cultural differences between the two groups but because, unlike Chinese exclusion, which was imposed rather suddenly, the U.S. government restricted Japanese immigration in stages, thereby allowing Japanese men more time to decide whether or not to bring women to America. After the Gentlemen's Agreement went into effect in 1908, those men who chose to set down roots in the United States had various options. Married men could send for their wives, while bachelors could either return to Japan to get married or ask relatives back home to find them brides. Two factors, however, deterred many men from returning to Japan: one was the cost of passage, the other was the fact that they would lose their deferred military draft status should they remain in Japan for more than thirty days. Thus, many men resorted to arranged marriages facilitated by an exchange of photographs.

Such an arrangement gave rise to the phenomenon of "picture brides."[4] These women went through wedding ceremonies with the grooms absent, had their names entered into their spouses' family registers, applied for passports, and then sailed for America to join husbands they had never met. The Japanese government controlled the exodus of picture brides rather strictly. Before 1915, the Japanese consuls in the United States denied permission to virtually all laborers who wished to send for picture brides. Only farmers who showed an annual profit of more than $400 and had savings of at least $1,000 and merchants who grossed more than $1,200 with savings of at least $1,000 were eligible to summon wives. One reason that the Japanese government encouraged farmers to send for wives was that it considered having settled agricultural communities in the Americas a desirable development, both in terms of Japan's foreign policy and as a means of relieving the country's population pressure. The immigrant farmers, for their part, found that having unpaid family labor helped them to be competitive.

In 1915 the criteria for summoning wives were liberalized: any male resident with savings of at least $800 could qualify, but husbands were required to receive their brides in person at the docks. Potential brides could not apply for passports until their names had been in their husbands' families' registers for six months or longer. They also could not be more than 13 years younger than their spouses. The government found it necessary to impose such an age restriction because in many instances, the aspiring husbands were much older than the women they hoped to marry, given the fact that it took them years to save up enough money to afford wives. Great attention was also paid to the women's health: they had to pass rigorous medical examinations before departure and upon arrival.

Controlled as the influx of picture brides was, it did allow Japanese in the United States to form families. According to statistics in Japanese-language sources, in 1900, of the 850 Japanese females among 18,000 men in the three

A *Japanese wedding, Oakland, California,* 1906.
Courtesy Visual Communications

Pacific Coast states (a sex ratio of 21:1), about 400 were married. Ten years later, the number of women had increased tenfold to over 8,000 with almost 5,600 married. The sex ratio in 1910 was 6.5:1. There were more than 22,000 married women among a total female population of 38,000 on the mainland by 1920. In that year, about half of the farmers, one-tenth of the farmworkers, and one-third of the urban dwellers in California had wives living with them. Japanese females numbered 48,000 in 1920 in Hawaii.[5]

Just as family formation was proceeding apace in the Japanese immigrant communities, anti-Japanese groups put a stop to the influx of Japanese women. They charged that the coming of picture brides was a violation of the Gentlemen's Agreement. As an increasing number of Japanese American children appeared, anti-Japanese leaders, such as California's U.S. senator James Phelan and publisher V. S. McClatchy, stirred up public sentiment against the alleged fertility of Japanese women. To mollify the agitators, the Japanese consul in San Francisco in 1919 recommended to the foreign ministry in Tokyo that it suspend the issuance of passports to picture brides. The Japanese Association of America, ever sensitive to American public opinion, supported the call for abolishing this form of marriage—a decision that caused a furor in the immigrant community. Despite the vociferous protests, no more passports were issued to picture brides after March 1920.

By the time the picture bride influx was cut off, there were almost 30,000 American-born children of Japanese ancestry in the continental United States, compared to only 4,500 ten years earlier. They comprised almost 27 percent of the total population of Japanese ancestry. In 1930, the number stood at over 68,000 in the mainland and more than 91,000 in Hawaii—49 and 65 percent, respectively, of the Japanese-ancestry population.

The number of Korean, Filipino, and Asian Indian women who immigrated was far smaller. During the first short phase of Korean immigration, about 600 women and a similar number of children accompanied their menfolk to Hawaii. They were followed by more than 1,000 Korean picture brides who came before 1924. In comparison, only a tenth of that number journeyed to join husbands on the mainland. The sex ratio among Koreans was approximately 10:1 in Hawaii in the early 1900s; two decades later, it was 3:1. Among Filipinos, the sex ratio in 1920 was roughly 19:1 on the mainland and 4:1 in Hawaii. Some 4,000 Filipinas resided in the islands in 1920 and more than 10,000 in 1930. Of the latter, 42 percent were married. Fewer than a dozen Asian Indian women made their way to the United States before World War II, but several hundred Asian Indian men married Mexican women in southern California; their children were called "Mexican-Hindus."

The arrival of children was at once joyful and burdensome: joyful because family life is such an important aspect of Asian cultures; burdensome because a very large percentage of the Asian women in nineteenth- and early twentieth-century America worked. Unlike the situation in their homelands, few female relatives were available to help with childcare. Almost all Asian immigrant working women—prostitutes, laundresses, farm women, cooks, and seamstresses—continued to work after their babies came. Even the wives of merchants often contributed to the family income by taking in sewing and fancy embroidery. Others provided unpaid family labor in their husbands' stores.

Asian immigrant women who survived were physically tough and emotionally resilient. On the plantations of Hawaii, the women earned money by working in the fields and by cooking and washing clothes for unattached men. They arose before dawn, cooked breakfast for their families and boarders, prepared dozens of lunch boxes, dressed their children for school, and then put in full days hoeing weeds, stripping leaves from the sugarcane stalks, or doing other kinds of field labor. Upon returning to their bunkhouses in the late afternoon, they cooked dinner and fed everyone. Then came washing, ironing, and mending into the middle of the night. In short, in the evening hours, while men relaxed, women continued to work at various chores.

Hard as the physical labor was, the women would have found it more tolerable were it not for the callous way in which they were treated. Recalled one Korean woman in Hawaii:

My mother had many maids in Korea, but at Kipahulu [*sic*] plantation she worked in the canefields with my older brother and his wife. I remember her hands, so blistered and raw that she had to wrap them in clothes [*sic*]. One morning she overslept and failed to hear the work whistle. We were all asleep—my brother and his wife, my older sister, and myself. I was seven years old at the time. Suddenly the door swung open, and a big burly luna burst in, screaming and cursing, "Get up, get to work." The luna ran around the room, ripping off the covers, not caring whether my family was dressed or not. I'll never forget it.[6]

Women treated this way determined to do everything possible to enable their families to leave the plantations as soon as possible. They took in laundry, grew vegetables, and undertook whatever additional work they could to help save up enough money to open their own stores, boardinghouses, bathhouses, or restaurants in Honolulu. Among both Koreans and Japanese, many of the picture brides were better educated than their husbands. Though brought up to obey their husbands, circumstances in the new environment forced them to take greater initiative in attempting to secure a better future for their children.

Many wives of tenant farmers and even farm owners in the continental United States lived under similarly harsh conditions and did heavy "men's work." As one picture bride who settled in the Pacific Northwest recounted,

I was one of the photo brides, and in June 1910, I went to my husband's . . . place . . . . The house, however, was just a slant-roofed shanty such as swine live in. . . . In 1913 . . . we moved. . . . [The new location] was still so wild that bears, wolves and wild cats came around, and of course there was no electricity or running water. . . . Before we could afford a machine to cut wood, my husband and I cut the trees with an eight-foot saw, split the wood with a wedgehammer and brought it to the house on a sled. At the time we had two children, aged three and one, and with them to take care of I couldn't do so much work, so when a friend of ours went back to Japan, I asked him to take them with him. Sending them away when they were so adorable and young made my milk run so! I thought of them on the boat, calling for their mother, and I couldn't sleep for sorrow and loneliness.[7]

Since mainland farms were scattered geographically, the women there suffered an additional hardship: they seldom enjoyed the emotional sustenance and physical assistance provided by female companionship. Life was especially hard during and immediately after the birth of a child. In many families, the husbands had to serve as midwives:

My husband had no experience as a midwife, but he had a friend who had once helped in an emergency and had safely delivered the baby, so my husband went to him to ask how he did it. The important thing is how to cut the umbilical cord. . . . When the time came, my husband and I, one way or another, cut the cord and delivered a beautiful baby. It was a Japanese custom for the mother to take a 21-day rest after delivery. . . . But as for me, I could only rest three days.[8]

Chinese immigrant women had their own unique problem. During the decades when tong wars raged and women were often kidnapped, it was extremely dangerous for women to appear in public. Some women saw other women only once a year—during Chinese New Year visits. Thus the women lived extremely isolated lives. The human beings to whom many Asian immigrant mothers were closest were their children.

One thing that enabled many women to play a more active public role was involvement in homeland politics. This was particularly true for Korean women—both the immigrant mothers and their American-born daughters. Because there were so few Koreans in the United States and in Hawaii, and those who were here felt so strongly about liberating their homeland, men and women alike worked indefatigably in the independence movement. As Eun Sik Yang has noted, in the wake of the 1919 Mansei Uprising, Korean women in California formed the Korean Women's Patriotic Society, while those in Hawaii established the Korean Women's Relief Society of Hawaii.[9] The Patriotic Society set up branches in Los Angeles, Delaney, Reedley, Dinuba, Sacramento, Willows, and San Francisco, while the Relief Society had branches in each of the main islands.

Members of both organizations raised funds to send to the Korean provisional government in Shanghai, the Korean Commission in Washington, D.C., Korean guerrilla forces in Manchuria, and the families of the 33 martyrs who had signed the Korean declaration of independence. They also organized a boycott of Japanese goods and learned first aid and nursing skills in anticipation of participating in anti-Japanese activities.

The most active women were picture brides, many of whom were quite well educated. Unfortunately, factional politics among Korean men spilled over into the women's organizations. Thus, for example, because Ahn Chang-ho had a great deal of influence on members of the Patriotic Society, female supporters of Syngman Rhee stayed away. When nationalist fervor waned in the mid-1920s, the women donated money to orphanages and Ewha Women's College in Korea as well as to community activities in Hawaii and the United States.

Both the Patriotic Society and the Relief Society found new life in the 1930s as Japanese armies advanced into Manchuria and North China. Koreans everywhere joined hands with the Chinese to oppose the Japanese. Chinese women in America formed the Chinese Women's Patriotic Association, whose primary goal was to "promote Chinese unity against Japanese aggression in China." They raised funds, spoke out against the KMT for its inaction, and called for improvements in the status of the Chinese in America.

By the 1920s and 1930s Asians in America had become more concerned than ever about their status because they were bringing up an increasing number of American-born children. More self-consciously than did any other Asian immigrant group, Japanese immigrants drew a clear distinction between themselves, the *Issei* (first generation), and their children, the *Nisei* (second generation). They also left a fuller written record than did any other Asian immigrant group of how they perceived their children's place in the world. Most Issei thought of themselves as sojourners, but they considered the Nisei to be Americans. According to Yuji Ichioka, immigrant leaders such as newspaper publisher Abiko Kyotaro, a strong advocate of permanent settlement, repeatedly urged their fellow Issei to make it possible for their children to adapt to American ways. The debate over the status of the Nisei focused on two issues—their education and their citizenship.[10]

In addition to public schools, many Nisei also went to Japanese schools after regular school hours and on weekends. At first these schools used text-books published in Japan to teach the Nisei the Japanese language as well as the history and geography of Japan, but in 1910 they started offering instruction in English to kindergarten pupils as well, in order to prepare them for entrance into first grade in the public schools. Instruction in Japanese thereafter was considered supplementary.

Immigrant educators who attended a California statewide conference in 1912 on Nisei education concluded that the Nisei should be educated for permanent residence in the United States, even as they were being taught to be proud of their heritage. They urged all parents to enroll their children in the public schools. At the same time, they thought it important to continue teaching children their ancestral tongue to enable them to talk to their parents, most of whom knew only a smattering of English. They also thought that the Japanese schools could provide moral education—something that the public schools did not offer, in their opinion. But instead of continuing to use textbooks published in Japan, immigrant educators wrote their own. These were in Japanese, but their contents focused on topics in American history and civic culture. The editions that appeared in 1923 contained no lessons on Japanese history or geography at all.

The issue of nationality or citizenship was more complex. Japan and the United States used two different doctrines—jus sanguinis and jus soli, respectively—for determining an individual's nationality. According to Japanese law, anyone born of a Japanese father, regardless of where the birth took place, was a Japanese citizen. In contrast, American law stipulated that anyone born on American soil, regardless of his or her parents' ethnicity or citizenship, is an American citizen. The existence of two doctrines gave rise to the phenomenon of dual citizenship among the Nisei.

The existence of dual citizenship gave anti-Japanese groups another axe to grind. They charged that no American of Japanese ancestry could be a loyal citizen of the United States if he or she were simultaneously a citizen of Japan. Recognizing this problem, Issei leaders urged Japan to amend its nationality law to enable Nisei to renounce the Japanese citizenship they automatically acquired at birth. The Japanese parliament did so in 1916, allowing the parents of Nisei 14 years and younger to renounce the latter's Japanese citizenship, while Nisei aged 15 and 16 could do so on their own behalf. Any male 17 and older, however, could not do so until he had completed his military service. As this fact continued to provide grist for the mills of the anti-Japanese spokespersons, a 1924 amendment to the Japanese Nationality Act finally abolished Japanese citizenship based on paternal descent for all Nisei.

Though the question of nationality was resolved, the issue of cultural affinity and identity remained. As in other immigrant families, a generational conflict existed in many Asian ones over parental authority and the freedom of those coming of age. Many American-born teenagers and young adults, especially females, resented most of all the restrictions on their social lives. Whatever time they had after school was spent either studying in Asian-language schools, where the teachers demanded the strictest obedience, or working in sewing factories, restaurants, or farms—without, however, being allowed to keep their earnings. Often, an impending marriage became a focal point of real friction. Virtually all Asian immigrant parents insisted on finding their children spouses—a prospect some second-generation members found so abhorrent that they ran away from home to make their own way in the world as best they could.[11]

One group of American-born youth whose lives were especially perplexing were the *Kibei*—Nisei sent to Japan for education. In families where both parents worked, sending the children to the homelands to be reared by grand-parents or other relatives was one way to deal with the absence of childcare facilities in the immigrant communities. But oftentimes, parents had a more explicit purpose in mind: they wanted their children to learn the language, culture, and moral values of the parents' own homeland. Kibei usually re-turned to the United States after they finished high school in Japan, but because the education they received in the Japan of the 1920s and 1930s was infused with militaristic and chauvinistic values, upon their return home many found it difficult to get along with their highly Americanized siblings. There are no accurate statistics on how many Kibei there were; one survey done in the early 1930s showed that Kibei comprised 13 percent of the total Nisei sample.

As for the children reared in America, the identity crisis they experienced was exacerbated by a racism that permeated many areas of public life.[12] Asian American youth were barred from public recreational facilities such as swim-ming pools and forced to sit at the back of movie theaters. As one Nisei woman interviewed by a member of the Survey of Race Relations project directed by sociologist Robert E. Park in the late 1920s recalled,

> Our . . . class went to Redondo Beach, where we planned to have a good time in the plunge [swimming pool]. We lined up at the ticket office and when I came to the window the girl said she wouldn't sell me a ticket. When I asked why, she snapped out that she had orders not to sell any tickets to Japs. That made me indignant. I told the girls to go in the plunge for a good time, while I stood by and watched them. I felt this keenly, but concluded it was best to say nothing and to act in a courteous manner.[13]

Her experience was quite representative. Those who participated in athletics usually had to join teams composed entirely of members of their own ethnic groups. A Chinese American young woman told her interviewer, "[i]n high school I did not enter into the different activities because I felt that I was not wanted and I was quite sensitive. . . . At times I have been called a "Chink" and I have resented it bitterly and would at times answer back, but recently I have not replied."[14]

Most troubling of all, very few second-generation college graduates could find jobs commensurate with their education and training. This fact was docu-mented not only by census data, by the writings of the older Nisei, Chinese Americans, and Filipino Americans, but also in a study done between 1929 and 1933 by several Stanford University professors who examined how the Nisei were adjusting to their environment.

In terms of educational achievement, Edward K. Strong, Reginald Bell, and their associates found that, in general, Nisei students were quite similar to their Euro-American peers.[15] Though they did not score as high as their Euro-American classmates in those sections of standardized tests that depended on reading and English comprehension, they outperformed the latter in terms of mathematics and spelling. Up to the seventh grade, relatively more Nisei received A's than did Euro-American students, but from the eighth grade on, their performance declined for no ostensible reasons.

With regard to vocational aptitude, the abilities of the two groups were also found to be quite parallel. However, they diverged in terms of occupational aspirations. Among high school students, whereas agriculture ranked first as the occupation that Nisei planned to enter, it ranked only seventh among Euro-Americans. Proportionately more Euro-American than Japanese American high school students planned to become engineers, chemists, and lawyers. Among college students, business was the first choice of 35 percent of the Nisei respondents in the survey; 22 percent hoped to become doctors, dentists, and pharamacists; 15 percent desired to become engineers; while only 9 percent looked to agriculture for a living. Smaller percentages of Euro-Americans were interested in business, but relatively more aspired to become engineers, lawyers, and physical scientists.

Strong and his associates thought the Nisei's strong desire for white-collar work was unrealistic and concluded that "the second generation are following their inclinations and not seriously considering as yet the occupations open to them or the chances of success in different occupations." In their eyes, it would be wiser for the Nisei to enter agriculture (not just the cultivation but also the sale and distribution of crops), to go into import-export businesses either by opening stores that sold Japanese goods to their coethnics or that specialized in novelties Euro-American customers fancied (such as goldfish stores and tea gardens), to run Japanese restaurants and boardinghouses, and to work as domestic servants in the homes of Euro-Americans.

The Stanford social scientists gave various reasons that Nisei should not aspire to become professionals. With regard to medicine and the other health professions, they noted that the Japanese-ancestry population was too small to support a large number of doctors and dentists. "Until it has been sufficiently demonstrated," they declared, that Nisei "can secure patients from other racial groups, it would seem hazardous for too many to specialize here." They also questioned the "advisability of many Japanese entering engineering and geology" because "these occupations necessitate the handling of white common and skilled laborers, who resent Japanese being placed over them." They further counseled the Nisei to "forgo any possible opportunity" in teaching, as the public schools would not hire them. As for becoming lawyers, they observed that "there seems to be a widespread feeling . . . that white judges and jurors are prejudiced against a Japanese lawyer." They thought, however, that Nisei might succeed as accountants and actuaries, because such work was "an inside activity in which there is little need to contact the general public."

In short, the Stanford researchers thought it best that the Nisei remain in the same occupational niches carved out by their fathers. They urged the Nisei to accept the existing barriers—obstacles created by white perceptions and reactions to them—and denied that Japanese Americans suffered from racism. Rather, they believed the so-called Japanese American problem was simply a reflection of the same existential condition faced by the children of all immigrants: "a chaotic state of mind," "a mind full of conflicting ideas, ideals, and aspirations." To deal with this situation, they called for more and better vocational counseling. They disapproved of the Nisei's presumptuousness—the assumption, as they put it sarcastically, that "the keys to the city" should be given to them. All immigrant groups had to start at the bottom, they said, for "life is like that."

Second-generation Asian Americans themselves tried hard to find a way out of their dilemma. What pained them was that having been educated in public schools where they learned the American creed, they thought they would enjoy all the rights, privileges, and duties of citizenship. Instead, they found themselves no better off than their parents. The latter, at least, could find solace in their heritage; moreover, as immigrants, they knew they could not expect equal treatment. But their children knew not where they belonged. They saw only two options available to them. These were best articulated by the winners of a debate sponsored by the Gin Hawk Club of New York in 1936. The winning statements were published in the *Chinese Digest*, a magazine founded by American-born Chinese and have been brought to light by Ling-chi Wang.[16]

The topic of the debate was "Does My Future Lie in China or America?" The winner, a student at Harvard University, concluded that his future lay in America, first, because he owed it as much allegiance as he did China; second, because jobs were hard to get in either place; and third, because being culturally American, he would feel more lonely and estranged in China than he did in America. The winner of the second prize, a student at the University of Washington, argued it would be best to go to China. He felt that after having "absorbed a bitter diet of racial prejudice," he could not live in the United States happily. In contrast to the United States, where his career advancement was limited, he believed that in China "every vocation is an open field."

In reality, second-generation Asian Americans could not work easily in Asia or America. Though they had attended Asian-language schools, not all of them had learned an Asian language sufficiently well or had absorbed enough of the subtleties of Asian culture to interact smoothly with people or to obtain good jobs in their parents' homelands. It was mostly engineers, aviators, or medical doctors who managed to use their skills in Asia. In the United States, only in those metropolitan areas with sizable Asian populations and in the East Coast, where prejudice was not as intense, could young college graduates practice their professions.

Quite apart from racial discrimination, second-generation Asian Americans also had the misfortune of entering the job market during the Great Depression. No one has yet studied in detail how the depression affected various Asian American communities. According to Thomas Chinn, in San Francisco's Chinatown about one-sixth of the population was receiving public assistance by 1933. At first relief came in the form of food baskets distributed through Chinese grocery stores, but after 1934 only cash relief was offered. Chinese and Filipinos on relief were given a food budget that was 10 to 20 percent lower than that given to whites, because the relief agencies believed that Asians could subsist on a less expensive diet. After the Works Progress Administration (WPA) was created in 1935, about 330 single Chinese men and 160 heads of families were put to work on WPA projects in San Francisco.[17]

In New York's Chinatown deprivation led some Chinese to take political action: they organized a Chinese Unemployed Council and sent delegates to a national demonstration in Washington, D.C. The group set out to provide emergency aid to the needy, to unite with unemployed people of other ethnic backgrounds, and to seek federal and local public assistance.[18]

Asian immigrant farmers also fared poorly during the depression. My preliminary analysis of the annual financial reports filed by white and Issei guardians of Nisei-owned farms in California—reports required by the state's 1920 alien land law—between 1921 and 1942 shows that in the 1930s, Japanese farm families barely managed to scratch a living from the soil. As the decade progressed, an increasingly large proportion of these farms showed negative incomes. Their owners survived only because they could grow their own food.

Compared to the Chinese and Japanese Americans, little is known about American-born children of other Asian ancestries. With regard to Korean Americans, bits of biographical information, such as those provided by Mary Paik Lee, indicate that because of the fierce nationalism that existed among Korean immigrants, their children felt less ambivalent about their heritage. As the Japanese colonial masters in Korea tried to wipe out Korean culture, Koreans abroad felt a special obligation to preserve it by teaching it to their children, who accepted such tutelage more willingly than did their Chinese or Japanese peers.[19]

The experiences of two other groups of Asian immigrants' children were quite different from those of Chinese, Japanese, and Korean Americans. Unlike the latter, to whom parents tried very hard to pass on aspects of their cultural heritage, the children of Punjabi fathers and Mexican mothers and of Filipino fathers and Euro-American mothers learned very little about their fathers' origins.

In the so-called Mexican-Hindu families, whose histories Karen Leonard has reconstructed, the mothers' culture predominated.[20] About the only concession the Mexican wives made to their Asian Indian husbands was to learn to cook Indian food, which in many ways resembles Mexican food. The mothers spoke to their children in Spanish and raised them as Catholics, rather than as Sikhs, Hindus, or Muslims. The women even persuaded their husbands (who were not Catholics) to become godfathers of each others' children. Conflicts arose in such families when the Sikh, Muslim, or Hindu fathers or godfathers proved stricter than the Catholic mothers or godmothers with their children or godchildren. The women often took the side of daughters who wanted to wear makeup and go out on dates, despite their husbands' strenuous objections to such practices.

One reason the Mexican mothers tended to support their children's desire for "freedom" was that they themselves demanded quite a bit of it. Even after marriage, some insisted on the right to go out in the evenings on their own, often with Mexican male friends. Moreover, being Catholics did not stop them from divorcing their husbands and remarrying others.

Many of the children born of Filipino men in the mainland United States were also of mixed parentage. Even though antimiscegenation laws existed, some Filipinos cohabited with Euro-American women, most of whom were themselves immigrants or daughters of immigrants. Other couples traveled to states without antimiscegenation laws to marry. Two studies by Barbara Posadas of racially mixed Filipino families in the Chicago area show that the mothers also exercised considerable influence over their children.[21] Some 300 of the almost 1,800 Filipinos who had settled in Chicago by 1930 worked for the Pullman Company as stewards in railroad club cars. Most were men who had originally come to the United States for higher education but for one reason or another could not continue in their studies.

Employment in the Pullman Company took them away from home for a week or more at a time. Their wives by default, if not by design, thus served as the chief disciplinarians at home. In terms of culture, the mestizo and mestiza children remember being encouraged by both their fathers and mothers to assimilate as much as possible into the general Euro-American culture. But in the case of the girls, one thing set them apart: almost invariably, their Filipino fathers, who were, for the most part, better educated than their Euro-American mothers, strongly encouraged them to go to college. This stood in stark contrast to the aspirations of their girlfriends in the working-class neighborhoods where they lived. Most of the latter looked forward only to a few brief years working in factories or in stores before getting married.

As more and more American-born Asians grew to adulthood, some among them began to see the need for collective action and formed organizations to meet their own needs. Musical groups, social clubs, and athletic teams enabled them to enjoy a life apart from the immigrant generation. YMCA and YWCA branches in the Asian immigrant communities, as well as Boy Scout troops, provided links with the wider society. A number of second-generation organizations formulated concrete plans to improve the lot of their members.

Again, relatively more information is available about the political activities of the Nisei than about the other groups. In the late 1920s and early 1930s, as Jerrold Takahashi has shown, Nisei proposed three strategies to cope with the conditions under which they lived.[22] The first, most clearly voiced by Kazuo Kawai, who was born in Japan but was educated in the United States from the age of six, envisioned the Nisei serving as a cultural bridge between East and West, interpreting one culture to the members of the other.

A second position argued that Nisei should become 200 percent American. Founders of the Japanese American Citizens League (JACL), most of whom were young professionals or in business, articulated this stance most forcefully. Concerned with economic success and social status, JACL members believed that the best way for them to prove their worthiness in the eyes of Euro-Americans was to be totally loyal to American ideals, which they understood to be individualism, free enterprise, and the ownership of private property. As loyal Americans, they never criticized racism, although they worked hard to challenge discriminatory laws. They successfully obtained naturalization rights for some 500 Issei veterans of World War I and helped to get the Cable Act, which affected Japanese as much as Chinese, repealed. So far as they participated in domestic electoral politics, a majority of JACL members were Republicans. With regard to the political and military situation in East Asia, they tried to excuse or explain away Japan's encroachment upon China's territory.

A third perspective was more leftist in orientation. Its advocates generally belonged to the Democratic party and came from more working-class backgrounds. Calling themselves "progressives," they were very interested in labor issues. A number of activists joined unions and helped to organize salmon cannery workers in Alaska. They were also very critical of racial discrimination and tried to promote solidarity with other minority groups. In terms of interna-

tional politics, unlike the JACL members, the Nisei progressives initially condemned Japanese militarism. However, as war clouds darkened, the more
astute members of both groups realized it was important for different segments
of the Japanese American community to close ranks. As a gesture of concilia-
tion, leaders among the progressives urged their peers to join the JACL.

Thus on the eve of World War II, among the Chinese, Japanese, and Koreans, second-generation Americans of Asian ancestry finally outnumbered their
immigrant parents, while the much smaller number of racially mixed progeny
of Asian Indians and Filipinos tried their best to fit into the mainstream. Young
and inexperienced though they were, members of the second generation were
beginning to find a voice of their own and to distinguish themselves from their
elders. Owing, however, to racial barriers in the labor market, which forced
them to work within their ethnic enclaves, they remained economically dependent on their fathers, grandfathers, and uncles for a far longer period than they
might have wished. The outbreak of war shattered the prevailing patterns and
brought new forces into play. During the war years, the lives of Japanese
Americans, on the one hand, and those of the other Asian immigrant groups,
on the other hand, moved in diametrically opposite directions.

*Japanese Americans being evacuated, 1942.*
Courtesy National Archives

*chapter seven*

---

# Changing Fortunes, 1941 *to* 1965

World War II affected the lives of all Americans, but it had an especially profound impact on Asian immigrants and their American-born children. The lot of persons of Chinese, Korean, Filipino, and Asian Indian ancestry improved because their ancestral lands were allies of the United States. Four positive changes took place: the images held by the general public of these groups improved, some of their members finally managed to get jobs in the technical professions and skilled trades, sizable numbers of Chinese and Filipinos joined and served in the armed forces, and immigration exclusion was lifted for the Chinese in 1943 and for Filipinos and Asian Indians in 1946 after the war ended. Individuals of Japanese ancestry along the Pacific Coast, in contrast, were confined in concentration camps, even as a very large percentage of draft-age Nisei served with distinction in the army and died for their country.

A Gallup poll taken in 1942 showed that the images of Chinese and Japanese had bifurcated. Respondents characterized the Chinese as "hardworking, honest, brave, religious, intelligent, and practical." Japanese, on the other hand, were said to be "treacherous, sly, cruel, and warlike" though also "hardworking and intelligent."[1] Obviously, this poll was a reflection of how newspapers and newsreels were covering the war in Asia. Particularly ironic was the fact that even though Chiang Kai-shek, China's wartime leader, had to be coerced into resisting Japan's advances, he was portrayed as a hero and a staunch ally of the United States in the world press. When Filipino forces fought side by side with American troops in defending Bataan and Corrigedor in the Philippines during the spring of 1942, the image of Filipinos in the United States similarly became more rosy.

There are no detailed statistics on the wartime employment of Asian Americans. However, changes between the 1940 and 1950 censuses, as analyzed by Ling-chi Wang, provide a rough indication of at least how the occupational status of the Chinese had changed. In 1940 only about 1,000 Chinese—a fifth of them women—held professional and technical jobs out of a gainfully employed population of 36,000. Ten years later, some 3,500—a third of them women—did so among 48,000 gainfully employed. Most of the professionals worked as engineers and technicians in war industries, which experienced an extraordinary boom and were desperately short of manpower. Among Chinese American women, the rise in the number of white-collar clerical workers was also noticeable—from 750 in 1940 to 3,200 in 1950. Like women of other ethnic backgrounds, Chinese American women entered the labor force in significant numbers in the 1940s: working women numbered 2,800 in 1940 and 8,300 ten years later.[2]

Meanwhile, large numbers of Chinese and Filipinos were inducted into the armed forces. Almost 40 percent of the Chinese inductees were foreign-born. The citizenship requirement for service was waived in some instances, while in other instances mass naturalization ceremonies were held before induction. The wartime need for manpower was apparently so urgent that the prohibition against the naturalization of Asians was brushed aside. Across the nation, according to Thomas Chinn, between 15,000 and 20,000 Chinese men and women served in all branches of the military, 70 percent of them in the army, with an additional 25 percent in the Army Air Force (at that time a part of the army). The Chinese inductees into the army saw action in Europe as members of the Third and Fourth Infantry Divisions and in Asia and the Pacific in the Sixth, Thirty-second, and Seventy-seventh Infantry Divisions. Those in the navy, Marines Corps, and Coast Guard similarly served in every theater of war. According to a survey of Chinese American veterans done in the late 1970s, 18 percent of them had been wounded in action.[3]

The anomalous status of Filipinos as U.S. "nationals" was also forgotten as thousands of them were inducted. As Fred Cordova has shown, mass naturalization ceremonies likewise made many of them citizens. The segregated First Filipino Infantry Regiment was activated in California in mid-1942 and the Second Filipino Infantry Regiment was formed later that year. Filipinos had long served as stewards in the U.S. Navy, and they continued to do so in large numbers throughout the war. In 1944 about 1,000 Filipino Americans were selected for a secret mission, taken to the Philippines by submarines, and landed in various spots throughout the archipelago to contact anti-Japanese underground groups and to gather intelligence for General Douglas MacArthur's headquarters in Australia.[4]

In the midst of the war in late 1943, as a gesture of goodwill toward China, Congress rescinded the Chinese exclusion laws, set a quota to allow 105 Chinese immigrants to be admitted each year, and granted Chinese the right of naturalization. Similar rights were not conferred on Filipinos and people from the Indian subcontinent until 1946, when each group received an annual quota of 100. (Japanese and Koreans, however, received no immigration quotas or the right of naturalization until 1952.)

Compared to the other groups of Asian Americans, the Japanese American wartime experience was traumatic. As soon as the United States declared war on Japan, following the latter's bombing of the American naval base at Pearl Harbor in Hawaii on 7 December 1941, more than 40,000 Japanese living on the Pacific Coast, along with their 70,000 American-born children—who were U.S. citizens—were removed from their homes and incarcerated in "relocation camps."[5]

As early as 1918, according to Gary Okihiro, military intelligence had begun to gather information on Japanese living in Hawaii and the continental United States.[6] Given this history of surveillance, it is not surprising that two years before the United States entered the Pacific war the Justice Department—through its Federal Bureau of Investigation (FBI)—the Office of Naval Intelligence (ONI), and the Military Intelligence Division of the army (called G-2) started investigating potentially "dangerous" persons. In 1941 the three intelligence agencies drew up a "delimitation agreement" among themselves whereby the FBI assumed overall responsibility for counterespionage and sabotage-security investigations of civilians. The FBI, however, agreed to share jurisdiction over the Japanese population in the continental United States with ONI, which, aside from this exception, was responsible only for navy personnel. G-2, meanwhile, would confine its investigations to army-employed civilians. Following this division of labor, the FBI drew up three lists, classifying people according to the degree of danger it thought they might pose. The work of these intelligence agencies was made easier when Congress passed an Alien Registration Act in June 1940 to enable the Justice Department to register some five million aliens aged 14 and above then residing in the United States.

As a result of the various lists compiled, and with the help of the Census Bureau—which turned over to the army information showing where persons of Japanese ancestry lived on the Pacific coast in 1940 (in violation of the confidentiality it promises everyone it enumerates, as Roger Daniels has pointed out[7])—the FBI was able to pick up more than 1,700 enemy aliens, including 736 Japanese, along the Pacific Coast on the very day that war was declared. (There were about a quarter million enemy aliens living in the western states at this time: 114,000 Italians, 97,000 Germans, and 40,000 Japanese.) Four days later, the FBI had 1,370 Japanese under detention. The number rose to over 2,000 on the mainland by March 1942—about half the total enemy aliens arrested. In addition, the bureau also picked up almost 900 Japanese in Hawaii who were detained in army-run camps in the islands until they were transferred to Justice Department camps on the mainland. One little-known fact is that Japanese in other parts of the Americas, especially Peru, were also arrested and sent for incarceration in the United States.

The individuals rounded up were officers of various community organizations, Japanese language school teachers, Shinto and Buddhist priests and priestesses, newspaper editors, and other identifiable leaders. They were arrested under a blanket presidential warrant (which did not specify any grounds for the arrests) and taken to camps run by the Immigration and Naturalization Service in Lordsburg and Santa Fe, New Mexico; Crystal City and Seagoville, Texas; Livingston, Louisiana; Fort Missoula, Montana; and Fort Lincoln, North Dakota.

Meanwhile, General John L. DeWitt, commander of the Western Defense Command headquartered at the Presidio in San Francisco, sought permission from the Justice Department to enter "all alien homes" without warrants in order to search for and seize contraband. The U.S. attorney general refused to grant authorization for such warrantless searches, but on 29 December 1941 the Justice Department itself ordered all enemy aliens in seven western states to surrender their radios, shortwave sets, cameras, binoculars, and any weapons they possessed. During these initial weeks of the war, enemy aliens of Japanese, German, and Italian ancestry were treated alike, but shortly afterward, the Japanese, together with their American-born children, were singled out for discriminatory treatment. In late December, three high-ranking members of the Justice Department met with three representatives of the War Department to discuss what further action might be taken with regard to enemy aliens. The officials from the Justice Department opposed mass evacuation, while those from the War Department favored it. Both sides agreed to hold off making a final decision until they had a chance to consult General DeWitt.

Feeling uneasy over the constitutionality of a possible mass evacuation, the attorney general consulted three lawyers outside of the Justice Department. They concluded that such a move might be justified if military necessity mandated it. Unlike individuals of German and Italian ancestry, said these private advisors, who could be individually recognized and kept under watch, "the Occidental eye cannot rapidly distinguish one Japanese resident from another." According to this logic, because of Euro-American failings, it might be necessary to evacuate en masse persons of Japanese ancestry. The secretary of war, who also had doubts, decided to put the question directly to his chief. President Roosevelt said he would back up whatever action his secretary of war decided to take.

As a result of these discussions, the Justice Department announced in late January that enemy aliens would be excluded from 86 prohibited zones in California—all of them chosen by DeWitt. These included areas around San Francisco Bay, the Los Angeles airport, several other airports, railroad stations, power plants, dams, gasworks, and the like. All enemy aliens were told they had to leave these localities no later than 24 February. A second proclamation specified 7 prohibited areas in Washington and 24 in Oregon. During the first part of February, some 10,000 enemy aliens—8,000 of them Japanese—left their homes in the prohibited areas. In addition, the entire coastal strip from the Oregon border to a point 50 miles north of Los Angeles and extending 30 to 150 miles inland was declared a restricted zone, in which enemy aliens had to abide by travel restrictions and a curfew. Meanwhile, on 14 January 1942 the president authorized a compulsory registration program for all enemy aliens.

Apparently at this stage DeWitt felt that the steps being taken would be sufficient safeguard against espionage and sabotage, so he did not yet advocate mass evacuation. The attorney general and secretary of war also were not convinced such a drastic measure was necessary or practical. However, the latter's subordinates—the assistant secretary of war and the provost marshal general and his assistant—wanted all persons of Japanese ancestry, including Nisei citizens, moved out of the Pacific Coast and interned inland.

The War Department officials' effort to realize their goal was aided by politicians and nativists who launched a campaign in mid-January to get persons of Japanese ancestry incarcerated. On 16 January California congressman Leland Ford sent identical letters to the secretary of war and the attorney general to urge that "all Japanese, whether citizens or not, be placed in inland concentration camps."[8] Ford made the same proposal on the floor of the Congress four days later. Then the entire congressional delegation from Washington, Oregon, and California, as well as the Native Sons of the Golden West, the California Joint Immigration Committee (a private organization, despite its name), and other anti-Japanese groups asked Roosevelt to remove "all persons of Japanese lineage . . . *aliens and citizens alike*" [italics added] from the West Coast.[9]

The report of a committee headed by Supreme Court Justice Owen J. Roberts to investigate the destruction of Pearl Harbor, which was released in late January, also helped to fuel hostility against persons of Japanese ancestry in the United States. The Roberts report blamed the islands' army and navy commanders for the lack of preparedness that made possible Japan's attack and charged that the enemy had been greatly aided by an alleged espionage network involving many American citizens of Japanese ancestry and centered at the Japanese consulate in Honolulu. No evidence has ever been offered for these charges, which were based entirely on racist rumors.

The conclusions of the Roberts Report no doubt unnerved DeWitt, who soon drafted a statement (referred to as his "Final Recommendation") calling for the removal of all persons of Japanese ancestry on racial grounds. The Japanese were "an enemy race," declared the document, whose "racial affinities [were] not severed by migration" and whose "racial strains" remained "undiluted" even among members of the second and third generations. Therefore, because the army had no ready means to separate out the disloyal from the loyal, all persons of Japanese ancestry, regardless of their citizenship status, must be removed from the coast.

At this point a number of journalists called national attention to the issue. Walter Lippmann, the highly influential columnist, published a column on 12 February entitled "The Fifth Column on the Coast," in which he deplored the unwillingness of the federal government to remove enemy aliens from what he called a "combat zone." He declared that there was "plenty of room elsewhere" for suspect persons to exercise their rights.[10] Lippmann's column was carried in hundreds of newspapers. Another journalist, Westbrook Pegler, wrote, "The Japanese in California should be under armed guard to the last man and woman right now—and to hell with habeas corpus until the danger is over."[11]

Upon receiving DeWitt's "Final Recommendation," the army's chief of staff immediately approved it, as did all the civilian heads of the War Department. They drafted an executive order for President Roosevelt's signature that would give the army complete power to remove Japanese aliens and citizens alike from the Pacific Coast. The draft was presented to Roosevelt on the afternoon of 19 February. He signed it as Executive Order 9066 the same evening, authorizing the secretary of war to designate military areas "from which any and all persons may be excluded as deemed necessary or desirable." The next day, the secretary appointed DeWitt to carry out the order as he saw fit.

Even as DeWitt and the Western Defense Command prepared to evacuate persons of Japanese ancestry, the army reclassified most Nisei who had registered for military service first as 4-F, the category for persons unfit to serve due to physical reasons, and later as 4-C, the classification for enemy aliens. It also relegated many already in the armed forces to kitchen or other menial duty. However, the changes did not apply to Nisei and Kibei recruited to teach in the Military Intelligence Service Language School. In Hawaii, Nisei soldiers were disarmed and put to work digging ditches under armed guard following the bombing of Pearl Harbor. Nisei in the Territorial Guards were expelled. Later these men were allowed to serve their country as members of the Varsity Victory Volunteers. When manpower shortage became severe, Hawaiian Nisei were finally activated as the One Hundredth Battalion of the U.S. Army.

Local and state government units in California also took action. Los Angeles County dismissed all its clerks of Japanese ancestry at the end of January, while the California State Personnel Board announced that all descendants of enemy aliens would be barred from civil service positions, but enforced that stricture only against Japanese Americans. When the House of Representatives Select Committee Investigating National Defense Migration (commonly referred to as the Tolan Committee) held hearings on the Pacific Coast in late February and early March, anti-Japanese spokespersons fanned the flames of prejudice further.

Under the authority granted him by Executive Order 9066, at the beginning of March DeWitt proclaimed the western halves of Washington, Oregon, California, and the southern half of Arizona as Military Areas 1 and 2, from which enemy aliens of German, Italian, and Japanese ancestry, as well as all persons of Japanese ancestry, should prepare to remove themselves. In an accompanying press release, he explained that the Japanese were scheduled to leave first. As it turned out, the Italians and most Germans were never ordered to move. A week before DeWitt's first proclamation, all persons of Japanese ancestry had already been evicted from Terminal Island (off San Pedro, California) by order of the U.S. Navy. On 16 March DeWitt designated Idaho, Montana, Nevada, and Utah as Military Areas 3, 4, 5, and 6. The following week, he ordered all persons of Japanese ancestry to leave Bainbridge Island, near Seattle, Washington. To allow DeWitt to enforce his orders with criminal penalties, on 19 March Congress passed Public Law 503 by voice votes, following only a half hour's debate in the House of Representatives and an hour's discussion in the Senate. Again, without hesitation, Roosevelt signed the bill into law two days later.

During March more than 3,000 persons moved from the prohibited to the restricted zones of California, while almost 5,000 left Washington, Oregon, and California altogether. Then suddenly on 27 March DeWitt announced voluntary moves would no longer be allowed. Thereafter, the Wartime Civil Control Authority (WCCA)—a unit created within the Western Defense Command to take charge of civilian affairs—took over the forced evacuation of more than 100,000 persons of Japanese ancestry. The WCCA asked several other federal agencies to help: the Federal Security Agency was responsible for social services, the U.S. Employment Service was to help evacuees find new jobs, the Farm Security Administration was to oversee the transfer of farms owned or leased by Japanese to other operators, while the Federal Reserve Bank was to aid evacuees in disposing of their property.

None of these bureaucracies, however, was able to aid the Japanese very much. Stripped of its leadership, its liquid assets frozen, the entire community was in a state of shock. Given no more than a week to sell, store, or otherwise dispose of their property, people sold their possessions at great loss. Each family was told to take bedding and linen, toilet articles, clothes, kitchen utensils, and whatever other personal effects they could hand carry. Nothing else was allowed, and people could not even send packages to themselves through the mail. The JACL urged everyone to cooperate, so with the exception of several individuals who defied the evacuation orders, there was virtually no resistance. People quietly stood in long lines, wore tags around their necks showing the numbers assigned their families, tried to keep their children from crying, allowed themselves to be examined by medical personnel and searched by soldiers, and traveled on buses and trains (often with the blinds drawn down the windows) to unknown destinations.

Before mass evacuation got very far, it turned into an internment program, because officials in ten inland western states declared in early April that they would not welcome any Japanese. The state officials agreed to allow the federal government to move the latter into their territories only if it placed the evacuees into guarded camps and guaranteed they would be "deported" after the war ended. Under such hostile conditions, virtually all persons of Japanese ancestry were uprooted from their homes in Military Areas 1 and 2 between April and August. Because incarceration was now the goal, many people had to move twice—first to temporary assembly centers and then to more permanent so-called relocation centers. Left behind were about 800 hospital patients too sick to travel, children in orphanages, and inmates of prisons and insane asylums, and around 600 non-Japanese spouses and mixed-blood children.

Sixteen assembly centers were set up at fairgrounds, race tracks, and other facilities able to hold 5,000 persons apiece. These were located at Puyallup, Washington; Portland, Oregon; Marysville, Sacramento, Tanforan, Stockton, Turlock, Salinas, Merced, Pinedale, Fresno, Tulare, Santa Anita, Manzanar, and Pomona, California; and Mayer, Arizona. The Army Corps of Engineers also built relocation centers on federal land in desolate places: Tule Lake and Manzanar, California; Minidoka, Idaho; Heart Mountain, Wyoming; Topaz, Utah; Poston and Gila River, Arizona; Amache, Colorado; and Rohwer and Jerome, Arkansas. The smallest housed 8,000 persons, the largest 20,000, with 10,000 being the average capacity. The last batch of evacuees moved from an assembly to a relocation center at the beginning of November. While all this was taking place, the Native Sons of the Golden West filed a law suit in June 1942 (*Regan v. King*) to attempt to strip all Japanese Americans of their citizenship. Fortunately, the U.S. Court of Appeals for the Ninth Circuit eventually dismissed the suit.

Japanese residents in Alaska were also uprooted. After the United States entered the war, the Alaska Defense Command was incorporated into the Western Defense Command and Alaska was designated as a combat zone. All persons of "Japanese race of greater than half blood"—fewer than 200 persons—were excluded from certain military areas and removed to the United States.

Though Hawaii was in much greater danger of being attacked and martial law was declared immediately following the bombing of Pearl Harbor, no mass evacuation of the 150,000 Japanese took place there, because to have removed them, when they comprised 37 percent of the islands' total population and an even larger proportion of its skilled labor force, would have disrupted the islands' economy too much and would, moreover, have tied up too many ships.

Once the Japanese were in the relocation camps, the War Relocation Authority (WRA), created by Roosevelt on 18 March 1942, took over supervision of the internees, though the army retained control over the camps. In addition to the civil servants who staffed it, the WRA hired Nisei to assist in a variety of capacities. Regardless of the degree of skill needed in a job, however, internees received wages ranging from only $12 to $19 a month. WRA officials especially favored members of the JACL, some of whom informed on their fellow internees in order to curry favor for themselves.

Camps were divided into blocks, each with fourteen barracks subdivided into apartments. Hastily constructed with green lumber and tar paper and unfinished on the inside, the barracks developed cracks in their walls when the lumber began to dry. Since the camps were located in semideserts, sand seeped through the cracks into the apartments whenever the wind blew. Summers were blistering hot, while winters were freezing cold. An average apartment housing a family of four to six persons measured 20 feet by 25 feet, was heated by a single stove, and was furnished only with army cots and straw mattresses. Internees used communal bathrooms with no partitions—a fact that caused some of the women great discomfort. They ate in mess halls in shifts. Complaints about food were rampant. To make their living conditions more tolerable, the more enterprising internees scrounged for scrap lumber and whatever else they could find, with which they constructed makeshift furniture.

Even more troubling than the poor food and unpleasant physical environment was the fact that the internees' families started to disintegrate, as Daisuke Kitagawa, Charles Kikuchi, Jeanne Wakatsuki Houston, and Yoshiko Uchida have documented.[12] The status and authority of the Issei fathers, whose average age was 55 in 1942, began to erode once they lost their role as breadwinners. The older Nisei, especially those earning salaries or who were block leaders, on the other hand, all of a sudden acquired independence and power. The younger children often preferred to eat meals with their friends rather than with their families and ran around the camps out of their parents' sight and control. More important, WRA policy with regard to education and social life helped to widen the cultural gulf between the Issei parents and their Nisei children: Japanese language schools and the practice of Shintoism were forbidden, while Euro-American teachers and WRA staff in the camps assiduously promoted Americanization. Political judgment and official policy now served to underpin the intense and almost desperate desire of Nisei to be accepted as Americans.

Internees were allowed to leave the camps only under very limited conditions. During 1942 some 9,000 evacuees left camp for short periods to help harvest crops. A National Japanese American Student Relocation Council aided about 250 college students whose studies had been interrupted to enroll in midwestern institutions for the fall term of 1942. In time, the council placed several thousand Nisei students, but only in colleges and universities where no war-related research was being done. And of the eligible institutions of higher learning, not all were willing to accept Japanese American students.

Those internees who wished to rejoin the outside world had to fill out a leave clearance form, which was carefully screened by WRA officials with the aid of the FBI to determine whether letting them out would endanger "national security" or the war effort. Individuals could apply for short-term leaves of thirty days or less to attend to urgent personal business, or work leaves to perform seasonal farm labor, or indefinite leave for permanent resettlement. Those in the last category had to demonstrate their ability to support themselves and to promise to report any change of address. Persons whose requests were granted received leave permits, but these were revocable at any time.

Within a few months of being moved into the camps, some internees began to show resentment against their lot. As Arthur Hansen and his associates, Gary Okihiro, Dorothy Thomas and her collaborators, and Douglas Nelson have shown, they dealt with the situation in a variety of ways.[13] First, some held demonstrations and engaged in strikes to protest the more repressive aspects of camp life. These incidents reflected the deep divisions within the internee population—divisions based on both social and political differences. The most fundamental cleavage was between Kibei and Issei, who were proud of their Japanese heritage and who deeply resented the injustice of their incarceration, on the one hand, and, on the other, Nisei—particularly leaders of the JACL—who wanted so badly to be accepted as Americans that they acted as the U.S. government's most ardent apologists.

A second set of responses developed in reaction to the army's decision to allow Nisei to serve. These ranged from outright refusal to register to eager acceptance of the chance to prove their loyalty in blood. Third, four individuals, who understood fully the meaning of the civil rights that all Americans are supposed to enjoy, doggedly used the legal system to challenge the constitutionality of the evacuation and internment. Finally, thousands of internees either requested repatriation to Japan or renounced their U.S. citizenship, as a way to show how they felt about a country that had rejected them.

The first large-scale protest occurred in Poston, Arizona, in November 1942, after camp police hauled in 50 persons for questioning and detained two of them as suspects in the beating of a Kibei. Family members of the suspects and representatives of the blocks where they lived insisted to camp authorities that the two men were innocent and requested that they be discharged. When the officials refused to comply, a crowd of 2,500 gathered and demanded their release. The authorities ignored this demand, whereupon an emergency committee of 72 persons called a general strike for the next day. Since many of the jobs in the camp were filled by the internees themselves, all but the most essential activities came to a halt. The strike lasted five days and ended only after the camp administrators and strikers reached agreement on important issues related to camp governance. Charges against one of the prisoners were dropped, while the second man was released pending his trial.

A more serious outbreak occurred in Manzanar, California, in early December. Unidentified assailants beat up Fred Tayama—a JACL leader who had turned over names of pro-Japan Issei and Kibei to the FBI—so badly that he had to be hospitalized. The camp police arrested several Kibei, among them Harry Ueno, who had tried to organize a Kitchen Workers' Union to obtain better working conditions. In response, more than 3,000 people held a demonstration. A delegation of five persons then presented the group's grievances to the camp director, as a crowd of 1,000 milled about, surrounded by armed military police. The crowd soon disbanded, but reassembled that evening in front of the jail. Soldiers on guard duty asked the protestors to disperse, but the latter ignored the orders. The soldiers then threw tear gas canisters and fired their rifles into the crowd, killing 2 internees and wounding at least 10 others. Angry internees beat up several persons branded as "informers" that night and threatened their family members. The next morning, camp police arrested the leaders of the protest and took them to an isolation camp at Moab, Utah. These individuals were later moved to Leupp, Arizona. In addition 65 JACL members were removed for their own safety. The army arrived and put Manzanar under martial law for more than a month.

In Topaz, Utah, a less violent but nevertheless telling incident took place during the spring of 1943. There, an old man was shot to death by a sentry as he walked toward the camp's barbed wire fence and did not stop when ordered to do so. No one witnessed the shooting but an autopsy showed that the man had been shot in his chest while facing the guard tower. The internees held a mass funeral to honor the memory of the deceased and to make a silent but eloquent statement about what they thought of the callousness of those who exercised power over them.

Far more complex, troubling, and explosive than these incidents at individual camps was internee reaction in all ten camps to the army's decision at the beginning of 1943 to induct Americans of Japanese ancestry into an all-Japanese combat team. Internees found the procedures set up to screen individuals for this purpose to be especially objectionable. The WRA, which had been trying to work out for some time a more efficient system for leave clearance, now combined efforts with the army to devise a questionnaire to separate the "loyal" from the "disloyal." Between early February and late March, all American citizens of Japanese ancestry and aliens over age seventeen, except those who had already requested repatriation to Japan, were required to fill out a Selective Service questionnaire as well as a WRA questionnaire. Both contained two "loyalty" questions.

Both questionnares asked male citizens, "Are you willing to serve in the armed forces of the United States on combat duty, wherever ordered?" and, "Will you swear unqualified allegiance to the United States of America and faithfully defend the United States from any or all attacks by foreign or domestic forces, and forswear any form of allegiance or obedience to the Japanese Emperor or any other foreign government, power or organization?" The WRA form for female citizens and aliens of both sexes inquired, "If the opportunity presents itself and you are found qualified, would you be willing to volunteer for the Army Nurse Corps or the W.A.C.?" while the second question was similar to that answered by male citizens. However, as soon as officials started helping people to fill out these forms, they realized that the second question, as worded, was inappropriate for aliens, who would become stateless persons if they forswore allegiance to Japan. So on the forms for aliens, officials hastily changed the question to read, "Will you swear to abide by the laws of the United States and to take no action which would in any way interfere with the war effort of the United States?" Those who wished to enlist had to fill out yet additional forms. At first, the army accepted only citizens. Several months later, it announced it would also take "loyal" aliens and make it possible for them to apply for citizenship, the existing naturalization laws notwithstanding.

The registration drive created real dilemmas for the camps' residents and split many families further apart. Answering yes to the question about forswearing allegiance to the Japanese emperor implied that one held such allegiance in the first place. A vast majority of the Nisei felt no attachment to Japan whatsoever and refused to be so impugned. On the other hand, by answering yes to both questions they became eligible for the draft. Many individuals resented being asked to serve a country whose government had imprisoned them and their families in concentration camps. Especially offensive was the fact that should they be inducted, they would be placed in a segregated unit. Some worried about what would happen to their aged parents, who had now been stripped of their possessions and had few remaining means of survival. Many Issei begged or cajoled their American-born children to answer no to both questions, as a means to keep their families together in a time of extreme uncertainty. Before registration began, over 3,000 individuals—mostly Issei and Kibei—had applied for repatriation or expatriation to Japan. As a result of the tensions engendered by registration, by the beginning of 1945 more than 20,000 persons—almost 7,000 foreign-born and over 13,000 American-born—had done so.

Altogether, 78,000 individuals were required to register—20,000 of them male Nisei between the ages of 17 and 37 subject to the draft. Over 4,000 of the latter refused to answer the two questions or gave negative or qualified answers. The percentage of internees registering and the proportion of affirmative versus negative answers varied considerably in the different camps, depending on how the WRA officials and army representatives dealt with the situation, as well as on the internal political dynamics among the internees at particular camps. The relocation centers at Minidoka, Idaho, and Tule Lake, California, represented two extremes in terms of internee reaction.[14]

Registration proceeded quietly and took less than a month at Minidoka, where the army and WRA authorities answered questions as forthrightly as they could and stressed that reinstating Selective Service procedures for Nisei was the first step towards the eventual restoration of other civil rights. Only 9 percent of the internees at Minidoka gave negative answers to the loyalty questions, and over 300 young men—a quarter of the volunteers from all the camps combined—were inducted.

Tule Lake was a different story. There, the WRA officials did not answer questions clearly and told the internees that only the army team due to visit the camp could do so. But this team did not arrive until the day before registration was scheduled to begin. Furthermore, the authorities at Tule Lake acted tough: they read the Espionage Act to the residents on several occasions and threatened those who refused to register with severe penalties—a $10,000 fine, 20 years in jail, or both. When internees tried to apply for repatriation or expatriation, the officials refused to take their petitions. They also called in the military police to arrest several young men who had demanded that their applications be accepted. MPs carrying machine guns and bayonets hauled the dissidents off to the county jail.

Efforts by the camp's JACL leaders, whom most internees distrusted enough as it was, to encourage voluntary enlistment also backfired. Rumors spread that it was the JACL that had pushed for registration in the first place. Three JACL leaders received anonymous threats, angry internees made plans for a general strike, and a delegation was chosen to negotiate with WRA officials to get the imprisoned men released.

Tule Lake's population polarized into those who favored cooperation and those who advocated resistance. The latter branded the former *inu* (literally "dog," but meaning "traitor") and threatened them. Several alleged inu, including a Christian minister, were beaten up. Resisters also circulated petitions, the signers of which swore not to register at all. At this point the WRA called in the FBI for help.

The FBI agents, after carefully scrutinizing the Selective Service Act, informed Tule Lake's WRA project director that mere refusal to fill out the questionnaire was not a violation of the act. But instead of conveying this information to the internees, the director instructed the camp police to continue arresting those who refused to register and charged them with violating WRA regulations, which carried a maximum penalty of ninety days in jail, a suspension of wages, or both. Taken aback by the stiff opposition at Tule Lake and several other camps, the WRA national office now decided that registration of female citizens and aliens of both sexes was no longer compulsory, but Tule Lake's director again kept this information from the internees.

As news of the resistance to registration leaked out, hostile public reaction developed, calling for punishment of the "disloyals." In July 1943 Congress passed a bill enabling the WRA to segregate them. Since the largest contingent of such persons was at Tule Lake, it was designated as the segregation center. Five categories of individuals were placed into Tule Lake: aliens who had requested repatriation to Japan; American citizens who desired to renounce their citizenship—even though there existed no procedure for doing so until July 1944—and requested expatriation to Japan; "disloyals" answering no; persons held in Justice Department camps who wished to join their families; and "old Tuleans" who did not wish to move yet one more time. There were about 6,000 persons in the last category, many of them people with large families containing small children. In September more than 6,000 "loyal" Tuleans moved out to other centers, while 12,000 "disloyal" persons from the other nine centers (both figures include family members) moved in. Thus Tule Lake now had 18,000 inhabitants cramped into facilities meant for 12,000.

Overt signs of repression immediately appeared. The army brought in an entire batallion and several outdated but prominently displayed tanks to guard Tule Lake and erected an eight-foot-high double "manproof" fence around its perimeter. Tuleans were denied leave privileges except under the most stringent conditions. However, the WRA allowed them to set up Japanese language schools and to participate in Japanese ceremonies in recognition of the fact that they had chosen "the Japanese way."

Two accidents that took place in October 1943 then ignited the underlying political, physical, and psychological tensions and culminated in the imposition of martial law. On 13 October a fire truck overturned, seriously wounding three of the 13 internee firemen riding in it. Two days later, a farm truck carrying 29 workers also overturned, bruising everyone and seriously injuring five who were pinned under the vehicle. One of the injured soon died. As news of the second accident spread, all 800 workers on Tule Lake's 2,900-acre farm, which grew produce to supply the camp as well as the military, decided to stop working until the authorities agreed to guarantee the workers' safety and compensated the injured workers and the family of the dead man adequately.

Block managers voted to support the farmworkers, while residents elected a 64-member committee to represent them in negotiations with the WRA officials. This large committee, in turn, selected a seven-man negotiating team to meet with the administration. They drew up a list of grievances and proposed remedies. These included demands for improved living conditions, better access to WRA officials, genuine community government, a clarification of the status of Tule Lake residents, a request for visits by the Spanish consul (who acted as a channel of communications between the Tokyo government and Japanese nationals in the United States during the war, in the absence of diplomatic relations between Japan and the United States), and fair compensation for the injured.

The internees held an elaborate outdoor public funeral for the dead man, even though the camp's director had denied permission for such an event.

Their sense of persecution grew when the U.S. Employment Compensation Commission announced that the widow of the deceased would receive a routine compensation equal to two-thirds the dead man's monthly salary. Calculated according to the meager wages paid by the WRA to interned workers, the sum came to only approximately $10. Then, when the WRA brought in people from other camps to harvest the crops on the Tule Lake farm at the wage of a dollar an *hour* (compared to internee farmworkers' wage of $16 a *month*) and fed the "strike breakers" with rations intended for Tule Lake's kitchens, the antagonism to the WRA stiffened. On 2 November Dillon Myer, WRA's national director, joined Tule Lake's director to talk to the negotiating committee. Two nights later a scuffle broke out between the camp's chief of internal security and several internees, whereupon the camp's director called in the army. Nine days after that, unable to quell the unrest, the army declared martial law, which remained in effect until mid-January 1944. The arrest of dissident leaders continued. The total number of persons put into a special stockade in one corner of the camp, imprisoned in the county jail, and sent to the isolation camp at Leupp rose to about 300. Conditions in the stockade were deplorable. Even though it was getting very cold, prisoners were sheltered only in tents. In protest, on 31 December stockade prisoners began a hunger strike, but to no avail. As the resistance was broken step by step, many of the internees who had participated in the work stoppage grudgingly returned to work because they found it difficult to continue without their wages, meager as they were. The WRA and the army also took the opportunity to weed out "trouble makers" by refusing to reinstate those thus identified. Work at the farm did not resume until spring.

Given the poor internee showing during registration, when only 1,200 Nisei volunteered for service (triple that number had been expected), the Selective Service reintroduced the draft for Japanese Americans at the beginning of 1944. To its surprise, this effort also met with resistance, especially at the camp in Heart Mountain, Wyoming.[15] Led by the Heart Mountain Fair Play Committee, formed by Kiyoshi Okamoto, a Nisei from Hawaii, and encouraged by the editorials of James Omura, editor of the *Rocky Shimpo*, a Japanese newspaper published in Denver, dozens of Nisei defied the draft orders.

At the beginning of March, 12 inductees refused to board buses to go to their physicals. In response, the director at Heart Mountain had 54 who had failed to appear for their induction arrested. Several religious leaders tried to persuade the draft resisters to comply, but they succeeded in getting only one of the 54 to change his mind. More significantly, 10 more individuals decided to join the ranks of the resisters. All these young men had answered yes to the two loyalty questions during registration and were thus deemed loyal. They insisted that they were resisting the draft out of patriotism: as good Americans, they felt morally obliged to challenge unconstitutional acts.

A federal grand jury nonetheless indicted them in May. They were tried in June and each of the 63 was sentenced to three years' imprisonment. Their attorneys appealed on the grounds that they had not acted out of malicious intent; rather, they were simply trying to get their status as internees clarified. Moreover, he pointed out, they had been deprived of their freedom without due process of law. The U.S. Court of Appeals for the Tenth Circuit, however, upheld the convictions in March 1945. Subsequently another 22 draft resisters from Heart Mountain were arrested, indicted, convicted, and jailed, making a total of 85.

Meanwhile, the Alien Property Custodian seized the files of the *Rocky Shimpo* and fired all the newspaper's staff. James Omura and seven leaders of the Fair Play Committee were arrested and indicted. The seven committee members were convicted and sentenced, but they were freed a year later when the circuit court decided that the judge in the district court had improperly instructed the jury. But Omura, accused of conspiracy—even though he never met the others until their joint arrest—was found not guilty.

In contrast to these various kinds of resisters, many Nisei eagerly grasped the chance offered by military service to prove their loyalty—in blood, if necessary—to the country of their birth. Approximately 25,000 Nisei served in the military during the war. The first and least-publicized group was trained at the Army's Military Intelligence Service Language School (MISLS). Established in November with temporary headquarters in San Francisco, this institution was moved first to Camp Savage and then to Fort Snelling in Minnesota. It trained 6,000 individuals, 3,700 of whom saw service in combat zones. To their dismay, MISLS instructors discovered that few Nisei knew Japanese well enough to translate and decode captured documents or to interpret for and interrogate prisoners. Ironically, it was the mistrusted Japan-educated Kibei who proved most valuable. Large numbers of MISLS graduates—working for the U.S. Army, Navy, and Marines, as well as within units of Allied forces— were stationed in Australia, India, Burma, China, and Hawaii. A few also served in the Pentagon in Washington, D.C. These men followed Allied troops into New Guinea, the Marianas, the Philippines, and Okinawa—all of which had been occupied by Japanese forces—to interrogate captured Japanese soldiers and to translate Japanese-language documents.[16]

Another group of Nisei who saw military service was the One Hundredth Battalion, made up largely of individuals expelled from the Hawaii Territorial Guard soon after Pearl Harbor. Although the War Department wanted to discharge the Hawaiian Nisei, the commanding general in Hawaii chose to retain them. He placed them into a separate battalion, which was sent to Camp McCoy, Wisconsin, and Camp Shelby, Mississippi, for training. The battalion departed for North Africa in September 1943. From there they proceeded to Italy, where they were joined by the third group of Nisei recruited for combat duty—the 442nd Regimental Combat Team, whose members came out of the mainland concentration camps and were trained at Camp Shelby. In June 1944 the 100th formally merged with the 442nd in central Italy, whence it proceeded to France. Its bloodiest engagement came when it was sent to save a "lost" battalion of Texans near Bruyeres, during which the 442nd suffered 800 casualties in a week. The total casualties at the end of this campaign numbered above 2,000, with 140 dead.

The 442nd gained fame as the most decorated unit of its size during World War II. It received seven Presidential Distinguished Unit Citations, while its members earned more than 18,000 individual decorations, including a Congressional Medal of Honor, 47 Distinguished Service Crosses, 350 Silver Stars, 810 Bronze Stars, and more than 3,600 Purple Hearts. But it paid dearly in lives for such honor, suffering almost 9,500 casualties (300 percent of its original

*Japanese American veterans of the 442ⁿᵈ Regimental Combat Team.*
Courtesy Katsuji Uranaka and Kats Nakamura

strength), including 600 killed. In all, 18,000 Nisei served in this unit during the war. Their exploits, publicized in newsreels and newspaper headlines, did a great deal to reduce, though not to erase, the prejudice against Japanese Americans, as President Harry S. Truman himself noted when he added the Presidential Unit banner to their regimental colors.[17]

During the same period that these visible forms of protest took place, a number of individuals fought a quieter but equally significant battle. Minoru Yasui, Gordon Hirabayashi, and Fred Korematsu challenged the constitutionality of the curfew and evacuation orders, while Mitsuye Endo questioned the WRA's right to keep her under custody. The history of their cases has been analyzed most fully by Jacobus tenBroek and Peter Irons.[18]

Yasui, a Methodist by upbringing, a second lieutenant in the U.S. Army Infantry Reserve, and a graduate of the University of Oregon Law School, immediately resigned his job with the Japanese consulate in Chicago when war broke out and returned to his native Oregon, where he attempted eight times to enlist for military service, despite the fact that his father, a leader of the Japanese immigrant community in Hood River, was taken to Fort Missoula to be interned. But the induction center at Fort Vancouver turned him down every time. When DeWitt put a stop to voluntary relocation and imposed a curfew on all persons of Japanese ancestry in late March, Yasui decided to test the constitutionality of the curfew order. Since no other citizens were similarly restricted, he felt it was discriminatory.

On 28 March 1942, the first day the curfew was in force, Yasui walked around the streets of Portland for hours trying to get himself arrested, but to no avail. Finally he went to a police station and insisted that he be detained. The grand jury indicted him in April and the federal district court tried him in June 1942. The judge who sentenced him in November ruled that the curfew was unconstitutional if applied to citizens. At the same time, however, he decided Yasui was guilty. In the judge's eyes, by working for the Japanese consulate and registering himself as an agent of a foreign government, Yasui had lost his citizenship and was thereby an enemy alien liable for criminal penalties for violating the curfew. Yasui received a sentence of one year's imprisonment. His attorneys appealed, but instead of hearing the case, the U.S. Court of Appeals for the Ninth Circuit certified it in March 1943 for review—along with the other three Japanese American test cases—by the U.S. Supreme Court.

Hirabayashi, a senior at the University of Washington and a Quaker who had received conscientious objector status before the war began, also deliberately violated the curfew and refused to report for evacuation when ordered to do so on 16 May 1942. He felt that having been born and educated as an American citizen, he should not be denied the privileges of citizenship on account of his racial origins. The grand jury in Seattle, however, indicted him for violating the curfew and for failure to report for evacuation.

Hirabayashi sat in jail for five months before he was tried in October 1942. He went through a full jury trial, at the end of which the judge sentenced him to one month's imprisonment for each count, the two sentences to run consecutively. Hirabayashi did not wish to spend any more time in jail, however, so he requested that he be sentenced to *three* months—the minimum term that would allow him to serve outdoors at a federal road camp. The judge agreed to let him do so and decided that the sentences could run concurrently. Hirabayashi's lawyers appealed, but the circuit court also declined to rule on it and likewise certified it for U.S. Supreme Court review.

Korematsu was a welder living in San Leandro, California. The navy had rejected him when he tried to enlist in June 1941, and he was dismissed from his job after the war began. He evaded evacuation because he wanted to remain with his non-Japanese girlfriend. He even used a false name on his draft card and underwent plastic surgery to change his features to conceal his identity. Beyond these personal concerns, however, he was also determined to fight the evacuation because he believed it was wrong.

Korematsu did not remain at large for long: the FBI found and arrested him on 30 May 1942. He was indicted for remaining in San Leandro and was tried and convicted in September, but the judge who heard his case placed him on probation for five years and refused to sentence him, which raised the question whether the case could be appealed. Though Korematsu was released on bail, as soon as he stepped out of the courtroom, military police rearrested him and forcibly took him to Tanforan Assembly Center. In certifying these cases, the circuit court asked the Supreme Court to deliberate the constitutionality of Public Law 503, which specified a penalty for those who disobeyed the army's evacuation orders, and DeWitt's curfew orders in the Hirabayashi case, the question of citizenship in the Yasui case, and the appealability of a probationary sentence in the Korematsu case. When the Supreme Court heard Hirabayashi's case, his lawyers argued that Public Law 503 unlawfully delegated legislative power to DeWitt and was so vaguely worded that it offered the general no clear guidelines in formulating his military orders. The U.S. solicitor general, responding on behalf of the government, said that the main issue in these cases was the power of the government to wage war successfully; that ability, in his view, was more important than the due process rights of citizens. Agreeing with the solicitor general, the justices unanimously upheld Public Law 503 so far as Hirabayashi's curfew violation was concerned, but they eschewed any pronouncement on the more sensitive issue of whether the evacuation itself was constitutional. They declared that since Hirabayashi's two sentences were concurrent, it was unnecessary to rule on the latter question.

Yasui's lawyers focused on the claim that neither Executive Order 9066 nor Public Law 503 authorized DeWitt to single out American citizens of Japanese ancestry for curfew and evacuation. By so doing, they pointed out, Yasui had been deprived of equal protection under the law. But the U.S. solicitor general once again stressed that the military must have "reasonable discretion" during wartime and that the Japanese, being nonassimilable, could not be trusted to be loyal. The government's lawyers conceded that the district court judge had erred in deciding that Yasui had lost his citizenship by virtue of his employment at the Japanese consulate, but the justices sustained Yasui's conviction for curfew violation, thus upholding the constitutionality of the evacuation. They sent his case back to the lower court, however, so that it could strike its findings on his loss of citizenship.

In the Korematsu case, the court decided that a probationary sentence was appealable, so they also returned it to the lower court for a rehearing. At the beginning of December 1943 the circuit court unanimously upheld Korematsu's conviction, but Korematsu's lawyer petitioned to have it retried by the U.S. Supreme Court. The high court considered the case for the second time in October 1944, at the same time that it heard the Mitsuye Endo case.

The Endo case differed from those of Yasui and Hirabayaski because it did not begin on her own initiative. Endo had lost her clerical job at the Department of Motor Vehicles when the California State Personnel Board dismissed all its employees of Japanese ancestry. The JACL national president persuaded a Sacramento lawyer to help the affected workers without fee. But before this lawyer could do anything, most of the dismissed workers were evacuated. A visit to those held at Tanforan Assembly Center so disturbed him—he thought the place had all the characteristics of a prison—that he decided to file a test case on behalf of someone willing to challenge his or her detention. After reviewing dozens of files, he picked Endo as an ideal plaintiff with all-American characteristics. She was a Methodist, did not speak any Japanese, had never visited Japan, and had a brother serving in the army.

Endo filed a writ of habeas corpus in July 1942, challenging the right of the government to prevent her from going home to California. The district court, however, failed to hand down a ruling for almost a year. Endo, meanwhile, remained behind barbed wire at Tule Lake Relocation Center. After the Supreme Court acted in the other three test cases, the district court judge had no more excuse to delay a decision. On 3 July 1943 he dismissed Endo's petition. Her lawyers then worked feverishly to attempt to get the case to the U.S. Supreme Court before it adjourned for that session.

The high court held off a decision for almost a year and a half because of complex maneuvers undertaken by both the plaintiff's attorneys and the American Civil Liberties Union (ACLU), on the one hand, and by lawyers representing the federal government, on the other. Moreover, President Roosevelt himself instructed his subordinates not to do anything final about the relocation program until after the November elections in order not to jeopardize his chances of being reelected to a fourth term, even though his staff had repeatedly told him from late 1943 onward that there was no longer any military necessity to keep the Japanese behind barbed wires.

During a second hearing in the Supreme Court, Korematsu's lawyers claimed that no real military necessity existed for evacuation and exclusion. They also argued that evacuation led inescapably to detention. They pointed out that DeWitt had issued two conflicting orders—one that forbade persons of Japanese ancestry to remain in the excluded areas and another that prohibited them from voluntary outmigration after 27 March 1942—which meant that the only alternative that Korematsu and others like him had was to allow themselves to be taken to an assembly or relocation center. The solicitor general, once again representing the government, stressed that if evacuation led to detention, it was done with a good purpose in mind. It was, according to him, a form of preventive detention or protective custody, undertaken to protect persons of Japanese ancestry from hostile public reception and to prevent potential racial outbreaks in society at large.

In the end, the justices upheld the evacuation order 6 to 3. They further stated that it was unnecessary to rule on the issue of detention in the Korematsu case, because on the same day they had reached a decision on the Endo case, declaring that she should be "unconditionally" granted her liberty—that is, without having to go through the WRA's leave clearance procedures. Unlike the Korematsu decision, over which the justices had profound disagreements, the Endo decision was unanimous. Even the solicitor general had conceded that Public Law 503 did not authorize the detention of "loyal" persons such as Endo who had not been charged with any crime.

In all four test cases, the justices rested their decisions on the narrowest legal grounds and failed to address the fundamental constitutional issues raised by the internment for a number of reasons, as Peter Irons has shown unequivocally.[19] For one thing, the government's lawyers concealed from the Supreme Court important analyses done by the FBI and the Federal Communications Commission—based on these agencies' own investigations—that General DeWitt's claims of Japanese American espionage and sabotage activities were simply unfounded. At the same time, the national board of the ACLU, whose lawyers played important roles in the four cases, made a policy decision not to attack the constitutionality of Executive Order 9066 out of loyalty to Franklin Delano Roosevelt. Finally, conflicts within various agencies of the federal government itself, and the sense of institutional loyalty certain individuals felt towards their agencies, forced some of them to acquiesce to decisions that their own consciences deplored.

A final form of resistance available to Japanese Americans was renunciation

of their American citizenship. The United States, however, had no denational-
ization law in its statute books. So in December 1943 Martin Dies, chairman of
the House Select Committee to Investigate Un-American Activities, summoned
the U.S. attorney general before his committee to ask how this might be done.
The latter responded that Congress would have to pass a law to make such an
act possible. Congress did so on 1 July 1944, and Roosevelt immediately signed
it into law. The willingness of the nation's lawmakers and president to so act
can be attributed in part, at least, to the long history of exclusionary sentiments
that most Americans have harbored toward Asians. What could be better than
for those already in the country to sever ties and to "go back"—a misnomer,
since most of them had never been there—to the land of their parents?

The Justice Department received over 6,000 applications for renunciation,
almost 5,600 of which it approved. As war drew to a close, however, many of
these individuals wrote the Justice Department asking to withdraw their petitions. After the war ended, San Francisco lawyer Wayne Collins, who had
defended Korematsu, filed two suits on behalf of 4,322 renunciants in an effort
to regain their citizenship, arguing that they had acted under duress and coercion. The federal district court in San Francisco issued a temporary injunction
to stop their deportation and in April 1948 canceled their renunciation and
declared them U.S. citizens. The federal government appealed but eventually
decided to rescind the outstanding orders against the 302 renunciants still
being held in its internment camps, whereupon Collins petitioned for a dismissal of the unsettled suits on the grounds that the cancellation had rendered
the issue moot. His petition was granted, but the renunciants did not regain
their citizenship.

At war's end in August 1945, 44,000 persons of Japanese ancestry were still
in camp, even though the federal government had revoked the mass exclusion
orders in December 1944. This population was so large because the dispossessed people had no place to go and were fearful of the hostile outside world.
But they were forcibly pushed back into a society that did not want them.
Those lucky enough to have children or other relatives who had resettled in the
Midwest or the East Coast joined them, while less fortunate ones received
nothing more than train fare to the locations where they had lived before the
war. Those who still owned property found their homes dilapidated and vandalized, their farms, orchards, and vineyards choked with weeds, their personal
belongings stolen or destroyed. Others with nothing left were sheltered for a
time by churches and a few social agencies as they looked for ways to eke out a
living. Issei men, now in their sixties, found work as gardeners and janitors;
their wives toiled as domestic servants. Despite such harsh circumstances, these
old pioneers picked up the broken pieces of their lives and carried on as their
children struggled to join postwar mainstream America.[20]

Several developments aided the second-generation Asian Americans' efforts.[21] At least half of the veterans of Japanese, Chinese, and Filipino ancestry
made use of the GI bill to get college educations or to buy homes. The rise in
the number of college graduates within the Asian-ancestry population, as well
as the slow but noticeable removal of racial barriers in certain sectors of the
labor market, which allowed some professionals to get jobs, made it possible
for a small middle class to emerge within Asian American communities. These
people wanted homes outside of the ethnic ghettos, and they persisted in their

efforts to buy them. Thus, although realtors often refused to sell them houses in "good" neighborhoods, the veterans did pioneer in integrating sections of various towns and cities.

Buying homes of their own was especially important because the 1945 War Brides Act, which had initially excluded veterans of Asian ancestry, was amended in 1947 to include them. That fact enabled Asian GIs to marry in Asia and to bring their brides back to the United States, where they started families. From the late 1940s through the 1950s and the first half of the 1960s, the number of Asian women entering the country exceeded the number of men.[22]

Wives of American servicemen fall roughly into two categories: those who married coethnics and those who married non-Asians. Chinese women were the main group admitted under the War Brides Act. The more than 6,000 who so entered married mainly Chinese American men and settled in metropolitan areas of the East and West coasts. During the 1950s, women made up 50 percent to 90 percent of the Chinese entries during particular years. Their presence pushed the skewed sex ratio of the Chinese-ancestry population closer to normalcy—it became 1.3:1 by 1960.

Japanese, Korean, and Filipina wives of GIs, on the other hand, more often than not married non-Asian men. They entered not as war brides but as non-quota immigrants (i.e., spouses of U.S. citizens) under the terms of the 1952 McCarran-Walter Act. The number of Japanese women admitted as dependents of U.S. citizens was largest until the early 1970s. American troops occupied Japan immediately after World War II; later, during the Korean and Vietnam wars, many went there for rest and recreation. In the 1950s the annual immigration of Japanese women ranged from 2,000 to 5,000 (comprising 80 percent of all Japanese immigrants); their number averaged 2,500 per year in the 1960s, declining to about 1,500 per year in the 1970s. These Japanese women went to live in the hometowns of their husbands all over the United States.

Korean women also started coming as a result of the American military presence in their homeland. American troops fought in Korea during the Korean War (1950–53); after armistice was declared, the United States continued to station more than 40,000 troops in the Republic of Korea (South Korea) until 1990, when the secretary of defense announced a small reduction. From 1953 to the end of the decade, almost 500 Korean women arrived annually as GI wives. They averaged about 1,500 a year in the 1960s and about 2,300 in the 1970s. Children, often of mixed parentage, adopted by American families also added to the Korean influx. There were more girls than boys among these youngsters. Women and girls represented more than 70 percent of all Korean immigrants in the 1950s and 1960s.

Filipinas likewise have entered as wives of American servicemen—including a sizable number of Filipino Americans serving in the U.S. Navy—stationed at major naval and air bases maintained by the United States in the Philippines or visiting the country on leave. In the late 1950s approximately 1,000 Filipinas a year immigrated as U.S. dependents; that number rose to an annual average of 1,500 in the 1960s and shot up to over 4,000 a year in the 1970s.

The entry of so many childbearing-age women led to a rapid rise in the number of Asian American as well as mixed-parentage Amerasian children.

When the women first arrived in the late 1940s and early 1950s, it was still well-nigh impossible for them and those husbands who were Asians to find housing outside the ethnic ghettos. Thus, for a time, the tenements in the Asian enclaves of major cities, which had up to then housed mainly single men, were occupied by entire families, all packed into one- or two-room apartments, many of which had only communal bathrooms and makeshift kitchens.

Political refugees comprised yet another group of Asians who came in under special legislation during the 1950s and 1960s. When a Communist government came to power in China in 1949, about 5,000 Chinese college and graduate students then studying in the United States sought political asylum.[23] The U.S. State Department allowed them to adjust their visa status, thereby enabling some of China's brightest intellectuals, most of them from well-to-do families, to remain in the country. These men and women sought work in universities, research laboratories, and private industries, bought homes in the suburbs, and had little to do with the old-time Chinese immigrants except for occasional meals in and shopping trips to the various Chinatowns of America. An additional 2,000 Chinese refugees came in under the 1953 Refugee Act, while the acts passed in 1957 and 1959 let in another 1,000. Between 1962 and 1967, 15,000 entered under the terms of a presidential directive signed by John F. Kennedy in 1962. The influx of some 23,000 highly educated and well-trained Chinese refugees greatly augmented the ranks of the Chinese American middle class.

The United States was willing to open its doors a crack because the cold war was on. Perceiving itself as the leader of the "Free World," the United States competed with the Communist bloc of countries for power and influence in the rest of the world. At the height of the cold war, refugee engineers were especially welcomed. After the Soviet Union successfully launched the first satellite into space, the United States tried hard to catch up.

Though Chinese American engineers and other professionals were admitted, it did not mean that they were let alone. The country's anticommunist paranoia found expression in the investigations of a subcommittee of the Senate Committee on Governmental Operations, chaired by Senator Joseph McCarthy; the House Un-American Activities Committee, chaired at various times by Congressmen Martin Dies, John Rankin, and Jay Parnell Thomas; the Senate Internal Security Subcommittee, chaired by Senator Pat McCarran; and the surveillance activities of the FBI. Individuals of Chinese ancestry were among those over whom the FBI kept watch: FBI director J. Edgar Hoover believed that Communist agents were slipping into the country under various guises. The Immigration and Naturalization Service (INS) attempted to deport suspects or, failing that, tried to "denaturalize" them. Meanwhile, agents of the government of the Republic of China on Taiwan, themselves full of anticommunist fervor, aided the U.S. government's efforts in order to silence dissenters or critics of the Nationalist regime.

While Chinese Americans were intimidated into silence and political inaction, Japanese Americans began their comeback into American society. As Japan became the most reliable ally of the United States in eastern Asia, the public perception of Japanese Americans grew more favorable. This change enabled the JACL to rise to even greater prominence. That organization lobbied hard to get an Evacuation Claims Act passed in 1948. Under it, at the end of more than a decade of litigation, a token 137 claims were settled, averaging $450 each. A more significant victory won by the JACL was the inclusion of a clause in the 1952 McCarran-Walter Act to allow Issei to be naturalized and to grant Japanese an immigration quota of 185 persons a year. (The provisions regarding people of Japanese ancestry were among the few liberal clauses in an otherwise repressive act, the main concern of which was to tighten U.S. national security measures.) Finally, the JACL also led efforts to remove a number of discriminatory laws: in 1948 the U.S. Supreme Court struck down one that had denied commercial fishing licenses to Japanese (*Takahashi* v. *Fish and Game Commission*), while in 1956 California's voters repealed all the alien land laws.[24]

More than any other period of Asian American history, the years between 1941, when the United States joined the war against the Axis powers, and 1965, when a new immigration law ushered in a resurgence of immigration from Asia, were ones during which the fate of Asian Americans depended largely on the changing fortunes wrought by war. The lives of people whose ancestors came from countries that were U.S. allies during World War II improved, while those identified with the enemy were ripped asunder. Then as a hot war turned into a cold one and a defeated Japan became America's "junior partner" in "containing" communism, while China went Communist and became a feared enemy, the perception and treatment of Japanese and Chinese Americans flip-flopped. Well-educated Japanese Americans finally began to enter the mainstream, while some Chinese Americans were spied upon and on occasion harassed and deported. Throughout those uncertain times, Asian Americans worked hard, complained little, and kept silent. In this unobtrusive manner, they managed to survive until renewed immigration after 1965 brought fresh vitality and new challenges to their communities.

*Vietnamese "boat people" being rescued at sea, ca. 1979.*
Courtesy U.S. Navy

# chapter eight

# New Immigrants and Refugees

C ontemporary Asian immigration and the refugee influx have been shaped by changes in U.S. immigration legislation and by the political, economic, and social ties forged between the sending countries and the United States since the end of World War II. The 1965 Immigration Act and its amendments, the 1975 Indochina Migration and Refugee Assistance Act, the 1980 Refugee Act, and the 1987 Amerasian Homecoming Act have provided the legal framework within which the Asian influx has occurred. These laws alone, however, do not explain why so many Asians have come to the United States in the last quarter century. Certain conditions in the Asian sending countries—especially as these have been shaped by the political, economic, and military relationships they have with the United States—have also helped to create the large supply of emigrants and refugees.

The 1965 Immigration Act, which removed "national origins" as the basis of American immigration legislation, has changed the pattern of immigration into the U.S. more profoundly than its architects ever expected. Until that year, the immigrant stream had been predominantly European, with sizable contributions from the western hemisphere, particularly Canada and Mexico, since the 1920s. But after the 1965 law went into effect, Asian immigration has increased so steadily that Asians now compose more than half of the total influx. While Mexico is the source of the largest number of immigrants, the next four most important sending countries are the Philippines, Korea, China (the People's Republic of China on the Asian mainland and the Republic of China in Taiwan each has its own quota), and Vietnam.

As David Reimers has revealed, this development is contrary to what proponents of the act had anticipated: they had predicted that European immigration would continue to predominate and that there would be only a slight increase in Asian immigration because they thought there were too few citizens of Asian ancestry in the country (who comprised only half of 1 percent of the U.S. population in the mid-1960s) to make wide use of the "family reunification" provisions of the new law. The same, it was said, would be true of African immigration, since Africans had "few family ties" to black Americans.[1]

In addition to such a projection—which mollified nativist groups opposed to immigration from areas of the world other than western Europe—other compelling reasons were advanced for passing the act. First, in terms of foreign policy considerations in the midst of the cold war, advocates for immigration reform argued that if the United States wished to portray itself as a leader of the "free world," the federal government had to eliminate racial discrimination not only in all domestic aspects of public life but also in its immigration policy. To win the hearts and minds of nonwhite peoples, first President John F. Kennedy and, after his assassination in November 1963, President Lyndon B. Johnson urged Congress to reform the country's immigration laws. At the same time, Johnson pushed through antipoverty and civil rights programs to convince the world that the United States is indeed a land of justice and equal opportunity for all people. Johnson succeeded because he had won a landslide victory in the 1964 elections, which also seated a larger number of Democrats in both the Senate and the House of Representatives and made possible changes in the composition of key committees. Private voluntary agencies that had been working with refugees and immigrants, meanwhile, helped to point out the humanitarian aspects of the act, which would enable families whose members had been separated for many years to be reunited.

Second, the act's supporters stressed that its implementation would benefit the United States by bringing in educated and skilled workers to fill labor needs in certain sectors of the economy, which was enjoying relative prosperity at the time. More important, organized labor, which had historically opposed immigration, decided to support the 1965 act because the U.S. Department of Labor would be given full control over labor certification, which meant that no immigrants would be admitted under the occupational preference categories in industries that already had a sufficient number of American workers.

The act that passed was framed as an amendment to the 1952 McCarran-Walter Act, under which the total quota for Asia had stood at 2,990, compared with 149,667 for Europe and 1,400 for Africa. (People from the western hemisphere were not subjected to a quota system at that time.) The 1965 act—fully implemented only in June 1968—abolished the "national origins" quota system, introduced a new preference system, set up a labor certification program, and imposed a ceiling on western hemisphere immigration. The eastern hemisphere received a total of 170,000 visas per year, with a maximum of 20,000 per country, while the western hemisphere got 120,000 a year, without any country ceilings. In addition, the spouses, unmarried minor children, and parents of U.S. citizens could enter as nonquota immigrants without any numerical limit.

The law specified seven preferences for eastern hemisphere quota immigrants: 1) unmarried children over age 21 of U.S. citizens; 2) spouses and unmarried children of permanent residents; 3) professionals, scientists, and artists of "exceptional ability;" 4) married children over age 21 of U.S. citizens; 5) siblings of U.S. citizens; 6) workers, skilled and unskilled, in occupations for which labor was in short supply in the U.S.; and 7) refugees. A percentage ceiling was given each preference; however, no one can be admitted under the third and sixth preferences unless the U.S. secretary of labor certifies that there are not enough qualified workers in that occupation in the United States and that the entry of the immigrants would not lower wages and otherwise lead to a deterioration of working conditions. The preference system did not apply to the western hemisphere, but all aspiring immigrants from there, with the exception of spouses, children, and parents of U.S. citizens, were also subject to a labor clearance.

The four family reunification preferences added up to 74 percent of the total number of quota immigrants allowed. In the early 1970s, a large number of highly trained professionals came in. Since the mid-1970s, however, the proportion of professionals has declined to less than a fifth of the total, while that of family members has increased to more than four-fifths of all quota immigrants. Overall, since 1965 about two million Asian quota immigrants, two million nonquota immigrants, and one million refugees admitted outside the provisions of the seventh preference have arrived. In addition, some 800,000 Asian students, tourists, and businessmen in the United States on temporary visas have adjusted their status and become permanent residents.

Several important amendments have modified the 1965 law, each of which has affected Asian immigration adversely. In 1976 Congress decided to restrict the number of professionals and other workers allowed in because the shortage of such persons had been alleviated and the U.S. economy was not doing as well as it had a decade earlier. After the change, instead of receiving a blanket labor certification, applicants under the third and sixth preferences needed actual job offers before they could obtain visas.

Congress also tightened the fifth preference, which large numbers of Asian Americans were using to sponsor the immigration of their siblings, thereby creating a huge backlog of visa applicants under this preference in certain Asian emigrant countries, especially the Philippines. U.S. citizens petitioning for the admission of brothers or sisters now had to be at least 21 years old. Other changes, which removed some of the differences in the regulations governing the eastern and western hemispheres, had less impact on Asian immigrants. One positive change was that the annual quota for Hong Kong—and for all other colonies—was raised from 200 to 600. Hong Kong's quota has subsequently been increased to 5,000.

As Gilbert Yochum and Vinod Agarwal have indicated, the 1976 Health Professions Educational Assistance Act reduced the number of health professionals by requiring the Department of Labor to remove physicians and surgeons from its Schedule A, which listed the fields with a shortage of practitioners.[2] But the Department of Labor went even further than Congress intended: it removed *all* the health professions from Schedule A. The law also allowed alien physicians and surgeons to apply for admission into the United States only if they passed parts 1 and 2 of the National Board of Medical Examiners Examination or its equivalent, the Visa Qualifying Examination, and demonstrated competence in written and oral English. Because of these changes, the influx of health professionals had dropped drastically by the early 1980s to only a tenth of the peak reached in 1977. And of the total number of certifications granted, three-quarters went to those who were already residing in the United States—a reversal of pre-1977 trends. Since Asians comprised a large percentage of the health professionals admitted before 1977, this law has curtailed their chances of getting an immigrant visa on the basis of their professional training. An increasing number of Asian doctors, nurses, and pharmacists, therefore, now attempt to enter under family reunification criteria instead.

The Eilberg Act of 1977 further constrained the immigration of professionals. It shifted major responsibility for labor certification from the U.S. Department of Labor to individual employers, who now had to file an Application for Alien Employment Certification for each alien professional they wished to hire.

Before they could obtain certification on behalf of future employees, employers had to prove they had tried to recruit U.S. citizens and to guarantee that they would not pay the alien professionals lower wages than the prevailing rates. The Eilberg Act had an immediately effect: whereas the Department of Labor received a combined total of 22,387 professional labor certification applications from aliens still abroad and those already resident in the United States in 1977, it only got 9,581 in 1978. As alien professionals and those who wished to hire them adjusted to the change, the number rose again, but with a different mix of applicants. The percentage of applications for professionals outside the United States dropped from more than half of the total in 1977 to only a tenth in 1982 (the last year for which data are available). Obviously, alien professionals already in the United States enjoyed a distinct advantage over those still living overseas. As a result of these changes, the so-called brain drain from Asia has definitely subsided.

Another major revision of the 1965 immigration law took place in 1986. The Immigration Reform and Control Act passed that year imposed civil and criminal penalties on employers who knowingly hire illegal aliens, granted temporary resident status to aliens who had resided in the United States since before 1 January 1982, and promised permanent resident status to these same aliens after eighteen months. Because there are fewer undocumented Asian than Mexican aliens in the United States, the 1986 law has affected Asians less than it has Mexicans. Nonetheless, Asian American civil rights groups paid close attention to the debates over the successive versions of the bill and managed to get a clause aimed at reducing the number of fifth-preference entrants deleted from its final version.

After taking care of illegal immigration, Congress turned its attention in 1988 to legal immigration. In March the Senate passed a bill that created a two-track preference system, one for family reunification and the other for independent immigrants—that is, those without relatives in the United States. It also raised the worldwide ceiling to 590,000 immigrants a year and reduced the quota allotted siblings of U.S. citizens and permanent residents from 24 percent to 10 percent. The House of Representatives, however, supported a more stringent bill, which both the Senate and House eventually approved in October.

Known as the Immigration Amendments of 1988, H.R. 5115 rectified what certain legislators had thought were unjust provisions of the 1986 act, under which people from certain countries could not take advantage of the family reunification provision because they had no immediate relatives in the United States. The 1988 amendments allowed the number of visas granted such persons residing in 36 designated countries to rise from 5,000 to 15,000 a year during 1989 and 1990. They also extended the coverage to the rest of the world for 1990 and 1991. The fifth preference was left intact, much to the relief of aspiring Asian immigrants, its major users.

Whereas changes in U.S. immigration legislation created the pull that brought millions of Asians here in the last quarter century, conditions in the major Asian sending countries have provided the necessary push. Since 1965 the largest emigrant streams have come from the Philippines (almost 450,000 quota and 400,000 nonquota immigrants) and South Korea (more than 350,000 quota and almost 240,000 nonquota immigrants). A majority of the refugees have poured out of Vietnam (more than 500,000 since 1975). In all three instances, the movement of their people to the United States has been part of a larger "American connection."

The ties created between the Philippines and the United States during almost half a century of colonial rule still exert enormous influence on the lives of Filipinos. The Philippine government as well as its educational system are both modeled after those of the United States. Most educated Filipinos speak a fair amount of English, which is the medium of instruction in secondary and higher education in their country. Thus, Filipinos do not experience as severe a language handicap as do immigrants from non-English-speaking countries; college students adjust somewhat more easily to American university life; and while professionals must pass certification examinations before they can practice, many have managed to do so, although some of them had to take the examinations several times before passing them.

A good number of Filipinos also have a chance to gain an intimate acquaintance with Americans before they leave their homeland. Today, two of the largest military installations maintained by the United States overseas are located at Clark Air Base and Subic Bay Naval Base in the Philippines, where the needs of the military personnel are served largely by Filipinos. Large numbers of Filipinas marry American soldiers and sailors every year. They and their children can enter the United States as the dependents of U.S. citizens. Others qualify for American citizenship after serving in the U.S. armed forces themselves.

Furthermore, the United States is the Philippines' major trading partner and more than half of the country's foreign investment belongs to American corporations, financial institutions, or individuals. These firms hire large numbers of Filipinos, who can thus gain work experience in an American-style corporate environment.

In addition to the social ties created by the presence of American military personnel, tourists, and businesses, American films, television programs, popular music, and printed materials, together with information sent back by friends and relatives already in the United States, all paint an alluring picture of life in the United States that generates strong incentives for emigration.

Such incentives are compelling because grave political, economic, and social problems beset the Philippines. The martial law regime of President Ferdinand Marcos, who was deposed in 1986, has been replaced by the more democratic rule of President Corazon Aquino, but her rivals for power, religious and ethnic minorities, and Communist insurgents all pose threats to political stability. Meanwhile, the Philippine economy is weighed down by the cost of servicing an increasingly intolerable foreign debt, continues to be heavily dependent on the export of agricultural products, suffers from massive unemployment and gross inequality in the distribution of income and wealth, and is saddled with a population growth rate of over 3 percent. As more and more peasants are driven off the land, they migrate to Manila in search of livelihood, but the city does not have enough industries to support its burgeoning urban population.

Under such conditions, opportunities for Filipinos to work abroad under short-term contracts and permanent emigration help to relieve part of the underemployment of professionals at home. An estimated one million Filipinos—construction workers, engineers, doctors, nurses—earn a living in the Middle East, where their contract wages are five to ten times higher than those in their homeland. The 50,000 or so Filipina nurses in the United States do better still: their salaries are twenty times those of nurses in the Philippines. Even the tens of thousands of Filipina maids and entertainers in Japan, Hong Kong, and Singapore manage to save enough money to send remittances home. Filipina domestics are also found in various European countries, while Filipino sailors serve on ships of many nations. In contrast to the estimated million Filipino contract workers scattered around the world, the vast majority of the emigrants have come to the United States. Regardless of whether they are contract workers or immigrants, they benefit the receiving countries by providing skilled labor at virtually no expense to their hosts, since the cost of their education has been borne by their families in the Philippines.[3]

The Republic of Korea (South Korea) has never been a U.S. colony, but it, too, has a dependent relationship with the United States as a result of the Korean War and the continued presence of some 40,000 American troops in the country. Serving as a northernmost outpost to the crescent of island nations—Japan, Taiwan, the Philippines, and Indonesia—that keep Soviet and Chinese communism at bay, South Korea has received billions of dollars of U.S. military aid to train and equip the country's armed forces and police and to help its rulers stay in power. Government officials, military officers, capitalists, and Christians, who have cause for concern should the Democratic People's Republic of Korea (North Korea) take over the South, or should reunification of the two halves of the country occur, favor a continued American military presence.

The South Korean economy is considerably healthier than that of the Philippines. Known as one of the "four little tigers" or NICs ("newly industrializing countries")—along with the Republic of China (Taiwan), Hong Kong, and Singapore—South Korea's gross national product has grown through the manufacture and export of textiles, apparel, footwear, electronic equipment, and more recently, vehicles. However, the apparent success of its export-led path of economic development camouflages some real costs. The South Korean economy is so dependent on the world market that price fluctuations and other economic changes in its major trading partners—Japan and the United States—produce severe and often adverse effects on large segments of the Korean working class. Korean workers are skilled and disciplined, but poorly paid and unorganized. As Bruce Cumings has documented, the American occupation forces that ruled the country between 1945 and 1948 clamped down on the incipient labor movement,[4] and the regimes that have been in power since 1948 have continued this antiunion policy, for the availability of cheap, non-unionized, but skilled labor is precisely what gives South Korea its competitive advantage in the world market.

Because of its successful population control program, South Korea's population growth rate is lower than that of the Philippines; still, it is the world's third most densely populated nation. Its capital, Seoul, which contains a quarter of the entire country's people, is bursting at the seams with migrants from the rural areas, for whom it is unable to provide adequate housing, transportation, social services, or employment.

According to Illsoo Kim, Hagen Koo and Eui-Young Yu, and Ivan Light and

Edna Bonacich, South Korea, more than any other Asian country, has since 1962 actively promoted emigration as part of its population control program. The government recognizes that emigration contributes to economic stability. Enterprising companies help aspiring emigrants cut through bureaucratic red tape, while vocational schools offer training in skills that are marketable abroad. Given the great demand for construction workers in the Middle East, schools that teach people how to operate heavy construction equipment, for example, are doing a booming business. Special training programs in automobile repair, television repair, metal working, computer programming, hairdressing, and a host of other skills also exist. Though less numerous than Filipina nurses, Korean nurses, too, are becoming increasingly visible in many countries around the world, including the United States. Like Filipinos, most of the Korean contract workers are going to the developing countries, while the emigrants have come mainly to the United States.[5]

The Republic of China in Taiwan (ROC), the People's Republic of China (PRC), and India are also sending large numbers of emigrants to the United States. After diplomatic relations between the United States and the ROC were severed in 1979 as those with the PRC were reestablished, Congress set up the American Institute in Taiwan to handle various matters in an unofficial manner. Visas for Taiwan Chinese are issued through the U.S. consulate in Hong Kong. When Hong Kong reverts to the PRC in 1997, new mechanisms no doubt will be found to deal with Taiwan's emigrants. Immigrants from the PRC, though less numerous than those from the ROC, are also flowing in. Most of them are family members of Chinese who have long resided in the United States. The number of Chinese quota immigrants from the PRC and ROC combined has been about 460,000 since 1965, while nonquota immigrants added up to approximately 150,000 for the same period.

As for India, although it was a British colony, the United States has maintained a significant presence there through economic aid and loans, technical assistance, and cultural exchange programs in the last forty years. Thus, many Indians have been exposed to the material allures of the "American way of life." Indian immigrants have been an especially elite group: doctors, scientists, engineers, and increasingly, businessmen, who are particularly visible in the New York metropolitan area. A total of about 360,000 quota and 70,000 nonquota Indian immigrants have arrived since 1965.

Japan is the only Asian country with close ties to the United States that has *not* sent large numbers of people to America since 1965—only a total of about 46,000 quota and 64,000 nonquota immigrants. As an industrialized nation itself, it is able to provide an adequate standard of living for its people. Japanese who go abroad these days tend to be employees or executives of banks and multinational corporations setting up branches overseas.

Contemporary Asian immigrants obviously differ in several significant ways from both the first wave of Asian men who came during the late nineteenth and early twentieth centuries, most of them without their families in tow, and the second wave of women and refugees who arrived in the mid-twentieth century. For the most part, Asians now come as intact families with the intention of settling here permanently and acquiring U.S. citizenship. They form a bimodal population: about a third of them are professionals, while the rest belong to the working class. They are entering a society that is less racist than the one their predecessors encountered, but many still face considerable discrimination.[6]

In addition to the arrival of quota and nonquota Asian immigrants under the post-1965 laws, the influx of almost a million refugees since 1975 has further swelled the number of persons of Asian ancestry in the United States. About three-quarters of the refugees have come from Vietnam and the rest from Laos and Kampuchea. Refugees differ from immigrants in that their exodus is not always voluntary and their path of escape is usually filled with peril. Psychologically, many exist in a state of limbo, reliving nightmarish experiences and not knowing whether they will ever see their homelands or loved ones again. They try to survive as best they can in a world where their presence is at best tolerated but seldom truly welcomed. More than half of the escapees from Vietnam, Laos, and Kampuchea have ended up in the United States because of American military involvement in the wars that ravaged those countries.

Americans showed little interest in those three Southeast Asian countries until the end of World War II, when the United States emerged as the world's most powerful nation. Postwar political settlements set the stage for the bloody wars and revolutions that followed, one result of which was a massive outflow of refugees. To understand why so many of them have landed in the United States, it is necessary to review briefly the history of American involvement there.[7]

In late July 1941 Japan and the collaborationist Vichy government in France signed a pact to permit Japanese troops to move freely through the Indochinese colonies. Even though Japan did not formally occupy Indochina during World War II, France was unable to maintain much contact with its colonies there. But the French colonial administration remained intact and the French flag continued to fly. After Free French forces liberated Paris in August 1944, General Charles de Gaulle, concerned that the Japanese might take over Indochina, ordered French commandos to parachute into the Plain of Jars in Laos to establish resistance bases. When Japanese intelligence discovered the presence of the commandos, Tokyo decided it was time to impose Japanese rule over the colonies, and in March 1945 Japanese troops arrested all French residents in Indochina.

Meanwhile, Vietnamese nationalists led by the Viet Minh (a Communist group formed by Ho Chi Minh in 1944) began to lay plans for the seizure of power in Vietnam. It also sent agents into Laos and Cambodia to work with nationalists there to forestall French reoccupation. By early 1945 Ho Chi Minh and Vo Nguyen Giap had organized an army of 5,000. In this period, Ho also made contact with U.S. Office of Strategic Services (OSS) agents, hoping to coordinate his own efforts at driving out the Japanese with those of American forces. When the Japanese surrendered, control of Vietnam, Laos, and Cambodia returned to France, in accordance with an agreement reached at the Potsdam Conference, despite Ho Chi Minh's declaration of Vietnamese independence on 2 September 1945. For more than a year after the French returned, the Viet Minh tried to work out a political settlement with them, but talks ended when a French cruiser shelled Haiphong (the port of Hanoi) in late

1946, killing some 6,000 civilians. For the next eight years, France and the Viet Minh forces fought a bitter war.[8]

Cambodia and Laos likewise declared their independence from France in 1945. Norodom Sihanouk of Cambodia, whom the French had placed on the throne in 1941 when he was 18 years old, did so under Japanese prodding, but in 1946 Cambodia became an associated state within the French Union, as did Laos in 1947. Meanwhile, pro-Viet Minh Laotian Prince Souphanouvong returned to his country and organized a liberation army.

Although initially the United States was not eager to see France retake its former colonies, in the end President Harry S. Truman did not oppose France's return, because the United States needed French cooperation to prevent the further spread of communism in Eastern Europe. Beginning in 1950 the U.S. government sent increasingly large arms shipments (totaling $2.6 billion during 1950–54) to the French. With the "fall" of China to Mao Zedong's forces in 1949 and the outbreak of war in Korea in 1950, Vietnam suddenly became vital to America's security in terms of "containing" the spread of communism. At that point, since U.S. economic investments in Vietnam were minimal, the main concerns were political and military.

In the midst of fierce fighting in Vietnam, Viet Minh forces invaded Laos in April 1953. Six months later, unable to do battle on so many fronts, France granted independence to both Laos and Cambodia. In Laos, three factions struggled for power, while the Pathet Lao (Laotian Communists) under Prince Souphanouvong built a stronghold in two northeastern provinces.[9] In Cambodia, Sihanouk skillfully played off rival groups—including Communists known as the Khmer Rouge—against each other and insisted that both Communist and "free world" countries respect Cambodian neutrality. He abdicated the throne in 1955 (his title thereby changing from *King* to *Prince* Sihanouk) in order to form his own political party, which captured 83 percent of the vote in the elections held that year.[10]

When the Viet Minh decisively defeated the French at Dien Bien Phu in 1954, the Geneva Agreements, which ended hostilities, partitioned Vietnam at the seventeenth parallel, pending a political settlement through a nationwide election scheduled for 1956. People from each half were given a chance to move. An estimated one million persons, two-thirds of them Catholics, migrated from the North to the South, some in American naval vessels, while about 120,000 civilians traveled in the opposite direction. Unlike Vietnam, Laos and Cambodia were not partitioned.

As the French withdrew, President Dwight D. Eisenhower sent a personal envoy to assure newly installed South Vietnamese prime minister Ngo Dinh Diem, a staunch anticommunist, that he had America's support, which came in the form of $100 million of aid. Early the following year the United States agreed to help train the South Vietnamese army. In October Diem proclaimed South Vietnam a republic, with himself as president, but he refused to hold the national elections that the Geneva Agreements had stipulated.

Communist insurgent activities began sporadically in 1957 in South Vietnam. North Vietnam formed a unit called Group 559 to send infiltrators to the South in 1959, while the National Liberation Front, commonly called the Viet Cong (South Vietnamese Communists) came into being in 1960. The United

States raised the number of American advisors in South Vietnam from 700 to 12,000 in 1962, making the U.S. mission in that country the largest in the world. Between 1955 and 1961 the United States poured more than $1 billion of aid—four-fifths of it military assistance—into South Vietnam. President Ngo Dinh Diem and his brother, Ngo Dinh Nhu, were murdered by their own generals in November 1963.[11]

The following August the North Vietnamese shelled the American destroyer *Maddox* in the Gulf of Tonkin. Within five days Congress passed a resolution that gave President Lyndon B. Johnson extraordinary powers to act as he saw fit in Vietnam. In February 1965 the United States began the first of many bombing raids on North Vietnam. The first American combat troops landed in March. From then on, the war escalated. By the end of 1967 there were half a million American troops in the country and the United States was spending $2 billion *per month* on the war. Undaunted by such numbers or by the most sophisticated and devastating weapons of modern warfare, Communist forces attacked and took several cities in central Vietnam during Tet (the lunar New Year) in 1968. An estimated 40,000 Communist troops died in the campaign, but their efforts forever destroyed the illusion that the United States and its South Vietnamese ally could win the contest with superior firearms.

In 1969 the United States started bombing neighboring Cambodia in order to deny sanctuary to the Viet Cong, dropping more than 100,000 tons of bombs over a 15-month period. President Richard M. Nixon managed to keep this fact hidden from the American public until spring of the following year. In April Cambodian prime minister Lon Nol led a coup and deposed Prince Sihanouk. During Long Nol's rule, American influence expanded.

In Laos, the U.S. Central Intelligence Agency, in violation of the agreements reached at the second Geneva Conference of 1962, which guaranteed Laotian neutrality, fought a war of its own against the Pathet Lao, using a mercenary army composed of 9,000 Hmong hill tribesmen led by General Vang Pao. But as increasing numbers of Hmong were killed, American generals relied more and more on air power to defeat the Communists. Between 1965 and 1973 the United States dropped more than 2 million tons of bombs on Laos in an attempt to destroy the Ho Chi Minh trail, the North Vietnamese supply route to South Vietnam that ran through Laotian jungles.[12]

At the same time that he widened the air war, Nixon announced a new policy to "Vietnamize" the ground war by gradually withdrawing American soldiers and leaving the Vietnamese themselves to do the fighting. Doing so was one way for the United States to get out of Vietnam "with honor." National Security Advisor (later Secretary of State) Henry Kissinger began meeting quietly outside of Paris with representatives of the North Vietnamese government. In October 1972 Kissinger and Le Duc Tho reached an agreement—one that President Nguyen Van Thieu of South Vietnam rejected, as he had not been party to the talks. Nevertheless, the United States and North Vietnam signed the cease-fire agreements in late January 1973. The remaining American troops began withdrawing from Vietnam at the end of March.

No sooner had American troops departed than the civil war between North and South flared once again. By March 1975, when Thieu's troops abandoned the highlands of central Vietnam, observers around the world realized that the Saigon government was about to fall. On 18 March President Gerald Ford authorized the attorney general to use his "parole" power to admit 130,000 refugees into the United States. He also created an Interagency Task Force, with representatives from 12 agencies, to oversee their resettlement. President Thieu left his country on 25 April 1975 as Americans, their Vietnamese dependents, and selected Vietnamese government and military personnel who had reason to fear for their lives were evacuated under chaotic conditions. South Vietnam surrendered on 30 April. Giant helicopters lifted out the last batch of evacuees the day before.

Communists also came to power in Cambodia and Laos in 1975. Khmer Rouge troops entered Phnom Penh, the Cambodian capital, on 17 April—*before* the fall of Saigon—but since the world's attention was riveted on South Vietnam, the change in government in Cambodia was less publicized. Several thousand military officers, government officials, the well-to-do, and the educated escaped to Thailand, from whence some made their way as refugees to the United States.

The change in government in Laos was the culmination of events that had been unfolding for more than two years. Under pressure from the United States, which had just signed the Paris agreement with North Vietnam, Laos's neutralist and Communist leaders in Vientiane signed a cease-fire accord of their own in February 1973. It then took fourteen months for them to hammer out the details for the coalition government that seated an equal number of Communists and noncommunists. When the Saigon and Phnom Penh governments collapsed in April 1975, the Laotian Communists also prepared to assume full control. Following a series of demonstrations, four rightist ministers resigned on 7 May 1975 and fled the country, as did General Vang Pao, commander of the Hmong mercenary army. "People's committees" replaced municipal and provincial administrations one after another until the process was completed with the takeover of the Vientiane city administration in August. Elections were held at the beginning of November, but on 28 November a huge crowd of demonstrators in Vientiane demanded that the coalition government be dissolved. The king abdicated and the neutralist prime minister retired the next day. A Lao People's Democratic Republic was established on 2 December.[13] Because what happened in Laos was not as precipitous as events in South Vietnam and Cambodia, refugees from Laos initially did not receive the same right to enter the United States by "parole." One of the few individuals allowed into the country was General Vang Pao, who arrived in the summer of 1975.

Although Clark Air Base in the Philippines was the most logical place to take the evacuees, it was used only as a transfer point because President Ferdinand Marcos announced he would not welcome Vietnamese refugees. So, as a humanitarian gesture, Governor Ricardo Bordallo of Guam offered his hospitality, and the entire military population on Guam (about 10,000 persons) worked around the clock to clear 1,200 acres of underbrush and erect a tent city with a capacity for housing 50,000 refugees at any one time. The first planeload landed two hours after orders were given to receive them. Troops in passing ships, civilians, and whoever else would volunteer—another 10,000 individuals—also pitched in to help. A massive airlift brought supplies from other bases in the Pacific Ocean and from the continental United States.

Smaller numbers of evacuees were also taken to Thailand, the Philippines

(Marcos's wishes notwithstanding), Wake Island, and Hawaii. Of the 130,000 refugees evacuated, 95 percent were Vietnamese and the rest Kampucheans. By August 1975 the ceiling of 130,000 refugees authorized for admission had already been exceeded by 1,000 persons, but the flow continued.

After the Immigration and Naturalization Service processed them in Guam, the refugees flew to four receiving centers in the United States: Camp Pendleton in southern California, Fort Chaffee in Arkansas, Fort Indiantown Gap in Pennsylvania, and Eglin Air Force Base in Florida. Upon landing, they were screened for security clearance and given medical examinations and identification numbers. They also had to register with one of the nine voluntary agencies (dubbed "volags") that had contracted with the federal government to resettle them.

The volags, which received a grant of $500 for each refugee they aided, were the United States Catholic Conference, the Lutheran Immigration and Refugee Service, the International Rescue Committee, the United Hebrew Immigrant Aid Society, World Church Service, the Tolstoy Foundation, the American Fund for Czechoslovak Refugees, the American Council for Nationalities Services, and Travelers' Aid–International Social Services. Since about 40 percent of the refugees were Catholics, the United States Catholic Conference played a major role. The staffs of a number of volags found the maximum of forty-five days allowed by the Interagency Task Force for finding the refugees sponsors was insufficient.

Refugees could leave the centers once they found sponsors who promised to provide them with food, clothing, and shelter until they could fend for themselves. The sponsors also agreed to help the refugees find jobs, to enroll their children in school, and to ease their traumatic entry into American society in other ways. Almost 60 percent of the sponsors were families, some 25 percent were churches and other organized groups, while the rest were individuals. The vast majority (121,610 out of the initial 130,000) of the refugees departed the camps under sponsorship.

Those with at least $4,000 per household member to ensure their self-sufficiency could leave without sponsors, but few had this kind of cash. Individuals could also choose to resettle in a third country; a small number joined relatives who had gone elsewhere—mostly France. A fourth route out was to request repatriation to Vietnam. Some 1,500 persons were sent back to Vietnam from Guam in October 1975, but the requests of those who had already reached the mainland were ignored. All the reception centers closed by the end of December 1975.

The resettlement process was financed by the Indochina Migration and Refugee Assistance Act of 1975, under which the federal government reimbursed state governments for the cash assistance and medical and social services that the refugees received. The Department of Health, Education, and Welfare (now the Department of Health and Human Services) also gave grants to public or nonprofit private agencies to provide the refugees with English instruction, employment counseling, and mental health services. When the 1975 act expired in 1977, a continuing resolution extended it for another year, but Congress did not appropriate any funds until March 1978, thus disrupting services in many states for more than half a year.

Federal policy encouraged the refugees to find gainful employment as quickly as possible. The government also tried to minimize the financial burden on any single locality by dispersing the refugees widely. But due to the importance of the extended family in Southeast Asian cultures, many refugees made determined efforts to reunite scattered family members and friends through secondary migration. California, with its sizable Asian population, warm climate, and generous public assistance programs, has been the favorite destination of a large number of secondary migrants. It initially received only 21 percent of the "first wave" refugees and 25 percent to 30 percent of the "second wave" (see following), but as a result of secondary migration, over 40 percent of all refugees from Vietnam, Kampuchea, and Laos now reside in California. Texas, with the second largest number, is home to only about 10 percent.

No sooner did government agencies, volags, and private individuals think the refugee problem was solved than a larger and more tragic exodus began. The more heterogeneous "second wave" of refugees who started arriving in 1978 can be divided into the "boat people" from Vietnam and the "land people" from Kampuchea and Laos. On the whole, they were poorer, less educated, less urbanized, more ethnically diverse—consisting of ethnic Chinese from Vietnam, Kampucheans, lowland Lao, highland Hmong, and smaller numbers of other groups—than the "first wave." Fewer of them are Catholics and more are Buddhists and animists.

The post-1975 outflow of refugees reflects developments in Vietnam, Kampuchea, and Laos since Communist governments came to power, as well as the legacy of 30 years of warfare, which not only killed hundreds of thousands—perhaps millions—of able-bodied people, but also demolished cities, destroyed farmland, denuded forests, poisoned water sources, and left countless unexploded mines. Despite the mind-boggling task of economic and ecological reconstruction that confronted them, the new rulers of Vietnam set their priorities on ridding their country of "bourgeois" elements, foremost among whom were thousands of Chinese petty traders whose families had lived in Vietnam for centuries. The government closed their businesses, Chinese language schools, and newspapers, confiscated their assets, removed them from civil service posts, denied them participation in certain occupations, forced them to register, and reduced their food rations.

Unable and unwilling to continue living under such harsh circumstances, the Sino-Vietnamese used every means available to escape. The People's Republic of China has taken in over a quarter million of them. Another estimated half million left in poorly equipped and grossly overcrowded small boats unfit for open seas. The plight of these "boat people," some 70 percent of them Sino-Vietnamese, captured the attention of the world, as they ran out of food, water, and fuel, were preyed upon by Thai pirates, and even after sighting shore, were sometimes forbidden to land by authorities in neighboring Malaysia, Indonesia, the Philippines, and Hong Kong.[14] Some estimates place the loss of lives at 50 percent or higher.

In addition to the Sino-Vietnamese, family members of former government officials and military personnel who have been sent to reeducation camps, from whence few have returned, have also tried to leave. They worry in particular about young men subject to conscription. People sent to "New Economic Zones"—remote regions of the country where, without any resources, they are expected to clear jungles, make the land arable, and eke out a living—are

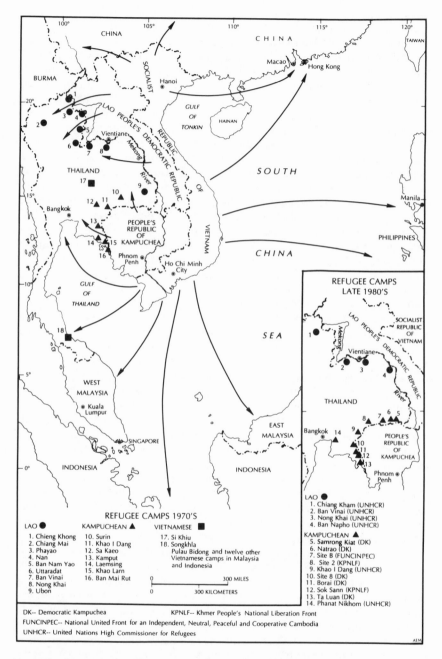

Map 6. *The refugee exodus from Vietnam, Laos, and Kampuchea and the location of refugee camps, 1970s and 1980s.*

likewise desperate. Even former high-ranking members of the Viet Cong have departed, feeling betrayed by Hanoi, which has included few of them in the national government established after 1975.[15]

An even greater calamity befell the people of Cambodia, now renamed Kampuchea. On the very day that the Khmer Rouge entered Phnom Penh, they ordered the entire population of the capital to evacuate to the countryside. This act was part of a program devised by Pol Pot, their ideological leader, to root out all undesirable "elements" in Cambodian society—particularly city people with their Westernized ways and former officials used to augmenting their income through corruption. Pol Pot ordered a second evacuation six months later, forcing people to march from one part of the country to another. In this period, the Khmer Rouge also executed an untold number of people. Estimates for the total death toll from executions, forced evacuation, starvation, exposure, and disease run from half a million to three million—in a country with a total population of no more than seven million in early 1975.[16] An invading Vietnamese army overthrew the Pol Pot regime at the end of 1978 and installed a new government under Heng Samrin and Hun Sen, pro-Vietnamese Communists. In retaliation, China (which supported Pol Pot) invaded Vietnam in early 1979 and fought a border war with it.

During the genocidal Pol Pot years, relatively few Kampucheans escaped because their movement was strictly controlled. In 1977 only about 20,000 Kampuchean refugees were in Thailand awaiting resettlement, but that number soon rose. The new regime installed by the Vietnamese in 1979 allowed much greater freedom of movement, so large numbers of refugees found their way to the Thai border. Some of them were not fleeing atrocities per se. They came, rather, to carry on a cross-border black market trade or with the hope of being resettled abroad. Others were nationalists biding their time as they prepared to launch a campaign to oust the Vietnamese from their country.

Alarmed by the size of the influx, the Thai government reacted harshly. In June 1979 Thai authorities loaded over 40,000 Kampucheans in trucks, drove them to a remote region with steep mountainous trails, forced them to get off the vehicles, and pushed them back into Kampuchea at gunpoint. After protests came from around the world, the Thai government placed the refugees in camps constructed under the auspices of the United Nations High Commissioner for Refugees. By the end of 1979 upwards of 600,000 Kampucheans— about 15 percent of Kampuchea's remaining population—were living in these camps along the Thai border.

After a ten-year occupation, Vietnam withdrew its forces from Kampuchea in October 1989. A civil war then raged until June 1990, when two of the three nationalist groups seeking to overthrow the Vietnam-backed Hun Sen government agreed to a cease-fire. The Khmer Rouge, however, refused to sign it. Since the Khmer Rouge is militarily the strongest group, its refusal to sign meant that war would very likely continue. But in July 1990, the United States unexpectedly announced a change in policy, indicating its willingness to talk to representatives of Vietnam as well as Hun Sen, instead of continuing to support the Khmer Rouge. This breakthrough may finally make possible a political settlement in Kampuchea.

In Laos, for over a year after the Communists assumed full control, they left the Hmong more or less alone. When General Vang Pao fled, his followers

A *recent Korean immigrant learning* English.
Photo by Shulee Ong

began trekking to Thailand, where eventually some 25,000 reached safety. Another 60,000 retreated to the Phou Bia massif south of the Plain of Jars, where they dug in and tried to survive. But the Laotian Communists, who regard the Hmong as traitors for the pro-American role they played during the war, soon sent troops to encircle and storm the Hmong stronghold. The fierce Hmong fighters repulsed the government forces, which then flew sorties over the massif, dropping bombs, napalm, and poisons known as trichothecene mycotoxins. Unable to withstand this onslaught, the Hmong descended from their hideout. An unknown number of them died; 3,000 refugees a month were still trying to cross the Mekong River into Thailand in late 1979.

Lowland Lao have also left their country for reasons very similar to those given by Vietnamese refugees. The Laotian government's policy of purging "cultural poisons" sent thousands to reeducation camps. In Thailand, lowland Lao refugees are generally housed in separate camps from the Kampucheans, the Hmong, and other groups. To deter any further influx, the Thai government in early 1981 placed most of the lowland Lao refugees in an "austerity camp" and told them they would not be eligible for resettlement. If they did not repatriate to Laos, they were warned, they would have to stay in that camp forever. The government charged that the people were not political refugees but economic migrants who did not deserve international compassion. Two years after this austerity camp was set up, only a little over 2,000 inmates had returned to Laos. Altogether, an estimated 300,000 Laotians—10 percent of the country's total population, lowlanders and highlanders combined—have become displaced persons.

In the face of the massive outflow of both boat and land refugees, the United States opened its doors in early 1979 to 7,000 refugees a month. Later that year President Jimmy Carter doubled the quota. Annual arrivals jumped from 20,400 in 1978 to 80,700 in 1979 to 166,700 in 1980. To deal with the situation, an international conference was convened in Geneva in 1979. The outcome was that the "first asylum" nations in Southeast Asia agreed not to turn refugees away if "second asylum" countries such as Australia, the United States, Canada, and France would accept them for resettlement. The conference participants also put strong pressure on the Vietnamese government to stop its eviction of Sino-Vietnamese.

To enable the United States to handle the refugee crisis in an organized manner, Congress passed the 1980 Refugee Act, which, as explained by Senator Edward Kennedy, one of its chief architects, has six goals. It adopted the United Nations definition of "refugee" as "any person who, owing to a well-founded fear of being persecuted for reasons of race, religion, nationality, membership of a particular social group or political opinion," seeks refuge outside of his or her country. It also set the annual quota for refugees at 50,000; established systematic procedures for admitting them; made Congress, rather than the executive branch, responsible for refugee policy; provided for asylum; and funded resettlement programs.[17] The federal government promised to reimburse states for refugee expenditures for a maximum of thirty-six months, but in March 1982 it reduced the time limit to eighteen months. "Time-expired" refugees are eligible for general welfare on the same basis as everybody else.

When resettlement efforts were decentralized, each state with a sizable refugee population set up mechanisms to serve the refugees' needs. The different organizational structures have been described by Paul Strand and Woodrow Jones, Jr.[18] In California, the state with the largest refugee population, several agencies share responsibility. The director of the Department of Social Services (DSS), which is housed in the state's umbrella Health and Welfare Agency, serves as the state's refugee services coordinator. DSS administers the Food Stamp and Aid to Families with Dependent Children programs, monitors the federal Supplementary Security Income/State Supplementary program, and oversees the provision of Title 20 social services—all of which eligible refugees may partake of. The Office of Refugee Services within DSS coordinates the various programs. Title 20 services available to refugees include instruction in English as a second language, vocational training, employment services, services to facilitate social adjustment, mental health services, and health assessment. Time-expired refugees can avail themselves of the Refugee Cash Assistance program, the Emergency Assistance program, and various county General Assistance programs. There is also an Office of Migration and Refugee Affairs, which coordinates programs offering services that are not reimbursed by federal allocations and which staffs the Governor's Refugee Task Force and Citizens' Advisory Committee.

Texas, which has the second-largest refugee population, has put the Department of Human Resources (DHR) in charge of its services to refugees. The associate commissioner of the Administration for Services to Families and Children coordinates all existing programs. To provide services effectively over its huge expanse, the state has divided itself into twelve regions, whose boundaries coincide with those of its health services areas. Within each, DHR contracts with various public and private organizations to deliver the needed services. The governor has a Refugee Resettlement Advisory Council and a Liaison for Voluntary Assistance. Because Texas does not have an Aid to Families with Dependent Children program or a General Assistance program, time-expired refugees in Texas receive a considerably smaller amount of aid than do those in California, but the employment rate of refugees in Texas was one of the highest in the nation during the years when the Texan economy was healthy.

The state of Washington has a Bureau of Refugee Assistance (BORA) within its Department of Social and Health Services and a full-time refugee coordinator. In each locality with a large concentration of refugees, BORA contracts with public and private agencies to offer the needed services. One of the most important contracts BORA has signed is with the Superintendent of Public Instruction to set up language classes under the state's English-as-a-second-language master plan. Washington is also known for its commitment to hiring bilingual staff. Owing to its depressed economy in the late 1970s and early 1980s, however, it has one of the highest refugee outmigration rates in the country.

A large number of refugees are in Pennsylvania, since Fort Indiantown Gap near Harrisburg was one of the original receiving stations. A variety of state agencies has been given responsibility for assisting refugees: first the Office of Income Maintenance, then the Office of Social Programs, and now the Office of Children, Youth and Families—all of which are units within the Department of Public Welfare, whose secretary serves as the state coordinator for refugee resettlement. As is true elsewhere, a great deal of the services is actually delivered by public and private agencies that have contracted to do so.

Minnesota is unusual in that about 40 percent of all the Hmong in the United States have resettled there, despite its bitterly cold winters. (In recent years, however, an increasing number of them have been moving to the San Joaquin Valley of California.) Its Refugee Program Office is a unit within the Bureau of Income Maintenance, which, in turn, is under the state Department of Public Welfare. A State Refugee Advisory Council, a Mutual Assistance Association Advisory Council, the Minnesota Consortium for Refugee Resettlement, and dozens of local bodies—especially in St. Paul and Minneapolis—also offer services. Faculty and staff at the University of Minnesota, meanwhile, have done research and disseminated information on the culture and special needs of the Hmong.

Within each state at the county level, the Welfare Department is responsible for processing refugee applications for assistance; determining their eligibility; providing cash, medical assistance, and other benefits and services; and referring refugees to other agencies when appropriate. Starting in 1984, counties assumed greater responsibility for refugee assistance under a new federally funded Targeted Assistance program. Because of all the attention and help refugees have received, they have aroused the jealousy of other needy groups, including Asian immigrants. One of the burdens they bear, therefore, is finding ways to cope with the intense animosity they often face.

Since 1981, when 132,500 refugees arrived from Vietnam, Laos, and

Kampuchea, the number entering has slowly fallen to about 50,000 a year. Today, slightly over 50 percent of them come from Vietnam, 40 percent from Kampuchea, and the rest from Laos. The Vietnamese government, for its part, established an Orderly Departure Program in 1980, under which approximately 5,000 Vietnamese and Sino-Vietnamese now come to the United States annually as bona fide immigrants.

The refugee population in Southeast Asia is still sizable: in 1989 more than 600,000 refugees were being held in camps awaiting resettlement. Camps in Thailand housed 437,000, in Malaysia 104,000, in the Philippines 27,000, and in Hong Kong 55,000.[19] Hard pressed to cope with the continual influx, the governments of these first-asylum countries took drastic action. In 1988 Thai officials pushed newly arriving "boat people" back to sea; the following year Malaysia did the same thing after giving them water and provisions. In late 1989 the Hong Kong government forcibly loaded 51 Vietnamese on a plane bound for Hanoi, but the action caused an international outcry. In defense of his government's action, Hong Kong's coordinator of refugees observed: "The U.S. screens people in south Texas and holds them in a detention center and repatriates them in one day. They do the same to the people from Haiti on a boat off the coast of Haiti. They pick them up, screen them on board the boat, deny them refugee status and then push them off. Now why are the Vietnamese different?"[20]

To bring some order to this difficult situation, a conference was once again convened in Geneva in June 1989. The participants agreed that "boat people" arriving in first-asylum countries after 14 March 1989 (and in Hong Kong after 16 June 1988) would be screened to see if they qualify for refugee status as defined by the United Nations. First-asylum countries agreed to shelter all arrivals, while resettlement nations promised to take everyone who had entered the camps before the cutoff dates as well as all legitimate refugees arriving thereafter.

One group of refugees, the children of American servicemen and Vietnamese women, has aroused especially mixed emotions. For almost a decade after the United States pulled its troops out of Vietnam, Congress ignored the plight of these youngsters, whom no one wanted. In their mothers' homeland, the mixed-blood progeny were often treated as pariahs, while in the United States, those fathers who wanted to send for their offspring faced innumerable obstacles. Even though Congress passed an Amerasian Immigration Act in 1982 to enable children known to have been fathered by Americans to immigrate, that law benefited only individuals in Korea, Thailand, the Philippines, and elsewhere, but not those in Vietnam, because there are no diplomatic relations between Vietnam and the United States. The number of persons who have entered under that act, in any case, has been small, because their mothers and half-siblings are not allowed to accompany them and their mothers must sign a document releasing them irrevocably before they are allowed to emigrate.

Between 1982, when Vietnam's Orderly Departure Program was expanded to cover American-Vietnamese, and the end of 1987, when Congress finally passed an Amerasian Homecoming Act, the only way such children could enter the United States was through the Orderly Departure Program. Approximately 4,500 of them did so during that five-year interval. The 1987 Amerasian Homecoming Act, which allows American-Vietnamese born between 1 January

1962 and 1 January 1976 and certain members of their families to be admitted into the United States as immigrants, so long as they apply for their visas before March 1990, has enlarged the influx—adding yet one more distinctive group to the increasingly heterogeneous Asian American population.

Political prisoners released from reeducation camps are the most recent group of refugees to be granted admission under special arrangements. Based on an agreement reached between the American and Vietnamese governments, they are allowed to emigrate to the United States if they have family members who will sponsor them. As many as 100,000 persons may enter under this provision, but U.S. officials estimate they can process a maximum of only 1,000 individuals per month.[21]

Political considerations, as well as humanitarian concerns, have prompted the United States to take in half of the refugees who have poured out of Southeast Asia. Looking at the refugee phenomenon globally (there are about ten million displaced persons in the world today), it is obvious that American generosity is quite selective and is based on ideological grounds: the United States favors escapees from communism above all others. America's doors are open primarily to refugees from Southeast Asian countries with Communist governments, to anti-Castro groups from Cuba, and increasingly, to Jews from the Soviet Union. Seekers of sanctuary from central American countries such as Haiti and El Salvador—whose rulers the United States supports—in contrast, have encountered no sympathy. There is yet another dimension to the politics of the refugee influx. By accepting escapees from communism, the United States can perhaps finally prove that the generals, presidents, legislators, and citizens who supported U.S. involvement in Vietnam were right, after all. The message the refugee influx imparts is that life under communism must indeed be atrocious if so many people are willing to risk everything to escape it. The moral victory thus won is probably helping to salve the wounds inflicted by military defeat. This fact, I suggest, is probably what helps to justify the financial costs incurred in extending public assistance to the refugees. Many taxpayers, however, deeply resent such largesse when it is given to the very people whom, just a short while ago, American troops were taught to hate and to kill.

Further evidence that political calculations underpin the U.S. policy on refugees is that there *is* an alternative to absorbing the seemingly endless outpour, and that is to aid Vietnam's economic recovery so that it can better support its people. The United States can end the trade embargo it has imposed on Vietnam since 1978 and stop blocking efforts by that country to get loans from the International Monetary Fund. Placed alongside these psychological and political factors, arguments that the United States has been willing to take in so many refugees because they add to the pool of cheap labor are simply not compelling. If all that American employers want is cheap labor, there are endless other sources of cheap labor upon which they can draw.

Refugees aside, even the more predictable flow of Asian immigrants has been generated by the political relationships that the United States has developed with the countries of origin. But regardless of what conditions impelled or enabled them to come, as soon as they arrive, most contemporary Asian newcomers quickly make themselves productive, as generations before them have done. This ability to find niches for themselves, however, is a double-edged sword: even as their achievements have brought them much public acclaim, their very success is resurrecting deeply ingrained prejudices and hostility. For that reason, the contradictions that have characterized Asian American history continue to circumscribe the lives of many Asian Americans today.

*University of California students who participated in the Spring Action '89 march on Sacramento, 1989.*
Courtesy Educational Opportunity Program, University of California, Santa Barbara, Sucheng Chan collection

# chapter nine

# Current Socioeconomic Status, Politics, Education, and Culture

While renewed immigration has made Asian Americans the fastest growing segment of the U.S. population, other changes have also transformed their communities. Among the most important are improvements in the socioeconomic status of certain groups within the Asian American
population, the increasing willingness of Asian Americans to participate in
politics, the much-publicized academic achievement of Asian American students, and the emergence of an Asian American artistic sensibility.

The current socioeconomic status of Asian Americans is a controversial
issue. The numerous scholarly studies on this topic can be grouped under two
contending schools of thought. One school paints a rosy picture of Asian Americans as a "model minority," while a second argues that the statistics presented
by the first are misleading and that many Asian Americans still suffer from
considerable discrimination in the labor market as well as in other areas of
public life.

The model minority thesis first surfaced in the mid-1960s when journalists
began publicizing the high educational attainment levels, high median family
incomes, low crime rates, and absence of juvenile delinquency and mental
health problems among Asian Americans.[1] This publicity served an important
political purpose at the height of the civil rights movement: proponents of the
thesis were in fact telling Black and Chicano activists that they should follow
the example set by Asian Americans who work hard to pull themselves up by
the bootstraps instead of using militant protests to obtain their rights.

Without question, the socioeconomic status of Asian Americans has improved since the early 1940s. Calvin Schmid and Charles Nobbe used 1960
national census data to compare systematically whites (Hispanics were not
separated out from the aggregate white figures in this study) with five nonwhite groups: Chinese, Japanese, Filipinos, Native Americans, and blacks. The
authors found that Japanese Americans ranked above whites in educational
attainment, as measured by three indicators: the percentage who had completed four years of college, the median years of schooling, and the percentage
of high school graduates. Chinese Americans outranked whites with regard to
the first, but trailed them in terms of the second and third indicators. However,
although relatively more Japanese and Chinese than whites had white-collar
occupations, the median income of both groups was lower than that of whites.[2]

Ten years later the U.S. Census Bureau released data that further undergirded the model minority image. According to these figures, Chinese and Japanese Americans had outpaced whites even in terms of median family income by 1970. Japanese American median family income was almost $3,000 higher, and Chinese American $1,000 higher, than the U.S. median family income.[3] But the federal government's study failed to place these figures alongside other relevant information, such as the fact that in 60 percent of the Japanese American and Chinese American families (compared to only 51 percent among the U.S. population as a whole), more than one person worked, which helps to account for their higher family income. If per capita income, rather than family income, had been used as the measure, then the public would have learned that Chinese Americans (though not Japanese Americans) were making considerably less than the national average. Moreover, if Hispanic groups, which earned much lower incomes than other whites, had been removed from the aggregate white figures, then Asian Americans would not have outranked whites.

Social scientists who analyzed the 1970 census data reached various conclusions, depending on whether they used statistics for the nation as a whole or for states with particularly high Asian concentrations, whether they separated the American-born from the foreign-born, and whether they distinguished between males and females. Studies based on national data, such as those by Barry Chiswick and by Charles Hirschman and Morrison Wong, invariably showed that American-born Chinese and Japanese men had a higher income than white men, but as Robert Jiobu, Amado Cabezas, and David Moulton have documented, such was not the case in California, where 58 percent and 45 percent, respectively, of the Japanese and Chinese in the contiguous states resided in 1970.[4] In that state, American-born Chinese and Japanese men indeed had significantly more years of schooling than non-Hispanic whites, but their median incomes were no higher than that of the latter, because their returns to education—that is, the additional income derived from increased years of schooling—were lower than those for whites. According to Robert Jiobu's 1976 study of American-born men in California in 1970, for each additional year of education, whites earned $522 more, compared to $438 for Japanese, $320 for Chinese, $340 for Mexican Americans, and $284 for blacks. Thus, the Asian-white parity in income was made possible mainly by the Asian Americans' higher levels of education.

Other criticisms have been raised against the model minority thesis, mainly by researchers associated with the Asian American community organization, ASIAN, Inc., in San Francisco.[5] First, more than half of the Asian/Pacific American population in the United States lives in only five metropolitan areas— Honolulu, San Francisco, Los Angeles, Chicago, and New York—and of these, more than nine-tenths are found in urban centers. These cities are not only high-income areas but also high-cost-of-living areas. Thus, while Asian Americans (and others) living there may earn more, they also have to spend more.

Second, in areas with the highest density of Asian Americans, the percentage of Asian Americans in low-status, low-income occupations—that is, service workers, laborers, farm laborers, and private household workers—is considerably higher than among whites. In 1970, for example, fully 25 percent of all gainfully employed Chinese men in the United States were cooks, waiters, busboys, dishwashers, and janitors. Such a figure gives an impression of Asian

American economic well-being that is quite different from one based on consideration of median income alone.

Third, a detailed study of the San Francisco-Oakland Standard Metropolitan Statistical Area (SMSA) showed that Asian Americans were unevenly distributed in the economy. Professionals clustered in accounting, dentistry, nursing, health technology, and engineering and were underrepresented in law, teaching, administration, social services, and the higher levels of the medical professions. Managers were more likely to be self-employed than employees of large firms. Salespersons were retail clerks but seldom brokers or insurance agents. Clerical workers were mostly file clerks, typists, or office machine operators, and not secretaries or receptionists. Few Asian Americans held jobs in the heavy-machine, electrical, paper, chemical, or construction industries. Most female operatives were garment workers. In short, Asian Americans were concentrated in occupations that did not pay as well as other jobs in the same industries.

Fourth, the low unemployment rate of Asian Americans—another measure often used to depict their economic success—merely camouflages high underemployment. Wary of being on welfare, many Asian American workers apparently would rather hold low-paid, part-time, or seasonal jobs than receive public assistance.

Fifth, the high labor force participation rate of Asian American women in both 1970 and 1980—supposedly a sign of their ready acceptance by employers—is in reality a reflection of the fact that more Asian American women are compelled to work because the male members of their families earn such low wages. It is true that working Asian American women earn a higher median income than do white working women, but they also have superior educational qualifications and live in localities with higher wages. Furthermore, compared to white women, a larger percentage of them work full time, which helps to drive their median income upward. But despite their high educational level, they receive lower returns to their education than do white women, while the disparity between their returns and those of white men is even greater. In other words, they are not receiving earnings that are commensurate with their years of schooling.

Sixth, with regard to the educational attainment of Asian Americans, the sizable influx of highly educated professionals after 1965 has inflated the average years of schooling completed. Critics of the model minority stereotype point out that the most important consideration should not be educational level, but returns to education, which more clearly reveal the existence of discrimination. For Asian Americans, even in 1980, these returns were still not on a par with those received by white men.

The entry of professionals has had another effect. Since some of them have not been able to find professional jobs, they have bought small businesses, thereby increasing the number of "managers" in the Asian American—particularly the Korean American—population. However, many of them operate only small mom-and-pop stores with no paid employees and very low gross earnings. Unlike journalists who tout Korean entrepreneurship as a sign of success, scholars who have examined the situation argue that the kind of business Korean immigrants engage in is, in fact, a disguised form of cheap labor: owners of small businesses run a high risk of failure and work long hours.[6] Many of them could not stay afloat were it not for the unpaid labor they extract from their spouses, children, and other relatives. Nonetheless, small business currently is an important channel of upward mobility open to nonwhite immigrants who face obstacles in obtaining well-paying and secure jobs.

Finally, other groups of Asian Americans do not share the improved economic standing achieved by Japanese and Chinese Americans. In 1970 in the San Francisco-Oakland SMSA, according to Amado Cabezas and his associates, Filipinos (lumping together foreign- and American-born) earned only 58 percent of what white men earned, while Filipinas earned only 38 percent. The respective figures in the Los Angeles-Long Beach SMSA were 62 percent and 47 percent. In 1980, in the San Francisco-Oakland SMSA, American-born Filipino men made 64 percent of what American-born white males made, while American-born Filipinas made 45 percent. In the Los Angeles-Long Beach SMSA, the comparable figures were 72 percent and 48 percent. Foreign-born men fared about the same as their American-born peers, while the foreign-born women did slightly better than their American-born sisters. A larger proportion of American-born Filipinos hold working-class jobs than do Chinese and Japanese Americans. They also seem to receive no discernible returns to schooling.[7]

Studies of Vietnamese refugees likewise paint contradictory pictures. In California, where some 40 percent of the refugees now live, about half of them remain on public assistance. (The percent on public assistance is lower in other states, where the welfare system is more stringent in terms of eligibility.) Even so, some authors still seem bent on extending the model minority image to this group of newcomers. Instead of using median family or per-capita income as measures, they focus on the relatively high labor participation rate of certain subgroups of refugees, on the rapid pace at which some refugee families have climbed out of poverty, and on the extraordinary academic performance of their children.[8]

There has been a lack of consensus on the current socioeconomic status of Asian Americans because, quite apart from methodological differences, scholars have used different theoretical models to guide their data analysis. The basic dichotomy is between those who use a human capital model and others who follow a variety of structural models. Human capital theorists believe that differences in earnings are the result of specific traits or abilities—such as education, work experience, number of weeks worked during the year—possessed by various *individuals*, whereas structural theorists posit that built-in features of the economy and sociopolitical *institutions* create barriers that prevent certain groups (principally nonwhites and females) from receiving equal rewards for their labor.

Most structuralists argue that the American economy is divided into core and peripheral sectors, while the labor market is divided into a primary and a secondary market. Wages in the primary labor market located in the core sector are higher and working conditions better, while wages in the secondary labor market in the peripheral sector are lower and working conditions worse. According to the structuralists, there is relatively little mobility between the two sectors or the two labor markets. Workers are distributed within these sectors and markets on the basis of race, ethnicity, gender, and nativity, rather than according to education, work experience, or other kinds of human capital. If this were not so, the structuralists argue, Asian Americans would be receiving the same returns to their education as non-Hispanic white males do.

Why do some scholars and journalists so eagerly highlight Asian American success while others keep harping on the continued existence of discrimination? To answer this question, it must be recognized that the debate is not just over economics but also over ideology. Put simply, those who depict Asian Americans as the model minority believe that American society is indeed an egalitarian one, with opportunities for all individuals who make the necessary effort to achieve a measure of material well-being. If someone or a certain group does not "make it," at least part of the fault lies with that person or group. Those who focus on continued inequality, on the other hand, believe the problem lies within the social, economic, and political system. In their view, before subordinated groups can improve their status, some aspect of the system must change. But systemic change can come about only with shifts in the present balance of power between different groups. For that reason, those Asian Americans who perceive reality in this manner advocate greater political activism.

Asians in America have a long, though until recently unrecognized, tradition of engaging in political action, but they never did so on a publicly visible scale until the 1960s. Those who became involved participated in two quite different kinds of politics: electoral politics, mainly in Hawaii, and mass protest politics, mostly on the West Coast and in a few metropolitan areas of the East Coast.

Asian participation in Hawaii's electoral politics goes back to 1922, when a Republican Nisei, James Hamada, ran for office in the territorial legislature. Neither he nor several others who tried in the late 1920s succeeded in winning a seat. The first successful candidates, two Republicans and a Democrat, were Noboru Miyake, who was elected county supervisor, and Tasaku Oka and Andy Yamashiro, who were elected to the House of Representatives of the territorial legislature. By 1936 there were nine Nisei among Hawaii's thirty-nine elected officials. Hiram Fong, a Hawaii-born Chinese, began serving in the House in 1938, rising to its speakership in 1949.[9]

The Asian, especially Japanese, presence in Hawaiian politics increased greatly in the late 1940s and early 1950s when a number of veterans of the famed 100th Battalion and 442nd Regimental Combat Team, who had gone to law school on the GI Bill, entered politics. In the words of Daniel K. Inouye, perhaps the best-known member of that cohort, "the time had come for us to step forward. We had fought for that right with all the furious patriotism in our bodies and now we didn't want to go back to the plantation. . . . We wanted to take our full place in society . . ."[10] The entry of veterans like Inouye into the political arena was part of a larger phenomenon, sometimes called Hawaii's "Democratic revolution" of 1954.

Up to that point, Hawaii's politics had been controlled by Euro-American Republican politicians who either came out of, or were firmly allied with, the old plantation elite. The latter's paramount status had been somewhat eroded during World War II, when the military ruled the islands. Then toward the end of the war, another important development occurred: the International Longshoremen's and Warehousemen's Union (ILWU) began organizing workers in the plantations and along the waterfront. Not only did the union successfully stage a strike in 1946 involving 28,000 workers and shut down 33 plantations for almost three months, but it also became involved in electoral politics.

As a new working- and middle-class constituency emerged, Democratic candidates, under the leadership of John Burns, who later became governor (1962–73), managed to sweep into office in both branches of the territorial government in 1954. These "New Democrats"—a large percentage of them of Japanese ancestry—retained their majority for more than three decades. Japanese Americans occupied 55 percent of the leadership positions in the legislature during this period as president of the Senate, Speaker of the House, and chairmen of key committees. Some 40 percent of the leaders, in turn, were veterans of the 100th Battalion or 442nd Regimental Combat Team.[11]

When Hawaii became a state in 1959, these Asian American politicians, who had cut their teeth in the territorial legislature, acquired national visibility. Hiram Fong, speaker of the territorial House from 1949 to 1953, was elected U.S. Senator. Dan Inouye, majority leader in the territorial House from 1954 to 1958 and a member of the territorial Senate in 1958–59, was elected to the U.S. House of Representatives. When Inouye won a seat in the U.S. Senate in 1962—where he still serves—his place in the U.S. House of Representatives was taken by Spark Matsunaga, a veteran of the 100th Battalion. When Hawaii's population increased sufficiently for it to be allocated a second seat in the House in 1964, Patsy Takemoto Mink, the first Hawaiian Nisei woman to receive a law degree, filled it. In 1976 Matsunaga was also elected to the U.S. Senate. Each of these members of Hawaii's Asian American delegation to Congress has served with distinction.

Not as well-known as Fong, Inouye, Matsunaga, and Mink are the Asian pioneer politicians on the mainland. The first person of Asian ancestry to win state office on the mainland was Wing F. Ong, a Chinese immigrant who came to the United States in 1918 at the age of 14. He joined relatives who wanted him to enter the laundry business, but he was determined to get an education. Denied admission even to the segregated "Oriental School" in San Francisco because he did not know any English, he went to Phoenix, Arizona, where one of his uncles had a grocery store. There he finished elementary and high school in six years, while working as a houseboy for Arizona's governor and catching a glimpse of American electoral politics. He attended the University of Arizona in Tuscon for a year, but had to drop out for lack of funds. During the next 15 years, he ran a grocery store and started a family. When he lost a bid for state office in 1940, he decided to study law. Three years after receiving a law degree, he ran again for office as a Democrat and became the first Asian to be elected to a state House of Representatives on the mainland. He served two terms. He unsuccessfully tried for a House seat again in 1950 and 1958 and a Senate seat in 1964. He was elected to the state Senate in 1966, but lost a reelection attempt in 1968.[12]

The first Asian immigrant from the mainland to win a seat in the U.S. House of Representatives was Dalip Singh Saund, a graduate of Punjab University who came to the United States in 1920 and eventually obtained a Ph.D. in mathematics. But having worked in the summers in the Imperial Valley, after obtaining his doctorate he decided to grow lettuce there, leasing land under the name of his wife, a Czech immigrant. When the 1946 Luce-Celler Bill made it possible for Asian Indians to be naturalized, Saund became a citizen. He ran for and was elected a judge in the town of Westmoreland in the Imperial Valley. He successfully ran for Congress in 1956 and was reelected in 1958; ill health forced him to retire before his second term expired.[13]

But Ong and Saund were exceptions. Unlike the situation in Hawaii, where Asian Americans have become a powerful political force, Asian American politicians are still relatively rare on the mainland. It was not until 1974 that another Asian American—Norman Mineta, mayor of San Jose, California—won a seat in the U.S. House of Representatives. He was joined by Robert Matsui, another Nisei and former member of the Sacramento City Council, in 1978. Both Mineta and Matsui are still in Congress. The first person of Asian ancestry from the mainland to enter the U.S. Senate was actually a Canadian—S. I. Hayakawa, a semanticist who served as president of San Francisco State University during the late 1960s. Hayakawa, who always wore a tam-o'-shanter, became a national symbol during the Third World student strike at San Francisco State in 1968: in the midst of a student demonstration against the university's administration, he leaped upon a truck and tore out the wires of the public address system, as a television crew filmed his action for a nationwide audience. His conservative politics helped get him elected on the Republican ticket to the U.S. Senate in 1976, where he served one term. When Chinese American physicist S. B. Woo won the lieutenant governorship of Delaware in 1984, he proved that an Asian American could be elected from a state without a large Asian population. However, Woo failed in his bid for a U.S. Senate seat in the 1988 elections.

A number of Asian American women office-holders have also gained considerable visibility. March Fong Eu, elected California's secretary of state in 1974, is still in office, having been repeatedly reelected by a large margin of votes. Jean King served as lieutenant governor of Hawaii from 1978 to 1982 and remains the highest-ranking Asian American woman ever to hold state office. Filipina American Thelma Garcia Buchholdt served in Alaska's House of Representatives from 1974 to 1983, surviving a smear campaign against "foreigners" in a primarily Euro-American district. At present, Patricia Saiki of Hawaii is the only Asian American woman in the U.S. House of Representatives. At a more local level, Carol Kawanami and Lily Chen have also made history: Kawanami was the first Japanese American woman in the nation to serve as mayor (in Villa Park, Orange County, California, in 1980), while Chen was the first Chinese American woman to be so honored (in Monterey Park, California, in 1983).[14]

Few in number though they are, these Asian American politicians have made a difference. Their effectiveness can perhaps be most clearly seen in the legislative history of the 1988 Civil Liberties Act. For some 30 years after World War II, Japanese Americans kept silent about the injustice of their internment, but in the mid-1970s a number of individuals began to talk openly about seeking reparations for their ordeal. A National Committee for Redress was formed within the JACL under the chairmanship of Clifford Uyeda of San Francisco. At its 1978 national convention, JACL adopted a resolution calling for $25,000 in reparations for each individual who was interned. When opposition to redress surfaced—not only from Euro-Americans but also from Japanese Americans who thought it best not to reopen old wounds—the JACL decided that, instead of seeking a monetary compensation, it would ask Congress to create a commission to "determine whether a wrong was committed against those American citizens and permanent residents relocated or interned as a result of Executive Order 9066."[15]

Congress agreed to set up such a body—the Commission on Wartime Relocation and Internment of Civilians, whose members and staff gathered and studied thousands of documents and held hearings across the country to hear testimony from 750 persons. After this exhaustive investigation, the commission concluded that the incarceration had indeed been "a grave injustice." More important, the commissioners decided that Executive Order 9066 and the evacuation and internment that it sanctioned resulted from "race prejudice, war hysteria and a failure of political leadership."[16]

Despite the commission's findings, it took extraordinary effort to marshal support for a redress bill that could pass both houses of Congress. The Japanese Americans in the U.S. Senate and House of Representatives prepared each step with care and bided their time. Finally, in September 1987 the House voted 243 to 141 to ask the nation to issue an official apology to Japanese Americans and to compensate each living internee the sum of $20,000. The Senate voted 69 to 27 in April 1988 for the bill.

President Ronald Reagan signed the bill into law before he left office, but it took almost a year of congressional wrangling over allocations to implement it. In August 1989 the House appropriated $50 million for redress payment in the 1990 fiscal year. But the following month the Senate recommended that no money be allocated in 1990, though its subcommittee on appropriations declared that funding for redress would be a "priority" in 1991. After outcries of "a second betrayal," in late November 1989 President George Bush finally signed into law an entitlement program scheduled to begin 1 October 1990 and end in 1993, with payment going to the oldest survivors first.

The redress movement has been a prime example of how Asian American elected officials have worked hand in hand with community activists toward a common end. Compared to those in electoral politics, who must work through established channels, community activists have more often engaged in protest politics at the grassroots level. Most of the early activists were young people who came of age during the 1960s.[17] Very few Asian Americans participated in the civil rights movement in the early 1960s, but the movement against U.S. involvement in the war in Vietnam caught their attention in the late 1960s. With the help of the television evening news, an increasing number of Asian American college and high school students realized with a shock that the "enemy" whom American soldiers were maiming and killing had faces like their own. A number of the more radical students began to think of the war not only as an imperialist but also as a racist one.

Young Asian Americans, as well as youth of other ethnic backgrounds, also drew inspiration from China's Great Proletarian Cultural Revolution, news of which sporadically filled the world's newspapers and television screens for the ten years between 1966 and 1976. The Cultural Revolution, an officially sanctioned campaign by young Red Guards against a segment of China's political establishment, fired the imagination of rebellious students everywhere. Bookstores in the United States that imported the red plastic-covered booklets containing the sayings of Mao Zedong did a thriving business. Like the Red Guards in China, many Asian American students, along with their black, Chicano, and white peers, waved the pocket-sized talismans as they marched in demonstrations against the war in Vietnam, for civil rights, for racial pride, and for the establishment of ethnic studies courses and programs.

The activists eagerly adopted the Chinese Communists' political work style: they held long meetings, practiced collective leadership, and engaged in sectarian struggles. But since there was no "countryside" to go to, where they might learn from "the masses"—as the Red Guards in China were doing—the Asian American activists descended on their surprised communities. Some members of these communities—especially the leaders of the traditional organizations—looked askance at the students' unkempt long hair, Mao jackets, and rude (and terribly un-Asian) manners.

Nonetheless, the activists tried to organize garment and restaurant workers; set up social service agencies; recruit individuals to leftist organizations, which mushroomed overnight; and protest against a variety of ills. These included not only those created by American racism and capitalism but also those spawned by the increasing presence of Asian "flight capital," which allowed entrepreneurs from Hong Kong, Taiwan, Tokyo, Bangkok, Singapore, and various other Asian metropolises to buy up buildings in the major Chinatowns and Japantowns of America, driving real estate prices sky high and causing severe hardship on the old residents.

The political activists were of two kinds: radicals who were mostly concerned with articulating the "correct" leftist political "lines" and reformers who put their energy primarily into setting up legal aid organizations, health clinics, and bilingual programs for the elderly and youth. In the long run, the former has had relatively little effect, but many of the agencies set up by the latter have remained. They continue to render important assistance to the needy and have been crucial in providing services to non-English-speaking new immigrants.

Within the political arena, the radicals were initially firmly opposed to "bourgeois" electoral politics, but a number of them later became actively involved in Jesse Jackson's Rainbow Coalition. Some of the reformers, meanwhile, have run for office or supported candidates. Ironically, those who paved the way for Asian American involvement in mainstream politics are now slowly outnumbered by more conservative individuals who support the domestic and foreign policies and programs of the Reagan and Bush administrations. The new immigrants who have come in search of a good life under capitalism, as well as the refugees who risked their lives to escape communism, are natural allies for the Republican party.

Nevertheless, there still exist issues that unite Asian Americans across political lines and across ethnic boundaries. One such issue is renewed violence against persons of Asian ancestry. Beginning in the early 1980s, instances of physical assault, harassment, vandalism, and anti-Asian racial slurs were reported to the U.S. Civil Rights Commission as well as to state and local civil rights bodies. In 1986, the Commission issued a report, in which it concluded that "the issue of violence against Asian Americans is national in scope."[18] The report listed many incidents in dozens of places around the country, described eight of them in some detail, and classified the victims into three categories: Southeast Asian refugees; immigrant entrepreneurs, especially Koreans; and various individuals.

A *Korean green grocer,* Los Angeles, 1980s.
Courtesy Visual Communications

Refugees from Vietnam, Laos, and Kampuchea in many parts of the country have been attacked. Adults as well as children have been beaten up. Refugee homes have been vandalized; the windows of their cars have been smashed and the tires slashed. In Texas and California, the boats of refugee fishermen have been burned. Said the attorney general of Massachusetts, "Racially motivated violence is a serious problem for Southeast Asian residents in our state. Often, these individuals cannot even walk along the public streets without being physically attacked and threatened because of their race or national origin."[19]

Tension has also erupted between Korean merchants and residents of the mostly black or Spanish-speaking neighborhoods where many of them have their stores. The local residents have accused the Koreans of treating them rudely—even roughly; some of the merchants' stores, meanwhile, have suffered from firebombings and defacement. In Washington, D.C., New York, and Los Angeles, human relations commissions have stepped in to mediate. "Treaties" of cooperation have been signed between the two groups and the situations have improved somewhat since the mid-1980s.

Of the many instances of harassment and violence, the one that has most incensed Asian Americans is the death in June 1982 of Vincent Chin, a 27-year old Chinese American draftsman in Detroit.[20] Chin, who was about to be married, was spending an evening out with several friends at a nightclub. Two

Euro-American men, Ronald Ebens and his stepson, Michael Nitz, taunted the group and a fist fight ensued. The manager evicted all of them. Once outside, Ebens and Nitz went to their car, took out a baseball bat from the trunk, and approached Chin and his companions, who were waiting in the parking lot to be picked up by another friend. Chin and his friends started running. Twenty minutes later, Ebens and Nitz caught up with Chin outside a McDonald's restaurant. With Nitz pinning back Chin's arms, Ebens hit him on the head, chest, and knees with the baseball bat. Chin fell bleeding to the pavement. Two off-duty policemen arrested the two assailants and called an ambulance. Chin died four days later from his wounds. Friends and relatives who had planned to attend his wedding came to his funeral instead.

Ebens was a foreman at an automobile plant. Nitz, who had been laid off, was going to school parttime. Soon after the incident, Ebens also lost his job. At that time, the American automobile industry was in a depression, facing stiff competition from cars imported from Japan. According to one witness, one of the things Ebens had said before the fight broke out in the nightclub was that it was because of people like Chin—Ebens apparently mistook him for a Japanese—that he and his fellow employees were losing their jobs.

The district attorney's office of Wayne County, Michigan, where Detroit is located, charged Ebens and Nitz with second-degree murder. In a plea bargain, Ebens pleaded guilty to manslaughter (a lesser charge), while Nitz did not contest his charge. Wayne County Circuit Judge Charles Kaufman sentenced both to three years' probation and a fine of $3,000 each plus $780 in fees.

Asian Americans in Detroit and eventually around the nation were outraged by the light sentences. When criticized, Judge Kaufman wrote a letter to a newspaper to defend the sentences. He said that in Michigan, sentences are tailored to the criminal and not just to the crime. According to him, since Ebens and Nitz had no previous criminal record, were longtime residents of the area, and were respectably employed citizens, he thought there was no reason to suspect they would harm anybody again. Hence, the light sentences. The judge's reasoning infuriated not only Asian Americans but non-Asians as well. One of the policemen who witnessed the beating said, "It's like nobody cares. It should have been first-degree murder." More important, another Michigan judge publicly declared that he also thought the charge should have been first-degree murder. A number of newspaper editorials pointed out that, in essence, the message Judge Kaufman was imparting to the public was that in the state of Michigan, as long as one was employed or was going to school, a license to kill cost only $3,000.[21]

A community group, American Citizens for Justice, which had been organized to ensure that justice would be done, demanded that the Michigan Court of Appeals vacate the sentences and order a retrial. The group also asked the U.S. Justice Department to investigate a possible violation of Chin's civil rights. Several California congressmen likewise wrote the U.S. attorney general requesting an investigation of the crime as well as the manner in which Wayne County officials had handled it. The Justice Department asked the FBI to carry out the investigation. Sufficient evidence of violation was found and a federal grand jury was convened in September 1983. Two months later the grand jury indicted Ebens and Nitz on two counts. The following year they were tried in a U.S. district court, whose jury convicted Ebens of violating Chin's civil rights but acquitted him of conspiracy, while acquitting Nitz of both charges. Ebens was sentenced to 25 years in jail and was told to undergo treatment for alcoholism, but he was freed after posting a $20,000 bond.

Ebens's attorney appealed the conviction and a federal appeals court overturned it in September 1986 on a technicality: one of the attorneys for Americans Citizens for Justice, who had interviewed several of the prosecution's witnesses, was said to have "improperly coached" them. The Justice Department ordered a retrial, which took place not in Detroit but in Cincinnati, a city whose residents not only had little exposure to Asian Americans in general but also were unfamiliar with the hostility that people in Detroit harbored against Japanese cars and Japanese-looking people. Much to the dismay of Asian Americans across the country, the Cincinnati jury acquitted Ebens of all charges. Neither he nor his stepson ever spent a day in jail. Lily Chin, Vincent's mother, was so upset by the final outcome that she left the United States—a country where, she felt, no justice existed—to live in China.

But the lesson learned in the Vincent Chin case was not lost. When a second Chinese American, 24-year-old Ming Hai Loo (commonly known as Jim Loo), was killed in late July 1989 in Raleigh, North Carolina, in a situation reminiscent of the Vincent Chin murder, Asian Americans immediately mobilized to monitor developments.

Loo was with five friends at a pool hall when two Euro-American men, Robert and Lloyd Piche, shoved them around while making racial slurs against Vietnamese. The Piche brothers, who had lost a third brother in Vietnam, had apparently mistaken Loo for a Vietnamese. The manager told the Piches to leave. They did, but when Loo and his friends came out, the two men assaulted them. Loo was hit on the back of his head with the shaft of a pistol and died two days later. Chinese Americans in the area quickly organized a Jim Loo American Justice Coalition to represent Loo's parents, who speak very little English, and to ensure that no travesty of justice would occur. Said a coalition leader, "We will do everything we can to avoid repeating the mistake with the Vincent Chin case."[22]

In late August, a grand jury indicted Robert Piche, the older of the two brothers, for second-degree murder. Lloyd Piche, who played an active part in aiding and abetting the attack, however, was only given a six-month sentence for assault and disorderly conduct. He was paroled after only six weeks because North Carolina's jails were overflowing. Leaders of the Jim Loo American Justice Coalition, in an effort to prevent plea bargaining in the Robert Piche case, sought and received a promise from the Wake County district attorney that they would be given ten days to present statements should the defense lawyers plead guilty, which would allow sentencing before 25 September, the date set for arraignment. The district attorney also assured the group that he would be willing to listen to evidence that might support a first-degree murder charge.

Though it was widely expected that the defendant would plead guilty in accordance with a plea bargain that his attorney had made with the court, at the arraignment Robert Piche surprised even his own lawyer by announcing that he was pleading not guilty. He also asked for a different court-assigned attorney and a change of venue. The general counsel for the Jim Loo Coalition was pleased by the unexpected turn of events because, by pleading not guilty,

Piche will have to go to trial. In the view of the coalition's leaders, this will allow the public to be "educated" about the nature of such racially motivated crimes.

In March 1990 the Wake County jury found Robert Piche guilty of second-degree murder, and Judge Howard Manning, Jr., sentenced him to 37 years in prison and told him he had "brought dishonor to North Carolina." Though Piche could be paroled after four years for good behavior, a spokesperson for the American Justice Coalition declared, "I think that this case shows that justice can be won if we as Asian Americans are willing to stand up and make clear in public that we will fight for justice."[23]

Asian Americans of various socioeconomic backgrounds and ethnic origins have also come together for action on another issue that concerns them deeply—the ability of their children to get a first-rate college education. In the mid-1980s community leaders, parents of college-bound students, and many students with straight A averages who had nevertheless been refused admission by some of the nation's most prestigious public and private universities, alleged that informal quotas were being imposed on Asian American university admissions. This development occurred at the same time that major periodicals (such as *Time, Newsweek, U.S. News & World Report*, the *New York Times Magazine*, the *New Republic*, and *Fortune*) and television programs (such as "20-20") were running stories about the dazzling academic achievements of Asian American students. To understand this contradiction, a brief review of the history of Asian Americans in American higher education is necessary.

Since the late nineteenth century, students from various Asian countries have come to the United States for higher education and practical training. In the 1920s these foreign Asian students were joined by a small number of American-born students of Asian ancestry—the sons and daughters of the first wave of immigrants. Most of the foreign students attended colleges and universities in various parts of the country, particularly where scholarships were available, but the bulk of the second-generation Asian Americans enrolled at universities on the Pacific Coast. The Berkeley and Los Angeles campuses of the University of California, first-rate public universities that charged no tuition, took in a majority of the latter. In comparison, relatively few second-generation Asian Americans went to the expensive Ivy League colleges on the East Coast.

But the pattern began to change in the late 1960s and early 1970s. With renewed immigration and the influx of large numbers of well-educated Asian parents eager to see their offspring receive the best education that money could buy, an increasing number of Asian-ancestry high school students began applying to the elite East Coast universities. Various affirmative action programs established in the wake of the civil rights movement had helped to open the doors of these institutions a crack to nonwhite students, including Asian Americans. By the late 1970s the number of Asian American applicants was rising so sharply that admissions officers and other university administrators worried aloud about the "overrepresentation" of Asian Americans in the student body. At universities such as Brown, Harvard, Princeton, and Yale, whereas Asian American applicants made up only 2 to 4 percent of the applicant pool in the early 1970s, they represented 10 to 15 percent a decade later. Despite this obvious increase, administrators at some of the Ivy League schools and at the University of California, Berkeley, have—under intense public pressure—

released figures that indicate that the admission *rate* of Asian American applicants has been lower than that for any other ethnic group. This revelation
seemed to substantiate charges that informal quotas must have been imposed
on Asian American university admissions for a number of years.

No university, however, has admitted any discriminatory intent, although
officials at several have acknowledged that existing policies and practices may
have had an unintentional adverse impact on Asian Americans. At the University of California, Berkeley, for example, under the scrutiny of a committee of
the California state legislature as well as the U.S. attorney general's office, the
school's officials revealed that, unbeknownst to the public, during the 1984
admissions cycle the school made two policy changes and proposed but did not
implement a third: 1) it raised the high school grade point average (GPA) for
regularly admissible applicants from 3.75 to 3.9; 2) Asian American Educational Opportunity Program (EOP) students would no longer be exempted
from "redirection" (i.e., be sent to other UC campuses); and 3) a minimum
score of 400 on the verbal part of the Scholastic Aptitude Test (SAT) was
proposed for permanent resident alien applicants (a very large proportion of
whom in northern California are of Asian ancestry). The effect of these changes
on Asian Americans were subtle but noticeable.

It is well known that students of Asian ancestry tend to have better GPAs
than standardized test scores and that, in particular, many recent immigrant
students do not do well on the SAT verbal test. Moreover, since a low family
income is one of the criteria that qualifies a student for EOP status, "redirect-
ing" Asian American applicants to other UC campuses away from the San
Francisco Bay area meant that most of them, who might have lived at home,
would have to live in dormitories, an added expense that their immigrant
families cannot afford. Thus the two changes negatively affected—and the
proposed one would have affected—Asian American applicants disproportion-
ately, even though on the face of it, Asian Americans were not singled out for
discriminatory treatment.

These revelations caused a furor. To restore amicable relations between his
university and the Asian American community, Berkeley's chancellor admitted
no guilt, but issued a public apology for the "insensitive" manner in which
members of his staff had responded to inquiries about the issue. Meanwhile, he
also appointed a committee to examine all aspects of Asian American life at
Berkeley. The committee issued a detailed report, but the campus did not act
speedily to implement the recommended changes. In February 1990 the board
of regents of the University of California announced that, on 1 July, Chang-lin
Tien, a Chinese American engineer, would become Berkeley's new chancellor,
making him the first Asian American to be chancellor of a major research
university in the United States. It remains to be seen whether the tensions
generated by the Asian American admissions controversy will finally be
soothed.[24]

Asian Americans from different walks of life and of varying political persua-
sions have joined hands to ensure that their educational rights would not be
abridged, because access to quality higher education, perhaps more than any
other issue, is something they feel very strongly about. It can be argued, in fact,
that many Asians now immigrate to the United States precisely to allow their
children to receive such education, even though coming to a new land means

they themselves will very likely suffer downward occupational mobility. Asian immigrants usually think in terms of the family and not of the individual: they are willing to sacrifice their own socioeconomic standing in exchange for giving the next generation a better chance to "make it" in the world.

The appearance of an increasing number of Asian American college students has had a positive impact on another educational issue: the growth of Asian American studies courses and programs. In the late 1960s and early 1970s such courses and programs were started at several dozen colleges and universities on the Pacific Coast. Those at San Francisco State University and at the University of California, Berkeley, began as part of the settlement of two long and militant student strikes. What that generation of students, as well as succeeding generations who filled the classes, wanted was a more "relevant" education—by which they meant that they wanted a curriculum that included an incisive analysis of the history of racism, sexism, and class oppression in the United States; an accurate portrayal of the contributions and struggles of people of color; and practical training to enable graduates to bring about fundamental social change in their ethnic communities as well as in society at large. Because of their radical agenda, the programs encountered stiff resistance from curriculum and personnel review committees. A number folded, while others managed to stay afloat but did not grow.

Then in the late 1980s these programs were given a new lease on life when students at an increasing number of colleges around the country began demanding a more multiethnic curriculum. Dozens of campuses, including five of the eight general campuses of the University of California, now have some version of an ethnic studies requirement. Students at East Coast and midwestern universities are also insisting that Asian American studies programs be set up. Ironically, more faculty positions are now available in ethnic studies—of which Asian American studies is a component—than there are candidates to fill them.

One reason that a new generation of Asian American students is now asking for more Asian American studies programs, courses, and faculty is that a new cultural awakening has occurred alongside rising political consciousness. Instead of being asked to choose between an "Asian" heritage, on the one hand, and "American" culture, on the other hand, young Asian Americans feel much more comfortable about forging a new culture of their own—one that goes beyond a formulaic "blending of East and West" to articulate sensibilities that arise directly out of the historical experience and contemporary life circumstances of Asians in America. Only in Asian American studies courses do they get a glimpse of this emerging culture and, more important, are encouraged to help create it.[25]

Since the 1970s Asian American themes have found their way into the novels, short stories, poems, plays, films, dances, paintings, and posters produced by Asian American artists. In their works the writers and artists express a unique identity that has been molded by one or more Asian traditions, by selected strands of the Euro-American heritage, and by a third legacy born of the struggles of nonwhite peoples to survive and to carve a place for themselves in a country whose culture is infused with a consciousness of color hierarchy.[26]

Of the different media that Asian American artists have used, film is perhaps the most accessible to a general audience. So far, most films produced by Asian Americans (as well as a number made by Euro-Americans on Asian American topics) have been documentaries that deal with the most painful aspects of the Asian American historical experience. Loni Ding's *Nisei Soldier: Standard Bearer for an Exiled People* (1984) and *The Color of Honor* (1987) are about the World War II experience of Japanese Americans who volunteered for service in the army while their families were incarcerated in internment camps. *The Color of Honor*, with its compelling vignettes of many individuals who served, as well as some who refused to do so, was aired on the Public Broadcasting System network in January 1989 in 11 major metropolitan areas across the United States. It introduced many American viewers, perhaps for the first time, to the human dimensions of the gross injustice that was perpetrated upon an entire ethnic group.

Another fine film, *Unfinished Business* (1984), by Steven Okazaki, juxtaposes interviews with Fred Korematsu, Min Yasui, and Gordon Hirabayashi, as these men reflect on the moral convictions that led to them to resist an order that so many others obeyed, with clips of the young lawyers who took up the former's cause. An important message imparted by the film is that it is never too late for the wrongs done to one generation to be righted by the next.

*Carved in Silence* (1988), by Felicia Lowe, explores the legacy of the immigration station on Angel Island in San Francisco Bay, where thousands of aspiring Chinese immigrants were held—sometimes for years—as their right to land was minutely investigated. Interviews with three detainees are interspersed with reenacted scenes of the interrogations to which every detainee was subjected. Especially telling is an interview with a former Euro-American immigration official, who recalled an experiment he had done with his own sons. He had questioned the two boys about how many windows there were in their bedroom, where the light switch was, and so forth, and found that even though they slept in the same room, they gave different answers. With this illustration, he pointed out how easy it was for members of the same family to disagree about minute details of their surroundings. For such "discrepancies," tens of thousands of aspiring immigrants were denied landing and sent back to China.

*Dollar a Day, Ten Cents a Dance* (1984), by Mark Schwartz and Geoffrey Dunn, graphically reveals the hardships experienced by old Filipino farm workers who toiled for decades in the fields and orchards along the Pacific Coast. Paid a pittance, deprived of any home life, and physically attacked for seeking the companionship of white female taxi dancers, these men nevertheless have retained a sense of dignity and humor that shines out in the film.

Although most documentaries focus on California, a number deal with the Asian experience elsewhere in the country. *In No One's Shadow* (1988), by Naomi and Antonio De Castro, portrays the history of Filipinos in many areas, including Louisiana, where dozens of Filipinos had settled in the 1780s, long before any Filipinos came to Hawaii and California. *Mississippi Triangle* (1983), by Christine Choy, looks at the descendants of Chinese men who settled in the Mississippi Delta and who, in many cases, married black women. The story of this group reminds us that the Asian American experience is by no means a homogeneous one.

The adaptation of new Asian immigrants to American life has also been the subject of films. *The New Puritans: The Sikhs of Yuba City* (1987), by Ritu Sarin and Tenzing Sonam, uses scenes of a traditional wedding ceremony taking place in the 1980s in a California town as a backdrop against which Asian Indian teenagers speaking accentless American English discuss how they see themselves. The struggle of Vietnamese refugee fishermen for survival can be seen in *Monterey's Boat People* (1982), by Spencer Nakasako, a balanced and fair exploration of a controversial subject: the conflicting concerns of ecologists and the desire of immigrant fishermen to stay off welfare and earn an honorable living. *Becoming American* (1982), by Ken Levine, follows a Hmong family as it finds its way from a refugee camp in Thailand to Seattle, recording for posterity the sense of bewilderment that these newcomers experience as they learn to cope with modern Western life.

Complex contemporary events have also become the subject of films. *Who Killed Vincent Chin?* (1988), by Christine Choy and Renee Tajima, presents not only the recollections and opinions of many individuals who knew Vincent Chin or witnessed the events that led to his death, but also devotes considerable footage to Ronald Ebens, the killer. By letting Ebens have his say, instead of editorializing about his motives and actions, Choy and Tajima allow viewers to make up their own minds about the fairness, or lack thereof, of the American judicial system. Especially riveting are scenes of Vincent's bereaved but courageous mother, who, out of indignation at the lenient way the courts dealt with her son's killers, overcame the hurdle imposed by her limited knowledge of English and gave many public speeches in English.

A number of Asian Americans have produced commercial films. Wayne Wang's *Chan Is Missing* (1981) offers an insider's view of a contemporary American Chinatown. As the audience is drawn into the efforts of a middle-aged man and his hip nephew to solve a mystery (the disappearance of a friend who made off with a goodly sum of money), a range of characters show that Chinese Americans are not all cut from the same cloth. Wang's second film with Asian American characters, *Dim Sum* (1987), sensitively portrays the relationship between a Chinese American mother and one of her daughters as well as changing Chinese American attitudes toward marriage, the family, and the community. Wang's most recent film, *Eat a Bowl of Tea* (1989), is an adaptation of Louis Chu's 1961 novel of the same title. To make the film commercially viable, Wang has turned it into a love story, even though the main focus of the novel was the social dynamics of the "bachelor society" in New York's Chinatown. Another commercial film, *The Wash* (1988), by Philip Kan Gotanda, author of half a dozen plays, portrays a 60-year-old Japanese American woman who leaves her husband for a younger man, but feels obligated, nevertheless, to return weekly to her former home to do her husband's laundry. These films pull at the heartstrings in ways that no scholarly studies of the Asian American experience can possibly do.

Asian American artists working in other media have used some of the same historical events that films have explored. Chinese American playwright Genny Lim's *Paper Angels* (1982) depicts the hardships experienced by Chinese immigrants on Angel Island. The characters in the play express notalgia for China, sigh over its weakness, and voice anger at the immigration officials who demean their existence. Another play by Lim, *Bitter Cane* (1989) blends naturalism with fantasy, as it unravels the relationship between a Chinese prostitute in Hawaii and several men in her life: the plantation foreman who owns her, a militant worker who visits her regularly, a naive young man who falls in love with her, and a ghost that is not seen but is nevertheless an important part of her life.

Chinese American jazz musician and composer Fred Ho (formerly Houn) interweaves Chinese classical music with American jazz to create an extraordinary bilingual opera, *Chinamen's Chance* (1987)—the first of its kind—which contains a scene of a coolie rebellion on a ship sailing across the Pacific. Although Ho's history is confused (he had in mind the rebellion on the *Robert Browne*, bound not for the United States but for Latin America), he effectively uses music and lyrics to evoke an intense, manly anger.

Japanese American short story writer and playwright Wakako Yamauchi likewise delves into some of the key elements in her cultural heritage. In *And the Soul Shall Dance* (1977) the audience meets the members of two Japanese immigrant farm families in the Imperial Valley during the Great Depression. The characters' nostalgia for Japan, which shimmers like a mirage on the desert horizon, serves as a counterpoint for the harsh realities they must daily endure. Another play by Yamauchi, *12-1-A* (1982) dramatizes the diverse responses, ranging from rebellion to superpatriotism, of an internment camp's residents to their incarceration.

Moving closer to more recent events, Filipino American playwright Mel Escueta explores the plight of a Vietnam War veteran who, upon his return home, continues to be tormented by the guilt of having killed fellow Asians. Escueta, himself a veteran of the Vietnam War, said that he wrote *Honey Bucket* (1979) in order to deal with the "whole wrenching sadness" of that experience.

Compared to the naturalistic works of artists like Lim, Ho, Yamauchi, and Escueta, pioneer Chinese American playwright Frank Chin, whose play *The Chickencoop Chinaman* (1972) was the first theatrical work by an Asian American to receive critical notice in New York, seems more intent on creating characters that embody certain qualities dear to Chin's heart—particularly an Asian American version of machismo. In many of his works, women serve only as foils for the posturing of tough-talking men. Calling himself the only "authentic" Asian American writer, Chin disparages immigrants, Chinatowns, and other Asian American writers such as Maxine Hong Kingston and Henry David Hwang who, like him, have enjoyed critical acclaim. Hwang's most recent play, *M. Butterfly* (1988), which won the Tony Award for the best American play of 1988, has generated considerable controversy among Asian Americans. The story is about a French diplomat who falls in love with a male Chinese opera singer impersonating a woman, who, in the end, unveils his disguise. Critics accuse Hwang of catering to the taste for Oriental exotica on the part of Euro-Americans, while defenders of the work view it as the playwright's vehicle for making certain statements about imperialism, racism, and sexism.

Unlike the female characters in Chin's works, the women found in the writings of most Asian American female writers are complex and fascinating. The female characters in Maxine Hong Kingston's *The Woman Warrior: Memoirs of a Childhood among Ghosts* (1976), though often abused, are nevertheless resourceful people who find ways to transcend the circumstances into which they were born. The Japanese war brides in playwright Velina Hasu Houston's 1985 trilogy, *Asa Ga Kimashita, American Dream,* and *Tea* are women who dare to break traditional boundaries and who, despite enormous difficulties, find ways to survive in strange, new environments. The wife and mother in *Clay Walls* (1986), by Korean American novelist Kim Ronyoung, ruins her eyes doing embroidery in order to support her family after her husband loses the family's savings in gambling and later dies. Nonetheless, she always retains her dignity and teaches her children to be proud of who they are. In *The Joy Luck Club* (1989), novelist Amy Tan unpeels, layer by layer, the intertwined lives of four Chinese immigrant women and their daughters, offering intimate glimpses of complicated personalities.

A number of works deal with women who live at the margins of society. In *Aw Shucks!* (1981) playwright Barbara Noda depicts three Asian American lesbians who struggle to make their sexual orientation public. In *The Legend of Miss Sasagawara* (1950) short story writer Hisaye Yamamoto juxtaposes the daydreams of two innocent Nisei girls in an internment camp with the bizarre behavior of a spinster who has gone mad. Another mad but poignant woman appears in "Crazy Alice," a poem by Janice Mirikitani that indirectly raises the question whether madness is in fact a rational way to escape the constrictions that bound women's lives.

Many of the works by Asian Americans are compelling because they shatter stereotypes and articulate hitherto suppressed sensibilities. They give form to the paradoxes faced by Asian Americans and provide artistic maps, as it were, that lead their readers, viewers, or listeners to a new terrain that Asian Americans finally can claim as their very own. Finding an Asian American voice is a kind of homecoming. In the words of Janice Mirikitani,

> There are miracles that happen
> she said,
> and everything is made visible.
>> We see the cracks and fissures in our soil:
> We speak of suicides and intimacies,
> of longings lush like wet furrows,
> of oceans bearing us toward imagined riches,
> of burning humiliations and
> crimes by the government.
> Of self hate and of love that breaks
> through silences.
>> We are lightning and justice.
>> Our souls become transparent like glass
> revealing tears for war-dead sons
> red ashes of Hiroshima
> jagged wounds from barbed wire.
>> We must recognize ourselves at last.
>> We are a rainforest of color
> and noise.
>> We hear everything.
>> We are unafraid.
>
> Our language is beautiful.[27]

# Conclusion

The history of Asians in America can be fully understood only if we regard them as both immigrants and members of nonwhite minority groups. As immigrants, many of their struggles resemble those that European immigrants have faced, but as people of nonwhite origins bearing distinct physical differences, they have been perceived as "perpetual foreigners" who can never be completely absorbed into American society and its body politic. To undergird their separateness, discriminatory laws and practices similar to those forced upon Native, African, and Latino Americans have likewise been imposed on Asian immigrants and their American-born progeny.

Thus the acculturation process experienced by Asians in America has run along two tracks: even as they acquired the values and behavior of Euro-Americans, they simultaneously had to learn to accept their standing as racial minorities—people who, because of their skin color and physiognomy, were not allowed to enjoy the rights and privileges given acculturated European immigrants and native-born Americans. In short, if they wished to remain and to survive in the United States, they had to learn to "stay in their place" and to act with deference toward those of higher racial status.

This was a new form of subordination, for though many of the early immigrants came from a low-class background and had lived in poverty, in their homelands most had not been racial or ethnic minorities. (Exceptions were the "untouchable" *eta* among Japanese immigrants and the Hakka among Chinese immigrants.) In the communities they established in the New World, social hierarchy based on class continued to exist, even though not all the Old World classes were represented. But in their relationship to the host society, well-to-do merchants and poor servants, landowning farmers and propertyless farm workers, exploitative labor contractors and exploited laborers alike were considered inferior to *all* Euro-Americans, regardless of the internal ethnic and socioeconomic divisions among the latter.

Only in the decades since World War II have various facets of the institutional structure upholding the racial division of American society been dismantled piece by piece. Today, discrimination based on race—as well as on sex and religion—is no longer legal, and those who feel the sting of injustice can go to court to challenge what de facto discrimination remains. Prejudice and systematic bias have not disappeared, however; instead, they have taken new forms. The present status of Asian Americans is a subject that requires serious study and incisive analysis precisely because Asian Americans, more so than black or Latino Americans, live in a state of ambivalence—lauded as a "successful" or "model minority" on the one hand, but subject to continuing unfair treatment, including occasional outbursts of racially motivated violence, on the other.

For that reason, no work of synthesis on the history of Asian Americans can be definitive: given the flux in which Asian Americans live, and given the incomplete knowledge we have of their history, what I present here is only a snapshot in time—one that reflects what is known about Asian Americans in the early 1990s in general and my interpretation of past and present events in particular.

There is no question that the status of Asians in America has dramatically improved. A larger question, however, remains: will Asian Americans work alongside their multiethnic neighbors to bring about a more egalitarian society in the United States? Intrepid Asian immigrants have proven their ability to resist oppression and to survive. Whether or not Asian Americans can now become full participants in American life depends in part on their own willingness to channel some of their energies into public service—activities that improve the larger commonweal. Indeed, if the United States wishes to be the beacon that shows the way to a more harmonious world, then the curtailment of racial tensions is a goal toward which all Americans must steadfastly work.

# Films about the Asian American Experience

Quite a number of films about Asian Americans are now available for classroom use. Most of them can be rented for a modest fee either in 16 mm or videocassette. Available catalogs include Bernice Chu, ed., *Asian American Media Reference Guide* (New York: Asian Cinevision, 1986), and National Asian American Telecommunications Association, *CrossCurrent Media: Asian American Audiovisual Catalog, 1990–91* (San Francisco: National Asian American Telecommunications Association, 1990). Distributors and their addresses are in brackets. Annotation is provided only for those films the contents of which are not self-evident from their titles.

*A Dollar a Day, Ten Cents a Dance* by Geoffrey Dunn and Mark Schwartz, 29 minutes, color. Filipino farm workers in California. [National Asian American Telecommunications Association (hereafter NAATA), 346 Ninth Street, 2nd floor, San Francisco, CA 94103]

*American Chinatown* by Todd Carrel, 30 minutes, color. [Extension Media Center, University of California, 2223 Fulton, Berkeley, CA 94720]

*Asian American New Wave* by Nancy Tong, 18 minutes, color. Interviews with Asian American performers and artists. [Apple TV, 11 Mercer Street, New York, NY 10013]

*Becoming American* by Ken Levine, 58 minutes, color. A Hmong family's journey from Laos to the United States. [New Day Films, 121 W. 27th St., #902, New York, NY 10001]

*Blue Collar and Buddha* by Taggart Siegel and Kati Johnston, 90 minutes, color. Reception of Laotian refugees in a small midwestern town. [NAATA]

*Carved in Silence* by Felicia Lowe, 45 minutes, color. Recollections of Chinese immigrants detained in the Angel Island immigration station. [NAATA]

*Chan Is Missing* by Wayne Wang, 80 minutes, black and white. A detective story set in San Francisco's Chinatown. [New Yorker Films, 16 W. 61st Street, New York, NY 10023]

*Children of the Railroad Workers* by Richard Gong, 40 minutes, black and white. Chinese construction workers in New York's Chinatown. [Amerasia Bookstore, 129 Japanese Village, Los Angeles, CA 90012]

*Chinese Gold: The Chinese of the Monterey Bay Region* by Mark Schwartz and Geoffrey Dunn, 42 minutes, color. [Chip Taylor Communications, 15 Spollett Drive, Derry, NH 03038]

*Color of Honor: The Japanese American Soldier in World War II* by Loni Ding, 90 minutes, color. Focuses on the Japanese American graduates of the Military Intelligence Service Language School who served as translators and interrogators in the Asian/Pacific theater during World War II. [Vox Productions, 2335 Jones Street, San Francisco, CA 94133 or NAATA]

*The Cutting Edge* by Judith Mann, 29 minutes, color. Three adolescents from Vietnam and Laos in America. [Judith Mann, 3006 S.E. Tibbetts, Portland, OR 97202]

*Days of Waiting* by Steven Okazaki, 18 minutes, color. The story of an Euro-American wife of a Japanese American internee. [NAATA]

*East of Occidental* by Lucy Ostrander and Maria Garguilo, 29 minutes, color. The residents of Seattle's multiethnic International District. [NAATA]

*The Fall of the I Hotel* by Curtis Choy, 57 minutes, color. The demolition of the International Hotel in San Francisco, where many old Filipinos lived. [NAATA]

*Family Gathering* by Lisa Yasui, 30 minutes, color. A chronicle of the Yasui family of Hood River, Oregon. [New Day Films]

*Farewell to Freedom* by WCCO-TV, 55 minutes, color. Hmong in Laos and America. [Audio-Visual Center, Indiana University, Bloomington, IN 47405]

*Forbidden City, U.S.A.* by Arthur Dong, 56 minutes, color. A Chinese American nightclub and the lives of men and women who defied tradition to dance and sing. [Deepfocus Productions, 4506 Palmero Drive, Los Angeles, CA 90065]

*Framed Out: The Challenges of the Asian American Actor* by John Esaki, 28 minutes, color. [Amerasia Bookstore]

*Freckled Rice* by Stephen Ning and Yuet-Fung Ho, 48 minutes, color. A Chinese American boy in Boston's Chinatown. [NAATA]

*From Spikes to Spindles* by Christine Choy, 50 minutes, color. Chinese immigrant workers from the 1860s to the present. [Third World Newsreel, 335 W. 38th Street, New York, NY 10018]

*Fujikawa* by Michael Uno, 30 minutes, color. Japanese immigrant fishermen in San Pedro, California. [GPN, Box 80669, Lincoln, NE 68501]

*Great Branches, New Roots: The Hmong Family* by Rita LaDoux, 42 minutes, color. [Hmong Film Project, 2258 Commonwealth Avenue, St. Paul, MN 55108]

*Hito Hata: Raise the Banner* by Bob Nakamura, 90 minutes, color. Japanese immigrants from the late nineteenth century to the present. [Visual Communications, 263 South Los Angeles Street, Room 307, Los Angeles, CA 90012]

*In No One's Shadow: Filipinos in America* by Naomi De Castro and Antonio De Castro, 58 minutes, color. [NAATA]

*Invisible Citizens* by Keiko Tsuno, 59 minutes, color. Three generations of Japanese Americans. [Downtown Community Television, 87 Lafayette Street, New York, NY 10013]

*Japanese Americans in Concentration Camps* by Visual Communications, 120 minutes, color. Hearings held by the Commission on Wartime Relocation and Internment of Civilians in Los Angeles. [Visual Communications]

*Mississippi Triangle* by Christine Choy, 110 minutes, color. Chinese in the Mississippi Delta. [Third World Newsreel]

*Mitsuye and Nellie: Asian American Poets* by Allie Light, 58 minutes, color. [Light-Saraf Films, 246 Arbor Street, San Francisco, CA 94131]

*Monterey's Boat People* by Spencer Nakasako and Vincent DiGirolamo, 29 minutes, color. Vietnamese fishermen in Monterey, California. [NAATA]

*The New Puritans: The Sikhs of Yuba City* by Ritu Sarin and Tenzing Sonam, 27 minutes, color. [NAATA]

*Nisei Soldier: Standard Bearer for an Exiled People* by Loni Ding, 29 minutes, color. Japanese American soldiers of the 442nd Regimental Combat Team. [Vox Productions]

*Perceptions: A Question of Justice* by Sandra Yep, 25 minutes, color. Korean American Chol Soo Lee's conviction, imprisonment, and community efforts to get him released. [KCRA-TV, 310 Tenth Street, Sacramento, CA 95814]

*The Price You Pay* by Christine Keyser, 29 minutes, color. Newcomers from Vietnam, Laos, and Kampuchea. [NAATA]

*Sewing Woman* by Author Dong, 14 minutes, black and white. Portrait of a Chinese immigrant seamstress. [Deepfocus Productions]

*Slaying the Dragon* by Deborah Gee, 60 minutes, color. Images of Asian women in American films and television. [NAATA]

*Two Lies* by Pam Tom, 24 minutes, color. The conflict between a Chinese American teenager and her recently divorced mother over standards of beauty. [NAATA]

*Unfinished Business: The Japanese American Internment Cases* by Steven Okazaki, 58 minutes, color. [NAATA]

*Wataridoro: Birds of Passage* by Robert Nakamura, 37 minutes, color. Portraits of three Japanese immigrants. [Amerasia Bookstore]

*Who Killed Vincent Chin?* by Christine Choy and Renee Tajima, 90 minutes, color. [Third World Newsreel]

*With Silk Wings: Asian American Women at Work* is a series of four films: *Four Women*, *On New Ground*, and *Frankly Speaking* by Loni Ding, and *Talking History* by Spencer Nakasako; 30 minutes each, color. [NAATA]

# Chronology

| | |
|---|---|
| 1600s | Chinese and Filipinos reach Mexico on the ships of the Manila galleon. |
| 1830s | Several Chinese "sugar masters" at work in Hawaii; Chinese sailors and peddlers show up in New York. |
| 1835 | Americans establish first sugar plantation in Hawaii. |
| 1844 | United States and China sign first treaty. |
| 1848 | Gold discovered in California; Chinese begin to arrive. |
| 1850 | California imposes Foreign Miners' Tax; Hawaii passes Masters and Servants Act and sets up Royal Hawaiian Agricultural Society to recruit plantation laborers. |
| 1851 | Chinese in San Francisco form Sam Yup and Sze Yup associations. |
| 1852 | First batch of 195 Chinese contract laborers land in Hawaii; over 20,000 Chinese enter California; Chinese first appear in court in California; missionary William Speer opens Presbyterian mission for Chinese in San Francisco. |
| 1854 | Chinese in Hawaii establish a funeral society, their first community association in the islands; *People* v. *Hall* rules that Chinese cannot give testimony in court; United States and Japan sign first treaty. |
| 1857 | San Francisco opens a school for Chinese children (changed to an evening school two years later); missionary Augustus Loomis arrives to serve the Chinese in San Francisco. |
| 1858 | California passes a law to bar entry of Chinese and "Mongolians." |
| 1860 | Japan sends a diplomatic mission to the United States. |
| 1862 | Six Chinese district associations in San Francisco form a loose federation; California imposes a "police tax" of $2.50 a month on every Chinese. |
| 1864 | Hawaiian plantation owners form Planters' Society and a Bureau of Immigration. |
| 1865 | Central Pacific Railroad Co. recruits Chinese workers for the first transcontinental railroad. |
| 1867 | Two thousand Chinese railroad workers strike for a week. |

| | |
|---|---|
| 1868 | United States and China sign Burlingame-Seward Treaty recognizing the right of their citizens to emigrate; Eugene Van Reed illegally ships 149 Japanese laborers to Hawaii; Sam Damon opens Sunday School for Chinese in Hawaii. |
| 1869 | Completion of first transcontinental railroad; J. H. Schnell takes several dozen Japanese to California to establish the Wakamatsu Tea and Silk Colony; Chinese Christian evangelist S. P. Aheong starts preaching in Hawaii. |
| 1870 | California passes a law against the importation of Chinese, Japanese, and "Mongolian" women for prostitution; Chinese railroad workers in Texas sue company for failure to pay them wages. |
| 1871 | Anti-Chinese violence in Los Angeles; San Francisco closes its evening school for Chinese children; Japan and Hawaii sign a friendship treaty. |
| 1872 | California's Civil Procedure Code drops law barring Chinese court testimony. |
| 1875 | Page Law bars entry of Chinese, Japanese, and "Mongolian" prostitutes, felons, and contract laborers. |
| 1876 | United States and Hawaii sign Reciprocity Treaty, providing that Hawaiian sugar may henceforth enter the United States duty-free. |
| 1877 | Anti-Chinese violence in Chico, California; Japanese Christians set up the Gospel Society in San Francisco, the first immigrant association formed by Japanese. |
| 1878 | *In re Ah Yup* rules Chinese ineligible for naturalized citizenship. |
| 1879 | California's second constitution prevents municipalities and corporations from employing Chinese; California state legislature passes law requiring all incorporated towns and cities to remove Chinese outside of city limits, but U.S. circuit court declares the law unconstitutional. |
| 1880 | United States and China sign treaty giving the former the right to limit but "not absolutely prohibit" Chinese immigration; Section 69 of California's Civil Code prohibits the issuance of marriage licenses for whites and "Mongolians, Negroes, mulattoes and persons of mixed blood." |
| 1881 | Hawaiian King Kalakaua visits Japan during his world tour; Sit Moon becomes pastor of the first Chinese Christian church in Hawaii. |
| 1882 | Chinese Exclusion Law suspends immigration of laborers for ten years; Chinese community leaders form Chinese Consolidated Benevolent Association (CCBA or Chinese Six Companies) in San Francisco; United States and Korea sign first treaty. |
| 1883 | Chinese in New York establish CCBA. |
| 1884 | Joseph and Mary Tape sue San Francisco school board to enroll their daughter Mamie in a public school; Chinese Six Companies sets up Chinese language school in San Francisco; United Chinese Society established in Honolulu; CCBA established in Vancouver; 1882 Chinese Exclusion Law amended to require a certificate as the sole permissible evidence for reentry. |

| | |
|---|---|
| 1885 | San Francisco builds new segregated "Oriental School;" anti-Chinese violence at Rock Springs, Wyoming Territory; first batch of Japanese contract laborers arrives in Hawaii under the Irwin Convention. |
| 1886 | Residents of Tacoma, Seattle, and many places in the American West forcibly expel the Chinese; end of Chinese immigration to Hawaii; Chinese laundrymen win case in *Yick Wo* v. *Hopkins*, which declares that a law with unequal impact on different groups is discriminatory. |
| 1888 | Scott Act renders 20,000 Chinese reentry certificates null and void. |
| 1889 | First Nishi Hongwanji priest from Japan arrives in Hawaii; *Chae Chan Ping* v. *U.S.* upholds constitutionality of Chinese exclusion laws. |
| 1892 | Geary Law renews exclusion of Chinese laborers for another ten years and requires all Chinese to register; *Fong Yue Ting* v. *U.S.* upholds constitutionality of Geary Law. |
| 1893 | Japanese in San Francisco form first trade association, the Japanese Shoemakers' League; attempts are made to expel Chinese from towns in southern California. |
| 1894 | Sun Yat-sen founds the Xingzhonghui in Honolulu; U.S. circuit court in Massachusetts declares in *In re Saito* that Japanese are ineligible for naturalization; Japanese immigration to Hawaii under Irwin Convention ends and emigration companies take over. |
| 1895 | *Lem Moon Sing* v. *U.S.* rules that district courts can no longer review Chinese habeas corpus petitions for landing in the United States; Hawaiian Sugar Planters' Association (HSPA) formed. |
| 1896 | Shinsei Kaneko, a Japanese in California, is naturalized; bubonic plague scare in Honolulu—Chinatown burned. |
| 1897 | Nishi Hongwanji includes Hawaii as a mission field. |
| 1898 | *Wong Kim Ark* v. *U.S.* decides that Chinese born in the United States cannot be stripped of their citizenship; Japanese in San Francisco set up Young Men's Buddhist Association; United States annexes Hawaii and the Philippines. |
| 1899 | Chinese reformers Kang Youwei and Liang Qichao tour North America to recruit members for the Baohuanghui; first Nishi Hongwanji priests arrive in California and set up North American Buddhist Mission. |
| 1900 | Organic Act makes all U.S. laws applicable in Hawaii, thus ending contract labor in the islands; Japanese plantation workers begin going to the mainland; bubonic plague scare in San Francisco—Chinatown cordoned and quarantined. |
| 1902 | Chinese exclusion extended for another ten years; immigration officials and the police raid Boston's Chinatown and, without search warrants, arrest almost 250 Chinese who allegedly had no registration certificates on their persons. |
| 1903 | First batch of Korean workers arrives in Hawaii; 1,500 Japanese and Mexican sugar beet workers strike in Oxnard, California; Kore- |

ans in Hawaii form Korean Evangelical Society; Filipino students (*pensionados*) arrive in the United States for higher education.

1904    Chinese exclusion made indefinite and applicable to U.S. insular possessions; Japanese plantation workers engage in first organized strike in Hawaii; Punjabi Sikhs begin to enter British Columbia.

1905    *U.S.* v. *Jue Toy* affirms that the commissioner-general of immigration has sole jurisdiction over Chinese immigration; Chinese in the United States and Hawaii support boycott of American products in China; Koreans establish Korean Episcopal Church in Hawaii and Korean Methodist Church in California; San Francisco School Board attempts to segregate Japanese schoolchildren; Korean emigration ends; Koreans in San Francisco form Mutual Assistance Society; Asiatic Exclusion League formed in San Francisco; Section 60 of California's Civil Code amended to forbid marriage between whites and "Mongolians."

1906    Anti-Asian riot in Vancouver; Japanese nurserymen form California Flower Growers' Association; Koreans establish Korean Presbyterian Church in Los Angeles; Japanese scientists studying the aftermath of the San Francisco earthquake are stoned.

1907    Japan and the United States reach "Gentlemen's Agreement" whereby Japan stops issuing passports to laborers desiring to emigrate to the United States; President Theodore Roosevelt signs Executive Order 589 prohibiting Japanese with passports for Hawaii, Mexico, or Canada to reemigrate to the United States; Koreans form United Korean Society in Hawaii; first batch of Filipino laborers arrives in Hawaii; Asian Indians are driven out of Bellingham, Washington.

1908    Japanese form Japanese Association of America; Canada curbs Asian Indian immigration by denying entry to immigrants who have not come by "continuous journey" from their homelands (there is no direct shipping between Indian and Canadian ports); Asian Indians are driven out of Live Oak, California.

1909    Koreans form Korean Nationalist Association; 7,000 Japanese plantation workers strike major plantations on Oahu for four months.

1910    Administrative measures used to restrict influx of Asian Indians into California.

1911    Chinese men cut off queues following revolution in China; Pablo Manlapit forms Filipino Higher Wages Assocation in Hawaii; Japanese form Japanese Association of Oregon in Portland.

1912    Sikhs build *gurdwara* in Stockton and establish Khalsa Diwan; Japanese in California hold statewide conference on Nisei education.

1913    California passes alien land law prohibiting "aliens ineligible to citizenship" from buying land or leasing it for longer than three years; Sikhs in Washington and Oregon establish Hindustani Association; Asian Indians in California found the revolutionary Ghadar Party and start publishing a newspaper; Pablo Manlapit forms Filipino Unemployed Association in Hawaii; Japanese form

Northwest Japanese Association of America in Seattle; Korean farmworkers are driven out of Hemet, California.

1914   Aspiring Asian Indian immigrants who had chartered a ship to come to Canada by continuous journey are denied landing in Vancouver.

1915   Japanese form Central Japanese Association of Southern California and the Japanese Chamber of Commerce.

1917   Arizona passes an Alien Land Law; 1917 Immigration Law delineates a "barred zone" from whence no immigrants (including Asian Indians) can come; Syngman Rhee founds the Korean Christian Church in Hawaii.

1918   Servicemen of Asian ancestry who had served in World War I receive right of naturalization; Asian Indians form the Hindustani Welfare Reform Association in the Imperial and Coachella valleys in southern California.

1919   Japanese form Federation of Japanese Labor in Hawaii.

1920   Ten thousand Japanese and Filipino plantation workers go on strike; Japan stops issuing passports to picture brides due to anti-Japanese sentiments; initiative in California ballot plugs up loopholes in the 1913 alien land law.

1921   Japanese farm workers driven out of Turlock, California; Filipinos establish a branch of the Caballeros Dimas Alang in San Francisco and a branch of the Legionarios del Trabajo in Honolulu; Washington and Louisiana pass alien land laws.

1922   *Takao Ozawa* v. *U.S.* declares Japanese ineligible for naturalized citizenship; New Mexico passes an alien land law; Cable Act stipulates that any American female citizen who marries an alien ineligible to citizenship would lose her citizenship.

1923   *U.S.* v. *Bhagat Singh Thind* declares Asian Indians ineligible for naturalized citizenship; Idaho, Montana, and Oregon pass alien land laws; *Terrace* v. *Thompson* upholds the constitutionality of Washington's alien land law; *Porterfield* v. *Webb* upholds the constitutionality of California's alien land law; *Webb* v. *O'Brien* rules that sharecropping is illegal; *Frick* v. *Webb* forbids aliens "ineligible to citizenship" from owning stocks in corporations formed for farming.

1924   Immigration Act denies entry to virtually all Asians; 1,600 Filipino plantation workers strike for eight months in Hawaii.

1925   Warring tongs in North America's Chinatowns declare truce; Hilario Moncado founds Filipino Federation of America.

1928   Filipino farm workers are driven out of Yakima Valley, Washington; Filipinos in Los Angeles form Filipino American Christian Fellowship.

1930   Anti-Filipino riot in Watsonville, California.

1931   Amendment to Cable Act declares that no American-born woman who loses her citizenship by marrying an alien ineligible to citizenship can be denied the right of naturalization at a later date.

1934   Tydings-McDuffie Act spells out procedure for eventual Philippine independence and reduces Filipino immigration to fifty persons a year; Filipino lettuce pickers in the Salinas Valley, California, go on strike.

1936 American Federation of Labor grants charter to a Filipino-Mexican union of fieldworkers.

1937 Last ethnic strike in Hawaii.

1938 One hundred and fifty Chinese women garmentworkers strike for three months against the National Dollar Stores (owned by a Chinese).

1940 AFL charters the Filipino Federated Agricultural Laborers Association.

1941 United States declares war on Japan following attack on Pearl Harbor; 2,000 Japanese community leaders along Pacific Coast states and Hawaii are rounded up and interned in Department of Justice camps.

1942 President Franklin D. Roosevelt signs Executive Order 9066 authorizing the secretary of war to delegate a military commander to designate military areas "from which any and all persons may be excluded"; Congress passes Public Law 503 to impose penal sanctions on anyone disobeying orders to carry out Executive Order 9066; incidents at Poston and Manzanar relocation centers.

1943 Incident at Topaz Relocation Center; registration crisis; Tule Lake Relocation Center made a segregation center; Hawaiian Nisei in the 100th Battalion sent to Africa; Congress repeals all Chinese exclusion laws, grants the right of naturalization and a small immigration quota to Chinese.

1944 Tule Lake is placed under martial law; draft reinstated for Nisei; draft resistance at Heart Mountain Relocation Center; 442nd Regimental Combat Team gains fame; exclusion orders are revoked.

1945 World War II ends.

1946 Luce-Celler bill confers the right of naturalization and small immigration quotas to Asian Indians and Filipinos; Wing F. Ong becomes first Asian American to be elected to state office in the Arizona House of Representatives.

1947 Amendment to 1945 War Brides Act allows Chinese American veterans to bring brides into the United States.

1949 Five thousand highly educated Chinese in the United States are granted refugee status after a Communist government comes to power in China.

1952 One clause of the McCarran-Walter Act grants the right of naturalization and a small immigration quota to Japanese.

1956 California repeals its alien land laws; Dalip Singh Saund from the Imperial Valley, California, is elected to Congress.

1959 Hawaii becomes the fiftieth state; Daniel K. Inouye and Hiram Fong are elected to represent Hawaii in Congress.

1962 Daniel K. Inouye becomes U.S. senator and Spark Matsunaga becomes U.S. congressman from Hawaii.

1964 Patsy Takemoto Mink becomes first Asian American woman to serve in Congress as representative from Hawaii.

| | |
|---|---|
| 1965 | Immigration Law abolishes "national origins" as basis for allocating immigration quotas to various countries—Asian countries are finally placed on an equal footing. |
| 1968 | Students go on strike at San Francisco State University to demand the establishment of ethnic studies programs. |
| 1969 | Students at the University of California, Berkeley, also go on strike for the establishment of ethnic studies programs. |
| 1970 | Asian American students join nationwide protests against the American invasion of Cambodia and the broadening of the war in Vietnam. |
| 1974 | March Fong Eu is elected California's secretary of state; *Lau* v. *Nichols* rules that school districts with children who speak little English must provide them with bilingual education. |
| 1975 | More than 130,000 refugees from Vietnam, Kampuchea, and Laos enter the United States as Communist governments come to power in their homelands. |
| 1976 | Health Professionals Education Assistance Act reduces influx of foreign doctors, nurses, and pharmacists; President Gerald Ford rescinds Executive Order 9066. |
| 1977 | Eilberg Act further restricts immigration of professionals. |
| 1978 | National convention of the Japanese American Citizens League adopts resolution calling for redress and reparations for the internment of Japanese Americans; massive exodus of "boat people" from Vietnam. |
| 1979 | Resumption of diplomatic relations between the People's Republic of China and the United States allows members of long-separated Chinese American families to be reunited. |
| 1980 | Refugee Act systematizes the admission of refugees; the government of the Socialist Republic of Vietnam and the United Nations High Commissioner for Refugees set up an Orderly Departure Program to enable Vietnamese to emigrate legally. |
| 1981 | Commission on Wartime Relocation and Internment of Civilians (set up by Congress) holds hearings across the country and concludes the internment was a "grave injustice" and that Executive Order 9066 resulted from "race prejudice, war hysteria and a failure of political leadership." |
| 1982 | Vincent Chin, a Chinese American draftsman, is clubbed to death with a baseball bat by two Euro-American men. |
| 1983 | Fred Korematsu, Min Yasui, and Gordon Hirabayashi file petitions to overturn their World War II convictions for violating the curfew and evacuation orders. |
| 1986 | Immigration Reform and Control Act is passed but affects Mexicans more than Asians. |
| 1987 | The U.S. House of Representatives votes 243 to 141 to make an official apology to Japanese Americans and to pay each surviving internee $20,000 in reparations. |
| 1988 | The U.S. Senate votes 69 to 27 to support redress for Japanese Americans; Amerasian Homecoming Act allows children in Vietnam born of American fathers to emigrate to the United States. |

1989    President George Bush signs into law an entitlement program to pay each surviving Japanese American internee $20,000; United States reaches agreement with Vietnam to allow political prisoners to emigrate to the United States.

# Notes and References

## Chapter 1

1. The institutional mechanisms that facilitated the Chinese diaspora are described in greatest detail in Robert Irick, *Ch'ing Policy toward the Coolie Trade, 1847–1878* (San Francisco: Chinese Materials Center, 1982), and Sing-wu Wang, *The Organization of Chinese Emigration, 1848–1888* (San Francisco: Chinese Materials Center, 1978). Among the vast literature on the Chinese in Southeast Asia, Victor Purcell, *The Chinese in Southeast Asia*, 2d ed. (London: Oxford University Press, 1965), though outdated, is still the most comprehensive survey.

2. The next six paragraphs are condensed from my study, *This Bittersweet Soil: The Chinese in California Agriculture, 1860–1910* (Berkeley and Los Angeles: University of California Press, 1986), 1–31. For Chinese emigration to the United States, see also Robert G. Lee, "The Origins of Chinese Immigration to the United States, 1848–1882," in *The Life, Influence and the Role of the Chinese in the United States, 1776–1960*, ed. Chinese Historical Society of America (San Francisco: Chinese Historical Society of America, 1976), 183–92; June Mei, "Socioeconomic Origins of Emigration: Guangdong to California, 1850–1882," *Modern China* 5 (1979): 473–501; and Zo Kil Young, *Chinese Emigration into the United States, 1850–1880* (New York: Arno Press, 1979).

3. Circumstances that made the initial Japanese exodus possible are recounted in Hilary F. Conroy, *The Japanese Frontier in Hawaii, 1868–1898* (Berkeley and Los Angeles: University of California Press, 1953), and Yasui Wakatsuki, "Japanese Emigration to the United States, 1866–1924," in *Perspectives in American History* 12 (1979): 389–516.

4. Yukiko Irwin and Hilary Conroy, "R. W. Irwin and Systematic Immigration to Hawaii," in *East Across the Pacific: Historical and Sociological Studies of Japanese Immigration and Assimilation*, ed. Hilary Conroy and Scott Miyakawa (Santa Barbara: ABC-Clio Press, 1972), 40–55.

5. For details, see Conroy, *Japanese Frontier*, 15–43.

6. Ibid., 65–80.

7. Alan Takeo Moriyama, *Imingaisha: Japanese Emigration Companies and Hawaii* (Honolulu: University of Hawaii Press, 1985), 13–24.

8. Ibid., 43–88.

9. The short-lived Korean emigration is covered in Wayne K. Patterson, *The Korean Frontier in America: Immigration to Hawaii, 1896–1910* (Honolulu: University of Hawaii Press, 1988), on which I rely for the next six paragraphs.

10. Ibid., 103–5.

11. U.S. Congress, Senate, *Charges of Cruelty in the Philippines*, Senate doc. 205, 57th Cong., 1st sess. (1902), and *Hearings on Affairs in the Philippine Islands before the Senate Committee on the Philippines*, Senate doc. 331, 3 vols., 57th Cong., 1st sess. (1902). A handy selection of testimony from these hearings is Henry F. Graff, ed., *American Imperialism and the Philippine Insurrection* (Boston: Little, Brown, 1969).

12. Stuart Creighton Miller, *Benevolent Assimilation: The American Conquest of the Philippines, 1899–1903* (New Haven: Yale University Press, 1982), is a good recent study of American policy in the Philippines.

13. Mary Dorita, *Filipino Immigration to Hawaii* (San Francisco: R & E Research Associates, 1975), 3–11, 16–17. See also Marvelino A. Foronda, Jr., "America Is in the Heart: Ilokano Immigration to the United States, 1906–1930," *Bulletin of the American Historical Collection* 4 (1976): 46–73.

14. Figures are computed from Bruno Lasker, *Filipino Immigration to Continental United States and to Hawaii* (1931; reprint, New York: Arno Press, 1969), 347–53.

15. Ibid., 354–55.

16. There is as yet no good study of Punjabi emigration based on Indian sources, but Sucheta Mazumdar, "Colonial Impact and Punjabi Emigration to the United States," in *Labor Immigration under Capitalism: Asian Workers in the United States before World War II*, ed. Lucie Cheng and Edna Bonacich (Berkeley and Los Angeles: University of California Press, 1984), 316–36, and Joan Jensen, *Passage from India: Asian Indian Immigrants in North America* (New Haven: Yale University Press, 1988), survey the global context of Punjabi emigration. John L. Gonzales, Jr., "Asian Indian Immigration Patterns: The Origins of the Sikh Community in California," *International Migration Review* 20 (1986): 40–54, and Bruce La Brack, *The Sikhs of Northern California, 1904–1975* (New York: AMS Press, 1988), 52–167, describe the several phases of Asian Indian immigration.

17. Romesh Dutt, *The Economic History of India in the Victorian Age*, vol. 2 (1904; reprint, New York: Augustus M. Kelley, 1969), 276.

18. Rajani Kanta Das, *Hindustani Workers on the Pacific Coast* (Berlin: de Gruyter, 1923), 3–4.

19. W. L. MacKenzie King, *Report of the Royal Commission Appointed to Inquire into the Methods by Which Oriental Labourers Have Been Induced to Come to Canada* (Ottawa: Government Printing Bureau, 1908).

20. Gerald N. Hallberg, "Bellingham, Washington's Anti-Hindu Riot," *Journal of the West* 12 (1973): 163–75.

## Chapter 2

1. Marina E. Espina, as reported in Fred Cordova, *Filipinos: Forgotten Asian Americans* (Seattle: Demonstration Project for Asian Americans, 1983), 1–7.

2.   Tin-Yuke Char, *The Sandalwood Mountains: Readings and Stories of the Early Chinese Immigrants in Hawaii* (Honolulu: University of Hawaii Press, 1975), 54–57, discusses the first Chinese sugarmakers in Hawaii.

3.   The best quick overview of changes in Hawaii's land tenure system is Edward D. Beechert, *Working in Hawaii: A Labor History* (Honolulu: University of Hawaii Press, 1983), 1–4, 29–34.

4.   Ronald Takaki, *Pau Hana: Plantation Life and Labor in Hawaii* (Honolulu: University of Hawaii Press, 1983), 19.

5.   John Wesley Coulter and Chee Kwon Chun, *Chinese Rice Farmers in Hawaii* (Honolulu: University of Hawaii Research Bulletin no. 16, 1937), 9.

6.   Edward C. Lydon, *The Anti-Chinese Movement in the Hawaiian Kingdom, 1852–1886* (San Francisco: R & E Research Associates, 1975).

7.   The statistics come from my article "Chinese Livelihood in Rural California: The Impact of Economic Change, 1860–1880," *Pacific Historical Review* 53 (1984): 299–306, and from my *This Bittersweet Soil*, 48–49.

8.   The activities of Chinese miners are recorded in J. D. Borthwick, *Three Years in California* [1851–1854], 1st ed. (Edinburgh and London: W. Blackwood and Sons, 1857), 117–19; David V. DuFault, "The Chinese in the Mining Camps of California: 1848–1870," *Historical Society of Southern California Quarterly* 41 (1959): 155–70; and Ping Chiu, *Chinese Labor in California, 1850–1880: An Economic Study* (Madison: State Historical Society of Wisconsin, 1967), 10–39.

9.   Despite their importance, no in-depth study of Chinese merchants has been done. A few large businesses are described in Eve Armentrout Ma, "The Big Business Ventures of Chinese in North America, 1850–1930," in *The Chinese American Experience*, ed. Genny Lim (San Francisco: Chinese Historical Society of America and Chinese Culture Foundation, 1984), 101-12. My discussion of merchants and the goods they imported is based on my examination of extant account books of Chinese stores held at the Bancroft Library, University of California, Berkeley.

10.   Alexander Saxton, "The Army of Canton in the High Sierra," *Pacific Historical Review* 35 (1966): 141–52, and Chiu, *Chinese Labor*, 40–51, provide the information for the next four paragraphs.

11.   Testimony by James Strobridge in U.S. Congress, Senate, Pacific Railway Commission, *Report and Testimony Taken*, 50th Cong., 1st sess. (1888), Senate exec. doc. 51, vol. 6, 3150, as quoted in Saxton, "The Army of Canton," 148.

12.   Varden Fuller, "The Supply of Agricultural Labor as a Factor in the Evolution of Farm Organization in California," in U.S. Congress, Senate, Committee on Education and Labor, *Hearings Pursuant to Senate Resolution 266, Exhibit 8762-A*, 76th Cong., 3d sess. (1940), 19777–898. For a critique of Fuller's thesis, see my *This Bittersweet Soil*, 273–80. The brief description of how Chinese participated in California's agricultural development is condensed from *This Bittersweet Soil*.

13.   Paul P. C. Siu, *The Chinese Laundryman: A Study in Social Isolation* (New York: New York University Press, 1987), is a classic study of how Chinese entered the laundry business in Chicago. Information from this source and from Paul M. Ong, "An Ethnic Trade: The Chinese Laundries in Early California," *Journal of Ethnic Studies* 8 (1981): 95–113, form the basis for the next five paragraphs. The numbers for Chinese laundrymen in California come from my *This Bittersweet Soil*, 54–55, 62–63, 68–69, 74–75.

14.   Siu, *Chinese Laundryman*, 46.

15.   Ibid., 21.

16.   On Japanese plantation workers and plantation life in general, see Takaki, *Pau Hana*; Beechert, *Working in Hawaii*; Moriyama, *Imingaisha*; and United

Japanese Society of Hawaii, *A History of Japanese in Hawaii* (Honolulu: United Japanese Society of Hawaii, 1971). The next nine paragraphs rely on these sources.

17. Virtually every study of Japanese Americans discusses their farming activities. The most succinct accounts of Japanese contributions to California agriculture are Masakazu Iwata, "The Japanese Immigrants in California Agriculture," *Agricultural History* 36 (1962): 25–37, and Adon Poli and Warren M. Engstrand, "Japanese Agriculture on the Pacific Coast," *Journal of Land and Public Utility Economics* 21 (1945): 352–64.

18. My tallies from the manuscript schedules of the 1910 U.S. Census of Population for the state of California are corroborated by Zaibei Nihonjinkai, *Zaibei nihonjinshi* (A History of the Japanese in America) (San Francisco: Zaibei Nihonjinkai, 1940), 182.

19. Japanese Agricultural Association, *The Japanese Farmers in California* (San Francisco: Japanese Agricultural Association, 1918), chart on ii.

20. Korean farming and other economic activities are described in Bong-Youn Choy, *Koreans in America* (Chicago: Nelson-Hall, 1979), 123–40, and Hyung June Moon, "The Korean Immigrants in America: The Quest for Identity in the Formative Years, 1903–1918" (Ph.D. diss., University of Nevada, Reno, 1976), 99–131, 169–217. Asian Indian employment is discussed in Das, *Hindustani Workers*; Sucheta Mazumdar, "Punjabi Agricultural Workers in California, 1905-1945," in *Labor Immigration under Capitalism*, ed. Cheng and Bonacich, 549–78, and Jensen, *Passage from India*, 28–40. Asian Indian reaction to the alien land laws is discussed in Karen Leonard, "The Pahkar Singh Murder Case," *Amerasia Journal* 11, no. 1 (1984): 75–88, and her "Punjabi Farmers and California's Alien Land Laws," *Agricultural History* 59 (1985): 549–61.

21. There is as yet no good study of Filipino livelihood; Lasker, *Filipino Immigration*, is still the main work available.

22. Yuji Ichioka, "Asian Immigrant Coal Miners and the United Mine Workers of America: Race and Class at Rock Springs, Wyoming, 1907," *Amerasia Journal* 6, no. 1 (1979): 1–24.

23. Yuji Ichioka, "Japanese Immigrant Labor Contractors and the Northern Pacific and the Great Northern Railroad Companies, 1898–1907," *Labor History* 21 (1980): 325–50.

24. Eve Armentrout Ma, "Chinese in California's Fishing Industry, 1850–1941," *California History* 60 (1981), 142–57, and Jack Masson and Donald Guimary, "Asian Labor Contractors in the Alaskan Canned Salmon Industry, 1880–1937," *Labor History* 22 (1981): 377–97.

25. U.S. Congress, Senate, Immigration Commission, *Reports of the Immigration Commission: Immigrants in Industries*, part 25, in 3 vols., "Japanese and Other Immigrant Races in the Pacific Coast and Rocky Mountain States," 61st Cong., 2d sess. (1911), Senate doc. 633, contain extensive statistics on the occupational distribution of Japanese and Asian Indian immigrants. On Japanese, see also H. A. Millis, *The Japanese Problem in the United States* (New York: Macmillan, 1915); Yamato Ichihashi, *Japanese in the United States* (1932; reprint, New York: Arno Press, 1969); and Yuji Ichioka, *The Issei: The World of the First Generation Japanese Immigrants, 1885–1924* (New York: Free Press, 1988), 57–175.

26. Scott Miyakawa, "Early New York Issei Founders of Japanese American Trade," in *East across the Pacific*, ed. Conroy and Miyakawa, 156–86.

## Chapter 3

1. Two older works—Mary Roberts Coolidge, *Chinese Immigration* (New York: Holt, 1909), and Elmer Clarence Sandmeyer, *The Anti-Chinese Movement in California* (Urbana: University of Illinois Press, 1939)—still provide the fullest analysis of the anti-Chinese movement. Gunther Barth, *Bitter Strength: A History of the Chinese in the United States, 1850–1870* (Cambridge: Harvard University Press, 1964), has been widely quoted by Euro-American historians but has been severely criticized by Asian American specialists for its blame-the-victim perspective. Alexander Saxton, *The Indispensable Enemy: Labor and the Anti-Chinese Movement in California* (Berkeley and Los Angeles: University of California Press, 1971), shows how the anti-Chinese campaign helped the labor movement to consolidate itself. Lydon, *The Anti-Chinese Movement*, examines the situation in Hawaii. The anti-Japanese movement may be divided into three phases: the passage of the alien land acts, the exclusion of Japanese, and the incarceration of persons of Japanese ancestry in so-called relocation camps during World War II. But few scholars have successfully analyzed all three in an integrated manner. One attempt was made in Jacobus tenBroek et al., *Prejudice, War, and the Constitution: Causes and Consequences of the Evacuation of the Japanese Americans in World War II* (Berkeley and Los Angeles: University of California Press, 1954); another is found in Daniels, *Asian America: Chinese and Japanese in the United States since 1850* (Seattle: University of Washington Press, 1988). Roger Daniels, *The Politics of Prejudice: The Anti-Japanese Movement in California and the Struggle for Japanese Exclusion* (Berkeley and Los Angeles: University of California Press, 1962), remains a standard work, while Ichioka, *The Issei*, 176–254, provides the only analysis based on Japanese-language sources. Since there were so few Koreans in the continental United States before World War II, no separate organized anti-Korean movement developed; a few sporadic incidents are briefly described in Choy, *Koreans in America*, 107–10, and Moon, "Korean Immigrants," 379–91. The anti-Filipino movement is investigated in the essays in J. M. Saniel, ed., *The Filipino Exclusion Movement, 1927–1935* (Quezon City, Philippines: Institute of Asian Studies, University of the Philippines, 1967). Anti-Asian Indian activities are best covered in Jensen, *Passage from India*, which stands alone in the entire literature on Asian Americans in its analysis of federal surveillance of dissident Asians in America.

2. Stuart Creighton Miller, *The Unwelcome Immigrant: The American Image of the Chinese, 1785–1882* (Berkeley and Los Angeles: University of California Press, 1969).

3. Hudson N. Janisch, "The Chinese, the Courts, and the Constitution: A Study of the Legal Issues Raised by Chinese Immigration to the United States, 1850–1902" (J.D. diss., University of Chicago, 1971), is an exhaustive study of the legal liabilities imposed on the Chinese. Frank F. Chuman, *The Bamboo People: The Law and Japanese Americans* (Del Mar, Calif.: Publisher's Inc., 1976), is a systematic survey of laws affecting the Japanese.

4. Reprinted in "The Wrongs to Chinamen," *Alta California*, 23 November, 1858, as quoted in Janisch, "The Chinese, the Courts, and the Constitution," 60, footnote 2.

5. Daniels, *Politics of Prejudice*, 46–64, and Chuman, *Bamboo People*, 39–42, 46–51, 76–89.

6. Dudley O. McGovney, "The Anti-Japanese Land Laws of California and Ten Other States," *California Law Review* 35 (1947): 7–54, covers states other than California. Studies of the alien land laws in Washington State include Jack D. Freeman, "The Rights of Japanese and Chinese Aliens in Land in Washington,"

*Washington Law Review* 6 (1930–31): 127–31, and Theodore Roodner, "Washington's Alien Land Law: Its Constitutionality," *Washington Law Review* 39 (1964): 115–33.

7. U.S. Congress, Senate, 40th Cong., 3d sess. (1868–69), *Congressional Globe*, pt. 2, 1030.

8. "A Chinese Citizen," San Francisco *Chronicle*, 28 November, 1878, as quoted in Janisch, "The Chinese, the Courts, and the Constitution," 205.

9. Janisch, "The Chinese, the Courts, and the Constitution," 227.

10. Roger Daniels, ed., *Anti-Chinese Violence in North America* (New York: Arno Press, 1978), is a collection of articles recounting violent incidents in various areas.

11. California State Legislature, "Report of the Joint Select Committee Relative to the Chinese Population of the State of California," *Journals of the Senate and Assembly*, Appendix, vol. 3 (Sacramento: State Printing Office, 1862), 7.

12. William R. Locklear, "The Celestials and the Angels: A Study of the Anti-Chinese Movement in Los Angeles to 1882," *Historical Society of Southern California Quarterly* 42 (1960): 239–56.

13. Chan, *This Bittersweet Soil*, 371–74.

14. Paul Crane and Alfred Larson, "The Chinese Massacre," *Annals of Wyoming* 12 (1940): 47-55, and Shih-shan Henry Tsai, *China and the Overseas Chinese in the United States, 1868–1911* (Fayetteville: University of Arkansas Press, 1983), 72–78, are the sources for the next three paragraphs.

15. Jules Alexander Karlin, "The Anti-Chinese Outbreak in Tacoma, 1885," *Pacific Historical Review* 23 (1954): 271–83; idem, "The Anti-Chinese Outbreaks in Seattle, 1885-1886," *Pacific Northwest Quarterly* 39 (1948): 103–29; and George Kinnear, "Anti-Chinese Riots at Seattle, Washington, February 8th, 1886," *Twenty-fifth Anniversary of Riots* (Seattle: n.p., 1911), provide information for the next five paragraphs.

16. Sacramento *Daily Record Union*, 4, 11, 26, and 27 January, 1, 2, 6, 12, 16, 19, 20, 23, and 26 February, 2, 5, 6, 8, 9, 10, 13, 15, 16, 17, 18, 19, 20, 23, 24, 29, and 31 March, 18 June, 10 August, 24, 25, and 28 October 1886.

17. Sacramento *Daily Record Union*, 15, 16, 18, 19, 20, and 21 August and 2, 3, 4, 5, 8, and 11 September 1893.

18. Daniels, *Politics of Prejudice*, 33.

19. Mazumdar, "Punjabi Agricultural Workers," 563.

20. The Hemet incident is told in Moon, "Korean Immigrants," 379–91. The telegram from the Koreans was sent on 29 June 1913 by Yi Tae-wi (David Lee), president of the Korean National Association, to Secretary of State William Jennings Bryan. Bryan's reply was sent out by the Associated Press and picked up by the Hemet *News*, 4 July, 1913, as cited in Moon, "Korean Immigrants," 390–91.

21. Yuji Ichioka, "The 1921 Turlock Incident: Forceful Expulsion of Japanese Laborers," in *Counterpoint: Perspectives on Asian America*, ed. Emma Gee (Los Angeles: Asian American Studies Center, University of California, Los Angeles, 1976), 195–201. Another incident is described in Stefan Tanaka, "The Toledo Incident: The Deportation of the Nikkei from an Oregon Mill Town," *Pacific Northwest Quarterly* 69 (1978): 116–26.

22. Emory S. Bogardus, "Anti-Filipino Race Riots" (San Diego: Ingram Institute of Social Science, 1930), reprinted in Jesse Quinsaat et al., eds., *Letters in Exile: An Introductory Reader on the History of Pilipinos in America* (Los Angeles: University of California, Los Angeles, Asian American Studies Center, 1976), 51–

62, and Howard A. De Witt, *Anti-Filipino Movements in California: A History, Bibliography and Study Guide* (San Francisco: R & E Research Associates, 1976), 46–66.

23.   Saxton, *Indispensable Enemy*, 74.

24.   George Anthony Peffer, "Forbidden Families: Emigration Experiences of Chinese Women under the Page Law, 1875–1882," *Journal of American Ethnic History* 6 (1986): 28–46.

25.   Coolidge, *Chinese Immigration*, has the most detailed account of the political and legislative maneuvers that led to the passage of the various Chinese exclusion laws.

26.   Daniels, *Politics of Prejudice*, 92–105, and Ichioka, *The Issei*, 244–54.

27.   Choy, *Koreans in America*, 87–88, reveals how a small number of Koreans managed to enter the country after 1910.

28.   Jensen, *Passage from India*, 101–20, 139–62.

29.   H. Brett Melendy, *Asians in America: Filipinos, Koreans, and East Indians* (Boston: Twayne, 1977), 27–28, 40–44.

30.   Sucheng Chan, "The Exclusion of Chinese Women, 1870–1943," in *Entry Denied: Exclusion and the Chinese Community in America, 1882–1943*, ed. Sucheng Chan (Philadelphia: Temple University Press, 1991).

31.   *Alta California*, 1 February 1861.

32.   Joan B. Trauner, "The Chinese as Medical Scapegoats in San Francisco, 1870–1905," *California History* 57 (1978): 70–87, and Charles J. McClain, "Of Medicine, Race, and American Law: The Bubonic Plague Outbreak of 1900," *Law and Social Inquiry* 13 (1988): 447–513, provide the information for the next two paragraphs.

33.   Charles M. Wollenberg, *All Deliberate Speed: Segregation and Exclusion in California Schools, 1855–1975* (Berkeley and Los Angeles: University of California Press, 1976), 8–27.

34.   Victor Low, *The Unimpressible Race: A Century of Educational Struggle by the Chinese in San Francisco* (San Francisco: East/West, 1982), 13–71.

35.   James W. Loewen, *The Mississippi Chinese: Between Black and White* (Cambridge: Harvard University Press, 1971), 65–69, is the basis for the next two paragraphs.

36.   *Rice et al. v. Gong Lum et al.*, 139 Mississippi Reports 763 (1925), as quoted in ibid., 67.

37.   *Gong Lum et al. v. Rice et al.*, 275 U. S. Reports 78 (1927), as quoted in ibid., 68.

38.   Ichioka, *The Issei*, 7–19, 22–28, describes the lives of the first immigrant students.

39.   Daniels, *Politics of Prejudice*, 31–45, documents efforts to segregate Japanese children.

40.   The most detailed study of anti-miscegenation laws against Asian immigrants is Megumi Dick Osumi, "Asians and California's Anti-Miscegenation Laws," in *Asian and Pacific American Experiences: Women's Perspectives*, ed. Nobuya Tsuchida (Minneapolis: Asian/Pacific American Learning Resources Center, University of Minnesota, 1982), 1–37. This study contains the information used in the next three paragraphs.

## Chapter 4

1. Rose Hum Lee, *The Chinese in the U.S.A.* (Hong Kong: Hong Kong University Press, 1960); Stanford Lyman, "Conflict and the Web of Group Affiliation in San Francisco's Chinatown, 1850–1910," *Pacific Historical Review* 43 (1974), 473–99; and Eve Armentrout Ma, "Urban Chinese at the Sinitic Frontier: Social Organizations in United States' Chinatowns, 1840–1898," *Modern Asian Studies* 17 (1983), 107–35, are general studies of Chinese immigrant communities on the mainland and the organizations within them. The next four paragraphs are based on these sources. Writings on cultural institutions in the older Chinese immigrant communities include Lois Rodescape, "Celestial Drama in the Golden Hills: The Chinese Theater in California, 1849–1869," *California Historical Society Quarterly* 23 (1944): 97–116; Ronald Riddle, *Flying Dragons, Flowing Streams: Music in the Life of San Francisco's Chinese* (Westport, Conn.: Greenwood Press, 1983); Wolfram Eberhard, "Economic Activities of a Chinese Temple in California," *Journal of the American Oriental Society* 82 (1962): 362–71; and Marianne Kay Wells, *Chinese Temples in California* (San Francisco: R & E Research Associates, 1971).

2. Clarence E. Glick, *Sojourners and Settlers: Chinese Immigrants in Hawaii* (Honolulu: University of Hawaii Press, 1980), 135–60, 185–268, provides details on organizations in Hawaii.

3. Him Mark Lai, "Historical Development of the Chinese Consolidated Benevolent Association/*Huiguan* System," *Chinese America: History and Perspectives, 1987* (San Francisco: Chinese Historical Society of America, 1987), 13–52, is the best study of the Chinese Six Companies and is the authority relied on in the next two paragraphs.

4. The most detailed descriptions of Japanese immigrant community associations are in Zaibei Nihonjinkai, *Zaibei nihonjinshi* (A history of the Japanese in America) (Los Angeles: Zaibei Nihonjinkai, 1940); Murai Ko, *Zaibei nihonjin sangyo soran* (A compendium of Japanese agriculture in America) (Los Angeles: Beikoku Sangyo Nipposha, 1940); and Noritake Yagasaki, "Ethnic Cooperativism and Immigrant Agriculture: A Study of Japanese Floriculture and Truck Farming in California" (Ph.D. diss., University of California, Berkeley, 1982).

5. Yukiko Kimura, "Locality Clubs as Basic Units of the Social Organization of Okinawans in Hawaii," in *Uchinanchu: A History of Okinawans in Hawaii*, ed. Ethnic Studies Oral History Project, United Okinawan Association of Hawaii (Honolulu: University of Hawaii, Ethnic Studies Program, 1981), 285.

6. Yuji Ichioka, "Japanese Associations and the Japanese Government: A Special Relationship, 1909–1926," *Pacific Historical Review* 46 (1977): 409–37, is the basis for the next four paragraphs.

7. Zaibei Nihonjinkai, *Zaibei nihonjinshi*, 280–96.

8. Yagasaki, "Ethnic Cooperativism," 49–57, 91–93, 130–41, 174–99, is the basis of the next four paragraphs.

9. Nihonjin Chuo Nokai, *Rono konshinkai kinen* (Record of a gathering of old and experienced farmers to promote friendship) (Sacramento: Nihonjin Chuo Nokai, 1909), 138–41, as quoted in ibid., 176.

10. Ibid., 56.

11. The attempt by immigrant leaders to wipe out gambling is covered in Ichioka, *The Issei*, 176–79.

12. Louise M. Hunter, *Buddhism in Hawaii: Its Impact on a Yankee Community* (Honolulu: University of Hawaii Press, 1971), and Tetsuden Kashima, *Bud-*

*dhism in America: The Social Organization of an Ethnic Religious Institution* (Westport, Conn.: Greenwood Press, 1977), are the sources for the next three paragraphs.

13.  Hunter, *Buddhism*, 33–36.

14.  Kashima, *Buddhism*, 6, 13–16.

15.  Wesley Woo, "Protestant Work among the Chinese in the San Francisco Bay Area, 1880-1920" (Ph.D. diss., Graduate Theological Seminary, Berkeley, 1983), is the only detailed study of Protestant proselytizing among Chinese immigrants.

16.  Hyung-chan Kim, "The History and Role of the Church in the Korean American Community," in *The Korean Diaspora*, ed. Kim, 47–63.

17.  Choy, *Koreans in America*, 99–101, 114–21, is the basis for the next three paragraphs.

18.  Don Chang Lee, "Korean Community Structures in America," *Korean Journal* 17 (1977): 48–60, and Hyung-chan Kim, "Korean Community Organizations in America: Their Characteristics and Problems," in *The Korean Diaspora*, ed. Kim, 65–83, describe Korean community organizations on the mainland. Kingsley K. Lyu, "Korean Nationalist Activities in Hawaii and the Continental United States, 1900–1945," part 1 (1910–19), *Amerasia Journal* 4, no. 1 (1977): 23–90, and part 2 (1919–45), *Amerasia Journal* 4, no. 2 (1977): 53–100, focus on the political activities that absorbed Koreans in America before World War II.

19.  Jensen, *Passage from India*, 41, and Ann Louise Wood, "East Indians in California: A Study of Their Organizations, 1900–1947" (M.A. thesis, University of Wisconsin, 1966).

20.  Jensen, *Passage from India*, 179–80.

21.  Mario P. Ave, *Characteristics of Filipino Organizations in Los Angeles* (1956; reprint, San Francisco: R & E Research Associates, 1974), provides the information used in the next three paragraphs.

22.  Severino F. Corpus, *An Analysis of the Racial Adjustment Activities and Problems of the Filipino-American Christian Fellowship in Los Angeles* (1938; reprint, San Francisco: R & E Research Associates, 1975).

23.  Cordova, *Filipinos*, 175–80.

## Chapter 5

1.  No in-depth study of the Chinese railroad workers' strike has been done, but there is a brief account in Thomas W. Chinn, H. Mark Lai, and Philip P. Choy, *A History of the Chinese in California: A Syllabus* (San Francisco: Chinese Historical Society of America, 1969), 45–46, based on information in *Alta California*, 1 July 1867; Sacramento *Record Union*, 1 and 3 July 1867; Stockton *Daily Independent*, 3 July 1867; and San Francisco *Commercial Herald and Market Review*, 10 July 1867.

2.  Lucy M. Cohen, *Chinese in the Post–Civil War South: A People without a History* (Baton Rouge: Louisiana State University Press, 1984), 82–132. The following five paragraphs are based on this source.

3.  J. C. B. Davis, assistant secretary of state, to C. M. Goulding, 20 January 1870, U. S. National Archives, Record Group 59, Instructions to Consuls, Department of State, as quoted in Cohen, *Chinese in the Post–Civil War South*, 76.

4.  San Francisco *Evening Bulletin*, 22 April 1875; Takaki, *Pau Hana*, 147–48.

5. The next fifteen paragraphs are culled from Beechert, *Working in Hawaii*, 161–76, 198–232; Takaki, *Pau Hana*, 145–76; and Alan Moriyama, "The 1909 and 1920 Strikes of Japanese Sugar Plantation Workers in Hawaii," in *Counterpoint*, ed. Gee, 169–80.

6. Karl Yoneda, "100 Years of Japanese Labor History in the USA," in Amy Tachiki et al., *Roots: An Asian American Reader* (Los Angeles: University of California, Los Angeles, Asian American Studies Center, 1971), 150–58, and Tomas Almaguer, "Racial Domination and Class Conflict in Capitalist Agriculture: The Oxnard Sugar Beet Workers' Strike of 1903," *Labor History* 25 (1984): 325–50.

7. Yoneda, "100 Years," 152.

8. Beechert, *Working in Hawaii*, 214–15. The next three paragraphs are based on 216–32.

9. Howard A. DeWitt, "The Filipino Labor Union: The Salinas Lettuce Strike of 1934," *Amerasia Journal* 5, no. 2 (1978): 1–22, and Cordova, *Filipinos*, 73–80, contain the information used in the next four paragraphs.

10. Peter Kwong, *Chinatown, New York: Labor and Politics, 1930–1950* (New York: Monthly Review Press, 1979), 116–30, is the basis for the following three paragraphs.

11. I arrived at these figures by going through the indexes of the *Federal Reporter* and *U.S. Reports* for the period 1878–1943 and picking out all cases with Asian plaintiffs or defendants.

12. Janisch, "The Chinese, the Courts, and the Constitution," 50–51.

13. Charles J. McClain, Jr., "The Chinese Struggle for Civil Rights in Nineteenth Century America: The First Phase, 1850–1870," *California Law Review* 72 (1984): 529–68; idem, "The Chinese Struggle for Civil Rights in Nineteenth-Century America: The Remarkable Case of *Baldwin* v. *Frank*," *Law and History Review* 3 (1985): 350–73; Charles J. McClain and Laurene Wu McClain, "The Chinese Contribution to the Development of American Law," in *Entry Denied*, ed. Chan; Christian G. Fritz, "Bitter Strength (k'u-li) and the Constitution: The Chinese before the Federal Courts in California," *Historical Reporter* 1 (1980): 2–15; and Linda C. A. Przybyszewski, "Judge Lorenzo Sawyer and the Chinese Civil Rights Decisions in the Ninth Circuit," *Western Legal History* 1 (1988):23–56.

14. My estimate is based on cases discussed in John R. Wunder, "Law and Chinese in Frontier Montana," *Montana* 30 (1980): 18–31; idem, "The Courts and the Chinese in Frontier Idaho," *Idaho Yesterdays* 25 (1981): 23–32; and idem, "The Chinese and the Courts in the Pacific Northwest: Justice Denied?" *Pacific Historical Review* 52 (1983): 191–211, and on a count derived from the index of *California Reports*.

15. Christian G. Fritz, "A Nineteenth-Century 'Habeas Corpus Mill': The Chinese before the Federal Courts in California," *American Journal of Legal History* 32 (1988): 347–72, and Lucy E. Salyer, "Captives of Law: Judicial Enforcement of the Chinese Exclusion Laws, 1891–1905," *Journal of American History* 76 (1989): 91–117. The next five paragraphs are based on these sources and on Chan, "The Exclusion of Chinese Women."

16. Chuman, *Bamboo People*, 6–7, 65–71.

17. The most succinct review of how various Asian nationalities were treated is in the "Petition for Rehearing" filed in the Supreme Court of Washington, 9 June 1921, in the brief of *Yamashita and Kono* v. *Hinkle*, 260 U.S. 199 (1922), reprinted in *Documental* [sic] *History of Law Cases Affecting Japanese in the United States, 1916–1924*, vol. 1 (San Francisco: Consulate-General of Japan, 1925), 128–

29. See also Jeff H. Lesser, "Always 'Outsiders': Asians, Naturalization, and the Supreme Court," *Amerasia Journal* 12, no. 1 (1985): 83–100.

18. Yuji Ichioka, "The Early Japanese Immigrant Quest for Citizenship: The Background of the 1922 Ozawa Case," *Amerasia Journal* 4, no. 2 (1977): 1–22, provides the information used in the next two paragraphs.

19. Harold S. Jacoby, "More Thind against than Sinning," *Pacific Historian* 2 (1958): 1–2, 8, and Jensen, *Passage from India*, 246–69.

20. I found these cases by reading over 1,000 reported cases involving Chinese plaintiffs and defendants in the lower federal courts.

21. John Gioia, "A Social, Political and Legal Study of *Yick Wo* v. *Hopkins*," in *The Chinese American Experience*, ed. Lim, 211–20, and McClain and Wu McClain, "Chinese Contribution," in *Entry Denied*, ed. Chan, provide the information for the next three paragraphs.

22. Kwong, *Chinatown*, 61–86, is the basis for the next two paragraphs.

23. Chuman, *Bamboo People*, 46–51, 76–89; the briefs and court decisions are compiled in *Documental History of Law Cases*, vol. 2.

24. Ibid., 80–81, 88.

25. Eve Armentrout Ma, *Monarchists, Revolutionaries, and Chinatowns: Chinese Politics in the Americas and the 1911 Revolution* (Honolulu: University of Hawaii Press, 1990); Robert Worden, "A Chinese Reformer in Exile: The North American Phase of the Travels of K'ang Yu-wei, 1899–1909" (Ph.D. diss., Georgetown University, 1972); Him Mark Lai, "China Politics and the U.S. Chinese Communities," in *Counterpoint*, ed. Gee, 152–59; and idem, "The Kuomintang in Chinese American Communities before World War II," in *Entry Denied*, ed. Chan.

26. Tsai, *China and the Overseas Chinese*, 104–23.

27. Delber L. McKee, "The Chinese Boycott of 1905–1906 Reconsidered: The Role of Chinese Americans," *Pacific Historical Review* 55 (1986): 165–91, and Linda Pomerantz, "The Chinese Bourgeoisie and the Anti-Chinese Movement in the United States, 1850–1905," *Amerasia Journal* 11, no. 11 (1984): 1–33, are the sources used in the next three paragraphs.

28. Mark Juergensmeyer, "The Ghadar Syndrome: Immigrant Sikhs and Nationalist Pride," in *Sikh Studies: Comparative Perspectives on a Changing Tradition*, ed. Mark Juergensmeyer and Gerald N. Barrier (Berkeley: Graduate Theological Union, 1979), 173–90; Jensen, *Passage from India*, passim; and Harish K. Puri, *Ghadar Movement: Ideology, Organization, and Strategy* (Amritsar, India: Guru Nanak Dev University Press, 1983). See also Kushwant Singh, *A History of the Sikhs* (Princeton: Princeton University Press, 1962), 168–92, and Kalyan Kumar Banerjee, "East Indian Immigration into America: Beginnings of Indian Revolutionary Activity," *Modern Review* 116 (1964): 355–61.

29. Hugh Johnston, *The Voyage of the Komagata Maru: The Sikh Challenge to Canada's Colour Bar* (New Delhi, India: Oxford University Press, 1979), and Jensen, *Passage from India*, 121–38, provide the information for the next two paragraphs.

30. The next three paragraphs are based on Choy, *Koreans in America*, 141–89, and Lyu, "Korean Nationalist Activities," Parts 1 and 2.

31. Kwong, *Chinatown*, 103–06, 110, 112, 141.

# Chapter 6

1. Overviews of Asian women immigrants include Lucie Cheng, "Chinese Immigrant Women in Nineteenth-Century California," in *Women of America: A History*, ed. Carol Ruth Berkin and Mary Beth Norton (Boston: Houghton Mifflin, 1979), 223–44; Judy Yung, *Chinese Women of America: A Pictorial History* (Seattle: University of Washington Press, 1986); Yuji Ichioka, "*Amerika-Nadeshiko*: Japanese Immigrant Women in the United States, 1900–1924," *Pacific Historical Review* 44 (1980): 339–57; Eun Sik Yang, "Korean Women of America: From Subordination to Partnership, 1903–1930," *Amerasia Journal* 11, no. 2 (1984): 1–28; Sun Bin Yim, "Korean Immigrant Women in Early Twentieth-Century America," in *Making Waves: An Anthology of Writings by and about Asian American Women*, ed. Asian Women United of California (Boston: Beacon Press, 1989), 50–59; Jovina Navarro, "Immigration of Filipino Women to America," in *Asian American Women* (Stanford, Calif.: Asian American Women, 1976), 18–22; and Dorothy Cordova, "Voices from the Past: Why They Came," in *Making Waves*, ed. Asian Women United of California, 42–49. Studies of Chinese and Japanese family life in the United States in the 1930s and 1940s include Norman S. Hayner and Charles H. Reynolds, "Chinese Life in America," *American Sociological Review* 2 (1937): 630–37; Lee, *The Chinese in the U.S.A.*, 185–251; and John Modell, "The Japanese American Family: A Perspective for Future Research," *Pacific Historical Review* 37 (1968): 67–81. Sylvia Junko Yanagisako, *Transforming the Past: Tradition and Kinship among Japanese Americans* (Stanford, Calif.: Stanford University Press, 1985), is the most sophisticated study of changing values and norms as they relate to family life.

2. Prostitutes were among the earliest Asian women to enter the country. Lucie Cheng Hirata, "Free, Indentured, Enslaved: Chinese Prostitutes in Nineteenth-Century America," *Signs: Journal of Women in Culture and Society* 5 (1979): 3–29, and Yuji Ichioka, "*Ameyuki-san*: Japanese Prostitutes in Nineteenth-Century America," *Amerasia Journal* 4, no. 1 (1977): 1–21, describe the lot of Chinese and Japanese prostitutes in California, while Joan Hori, "Japanese Prostitution in Hawaii during the Immigration Period," in *Asian and Pacific American Experiences*, ed. Tsuchida, 56–65, looks at those in Hawaii.

3. The following five paragraphs are condensed from Chan, "The Exclusion of Chinese Women."

4. The lives of picture brides are described in Ichioka, "*Amerika Nadeshiko*" and idem, *The Issei*, 164–75. Akemi Kikumura, *Through Harsh Winters: The Life of a Japanese Immigrant Woman* (Novato: Calif.: Chandler and Sharp, 1983), is the life history of a woman who was not a picture bride but who lived and worked in California. Korean women's lives are recorded in Harold Hakwon Sunoo and Sonia Shinn Sunoo, "The Heritage of the First Korean Women Immigrants in the United States, 1903–1924," *Korean Christian Scholars Journal* 2 (1977): 142–71, and Alice Chai, "Korean Women in Hawaii, 1903–1945," in *Asian and Pacific American Experiences*, ed. Tsuchida, 75–87.

5. The only statistics on Japanese family formation according to occupational grouping that I have found are in Oka Naoki, *Hoku-Bei no Kochi kenjin* (Japanese from Kochi Prefecture in North America) (San Francisco: Oka Naoki, 1921), 82–83.

6. *75th Anniversary of Korean Immigration to Hawaii, 1903–1978* (Honolulu: n.p., 1978), 50, as quoted in Yang, "Korean Women of America," 5.

7.   Kazuo Ito, *Issei: A History of Japanese Immigrants in North America*, trans. Shinichiro Nakamura and Jean S. Gerard (Seattle: Executive Committee for the Publication of *Issei*, 1973), 252–54.

8.   Ibid., 250.

9.   The political activities of Korean women are described in Yang, "Korean Women of America," 12–22.

10.   Ichioka, *The Issei*, 196–210, provides the information for the next four paragraphs.

11.   Autobiographical glimpses of Asian American childhood are found in Jade Snow Wong, *Fifth Chinese Daughter* (1945; reprint, Seattle: University of Washington Press, 1988); Pardee Lowe, *Father and Glorious Descendant* (Boston: Little, Brown, 1943); Monica Sone, *Nisei Daughter* (Boston: Little, Brown, 1953); Daniel I. Okimoto, *American in Disguise* (New York: Walker/Weatherhill, 1970); Eleanor Wong Telemaque, *It's Crazy to Stay Chinese in Minnesota* (Nashville, Tenn.: Nelson, 1978); Gene Oishi, *In Search of Hiroshi: A Japanese-American Odyssey* (Tokyo: Tuttle, 1988); Kartar Dhillon, "The Parrot's Beak," in *Making Waves*, ed. Asian Women United of California, 214–22; and Mary Paik Lee, *Quiet Odyssey: A Pioneer Korean Woman in America*, ed. Sucheng Chan (Seattle: University of Washington Press, 1990).

12.   William C. Smith, "The Second Generation Oriental-American," *Journal of Applied Sociology* 10 (1925): 160–68, and a series of short articles in *Sociology and Social Research*: Kit King Louis, "Problems of Second Generation Chinese," 16 (1932): 250–58; idem, "Program for Second Generation Chinese," 16 (1932): 455–62; Francis Y. Chang, "An Accommodation Program for Second-Generation Chinese," 18 (1934): 541–53; Isamu Nodera, "Second Generation Japanese and Vocations," 21 (1937): 454–66; Severino F. Corpus, "Second Generation Filipinos in Los Angeles," 22 (1938): 446–51; Robert H. Ross and Emory Bogardus, "The Second-Generation Race Relations Cycle: A Study in Issei-Nisei Relationships," 24 (1940): 357–63; and Jitsuichi Masuoka, "Race Relations and Nisei Problems," 30 (1946): 452–59.

13.   *Orientals and Their Cultural Adjustment* (Nashville, Tenn.: Fisk University Social Science Institute, 1946), 107–8. The life histories in this publication were actually collected by researchers of the Survey of Race Relations Project in 1925–27.

14.   Ibid., 41.

15.   Edward K. Strong, Jr., *The Second-Generation Japanese Problem* (Stanford, Calif.: Stanford University Press, 1934), summarizes three separate monographs—Edward K. Strong, Jr., and Reginald Bell, *Vocational Aptitudes of Second-Generation Japanese in the United States* (Stanford, Calif.: Stanford University Press, 1933); Edward K. Strong, Jr., *Japanese in California* (Stanford, Calif.: Stanford University Press, 1933); and Reginald Bell, *Public School Education of Second-Generation Japanese in California* (Stanford, Calif.: Stanford University Press, 1935)—and places their findings in a broader discussion of race prejudice and the problem of adjustment by second-generation Americans. The next five paragraphs are based on these studies.

16.   L. Ling-chi Wang, "The Politics of Assimilation and Repression: The Chinese in the United States, 1940–1970," unpublished manuscript on file at the University of California, Asian American Studies Library. The texts of the essays in *The Chinese Digest* are reprinted in Thomas W. Chinn, *Bridging the Pacific: San Francisco Chinatown and Its People* (San Francisco: Chinese Historical Society of America, 1989), 138–42.

17. Chinn, *Bridging the Pacific*, 136–38.

18. Kwong, *Chinatown*, 55–61.

19. Lee, *Quiet Odyssey*.

20. Karen Leonard, "Marriage and Family Life among Early Asian Indian Immigrants," *Population Review* 25 (1982): 67–75; Karen Leonard and Bruce La Brack, "Conflict and Compatibility in Punjabi-Mexican Immigrant Families in Rural California, 1915–1965," *Journal of Marriage and the Family* 46 (1984): 527–37; and Leonard, *Ethnic Choices: California's Punjabi-Mexican-Americans, 1910–1980* (Philadelphia: Temple University Press, 1991).

21. Barbara M. Posadas, "Crossed Boundaries in Interracial Chicago: Pilipino American Families since 1925," *Amerasia Journal* 8, no. 2 (1981): 31–52, and idem, "Mestiza Girlhood: Interracial Families in Chicago's Filipino American Community since 1925," in *Making Waves*, ed. Asian Women United of California, 273–82.

22. Jerrold H. Takahashi, "Japanese American Responses to Race Relations: The Formation of Nisei Perspectives," *Amerasia Journal* 9, no. 1 (1982): 29–58, and idem, *Identity, Culture, and Politics: Japanese Americans and Social Change, 1920s to 1970s* (Philadelphia: Temple University Press, 1991).

## Chapter 7

1. Harold R. Isaacs, *Images of Asia: American Views of China and India* (New York: Harper & Row, 1972), xviii–xix (originally published in 1958 under the title *Scratches on Our Minds*).

2. Wang, "The Politics of Assimilation and Repression" (unpublished manuscript).

3. Chinn, *Bridging the Pacific*, 147–50.

4. Cordova, *Filipinos*, 217–24.

5. There is an extensive literature on the evacuation and internment of persons of Japanese ancestry. The War Relocation Authority staff produced many volumes to justify their deeds; Richard Drinnon, *Keeper of Concentration Camps: Dillon S. Myer and American Racism* (Berkeley and Los Angeles: University of California Press, 1987), counters the benign "official" literature with an extremely critical look at the values, motivations, and actions of the director of the WRA. The account in this chapter relies most heavily on tenBroek et al., *Prejudice, War, and the Constitution;* Roger Daniels, *Concentration Camps North America: Japanese in the United States and Canada during World War II* (Malabar, Fla.: Krieger, 1981); idem, *The Decision to Relocate the Japanese Americans* (1975; reprint, Malabar, Fla.: Krieger, 1986); *Personal Justice Denied: Report of the Commission on Wartime Relocation and Internment of Civilians* (Washington, D.C.: Government Printing Office, 1982); Roger Daniels et al., eds., *Japanese Americans: From Relocation to Redress* (Salt Lake City: University of Utah Press, 1986); Michi Weglyn, *Years of Infamy: The Untold Story of America's Concentration Camps* (New York: Morrow, 1976); Peter Irons, *Justice at War: The Story of the Japanese American Internment Cases* (New York: Oxford University Press, 1983); and idem, *Justice Delayed: The Record of the Japanese American Internment Cases* (Middletown, Conn.: Wesleyan University Press, 1989).

6. Gary Y. Okihiro, *Cane Fires: the Anti-Japanese Movement in Hawaii* (Philadelphia: Temple University Press, 1991), traces how military intelligence began

surveillance of Japanese Americans more than two decades before World War II began.

7.   Roger Daniels, "The Bureau of the Census and the Relocation of Japanese Americans: A Note and a Document," *Amerasia Journal* 9, no. 1 (1982): 101–5.

8.   Leland Ford to Henry L. Stimson, 16 January 1942, U.S. National Archives, record group 107, as quoted in Daniels, *Decision*, 23.

9.   TenBroek, *Prejudice, War, and the Constitution*, 77–80.

10.   Daniels, *Decision*, 47.

11.   Ibid., 47–48.

12.   Daisuke Kitagawa, *Issei and Nisei: The Internment Years* (New York: Seabury Press, 1967); Charles Kikuchi, *The Kikuchi Diary: Chronicle from an American Concentration Camp*, ed. John Modell (Urbana: University of Illinois Press, 1973); Jeanne Wakatsuki Houston and James D. Houston, *Farewell to Manzanar* (Boston: Houghton Mifflin, 1973); and Yoshiko Uchida, *Desert Exile: The Uprooting of a Japanese American Family* (Seattle: University of Washington Press, 1982).

13.   Arthur Hansen and Betty E. Mitson, eds., *Voices Long Silent: An Oral Inquiry into the Japanese American Evacuation* (Fullerton, Calif.: Japanese American Project, California State University, Fullerton, 1974); Gary Y. Okihiro, "Japanese Resistance in America's Concentration Camps: A Re-evaluation," *Amerasia Journal* 2, no. 1 (1973): 20–34; Dorothy S. Thomas and Richard Nishimoto, *The Spoilage: Japanese American Evacuation and Resettlement during World War II* (Berkeley and Los Angeles: University of California Press, 1946); and Douglas W. Nelson, *Heart Mountain: The History of an American Concentration Camp* (Madison: State Historical Society of Wisconsin, 1976). Also of interest are Alexander H. Leighton, *The Governing of Men* (Princeton, N.J.: Princeton University Press, 1945), and Morton Grodzins, *Americans Betrayed: Politics and the Japanese Evacuation* (Chicago: University of Chicago Press, 1949). John Tateishi, *And Justice for All: An Oral History of the Japanese American Detention Camps* (New York: Random House, 1984); Sue Kunitomi Embrey et al., *Manzanar Martyr: An Interview with Harry Y. Ueno* (Fullerton, Calif.: Oral History Program, California State University, Fullerton, 1986); and Deborah Gesensway and Mindy Roseman, *Beyond Words: Images from America's Concentration Camps* (Ithaca, N.Y.: Cornell University Press, 1987), are based on interviews, and "Rite of Passage: The Commission Hearings, 1981," *Amerasia Journal* 8, no. 2 (1981): 53–106, are transcripts of testimony by former internees. Paul Bailey, *City in the Sun: The Japanese Concentration Camp at Poston, Arizona* (Los Angeles: Westernlore Press, 1971); John Armor and Peter Wright, *Manzanar: Photographs by Ansel Adams, Commentary by John Hersey* (New York: Times Books, 1988); Thomas James, *Exile Within: The Schooling of Japanese Americans, 1942–1945* (Cambridge: Harvard University Press, 1987), depict other aspects of camp life.

14.   The next twelve paragraphs are based on Thomas et al., *Spoilage*, and Okihiro, "Japanese Resistance."

15.   The following three paragraphs rely on Nelson, *Heart Mountain*, 116–50.

16.   Tad Ichinokuchi, *John Aiso and the M.I.S.: Japanese-American Soldiers in the Military Intelligence Service, World War II* (Los Angeles: MIS Club of Southern California, 1988), recounts the experiences of Nisei soldiers who served in the Pacific theater.

17.   Tamotsu Shibutani, *The Derelicts of Company K: A Sociological Study of Demoralization* (Berkeley and Los Angeles: University of California Press, 1978); Joseph D. Harrington, *Yankee Samurai: The Secret Role of Nisei in America's Pacific*

*Victory* (Detroit: Pettigrew, 1979); Chester Tanaka, *Go for Broke: A Pictorial History of the Japanese American 100th Battalion and the 442nd Regimental Combat Team* (Richmond, Calif.: Go for Broke, 1982); and Masayo Umezawa Duus, *Unlikely Liberators: The Men of the 100th and 442nd* (Honolulu: University of Hawaii Press, 1987), contain the information used in the preceding two paragraphs.

18. TenBroek, *Prejudice, War, and the Constitution;* Irons, *Justice at War;* and idem, *Justice Delayed,* are the main sources used in the next eleven paragraphs. Also of interest is William Minoru Hohri, *Repairing America: An Account of the Movement for Japanese-American Redress* (Pullman: Washington State University Press, 1988), which describes one segment of the Japanese American redress and reparations movement.

19. Irons, *Justice at War,* 286.

20. Compared with the internment, resettlement is the subject of relatively few studies. Dorothy S. Thomas, Charles Kikuchi, and James Sakoda, *The Salvage* (Berkeley and Los Angeles: University of California Press, 1952); Leonard Broom and Ruth Riemer, *Removal and Return: The Socio-Economic Effects of the War on Japanese Americans* (Berkeley and Los Angeles: University of California Press, 1949); and Mitziko Sawada, "After the Camps: Seabrook Farms, New Jersey, and the Resettlement of Japanese Americans, 1944–1947," *Amerasia Journal* 13, no. 2 (1986): 117–36, are among the handful available.

21. Very little has been written about Asian Americans other than Japanese during World War II or about the experience of any group at all for the period 1945–65. Daniels, *Asian America,* 283–316, is the only available synthesis; Kwong, *Chinatown,* records developments in New York; Lee, *The Chinese in the U.S.A.,* examines the status of Chinese Americans in the 1940s and 1950s. The best framework for understanding these years is Wang, "The Politics of Assimilation and Repression," which, though completed in 1980, remains unpublished.

22. Anselm L. Strauss, "Strain and Harmony in American-Japanese War Bride Marriages," *Journal of Marriage and Family Living* 16 (1954): 99–106; Gerald J. Schnepp and Agnes Masako Yui, "Cultural and Marital Adjustment of Japanese War Brides," *American Journal of Sociology* 61 (1955): 48–50; Rose Hum Lee, "The Recent Immigrant Chinese Families of the San Francisco–Oakland Area," *Journal of Marriage and Family Living* 18 (1956): 14–24; and three works by Bok-Lim C. Kim, "Casework with Japanese and Korean Wives of Americans," *Social Casework* 53 (1972): 273–79; "Asian Wives of U.S. Servicemen: Women in Shadows," *Amerasia Journal* 4, no. 1 (1977): 91–115; and *Women in Shadows: A Handbook for Service Providers Working with Asian Wives of U.S. Military Personnel* (La Jolla, Calif.: National Committee Concerned with Asian Wives of U.S. Servicemen, 1981), are studies of Asian war brides and military wives. Sil Don Kim, "Interracially Married Korean Women Immigrants: A Study in Marginality" (Ph.D. diss., University of Washington, 1979); Daniel B. Lee, "Military Transcultural Marriage: A Study of Marital Adjustment between American Husbands and Korean-born Spouses" (D.S.W. diss., University of Utah, 1980); and Young In Song, "Battered Korean Women in Urban America" (Ph.D. diss., Ohio State University, 1986), provide more details on their lot. The next four paragraphs are based on these studies. Research on war orphans and adopted Asian (mainly Korean) children who have entered in sizable numbers since the early 1950s include Won Moo Hurh, "Marginal Children of War: An Exploratory Study of American-Korean Children," *International Journal of Sociology of the Family* 2 (1972): 10–21; Chim Kim and Timothy G. Carroll, "Intercountry Adoption of South Korean Orphans: A Lawyer's Guide," *Journal of Family Law* 14 (1977): 223–53; Dong Sil Kim, "How They Fared in American

Homes: A Follow-Up Study of Adopted Korean Children," *Children Today* 6 (1977): 2–6, 31; and idem, "Intercountry Adoption: A Study of Self-Concept of Adolescent Korean Children Who Were Adopted by American Families" (Ph.D. diss., University of Chicago, 1978).

23.   Robert A. Burton, "The New Chinese in America," *American Universities Field Staff Reports Service*, East Asia Series 7 (1959): 105–16, is about the Chinese refugees who entered under the 1953 Refugee Act.

24.   Chuman, *Bamboo People*, 198–331.

## Chapter 8

1.   David M. Reimers, *Still the Golden Door: The Third World Comes to America* (New York: Columbia University Press, 1985), 63–90. The next five paragraphs are based on it and on the essays in James T. Fawcett and Benajamin V. Carino, eds., *Pacific Bridges: The New Immigration from Asia and the Pacific Islands* (Staten Island, N.Y.: Center for Migration Studies, 1987). Other works that provide frameworks for understanding the phenomenon include Monica Boyd, "The Changing Nature of Central and Southeast Asian Immigration to the United States, 1961–1972," *International Migration Review* 8 (1974): 507–19; Tai K. Oh, *The Asian Brain Drain: A Factual and Casual* [sic] *Analysis* (San Francisco: R & E Research Associates, 1977); Thomas K. Morrison, "The Relationship of U.S. Aid, Trade, and Investment to Migration Pressures in Major Sending Countries," *International Migration Review* 16 (1982): 4–26; Tomoji Ishi, "International Linkage and National Class Conflict: The Migration of Korean Nurses to the United States," *Amerasia Journal* 14, no. 1 (1988): 23–50; Luciano Mangiafico, *Contemporary American Immigrants: Patterns of Filipino, Korean, and Chinese Settlement in the United States* (New York: Praeger, 1988); and Fred Arnold et al., "Estimating the Immigration Multiplier: An Analysis of Recent Korean and Filipino Immigration to the United States," *International Migration Review* 23 (1989): 813–38.

2.   Gilbert Yochum and Vinod Agarwal, "Permanent Labor Certifications for Alien Professionals, 1975–1982," *International Migration Review* 22 (1988): 265–81, is the basis for the next two paragraphs.

3.   Mangiafico, *Contemporary American Immigrants*, 41–48; Pido, *Pilipinos in America*, 5–13; Sun-Hee Lee, *Why People Intend to Move: Individual and Community-Level Factors of Out-Migration in the Philippines* (Boulder, Colo.: Westview Press, 1975); and Benjamin V. Carino, "The Philippines and Southeast Asia: Historical Roots and Contemporary Linkages," in *Pacific Bridges*, ed. Fawcett and Carino, deal with Filipino emigration.

4.   Bruce Cumings, *The Origins of the Korean War: Liberation and the Emergence of Separate Regimes, 1945–1947* (Princeton, N.J.: Princeton University Press, 1981), 76–81, 193–201, provides the historical background for understanding the current status of workers in South Korea.

5.   The most illuminating studies of the relationship between conditions in South Korea and emigration are Illsoo Kim, *Urban Immigrants: The Korean Community in New York* (Princeton, N.J.: Princeton University Press, 1981), 48–98; Hagen Koo and Eui-Young Yu, *Korean Immigration to the United States: Its Demographic Pattern and Social Implications for Both Societies* (Honolulu: East West Center Population Institute, 1981); and Ivan Light and Edna Bonacich, *Immigrant Entrepreneurs:*

*Koreans in Los Angeles, 1965–1982* (Berkeley and Los Angeles: University of California Press, 1988), 25–125.

6. The arrival of several million newcomers has affected the existing Asian immigrant communities in profound ways. D. Y. Yuan, "Social Consequences of Recent Changes in the Demographic Structure of New York's Chinatown," *Phylon* 35 (1974): 15–64; Chia-ling Kuo, *Social and Political Change in New York's Chinatown: The Role of Voluntary Associations* (New York: Praeger, 1977); and Peter Kwong, *The New Chinatown* (New York: Hill and Wang, 1987), analyze the social change that has transformed New York's Chinese community. Kim, *New Urban Immigrants*; Light and Bonacich, *Immigrant Entrepreneurs*; Won Moo Hurh and Kwang Chung Kim, *Korean Immigrants in America: A Structural Analysis of Ethnic Confinement and Adhesive Adaptation* (Cranbury, N.J.: Associated University Presses, 1984); and Pyong Gap Min, *Ethnic Business Enterprise: Korean Small Business in Atlanta* (Staten Island, N.Y.: Center for Migration Studies, 1988), discuss the impact that new Korean immigrants have made, focusing in particular on their tendency to enter small business. Edwin B. Almirol, *Ethnic Identity and Social Negotiation: A Study of a Filipino Community in California* (New York: AMS Press, 1985), examines those Filipinos who have arrived since the early 1970s. Maxine P. Fisher, *The Indians of New York City: A Study of Immigrants from India* (Columbus, Mo.: South Asia Books, 1980); Parmatma Saran and Edwin Eames, eds., *The New Ethnics: Asian Indians in the United States* (New York: Praeger, 1980); and Parmatma Saran, *The Asian Indian Experience in the United States* (Cambridge, Mass.: Schenkman, 1985), examine Asian Indian ones. John Y. Fenton, *Transplanting Religious Traditions: Asian Indians in America* (New York: Praeger, 1988), and Raymond Brady Williams, *Religions of Immigrants from India and Pakistan: New Threads in the American Tapestry* (Cambridge: Cambridge University Press, 1988), focus on the transplantation of Asian Indian religious traditions.

7. The literature on American involvement in the war in Vietnam is large and growing. Four works of synthesis that espouse different perspectives are George E. Herring, *America's Longest War: The United States in Vietnam, 1950–1975* (1979; 2d ed., New York: Alfred A. Knopf, 1986); Gabriel Kolko, *Anatomy of a War: Vietnam, the United States, and the Modern Historical Experience* (New York: Pantheon, 1985); George McT. Kahin, *Intervention: How America Became Involved in Vietnam* (New York: Alfred A. Knopf, 1986); and Andrew J. Rotter, *The Path to Vietnam: Origins of the American Commitment to Southeast Asia* (Ithaca, N.Y.: Cornell University Press, 1987). Arnold R. Isaacs, *Without Honor: Defeat in Vietnam and Cambodia* (Baltimore: Johns Hopkins University Press, 1983), and James Fenton, "The Fall of Saigon," in *Granta: A Paperback Magazine of New Writing* 15 (1985): 28–116, are two gripping accounts of the final days of the American presence.

8. A great deal has also been published on the first Indochina War. Among the classics are Bernard B. Fall, *The Two Viet-Nams: A Political and Military Analysis* (1963; 2d rev. ed., New York: Praeger, 1967); idem, *Hell in a Very Small Place: The Siege of Dien Bien Phu* (New York: Vintage, 1966); and Ellen J. Hammer, *The Struggle for Indochina, 1940–1955* (Stanford, Calif.: Stanford University Press, 1954).

9. Far less has been published about Laos. Nina S. Adams and Alfred W. McCoy, eds., *Laos: War and Revolution* (New York: Harper & Row, 1970), is a collection of essays by scholars opposed to the American involvement there.

10. Michael Leifer, *Cambodia: The Search for Security* (New York: Praeger, 1967), and the essays in Malcolm Caldwell and Lek Tan, eds., *Cambodia in the*

*logical Perspectives* 28 (1985): 307–38; and Eui Hang Shin and Kyung-Sup Chang, "Peripherization of Immigrant Professionals: Korean Physicians in the United States," *International Migration Review* 22 (1988): 609–26. The current socioeconomic status of Asian immigrant working women is discussed in Don Mar, "Chinese Immigrant Women and the Ethnic Labor Market," *Critical Perspectives of Third World America* 2 (1984): 62–74, and Paul M. Ong, "Immigrant Wives Labor Force Participation," *Industrial Relations* 26 (1987): 296–303. The noneconomic needs of Asian Americans are addressed in Bok-Lim C. Kim, *Asian Americans: Changing Patterns, Changing Needs* (Montclair, N.J.: Association of Korean Christian Scholars in North America, 1978), and Stanley Sue and James K. Morishima, *The Mental Health of Asian Americans: Contemporary Issues in Identifying and Treating Mental Problems* (San Francisco: Jossey-Bass, 1982).

5.   The following six paragraphs are culled from Cabezas and Yee, *Discriminatory Employment*; Moulton, *Socioeconomic Status*; and Cabezas, "Myths and Realities."

6.   Hurh and Kim, *Korean Immigrants in America*, and Light and Bonacich, *Immigrant Entrepreneurs*, take very critical looks at the true meaning of Korean immigrant participation in small business.

7.   Amado Cabezas et al., "New Inquiries into the Socioeconomic Status of Filipino Americans in California," *Amerasia Journal* 13, no. 1 (1986): 1–21, and idem, "Income Differentials between Asian Americans and White Americans in California, 1980," in *Income and Status Differences between Minority and White Americans*, ed. Sucheng Chan (Lewiston, N.Y.: Mellen Press, 1990), 55–98.

8.   Nathan Caplan et al., *The Boat People and Achievement in America: A Study of Family Life, Hard Work, and Cultural Values* (Ann Arbor: University of Michigan Press, 1989), is a prime example of the effort to extend the model minority image to a refugee population.

9.   Brief glimpses of Asian American, particularly Japanese American, involvement in electoral politics in Hawaii are found in Bill Hosokawa, *Nisei: The Quiet Americans, the Story of a People* (New York: Morrow, 1969), 457–72, and in George Cooper and Gavan Daws, *Land and Power in Hawaii* (Honolulu: Benchmark Books, 1985).

10.   Daniel K. Inouye, as quoted in Hosokawa, *Nisei*, 468.

11.   Cooper and Daws, *Land and Power*, 43.

12.   Richard Nagasawa, *Summer Wind: The Story of an Immigrant Chinese Politician* (Tucson, Ariz.: Westernlore Press, 1986).

13.   Leona B. Bagai, *The East Indians and the Pakistanis in America* (Minneapolis: Lerner, 1972), 35–37, and Dalip Singh Saund, *Congressman from India* (New York: Dutton, 1960).

14.   Judy Chu, "Asian Pacific American Women in Mainstream Politics," in *Making Waves*, ed. Asian Women United of California, 405–21, is the only study of Asian American female politicians.

15.   Daniels, *Asian America*, 334. Yasuko I. Takezawa, "Breaking the Silences: Ethnicity and the Quest for Redress among Japanese Americans" (Ph.D. diss., University of Washington, 1989), analyzes the meaning that the redress movement has had for two generations of Japanese Americans in Seattle.

16.   *Personal Justice Denied*, 18.

17.   The Asian American political movement that began in the 1960s has received little scholarly analysis. The articles and memoirs in *Amerasia Journal* 15, no. 1 (1989): 3–158, reflect both the temper of the times and the nostalgia of the

participants. The account here is based on my personal experience, observations, and evaluation.

18. U.S. Commission on Civil Rights, *Recent Activities against Citizens and Residents of Asian Descent* (Washington, D.C.: Clearinghouse Publication no. 88, 1986), 56.

19. Press release by Massachusetts Attorney General Francis X. Bellotti, 1984, as quoted in ibid., 46.

20. There is no scholarly study of the Vincent Chin case. The account here is culled from newspaper stories: *East/West*, 11 and 18 May, 8 June, 14 September, and 9 November 1983; 21 March, 4 April, 13 and 20 June, 25 and 27 July, and 8 August 1984; and 7 May 1987. *AsianWeek*, 26 May, 23 June, 6 July, 10 August, and 11 November 1983; 20 January, 8 and 22 June, and 6 July 1984; 8 May and 6 November 1987. *Hokubei Mainichi*, 13, 18, and 21 May, and 8 and 16 July 1983; 9, 19, and 30 June, 10 July, and 20 September 1984. *Pacific Citizen*, 6 May, 3 and 10 June, and 2 December 1983; 16 March, 29 June, 6 and 27 July, and 10 August 1984; and 19 September 1986.

21. Cecil Suzuki, "Detroit's Asian Americans Outraged by Sentence Given in Murder Case," *Hokubei Mainichi*, 13 May 1983.

22. *AsianWeek*, 1 September 1989.

23. *AsianWeek*, 23 March 1990.

24. The account here is abbreviated from Sucheng Chan and L. Ling-chi Wang, "Racism and the Model Minority: Asian Americans in American Higher Education," in *The Racial Crisis in American Higher Education*, ed. Philip Altbach and Kofi Lomotey (Albany: State University of New York Press, 1991), and the sources cited therein.

25. The essays in Okihiro et al., eds., *Reflections on Shattered Windows*, are retrospective assessments of how Asian American studies has fared in the twenty years of its existence. Several other educational issues concern Asian Americans. Don Nakanishi and Marsha Hirano-Nakanishi, eds., *The Education of Asian and Pacific Americans: Historical Perspectives and Prescriptions for the Future* (Phoenix, Ariz.: Oryx Press, 1983); Nobuya Tsuchida, ed., *Issues in Asian and Pacific American Education* (Minneapolis: Asian/Pacific American Learning Resources Center, University of Minnesota, 1986); and Jayjia Hsia, *Asian Americans in Higher Education and at Work* (Hillsdale, N.J.: Erlbaum, 1988), provide overviews. L. Ling-chi Wang, "*Lau v. Nichols*: The Right of Limited-English-Speaking Students," *Amerasia Journal* 2, no. 2 (1974): 16–45; John H. Koo and Robert N. St. Clair, eds., *Bilingual Education for Asian Americans: Problems and Strategies* (Hiroshima, Japan: Bunka Hyoron, 1980); Mae Chu-Chang, ed. *Asian- and Pacific-American Perspectives on Bilingual Education* (New York: Columbia University Teachers College Press, 1983); and Sandra Lee McKay and Sau-ling Cynthia Wong, eds., *Language Diversity: Problem or Resource?* (New York: Newbury, 1988).

26. Most of the available writings on Asian American culture are on literature. Apart from brief reviews, there is as yet no full-length critical study of films and plays written and produced by Asian American artists. Even less has been said about painting, sculpture, dance, and other art forms. Frank Chin et al., eds., *AIIIEEEEE! An Anthology of Asian American Writers* (Washington, D.C.: Howard University Press, 1974), first defined "Asian American literature" and "Asian American sensibility"; Elaine H. Kim, *Asian American Literature: An Introduction to the Writings and Their Historical Context* (Philadelphia: Temple University Press, 1982), is the first comprehensive survey of works published up to 1980; Cheung and Yogi,

*Asian American Literature*, is the most exhaustive bibliography; and Marlon K. Hom, *Songs of Gold Mountain: Cantonese Rhymes from San Francisco Chinatown* (Berkeley and Los Angeles: University of California Press, 1987), introduces a body of Asian American literature written in Chinese. Literary criticism of Asian American writings is a burgeoning field, with the books of Maxine Hong Kingston, particularly *The Woman Warrior: Memoirs of a Childhood among Ghosts* (New York: Random House, 1975), having received more critical scrutiny than those of any other Asian American author. For a full listing of critical studies, see Cheung and Yogi, eds., *Asian American Literature*. Individual pieces of creative writing are too numerous to list and some are difficult to locate. Accessible anthologies containing the works of multiple authors include Kai-yu Hsu and Helen Palubinskas, eds., *Asian American Authors* (Boston: Houghton Mifflin, 1972); David Hsin-Fu Wand, ed., *Asian-American Heritage: An Anthology of Prose and Poetry* (New York: Washington Square Press, 1974); Chin et al., eds., *AIIIEEEEE!*; Fay Chiang et al., eds., *American Born and Foreign: An Anthology of Asian American Poetry* (New York: Sunbury Press Books, 1979); Janice Mirikitani et al., eds., *Ayumi: A Japanese American Anthology* (San Francisco: Japanese American Anthology Committee, 1980); Joseph Bruchac, ed., *Breaking Silence: An Anthology of Contemporary Asian American Poets* (New York: Greenfield Review Press, 1983); Shirley Ancheta et al., eds., *Without Names: A Collection of Poems by Bay Area Pilipino American Writers* (San Francisco: Kearney Street Workshop Press, 1985); *The Hawk's Well: A Collection of Japanese American Art and Literature* (San Jose: Asian American Art Projects, 1986); Shirley Geok-lin Lim and Mayumi Tsutakawa, eds., *The Forbidden Stitch: An Asian American Women's Anthology* (Corvallis, Ore.: Calyx Books, 1989); and Sylvia Watanabe and Carol Bruchac, eds., *Home to Stay: Asian American Women's Fiction* (New York: Greenfield Review Press, 1990). For individual works, consult Cheung and Yogi, eds., *Asian American Literature*. Only a small number of plays has been published: Jessica Hagedorn, *Chiquita Banana*, in *Third World Women* (San Francisco: Third World Communications, 1972), 118–27; Mei-Mei Berssenbrugge, *One, Two Cups*, in Mei-Mei Berssenbrugge, *Summits Move with the Tide* (New York: Greenfield Review Press, 1974); Momoko Iko, *The Gold Watch* (act 1 only), in *AIIIEEEEE!*, ed. Chin et al., 163–98; Frank Chin, *The Chickencoop Chinaman* and *The Year of the Dragon* (two plays in one volume) (Seattle: University of Washington Press, 1981); Wakako Yamauchi, *And the Soul Shall Dance*, in *West Coast Plays* 11–12 (1982): 117–64; David Henry Hwang, *Broken Promises: Four Plays* (New York: Avon, 1983); Philip Kan Gotanda, *The Dream of Kitamura*, in *West Coast Plays* 15–16 (1983): 191–223; Genny Lim, *Pigeons*, in *Bamboo Ridge* 30 (1986): 57–79; Laurence Yep, *Daemons*, in *Bamboo Ridge* 30 (1986): 80–94; and Misha Berson, ed., *Between Worlds: Contemporary Asian-American Plays* (New York: Theatre Communications Group, 1990), which contains plays by Ping Chong, Philip Kan Gotanda, Jessica Hagedorn, David Henry Hwang, Wakako Yamauchi, and Laurence Yep. Drama review sections of newspapers in East and West Coast metropolitan areas often contain reviews of new Asian American plays.

    27. Janice Mirikitani, "Breaking Silence," in *Shedding Silence: Poetry and Prose* (Berkeley: CelestialArts, 1987), 36.

# Bibliograhic Essay

The most important studies I have relied on in this book are given in the endnotes, and will not be repeated here. This list of additional references is of necessity very selective, since the literature in Asian American history is now sizable. After its first appearance, an item is cited in short form. During a number of years, the University of Hawaii Press was called the University Press of Hawaii, but for the sake of consistency, the former is used throughout. For journal articles, the issue number is given only for *Amerasia Journal*, which does not use continuous pagination for the successive issues of each volume.

## General

Hyung-chan Kim, ed., *Dictionary of Asian American History* (Westport, Conn.: Greenwood Press, 1986), contains entries on a wide range of topics. Hyung-chan Kim, ed., *Asian American Studies: An Annotated Bibliography and Research Guide* (Westport, Conn.: Greenwood Press, 1989), is an extensive but by no means complete bibliography on historical and sociological writings and contains two essays by Shirley Hune that assess works published before the mid-1970s. It should be used in conjunction with another lengthy bibliography: Asian American Studies Program, University of California, Davis, *Asians in America: A Selected Annotated Bibliography—an Expansion and Revision* (Davis: University of California, Asian American Studies, 1983). My "Asian Americans: A Selected Bibliography of Writings Published since the 1960s," in *Reflections on Shattered Windows: Promises and Prospects for Asian American Studies*, ed. Gary Y. Okihiro et al. (Pullman: Washington State University Press, 1988), 214–37, is a relatively short listing, divided by topics and by ethnic groups. For annual bibliographical updates, see the spring issues of *Amerasia Journal*.

Four somewhat dated but nonetheless useful bibliographies on Asians in Hawaii are Arthur L. Gardner, *The Koreans in Hawaii: An Annotated Bibliography* (Honolulu: University of Hawaii, Social Science Research Institute, 1970); Nancy Foon Young, *The Chinese in Hawaii: An Annotated Bibliography* (Honolulu: University of Hawaii, Social Science Research Institute, 1973); Mitsugi Matsuda, revised by Dennis M. Ogawa and Jerry Y. Fujioka, *The Japanese in Hawaii: An Annotated Bibliography of Japanese Americans* (Honolulu: University of Hawaii, Social Sciences and Linguistics Institute, 1975); and Reuben R. Alcantara et al., *The Filipinos in Hawaii: An Annotated Bibliography* (Honolulu: University of Hawaii, Social Sciences and Linguistics Institute, 1977).

Asian Indians are often slighted in general bibliographies on Asian Americans, but Jane Singh et al., eds., *South Asians in North America: An Annotated and Selected*

*Bibliography* (Berkeley: Center for South and Southeast Asian Studies, University of California, Berkeley, 1988), fills this lacuna. My "Koreans in America, 1903–Present: A Selected Bibliography," *Immigration History Newsletter* 20 (1988): 11–15, is a relatively up to date listing on Korean Americans.

Bibliographies on refugees from Vietnam, Laos, and Kampuchea include *Refugee Materials Center Bibliography*, rev. ed. (Kansas: Kansas City, Department of Education, 1986); *Bibliography of the Hmong*, 2d ed. (Minneapolis: University of Minnesota, Southeast Asian Refugee Studies Project, 1983); J. Christina Smith, *The Hmong: An Annotated Bibliography, 1983–1987* (Minneapolis: University of Minnesota, Southeast Asian Refugee Studies Project, 1988); John Marston, comp., *An Annotated Bibliography of Cambodia and Cambodian Refugees* (Minneapolis: University of Minnesota, Center for Urban and Regional Affairs, 1987); J. Kirk Felsman et al., *Selected Bibliography on Indochinese Refugee Children* (Hanover, N.H.: Amerasian Project, 1985); Ruth E. Hammond and Glenn L. Hendricks, comps., *Southeast Asian Refugee Youth: An Annotated Bibliography* (Minneapolis: University of Minnesota, Center for Urban and Regional Affairs, 1988); C. L. Williams, *An Annotated Bibliography on Refugee Mental Health* (Rockville, Md.: National Institute of Mental Health, 1987); and U.S. Department of Health and Human Services, *An Annotated Bibliography on Refugee Mental Health*, vol. 2 (Washington, D.C.: Government Printing Office, 1989).

An exhaustive listing of creative writings and literary criticism is found in King-Kok Cheung and Stan Yogi, *Asian American Literature: An Annotated Bibliography* (New York: Modern Languages Association of America, 1988). Yuji Ichioka et al., comps., *A Buried Past: An Annotated Bibliography of the Japanese American Research Project Collection* (Berkeley and Los Angeles: University of California Press, 1974), and Him Mark Lai, *A History Reclaimed: An Annotated Bibliography of Chinese Language Materials on the Chinese of America* (Los Angeles: Asian American Studies Program, University of California, Los Angeles, 1986), list Asian-language sources.

## Multigroup Studies

Books and anthologies that cover the history of several groups of Asian immigrants and their descendants are Norris Hundley, Jr., ed., *The Asian American: The Historical Experience* (Santa Barbara, Calif.: ABC-Clio Press, 1976); H. Brett Melendy, *Asians in America: Filipinos, Koreans, and East Indians* (Boston: Twayne, 1977); Tricia Knoll, *Becoming Americans: Asian Sojourners, Immigrants, and Refugees in the Western United States* (Portland, Ore.: Coast to Coast Books, 1982); Ronald Takaki, *Pau Hana: Plantation Life and Labor in Hawaii* (Honolulu: University of Hawaii Press, 1983); Lucie Cheng and Edna Bonacich, eds., *Labor Immigration under Capitalism: Asian Workers in the United States before World War II* (Berkeley and Los Angeles: University of California Press, 1984); Edward D. Beechert, *Working in Hawaii: A Labor History* (Honolulu: University of Hawaii Press, 1985); Harry H. L. Kitano and Roger Daniels, *Asian Americans: Emerging Minorities* (Englewood Cliffs, N.J.: Prentice-Hall, 1988); Roger Daniels, *Asian America: Chinese and Japanese in the United States since 1850* (Seattle: University of Washington Press, 1988); and Ronald Takaki, *Strangers from a Different Shore: A History of Asian Americans* (Boston: Little, Brown, 1989).

## Surveys of Single Groups

Available surveys of Chinese and Japanese Americans are Stanford M. Lyman, *Chinese Americans* (New York: Random House, 1974); Shih-shan Henry Tsai, *The*

*Chinese Experience in America* (Bloomington: Indiana University Press, 1986); Harry H. L. Kitano, *Japanese Americans: The Evolution of a Subculture* (Englewood Cliffs, N.J.: Prentice-Hall, 1969); William Petersen, *Japanese Americans: Oppression and Success* (New York: Random House, 1971); and Robert A. Wilson and Bill Hosokawa, *East to America: A History of the Japanese in the United States* (New York: Quill, 1982).

Textbooks on Filipino, Korean, and Asian Indian Americans do not exist, but there are general surveys. Bong-Youn Choy, *Koreans in America* (Chicago: Nelson-Hall, 1979); Hyung June Moon, "The Korean Immigrants in America: The Quest for Identity in the Formative Years, 1903-1918" (Ph.D. diss., University of Nevada, Reno, 1976); Lee Houchins and Chang-su Houchins, "The Korean Experience in America, 1903–1924," *Pacific Historical Review* 43 (1974): 548–75; Melendy, *Asians in America*, 111–72; and Eui-Young Yu, "Korean Communities in America: Past, Present, and Future," *Amerasia Journal* 10, no. 2 (1983): 23–52, tell the story of Koreans in America, while Hyung-chan Kim, ed., *The Korean Diaspora: Historical and Sociological Studies of Korean Immigration and Assimilation in North America* (Santa Barbara, Calif.: ABC-Clio Press, 1977), is a good collection of articles.

Bruno Lasker, *Filipino Immigration to Continental United States and to Hawaii* (1931; reprint, New York: Arno Press, 1969), and Melendy, *Asians in America*, 17–108, are the two most reliable surveys of the Filipino experience in America. Antonio J. A. Pido, *The Pilipinos in America* (Staten Island, N.Y.: Center for Migration Studies, 1986), though framed broadly, is marred by some factual errors. Jesse Quinsaat et al., eds., *Letters in Exile: An Introductory Reader on the History of Pilipinos in America* (Los Angeles: Asian American Studies Center, University of California, Los Angeles, 1976), is a good collection of essays.

On Asian Indians, see Joan Jensen, *Passage from India: Asian Indian Immigrants in North America* (New Haven, Conn.: Yale University Press, 1988); Melendy, *Asians in America*, 175–248; Gary R. Hess, "The Forgotten Asian Americans: The East Indian Community in the United States," *Pacific Historical Review* 43 (1974): 576–96; and S. Chandrasekhar, ed., *From India to America: A Brief History of Immigration, Problems of Discrimination, Admission, and Assimilation* (La Jolla, Calif.: Population Review Publications, 1982).

There are no works of synthesis on the one million refugees from Vietnam, Laos, and Kampuchea, but their influx has spawned a sizable literature. Paul J. Strand and Woodrow Jones, Jr., *Indochinese Refugees in America: Problems of Adaptation and Assimilation* (Durham, N.C.: Duke University Press, 1985), 32–68, and Edward M. Kennedy, "Refugee Act of 1980," *International Migration Review* 15 (1981): 141–56, discuss the legal framework within which the refugee influx has taken place.

Knoll, *Becoming Americans*, 171–300, provides a textbook overview of the various ethnic groups within the refugee population. Darrel Montero, *Vietnamese Americans: Patterns of Resettlement and Socioeconomic Adaptation in the United States* (Boulder, Colo.: Westview Press, 1977); Gail P. Kelly, *From Vietnam to America: A Chronicle of the Vietnamese Immigration to the United States* (Boulder, Colo.: Westview Press, 1978); and William T. Liu et al., *Transition to Nowhere: Vietnamese Refugees in America* (Nashville, Tenn.: Charter House, 1979), are studies of conditions in the holding camps that housed those who arrived in the spring of 1975.

The only three works in which the voices of individual Vietnamese refugees themselves are heard are Nathan Caplan et al., *The Boat People and Achievement in America: A Study of Family Life, Hard Work, and Cultural Values* (Ann Arbor: University of Michigan Press, 1989); James A. Freeman, *Hearts of Sorrow: Vietnamese-American Lives* (Stanford, Calif.: Stanford University Press, 1989); and Le Ly Hayslip with Jay Wurts, *When Heaven and Earth Changed Places: A Vietnamese Woman's Journey from War to Peace* (New York: Doubleday, 1989).

The Hmong of Laos, who have fascinated anthropologists, have received separate scholarly treatment. Available anthologies include Bruce T. Downing and Douglas P. Olney, eds., *The Hmong in the West: Observations and Reports* (Minneapolis: University of Minnesota Center for Urban and Regional Affairs, 1982), and Glenn Hendricks, ed., *The Hmong in Transition* (Staten Island, N.Y.: Center for Migration Studies, 1985). Keith H. Quincy, *Hmong: History of a People* (Cheney: Eastern Washington University Press, 1988), provides a historical perspective on this people. Other studies are Timothy Dunnigan, "Segmentary Kinship in Urban Society: The Hmong of St. Paul and Minneapolis," *Anthropological Quarterly* 55 (1982): 126–34; George M. Scott, Jr., "The Hmong Refugee Community in San Diego: Theoretical and Practical Implications of Its Continuing Ethnic Solidarity," *Anthropological Quarterly* 55 (1982): 146-60; Banjerd B. Ukapatayasakul, "Hmong Refugee Economic Adjustment in a California Community" (Ph.D. diss., United States International University, 1983); George M. Scott, Jr., "Migrants without Mountains: The Politics of Sociocultural Adjustment among the Lao Hmong Refugees in San Diego" (Ph.D. diss., University of California, San Diego, 1986); William H. Meredith and George P. Rowe, "Changes in Lao Hmong Marital Attitudes after Immigrating to the United States," *Journal of Comparative Family Studies* 17 (1986): 117–26; Simon Fass, "Innovation in the Struggle for Self-Reliance: The Hmong Experience in the United States," *International Migration Review* 20 (1986): 351–80; Frank Viviano, "Strangers in the Promised Land," *Image* (31 August 1986): 15–21, 36; Srila Sen, "The Lao in the U.S. since Migration: An Anthropological Inquiry of Persistence and Accommodation" (Ph.D. diss., University of Illinois, Urbana, 1987); and Karen L. Muir, *The Strongest Part of the Family: A Study of Lao Refugee Women in Columbus, Ohio* (New York: AMS Press, 1988).

With the exception of a handful of psychiatric analyses, there are few substantial scholarly studies of Kampuchean refugees. Herbert W. Hemmila, "The Adjustment and Assimilation of Cambodian Refugees in Texas" (Ed.D. diss., East Texas State University, 1984), and Florence S. Mitchell, "From Refugee to Rebuilder: Cambodian Women in America" (Ph.D. diss., Syracuse University, 1987), are two available dissertations. Items in David W. Haines, ed., *Refugees as Immigrants: Cambodians, Laotians, and Vietnamese in America* (Totowa, N.J.: Rowman and Littlefield, 1989), and M. A. Bromley, "New Beginnings for Cambodian Refugees or Further Disruptions?" *Social Work* 52 (1987): 236–39, are articles on this group. At a nonacademic level, several personal accounts of their harrowing escape have been published, including Someth May, *Cambodian Witness: The Autobiography of Someth May* (New York: Random House, 1986); Molyda Szymusiak, *The Stones Cry Out: A Cambodian Childhood, 1975–1980* (New York: Hill and Wang, 1986); Joan Criddle and Teeda Butt Mam, *To Destroy You Is No Loss: The Odyssey of a Cambodian Family* (New York: Atlantic Monthly Press, 1987); Haing Ngor with Roger Warner, *Haing Ngor: A Cambodian Odyssey* (New York: MacMillan, 1987); and Pin Yathay, *Stay Alive, My Son* (New York: Free Press, 1987).

## Local Histories

Before 1965, a majority of the Chinese in the United States lived in California and Hawaii. Otis Gibson, *The Chinese in America* (Cincinnati: Hitchcock and Walden, 1877); William W. Bode, *Lights and Shadows of Chinatown* (San Francisco: Crocker, 1896); Charles C. Dobie, *San Francisco's Chinatown* (New York: Appleton-Century, 1936); Alexander McLeod, *Pigtails and Gold Dust* (Caldwell, Idaho: Caxton Printers, 1947); and Thomas W. Chinn, *Bridging the Pacific: San Francisco's Chinatown and Its*

*People* (San Francisco: Chinese Historical Society of America, 1989), offer glimpses of the metropolis of Chinese America at different points in time.

Sandy Lydon, *Chinese Gold: The Chinese in the Monterey Bay Area* (Capitola, Calif.: Capitola Book Co., 1985); Sylvia Sun Minnick, *Samfow: The San Joaquin Chinese Legacy* (Fresno, Calif.: Panorama West, 1988); and Great Basin Foundation, ed., *Wong Ho Leun: An American Chinatown* (San Diego, Calif.: Great Basin Foundation, 1988), are studies of California's rural Chinatowns. (The last item is about Riverside, California.)

The best account of the Chinese in Hawaii is Clarence E. Glick, *Sojourners and Settlers: Chinese Immigrants in Hawaii* (Honolulu: University of Hawaii Press, 1980). Also useful are Tin-Yuke Char, ed. and comp., *The Sandalwood Mountains: Readings and Stories of the Early Chinese Immigrants in Hawaii* (Honolulu: University of Hawaii Press, 1975), and Steven B. Zuckerman, "Pake in Paradise: A Synthetic Study of Chinese Immigration to Hawaii," *Bulletin of the Institute of Ethnology, Academia Sinica* 45 (1978): 39–79.

The most important Chinese immigrant community outside California and Hawaii is in New York. Two nineteenth-century accounts are Helen F. Clark, "The Chinese of New York," *Century Magazine* 53 (1896): 104–13, and Louis J. Beck, *New York's Chinatown: An Historical Presentation of Its People and Places* (New York: Bohemia, 1898). I. Hsuan Julia Chen, "The Chinese Community in New York, 1920–1940" (Ph.D. diss., American University, 1942); Virgina Heyer, "Patterns of Social Organization in New York City's Chinatown" (Ph.D. diss., Columbia University, 1953); D. Y. Yuan, "Voluntary Segregation: A Study of New York Chinatown," *Phylon* 24 (1963): 255–65; Cheng Tsu Wu, "Chinese People and Chinatown in New York City" (Ph.D. diss., Clark University, 1969); Peter Kwong, *Chinatown, New York: Labor and Politics, 1930-1950* (New York: Monthly Review Press, 1979); and Bernard Wong, *Patronage, Brokerage, Entrepreneurship and the Chinese Community of New York* (New York: AMS Press, 1988), describe largely the pre-1965 period.

Less has been published about Chinese elsewhere in the United States. The more substantial works include Nelson Chia-chi Ho, "Portland's Chinatown: The History of an Urban Ethnic District," in *Annals of the Chinese Historical Society of the Pacific Northwest* (1984): 30-39; Douglas W. Lee, "Sojourners, Immigrants, and Ethnics: The Saga of the Chinese in Seattle," in *Annals of the Chinese Historical Society of the Pacific Northwest* (1984): 51–58; George M. Blackburn and Sherman L. Ricards, "The Chinese of Virginia City, Nevada, 1870," *Amerasia Journal* 7, no. 1 (1980): 51–72; Russell M. Magnaghi, "Virginia City's Chinese Community, 1860–1880," *Nevada Historical Society Quarterly* 24 (1981): 130–57; Rose Hum Lee, *The Growth and Decline of Chinese Communities in the Rocky Mountain Region* (New York: Arno Press, 1979); James W. Loewen, *The Mississippi Chinese: Between Black and White* (Cambridge: Harvard University Press, 1971); and Lucy M. Cohen, *Chinese in the Post-Civil War South: A People without a History* (Baton Rouge: Louisiana State University Press, 1984).

Yuji Ichioka, *The Issei: The World of the First Generation Japanese Immigrants, 1885–1924* (New York: Free Press, 1988); John Modell, *The Economics and Politics of Racial Accommodation: The Japanese of Los Angeles, 1900–1942* (Urbana: University of Illinois Press, 1977); and Cheryl L. Cole, *A History of the Japanese Community in Sacramento, 1883–1972: Organizations, Businesses, and Generational Response to Majority Domination and Stereotypes* (San Francisco: R & E Research Associates, 1974), deal with the three most important Japanese immigrant communities in California—San Francisco, Los Angeles, and Sacramento.

Studies of California rural Japanese immigrant communities include Kesa Noda, *Yamato Colony, 1906–1960: Livingston, California* (Livingston, Calif.: Japanese American Citizens League, 1981); Timothy J. Lukes and Gary Y. Okihiro, *Japanese Legacy:*

*Farming and Community Life in California's Santa Clara Valley* (Cupertino: California History Center, 1985); and Valerie Matsumoto, *The Cortez Colony: Family, Farm and Community among Japanese Americans, 1919–1982* (Ithaca, N.Y.: Cornell University Press, forthcoming).

The story of Japanese in Hawaii is told in Hilary F. Conroy, *The Japanese Frontier in Hawaii, 1868–1898* (Berkeley and Los Angeles: University of California Press, 1953); Alan Takeo Moriyama, *Imingaisha: Japanese Emigration Companies and Hawaii, 1894–1908* (Honolulu: University of Hawaii Press, 1985); United Japanese Society of Hawaii Publications Committee, *A History of Japanese in Hawaii* (Honolulu: United Japanese Society of Hawaii, 1971); Dennis M. Ogawa, *Kodomo no tame ni: For the Sake of the Children* (Honolulu: University Press of Hawaii, 1978); and Yukiko Kimura, *Issei: Japanese Immigrants in Hawaii* (Honolulu: University of Hawaii Press, 1988). Ethnic Studies Oral History Project, *Uchinanchu: A History of Okinawans in Hawaii* (Honolulu: Ethnic Studies Program, University of Hawaii and United Okinawan Association of Hawaii, 1981), is a collection of essays on the Okinawans.

Relatively little has been written about Japanese elsewhere in the country. Of the available studies, Marjorie R. Stearns, "The History of the Japanese People in Oregon" (M.A. thesis, University of Oregon, 1937); John A. Rademaker, "The Ecological Position of the Japanese Farmers in the State of Washington" (Ph.D. diss., University of Washington, 1939); Kazuo Ito, *Issei: A History of Japanese Immigration in North America*, trans. Shinichiro Nakamura and Jean S. Gerard (Seattle: Executive Committee for Publication of *Issei*, 1973); S. Frank Miyamoto, *Social Solidarity among the Japanese in Seattle* (1939; reprint, Seattle: University of Washington Press, 1981); Jack August, "The Anti-Japanese Crusade in Arizona's Salt River Valley," *Arizona and the West* 21 (1977): 113–36; T. Scott Miyakawa, "Early New York Issei Founders of Japanese American Trade," in *East Across the Pacific: Historical and Sociological Studies of Japanese Immigration and Assimilation*, ed. Hilary Conroy and T. Scott Miyakawa (Santa Barbara, Calif.: ABC-Clio Press, 1972), 156–86; George E. Pozzeta and Harry A. Kersey, Jr., "Yamato Colony: A Japanese Presence in South Florida," *Tequesta* 36 (1976): 66-77; and Thomas K. Walls, *The Japanese Texans* (San Antonio: Institute of Texan Cultures, University of Texas, San Antonio, 1987), are of the greatest interest.

Bernice B. H. Kim, "The Koreans in Hawaii" (M.A. thesis, University of Hawaii, 1937), is the most detailed study of old Korean immigrants in the islands. Other local studies of the pre-1965 arrivals include Helen Given Lewis, *The Korean Community in Los Angeles County* (1939; reprint, San Francisco: R & E Research Associates, 1974), and Kyung Sook Cho Gregor, "Korean Immigrants in Gresham, Oregon: Community Life and Social Adjustment" (M.A. thesis, University of Oregon, 1963). Jay Kun Yoo, *The Koreans in Seattle* (Elkins Park, Pa.: Philip Jaisohn Memorial Foundation, 1979); Kyung Soo Chol, "The Assimilation of Korean Immigrants in the St. Louis Area" (Ph.D. diss., St. Louis University, 1982); Won Moo Hurh et al., *Assimilation Patterns of Immigrants in the United States: A Case Study of Korean Immigrants in the Chicago Area* (Washington, D.C.: University Press of America, 1978); and Don Chang Lee, *Acculturation of Korean Residents in Georgia* (San Francisco: R & E Research Associates, 1975), examine recent immigrants.

Most of the studies of the older Filipino communities in California are rather slim unrevised M.A. theses and Ph.D. dissertations. The two most substantial are Valentine R. Aquino, *The Filipino Community in Los Angeles* (San Francisco: R & E Research Associates, 1974), and Mario P. Ave, *Characteristics of Filipino Organizations in Los Angeles* (San Francisco: R & E Research Associates, 1974). Adelaid Castillo, "Filipino Migrants in San Diego, 1900–1946," *Journal of San Diego History* 22 (1976): 26–35, and Carol Hemminger, "Little Manila: The Filipino in Stockton

Prior to World War II," parts 1 and 2, *Pacific Historian* 24 (1980): 21–34, 207–20, are also of some interest.

Roman R. Cariaga, *The Filipinos in Hawaii: Economic and Social Conditions, 1906–1936* (Honolulu: Filipino Public Relations Bureau, 1937); Ruben R. Alcantara, *Sakada: Filipino Adaptation in Hawaii* (Washington, D.C.: University Press of America, 1981); Luis V. Teodoro, Jr., ed., *Out of This Struggle: The Filipinos in Hawaii* (Honolulu: University Press of Hawaii, 1981); and Robert N. Anderson with Richard Collier and Rebecca F. Pestano, *Filipinos in Rural Hawaii* (Honolulu: University of Hawaii Press, 1984), are about Filipinos in Hawaii, while Fred Cordova, *Filipinos: Forgotten Asian Americans, a Pictorial Essay, 1763–ca. 1963* (Seattle: Demonstration Project for Asian Americans, 1983), contains vignettes about Filipinos elsewhere in the country.

On the early Asian Indian communities, besides Jensen, *Passage from India*, see Bruce La Brack, *The Sikhs of Northern California, 1904–1975* (New York: AMS Press, 1988), and Lawrence A. Wenzel, "The Rural Punjabis of California: A Religio-Ethnic Group," *Phylon* 40 (1968): 245-56. Karen Leonard, *Ethnic Choices: California's Punjabi-Mexican Americans, 1910–1980* (Philadelphia: Temple University Press, 1991), deals with an interesting interracial subcommunity among the Asian Indians.

Barry N. Stein, "Occupational Adjustment of Refugees: The Vietnamese in the United States," *International Migration Review* 13 (1979): 25–45; Kenneth A. Skinner, "Vietnamese in America: Diversity in Adaptation," *California Sociologist* 3 (1980): 103–24; W. Gim and T. Litwin, *Indochinese Refugees in America: Profiles of Five Communities* (Washington, D.C.: U.S. State Department, 1980); Bruce B. Dunning and Joshua Greenbaum, *A Systematic Survey of the Social, Psychological and Economic Adaptation of Vietnamese Refugees Representing Five Entry Cohorts, 1975–1979* (Washington, D.C.: Bureau of Social Science Research, 1982); Paul D. Starr and Alden E. Roberts, "Community Structure and Vietnamese Refugee Adaptation: The Significance of Context," *International Migration Review* 16 (1982): 595–618; Christine R. Finnan, "Community Influences on the Occupational Adaptation of Vietnamese Refugees," *Anthropological Quarterly* 55 (1982): 161–69; Anh T. Nguyen and Charles C. Healy, "Factors Affecting Employment and Job Satisfaction of Vietnamese Refugees," *Journal of Employment and Counseling* 22 (1985): 522–38; Strand and Jones, *Indochinese Refugees*, 69–138; Robert Bach and Rita Carroll-Seguin, "Labor Force Participation, Household Composition and Sponsorship among Southeast Asian Refugees," *International Migration Review* 20 (1986): 381–404; Jacqueline Desbarats, "Ethnic Differences in Adaptation: Sino-Vietnamese Refugees in the United States," *International Migration Review* 20 (1986): 405–27; David W. Haines, "Patterns in Southeast Asian Refugee Employment: A Reappraisal of the Existing Research," *Ethnic Groups* 7 (1987): 39–63; and Nathan Caplan et al., *The Boat People and Achievement in America: A Study of Family Life, Hard Work, and Cultural Values* (Ann Arbor: University of Michigan Press, 1989), assess how several waves of refugees have fared since their arrival.

# Index

Abiko Kyotaro, 111
academic achievements, 167, 169, 179–80
affirmative action programs, 179
African Americans. *See* black Americans
Africans, enslaved, 4, 5, 42, 45
Agarwal, Vinod, 147
agricultural associations, 69–70, 71
agriculture, 32, 35
  and desire for cheap labor, 4-5, 37
  as foundation of Japanese immigrant economy, 69–70
  *See also* farmers and farm workers; tenant farming
Aguinaldo, Emilio, 17
Aheong, S. P., 73
Ahn Chang-ho, 74, 98–99, 111
Alabama and Chattanooga Railroad Company, 82
Alaskan salmon canneries, 39, 89, 117
alien land laws, 38, 39, 47, 69, 95–96, 142
Alien Registration Act (1940), 123
Alipay, Gregorio, 77
Alipayan Church, 77
All-Chinatown Anti-Japanese Patriotic Association, 100
Allen, Horace N., 13, 15
Almaguer, Tomas, 86
Amerasian children, 140, 163–64
Amerasian Homecoming Act (1987), 145, 163–64
Amerasian Immigration Act (1982), 163
American Citizens for Justice, 177, 178
American Civil Liberties Union (ACLU), 138
American Civil War, 27, 30
American Council for Nationalities Services, 156
*American Dream*, 184–85

American Federation of Labor (AFL), 85, 86–87, 88, 89, 90
American Fund for Czechoslovak Refugees, 156
Americanization, 59, 128
American Magazines and Books Commercial Association, 69
*And the Soul Shall Dance*, 184
animism, 64, 157
Anti-Imperialist Alliance, 100
antimiscegenation laws, 59–61, 116
Aquino, Corazon, 149
armed forces, service in, 117, 121, 130–31
  and citizenship, 122, 130, 149
  by Nisei, 121, 125, 129, 133–35
Armenians, 93
arranged marriages:
  generational conflict over, 112–13
  to "picture brides," 46, 107–109, 110, 111
Art Goods and Notions Commercial Association, 69
artists, 146, 167, 181–85
*Asa Ga Kimashita*, 184–85
Asian Americans, contemporary, 187–88
  academic achievements of, 167, 169, 179–80
  artistic sensibility of, 167, 181–85
  and discrimination in higher education, 179–81
  political participation and activism of, 167, 171–81
  and renewed anti-Asian violence, 175–79, 188
  socioeconomic status of, 167–71
Asian Americans, second-generation, 100
  and arranged marriages, 112–13
  and discrimination in higher education, 179–81

*230*

# The Author

Sucheng Chan is professor of history and chair of the Asian American Studies Program at the University of California, Santa Barbara. She received her B.A. from Swarthmore College in 1963, her M.A. from the University of Hawaii in 1965, and her Ph.D. from the University of California, Berkeley, in 1973.

She is the author of *This Bittersweet Soil: The Chinese in California Agriculture, 1860-1910* (1986), which won the 1986 Theodore Saloutos Memorial Book Award in Agricultural History, the 1987 American Historical Association Pacific Coast Branch Book Award, and the 1988 Association for Asian American Studies Outstanding Book Award. Her essay, "Chinese Livelihood in Rural California, 1860–1880: The Impact of Economic Change," received the Louis Knott Koontz Prize for the "most deserving article" published in the *Pacific Historical Review* in 1984. She has also edited four books.

She received a Distinguished Teaching Award from the University of California, Berkeley, in 1978 and held a John Simon Guggenheim fellowship in 1988–89.

## The Editor

Thomas J. Archdeacon is professor of history at the University of Wisconsin–Madison, where he has been a member of the faculty since 1972. A native of New York City, Archdeacon earned his doctorate from Columbia University, under the direction of Professor Richard B. Morris. His first book, *New York City, 1664–1710: Conquest and Change* (1976), examines relations between Dutch and English residents of that community during the late seventeenth and early eighteenth centuries. Building on that work, Archdeacon increasingly concentrated his research and teaching on topics related to immigration and ethnic-group relations. In 1983 he published *Becoming American: An Ethnic History.*